D1595114

True or False

Judging Doctrine and Leadership

True or False

Judging Doctrine and Leadership

Guy Duininck

Master's Touch Publishing Company

Tulsa, Oklahoma

Unless otherwise indicated, all scriptural quotations are from the *King James Version* of the Bible.

Scripture quotaions marked (NIV) are from the Holy Bible, New International Version. Copyright © 1973, 1978, 1984 International Bible Society. Used by permission of Zondervan Bible Publishers.

Scripture quotations marked (AMP) are from the Ampliphied Bible. Old Testament copyright © 1965, 1987 by the Zondervan Corporation. The Ampliphied New Testament copyright © 1958, 1987 by the Lockman Foudation. Used by permission.

True or False – Judging Leadership and Doctrine
ISBN 0-929400-03-8
Copyright © 1992 by
Guy Duininck
P.O. Box 54026
Tulsa, OK 74155

Published by
Master's Touch Publishing Co.
P.O. Box 54026
Tulsa, OK 74155
U.S.A.

Cover design and book production by
DB & Associates Design Group, Inc.
P.O. Box 52756
Tulsa, OK 74152

Dedication

When I began to write this my fourth book, I knew that I would dedicate it to my parents. Because they have dedicated so much effort to my success, I wanted to dedicate the fruit of this effort to them. But what could I say to convey my feelings of thanks?

You see, since the beginning of time, men have sought to employ words in the task of transmitting their feelings. Their attempts have, almost without exception, failed. Words simply do not have the ability to convey the intensity, the weight, or the depth of human feeling. Though words cannot adequately convey my feelings of gratitude, to say nothing is wrong. To my parents I say simply, but with the deepest of feeling:

Mom, Dad, this book represents the completion of one of the most significant efforts of my life. I dedicate it to you in thanks for your many years of unwavering support.

Always grateful, your son,

Guy

Contents

Preface

This book is the culmination of more than three years of concentrated study on the subject of judging doctrine and spiritual leadership. I was first alerted to the importance of this subject by the many tangents of doctrine I observed in the body of Christ and by the instability I recognized in spiritual leadership. Almost weekly I heard or read of some new revelation, some new move of God, or some unusual spiritual activity. I began to realize that Christians either were not qualified or not willing to make judgments about doctrine and spiritual leadership. Recognizing a weakness in this important area of spiritual life, I felt inspired to write this book.

The message of this book is not only timeless; it is also very timely. The rise of false spiritual leaders and the infiltration of unsound doctrine is a problem right now and will become an even greater problem as we approach the last of the last days. This may surprise you, but a careful study of the gospels and the epistles reveals numerous warnings which foretell the latter day rise of unsound doctrine and false leadership.

It is imperative that believers learn how to judge doctrine and spiritual leadership. Their own spiritual stability, the soundness of local churches, and the plans and purposes of God can all be undermined if believers do not know how to judge. Learning how to judge doctrine and spiritual leadership will save believers and local churches from spiritual disaster!

PURPOSE

It is my intention that this book be both a guide-book for believers and an excellent source-book for those who are called to the full-time ministry. Every page deals either with doctrine or with spiritual leadership. These are two areas of spiritual life that believers and ministers **must** be experts in. Along with this general goal there are several specific goals I hope to accomplish.

First: I hope to make you aware that there has been, is now, and will be as we approach the last days, a growing influence in the church of false and unsound doctrine and false and unsound spiritual leadership. Unlearned, unstable, and wrongly motivated individuals will continue to secure positions of spiritual leadership. They will twist the scriptures and promote unsound doctrine, drawing believers away from sound doctrine and healthy local bodies unto themselves. Seducing spirits will also endeavor to introduce doctrines of demons to unsuspecting believers and ministers, especially those who are hungry for spiritual things.

Second: By sounding out a warning, I hope to put you in a defensive and watchful spiritual posture. I will warn you to take heed, to beware, and to be on guard so that you will not be seduced into false doctrines or taken advantage of by unsound spiritual leaders. When you become aware of the potential spiritual danger of false doctrine and false spiritual leadership, you will want to prepare yourself to judge.

Third: I will give you clear and straightforward Bible teaching about the important spiritual activity called judging. You will learn that the teaching, "Judge not that ye be not judged," does not apply to the examination, evaluation, and scrutiny of doctrine and spiritual leadership. You will learn, rather, that you are not only permitted to judge, but that you are responsible to judge and capable of judging in these areas. You will also learn *how* to judge doctrine and spiritual leadership. Knowing how to judge will enable you to avoid the deception, instability, and spiritual sickness that is inevitable if believers become involved in unsound doctrine or follow false spiritual leadership.

OUTLINE

In Section One, you will learn what the church situation will be like in the latter days. The Word of God contains many prophetic words about these last days, especially concerning the rise of unsound doctrine and false spiritual leadership. I will expose Satan's latter day strategy to infiltrate the church with unsound doctrine and unsound spiritual leadership. He hopes, by influencing these two strategic areas of spiritual life, to undermine believers and local churches, and thus, the will of God. You will also be introduced to the serious warnings of four great New Testament teachers — Jesus, Paul, Peter, and John — concerning the end time rise of unsound doctrine and false spiritual leadership.

In Section Two, you will learn about the often misunderstood spiritual activity called judging. You will learn that there is a difference between being judgmental and objective judging. You will learn that judging doctrine and spiritual leadership is a necessary spiritual activity. You will also learn that your own spiritual health and stability is contingent upon your *willingness* and your *ability* to judge both spiritual leadership and doctrine.

In Section Three, you will learn about doctrine. First, you will learn about the significant place of sound doctrine in the spiritual life of the church. Then you will learn about different categories of unsound doctrine. Next, you will learn where unsound doctrine comes from and the unhealthy spiritual consequences which result from its promotion. Finally, you will learn how to judge doctrine.

In Section Four, you will learn about spiritual leadership. First, you will learn about different categories of false spiritual leaders. Then you will learn where they come from, what they want, how they gain places of leadership, and the dangerous results of their activities. Finally, you will learn how to judge spiritual leadership.

In Section Five, our study will be concluded and you will receive instructions about what specific actions to take after you have judged doctrine and spiritual leadership.

FINAL NOTE

I wrestled over whether or not to use modern day examples of unsound doctrine and unsound spiritual leadership to clarify the principles I was teaching. I decided to use some examples, but purposely avoided calling of any names. Although you may recognize individuals I refer to and be able to identify sources of the unsound doctrines I mention, it is not my intention to pick out any doctrine or person for ridicule. I do not fear, however, to question doctrine or leadership. Whoever and whatever is truly of God should stand the test of careful scrutiny.

It is my heartfelt desire that the spiritual health of believers, ministers, and local churches be preserved and enriched through the teachings of this book. Please read the following scripture prayerfully and ask the Holy Spirit to guide you as you study.

> *"They that are unlearned and unstable wrest...the scriptures, unto their own destruction. Ye therefore, beloved, seeing ye know these things before, beware lest ye also, being led away with the error of the wicked, fall from your own steadfastness. But grow in grace, and in the knowledge of our Lord and Saviour Jesus Christ. To him be glory both now and for ever. Amen."*

> *II Peter 3:16-18*

True or False

Judging Doctrine and Leadership

Section One

The Spiritual Scene of the Latter Days

II Timothy 3:1

*"This know also, that in the last days
perilous times shall come."*

·∽ 1 ∾·

Warning! Now Entering the Last of the Last Days

T here is no doubt that we are living in the last days. Nearly 2000 years ago the apostle John told his spiritual children, "Little children, it is the last time" [I John 2:18]. The apostle Peter reported that the outpouring of the Holy Spirit in Jerusalem was a fulfillment of Joel's prophesy that in the last days God would pour out His Spirit [Acts 2:7]. The whole church age, from the day of Pentecost till Jesus comes again, is considered to be the last days. We are perfectly correct, therefore, when we say that we are living in the last days.

Not only are we living in the last days, however. We are living in the *last* of the last days. We are nearing that moment when time as we know it will be no more. Foreboding signs have crested the horizon. Eternity is waiting in the wings. The kingdom of God is coming. Satan's days are numbered and his demise is eminent. The whole world, both Christian and non-Christian, senses the advent of significant change.

These final days will be different than former days. Of the final days the apostle Paul wrote, "This know also, that in the last days perilous times shall come" [II Timothy 3:1]. The word "perilous" means grievous, fierce, and hard to bear. The Amplified Bible says,

> "But understand this, that in the last days will come (set in) perilous times of great stress and trouble [hard to deal with and hard to bear]."
>
> II Timothy 3:1 Amp

Believers of this generation, believers of the last, last days, must understand that they will face difficulties and experience perilous times that believers in past generations did not face. In these final days there will be tribulation such as there has never been before and will never again be [Matthew 24:21]. Men's hearts will fail them because of fear. Because iniquity will abound, the love of many will grow cold. If these last days were not shortened, none would endure, not even the elect [Matthew 24:22].

One of the most significant last day's perils for believers will be the unprecedented rise of false spiritual leadership and the infiltration of unsound doctrine. This is a very serious hour for the church. It is a time to watch, to be aware, and to be prepared!

THE LATTER DAYS AND SPIRITUAL HUNGER

We are living at a time when there is a strong resurgence of spiritual hunger. Societies that have been built by human wisdom are realizing that their achievements and advances have produced no true or lasting satisfaction. Whole nations are being turned up side down, their ideologies exposed as failures. Questions are being pondered. People are searching for answers, hungry for the truth. Individuals are turning inward, looking for purpose and reality. Everywhere in the world there is a quest for truth. This is a season of spiritual hunger.

Spiritual hunger creates a vacuum which tends to draw all manner of spiritual leaders, teaching, and spiritual activity onto the scene. Wherever and whenever there are seekers, there will be men with answers to accommodate them. Self-appointed gurus of truth welcome searching individuals with open arms. Unless people are very careful, their own spiritual hunger will make them prey to self-appointed spiritual leaders who would love to have them as disciples in their movements.

In the church community there is a renewed hunger for spiritual reality. Men and women who have been bound for years in religion and dead churches are looking for something different. Some are experimenting with New Age doctrine and other spiritual teachings. Others, claiming to be Christians, are no longer committed to the teachings of the scriptures either in doctrine or Christian lifestyle. Some have drifted so far away from sound doctrine that they deny the virgin birth and doubt that Jesus was God in the flesh. Others hold to and endorse lifestyles that are far outside the boundaries of God's written Word. Some so-called Christians and so-called ministers are so "spiritually enlightened" that they no longer believe the Bible is the inspired Word of God!

Other believers are searching for supernatural experiences. Some who call themselves full gospel have gone well beyond the gospel by attempting to enter into more spiritual experiences. Some ministers, declaring, "God is doing a new thing," are seriously pushing the edge, sometimes going well over the edge, of what can be classified as sound doctrine. All these happenings are evidence that we are living in a season of spiritual hunger.

In 1989, I ministered in a country that had just reopened its doors to the gospel. Although I was ministering for one particular denomination, I met pastors from many other denominations. Almost without exception these pastors invited me to speak in their local churches. Without asking me any questions about what I believed or taught, they opened wide the doors to their sheepfolds. Why were they so anxious and so careless? It was because I was an American preacher and they were hungry for spiritual instruction. It did not surprise me to learn that many unsound men were vying for spiritual leadership in that country and that many unsound and strange doctrines had already been introduced there.

In a time of spiritual hunger the doors are wide open for individuals to come on the scene and promote their brand of spirituality. Everyone, including false spiritual leaders and the devil himself, will attempt to market their "goods" during this time. The unsound spiritual leaders and unsound doctrines that arise on the scene during a season of spiritual hunger are very detrimental to the stability and spiritual health of the church.

A time of spiritual hunger can be wonderful, but a time of spiritual hunger can also be very dangerous. If people are too hungry, they will eat anything! **If believers are too hungry for spiritual things, they will swallow anything and follow anyone!** A time of spiritual hunger, although exciting, is also a time for great caution.

THE LATTER DAYS AND SATAN'S STRATEGY

In this dispensation called the church age, God brings His will to pass through the church. Jesus revealed the tremendous potential of the church when He said,

> "...I will build my church; and the gates of hell shall not prevail against it."
> Matthew 16:18

The Amplified Bible says,

> "...I will build my church, and the gates of Hades (the powers of the infernal region) shall not overpower it [or be strong to its detriment, or hold out against it]."
> Matthew 16:18 Amp

When the church is mature and strong, it is effectual both in building the kingdom of God and in working against the kingdom of Satan. When the church is properly built, the power of Satan's kingdom will not overpower it, will not deter it, and will not hold out against it. This is a powerful truth! **When the church is built, it will prevail!**

Absolutely essential, however, to the proper building and maintaining of a sound and strong church is the guidance of sound spiritual leaders and the anointed teaching of sound doctrine. When the church is properly built upon sound doctrine and guided by mature spiritual leaders, it will come to maturity, remain strong, and be effective in its work.

The devil is worried because he understands this. He knows that when the church is properly built it will prevail against his kingdom. He also knows that the church is built by the anointed teaching of sound doctrine and the guidance of mature and sound spiritual leaders. A very important part of his ongoing strategy against the church, therefore, is to infiltrate it with unsound spiritual leaders and unsound doctrine. If Satan can succeed in this endeavor, the church will be weakened. If the church is weakened, it will not be able to prevail against his kingdom and it will not be able to fulfill the plan of God.

The Bible says that when the enemy comes in like a flood, the Spirit of the Lord raises up a standard against him [Isaiah 59:16]. It is also true, however, that when God begins to move by His Spirit, Satan will try to raise up a flood! When Moses, God's instrument of deliverance in his generation, was about to be born, Satan made sure that the king was stirred up to destroy all the babies. When Jesus was about to be born, Satan made sure that king Herod was stirred up to destroy all the babies. In these last days, when God purposes to bring deliverance to the world through the church, Satan will be at work to destroy her or, at least, to keep her from coming to maturity, so that she cannot fulfill the will of God.

You see, Satan cannot directly oppose God. He already tried that and was thrown out of heaven. Satan can, however, oppose the church. Because he is the god of this world and the church is in this world, he has a legal right to attempt to deceive, mislead, tempt, persecute, and do anything else to hinder the church from being what God wants it to be and from doing what God wants it to do. **The way that Satan opposes God's plans and purposes in the earth is by attempting to undermine the growth and spiritual stability of the church.**

Satan's Strategy To Infiltrate The Church

In these last days, God plans to pour out His Spirit upon the church and move through her to bring in the final harvest of souls. In these last days, however, Satan will endeavor to thwart God's plan by weakening the church. How does Satan plan to weaken the church of the last days? Will he do it through persecution? Will he do it through confrontation? Will he do it through warfare? All these methods may be a part of his plan, but they are **not** the primary or most effective part.

In these latter days, Satan will employ a strategy that is calculated to weaken the church without raising the suspicion of the church. His strategy is to undermine, infiltrate, and in any way possible negatively affect the two most necessary elements for the growth and healthy spiritual life of the church. **These two elements necessary for building and maintaining the spiritual life of the church are sound spiritual leadership and sound doctrine.**

The option of confronting the church or persecuting the church is not advantageous for the devil. First, confrontation is too obvious. When Satan confronts the church, he exposes himself and his strategies. If his strategies are exposed, the church will be able to wage effective war against him. Second, when Satan confronts the church, believers bind together against him. One of the most universally unifying factors in life is attack. A family at war with itself will quickly unify if one of its members is attacked from the outside. A divided nation will quickly unify if it is attacked by another nation. This same principle is true concerning the church. If it is confronted, it will unify. A united church is strong and will prevail!

The careful introduction of unsound doctrine and the covert infiltration of false spiritual leadership, on the other hand, has several key advantages for the devil. First, careful infiltration is not obvious. It is very possible that believers will accept, without question, carefully disguised false spiritual leaders and carefully introduced unsound doctrines. Second, infiltration will divide the church. Some believers will join the unsound leaders who desire to build their own followings. Some will join themselves to divisive and unsound doctrines. Any kingdom (including the church) that is divided against itself cannot stand.

Many years ago, Russian strategists who were scheming the rise of the Russian empire and the overthrow of other nations said that they would destroy the United States, not through military might, but through the slow and careful introduction of propaganda. By carefully introducing and promoting their doctrines, they intended to weaken and cripple the United States without raising her suspicion.

This same strategy can be effectively applied in the spiritual realm. Since Satan will not be able to cause dedicated believers of the last days to *backslide* through confrontation, he will attempt to cause them to *sideslip* into spiritual error by seducing them away from sound spiritual leadership, sound doctrine, and sound local churches. **It will be just as difficult for the church to win her race if she falls into the spiritual ditch as it would be if she quit running!**

Satan will try to weaken the church of the last days by infiltrating it with unsound spiritual leaders and unsound doctrine. If unsound spiritual leaders gain a foothold and unsound doctrine gains acceptance, the church will become unsound. **An unsound church cannot work effectually or wage a winning war.**

WHAT ABOUT SPIRITUAL WARFARE?

In the past few years there has been a strong emphasis on the teaching called Spiritual Warfare. This teaching encourages believers to become aggressive and offensive, doing warfare with the devil and his demons. This teaching asserts that the devil is warring aggressively against the church and that believers should resist him just as aggressively. Some Christians are "pulling down demonic strongholds" through the avenue of aggressive prayer and militant worship. Some are even wearing military fatigues while they spend hours "warring" (shouting, praying loud in other tongues, shaking fists, and stomping) against the devil.

The truth of the matter, however, is that confrontation has never been Satan's forte. **The devil is first and foremost a deceiver!** The strong emphasis on spiritual warfare may well be turning the church's attention away from Satan's real strategy. While believers are busy shaking their fists at him, shadow boxing with him, and shouting at him, he is scheming to lure believers, churches, and even ministers away from sound doctrine and sound spiritual leadership. Mature believers should realize that when dealing with the Deceiver, it is not wise to give their full attention to the obvious. While some ministers and believers are transfixed with the obvious, Satan is invading the church and undermining her true defenses.

Two Old Testament Battles

In the Old Testament, there are two battles that illustrate the last day's strategy of the devil against the church. The accounts of these two battles can be found in Joshua 8:10-29 and Judges 20:28-48.

Joshua verses Ai

In the battle that Joshua fought against Ai, he devised a specific offensive strategy. On the night before the planned attack, he secretly positioned a small band of men called "liars in ambush" behind the city. Then he set the majority of his army in an obvious attacking position in front of the city. When morning arrived, the king of Ai saw the large part of Joshua's army encamped against the city in striking position. Without hesitation, the army of Ai marched out against Joshua's army and engaged them in battle. Let's read how this battle unfolded,

"...when the king of Ai saw it...the men of the city went out against Israel to battle...but he wist (knew) not that there were liars in ambush against him behind the city. And Joshua and all Israel made as if they were beaten before them, and fled by the way of the wilderness. And all the people that were in Ai were called together to pursue after them: and they pursued after Joshua, and were drawn away

*from the city. And there was not a man left in Ai or Bethel, that went not out after
Israel: and they left the city open, and pursued after Israel."*

Joshua 8:14-17

When the men of Ai beheld the obvious frontal attack Joshua had set
in place, they were stirred to action and rushed out immediately to engage
the battle. In fact, "all the people that were in Ai were called together to
pursue." As a result of their aggressive pursuit, they, "were drawn away from
the city." Once the inhabitants of Ai had been drawn away from their city
and completely engrossed in the frontal attack, Joshua gave a pre-arranged
signal to the "liars in ambush" hiding behind the city. These men arose out
of their place, entered into the deserted city, plundered it, and set it on fire.
Notice the response of the men of Ai when they realized what had happened,

*"And when the men of Ai looked behind them, they saw, and, behold, the smoke
of the city ascended up to heaven, and they had no power to flee this way or that
way..."*

Joshua 8:20

The inhabitants of Ai failed to discern Joshua's strategy. They did not
realize that there were liars in ambush secretly positioned behind their city.
Consequently, they, "left the city open." They abandoned their most important position and left their most valued possessions unguarded. This proved
to be a fatal error.

The disastrous decision to abandon the city was primarily the responsibility of the king of Ai. Unfortunately, he was a poor leader, a terrible tactician, and a gullible warrior. When he saw the armies of Israel and heard
the sound of battle, he could not restrain himself from plunging into the
conflict. While his head was in the conflict, however, his city was plundered
and overtaken.

Israel verses the Children of Benjamin

In a similar battle story, the army of Israel attacked the children of Benjamin. Like Joshua, they secretly set "liars in wait" behind the city on the
night before the frontal attack. When they brought their obvious frontal
attack against the city, the children of Benjamin responded and engaged the
battle. As soon as the children of Benjamin were thoroughly committed to
the battle, the people of Israel said this,

"...Let us flee, and draw them from the city unto the highways."

Judges 20:32

When the army of Israel began to retreat as if being defeated, the children of Benjamin began to pursue them. Once the children of Benjamin

had completely abandoned their city, the children of Israel gave a pre-determined signal and the "liars in wait" rose up and ambushed the unde-fended city.

While the children of Benjamin pursued a diversion, their city was ambushed and set on fire. When they turned around and saw what had happened, "they were amazed: for they saw that evil was come upon them" [Judges 20:41]. Because they had carelessly rushed into battle, the children of Benjamin lost their city and, being surrounded in front and behind by the armies of Israel, lost the battle. The Bible records of the children of Benjamin that,

> "*...they knew not that evil was near them.*"
>
> Judges 20:34

The Amplified Bible says,

> "*...the Benjamites did not know disaster was close upon them.*"
>
> Judges 20:34 Amp

The Benjamites knew they were in a battle. They failed, however, to discern the strategy of the enemy! If they had known about the liars in wait, they would not have foolishly given all their attention to the obvious frontal attack. They would have stayed in their city.

Defending Our City

In both of these battles the offensive strategy was the same. The attacking army drew the defending army out of its city by the means of a diversionary frontal attack. Once the city was abandoned, a few hidden men plundered it from the rear.

The key to this offensive strategy was drawing the defending army out of its city. If the defending army remained in its city, the odds would be against the attacking army. If, however, the defending army could be drawn out, the city could be plundered from behind and the battle won. Drawing a defending army out of its city by the means of a diversionary frontal attack was a very wise and deceptive military strategy.

The church could learn a very valuable lesson from these two stories. Most of us realize that we are in a war with Satan and his hosts. Often, however, we fail to discern the strategies of the devil. Like the men of Benjamin, we do not realize how dangerous and perilous our situation really is. We discern Satan's obvious attacks (like drug problems, sexual promiscuity, demonic possession, and disease), but fail to realize that the devil is a Liar in wait!

The strategy that Joshua employed against Ai and that Israel employed against Benjamin is one strategy the devil will employ against the church. He will attack in obvious ways, hoping that believers give full attention to what is, unbeknownst to them, a diversionary tactic. If complete attention is given to the frontal attack, he will be able to successfully launch his secret rear assault. He will signal his "liars in wait" and they will attack from their hiding place. By the time believers "turn around" and realize what is happening, it will be too late. We will have been deceived by a keen strategist and, by his strategy, defeated.

The strong "city" that Satan wants to draw believers away from is sound spiritual leadership and sound doctrine. As long as believers remain **in the truth** and **with** sound spiritual leaders, the church will be safe and sound. If, however, believers abandon these two essential areas of safety, Satan will have success against the church. His secret attack against the church is a two-pronged rear assault upon spiritual leadership and sound doctrine.

The church of this generation may be in danger of making the same mistake that Ai and the children of Benjamin made when they allowed themselves to be deceived and drawn away from their city. We are not carefully guarding our most important position and our most valuable assets. Some believers, in their aggressive and heated pursuit of the devil's frontal attacks, have abandoned the **"Not to be abandoned!"** areas of sound doctrine and sound spiritual leadership. If these two areas of spiritual life are "plundered," the church will have lost her greatest place of refuge and her greatest source of direction and spiritual strength!

King David, normally a brilliant commander in chief, once made the tragic error of abandoning his city. Errantly, he committed himself and all his mighty men to king Achish for a battle that was not even theirs. By so doing, he left his own city of Ziklag undefended. While David and his men were out preparing for another man's war, their own city was plundered and burned and their women and children carried away [I Samuel 29:1-30:19]. When David and his men returned to Ziklag and saw the devastation of their city, they were overcome with grief. The Bible says,

> "...*David and the people that were with him lifted up their voice and wept, until they had no more power to weep.*"
>
> I Samuel 30:4

David's men wanted to stone him because of his foolish decision to leave their city undefended. Fortunately, he was able to encourage himself in the Lord and go forth to recover all that was lost.

Could it be that the church of this generation is looking the wrong direction? Yes, there are obvious Satanic attacks at our front door. But is there a more subtle, yet devastating, conflict at our back door? While we are busy responding to Satan's obvious maneuvers, is he positioning himself for his main maneuver? The church of this hour must be careful not to be deceived by Satan's obvious frontal attacks. We must not abandon our "city." We must not abandon the very important areas of sound doctrine and sound spiritual leadership!

Hopefully the church of this generation will not have to wonder how she could have failed to discern the schemes of the devil. Hopefully the church of the future will not look back to the church of this generation and ask, "Why couldn't they see the strategy of Satan?" Hopefully the church of the next generation will not have to be re-built because the spiritual leaders and believers of this generation, "left the city open" [Joshua 8:17].

Anyone can discern the strategy of an enemy when it has fully unfolded. But that is too late! The church must discern the strategy of the enemy **before** it unfolds and prepare her defenses accordingly! Let us not "get off" in an attempt to "go on!" Stay in the city! Stay with the sound doctrines of the Word of God! Stay submitted to sound spiritual leadership! And stay ready to defend the church, both against obvious frontal attacks and against secret ambushment!

DECEPTION — THE DEVIL'S MAIN TACTIC

Never forget this: The devil is a deceiver! He is a clever tactician, a skilled strategist. Concerning his method of warfare, Satan should not be thought of as some muscled hulk that lumbers into battle with both arms swinging. He doesn't put guns in both hands and blow himself into our midst like some kind of Rambo character. Satan is more like the wizard in the Wizard of Oz. He watches from his well chosen vantage point and manipulates his forces in carefully planned strategies. He is more like a man at the chess board than a man in the boxing ring. His greatest chance for victory is to outwit and outmaneuver his opponent.

Concerning Satan and his strategies God warns believers to, "Be sober, be vigilant" [I Peter 5:8]. To be vigilant means to be watchful, to be aware, and to be wide awake. The church must remain spiritually sharp. Her conflict with the devil is more comparable to a battle of the wits than to a battle of strength. That is why the Word of God warns believers to be aware of the schemes, or wiles, of the devil. If Satan only attempted obvious frontal attacks, we would not need to be cautious of his tactics. Interestingly, however, the Word of God never cautions believers to beware of the power of the enemy. Rather, it warns believers to beware of his tactical and scheming ability!

Make no mistake. A significant part of Satan's last days strategy is to mislead and weaken the church by the infiltration of false leadership and the promotion of unsound doctrine. Deception is not a new strategy for the devil. It has always been his favorite tactic. No doubt he employed deception in leading one third of the angels of God in his revolt. He certainly employed deception in the Garden of Eden. Through it he gained power over the human race. Satan will definitely employ this favorite strategy in these last days. At the end of this age he will be known as, "that old serpent, called the Devil, and Satan, which deceiveth the whole world" [Revelation 12:9].

Church, watch out! Direct confrontation is not the devil's primary *modus operandi*! His strategies against the people of God have **always** been based on deception. In these last days when God wants to move in a powerful way to bring in the final harvest of lost souls, it should not surprise us that the devil will attempt to mislead the church through false leadership and unsound doctrine.

THE CHURCH OF THE LAST DAYS

The church of this generation is living in exciting times. The curtain is being drawn on time as we know it. God is planning to move in great ways to bring in the final harvest. These are days of excitement, but they must also be days of great caution.

The last days are a time of renewed spiritual hunger. Spiritual hunger can be good, but it can also be very dangerous. There will be plenty of tempting "food" in this generation. If believers are too hungry, they will eat anything. In these last days, Satan and his cohorts will employ every strategy they know against the church. The strategy of deception, however, one of the devil's favorites, will be on the **forefront** of his end-time warfare agenda.

The combination of the spiritual hunger of this generation and the last days strategy of the devil makes for a very dangerous spiritual climate. **Believers: Be excited! BUT BEWARE!**

·~2~·
Four Men's Warnings!

I t is no coincidence that the four most prominent spiritual leaders of the New Testament — Jesus, Paul, Peter, and John — each issued distinct and strong warnings about the dangers of false doctrine and false spiritual leadership. Not only did they alert believers of their own generation to this impending danger; they prophesied of its proliferation in the last days. These true spiritual leaders were very aware of the potential dangers of false doctrine and unsound spiritual leadership, straightforward and candid in their warnings about it, and clear in their teachings on how to deal with it. Repeatedly, they used words like, "beware," "take heed," and, "watch," fully intending to put their hearers in a defensive spiritual posture. The reason these New Testament leaders dealt so pointedly and forthrightly with this problem was because they understood that more than any outside force, false spiritual leaders and unsound doctrine have the potential to ruin believers and devastate local churches.

Recently, there was a prediction of an earthquake within a few hundred miles of where I live. On the basis of this prediction, my insurance agent called to ask me if I would like to buy earthquake insurance. I decided to heed the warning and insured myself against earthquake damage. Fortunately, the prediction was wrong and the earthquake never occurred. If I had not been warned and the earthquake had occurred, I could have suffered catastrophic losses. Because I was forewarned, however, I had the opportunity to prepare. If the earthquake had occurred, my losses would have been covered.

Warnings are issued so that people can prepare themselves against the dangers predicted. If warnings are not issued, people will be taken by surprise. Trouble will be eminent and destruction probable. This is why the four most prominent spiritual leaders of the New Testament sounded forth strong warnings concerning unsound doctrine and unsound spiritual leadership. It was so that believers and local churches in every generation would **be aware** and **could prepare!**

Is it possible for believers to be misled by false spiritual leaders or seduced into unsound doctrine? Yes, absolutely! This is precisely the reason Jesus and other New Testament church leaders gave such strong warnings. They knew that if believers were not warned, they could come under the dangerous influence of false doctrine and fall victim to the wiles of false and unsound spiritual leaders.

It is significant that the strongest caution words in the Bible are reserved for warnings of false spiritual leadership and false doctrine. Concerning false spiritual leadership the Word of God says, "**beware!**" Concerning unsound doctrine the Word of God says, "**beware!**" Why does the Word of God say to, "**beware?**" So that believers can be aware, watchful and prepared.

It is imperative that believers heed the serious warnings concerning unsound doctrine and false spiritual leadership. Foreknowledge of a potential disaster offers an opportunity to educate and properly prepare one's self so that the dangers which lie ahead can be avoided! If believers heed the warnings concerning unsound doctrine and false spiritual leadership and prepare themselves accordingly, they will not be the victims of deception. Let's look now at the specific warnings of four great spiritual leaders concerning the latter day rise of unsound doctrine and false spiritual leadership.

JESUS' WORDS OF WARNING

Early in His teaching ministry, Jesus spoke a solemn warning concerning false spiritual leadership. He said to His disciples,

"**Beware** of false prophets, which come to you in sheep's clothing, but inwardly they are ravening wolves."

Matthew 7:15

Jesus used the strong and attention grabbing word "beware" to put His disciples on alert. This word comes from the Greek *prosecho* and means to give attention to something by being on guard against it. It means to be alert and aware. It means to pay attention so as not to be snared, captured, taken advantage of, or abused. "Beware" is a strong term. Equally strong was Jesus' unabashed categorization of false spiritual leaders as ravening wolves. He intended to raise an immediate concern and a posture of defensiveness within the disciples. You see, some false spiritual leaders and false doctrines will look so right and sound so spiritual that without warnings to put us on guard, we would not suspect or detect them. Believers are not to be *unaware*, but are to *beware*. They are to keep alert and watch out for false spiritual leaders and unsound doctrine.

Later in His ministry, near the time of His departure from earth, Jesus began to instruct His disciples of several important matters they would need to remember after He had left. One question the disciples asked Jesus during this time concerned when the end would come and when He would return to earth. They said to Jesus,

> "...when shall these things be? and what shall be the sign of thy coming, and of the end of the world?"
>
> *Matthew 24:3*

Jesus' first response to the disciples concerning the signs of His coming and of the end of time is very revealing. His first words were a warning of false spiritual leadership. He said,

> "...**Take heed** that no man deceive you. For many shall come in my name, saying, I am Christ; and shall deceive many."
>
> *Matthew 24:4-5*

When the disciples asked Jesus about the signs of the end times, His **first response** was a warning about false leaders and their deceptive teachings. This response not only put His disciples on guard, but revealed that one of the most significant spiritual dangers of the last days is the proliferation of false spiritual leadership.

Jesus also said this to His disciples,

> "And **many false prophets shall rise, and shall deceive many**."
>
> *Matthew 24:11*

In this warning there are two points we cannot ignore. First, Jesus said, "*many false prophets shall arise*." Second, He said they, "shall deceive *many*." As we move toward the last days, the uprising of false spiritual leadership will be a significant problem. Many shall come in Jesus' name claiming to be called and anointed of God. Many false prophets shall arise. These many false spiritual leaders will deceive many. **The uprising of false spiritual leaders and the infiltration of unsound doctrine is going to be a major problem for the church of the last days.** This is why Jesus issued such forthright and strong warnings.

The same conversation between Jesus and His disciples is recorded in the gospel of Mark. When the disciples asked Jesus, "what shall be the sign when all these things shall be fulfilled," Jesus answered,

"...Take heed lest any man deceive you...For false Christs and false prophets shall rise, and shall show signs and wonders, to seduce, if it were possible, even the elect. But take heed: behold, I have foretold you all things."

Mark 13:5; 22-23

Jesus said, "Take heed." These words imply an intent and earnest contemplation. They mean to stay awake, to keep one's spiritual eyes open, to watch out. The Amplified Bible says, "Be careful and watchful." The words, "Be careful," are reserved for situations that are potentially dangerous. "Be careful," says a mother when her young daughter crosses the street. "Be careful," says a father when his son uses the chain saw. "Be careful," say parents when their children walk to school. And, "Be careful," says our Father, our Lord, and the Holy Spirit, concerning the end time rise of false spiritual leadership and unsound doctrine.

Disciples Beware

It is significant that Jesus was speaking to His own disciples when He gave these warnings. Even though they had been carefully selected and trained and were destined to be spiritual leaders in the church, Jesus warned them to beware of false spiritual leaders and their deceptive teachings! The fact that Jesus warned His own disciples does not mean that only Christians will be deceived by unsound doctrine and false spiritual leaders. Jesus' warnings do, however, apply to disciples!

Jesus' warnings not only applied to the disciples of His day. They also apply to disciples who live in these last days. His warnings have travelled the corridors of time right up to this present hour. In fact, they are more pertinent now than ever before in view of the nearness of the end of time. According to Jesus, the last days will be characterized by the rise of dangerous false spiritual leaders and their deceptive teachings. False christs and false prophets will not only target sinners, but will attempt to deceive, "even the elect." Even sound believers from sound local churches will be targets for demonic doctrines and false spiritual leaders.

Jesus concluded His words of warning to His disciples by saying, "behold, I have foretold you." These words were a final note of caution. He was saying, "I have warned you ahead of time of what will happen, so be careful!" With His warnings, Jesus awakens all believers to the reality that ungodly men will put on sheep's clothing and speak good sounding words to gain positions of spiritual leadership. He also awakens believers to the reality that deceptive teaching will rise up in the church. Christians, we have been foretold. With the early disciples, we must be alert and prepared so that we are not deceived and misled by false spiritual leaders or unsound doctrines.

Believers of the last days should expect to encounter false spiritual leaders who make claims like, "I am anointed," or, "I have a special calling from God," or, "God gave me a vision and told me to tell you." Believers of the last days should also expect to encounter unsound doctrine. Not only unsound ministers, but also seducing spirits will promote it in these last days. Believers who do not expect to encounter false spiritual leadership and unsound doctrine are prime candidates for deception. If, however, believers watch out for and, without being paranoid, judge doctrine and judge those who claim to be spiritual leaders, they will remain safe, sound, and steadfast in the faith and in Christian life.

PAUL'S WORDS OF WARNING

Paul gave us a foretaste of the spiritual climate of the last days in his second letter to Timothy. There he wrote,

> "This know also, that in the last days perilous times shall come...evil men and seducers shall wax worse and worse, deceiving and being deceived."
>
> II Timothy 3:1,13

Paul said, "This know also, that in the last days." There are some facts Christians **must** know about the last days. We must know that perilous times will come, not only because of natural calamity, but also because of evil men. We must know that spiritual seducers will get worse and worse. We must know that Satan will dispatch false spiritual leaders who will give every appearance of being ministers of light. We must know that wolves in sheep's clothing will endeavor to lead the church into spiritual bankruptcy through false teaching. We must know that seducing spirits will endeavor to draw believers away from sound doctrine and into doctrines of demons. We must know that believers will be deceived and will become deceivers of others. The Amplified Bible renders Paul's words to Timothy this way,

> "But understand this, that in the last days will come (set in) perilous times of great stress and trouble [hard to deal with and hard to bear]...wicked men and impostors will go on from bad to worse, deceiving and leading astray others and being deceived and led astray themselves."
>
> II Timothy 3:1,13 Amp

Believers must understand that the last days will be days of, "great stress and trouble." Impostors, said Paul, those pretending to be spiritual leaders, "will go from bad to worse." They will deceive. They will be deceived. They will lead believers astray. They will be led astray themselves.

Spiritually, the last days will be perilous days. They will be exacting days, "hard to deal with and hard to bear." They will be days that test men's spiritual mettle. All will not be so clear as it was before. What were once clear boundaries concerning doctrine and Christian lifestyle will be smeared. Men who could once be trusted because they claimed to be called of God may be impostors. Believers, be ready! You have been forewarned!

Paul not only *warned* Timothy about deceivers and deception. He also *taught* him how to remain steadfast and unaffected. Immediately following his warning, Paul offered Timothy these words of positive instruction,

> *"But continue thou in the things which thou hast learned…And that from a child thou has known the holy scriptures…"*
>
> II Timothy 3:14-15

Rather than following spiritual seducers or new doctrines that came on the scene, Timothy was to continue steadfast in what he had already learned. He was to hold fast to the holy scriptures. If he maintained a firm grasp on the written Word of God, he would remain free from seducers and deceivers.

Paul also penned these very somber words to Timothy concerning the last days,

> *"Now the Spirit speaketh expressly, that in the latter times some shall depart from the faith, giving heed to seducing spirits, and doctrines of devils; Speaking lies in hypocrisy…"*
>
> I Timothy 4:1

The Spirit of God, said Paul, "speaketh expressly" about the latter days. He has sounded forth a very clear and unmistakable warning. His message is distinct; it cannot be misinterpreted or misunderstood. What is it that the Holy Spirit has so clearly declared?

The Holy Spirit has declared that in the latter days seducing spirits will attempt to seduce believers away from sound faith by the means of doctrines of demons. Some believers, perhaps even sound ministers, will pay attention to the demons and seducing spirits Satan has commissioned to lead them into unsound doctrine. They will leave the body of sound believers and the body of sound teaching in which they were once established. Then they will become the promoters of the false teachings they have accepted, "speaking lies in hypocrisy." They will mix truth with error, teach doctrines that sound spiritual but are false, and hide their lies behind a hypocritical lifestyle so that their deception will not be detected.

Paul prefaced this prophetic declaration concerning the last days with the words, "The Spirit speaketh expressly," to insure that Timothy would pay very strict attention to the message which followed. This prophetic message of the Holy Spirit concerning the latter days was not, however, only for Timothy. This message was safeguarded by God, recorded in the scriptures, and delivered to us who live in this present hour. Believers of this generation must seriously consider this message. What the Holy Spirit prophesied concerning the latter days **will** happen! But will we be ready?

To the Church in Ephesus

Before leaving the church at Ephesus, a church he had ministered to for three years, Paul issued a very strong warning concerning false spiritual leadership. In his final address to the elders of this church, he said,

> "For I have not shunned to declare unto you all the counsel of God. **Take heed** therefore unto yourselves, and to all the flock...**For I know this**, that after my departing shall grievous wolves enter in among you, not sparing the flock...Therefore **watch**, and remember, that by the space of **three years I ceased not to warn every one night and day with tears.**"
>
> Acts 20:27-31

Paul said, "Take heed...for I know this." Why was Paul concerned? Why did he give this warning? What did Paul know? Paul knew that false spiritual leaders, grievous wolves, would attempt to infiltrate the local church in Ephesus. How did he know this? Had the Holy Spirit given him a vision of the future? Had God revealed something special to him about this particular church? Was Paul's message a specific word of prophesy or was it a general warning?

Most likely, Paul was not delivering a word of personal prophesy to these elders. Rather, he was delivering a general warning. He knew from past experiences that when he left this local church, false spiritual leaders would attempt to infiltrate it. Paul's warning was a prediction of what would happen if the Holy Ghost chosen leaders and the rest of the church did not, "Take heed." Paul anticipated trouble from false spiritual leaders and, therefore, warned the local church at Ephesus.

Paul exhorted the elders in Ephesus to a two-fold course of action. First, they were to *feed the flock* with sound doctrine. This would mature the believers, making them strong and steadfast. Second, they were to *guard the flock* from the intrusion of wolves. Evidently, the elders in Ephesus listened well to Paul's warning because at a later time Jesus commended this local church for judging those who claimed to be apostles, but were liars [Revelation 2:2].

Paul warned a local church in his generation of the danger of wolves, of false spiritual leaders. The activity of false spiritual leadership and the infiltration of unsound doctrine is, however, an issue for the church in every generation. Paul knew it and we should know it. **False spiritual leaders and**

unsound doctrine will come! For this reason true spiritual leaders and all believers must remain cautious, sober, and vigilant.

To Other Local Churches

To the believers in Colosse, Paul wrote,

*"And this I say, lest any man should beguile you with enticing words...**Beware** lest any man spoil you..."*

Colossians 2:4, 8

Paul warned the believers in Colosse that men would attempt to beguile them by the means of enticing words. What word did Paul use to caution these believers? He said, "Beware!" This word is used repeatedly by New Testament spiritual leaders concerning false spiritual leadership and unsound doctrine.

Paul addressed the local church at Corinth concerning false apostles and false teachers in their midst. To them he said,

*"I write not these things to shame you, but as my beloved sons **I warn you**. For though ye have ten thousand instructors in Christ, yet have ye not many fathers..."*

I Corinthians 4:14-15

Again, we find words that are obviously intended to grasp attention. "I warn you," Paul said to the believers at Corinth. A true servant and apostle of Christ, Paul was afraid that these believers would follow wrong teaching and be misled by false spiritual leaders.

Warnings of false spiritual leadership and unsound doctrine were a prominent theme in all Paul's letters. He reprimanded and warned the churches of Galatia of their involvement with false spiritual leaders and the false gospel they promoted [Galatians 1:8; 3:1-3; 5:7-12]. He encouraged the church at Thessalonica not to be deceived, "by any means" [II Thessalonians 2:3]. He instructed the church at Rome to mark those who caused divisions contrary to the doctrine they had learned [Romans 16:17]. In almost every epistle, Paul brought believer's attention to the dangers of false spiritual leadership and unsound doctrine. He informed them to *be aware* and to *beware* of false spiritual leaders and of unsound teaching.

PETER'S WORDS OF WARNING

In his second epistle, Peter penned these words concerning false teachers and their heretical doctrines,

*"But there were false prophets also among the people (in the Old Testament), even as **there shall be false teachers among you**, who privily shall bring in*

damnable heresies...*And many shall follow their pernicious ways...And through covetousness shall they with feigned words make merchandise of you...*"

II Peter 2:1-3

Although Peter's words were written to a specific group of believers in a specific place at a specific time, they are a *now word* for the church of every generation and in every place. Peter said, "there **shall** be false teachers among you." He said they, "**shall** bring in damnable heresies." He said, "many **shall** follow their pernicious ways." He said, "through covetousness **shall** they...make merchandise of you." Peter's warning is clear, direct, and absolute. **It shall be so!**

Peter's words concern something that has always been and will always be a problem among the people of God. There were false prophets among God's people in the Old Testament. There were false teachers among the New Testament churches. And there **will** be false leaders among the churches or this generation. Human nature and the schemes of Satan insure it. Wherever you find the people of God, you will find those who will, through claims of spiritual superiority and by handling the Word of God deceitfully, infiltrate the church with false doctrine and make merchandise of the people of God.

Peter's warning is a word of wisdom to believers in this generation just as it was a word of wisdom to the believers of his day. There will be false teachers and other false spiritual leaders, not only in our time, but also in our midst! They will introduce unsound doctrines, perhaps even damnable heresies, into the church. Although they are false and their doctrine is unsound, "many shall follow their pernicious ways." Many of the many who follow unsound doctrine and unsound spiritual leaders will be those who have not *heard* or have not *heeded* the clear New Testament warnings concerning false doctrine and false leadership or who have not *learned* how to judge doctrine and leadership. Precaution in these last days concerning doctrine and spiritual leadership will prove to be a priceless boon to those who exercise it.

What Peter wrote in this scripture, although he did not use the specific word "warning" is clearly a warning to the church. The issue of unsound doctrine and unsound spiritual leadership is not to be taken lightly. Spiritual stability and wholeness are at stake. Truth is at stake. The reputation of Christianity and the Truth is at stake! In every generation and in every place believers must be warned about false spiritual leadership and unsound doctrine and instructed how to judge.

JOHN'S WORDS OF WARNING

In his first epistle, the apostle John made a statement which identified one of his main purposes for writing. He said,

"These things have I written unto you concerning them that seduce you."
I John 2:26

One of the primary reasons John penned his epistle to his beloved spiritual children was to warn them of the seductive activities of false spiritual leaders. He wanted to be sure that they were aware of what was going on. His intention was not to make these believers afraid, but to bring them to spiritual attention. In this same epistle, John wrote,

"Little children, it is the last time: and as ye have heard that antichrist shall come, even now there are many antichrists; whereby we know that it is the last time."
I John 2:18

According to the apostle John, the presence and influence of antichrists, of false spiritual leaders, is one of the characteristics of the last days. He said, "whereby (because of the presence of antichrists) we know that it is the last time." In the last days there will be "many antichrists." These many antichrists will attempt to seduce sound believers *away from* sound spiritual leadership, sound doctrine, and sound local churches and *into* their erroneous teachings and unsound spiritual life.

Some false spiritual leaders, according to John, will be those who, "went out from us" [I John 2:19]. Not all false spiritual leaders will be unconventional or eccentric gurus. Some will be former members or even former sound leaders in the church! If believers do not carefully examine those who claim to be spiritual leaders, some once sound, but now unsound spiritual leaders could slip undetected into the church.

John not only warned his spiritual children to beware of false spiritual leaders and unsound doctrine, he also instructed them to test spiritual leaders and doctrine. He wrote,

*"Beloved, **believe not** every spirit, but **try** (test) the spirits whether they are of God: because many false prophets are gone out into the world."*
I John 4:1

John's message to his spiritual children was, "Don't believe everyone and everything you hear!" What then should be their attitude? They should test, try, weigh, and evaluate what was said and who was saying it to determine whether it or they be of God, of the devil, or of men. John's warning not only reveals that believers are *permitted* judge, but implies that they are *expected* to judge.

The Holy Spirit, knowing that believers in every generation would encounter false spiritual leadership and unsound doctrine, inspired John to sound forth a note of warning. False ministers and their unsound doctrines will be part of the spiritual scene of the church, especially in the last days. They are, according to John, one of the signs of the times. If you know this, you can be aware and beware!

FINAL WARNING!

Warning! There will be, in these last days, a rise in false doctrine! **Warning!** There will be, in these last days, a proliferation of false spiritual leaders who will endeavor to mislead you!

The infiltration of false spiritual leaders and false doctrine into the church has always been and will always be a problem. This problem was already prevalent when the first epistles were written. Already, at her young age, the church was having to deal with the grim reality of the invasion of false teachers and false doctrine. At a time when she should have been spiritually sound and unshakable from the excellent foundational teachings and spiritual leadership of Jesus, Paul, Peter, and John, warnings had to be given and action had to be taken.

The infiltration of false leadership and false doctrine was not only a problem for the early churches; it will be a problem for the church in this generation. For this reason, believers who live in these latter days must pay special attention to the clear warnings concerning false spiritual leadership and unsound doctrine. Acquaintance with these warnings will set believers in a posture of carefulness and watchfulness.

To *watch* does not mean to launch a covert operation against every teacher, pastor, and evangelist in the body of Christ. To *watch* does not mean to scrutinize everything every person says hoping to find something wrong. To *watch* simply means to stay alert so that if you do encounter something false, you will recognize it. Carefulness and watchfulness concerning doctrine and spiritual leadership will position believers of these last day in a place of spiritual safety.

Believers of this generation must be prepared without being paranoid. They must be alert without being afraid. They must be on guard without being on edge. They must be watchful without being worried. The church of this generation, nearer the end of time than ever before, must beware of unsound doctrine and false leadership and know how to judge them.

If believers of this generation do not watch for unsound doctrine and false leadership and learn how to judge, they will be candidates for spiritual instability and potential victims of deception. If, however, believers heed the warnings of Jesus, Paul, Peter, and John, the warnings of the Holy Spirit, and the warnings of the Word of God, they will have the *opportunity* and the *knowledge* to judge and will be able, thereby, to avoid the sure danger and possible destruction which results from of the infiltration of unsound doctrine and false spiritual leadership.

Believers beware! Watch for false spiritual leadership and unsound doctrine. Jesus issued this serious warning. Every important New Testament teacher issued this warning. The Spirit of God sounded forth this prophetic warning. This is a fact of the written scriptures. "Watch," "beware," and, "take heed," are the expressions of true spiritual leaders, of the Holy Spirit, and of the Word of God concerning unsound doctrine and false spiritual leadership. Do not be surprised if you encounter false doctrine and false leadership. You have been foretold!

Section Two

Preparing to Judge

I Corinthians 2:15

"But he that is spiritual judgeth all things."

·~3~·
Judge Not?

If you asked most believers, "Is it right for Christians to judge?" they would answer with a simple but firm, "No." Because the church has concentrated primarily on the teaching, "Judge not that ye be not judged," believers are often afraid to judge. They think that if they judge others, they will reap judgement from God.

What many Christians fail to realize, however, is that more than one activity can come under the heading of judging. It cannot be concluded that because one kind of judging is wrong, all kinds of judging are wrong. Neither can it be concluded that because judging is wrong in some situations, judging is wrong in every situation. Consequently, the answer to, "Is it right for Christians to judge?" depends upon what kind of judging one is asking about.

Some questions can be answered both yes and no. One question that could be answered both yes and no is, "Can you walk through a door?" If the door is to your own home or to a public restaurant, the answer would be, "Yes." If the door is to another person's home or to a bank vault, the answer could be, "No." Another question that could be answered both yes and no is, "Can you drive 55 mph?" Yes, you can drive 55 mph on a state highway. No, you cannot drive 55 mph on a city street.

Like the answer to these two questions, the answer to, "Is it right for Christians judge?" can be both No and Yes. No, Christians are not permitted to judge in the sense of criticizing and condemning other believers. Yes, Christians are permitted to judge in the sense of discerning, examining, and testing all things that pertain to the soundness of their own spiritual life. Yes, Christians can judge doctrine and spiritual leadership.

Christians must recognize the difference between the kind of judging the Word of God prohibits — that of being a self-appointed judge that pronounces guilty verdicts on other believer's lives — and the kind of judging the Word of God encourages — that judging which means to weigh, discern, search out, assess, and evaluate teachers and teaching to determine their true spiritual value. If Christians don't understand the difference between these two kinds of judging, they will either judge when they should not judge or fail to judge when they must judge!

In this chapter, you will learn the difference both in *attitude* and in *activity* between the kind of judging believers must not do and the kind of judging believers are responsible to do. To help separate between these two kinds of judging, I am going to designate the judging that Christians are not to engage in "Being Judgmental" and designate the judging Christians must engage in "Objective Judging." We will look briefly at the differences in attitude and activity between these two kinds of judging and then proceed to learn more specifically about believer's responsibility to judge doctrine and spiritual leadership.

BEING JUDGMENTAL

In Matthew 7:1-2, Jesus spoke these very familiar words,

> *"Judge not, that ye be not judged. For with what judgement ye judge, ye shall be judged..."*
>
> Matthew 7:1-2

The word "judge" Jesus used in this scripture comes from the Greek word *krino*. The meaning of this word includes both the examination of evidence and the pronouncement of a judgment. The uses of this verb in the New Testament include assuming the office of a judge [Matthew 7:1; John 3:17]; undergoing the process of a trial [John 3:18, 16:11; James 2:12]; giving sentence [Acts 15:19]; condemning [John 12:48; Acts 13:27]; and executing judgement [II Thessalonians 2:12; Acts 7:7]. This word is used primarily in the New Testament of the action of a judge in pronouncing a sentence.

In the Amplified Bible, Jesus' words are rendered this way,

> *"Do not judge, criticize, and condemn..."*
>
> Matthew 7:1-2 Amp

In these three words — judge, criticize, and condemn — we find the kind of judging that believers must **not** do. This kind of judging begins with a critical attitude and concludes with a negative judgement. According to Jesus, no believer has the right to investigate his brother from a hypocritical and self-righteous motivation, discover his faults, and then criticize and condemn him.

A more complete understanding of what Jesus really meant by, "Judge not," comes from reading the verses that follow this instruction. Jesus continued on to say,

> *"And why beholdest thou the mote that is in thy brother's eye, but considerest not the beam that is in thine own eye? Or how will you say to thy brother, Let me pull out the mote out of thine eye; and behold, a beam is in thine own eye? Thou hypocrite, first cast out the beam out of thine own eye, and then shalt thou see clearly to cast out the mote out of thy brother's eye."*
>
> *Matthew 7:3-5*

The judgmental man that Jesus described in these verses has serious spiritual problems. He recognizes others' faults and condemns them, but refuses to acknowledge his own faults which are far worse. The beam in this man's eye makes it difficult for him to see at all, much less to evaluate his brother's spiritual condition.

The judgmental man is a hypocrite. He turns attention away from the problems in his own life by pointing a finger at others. Rather than correcting himself, he critically judges others. He has no plan to make changes in his own life. He only wants to *appear* as spiritual. By pointing out problems in others, he hopes to be perceived as a spiritual man.

A person who is judgmental does not look at others objectively, open to finding either good or bad. He looks for and hopes to find incriminating evidence. Something in his personality leads him to hone in on the faults and weaknesses of others. Those who are judgmental **always** look for and find faults in others and **always** render a pre-determined guilty verdict.

In the scenario Jesus painted in Matthew seven, the man who judged his brother had appointed himself the investigator, the prosecutor, the jury, and the judge. He had examined evidence against his brother from his own unhealthy spiritual condition, found his brother guilty, and pronounced a guilty verdict. No Christian is authorized to judge with this attitude and in this way. God's Word forbids it.

The person who is judgmental not only looks for problems in others, he also broadcasts his findings to the brethren. He wants others to perceive him as spiritually keen. When he finds a problem he can say, "Yes, I saw something wrong with so and so," or, "I knew about so and so's problem first," or, "How could so and so do such a thing; I sure wouldn't." Being judgmental always includes broadcasting a guilty verdict.

When Jesus taught, "Judge not," He was warning believers not to pass critical judgement on their brethren as if they had a right to do so. He was warning those who think it is their duty to discover and then report on others' less than perfect spiritual condition. Jesus made it clear that if believers judge with the intent to criticize and condemn, then with that same unmerciful judgement they will be judged by God. This clearly reveals that God does **not** approve of this kind of judging.

James also prohibited this kind of judging when he said,

> *"Speak not evil of another, brethren...who art thou that judgest another?"*
>
> James 4:11

James' warning, like Jesus' warning, prohibits judging in the sense of being critical and speaking evil about a brother. Of the person who judges, James essentially asks, "Who do you think you are?" By asking this question, he makes it clear that the person who judges and speaks evil of another is in spiritual error.

The Word of God forbids the self-righteous, critical, and hypocritical assuming of the seat of a judge and passing critical judgement on others. This searching for incriminating evidence, criticizing, and speaking evil of others is not an allowable activity for believers. This is the kind of judging that believers must **not** do.

OBJECTIVE JUDGING

In his first letter to the church at Corinth, Paul said,

> *"But he that is spiritual judgeth all things..."*
>
> I Corinthians 2:15

The word "judgeth" that Paul used in this scripture comes from the Greek *anakrino*. This word means to examine by looking throughout, to investigate, to scrutinize, or to question. It indicates a careful, even intensive searching out of a matter and the making of a decision concerning that matter. It refers to the exercising of discerning judgement of all things to ascertain their true value. This kind of judging includes determining the excellence or defects of a person or a teaching.

This kind of judging is an allowable and expected *spiritual activity*. It is not motivated by a critical attitude or by a desire to find faults, but is motivated by a sincere desire to maintain personal and corporate spiritual stability. It is motivated by a heartfelt concern to be "on the mark" doctrinally and spiritually. There is no critical attitude, spiritual pride, or naughtiness in this spiritual activity called judging.

To judge in this sense means to discern by the means of examination. It means to test the true spiritual value of a person, of a message, or of a messenger. It includes the objective personal assessment of persons who claim to be a spiritual leaders and the objective personal assessment of particular doctrines. This spiritual activity called judging includes gathering evidence about a person or teaching, objectively assessing that evidence, and then deciding whether or not the person who claims to be a spiritual leader is true or false and whether or not the particular doctrine being examined is true or false.

This kind of judging is *objective*. It is not based upon opinion or personal preference. It is not based upon one's upbringing or spiritual background. It is not colored by opinion, prejudice, or a critical spirit. Objective judging is based upon the Word of God, upon the witness of the Spirit, and upon the fruit that is brought forth. If a person or message is in agreement with the Word of God, in agreement the witness of the Holy Spirit, and consistently brings forth good fruit, then they or it can be judged as sound. If, however, a person or message is not in agreement with the Word of God or the witness of the Holy Spirit and consistently brings forth bad fruit, then they or it should be judged as unsound.

Objective judging is a *personal* assessment. One who judges in this way has no premeditated plan to report his findings or to condemn a minister or teaching (although there is a place for exposing false doctrine and marking false ministers). When one judges to discern the true value of a teacher or a teaching, his judgement will primarily affect his own involvement with that teacher or teaching.

The believer who objectively judges is not looking for evidence to support a pre-determined guilty verdict. He does not settle the verdict before he has examined the evidence. In this kind of judging, a believer is looking for the truth. Consequently, he investigates with an open mind and a non-premeditated position. A believer who judges objectively will not find every teaching and every teacher guilty. He may examine evidence and conclude that a teaching or a teacher is sound and accurate. If he comes to this conclusion, he rejoices. If he concludes, however, that a teaching or a teacher is false or unsound, he will separate himself.

BEING JUDGMENTAL VERSES OBJECTIVE JUDGING

There is a significant difference between judging with a self-righteous and critical attitude and judging because of a sincere desire to remain spiritually sound. There is a significant difference between judging with the intent to support a pre-meditated guilty verdict and judging because of an honest desire to find the truth. There is a significant difference between judging from a subjective position with the intent to condemn a brother and judging from an objective position with the intent to discern the true value of a person or a message. There is a significant difference between judging with the intent to broadcast the faults of others and judging with the intent to reach a decision that will affect one's own spiritual life. There is a significant difference between *being judgmental* and *objective judging*. One is a wrong critical attitude. The other is a necessary spiritual activity.

There is a difference between judging and condemning a brother who, because of personal faults or by falling into sin, has damaged *his own* spiritual life and judging a person or a message that could damage *your* spiritual life. The person who has faults or who has fallen into sin needs no condemning; he knows he is wrong. He needs mercy and restoration. A person, however, who would purposely lead you into sin, wrongly influence you in doctrine, or take advantage of you by claiming to be a spiritual leader **must be judged** because he could greatly affect the affairs and the outcome of your spiritual life.

For those who have faults, who have made mistakes, who have fallen into sin, or who have unregenerate ways in their lives (which we all do, by the way), we must show the mercy of God and the love of God. The Bible teaches us that if a brother is overtaken in a fault, those who are truly spiritual should restore him (not judge him) with a meek attitude, realizing that the same thing could happen to them. The apostle Paul wrote,

> "Brethren, if a man be caught in any trespass, ye which are spiritual, restore such a one in a spirit of meekness; considering thyself, lest thou also be tempted."
>
> Galatians 6:1

This is how believers help each other with problems and so fulfill the New Testament law of love. Believers are not to judge one another because of shortcomings, but, "bear ye one another's burdens, and so fulfill the law of Christ" [Galatians 6:2]. If we deal in this way, when our own faults come to light, we will also receive mercy.

There are areas of spiritual life where Christians **are not** permitted to judge. Christians **are**, however, permitted to examine and judge the soundness and true value of the doctrines they encounter and the soundness and true value of those who claim to be spiritual leaders. It is concerning judging in these two important areas of spiritual life that we will concentrate for the rest of our study.

·~4~·
Judging Doctrine and Leadership

oncerning judging doctrine and leadership, most Christians have two over-riding thoughts. First, they think that it is *not right* for them to judge. As we learned in the previous chapter, most Christians believe that any kind of judging is wrong. Second, they think that they are *not capable* of judging. They think that they are not equipped to judge doctrine and certainly feel unqualified to evaluate spiritual leadership. Every believer, however, has certain responsibilities concerning their own spiritual life. One responsibility believers must fulfill is the responsibility to judge doctrine and spiritual leadership. In this chapter, we will learn that believers are not only permitted to judge doctrine and spiritual leadership, but that they are responsible to judge doctrine and spiritual leadership.

WHAT DOES IT MEAN TO JUDGE DOCTRINE AND LEADERSHIP?

To judge doctrine and spiritual leadership means to examine in order to assess true spiritual value. It means to investigate those who present themselves as spiritual leaders and test the doctrines they teach to determine their excellence or their defects. It means to assess the accuracy of something written or spoken and to determine the soundness of the one who wrote it or spoke it. Judging in this sense is the careful exercising of spiritual discernment concerning doctrine and spiritual leadership to ascertain whether they are true or false, sound or unsound, valid or invalid. Paul expressed this concept of judging in his first letter to the church at Corinth when he said,

> *"...he that is spiritual judgeth (examines and discerns) all things."*
>
> I Corinthians 2:15

The same word translated "judgeth" in the above scripture is used of the daily searching of the scriptures done by the Berean Christians in the days of Paul. We read of these believers,

"These were more noble than those in Thessalonica, in that they received the word with all readiness of mind, and searched (judged) the scriptures daily, whether those things were so."

Acts 17:11

Believers are not to judge doctrine and spiritual leaders in the sense of criticizing and condemning. They are not to be fault finding, down-grading, or high-minded. They are not to look for problems so that they can expose them to the whole body of Christ. Believers are, however, encouraged to, responsible for, and capable of judging doctrine and spiritual leadership to determine whether they are true or false, sound or unsound, valid or invalid.

Don't Be Children

Paul challenged the believers in Corinth about discerning in spiritual matters with these words,

"Brethren, be not children in understanding...but in understanding be men."

I Corinthians 14:20

Too often Christians are like children. They are trusting and gullible, ready to accept anything, including unsound doctrine, and willing to follow anyone, including unsound spiritual leaders. Often, like nice children raised in a small rural town, they don't suspect others of not being nice. They don't realize that not every so-called minister is a godly person. They don't realize that not every sheep is a sheep. They don't suspect that men may have evil motives or that their teachings may be unsound.

It is unfortunate, but in this generation parents must instruct their children in matters of life that children never had to be instructed about in the past. Today, children must be taught not to accept rides from strangers. They must be told not to answer the door when their parents are not home. They must be warned not to eat Halloween candy unless it has been carefully inspected. They must even be cautioned, at times, concerning their own relatives! Because of the rise of evil men and the greater possibility of danger, children of this generation must be warned and carefully educated.

In a similar way, believers in these latter days must be instructed concerning potential spiritual dangers. Paul said that when he was a child he thought like a child and acted like a child, but that when he became a man he put away childish things [I Corinthians 1:11]. In these latter days, believers must put away childlike thinking and become adults in spiritual understanding. One aspect of spiritual life that believers **must** become adults in is judging doctrine and spiritual leadership. If believers remain children in this area, they will be tossed to and fro by every wind of doctrine and manipulated by cunning unsound spiritual leaders.

Be Wise

Paul issued this very important exhortation to the local church at Ephesus,

"See then that ye walk circumspectly, not as fools, but as wise."

Ephesians 5:15

The Amplified Bible clarifies Paul's exhortation saying,

"Look carefully then how you walk! Live purposefully and worthily and accurately not as the unwise and witless, but as wise (sensible, intelligent people)."

Ephesians 5:15 Amp

The word "walk," commonly used in the New Testament, refers to the daily Christian life. The word "circumspectly" could be translated "accurately." To "walk circumspectly" means to live the Christian life accurately. To live accurately in spiritual life, especially in these last days, believers must be *willing to* and must *know how to* judge doctrine and spiritual leadership.

It is very significant that Paul instructed the believers in Ephesus not to be fools, but to be wise. Evidently, being wise in Christian life is **not** automatic. Believers can be born-again, filled with the Spirit, and go to a good church, but be ignorant in spiritual matters. Paul continued to exhort the believers in Ephesus saying,

"...be ye not unwise, but understanding what the will of the Lord is."

Ephesians 5:17

In a similar address to the church at Colosse, Paul informed them of his desire and his prayers that they might be,

"...filled with the knowledge of his will in all wisdom and spiritual understanding."

Colossians 1:9

Being filled with wisdom and spiritual understanding includes recognizing the importance of examining doctrine and spiritual leadership. Wise Christians weigh, test, and examine the doctrines they are taught, realizing that it is foolish to believe everything they hear. Wise Christians examine and investigate those who claim to be spiritual leaders because they understand that not every person who claims to be a spiritual leader is, in fact, called of God and qualified. Wise Christians discern between true and false, right and wrong, sound and unsound, and even between good and best. Christians must not only be harmless as doves; they must also be wise as serpents!

Judging doctrine and spiritual leadership is not just the responsibility of the Father God, of Jesus, of the Holy Spirit, or of true spiritual leaders. Every believer is responsible to judge. That is why *believers* are warned. It is so that *believers* will be prepared to judge. In one fashion or another true spiritual leaders express this reality all throughout the New Testament. Let's examine what these spiritual leaders said about judging and establish the truth that every believer is *responsible* to and *capable* of judging doctrine and spiritual leadership.

JESUS' WORDS ABOUT JUDGING

Early in His ministry, Jesus told His disciples,

"Beware of false prophets, which come to you in sheep's clothing, but inwardly they are ravening wolves, Ye shall know them by their fruits..."

Matthew 7:15-16

With this warning, Jesus alerted His disciples to the activity of false prophets. He said that they would come in sheep's clothing and, therefore, be difficult to recognize. Jesus expected, however, that His disciples would examine the fruits of those who claimed to be spiritual leaders. By teaching, "by their fruits ye shall know them," Jesus implied that they were responsible to and capable of judging.

Prior to the time of His death, Jesus responded to His disciples' question concerning the end times by saying,

"For false Christs and false prophets shall rise, and shall show signs and wonders, to seduce, if it were possible, even the elect. But take heed: behold, I have foretold you all things."

Mark 13:22

Jesus warned His disciples that in the last days there would be an increase of false spiritual leaders. He told them, "take heed; behold I have foretold you all things." Why did Jesus forewarn His disciples of false spiritual leaders and their deceptive activities? He forewarned them so that they could be forearmed. He warned them because they would be responsible for their own spiritual stability. He warned them so they could prepare themselves to judge. The responsibility of recognizing false spiritual leaders and their false doctrines belonged to the disciples.

The Church at Ephesus

In Revelation two, Jesus commended the believers in Ephesus because they judged men who claimed to be apostles. He said,

"...and thou hast tried (judged) them which say they are apostles, and are not, and hast found them liars..."

Revelation 2:2

Jesus commended the believers in this local church because they did what was right. They did what spiritually mature believers and local churches must do when someone comes into their midst claiming to be a spiritual leader. They judged! They examined and evaluated these men and their teachings. Their examination uncovered clear evidence that these men were not apostles, but were liars. This church judged these men as false, pronounced them liars, and refused to give them a place in their midst.

Two important facts can be noted from Jesus' message to this church. First, Jesus expected these believers to examine those who claimed to be apostles or to be any other kind of spiritual leader. His word of praise reveals that they did what was right; they did what they were supposed to do. By judging, they fulfilled their responsibility in maintaining their own spiritual health and the spiritual health of the local body. Second, Jesus commended not only the pastor, or pastors, at Ephesus. He commended the whole body because they, as a body, fulfilled their responsibility to judge.

The Church at Pergamos

In Revelation two, Jesus spoke to the church at Pergamos concerning the false doctrine they had allowed in their midst. He said,

"...I have a few things against thee, because thou hast there them that hold the doctrine of Balaam...so hast thou also them that hold the doctrine of the Nicolaitanes, which thing I hate. Repent..."

Revelation 2:14-16

Jesus issued strong words of correction to this local church. He said, "I have a few things against thee." Concerning the false doctrine in their midst, He said, "which thing I hate." Jesus was angry with this local church because they allowed individuals who held to unsound doctrine to remain in their local body. The sound believers in this church should have judged the unsound doctrine in their midst and judged those who promoted and held to it. If those who were holding to or promoting unsound doctrine would not accept correction and make a change, they should have been put out of that local body.

If the believers in this local church had been responsible and to judge the false doctrine in their midst, Jesus would not have had to speak His strong words of reproof. After showing this church their error, He admonished them to, "Repent." They were to repent of their failure to judge the false doctrine in their midst and repent of the ungodly lifestyle it gendered. If they did not repent and judge the false doctrine in their midst, Jesus said,

> "...else I will come unto thee quickly, and will fight against them with the sword of my mouth."
>
> Revelation 2:16

Notice that Jesus said, "I will come unto *thee* and will fight against *them*." By "thee," Jesus was referring to the whole local church. By "them," He was referring to those believers who held to and were promoting false doctrine. If this local church failed to heed the corrective word of Jesus and judge, then He would visit them and bring judgement Himself. He would fight against those who held to false doctrine with the sword of His mouth. He would put the doctrine of this church in order by the sword of the Spirit which is the Word of God.

We can note two important truths from Jesus' message to this local church. First, Jesus expected this church to police itself by judging both the false doctrine in their midst and the individuals that held to it. He was angry because they had failed in their responsibility to do so. Second, this church's failure to judge was such a serious issue that if they did not take immediate action, Jesus would act Himself.

The Church at Thyatira

In Revelation two, Jesus spoke these words to the church at Thyatira concerning a false prophetess they had permitted to teach in their midst,

> "...I have a few things against thee, because thou sufferest that woman Jezebel, which calleth herself a prophetess, to teach and to seduce my servants to commit fornication...But unto you I say, and unto the rest in Thyatira, as many as have not this doctrine...I will put upon you none other burden. But that which ye have already hold fast till I come."
>
> Revelation 2:20-25

In this passage, as in the previous two passages, Jesus was speaking to a specific local church. He commended this church for their, "charity, and service, and faith and patience," but corrected them because they failed to judge the false prophetess in their midst. To this church at Thyatira, Jesus said, "I have a few things against thee."

Jesus reprimanded the believers in this local church because they allowed the false prophetess Jezebel to operate in their midst and promote false doctrine. Jezebel contaminated this church with false doctrine and led some of Jesus' servants (perhaps ministers) into reprobate activity. Her presence not only introduced spiritual sickness into the local body and caused spiritual decline in some of the members; it put the whole local body at risk.

The believers in Thyatira should have investigated Jezebel's claim to be a prophetess, found her false, and taken the necessary course of action. They should have investigated her teaching, found it to be unsound, and refused it. They should have examined her lifestyle, found it ungodly, and demanded repentance. This church, however, did none of these things. Jesus reprimanded them because of what they allowed!

Because the believers in Thyatira failed to judge this false prophetess, Jesus judged her Himself. He dealt with Jezebel's heart and gave her time to repent. Jezebel, however, did not want to change. For the sake of the spiritual soundness of the whole church in Thyatira, Jesus pronounced judgement on her and her followers.

We can note two important truths from Jesus' message to this local church. First, Jesus reprimanded this local body because they failed in their responsibility to judge a women who claimed to be a prophetess. They also failed in their responsibility to rightly discern her unsound doctrine and to discipline her ungodly lifestyle. This local body should have examined Jezebel, judged her to be a false prophetess, and refused her a position of spiritual leadership in their assembly. Second, what believers allow will be allowed! Jezebel was able to gain a place of leadership in this local church and introduce her unsound doctrine and ungodly lifestyle because the church members allowed it.

PAUL'S WORDS ABOUT JUDGING

In I Thessalonians 5:21, Paul penned a very short message of spiritual wisdom to the church at Thessalonica. Before we look at this instruction, let's read the two verses that precede it. In verses 19 and 20, Paul said,

"Quench not the Spirit. Despise not prophesyings."

I Thessalonians 5:19-20

Paul instructed the local church at Thessalonica not to quench the moving of the Holy Spirit and not to despise prophesying. Notice, however, the instruction which follows in verse 21,

"Prove all things; hold fast that which is good."

I Thessalonians 5:21

The spiritual instructions in these three verses are given in divine order. Paul's instruction to, "Prove all things," follows his instruction not to quench the Spirit and not to despise prophesyings for a reason. Believers are not to quench the real move of the Holy Spirit or to despise the gift of prophesy (or any other gift of the Spirit for that matter). On the other hand, however, believers must, "Prove all things," and, "hold fast that which is good."

What does Paul mean by, "Prove all things?" The word "prove" comes from the Greek *dokimazo*. This word was used in the Greek language primarily of testing metals by fire to determine whether they were pure, flawed, or totally corrupt. In the New Testament the word "prove" means to test, to try, or to examine a person or a thing with a view toward approval. It is used in I Corinthians 3:13 of the fire that will test every man's work to see what sort it is; whether wood, hay, stubble, precious stones, silver, or gold. It is used both in I Corinthians 11:28 and II Corinthians 13:5 of believers judging themselves. It is used in I Timothy 3:10 of the stringent testing a man must undergo to determine if he is qualified to be a deacon in the church. To "prove" something means to test it very carefully to determine its quality.

What does Paul mean by, "hold fast that which is good?" To "hold fast" means to grip something tightly. It is the opposite of letting something go or letting something slip away. Paul exhorted believers to hold fast to that which is good. By, "that which is good," he was referring specifically to what is spiritually viable, what is spiritually sound, what is spiritually healthy, and what is spiritually right and true. Paul exhorted the believers in Thessalonica to keep a firm grip on and maintain a tight and strong relationship with what was spiritually good.

What Paul wrote in I Thessalonians 5:21 is a very significant two-part spiritual directive. First, believers are to prove, or judge, all things. They are to test all things that relate to spiritual life to determine their spiritual value. Are the things they are testing excellent, mediocre, useless, or dangerous? Second, believers are to hold fast to what they have judged to be excellent and spiritually valuable and let go of what they have judged to be of no spiritual value or spiritually dangerous. Paul's instructions could be rendered this way,

> *"Christians, don't quench the move of the Spirit of God. Don't despise the gift of prophesy or any other spiritual gift. On the other hand, however, test everything! Don't refuse what is truly of God, but don't believe everything or everyone. Test what you hear and see. Examine those who claim to speak and act for God. After you have tested and determined the validity of what or who you have heard or seen, hold fast to what is good and let go of the rest."*

Believers must realize that concerning doctrine and spiritual leadership there is always a possibility of both error and deception. This is a consequence of the mingling of the human and the divine. There is never, of course, a possibility of error from the divine side. But there is always the possibility of honest error or purposeful deceit on the human side. Believers should neither dismiss everything as not of God or accept everything as from God. Rather, they must examine and weigh everything and then hold fast to that which they judge to be of God.

I recall hearing the story of a woman who prophesied this in her local church: "My children, My children, don't be afraid. Even I am afraid sometimes. Thus saith the Lord." We know, of course, that God is never afraid. This woman obviously missed it. She made an honest mistake. Her message, however, should have been judged as false.

In the past 15 years, several individuals have given me words of personal prophesy. Of the four prophesies I have been given, two were at the insistence of the person giving the word and at my hesitation. Of the four prophesies, only one bore witness with my own spirit.

At one church where I ministered there was a person who very much wanted to give me a word of prophesy. The pastor of the church encouraged me to allow this person to prophesy to me. I had no witness in my spirit that I should accept this offer, but being a guest at the church I did not want to be rude. I allowed this person to give their word. When they finished the "prophesy," I knew that it was not accurate. It was not even close. In fact, when I evaluated the various elements of the total prophesy, I realized that it disagreed almost completely with the general direction God had been leading me.

I'm sure this person was sincere, but their prophesy did not bear witness with my own spirit. I did not quench the Spirit of God or despise the gift of prophesy. I did, however, prove what this person said and did not hold fast to what did not bear witness with my own heart. When this person finished their word to me, I did not say, "Praise the Lord. Thank you so much for that encouraging word." I just slipped away as smoothly as possible.

It can be difficult in these situations to find a balance between being open and being gullible. It can also be difficult to find a balance between being gracious and being honest. Those, however, who confidently claim to be moving in the gifts of the Spirit must also be prepared to be judged by those to whom they speak. They do not have a corner on what the Spirit of God is saying. All believers have the same Holy Spirit. If what one person prophesies does not bear witness with someone else's spirit, the other person should not feel obligated to accept what has been prophesied as if it was from the Lord.

"Prove **all** things," said Paul. Believers are expected to judge. They must test all things that relate to their own spiritual life including doctrine and spiritual leadership. Whatever and whoever believers judge to be of God and to be spiritually sound, they should hold fast to. Whatever and whoever they judge to be not of God and to be spiritually unsound, they must let go of.

The Spiritual Man Judges All Things

In I Corinthians 2:15, the apostle Paul made a very concise statement that settles once and for all that believers are not only *permitted* to judge in spiritual matters, but are *responsible* to judge. He wrote,

"But he that is spiritual judgeth all things…"

I Corinthians 2:15

To whom was Paul referring when he wrote, "he that is spiritual?" We know he was referring to a person who was at least born-again because he was comparing the natural man (the man without the Spirit) to the spiritual man (the man who has received the Spirit of God through the new birth). By the designation, "he that is spiritual," however, Paul was referring even more specifically to the born-again Christian who has grown beyond the baby stage and developed in the Word of God and in spiritual matters. We know this is true because only two verses after writing about the spiritual man, Paul said this to the born-again believers at Corinth,

"…I…could not speak unto you as unto spiritual, but as unto carnal, even as unto babes in Christ."

I Corinthians 3:1

Paul said that he could not address the believers in Corinth as spiritual, but as carnal, or as babes in Christ. Although the baby Christian is, in one sense, a spiritual man because he is born-again and has the Holy Spirit, he is more accurately designated as carnal, or as a babe, because he has not grown up in spiritual matters. He is still in the milk stage and needs careful supervision. He cannot yet function as a "spiritual man."

By, "he that is spiritual," Paul was most specifically referring to that believer who has advanced beyond initial salvation by exercising himself in spiritual growth. The spiritual man is not a babe that has to be addressed as carnal [I Corinthians 3:1-3]. Neither is he a child who is tossed to and fro by winds of doctrine and the cunning ways of false spiritual leaders [Ephesians 4:14]. The spiritual man is moving toward "full age" as he exercises himself to discern both good and evil [Hebrews 5:11]. He is grown up in every way and in all things.

According to Paul, one of the primary characteristics of the spiritual man, of the mature believer, is that he, "judges all things." By, "judges all things," Paul obviously does not mean that the spiritual man judges in a court of law or judges runners in a foot race. What Paul means by, "judges all things," is very clear in the Amplified Bible. It renders Paul's words this way,

> *"But the spiritual man tries all thing — [that is] he examines, investigates, inquires into, questions, and discerns all things...He can read the meaning of everything..."*
>
> I Corinthians 2:15 Amp

The spiritual man — one who has been born again, has the indwelling of the Spirit of God, and is growing up in spiritual life — is qualified to investigate, examine, inquire into, question, and discern all things that relate to spiritual life. The spiritual man, "can read the meaning of everything." He has the spiritual capacity not only to search out spiritual matters, but to come to a correct conclusion concerning what he searches out. The spiritual man is capable of examining, investigating, and discerning all things that relate to his spiritual life to determine their true spiritual value. The spiritual man is *responsible to* and *capable of* judging doctrine and spiritual leadership.

PETER'S WORDS ABOUT JUDGING

Peter was one of the chief apostles in the early church. He followed Jesus throughout His whole earthly ministry and was chosen to fulfill a place of significant leadership in the early church. The apostle Peter had a deep compassion for believers. He had been commissioned by Jesus to, "feed my sheep." Peter, a true shepherd, an elder, and a chief apostle, introduced his second epistle this way,

> *"Simon Peter, a servant and an apostle of Jesus Christ, to them that have obtained like precious faith with us..."*
>
> II Peter 1:1

Peter's second epistle was clearly written to believers. It was not written only to the pastor of a particular congregation or to other spiritual leaders. This is clarified in the third chapter where, preparing to conclude this epistle, Peter said,

> *"This second epistle, beloved, I now write unto you..."*
>
> II Peter 3:1

The fact that Peter's second epistle was written to believers is significant. It means that the instructions found in it are pertinent to all believers. If this letter was written to another spiritual leader, as were Paul's letters to Timothy and Titus, then believers could ignore some of the instructions. The words of Peter's epistle, however, pertain to every Christian.

In his second epistle, Peter spoke of false teachers and the damnable heresies they promoted. From his words, inspired by the Holy Spirit and preserved up to this generation, believers can take spiritual counsel. After recounting his experience on the mount of Transfiguration, Peter wrote,

> *"We have also a more sure word of prophecy; whereunto ye do well that ye take heed, as unto a light that shineth in a dark place, until the day dawn, and the day star arise in your hearts: Knowing this first, that no prophecy of the scripture is of any private interpretation. For the prophecy came not in old time by the will of man: but holy men of God spake as they were moved by the Holy Ghost. But there were false prophets also among the people, even as there shall be false teachers among you, who privily shall bring in damnable heresies..."*

> *II Peter 1:16-2:1*

With these informative words, Peter entrusted the responsibility for examining doctrine and recognizing false teachers to believers. He directed believers to the written scriptures, calling them, "a more sure word of prophesy." Peter did this to insure that impostors would not gain positions of spiritual authority by claiming to have seen visions and heard God speak. Peter informed believers that the written scriptures were "more sure" than any person's claim of supernatural experience. The clear implication of his exhortation is that believers were to judge those who claimed to be spiritual leaders and judge their teaching by the "more sure word of prophesy."

Peter taught these believers that a primary spiritual principle they needed to know was that they could understand the scriptures themselves. He said,

> *"Knowing this first, that no prophecy of the scripture is of any private interpretation."*

> *II Peter 1:20*

If these believers were not confident of their ability to understand the scriptures, they would not be confident to judge teachers, would not be equipped to judge doctrine, and would, therefore, be susceptible to all manner of error. By teaching them that, "no scripture is of any private interpretation," Peter laid the responsibility for spiritual stability and doctrinal soundness at the feet of believers.

Believers in every generation must realize that they can understand the Word of God themselves and are, thereby, equipped to judge. If believers assume that the Word of God can only be interpreted and understood by spiritual leaders, they will be easy prey for all manner of fraud and mischief from false teachers and gullible to unsound doctrine.

JOHN'S WORDS ABOUT JUDGING

Like Peter, the apostle John followed Jesus closely and held a place of spiritual leadership in the early church. He had a true compassion for believers and a deep concern for local churches. In all three of his epistles, he revealed this deep concern by addressing the issues of unsound spiritual leadership and false doctrine.

In his first epistle, John warned that antichrists had arrived on the spiritual scene and would attempt to draw believers into their false doctrines. In the typical style of a true spiritual leader, John placed the responsibility for judging these false spiritual leaders and their teachings into the care of individual believers. Notice his pertinent words,

> "But the anointing which ye have received of him abideth in you, and ye need not that any man teach you: but as the same anointing teacheth you of all things, and is truth, and is no lie, and even as it hath taught you, ye shall abide in him."
>
> *I John 2:27*

John told these believers, "ye need not that any man teach you." By these words, John was not implying that believers do not need to be taught by those who are truly called to the ministry. He meant that it was wrong for believers be completely dependent upon other men; even those who claimed to be spiritual leaders. If these believers were completely dependent upon spiritual leaders, they would be susceptible to any person who claimed to be a spiritual leader. Their absolute confidence, instead, was to be in the Indwelling Anointing that taught them all things. They were to be confident in and work together with the Holy Spirit. By following the witness of the Spirit of Truth, they could remain in Christ and free from false spiritual leaders and false doctrines.

Beloved, Believe Not

At another place in his first epistle, John wrote these somber words,

> "Beloved, believe not every spirit, but try the spirits whether they are of God: because many false prophets are gone out into the world."
>
> *I John 4:1*

John said, "Beloved, **believe not** every spirit." Christians should not believe everyone and everything they hear. False spiritual leaders will not wear signs that say: "Hello, I am a false spiritual leader." They will come in sheep's clothing, hoping believers will not suspect them or detect them. Unsound doctrine will not always be obvious. Sometimes it will sound very spiritual. There may even be scripture to "support it." Rather than believing everything, believers should "try the spirits" behind teachers and their teachings to determine whether or not they are of God. We could encapsule John's instructions this way: "Beloved, believe not...but try."

The word "try" that John used when he wrote, "*try* the spirits," is the same Greek word that Paul used in his instruction to, "*Prove* all things" [I Thessalonians 5:21]. To "try" means to test or to evaluate something with a view toward approval. It includes both examining and making a final determination about whether or not what is examined is true or false, sound or unsound. In this particular scripture, "try" meant to evaluate and judge whether or not those who claimed to be speaking for God were truly of God or were false prophets. Rather than embracing everything that those who claimed to be speaking by divine inspiration were saying, believers were to examine and determine whether what they were hearing was really from God and worthy of acceptance.

What John wrote in I John 4:1 was not only a warning to beware of false prophets, but is a clear indication that believers were *expected to* and *capable of* judging. John would not have instructed these believers to test if they were not responsible to test. His exhortation clearly discloses that believers are responsible to examine those who claim to be spiritual leaders and responsible to examine the doctrines they teach.

By the inspiration of the Holy Spirit, John instructs believers in every generation to judge what they hear and judge those who are speaking. **Believers are responsible for putting teachings and teachers on trial!** They must examine what is said and examine those who say it to determine if they be of God or not. If believers do not *test*, they will *accept* whatever comes. It is spiritual suicide, however, to accept, without reservation, every teacher and every teaching.

THE BEREAN CHRISTIANS

In Acts seventeen, we find the testimony of a group of believers who did what believers in every place and in every generation must do. These believers took the time and made the effort to examine the teachings they were hearing. Here is what the Word of God says about them,

"These were more noble than those in Thessalonica, in that they received the word with all readiness of mind, and searched (judged) the scriptures daily, whether those things were so."

Acts 17:11

The scriptures classify the Berean Christians as, "more noble." The word "noble" refers to being well-born, of being in a higher class. The Berean Christians were considered more noble, more intelligent, and of higher Christian character than those in Thessalonica not only because they received the word with readiness of mind, but also because they searched the Old Testament scriptures to see if what they were being taught was true.

The Berean Christians "searched." This word "searched" comes from the Greek *anakrino* which, as we have learned, means to examine, to investigate, or to inquire into something in order to make a determination. The Amplified Bible says of the Berean Christians that they were, "searching and examining." "Searching" implies an attitude of seriousness and concern and reveals that effort was being put forth. "Examining" implies close and careful scrutiny.

The spiritual attitude of these believers was revealed by their diligent examination of what they were being taught. They took responsibility for their own spiritual lives. They were not content to let words slip into their minds and hearts, but were serious about being accurate and sound in what they believed. They were not content to assume that everything Paul and others ministers taught and did was right. They realized that their own spiritual stability and spiritual destiny was at stake. With this in mind, they diligently examined *what* was said and examined *who* said it. They searched till they reached a personal conclusion.

The Berean Christians did not confer with other leaders or call around to see what brother so-and-so believed. They went directly to the scriptures and searched things out themselves. They compared what they were being taught to what God had already said. They listened to the witness of the Spirit. They judged in order to confirm the true value of the teaching they were hearing and to determine the soundness of those who were teaching.

What the Berean Christians did is illustrative of the responsibility of every Christian in every place and in every generation. Christians who are noble, who have a good spiritual constitution, will exercise themselves in spiritual discretion when it comes to doctrine and leadership. If they don't, they are missing something in their spiritual character.

JUDGING IS EVERY BELIEVER'S RESPONSIBILITY

The responsibility for judging doctrine and spiritual leadership, although certainly entrusted to those called to be spiritual leaders, falls finally upon the shoulders of each believer. The teachings and warnings of the New Testament concerning unsound doctrine and false spiritual leadership clearly substantiate the reality that Christians must be *ready* and *able* to judge. Through investigation they can come to a correct conclusion concerning the soundness of the doctrine they hear and the validity of those who claim to be true spiritual leaders.

The spiritual man will carefully investigate the teachings he hears. Are they sound? Are they Truth? He will question popular doctrines, examining them in light of the scriptures. He will also listen carefully for the confirming witness of the Spirit of Truth. Is the Holy Spirit bearing witness with a certain teaching or not? If a teaching does not agree with the Word of God or the witness of the Spirit of Truth, the spiritual man will refuse to follow. The spiritual man will judge all doctrines to determine whether they are true, unsound, or false.

The spiritual man will also examine those who claim to be spiritual leaders. He will try the spirits operating behind those who claim to be called of God to determine whether they are truly of God or not [I John 4:1]. He will search the scriptures to discover if a teacher's message is sound. He will "take heed," as Paul warned, so that no man deceives him [Colossians 2:4,8]. He will investigate a spiritual leader's past to see what kind of fruit he has born in other places. He will listen to the anointing that abides within him so that he will not be misled by those who want to seduce him [I John 2:26-27]. The spiritual man will judge all spiritual leaders to determine whether they are true, unsound, or false.

·~5~·

Contending for the Faith

In his epistle, Jude sounded forth a very clear and urgent exhortation to judge. The spiritual soundness of a local church was in jeopardy because certain unsound men had crept into their midst and were promoting unsound doctrine. Because the believers in this local body had allowed false teachers and unsound teaching to creep in, they risked forfeiting their blessings, their stability, and their spiritual strength. If they did not take immediate action by judging and contending, their faith and spiritual soundness would be destroyed. Jude wrote his letter to warn these believers of their potentially dangerous situation and to exhort them to action. He said,

> *"Beloved, when I gave all diligence to write unto you of the common salvation, it was needful for me to write unto you, and exhort you that ye should earnestly contend for the faith which was once delivered unto the saints. For there are certain men crept in unawares..."*

Jude 3-4

THE NECESSITY OF JUDE'S EPISTLE

Jude introduced his epistle with these words,

> *"I gave all diligence to write...it was needful for me to write..."*

Jude 3

Jude wrote his epistle for a specific reason. He said, "I gave all *diligence* to write." Diligence means prudence in fulfilling a responsibility. By writing to these believers concerning their critical situation, Jude was fulfilling a responsibility, not just an urge to write. As a spiritual leader, he was responsible to alert these believers to the danger of their situation and exhort them to action.

"It was *needful* for me to write," Jude said. The Amplified Bible renders Jude's words this way,

"*...I found it necessary and was impelled to write you and urgently appeal to and exhort you to contend for the faith...*"

Jude 3 Amp

Jude did not write these believers to pass along some unimportant information or to say a casual, "Hi, how are you?" Jude was impelled to write. He felt constrained, pushed, driven. There was an urgency in his spirit. There was a strong compelling witness of the Holy Spirit that he needed to act swiftly. The situation was critical; the spiritual welfare of God's people was at risk; the spiritual soundness of a local church was at stake. It was imperative that these believers be made aware that unsound teaching and ungodly activity was being promoted in their midst. Jude's message to these believers was both a necessary cry of alert and an urgent appeal to action.

CERTAIN MEN HAVE CREPT IN UNAWARES

Jude informed this local body that certain men had, "crept in unawares." Whenever someone creeps in, it means they don't want anyone to know they are there! Creeping in guarantees that mischief and foul play are involved. The kind of men that creep into local bodies are like a cancer. They begin to attack the body in such subtle ways that the body may not even sense their presence at first. If these kind of men are allowed to operate uncontested, their false teaching and negative spiritual influence will increase and the whole body will be corrupted. The Amplified Bible says concerning these men that they,

"*...have crept in stealthily [gaining entrance secretly] by a side door.*"

Jude 4 Amp

The believers Jude wrote to did not realize that false teachers and unsound doctrine had slipped into their midst. That is precisely why their situation was so dangerous! False teachers were operating in their midst, carefully introducing unsound doctrines, heretical teachings, and ungodly lifestyle, and they were unaware of it. In time, the whole local church could be subverted!

EARNESTLY CONTEND FOR THE FAITH!

Jude wrote his epistle not only to *inform* these believers of their dangerous situation, but also to *exhort* them to a course of action. The word "exhort" means to call people to a path that leads to a successful future. Jude hoped that his exhortation would motivate these believers toward a course of action that would preserve their spiritual stability. What was the course of action Jude pointed them toward? They were to earnestly contend for the sound doctrine and the sound spiritual lifestyle that was first delivered to them and in which they had been established. They were to engage themselves in a spiritual activity that would preserve their soundness and the purity of their faith. Jude told them,

> *"...it was needful for me to write unto you, and exhort you that ye should earnestly contend for the faith which was once delivered unto the saints."*
>
> Jude 3

These believers were to contend for "the faith." By "the faith" Jude was not referring to that heart conviction and corresponding action by which a person is saved or by which one receives a promise of God such as healing. By "the faith" Jude was referring to that body of Christian doctrine which expresses the fullness of salvation in Christ and contains the teachings of Christian responsibility. The term, "the faith," represented the complete set of Christian doctrines which had been delivered to these believers by true spiritual leaders. The Amplified Bible clarifies this for us, rendering Jude's words this way,

> *"...contend for the faith which was once for all handed down to the saints [the faith which is that sum of Christian belief]..."*
>
> Jude 3

Jude also referred to that body of teaching which was the sum of Christian belief as, "the common salvation" [Jude 3]. The words, "the common salvation," denote those doctrines and spiritual experiences that are common to all believers. Paul used this same phrase in his letter to Titus calling him, "mine own son after the common faith" [Titus 1:4]. Paul and Titus had a common salvation. They had the same promises, the same inheritance, and the same teachings concerning the Christian life. This sum of Christian belief called "the faith" or "the common salvation" was being challenged in the body of believers that Jude wrote to.

The believers Jude wrote to were to "earnestly contend" for the sound doctrines they had first been established in. The words "earnestly contend" came from the Greek *epagonizomai*. This word meant to struggle, to fight, or to debate over a thing like a combatant. It represented an impassioned activity, an intensive contest, a vigorous debate. It is from this Greek word that we get our English word "agonize."

A familiar story from the book of Acts will help us understand what it means to contend. When Peter returned from Cornelius' house, having gone there by the special direction of God, he was confronted by the other leaders. The Bible tells us that they, "contended with him saying" [Acts 11:2-3]. How did they contend with Peter? They contended with words. They contended by passionately arguing their religious convictions.

Peter also contended, however. He contended by, "rehearsing the matter from the beginning and expounding it in order unto them saying" [Acts 11:1-18]. Peter gave a detailed account of his vision, told of how the Spirit of God had spoken to him, and recounted how God poured out His Spirit on the Gentiles. Peter *contended* by presenting a vigorous, but orderly argument. Each side contended, not with physical force or with natural weapons, but with vigorous words which conveyed their spiritual convictions.

The believers Jude wrote to were to *contend* for the faith. First, they were to examine and judge the leadership, doctrine, and lifestyle that had trespassed into their midst. They were to compare the doctrines that were being promoted with the teachings in which they had first been established. After carefully examining the teachings of the men that had sneaked into their midst, they were to speak boldly what they believed and separate themselves from any teaching or teacher that did not agree with what had first been delivered to them. They were to expound the truth and expose the error. They were to judge and then rigorously expose what was faulty with the new teaching. All this they were to do with energy, effort, and zeal.

BELIEVERS IN EVERY GENERATION MUST CONTEND!

All the great New Testament leaders issued serious warnings concerning false spiritual leaders and unsound doctrine. They said, "Beware." How does one, "beware?" First, by being aware! Believers must be aware that false spiritual leadership and unsound doctrine will be part of the spiritual scene of the last days.

"Bewaring" also demands, however, that believers be ready to judge both doctrine and spiritual leadership. The kind of judging I am speaking about is that examining, searching, and discerning of doctrines and leadership which is motivated by a desire to maintain spiritual soundness. Believers must be prepared to assess, evaluate, and decide whether or not to believe and follow a particular person or a particular teaching. It is not only permissible for believers to judge doctrine and spiritual leadership. **Believers are responsible to judge!**

Too often believers are bound by the attitude that to ask questions, to disagree, or to not follow one who claims to be a spiritual leader is to be in rebellion. There are times, however, when believers must ask questions and must examine both teachers and their teaching. If believers do not examine teachers and teaching, they risk falling into error and may even be devastated in their spiritual lives. My friends, there is nothing wrong with asking questions! Only a foolish Christian would commit spiritual suicide by never asking a question!

Believers in every generation and in every place are responsible to earnestly contend for that body of sound doctrine which is the sum of Christian belief and which governs Christian lifestyle. They are also responsible to contend with those who call themselves spiritual leaders, but are unsound and teaching unsound doctrine. This spiritual exercise called judging does not mean that believers go about as judges, correcting and criticizing everyone and everything. It does mean, however, that believers examine, test, and question and then come to a correct conclusion concerning the soundness of doctrine and leadership.

Doctrines must be judged to determine whether they are true or false, scriptural or unscriptural, sound or unsound, accurate or inaccurate. Even at this time in church history there are questionable doctrines in the church. There is false doctrine; it is wrong. There is unsound doctrine; it is difficult to support from scripture. Too much of what our modern day "cutting-edge" ministers teach is questionable. There may be truth in what they teach, but their doctrines are certainly not foundational scriptural principles upon which strong lives and strong local churches are built.

Those who claim to be spiritual leaders must also be tested and tried. Are they true spiritual leaders or false? What is their fruit like? What witness do you have in your spirit about that person? Maybe they are pretending to be a spiritual leader in order to take advantage of you. Perhaps they are wrong and don't even know themselves they are wrong. If you follow an unsound spiritual leader and end up in the spiritual ditch, it is your own fault. You should have taken the time and made the effort to judge the man.

Christians friends, we are responsible for our own spiritual stability! If we allow false or unsound doctrine to prevail, our lives and our churches will be on shaky ground. If we allow false or unsound spiritual leaders to operate in our midst, we will be misused and the church will be misled. If we do not fulfill our responsibility to judge doctrine and spiritual leadership, we will not grow up into the measure of the stature of the fullness of Christ, but will remain children, tossed to and fro by every wind of doctrine and by the sleight of men.

Section Three

Judging Doctrine

I Thessalonians 5:21

"Prove all things; hold fast that which is good."

·~6~·
The Significant Place of Sound Doctrine

In 1988, the Lord spoke these simple, but very important words to my heart, *"The more I move by my Spirit in these last days the more established you must be in sound doctrine."*

Some Christians may wonder whether there is time to concern themselves with doctrine when so many people need to hear the message of salvation? Why should we fuss over doctrine when there is so much work to do? Isn't the outpouring of the Spirit and the increase of supernatural manifestations what we need to concentrate on in these last days? Does the Word of God even say anything about the place of doctrine in the church? Is doctrine really important?

In this section we will learn that sound doctrine is absolutely essential to the spiritual life of the church. Without sound doctrine there can be no sound believers and no sound local churches. Without sound believers and sound local churches the plans and purposes of God cannot be accomplished. It is essential, therefore, that believers become established in sound doctrine and know how to recognize and avoid unsound doctrine.

WHAT IS DOCTRINE?

The word "doctrine" often intimidates Christians. It can evoke images of boring seminars, of little professors with round glasses, and of thick books on systematic theology. Often believers negatively associate the word doctrine with a very intellectual approach to the Word of God. These attitudes cause Christians to shy away from doctrine.

A correct attitude toward doctrine is essential, however, because doctrine is the foundation upon which Christian faith, hope, and lifestyle is based. Without sound doctrine the church will be either undirected or misdirected in every aspect of spiritual life.

The word *doctrine* should not be intimidating. It simply means teachings. In Proverbs 4:2, a father instructing his son said,

> "*Hear, ye children, the instruction of a father, and attend to know understanding. For I give you good doctrine...*"
>
> Proverbs 4:2

In this case, doctrine was the instructions of wisdom from a father to his son. If you have ever read the book of Proverbs, you know it is comprised of hundreds of one sentence nuggets of divine wisdom. These words of wisdom are called doctrine.

In Mark 4, Jesus was teaching the multitudes at the seaside. Verse two says,

> "*And he taught them many things by parables, and said unto them in his doctrine.*"
>
> Mark 4:2

Jesus' doctrine was not a 25 hour lecture on one particular Old Testament scripture. His doctrine was the spiritual truths He taught as He travelled from place to place. His doctrine was the very simple, yet profound teachings of God that even the simple could comprehend and adhere to. For example, when Jesus finished His teaching called the Sermon on the Mount, the Bible says,

> "*And it came to pass, when Jesus had ended these sayings, the people were astonished at his doctrine.*"
>
> Matthew 7:28

The three thousand individuals who were saved on the day of Pentecost, "continued steadfastly in the apostles' doctrine" [Acts 2:42]. What was the apostles' doctrine? It was the teachings and prophesies of the Old Testament scriptures, the teachings of Jesus, and the recently revealed New Covenant message of salvation through Jesus Christ.

The word "doctrine" signifies that body of teaching, or any teaching within that body, that a particular group believes in, adheres to, and governs their lives by. Christian doctrine is that body of teaching, or any specific teaching within that body, that is inspired by the Holy Spirit and contained in the written Word of God called the Bible. It is the words of God transmitted through chosen human vessels that Christians believe in and adhere to.

Christian doctrine includes a broad history of the human race, commandments from God, promises from God, and prophesies of the coming Christ. It also includes a record of the life, death, resurrection, and ascension of Jesus, New Covenant realities, instructions for Christian living, and predictions of the future. Christian doctrine sets parameters for believer's lives and provides revelation of the One they believe in. It furnishes believers with a knowledge of the past, faith for the present, guidelines for living, and hope for the future.

WHAT IS SOUND DOCTRINE?

The word "sound" comes from the Greek word *hygiaino* and means healthy, sound in health, and whole. The English word "hygiene" comes from this Greek word. "Hygiene," according to Webster's dictionary, is, "The science concerned with maintenance of sound health and prevention of disease." It also designates, "those practices that contribute to disease prevention."

Sound doctrine is hygienic doctrine. It is the healthy teachings of the written scriptures that produce and maintain spiritual health. It is the instructions of life that prevent spiritual sickness and assist in sustaining spiritual health. In Luke 15:27 the Greek word *hugianino* is translated, "Safe and sound." Sound doctrine is accurate teaching from the Bible that will keep believers safe and sound!

Sound doctrine is, very simply, the truths of the Word of God. Paul confirmed this when he told Timothy,

> *"Preach the Word...with all longsuffering and doctrine. For the time will come when they will not endure sound doctrine...And they shall turn away their ears from the truth..."*
>
> II Timothy 4:2-4

To, "not endure sound doctrine," is the same as to, "turn away...from the truth." In John 17, Jesus said, "Thy Word is truth." Jesus also said, "If ye continue in My Word...Ye shall know the truth" [John 8:31-32]. The Word of God is truth and sound doctrine is the truth. Sound doctrine, then, could simply be defined as the truths of the written Word of God.

Sound doctrine is that sacred and sound body of teaching inspired by the Holy Spirit and presented in the written scriptures upon which Christian faith, hope, and lifestyle is established. It is the whole and healthy teachings of God's written Word that produce spiritual health, strength, and wholeness. It is the core and foundation of the Christian faith and the measuring line for Christian lifestyle and ministry. Sound doctrine includes a right interpretation of God's Word and a right application of God's Word.

THE IMPORTANT PLACE OF SOUND DOCTRINE IN THE CHURCH

The place of sound doctrine in the spiritual life of the church is very significant. Paul and other New Testament spiritual leaders not only leaned upon the sound teachings of the scriptures as the standard of truth themselves, but exhorted believers, local churches, and other upcoming spiritual leaders to give serious attention to sound doctrine and to beware of unsound doctrine. These spiritual leaders expressed serious concern that local churches maintain doctrinal purity. Their emphasis upon sound doctrine and their warnings of unsound doctrine not only applied to the spiritual life of the early church, but applies to believers, to local churches, and to spiritual leaders in every generation.

Sound faith cannot be separated from sound doctrine. Clear thinking cannot be separated from sound doctrine. Healthy spiritual life cannot be separated from sound doctrine. Godly living cannot be separated from sound doctrine. No matter where the church is in time or what specific truths God is emphasizing, believers and local churches cannot afford to let go of the sound doctrines of the Word of God or involve themselves with false, unsound, or extreme doctrines!

We will begin learning about the important place of sound doctrine by studying the instructions Paul gave to Timothy and Titus in what we call the pastoral epistles. When you read what Paul wrote to these young spiritual leaders, you will understand what matters most for believers, for local churches, and for spiritual leaders. We will then study what Jesus said to two local churches in Revelation two. His attitude toward the unsound doctrine in these two local churches give us clear insight into how the Head of the Church, the Lord Jesus, perceives the place of doctrine in the church. What we study in the next few pages will clearly expose and strongly underscore the significant place doctrine holds in the spiritual life of the church.

PAUL'S INSTRUCTIONS TO TIMOTHY AND TITUS

We can gain a deep appreciation of the significant place of sound doctrine and the danger of unsound doctrine by studying the letters Paul wrote to his two young proteges. Both Timothy and Titus were maturing to a place of spiritual leadership. They were not only elders themselves, but were responsible for ordaining and watching over other elders. By noting what

Paul stressed in his letters to these two young spiritual leaders, we become aware of what is most important for the church.

In his second letter to Timothy, Paul, referring to his imminent departure, said,

"...the time of my departure is at hand. I have fought a good fight, I have finished my course, I have kept the faith."

II Timothy 4:6-7

The letters Paul wrote to Timothy and Titus are significant not only because these two young men were called to spiritual leadership. They are also significant because of the immanency of Paul's departure. Paul was preparing to pass the baton of spiritual leadership. He would no longer be able to protect the purity of the faith. He would no longer be able to watch over local churches as he did with the church at Ephesus, the churches of Galatia, the church at Thessalonica, the church at Corinth, and many other local churches. His challenges to Timothy and Titus were not casual words to friends, but were strong directives to those who would play a leading role in governing the affairs of the church, guiding her into the future. The instructions Paul gave to these two young spiritual leaders reveal what is **most important** for the ongoing sound spiritual life of the church.

The issue Paul dealt with the most in his letters to Timothy and Titus was the significant place of doctrine. He not only stressed the importance of developing and maintaining sound doctrine, but also issued strong warnings against involvement with unsound doctrine. Paul never instructed either Timothy or Titus to cast out devils. He never directed them to lay hands on the sick. He never told them how much to pray in tongues or how to believe God for finances. He never taught them how to prepare a sermon or how to conduct church services. He never informed them how to set up their offices or how to promote their meetings.

Although all these areas of ministry are important, Paul's overriding concern for these young spiritual leaders was that they develop and maintain sound doctrine. They were to attain to good doctrine, hold fast to sound words, and teach sound doctrine to others. They were to avoid any teaching that resembled unsound doctrine. They were to be prepared to confront unsound doctrine and those who were promoting it. There were many recommendations Paul could have made to these young spiritual leaders. No topic of instruction, however, even distantly approached the amount of instruction he gave them concerning doctrine. Not once, not twice, not even a few times, Paul communicated to these young spiritual leaders in the clearest terms the absolute necessity of maintaining sound doctrine!

Paul's instructions to Timothy and Titus disclose what is most important for the strength and stability of local churches and the church in general. By knowing Paul's concerns for the spiritual leaders and churches of his day, we can know the concerns of the Holy Spirit and of the Head of the church for the spiritual leaders and churches of our generation. There is no doubt about it, sound doctrine is absolutely essential! Let's proceed to study five specific areas of instruction Paul gave to Timothy and Titus concerning doctrine.

ONE: HOLD FAST TO SOUND DOCTRINE

In his second letter to Timothy, Paul exhorted him to,

"Hold fast the form of sound words, which thou has heard of me, in faith and love which is in Christ Jesus."

II Timothy 1:13

Why would Paul exhort Timothy to hold fast to sound words? Why even bring this issue up? The reason Paul exhorted Timothy to *hold fast* to sound words was because there would be temptations to *let go*. If Timothy let go of sound words, he would eventually end up on the spiritual junk heap. It would not only lead to his own spiritual ruin, but also to the ruin of those for whom he was responsible. He would shipwreck in faith as did Hymaneaus and Alexander [I Timothy 1:20] and become a cause of spiritual sickness as were Hymaneaus and Philetus [II Timothy 2:17-18].

Paul did not casually write this instruction to Timothy. He wrote it with serious intent. He did not just happen to mention to Timothy, "Oh, by the way, there is a place for doctrine somewhere in your life and ministry." No! Timothy was to, as the NASB translation says, "Retain the standard of sound words." He was to be like a retaining wall in the spirit. He was to safeguard that high standard of truth called sound doctrine. He was to be a bulwark against the unsound spiritual influences of his generation. He was not to yield to unsound spiritual leaders or follow the spiritual appetites and whims of those he led. He was to remain securely attached the sound doctrine of the Word of God himself and hold that standard high for others to follow.

Imagine that you were journeying across the ocean and a storm arose that threatened the safety of the ship. You would not let go of your life preserver, would you? Of course not. The life preserver would be your only hope. It would be your guarantee against sinking. It would be your deliverance from the deep. It would be your guarantee of life. You would be less than a fool if you let go!

Spiritual life is like a journey across a great ocean. You can be sure that threatening storms will confront you. You can be sure that tests and temptations will come. Without a doubt you will be interrogated by the devil. What is your safety? What is your deliverance? What is your anchor? What is your answer? It is the sound doctrine of the good Word of God! The writer of Proverbs gave this weighty counsel,

"Take fast hold of instruction; let her not go: keep her; for she (instruction) is thy life."

Proverbs 4:13

The prophet Isaiah said this,

"And wisdom and knowledge shall be the stability of thy times..."

Isaiah 33:6

Spiritual life is serious business. It should not be approached with a careless attitude. If, however, you have no concern for doctrinal soundness, then you **are** approaching spiritual life with a care-less attitude. Sound doctrine will be the stability of the church of these last days. It must be gripped like a life preserver. The sound doctrines of the Word of God are the wisdom and instruction believers must hold fast to. Don't let go of sound doctrine. It is your life!

Giving Attention to Doctrine

"Till I come, give attendance to reading, to exhortation, to doctrine...Meditate upon these things; give thyself wholly to them; that thy profiting may appear to all. Take heed unto thyself, and unto the doctrine; continue in them: for in doing this thou shalt both save thyself, and them that hear thee."

I Timothy 4:13-16

Paul admonished Timothy to give attention to reading, to exhortation, and to doctrine. He was to read the scriptures, exhort people with the Word of God, and pay close attention to doctrine. He was to meditate upon "these things." He was to meditate upon what he read and meditate on doctrine. He was to, "give [himself] wholly to them." This phrase literally means to, "be *in* these things." Timothy was to get into sound doctrine. It was to be his atmosphere. If he lived and breathed in the atmosphere of sound doctrine, he would stay spiritually healthy.

Paul continued his exhortation to Timothy saying, "Take heed unto thyself and unto the doctrine." Timothy was to pay careful attention to doctrine. By attending to doctrine, giving himself to doctrine, taking heed to doctrine, and continuing in doctrine, he would be attending to his own and to others' spiritual stability. What would result when Timothy paid careful attention to doctrine? Paul told him,

"Thou shalt both save thyself and them that hear thee."

I Timothy 4:16

If Timothy continued in sound doctrine, he would save himself and those he ministered to. When ministers, believers, and local churches give attention to reading the Word and to doctrine; when they meditate on doctrine and give themselves wholly to it; when they take heed unto doctrine and continue in it; then their spiritual stability and spiritual progress will be evident. Sound doctrine leads to sound faith, sound works, sound life, and sound ministry. If you want to help yourself and help those who hear you, give careful attention to sound doctrine.

Perilous Times and the Place of Sound Doctrine

In his second letter, Paul warned Timothy of the perilous times of the last days. They would be times, he said, when men would love themselves and be unholy; times when men would be lovers of pleasures more than lovers of God. In those days, men, though they were always studying, would never come to the knowledge of the truth. They would withstand true spiritual leaders and resist the truth. "But," Paul comforted Timothy, "Thou has fully known my doctrine" [II Timothy 3:10]. He then proceeded to tell Timothy,

"But evil men and seducers shall wax worse and worse, deceiving, and being deceived. But continue thou in the things which thou hast learned and hast been assured of...And that from a child thou hast known the holy Scriptures, which are able to make thee wise unto salvation through faith which is in Christ Jesus. All scripture is given by inspiration of God, and is profitable for doctrine, for reproof, for correction..."

II Timothy 3:13-16

Paul did not hide the truth from Timothy. Evil men and seducers would get worse and worse. They would be deceived and would deceive others. How could Timothy maintain soundness and spiritual stability in such perilous times? By continuing in what he had already learned and was assured of. What was this? It was the holy scriptures. From a young age Timothy had known and been established in the Word of God.

Paul admonished Timothy to hold fast to the scriptures. They would keep him from being misled. They would keep him sound in the faith. They would bring him to personal maturity and thoroughly furnish him for every good work [II Timothy 3:17]. They would also be profitable to him for establishing and maintaining sound doctrine. "All scripture," said Paul, "is profitable for doctrine" [II Timothy 3:16].

Isn't it interesting that when Paul picked a young man to train for the ministry, perhaps even to carry on his work of founding and guiding local churches, he picked a young man who was established from his childhood in the scriptures? Being established in the scriptures not only made Timothy a sound young man, it also made him an excellent candidate for an important ministry.

Two: Refuse Unsound Doctrine

Paul not only instructed Timothy and Titus what to give attention to. He also warned them what to beware of. In his first letter to Timothy, he said,

"...*refuse profane and old wives' fables, and exercise thyself rather unto godliness.*"

I Timothy 4:7

Timothy was to "refuse" — to avoid and turn away from — teachings which were unsound. Rather than getting involved in profane doctrines, unsound doctrines, and old wives' fables, he was to exercise himself unto godliness. It is apparent from what Paul wrote to Timothy that exercising himself unto godliness included both avoiding unsound doctrine and persisting steadfastly in sound doctrine.

Paul also instructed Timothy about the kind of relationship he was to have with individuals who promoted unsound doctrine. He said,

"*If any man teach otherwise, and consent not to wholesome words...from such withdraw thyself.*"

I Timothy 6:3-5

The word "withdraw" comes from the Greek *aphistemi*. It means to stand aloof, to depart, or to absent oneself. Timothy was not to associate with men who taught anything that could not be classified as "wholesome words." If he associated with them, he might get the same disease. If an individual is physically ill, those who are healthy should abstain from physical contact. This same principle holds true in the spiritual realm. If you know that a person is a carrier of spiritual sickness, you should abstain from contact.

THREE: TEACH SOUND DOCTRINE

In his first letter to Timothy, Paul shared something with him that the Spirit of God had revealed to him. He wrote,

> *"Now the Spirit speaketh expressly, that in the latter times some shall depart from the faith, giving heed to seducing spirits, and doctrines of devils; Speaking lies... Forbidding to marry, and commanding to abstain from meats..."*
>
> I Timothy 4:1-3

The Holy Spirit testified that in the latter times some believers would depart from the faith — from that body of teaching called sound doctrine — and give heed to seducing spirits and doctrines of devils. Two specific examples of false doctrine that Paul mentioned were forbidding to marry and commanding to abstain from meats. Paul gave Timothy correct instructions concerning these two unsound doctrines and then told him,

> *"If thou put the brethren in remembrance of these things thou shalt be a good minister of Jesus Christ, nourished up in the words of faith and of good doctrine, whereunto thou has attained."*
>
> I Timothy 4:6

Timothy was to be "nourished up in the words of faith and of good doctrine" and correct those who wandered from it. If he did this, he would be, "a good minister of Jesus Christ." Being a good minister does not mean being wild, preaching loud and jumping, having a "deep" revelation, or promoting some new move. Simply putting the brethren in remembrance of sound doctrine makes one a good minister!

If you look back to the previous scripture, you will notice that Paul said, "good doctrine, whereunto thou has attained." Believers and ministers do not just *wander* into good doctrine. Sound doctrine must be *attained* through careful study, faithful adherence to the scriptures, and shunning unsound teaching. Timothy was spiritually sound because he had attained to sound doctrine.

Uncorrupt Doctrine

Paul gave these potent instructions to Titus concerning teaching and doctrine,

> *"In all things shewing thyself a pattern of good works: in doctrine shewing uncorruptness, gravity, sincerity, Sound speech, that cannot be condemned; that he that is of the contrary part may be ashamed, having no evil thing to say of you."*
>
> Titus 2:7-8

The Amplified Bible says,

"And show your own self in all respects to be a pattern and a model of good deeds and works, teaching what is unadulterated, showing gravity [having the strictest regard for truth and purity of motive], with dignity and seriousness. And let your instruction be sound and fit and wise and wholesome, vigorous and irrefutable and above censure, so that the opponent may be put to shame, finding nothing discrediting or evil to say about us."

Titus 2:7-8 Amp

Titus' doctrine was to show "uncorruptness." This word comes from the Greek *aphthoria* which means to be brought to an inferior or worse condition. Some texts have the word *adiaphthoria*, which means, "a thorough corruption." Titus' doctrine was to be unadulterated. It was to be free from any taint of untruth, speculation, or tradition. He should not color it or add anything to it to make it more attractive. His doctrine should contain nothing that would lead to any kind of spiritual instability, any eroding of faith or hope, or any ungodly lifestyle.

Titus was to approach both his formulation and his presentation of doctrine with gravity, sincerity, and extreme care. He was to have, "the strictest regard for truth." He was to maintain dignity and high standards. Dignified people will not lower their standards to the level of the common folk. Neither should ministers of the Truth or any member of the body of Christ lower their standards concerning the sound doctrines of the Word of Truth.

Paul challenged Titus to have, "Sound speech, that cannot be condemned." Currently, I live across from a large building that is condemned. This building was inspected and found to be structurally unsound. When it was discovered to be unsound and a potential hazard, the residents were evacuated. A sign of caution was put out front so that no one would come near the building and be hurt. Soon a demolition crew will tear the building down. It is much too dangerous to be left standing.

Sound doctrine, when inspected, should pass the test without a hint of trouble. If, when inspected, doctrine is found to be unsound, it is best to evacuate people and put a sign on it that says, "Danger! Do not come near!" As soon as possible unsound doctrine should be confronted, refuted, and condemned. In this way the least amount of people will be hurt.

Titus' doctrine was to be sound, fit, wise, wholesome, vigorous, and irrefutable. If something is irrefutable, it is unquestionably right; it cannot be proved wrong. If something can be refuted, however, it means that it has a weakness. **Any teaching that can be refuted with the scriptures is not sound doctrine.** Titus' teaching was to be so sound and solid that it could never be proved wrong. It was to be indisputable.

Titus' doctrine was also to be "above censure." A censure is an official rebuke or a strong declaration of disapproval. When, for example, a particular movie or musical lyric is judged to be socially unwholesome, it is censured. It is declared unfit and not permitted free expression in society. Titus' doctrine was to be above censure. He was to teach nothing but truth. Then God would not have to rebuke him or disapprove his doctrine.

Preach the Word

In his strongest admonition to Timothy concerning teaching sound doctrine, Paul said,

> *"I charge thee therefore before God, and the Lord Jesus Christ, who shall judge the quick and the dead at his appearing and his kingdom; Preach the word; be instant in season, out of season; reprove, rebuke, exhort with all longsuffering and doctrine."*

> II Timothy 4:1-2

The word "charge" used in this text means to testify through and through or to bear a solemn witness. When Paul charged Timothy to preach the Word, he was not lacing his letter with cute rhetoric or coining a Christian phrase. He was not making a suggestion to Timothy as a friend would make a suggestion to a friend. He was not instructing Timothy as a teacher would instruct a student. He was not admonishing Timothy as a father would admonish a son.

Paul was **charging** Timothy from his position as a chief apostle and veteran spiritual leader who had for many faithful years experienced the power of the gospel, felt the pain of obedience, and seen the true needs of the church. He was **charging** Timothy as if Timothy was standing before God and before the Lord Jesus Who would one day judge his obedience. Paul's charge to Timothy was more than a challenge; it was a commandment! He raised the standard high and implied danger for disobedience. He charged Timothy with a most solemn charge and entrusted him with a noble commission.

Paul's charge to Timothy was, "Preach the Word." Timothy was not to preach a new move of the Spirit or a new revelation from heaven. He was not to preach what people wanted to hear or even what he wanted to preach. He was to preach the Word of God! In verses three and four, Paul explained why he gave Timothy this very solemn charge. He said,

> *"For the time will come when they (believers) will not endure sound doctrine...they shall turn away their ears from the truth, and shall be turned unto fables."*

> II Timothy 4:3-4

Paul foretold of a time when believers would not endure sound doctrine. They would not be interested in hearing and doing the Word. They would rather have jokes and poems. They would prefer to be entertained. They would rather see miracles. Instead of listening to sound teaching and sound teachers who would correct them, reprove them, encourage them, and accurately and patiently teach them sound doctrine, they would, "turn away their ears from the truth." Paul not only *predicted* the future spiritual condition of the church, however. He also *instructed* Timothy how to stem the tide that would flow in the direction of spiritual weakness. Timothy was to,

> **"Preach the Word**...*reprove, rebuke, exhort with all longsuffering and doctrine."*
>
> II Timothy 4:2

Timothy was not to build his own ministry by collecting contributors, developing a mailing list, and soliciting followers. He was not to be governed by whether or not people liked his teaching. He was not to be motivated by concerns of whether he would be hired, kept, or fired. Rather, Timothy was to be a **guiding force** in the church. He was to lead God's people, not follow their whims. He was to teach God's people, not scratch their itching ears. He was to reprove, rebuke, and exhort with all longsuffering and doctrine.

Timothy was to use sound doctrine to "reprove." This word comes from the Greek *elencho*. It represents strong preaching of the Word directed toward those who are living in sin or error, but are open to correction. The intention of this kind of preaching is to put a person to shame.

Timothy was to use sound doctrine to "rebuke." This word is even stronger than reprove and is used primarily in the gospels of Jesus' rebuking of evil spirits, fevers, winds, and people. This word is reserved as a chastisement for those who are purposely living in error.

Timothy was to use sound doctrine to "exhort." This word comes from the Greek *parakaleo*. *Parakaleo* is made up of two words which mean, "the side," and, "to call." To exhort means to call to a particular place or to a particular path. It means to encourage a person to pursue a designated course. Exhortation is always prospective, looking to the future.

Timothy was to reprove, rebuke, and exhort with all longsuffering and doctrine. To rebuke and reprove meant that he was to preach strong words in order to get individuals *off* a wrong path that they were on. He was to use sound doctrine to reprove and rebuke those who were in error either in life or in doctrine. To exhort meant that he was to speak strong words of encouragement to get people *on* a sound path that would lead to a sound future. He was to use sound doctrine to put people on a path of truth and light that would lead them to sound thinking, sound lifestyle, and sound faith. Sound doctrine was Timothy's tool both of correction and of encouragement.

The prevailing attitude Timothy was to maintain toward those to whom he ministered was "longsuffering." This meant that he should be prepared to suffer long! He may be required to minister the same doctrines to the same people over and over while they, at times, rejected what he said, ignored what he said, or failed to follow through on what he said. Timothy would have to be patient with them. He could not become frustrated if they didn't immediately change or correct their actions.

These Things Speak

After writing about unsound teachers and their unsound teaching, Paul exhorted Titus,

> *"But speak thou the things which become sound doctrine..."*
>
> Titus 2:1

Titus' responsibility, in stark contrast to the false teachers' activity of promoting false teaching, was to, "speak...things which become sound doctrine." The phrase, "things which *become* sound doctrine," signified teaching which agreed with or conformed to sound doctrine. Any teaching that could not with certainty be placed under the heading "Sound Doctrine" should not be taught. Any teaching that did not agree with sound words should be put in the reject pile. Titus was to speak only words that could, with certainty, be qualified as and come under the heading "Sound Doctrine!"

Titus' teachings were to, "become sound doctrine." His teachings must not only agree with sound doctrine; his teachings would literally *become* the sound doctrines that believers lived by. His careful study of the Word of truth, his right dividing of it, and his excellent presentation of the teachings contained therein, would become the sound doctrines that believers and churches would govern their lives by.

At a later point in his letter to Titus, Paul told him,

> *"These things speak, and exhort, and rebuke with all authority. Let no man despise thee."*
>
> Titus 2:15

What were the "these things" Titus was to speak, exhort, and rebuke? The "these things" Titus was to speak were the teachings Paul had just instructed him in. They were the sound doctrines and the faithful sayings of the Word of God. The Amplified Bible renders Paul's words to Titus this way,

> "Tell [them all] these things. Urge (advise, encourage, warn) and rebuke with full authority. Let no one despise or disregard or think little of you — conduct yourself and your teaching so as to command respect."
>
> Titus 2:15 Amp

In Titus 3:8, Paul again advised Titus,

> "This is a faithful saying, and these things I will that thou affirm constantly...these things are good and profitable unto men."
>
> Titus 3:8

What were the, "these things," Titus was to affirm constantly? "These things" were the sound doctrines and the trustworthy teachings Paul had been writing to him about. Paul wanted Titus to constantly affirm the teachings of sound doctrine because, "these things are good and profitable unto men." Again, let's note how the Amplified Bible renders this text,

> "This message is most trustworthy, and concerning these things I want you to insist steadfastly..."
>
> Titus 3:8 Amp

Titus was to "insist steadfastly" concerning sound doctrine. He was to be unmoved in this particular course of action. He was to be persistent and unswayed, urging believers and other ministers to become established in and to hold fast to the trustworthy messages of the scriptures. Why was Titus to "insist steadfastly?" Was it to be obnoxious or offensive? Was it to be boringly redundant? No, Titus was to continue to insist steadfastly because sound doctrine is **good** and **profitable** for believers! Sometimes, like a sincere and caring doctor, spiritual leaders must **insist** that Christians take the medicine that will save their lives!

Paul gave these very same instructions to Timothy. In his first letter, he wrote,

> "...These things teach and exhort...If any man teach otherwise, (something different) and consent not to wholesome words, even the words of our Lord Jesus Christ, and to the doctrine which is according to godliness..."
>
> I Timothy 6:3,4

Paul put strict limitations on what Timothy could teach. He told him, "These things teach." Timothy was to teach wholesome words, the words of Jesus, and other teachings which Paul called, "the doctrine which is according to godliness." Wholesome words would produce wholesome people. Godly doctrine would produce godly people. Sound doctrine would produce sound people.

Paul told Timothy and Titus what they **could** and **should** teach and what they **must not** teach. They were to teach the sound doctrines Paul taught, teach the words of Jesus, and teach doctrines that were in accordance with godliness. They must not teach doctrine that was not wholesome, not in agreement with the teachings of Jesus, or not according to godliness. Sound teaching would lead to right thinking, right acting, and godly living. Wrong doctrine would produce wrong thinking, wrong action, and ungodly living.

FOUR: SOUND DOCTRINE REQUIRED FOR SPIRITUAL LEADERS

At the beginning of his letter to Titus, Paul reminded him of why he had left him in Crete. He said,

"For this cause left I thee in Crete, that thou shouldest set in order the things that are wanting, and ordain elders in every city, as I had appointed thee…"

Titus 1:5

Titus had remained in Crete to establish spiritual order in that region and to ordain elders in every city. The elders he ordained would be responsible to govern and teach in the churches. Paul informed Titus that in order for a man to qualify as an elder and be ordained to govern and teach in a local church he had to meet a list of specific requirements. One of these essential requirements was that he must,

"[Hold] fast the faithful word as he hath been taught, that he may be able by sound doctrine both to exhort and convince the gainsayers."

Titus 1:9

For Titus to even consider a man for a place of spiritual leadership, that man had to meet the very specific requirement of holding tightly to sound doctrine. An elder was not to be chosen on the basis of his charisma or oratorical skills. Only if he was a faithful man who maintained and promoted sound doctrine would he be qualified to help maintain spiritual stability in the church. Only then would he be qualified to instruct believers. Only then would he be able to contend with and "convince the gainsayers." With sound doctrine as his weapon, this elder could convince and win over even those who opposed the truth.

In the next verse, Paul expounded further on why a potential elder must hold fast to sound doctrine. He said,

"For there are many unruly and vain talkers and deceivers, specially they of the circumcision: Whose mouths must be stopped, who subvert whole houses, teaching things which they ought not..."

Titus 1:10-11

Sound doctrine was (and is) the bedrock of solid spiritual life. If the men Titus confirmed to leadership positions in the church did not hold fast to sound doctrine, whole local churches would be put in spiritual jeopardy. If these who became spiritual leaders were not firmly established in sound doctrine, they would not be able to stem the tide of unsound doctrine that would undoubtedly confront the church. By knowing and using sound doctrine, however, those who became elders would be able to stop the mouths of unsound teachers and halt the advance of unsound doctrine.

When looking for men to guide the church and teach in the church, Titus was to look for men who were firmly established in sound doctrine. If a man was not sound in doctrine, he was **automatically disqualified** for a position of spiritual leadership.

Faithful Men and Sound Doctrine

Paul gave similar instructions to Timothy concerning who to entrust with the responsibility of teaching. He said,

"And the things that thou hast heard of me among many witnesses, the same commit thou to faithful men, who shall be able to teach others also."

II Timothy 2:2

Timothy was to commit Paul's teachings to faithful men who were able to teach. These men were required first of all to be faithful because it was essential that the sound teachings of Paul and other men of God not be ignored or distorted. If the men entrusted with the responsibility of teaching were able to teach, but not faithful, they might teach their own opinions and their own doctrines. Yes, it was important that these men be *able* to teach, but it was more important that they be *faithful* in what they taught!

There will always be men in the church who are willing and able to teach. It was a concern of Paul, however, and I'm sure it is a concern of Jesus and the Holy Ghost, that those who teach be first of all faithful. Paul said that it is required of stewards that they be faithful [I Corinthians 4:2]. Stewards of the mysteries of God's Word must not only be faithful *to* teach, but faithful in *what* they teach! Faithful men will not ignore, distort, or stretch what has already been established as sound doctrine.

Spiritual Leaders Must Labor in the Word and in Doctrine

Those who are called to be spiritual leaders in the church must give significant effort to searching out, teaching, and maintaining sound doctrine. Spiritual leaders must, "labor in the word and in doctrine." This is part of ruling well. Paul told Timothy,

> *"Let the elders that rule well be counted worthy of double honor, especially they who labor in the word and in doctrine."*
>
> I Timothy 5:17

The Amplified Bible says,

> *"Let the elders who perform the duties of their office well be considered double worthy of honor...especially those who labor faithfully in preaching and teaching."*
>
> I Timothy 5:17 Amp

A significant duty of spiritual leadership is to teach and preach sound doctrine. Yes, supernatural manifestations are needed. Yes, healing the sick is important. Yes, saving the lost is imperative. Yes, wild services are fun. Yes, jokes and stories are interesting. Paul's instructions to Timothy clearly reveal, however, that a primary responsibility of spiritual leaders is to labor in the Word and in doctrine.

Spiritual leaders must be capable of presenting the doctrines of the Word of God in a way that believers can receive them. They must be able to "break down" the Word of God into sound teachings, into sound doctrine. Ruling well, or being a good spiritual leader, demands work both in hewing out sound doctrine through diligent study and in teaching it. Before the corn can be fed to the hungry, it must be treaded out.

According to Paul, those who faithfully labor in the Word of God by treading out and teaching sound doctrine should be paid double. Why should these individuals receive double pay? They should receive double pay because the labor of studying the Word of God and then teaching sound doctrine is doubly significant! Without elders who labor in the Word there can be no sound doctrine. Without sound doctrine believers and local churches will be sick. Although there are many aspects of ministry that are important for the sound spiritual life of a local church, none is more important than the expert instruction of sound doctrine! **In the church, instruction in sound doctrine is premier — first and foremost — in importance!**

FIVE: REPROVE UNSOUND TEACHERS

Paul introduced his first letter to Timothy by reminding him of the reason he had asked him to remain at Ephesus. He wrote,

> *"...I besought thee to abide still at Ephesus...that thou mightest charge some that they teach no other doctrine, Neither give heed to fables and endless genealogies, which minister questions, rather than godly edifying which is in faith...some having swerved have turned aside unto vain jangling."*
>
> I Timothy 1:3-6

For some reason the church at Ephesus was a hot spot for wrong doctrine and false teachers. When Paul left that church after teaching there for three years, he warned the elders to guard it against wolves that would come from the outside and false teachers that would arise from within [Acts 20:29-31]. Jesus spoke at a later time to this same church and commended it for testing false apostles who tried to infiltrate [Revelation 2:2]. Paul knew that unsound doctrine could ruin the church in Ephesus. Knowing this, he wrote to Timothy to remind him of his responsibilities in regards to that local church.

Timothy was left in Ephesus to assist in maintaining the spiritual health of the church there. He was to be a guard — a hindering force. In order to fulfill this responsibility, he had to take a strong defensive position against unsound doctrine and against those who wanted to teach it. He was to, "charge some that they teach no other doctrine." The word "charge" was used strictly of commands received from a superior and transmitted to subordinates. Timothy, a true spiritual leader, was to command observance to sound doctrine. He was to inform other so-called or want-to-be spiritual leaders not to pay attention to fables, genealogies, or any other form of unsound doctrine.

Paul gave similar, but even stronger instructions to Titus. He told him,

> *"...rebuke them (false teachers) sharply, that they may be sound in the faith..."*
>
> Titus 1:13

The word "rebuke" comes from the Greek *elencho*. This word signified a deserved reprimand which carried conviction. The word "sharply" comes from the Greek *apotomos* and meant, "abruptly or curt, in a manner that cuts." A sharp rebuke could be likened to slapping the face of a person who is completely out of control. The slap is intended to jerk them back into reality. Titus' reproof of false teachers was to be a vigorous confrontation. By forthright speech, he was to bring them to quick attention, clearly and pointedly exposing the folly of their error.

Titus was not to dialogue with false and unsound teachers. He was not to become good friends with them, hoping to eventually persuade them to abandon their unsound doctrines. He was to aggressively confront false teachers and their unsound doctrines in the hope that they would be jerked out of their spiritual stupor and come to their senses. In the William's translation, Paul's instructions to Titus were, "continue correcting them severely" [Titus 1:13 Williams]. Goodspeed's translation says, "correct them rigorously" [Titus 1:13 Goodspeed].

Paul delivered a very serious and difficult assignment to Titus. He was to reprove those who taught unsound doctrine and do so sharply! The hope of such a reproof was that the unsound teacher would repent and become "sound in the faith." Anywhere unsound doctrine was found, it was to be confronted and cut out!

Sound Doctrine is Essential

The most significant theme of Paul's letters to Timothy and Titus were his instructions concerning doctrine. **This was what mattered most!** Again and again he stressed to Timothy and Titus the necessity of developing, holding fast to, and teaching sound doctrine. These young ministers were to take hold in their hearts and put in their mouths the established teachings of the Old Testament, of Jesus, and of Paul. They were to teach that sure word, that sound doctrine, those faithful sayings worthy of total acceptance [I Timothy 1:15]. They were to hold to them, speak them, and preach them patiently, faithfully, and continuously. They were also to ignore unsound doctrine and reprove those who flirted with it or taught it. This was not only for their own sakes, but for the sake of those who would hear them and for the safe and sound advancement of the church. Paying careful attention to doctrine was essential in order for Timothy and Titus to be strong and stable spiritual leaders who could establish and maintain strong and stable churches.

JESUS' WORDS TO LOCAL CHURCHES CONCERNING DOCTRINE

The important place of sound doctrine in the church and the danger of unsound doctrine can be further appreciated by studying what Jesus *commended* and what He *corrected* in His messages to the seven churches in Revelation two and three. His directives to these local churches not only forcefully convey the high priority He places on sound doctrine, but also reveal the hate He has for false doctrine. Let's examine what Jesus said to two of these churches concerning doctrine.

The Church at Pergamos

The way Jesus introduced Himself to each of the seven local churches revealed something of His thoughts concerning that church's spiritual condition. This is how He introduced Himself to the local church in Pergamos,

"And to the angel of the church in Pergamos write; These things saith he which hath the sharp sword with two edges..."

Revelation 2:12

Because the church at Pergamos had a problem with unsound doctrine, Jesus introduced Himself as the One Who had the sharp two-edged sword of the Word of God. With this introduction, Jesus not only revealed that He held fast to the Word of God Himself, but made it clear that He expected this church to do the same.

Following His introduction, Jesus spoke about the spiritual forces operating over Pergamos. He said,

"I know...where thou dwellest, even where Satan's seat is...where Satan dwelleth."

Revelation 2:13

Evidently, Satan had chosen the spiritual atmosphere over Pergamos as a temporary headquarters. He had his "seat" there. Interestingly, however, Jesus said nothing to this church about confronting Satan. He said nothing about any kind of spiritual warfare. He said nothing about pulling down strongholds or warring with ruling territorial spirits. If some charismatic Christians of our day were privy to this kind of information about a modern day city, they would gather a group of "prayer warriors" together and travel there to pull down the satanic strongholds.

Jesus gave no particular instruction to this church concerning Satan and his stronghold over their city. He did, however, speak very forcefully to this church about their doctrine! After commending them for holding fast to His name and not denying the faith, Jesus proceeded to address the problem of unsound doctrine in their midst. He said,

"But I have a few things against thee, because thou hast there them that hold the doctrine of Balaam...So hast thou also them that hold the doctrine of the Nicolaitanes, which thing I hate."

Revelation 2:14-15

Jesus was very concerned with this church's acceptance of unsound doctrine because local churches can be destroyed more subtly, swiftly, and completely from the inside than from the outside. Jesus did not direct the church at Pergamos to do spiritual warfare against Satan and his forces. He instructed them to correct the two false doctrines they had allowed to have a place in their congregation. These two false doctrines were the doctrine of Baalam and the doctrine of the Nicolaitanes.

The doctrine of Balaam can refer to several spiritual errors. First, Balaam, an Old Testament seer, loved money and was willing to compromise the Word of the Lord to get it. The doctrine of Balaam could refer, in part, to an emphasis on money and a willingness to compromise the Word of God to get it. Second, Balaam taught Balak to give beautiful women to the men of Israel in order to seduce them away from God. In this way, Israel would bring a curse upon themselves since Balaam did not have permission from God to curse them. Third, Balaam taught that fornication and eating meat offered to idols was not sin. All of these elements were part of the "doctrine of Balaam."

The doctrine of the Nicolaitanes was also false. The Nicolaitanes were a sect of gnostics who followed a heretic named Nicolaus. They taught impure and immoral doctrines such as the community of wives, that adultery and fornication were not sin, and that eating meats offered to idols was permissible. Concerning the doctrine of the Nicolaitanes, Jesus went so far as to say, "which thing I hate."

Why does Jesus hate unsound doctrine? He hates unsound doctrine because it produces unsound believers, ungodly lifestyle, and unstable local churches. He hates false doctrine because it disagrees with the Word of God. He hates unsound doctrine because it leads to perverse lifestyle and a spoiled spiritual harvest. Corrupt doctrine leads to corrupt thinking which leads to corrupt living. Wrong teaching will eventually cause spiritual decay and perhaps even the collapse of once stable local churches.

What did Jesus admonish the church at Pergamos to do concerning the unsound doctrine in their midst? He told them, "Repent!" Listen to His words,

> *"Repent; or else I will come unto thee quickly, and will fight against them with the sword of my mouth."*
>
> Revelation 2:16

Jesus offered the local church at Pergamos two alternatives. First, they could repent by acknowledging the false doctrine in their midst and purging it out themselves. Second, if they did not repent, Jesus would come Himself and fight against those who held to the false doctrines. Notice what Jesus said He would do if this church did not correct the wrong doctrine in their church,

> "...else I will come unto thee quickly and will fight against them with the sword of my mouth."
>
> Revelation 2:16

Notice that Jesus said, "I will come unto *thee* and fight against *them*." This meant that Jesus would visit the whole local church (thee) and purge out those members who held to false doctrine (them). If this church would not judge the members who were holding to unsound doctrine, Jesus would. And He would do so for the well being of the whole body. This church's adherence to unsound doctrine was no minor concern to Jesus. He had already made plans to fight against those who were holding to it!

Why would Jesus fight against those in the church at Pergamos who held to unsound doctrine? He would fight against them because if they refused to turn loose of unsound doctrine, they would remain spiritually sick and contaminate the rest of the church. The Head of the church is strict concerning doctrine because He is concerned for the spiritual health of His body.

Unless the believers in Pergamos repented of their unsound doctrine, Jesus would fight against those who held to it with the sword of His mouth. The "sword of my mouth" that Jesus would use was the Word of God. He would use *The Word* to fight against *their word*. He would use Truth to purge out error. The Head of the church hates false doctrine, commands repentance from it, and promises that He will purge it out if churches do not judge themselves. Jesus concluded His message to the church at Pergamos by saying,

> "He that hath an ear, let him hear what the Spirit saith unto the churches; to him that overcometh will I give to eat of the hidden manna..."
>
> Revelation 2:17

The Church at Thyatira

Jesus also issued very stern words of correction to the church in Thyatira. This local body had permitted someone who was teaching false doctrine and drawing church members into unholy lifestyle to have a place of leadership in their midst. To this church, Jesus said,

> "Notwithstanding I have a few things against thee, because thou sufferest that woman Jezebel, which calleth herself a prophetess, to teach and to seduce my servants to commit fornication, and to eat things sacrificed unto idols."
>
> Revelation 2:20

Jesus told this local church, "I have a few things against thee, because thou sufferest." "Thou sufferest" means, "You allowed." Jesus was angry with this church because they allowed a false prophetess to promote unsound teaching in their midst. Their failure to take correct spiritual action meant that the Head of the church had to do so Himself. Jesus dealt with Jezebel's heart and gave her an opportunity to repent — to change her doctrine and her lifestyle — but she would not. He said,

> "And I gave her space to repent of her fornication; and she repented not."
>
> *Revelation 2:21*

Because Jezebel and her followers refused to repent of their wrong doctrine and perverse lifestyle, Jesus took very decisive and strong action against them. Listen to the judgement He gave,

> "And I will kill her children (her spiritual offspring and followers) with death; and all the churches shall know that I am he which searcheth the reins and hearts: and I will give unto every one of you according to your works."
>
> *Revelation 2:23*

After pronouncing this judgement on Jezebel and her followers, Jesus spoke these words of encouragement to those believers who had not followed Jezebel or embraced her doctrine,

> "But unto…the rest in Thyatira, as many as have not this doctrine…I will put upon you none other burden. But that which ye have already hold fast till I come."
>
> *Revelation 2:24*

It is essential that local churches be sound in doctrine. If doctrine becomes perverted and unsound, it will not be long before lifestyle will have regressed to the place where a part of the church will have to repent or be judged by Jesus. If, however, believers will judge themselves, Jesus will not have to judge them.

Churches must repent if they have allowed unsound doctrine to become established in their midst. Unsound doctrine can be the beginning of the end. It is a weakness in spiritual armor. If doctrine is corrupt, the shield of faith will have holes in it. If doctrine is perverse, the sword of the Spirit will be dull. If doctrine is excessive in one area, believers will go out into the fight of faith with nothing on but one piece of armor. If doctrine is unsound, churches must repent and make a change.

CONCLUSION

Sound doctrine is absolutely essential for believers, for local churches, and for the church as a whole. It commands a very significant place in the spiritual life of the church. If there was a list called, "What is most important for the church?" the development and teaching of sound doctrine would be at the top! Because sound doctrine is so essential, the formulation and teaching of doctrine must be approached with sincerity and care.

The attitude that believers have toward doctrine should not be one of indifference or disinterest. The doctrines that believers and local churches hold to will determine their spiritual condition and their spiritual outcome. If they hold fast to sound doctrine, they will have a solid foundation for strong faith, healthy thinking, and sound spiritual activity. If, however, they delve into and persist in unsound doctrine, their foundation will begin to erode and their spiritual life will be in jeopardy.

·~7~·

What is Unsound Doctrine?

In the previous chapter we learned what sound doctrine is and discovered its significant place in the spiritual life of the church. In this chapter we will learn about unsound doctrine. We will discover that not all unsound doctrine is the same, but that there are different categories of unsound doctrine. Let's start this chapter by defining unsound doctrine.

GANGRENE OR CANCER

The word "unsound" is the opposite of the word "sound." Unsound simply means unhealthy, unwholesome, or unhygienic. Unsound doctrine is unhygienic teaching. It is any teaching that, rather than contributing to spiritual health and preventing spiritual decline, is a source of spiritual sickness and weakness.

Paul exposed the nature and the ill effects of unsound doctrine when he wrote to Timothy of the errant doctrine of Hymenaeus and Philetus. He said,

> "And their word will eat as doth a canker..."
>
> II Timothy 2:17

Paul said that the unsound doctrine of these men would, "eat as doth a canker." The word "eat" comes from the Greek phrase *nomen echo*. This phrase depicts the growth or spread of something. It was used in Greek writings of the spread of fire or of ulcers. Unsound doctrine eats. It spreads like a fire, devouring spiritual health and strength. The Amplified Bible renders Paul's words this way,

> "And their teaching [will devour; it] will eat its way like cancer or spread like gangrene..."
>
> II Timothy 2:17 Amp

Unsound doctrine could be likened to gangrene. Gangrene is the modern medical term for what Paul called, "a canker." It is a disease that results when bacteria hosts on dead tissue. The bacteria which causes gangrene most often attaches itself to a body member that has died because it was cut off from the blood supply. This is often a frostbitten toe or finger. After attaching itself to dead tissue, the bacteria multiplies producing an eating sore. Gangrene is not, however, a minor local problem. It is highly toxic and can spread swiftly to living tissue. Because gangrene is a serious threat to the whole body, it must be confronted immediately. Although the bacteria can be combated with medicine, if the dead tissue it originally attached itself to is not amputated, the whole process will recur.

Unsound doctrine could also be likened to cancer. Unlike gangrene, cancer is a disease that originates within the body. It is the dangerous mutation of once healthy cells. After mutating, newly formed cancer cells begin to divide in a rapid and crazy manner. These mutant cells rob strength and energy from healthy cells. Soon the number of mutant cancer cells have multiplied so greatly that they overtake healthy cells. Whole organs and even the whole body can be dominated. Unless the cancer cells can be isolated and exterminated, they will ravage the whole body and may even cause death. Often, the only way to eliminate cancer from the body is to remove the members or the organs that are infected.

Unsound doctrine can be likened to gangrene or cancer. Like gangrene, unsound doctrine can come from outside the body and take advantage of "dead tissue" (members who have isolated themselves from the sound body). Once it gains a foothold it grows, spreading its toxic poison until it has infected the whole body. Like cancer, unsound doctrine can begin from the inside. Aggressively multiplying mutant cells (unsound teachers who promote unsound doctrine) rob strength from the body and begin to starve out healthy cells. Eventually, the whole body can be weakened and crippled. The effects of unsound doctrine can be debilitating and even devastating. It can put not only individuals, but whole local bodies, and, thus, the whole body of Christ, in jeopardy.

Unsound doctrine is a **primary cause** of spiritual decay and spiritual sickness. It does not add to spiritual life, but takes away. Unsound doctrine is not spiritual food, but spiritual poison. It is unhealthy for individuals, unhealthy for local churches, and unhealthy for the whole church. If allowed to persist, unsound doctrine can lead to the complete corruption of spiritual life.

UNWHOLESOME WORDS

After instructing Timothy in sound teaching, Paul told him,

"...These things teach and exhort. If any man teach otherwise, and consent not to wholesome words, even the words of our Lord Jesus Christ, and to the doctrine which is according to godliness..."

I Timothy 6:2-3

Any teaching that is contrary to "wholesome words," contrary to what Jesus taught, contrary to what Paul taught, or contrary to "the doctrine which is according to godliness" is unsound doctrine! It comes from "men of corrupt minds, and destitute of the truth" [I Timothy 6:5]. These are stought words, but the Holy Spirit inspired Paul to make very strong and clear statements concerning doctrine that is not sound. Concerning the false doctrine of Hymenaeus and Philetus, Paul said,

"...concerning the truth (they) have erred...and overthrow the faith of some."

II Timothy 2:18

Unsound doctrine is any teaching that has erred from the truth. It is any teaching that is not in perfect accord with the doctrines of Christ, the teachings of the apostles, and with the written scriptures which God made sure were accurately recorded for our benefit. Any teaching that could not be **surely** classified as sound doctrine falls into the category of unsound doctrine.

Unsound doctrine is any teaching that cannot be fully supported by the written scriptures. It is not the truth that sets men free, but is the error that leads men to error. It does not establish individuals in the faith, but undermines faith, stirs up fear, dashes hope, causes confusion, leads to division, produces ungodly living, and may even result in the abandonment of the Christian faith. Any teaching that shakes you in your mind, undermines your confidence, subverts your soul, unsettles you, or raises more questions than it gives answers, is unsound doctrine.

CATEGORIES OF UNSOUND DOCTRINE

Not all unsound doctrine is the same. Some is blatantly false — there is no truth in it. Some is a distortion or twisting of truth. Some is simply an excess of a particular truth or the substituting of religious tradition for the words of God. All unsound doctrine, however, is dangerous. In fact, the most dangerous kind of unsound doctrine is that which most closely resemble the truth.

I have classified unsound doctrine into four different categories ranging from blatant false doctrine to tangents in true doctrine. For each of these categories, I have defined the nature of that unsound doctrine and given some examples of it.

ONE: BLATANT FALSE DOCTRINE

Blatant false doctrine is teaching that is obviously opposed to the written Word of God. It is not a slight deviation from truth or an accidental misinterpretation of God's Word. Blatant false doctrine is a lie against the truth and contrary to the scriptures. In it there are no trick questions. Along this line, Paul told Timothy,

> "...if there be any other thing that is contrary to sound doctrine."
>
> I Timothy 1:10

The word "contrary" that Paul used here comes from the Greek *antikeima* and literally means, "to lie against." The same construction of this word is used of the "man of sin" (the antichrist to come) in II Thessalonians 2:4 who, "opposeth and exalteth himself above all that is called God." Blatant false doctrine is not a mistake. It is teaching that is opposed to the truth. If you have even an elementary knowledge of the Word of God, you can recognize it.

Destitute of Truth

In I Timothy 6:1-2, Paul instructed Timothy concerning the correct relationship of servants and masters. Paul called his teaching, "wholesome words" [I Timothy 6:3]. He made it clear, however, that others may teach doctrines contrary to his. Paul did not condone any other teaching in this matter and told Timothy,

> "If any man teach otherwise, and consent not to wholesome words, even the words of our Lord Jesus Christ, and to the doctrine which is according to godliness; He is proud, knowing nothing...Perverse disputings of men of corrupt minds, and destitute of the truth..."
>
> I Timothy 6:3-5

To "consent not" means to not come in agreement with. Blatant false doctrine is teaching that is in obvious disagreement with wholesome words, with the words of Jesus, and with godly doctrine. It originates from men who are "destitute of the truth" and is itself "destitute of the truth." The word "destitute" means totally impoverished. Blatant false doctrine is totally impoverished. There is no truth in it.

This false doctrine, said Paul, comes from men of "corrupt minds." The word "corrupt" he used comes from the Greek *diaphtheiro*. This is an intensified form of the word *phtheiro* which itself means, "utterly corrupt." Blatant

false doctrine comes from those who are fully corrupt and is, itself, completely spoiled and thoroughly rotten. Nothing can be salvaged from the refuse
of blatant false doctrine. It must be discarded!

The unsound doctrine in the church at Thyatira is a pertinent example
of blatant false doctrine. To this church, Jesus said,

> *"Notwithstanding I have a few things against thee, because thou sufferest that*
> *woman Jezebel, which calleth herself a prophetess, to teach and to seduce my ser-*
> *vants to commit fornication...But unto you I say, and unto the rest in Thyatira,*
> *as many as have not this doctrine..."*
>
> Revelation 2:20,24

Jezebel, a woman who called herself a prophetess, was allowed to teach
in the church at Thyatira. She was likely one of the gnostic women who
taught that sexual involvement led to deeper spiritual experiences. These
gnostic women believed that in the beginning Eve was not deceived, but led
the way into greater spiritual knowledge by partaking of the tree of the
knowledge of good and evil.

Jezebel's doctrine, however, was blatantly false. She taught that fornication was permissible in the Christian experience. Her teaching was not
a slight deviation from the truth or a mix of truth and error. It was 100%
wrong! Adultery and fornication are clearly forbidden by the Word of God.
Jezebel was allowed to teach in the church at Thyatira, however, and was
successful in persuading some members, perhaps even elders in the church,
to participate in her ungodly lifestyle.

The church of this generation is also guilty of embracing blatantly false
doctrine. Some so-called spiritual leaders deny the virgin birth of Jesus.
By so doing, they deny His deity. This is the spirit of antichrist and in
direct opposition to the truth. Others teach that the Bible is not inerrant
and say that certain teachings do not apply to the times we are living in.
By taking these positions, individuals make themselves greater than God.
They give themselves authority to choose which words of God are and are
not acceptable.

Some liberal churches of this generation teach that homosexuality is
acceptable. They say it is not sin, but a lifestyle preference. They teach that
God accepts homosexuals just as He accepts everyone else. This is contrary
to the written scriptures and is blatant false doctrine. God's Word says that
"women who change the natural use into that which is against nature" and
"men, leaving the natural use of the woman [and] burn[ing] in their lust one
toward another...working that which is unseemly" are those who have
"changed the truth of God into a lie" [Romans 2:25-27]. Not only have they

changed the truth into a lie, however. They have also tried to make their lies the truth. Individuals who do this are vain in their imaginations; their hearts have been darkened. They profess to be wise, but are fools. Because they choose not to retain God in their knowledge, they have been given over to a reprobate mind [Romans 2:21, 22, 28].

"But," you may ask, "doesn't God accept everyone?" No, He does not. God accepts every repentant sinner. Those who approach God on their own terms and expect to be accepted with open arms will be bitterly disappointed. Paul preached this great truth in his address to the men of Athens when he said,

> "And the times of this ignorance God winked at; but now commandeth all men everywhere to repent..."
>
> Acts 17:30

In times past, God winked at the sins of the ignorant. Now, however, through the gospel message, He commands men to repent of their sin and accept deliverance in Christ. Paul reported to king Agrippa that the gospel message he preached was,

> "...they should repent and turn to God, and do works meet for repentance."
>
> Acts 26:20

If the Word of God is contrary to our personal value systems, then our value systems must be rejected. This is not easy for any one of us. The Word of God is not, however, a soft pillow that can be shaped to fit our fancy. Rather, it is a sharp two-edged sword that cuts to the heart and exposes sin and self. If anyone desires to **accept** the message of salvation through faith in Jesus Christ, he must also be willing to **reject** teachings and activities that are contrary to the Word of Truth. It is not only God's will, "to have all men to be saved," but also to have all men, "come unto the knowledge of the truth" [I Timothy 2:4].

Heresies

Blatant false doctrine includes what the Bible calls heresies. A heresy, according to W. E. Vine, is a self-willed opinion which is substituted for submission to the power of truth. These erroneous opinions are frequently the result of personal preference or the prospect of advantage. They are the inventions of self-willed individuals who will not submit themselves to the truth. They fit the preferences of ungodly men instead of fitting with the holy scriptures. Heretical doctrines are plain error. They are not just twisted truths, but are false teachings purposely substituted for the truth.

Some false spiritual leaders of our generation are promoting the heresy of reincarnation. They teach that people will be incarnated again after they die and given a chance to do better the second, third, or one hundredth time around. This is absolutely false doctrine. It is a heretical teaching substituted for the Word of God. The scriptures clearly declare that, "it is appointed unto men once to die, but after this the judgement" [Hebrews 9:27]. Although the doctrine of reincarnation is obviously false, there remains a possibility that it will gain entrance into and affect local churches.

In II Peter 2:1-2, Peter wrote of false teachers who,

"...privily shall bring in (into the body) damnable heresies, even denying the Lord that bought them, and bring upon themselves swift destruction. And many shall follow their pernicious ways..."

II Peter 2:1-2

The false teachings Peter called "damnable heresies" included denying the Lord Jesus. The doctrine of salvation through faith in Jesus Christ is the cornerstone of the Christian faith. To deny Christ and His saving work is obvious and completely false doctrine.

In his first epistle, the apostle John warned his spiritual children of false spiritual leaders he called antichrists. These men had once been part of the sound body, but had departed from the faith. Now they taught lies [I John 2:21]. One of their blatant lies was their teaching that Jesus of Nazareth was not the Christ. Of these teachers and their teaching, John wrote,

"Who is a liar but he that denieth that Jesus is the Christ? He is antichrist, that denieth the Father and the Son. Whosoever denieth the Son, the same hath not the Father..."

I John 2:22-23

The teachings of these antichrists were blatantly false. John was concerned, however, that these false teachings would influence the church. Because he was concerned, he reminded his spiritual children to,

"Let that therefore abide in you, which ye have heard from the beginning..."

I John 2:24

Profane Teaching

In his first letter to Timothy, Paul warned him,

"...refuse profane and old wives' fables, and exercise thyself rather unto godliness."

I Timothy 4:7

W. E. Vine says that the word profane (from the Greek *bebelos*) signifies that which lacks all relationship or affinity to God. It is the opposite of divine or holy. Paul called the teachings of God's Word, "the holy scriptures," and said that they were given by Divine inspiration [II Timothy 3:15-16]. Peter reported that the prophesy of scripture came when, "holy men...were moved by the Holy Ghost" [II Peter 2:21]. The Word of God is holy. It came from the Holy Spirit through holy men. Blatant false doctrine, on the other hand, is profane. It lacks all relationship with and affinity to God. It does not come from God, it is not condoned by God, and it will not lead men to God.

Paul told Timothy to refuse profane teaching. The word "refuse" comes from the Greek *katapheugo* and is a strengthened form of *pheugo* which means, "to flee away from." Timothy was to quickly and decidedly flee from any teaching which lacked affinity to God and run, rather, unto godliness. This was a significant part of obeying Paul's instruction to, "exercise thyself rather unto godliness."

In I Timothy 6:20-21, Paul repeated his instructions to Timothy concerning profane teaching saying,

> "O Timothy, keep that which is committed to thy trust, avoiding profane and vain babblings, and oppositions of science falsely so called: Which some professing have erred concerning the faith..."
>
> I Timothy 6:20-21

Paul instructed Timothy to, "keep that which is committed to thy trust." Committed to Timothy's trust was the responsibility to maintain sound doctrine and sound spiritual life in the church by preaching and teaching the sound Word of God. Keeping what had been committed to his trust included avoiding "profane and vain babblings." To avoid means to make a conscious effort to prevent something. If Timothy did not consciously keep his distance from profane and vain babblings, he would risk losing what had been committed to his trust. And he would not have been the first! Notice what happened to some individuals because they gave heed to profane and vain babblings,

> "...profane and vain babblings, and oppositions of science falsely so called: **Which some professing have erred** concerning the faith..."
>
> I Timothy 6:21

Some, because they followed profane and vain babblings, had already deviated from the purity of the Word of God, slipped in their responsibility concerning ministry, and erred concerning the faith. Blatant false doctrine is error that leads men into error and spiritual shipwreck!

Paul issued another warning to Timothy in his second letter saying,

"But shun profane and vain babblings: for they will increase unto more ungodliness. And their word will eat as does a canker: of whom is Hymenaeus and Philetus; Who concerning the truth have erred, saying that the resurrection is past already; and overthrow the faith of some."

II Timothy 2:16-18

The profane babblings of Hymenaeus and Philetus included their teaching that the resurrection was already past. This was not just questionable or "ify" doctrine. This was blatant false doctrine. Concerning the truth, these men had erred. To err means to miss the mark. These men not only missed the bullseye; they completely missed the target! Although they were speaking about a subject that was valid, their teaching on that subject was completely erroneous. Their doctrine, though blatantly false, influenced the church. The faith of some was overthrown because of it. It is possible for believers to be drawn away and overthrown even by blatant false doctrine.

Believers should be well enough established in the Word of God that they don't embrace blatant false doctrine. It is, however, possible to be a Christian and yet be unskilled in the word of righteousness [Hebrews 5:13]. If you are in that spiritual condition, if you are a baby Christian, you must be very cautious concerning doctrine. Blatant false doctrine, although obviously wrong, is especially dangerous to young believers.

TWO: ERRONEOUS DOCTRINE

Unsound doctrine is not always, or only, blatant false teaching. It can also include teachings which are a dangerous mix of truth and error, teachings that result from twisting or perverting the truth, or teachings that go beyond the truth as laid out in the written scriptures. This second category of unsound doctrine, Erroneous Doctrine, is comprised of corrupt doctrine, twisted doctrine, perverted doctrine, and doctrine that has trespassed beyond the boundaries of the written scriptures. This category of unsound doctrine is more prevalent in the church than blatant false doctrine and can be extremely dangerous for believers and local churches.

Corrupt Doctrine

Corrupt doctrine is a mixture of truth and error. It often results when the influences of the times or the aspirations, wishes, and opinions of men mix with what God has said. There is a temptation for men in every generation to mix popular philosophies with the Word of God in an attempt to keep the church "updated." Corrupt doctrine could be nine parts true and one part false. It could be one half the Word of God and one half personal opinion. It could be a mix of scripture and religious tradition.

Paul spoke of the corrupting influence of unsound teaching in his second letter to the church at Corinth. He wrote,

> *"But I fear, lest by any means, as the serpent beguiled Eve through his subtilty, so your minds should be corrupted from the simplicity that is in Christ."*
>
> II Corinthians 11:3

The word "corrupt" Paul used here comes from the Greek *phtheiro*. This word means to destroy by the means of corruption and bring into a worse state. According to Webster, to corrupt means to introduce deceiving information into something originally sound. Other words that correspond to corrupt are rotten, infected, tainted, spoiled, perverted, and impure. Corrupt doctrine results when deceiving information is introduced into and mixed with the sound Word of God.

An interesting illustration of corrupt doctrine can be taken from the early days of statue making. Some sculptors, rather than putting forth the effort to correct errors in their workmanship, used wax to fill in cracks and holes and to hide faults in their statues. Over time, however, the heat of the sun, the penetration of light, and the force of nature broke down the wax and the faults began to appear. In time the statue crumbled revealing that it was corrupt from the start.

Corrupt doctrine is partially based in the written scriptures, but severely tainted by the thoughts and opinions of man. It contains the Word of God and may even be primarily the Word of God, but is not the pure Word of God. Truth is like gold refined seven times in the furnace. Corrupt doctrine, however, contains dangerous impurities.

Paul wrote this to Titus concerning the kind of doctrine he was to formulate and teach,

> *"...in doctrine shewing uncorruptness, gravity, sincerity, Sound speech, that cannot be condemned..."*
>
> Titus 2:7-8

The word "uncorruptness" that Paul used here is the Greek *aphthoria*. It means to be free from any taint. There was to be no personal opinion or worldly philosophy in Titus' doctrine. His doctrine was to be purely the Word of God. Nothing was to be added to it and nothing was to be taken away from it. His doctrine was to be sound, sure, and clear, leaving no chance that someone would find a weakness and condemn it.

In his doctrine Titus was to show "gravity." This word comes from the Greek *semnotes* and denotes dignity and respectability. Sound doctrine is teaching that conforms to the very highest standards of purity as represented by the written Word of God. Corrupt doctrine, on the other hand, is teaching that has slipped from the very high standards that are required for a teaching to qualify as sound doctrine.

In his doctrine Titus was to show "sincerity." This word comes from the Greek *eilikrines* and denotes purity. It was used of unalloyed, pure, and unmixed substances. Doctrine is to be unalloyed. There is to be no mixing of human opinion, personal preference, worldly philosophy, or any other teaching with the Word of Truth. Adding anything to the Word of God leads to corrupt doctrine.

Titus' doctrine was to be, "sound speech that cannot be condemned." Sound doctrine, when inspected by the searchlight of the Word of God, will be found to be completely reliable. Corrupt doctrine, on the other hand, is teaching that can be condemned. When inspected, it is found to contain dangerous weaknesses. This kind of doctrine must be judged as unsound and declared unsafe.

The Amplified Bible renders Paul's instructions to Titus concerning doctrine this way,

> "...*teaching what is unadulterated*...let your instruction be sound and fit...irrefutable and above censure, so that the opponent may be put to shame, finding nothing discrediting or evil to say..."
>
> *Titus 2:7-8*

Sound doctrine is unadulterated. There is nothing "sleeping" with the Word of God in sound doctrine. It is pure and uncorrupted, unmixed with lies, human philosophy, or opinion. Sound doctrine is above censure and irrefutable. It is not possible to argue against sound doctrine from the written scriptures.

Corrupt doctrine is adulterated. It is the offspring of the Word of God and the opinions of men. Corrupt doctrine is refutable. It is not blatantly false, but it is full of weak spots. Even a young believer will have questions surface in his mind when he encounters corrupt doctrine. In a short time, he will be able to think of three or four scriptures that disagree with what is being taught.

God's Word, said the Psalmist, is very pure [Psalms 119:140]. Proverbs 30:5 says, "Every Word of God is pure." Adding anything to God's Word corrupts and weakens it just as adding a foreign substance to metal causes it to be weak. If metal is corrupt, it will crumble either in a time of stress or just over time. If doctrine is corrupt, it will crumble when the Light of God's Word and the fire of the Truth is brought to play upon it.

God Hates a Mix

There is an interesting Old Testament scripture which very aptly illus-trates the danger of corrupting doctrine by mixing truth with error. In this scripture God was instructing Israel concerning the purity of their vineyards. He said,

"Thou shalt not sow thy vineyard with divers (different) seeds; lest the fruit of thy seed which thou hast sown, and the fruit of thy vineyard, be defiled."

Deuteronomy 22:9

In this instruction God expressed His high standards concerning mixing different seeds. He also revealed the results of such activity. If a vineyard was sown with diverse seeds, the fruit would be defiled. If the fruit was defiled, then the new seeds in the fruit would be defiled. If these defiled seeds were planted and mixed again with other seeds, the purity of the strain would be further weakened. The original mixing of seeds would start a downward spiral of corruption.

Jesus compared the human heart to ground and compared the Word of God to seed [Mark 4]. When a mixture of seed, some incorruptible (the Word of God) and some corruptible (man's word), is planted in the human heart, the harvest will be defiled. Not only will the fruit be spoiled, but the new seed in the fruit will be corrupted. When this corrupted seed is replant-ed and mixed again with other corrupt seed, it will be weakened even more. By the second generation of planting, the pure strain of God's Word will have been dangerously corrupted.

In the world system scientists and farmers cross-pollinate in order to achieve superior strains of seed. In the spiritual realm, however, God has already provided the perfect seed. This perfect and incorruptible seed is the Word of God. Anytime this Incorruptible Seed is mixed with something else, its perfection, strength, and every other superior quality will be dimin-ished.

Another Old Testament admonition concerning the danger of a mixture can be found in Leviticus 19:19. Here God said,

"...Thou shalt not let thy cattle gender with a diverse kind: thou shalt not sow thy field with mingled seed: neither shall a garment mingled of linen and woolen come upon thee."

Leviticus 19:19

God forbade mixing because mixing produced weakness. If cattle were mixed, the strain would be tainted and the offspring weakened. If seeds were mixed in the field, the fruit would be defiled and the harvest diminished.

If a garment was made by the mingling of linen and woolen, it would not hold together over time and under stress.

Were these instructions written only for Israel concerning natural things or is there a spiritual application? No doubt there is a spiritual application. These instructions illustrate God's thinking concerning doctrine. God loves purity. He does not like a mix. A mix is dangerous. It is not strong. It is not pure. The offspring of a mixture is weakness. The harvest of a mixture is defiled fruit. It is not God's will that His Incorruptible Seed be mixed with corruptible seed.

Example of Corrupt Doctrine

A teaching that could easily become part of this category called corrupt doctrine is the teaching on financial prosperity. A very popular doctrinal position says that if a believer is faithful in giving, God will give them up to a one hundred-fold return and will continue to increase their financial standing. There is an emphasis in this teaching on giving to get (especially giving to get out of financial debt) and a strong impression left that God wants each person to be rich.

Certainly, God is a God of increase. Certainly, the man who meditates in the law of the Lord will prosper at whatever he sets his hands to do [Psalms 1:3]. Certainly, if a man sows bountifully, he will reap bountifully [II Corinthians 9:6]. Certainly, the man that gives finances will have finances returned to him full measure, pressed down, shaken together and running over [Luke 6:38]. Without a doubt, the New Testament teaches that a man who gives will be blessed in proportion to his giving. We must not fail, however, to consult and teach the whole counsel of God's Word concerning finances. We must also be careful not to add our own wishes and opinions to the pure Word of God.

Paul warned Timothy on many occasions about money, especially concerning the pursuit of riches. Evidently there was a popular doctrine in Timothy's day which equated financial gain with spirituality. This teaching said, "gain is godliness." In other words, prospering financially was a sign that God was pleased with one's life. Paul differed with this doctrine and those who taught it and told Timothy, "from such withdraw yourself." Paul then corrected this corrupt doctrine saying,

> *"But godliness with contentment (being content with what you have) is great gain. For we brought nothing into this world, and it is certain we can carry nothing out. And having food and raiment let us be therewith content. But they that will (want to) be rich fall into temptation and a snare...some (who) coveted after (money)...have erred from the faith..."*
>
> I Timothy 6:6-10

Who would dare to preach in this generation the warning Paul preached to Timothy about desiring to be rich? Who would dare to teach in this day of Success Seminars that Christians should be content with food and clothes and be content with what they already have [I Timothy 6:8; Hebrews 13:5]? Certainly not the preachers. They like to preach, "Give generously to me and God will give generously to you." People love to hear this message because they too want to prosper.

Some ministers, in an attempt to validate their teaching on money, have gone so far as to use the Parable of the Sower and the Seed to teach that if believers give their finances into good ground (they say this means a good ministry), they will receive a hundred-fold return on their giving. The parable of the Sower and the Seed is not, however, a teaching about how to get rich, but is the revelation of how the Word of God bears spiritual fruit when it is planted in a good heart. Jesus did not say, "The seed is money." He clearly stated, "The seed is the Word of God" [Luke 8:11]. In this parable, the seed is God's Word, the ground is the human heart (not a ministry), and the one hundred-fold harvest depicts the fruits of righteousness which richly abound when Incorruptible Seed is planted in good ground and carefully tended. To teach that believers will get a one-hundred fold financial return if they give into a good ministry on the basis of this parable is corrupt doctrine. It is a mixture of the Word of God and the wishes of men.

"But," you may ask, "where in the Bible can we find the doctrine of the one hundred-fold return?" I'm sorry, there is no Bible doctrine of a one hundred-fold return concerning finances. Yes, if you sow abundantly you will reap abundantly. Even if you sow sparingly, you will reap! But nowhere does the Bible teach that if you give one dollar, you will get one hundred back.

If ministers are not careful about what they teach in the areas of finances and success, they will be guilty of *purporting* in their teaching what cannot be *supported* by the Word of God. At that point their doctrine will be corrupt. It will be a mix of truth and opinion.

Ministers who are pushing these unsound doctrines concerning finances and success are guilty of motivating people in the very direction the Word of God warns against! Paul told Timothy that believers who desire to be rich, "fall into temptation and snare and into many foolish and hurtful lust which drown men in destruction." He continued on to say, "the love of money is the root of all evil." Then he told Timothy,

"But thou, O man of God, flee these things..."

I Timothy 6:11

What was Timothy to flee? He was to flee riches and the love of money!

When modern ministers instruct believers how to prosper, but fail to balance this message with the rest of the counsel of God's Word, they only stir up people's carnal desire to be rich. Believers begin to think that if they can just get a little more money, they will be content. This is precisely the "deceitfulness of riches" Jesus warned against in the parable of the Sower and the Seed! To teach sound doctrine concerning money or any other area, ministers must include the whole counsel of the Word of God. No scripture should be neglected and no personal opinions, aspirations, or wishes should be added.

Twisted Doctrine

In II Peter, the apostle Peter remarked to his readers that because Paul's epistles were difficult to understand, some twisted his teachings. He said,

"As also in all his (Paul's) epistles, speaking in them of these things; in which are some things hard to be understood, which they that are unlearned and unstable wrest, as they do also the other scriptures, unto their own destruction."

II Peter 3:16

Unsound doctrine often results when the unlearned or the unstable twist the scriptures. The *unlearned* are individuals who have not devoted time and effort to establish themselves in sound doctrine. Because they have not committed themselves to study, they cannot consistently and accurately divide the Word of truth. Consequently, they twist the scriptures in their effort to explain the scriptures. The *unstable* are individuals who are not spiritually sound themselves and, therefore, take careless liberties with the Word of God. If they have a personal theory they want to teach, but don't have enough scriptural support, they will twist some Bible verse or take it out of context to support what they are teaching. Because they want their teachings to appear Biblically sound, they will twist scriptures to support their opinions.

Those who teach the Word of God should be, at least to some degree, particular and technical. To even slightly misquote or misapply a scripture is to step away from the pure Word of God. Ministers should not be so technical that they miss the spirit of what God is saying, but neither should they be so relaxed that they mishandle the Word of God. There is a healthy balance between a stiff, intellectual approach to the scriptures and a sloppy, careless approach.

Example of Forbidding to Marry

In his first letter to Timothy, Paul wrote,

"Now the Spirit speaketh expressly, that in the latter times some shall depart from the faith, giving heed to seducing spirits, and doctrines of devils...Forbidding to marry..."

I Timothy 4:1-3

The Spirit of God has foretold that in the last days there will be a doctrine promoted which teaches that it is not right to marry. Paul called this a doctrine of demons, but reported that some believers would follow it. How will a doctrine like this get started?

Perhaps some young, zealous minister will read that Paul said concerning the unmarried and widows, "It is good if they abide even as I" [I Corinthians 7:8]. Paul taught that it was good if an unmarried person remained unmarried. He made it clear, however, that he taught this by permission and not by commandment of the Lord. In verse six, he said, "But I speak this by permission, and not of commandment [I Corinthians 7:6]. In verse 10, addressing those who were married, Paul said, "And unto the married I command, yet not I, but the Lord." This statement itself implies that what he had written to the unmarried was by permission, not by commandment. Paul's teaching that it was better for the unmarried not to marry could not be considered a, "Thus sayeth the Lord," but a, "Thus suggesteth Paul." It is very possible, however, that an unlearned or unstable individual could twist these scriptures and use them to to support an erroneous doctrine that forbade single believers to marry.

A person might also use the response the disciples made to Jesus' teaching about marriage to support a teaching that forbade marriage. The disciples said,

"If the case of the man be so with his wife, it is not good to marry."

Matthew 19:10

Jesus responded to this remark about marriage by saying that there would, in fact, be some who would make themselves eunuchs for the sake of the kingdom of God. He clarified His remark, however, saying that only those who were first called to that lifestyle would be able to receive and obey that instruction [Matthew 19:11-12]. By saying this, He clearly implied that marriage is the norm. Paul agreed with this when he said concerning some not marrying that,

*"...every man hath his proper **gift of God**, one after this manner, and another after that."*

I Corinthians 7:7

An individual might also use Jesus' promise that those who left family, house, and wives would receive a one-hundred-fold reward [Matthew 19:29]. If a person concentrated on this scripture, twisting it and removing it from its context, he could formulate and promote a new doctrine about not marrying or even about leaving one's wife.

If a minister or any other person wanted to teach believers not to marry because, "it's more spiritual to serve only the Lord," he could twist any one of these scriptures and support his theory. He could even say, "This is a now word for young believers who want to be in the end-time army of the Lord!" You may ask me, "Do you really think someone would teach as a Bible doctrine that believers should not marry?" No, I don't *think* they will. I *know* they will! The "Spirit speaketh expressly" to us concerning this very teaching and the last days. This unsound doctrine **will** arise in the last days because the unlearned or unstable will twist the scriptures concerning marriage.

Example of Pulling Down Strongholds

Another modern day example of twisting the scriptures to make them say something they were not intended to say is the use of II Corinthians 10:3-5 to teach spiritual warfare and mind renewal. Many ministers of this generation are using this scripture as a launching pad to teach all manner of things including pulling down strongholds of territorial demonic principalities over cities, warring in prayer against the devil, and renewing the mind. If you take time to check the context of this scripture, however, you will discover that Paul was not teaching on prayer, not teaching on spiritual warfare, not teaching on demonic strongholds, and not teaching on the renewing of the mind.

In this portion of his second letter to the church at Corinth, Paul was answering the attack of the false apostles in Corinth who accused him of being a false apostle and operating in the flesh. Paul wrote to the church at Corinth and defended himself against his accusers by saying,

> "...I think to be bold against some (the false apostles in Corinth), which think of us as if we walked according to the flesh. For though we walk in the flesh, we do not war after the flesh..."
>
> II Corinthians 10:2-3

Paul was continuing here the defense of his apostleship which he began in chapter three saying,

"Do we begin again to commend ourselves? or need we, as some others (speaking of false apostles), epistles of commendation to you, or letters of commendation from you?"

II Corinthians 3:1

A great part of Paul's second letter to the church at Corinth was a defense of his apostleship. In chapter five he wrote that he was an ambassador for Christ. In chapter six he defended his apostleship by speaking of his total commitment to fulfill his divine calling. He picked up this theme again in chapter ten arguing that he did not war after the flesh as he had been accused of by false apostles, but that the weapons of his warfare were mighty through God. He continued on for the rest of chapters ten and eleven and the first part of chapter twelve defending his apostleship and challenging the false apostles in Corinth. In II Corinthians 10:4-5, Paul wrote,

"(For the weapons of our warfare are not carnal, but mighty through God to the pulling down of strongholds;) Casting down imaginations, and every high thing that exalteth itself against the knowledge of God, and bringing into captivity every thought to the obedience of Christ."

II Corinthians 10:4-5

The "weapons" Paul wrote of did not refer to prayer or praise, but to the preaching of God's Word by the inspiration of the Holy Spirit. Through this kind of preaching he refuted the unregenerate thinking of men and brought them into submission to the truth. Prayer may be a weapon, but it is not suggested in this context. Praise may be a weapon, but neither is it suggested in this context. Paul's weapon against the strongholds, imaginations, and high things that exalted themselves against the knowledge of God was the proclamation of Truth. The "weapons of his warfare" were his speech and preaching which were not with enticing words of men's wisdom, but a demonstration of the Spirit and power [I Corinthians 2:3-5]. This weapon of anointed preaching was powerful through God to pull down the strongholds of men's thinking by producing a revolution in their hearts!

The "strongholds" Paul wrote of were not demons that had control over cities. They were not prevailing territorial spirits that had control over specific geographic territories. Demons are not even suggested in this context. By "strongholds" Paul was also not referring to the unrenewed thoughts of believers. Mind renewal is not mentioned in this context. The strongholds, imaginations, and high things Paul spoke of in this context were the philosophies and reasonings of unregenerate men.

You may say to me, "Now, brother Guy, don't you think we have power in prayer? Don't you think we can affect our cities through prayer? Isn't prayer one of the weapons we can use to fight our good fight of faith?" Of course, I believe we have power in prayer. I believe we can affect our cities through prayer. Yes, prayer could be considered a weapon in spiritual life. But you have missed the point. The point I am making is that this particular scripture does not teach that believers should war in prayer against demonic principalities that rule over cities.

You may also say to me, "Now, brother Guy, don't you think believers need to renew their minds with the Word of God and pull down vain imaginations and wrong thinking?" Absolutely! And I can prove the importance of mind renewal from numerous scriptures, both Old and New Testament. Again, however, you have missed the point. The point is that this scripture does not teach about renewing our minds. "But," you may say, "I know leading ministers who use this scripture to teach spiritual warfare and to teach about pulling down territorial demonic strongholds over cities." Or you may say, "I know leading ministers who use this scripture to teach on the renewing of the mind."

Christians must realize that just because someone has a Television ministry, has written a book, has a newsletter, or advertises in a magazine, is no proof that his teaching is accurate and has been approved by God. What Paul meant in II Corinthians 10:3-5 is exactly what I said he meant. He was defending himself against false apostles who had gained entrance to the church at Corinth and were accusing him of being a false apostle and operating in the flesh. He was not teaching about militant prayer. He was not teaching about demonic strongholds over cities. And he was not teaching on mind renewal. He was defending his God-ordained and God-anointed ministry of preaching and teaching!

Ministers (and other believers) must not add their own twists to the Word of God. Anytime a minister twists a scripture to support his theory or even to support a true doctrine, he is on very dangerous ground. If one has to hunt extensively for scripture verses to support their theory or has to twist the Word of God even a little to fit their sermon, they don't have enough Word to preach their subject!

Example of Every Christian Has a Demon

Another twisted doctrine that is again popular in our day is the teaching that every Christian has a demon and needs deliverance. Those who teach this twisted doctrine attribute every disease, every sin, and every negative thought to demonic activity. This teaching can be extremely radical. I heard about one man who ate breakfast cereal before an evening church meeting. When the leadership in the church heard about this, they said he had to be delivered of a spirit of gluttony because he lusted after breakfast food in the evening. They interceded over him and the "demon" came out. The evidence of his deliverance was that he vomited up the breakfast cereal! Yes, unsound doctrine can go this far!

Surely, people can have demons. This is clear from the Word of God and from the experiences of life. Jesus Himself taught that believers must cast out demons. Demons can cause problems, both mental and physical. The lunatic boy that Jesus ministered to was tormented by a demon. The crazy man of Gadare, when set free from Legion, was instantly right in his mind. On one occasion, Jesus pointed out a bowed over woman and said that she had been subject to a spirit of infirmity for 18 years. A deaf and dumb boy was immediately able to hear and speak when the demon was cast out of him. These scriptures make it clear that people can be demonized. The Word of God cannot, however, be twisted to prove that every Christian has a demon.

Nowhere does the Word of God teach or even suggest that every Christian has a demon. Nowhere does the Bible teach or suggest that every physical, mental, and spiritual problem can be attributed to a demon. Nowhere do any of the writers of the epistles attribute believers' sin problems or emotional problems to demonic possession. To teach this doctrine or to even imply it is a severe twisting of both the teachings and the examples of the scriptures.

The whole Word of God must be consulted concerning this doctrine. For example, what about the young man who was living in incest with his mother in the church at Corinth? Did Paul say this young man was possessed with a lust demon? No, Paul chided the whole church at Corinth for their lack of discipline and then instructed them, not to cast out a demon, but to turn this young man over to Satan for the destruction of his flesh [I Corinthians 5:1-5]. If this young man was already demonized, why would they turn him over to Satan? The fact is that this young man's sexual sin was a flesh problem!

When Paul wrote over and over again to various local churches about being careful of strife, did he ever warn them about a spirit of strife? No, Paul classified strife as a work of the flesh. What about other sins like adultery, lust, gluttony, and drunkenness. Are these caused by demons? There is no doubt that demons can attempt to stir people in these areas of sin, but Paul calls them, "works of the flesh" [Galatians 5:19-20]. The overriding emphasis of the New Testament concerning sin problems is that Christians must mortify their flesh and discipline their bodies [Romans 8:13]! Read and learn!

Example of Warring Tongues

Another current doctrine that often accompanies the excessive teaching on demons and deliverance is the "new revelation" that there is warring tongue for tormenting and driving out devils. One scripture used to support this erroneous theory is I Corinthians 12:28 which says there are, "diversities of tongues." This scripture has been severely twisted and wrongly interpreted to teach that one of the tongues believers possess is for the purpose of tormenting and casting out devils.

The context of I Corinthians 12:28 does not in any way support this postulated theory and errant teaching. By, "diversities of tongues," Paul was not referring to believer's power against demons through praying in other tongues, but was teaching about one aspect of the diversities of ministries within the church. The phrase, "diversities of tongues," in this passage refers specifically to that manifestation of the Spirit where one individual speaks forth a message in an unknown tongue and another individual (or sometimes the one who gave the tongue) interprets that message. The combination of the diversity of tongues and the interpretation of tongues is equal to prophesy.

The Word of God clearly teaches certain truths concerning speaking in other tongues. First, speaking in other tongues is one of the initial signs of the baptism of the Holy Spirit [Acts 2:4; 19:6]. Second, speaking in other tongues is a special language by which believers can speak mysteries with God in prayer and build themselves up [I Corinthians 14:2,4]. Third, speaking in other tongues can be one half of a manifestation of the Holy Spirit by which God speaks to men. The other half of this manifestation is the interpretation of the unknown tongue either by the one who spoke in the unknown tongue or by another individual [I Corinthians 12:10,28]. Nowhere does the Word of God mention casting out or tormenting demons in other tongues. Speaking in tongues is **never** connected with anything called spiritual warfare or with any kind of speaking to the devil.

It is impossible to deduce or even support from I Corinthians 12:28 or from any other New Testament scripture the theory that there is a tongue for battling evil principalities or casting out demons. Even if it was suggested in this text, it would be doctrinal suicide to base this teaching on one-fifth of one scripture lifted out of its context. Ministers are on very dangerous ground when what they teach is based on twisted and lifted scriptures!

Some of these modern "doctrines" are nothing more than what wish-to-be spiritual leaders are setting forth in order to appear as spiritually knowledgeable. Some of these ministers are not even aware that what they are teaching is unsound doctrine! Some know their teaching is unsound, but love the power and attention it brings them. At best, these errant teachings are invalid. At worst, they will produce spiritual weakness and confusion in the church and in local churches.

Perverted Doctrine

Perverted doctrine is unsound teaching which results when individuals transform a truth from the Word of God into something completely different than what it was intended to mean. The word "perverted" used in the New Testament usually means to change something into its opposite. In the book of Acts this word is used of the sun being turned to darkness [Acts 2:20]. James used this word to describe laughter being turned into mourning [James 4:9]. When a teaching is perverted, it is usually changed into the opposite of what it was intended to mean. Paul used this word "perverted" to describe the unsound teaching of false ministers who were negatively influencing the churches in Galatia. To these churches he wrote,

"*...there be some that trouble you, and would pervert the gospel of Christ.*"
Galatians 1:7-8

Paul constantly dealt with false ministers who perverted the truth in order to gain control in local churches. One perversion of truth he addressed in the churches of Galatia was the issue of Christian liberty. He wrote,

"*...brethren, ye have been called unto liberty; only use not liberty for an occasion to the flesh...*"
Galatians 5:13

Why did Paul have to warn these believers not to use their liberty in Christ as an opportunity to sin? Because there were those who perverted the doctrine of liberty, using it as an excuse to indulge the passions of the flesh. What was a wonderful truth about liberty in Christ was perverted into a license to sin.

In his letter to the church at Rome, Paul instructed believers about the grace of God. He taught them the New Covenant truth that because they were under grace, they were free from the law. He warned them, however, not to use this doctrine of grace as a license to sin, but to be self disciplined by reckoning themselves dead to sin and alive to God [Romans 6:1-23]. The true doctrine of grace could have easily been perverted into a license to sin. In fact, Jude wrote of false teachers who were perverting this very doctrine.

He said they were, "ungodly men, turning the grace of our God into lasciviousness" [Jude 4]. These ungodly men, posing as ministers, perverted the revelation of God's grace through Christ. When perverted, the teaching about God's grace was no longer a reason for rejoicing and a motivation to please God by living righteously. Instead it, became a teaching that authorized believers to exercise lust through excess and indecency.

Is perverted doctrine dangerous? Listen to what Paul said concerning those who perverted the gospel he preached,

> "...some...pervert the gospel of Christ. But though we, or an angel from heaven, preach any other gospel unto you than that which we have preached unto you, let him be accursed."
>
> Galatians 1:7-8

To "be accursed" means to be damned to hell. Those who pervert the truth are in danger of damnation. God does not like perverted doctrine. The spiritual results are too debilitating!

Trespassing Doctrine

Sound doctrine has boundaries. Some individuals, however, trespass these boundaries. They go beyond the limitations of the written scriptures and, thus, go beyond the truth. When individuals stretch beyond what is written in the Word, unsound doctrine results. The apostle John, a great lover of the truth, said,

> "Whosoever transgresseth and abideth not in the doctrine of Christ, hath not God. He that abideth in the doctrine of Christ, he hath both the Father and the Son."
>
> II John 9

The best manuscripts of II John have the Greek word *proago* for "transgresseth." This word is often translated, "go." It means, "to go before," or, "to lead the way." The Revised Version's marginal reading of II John 9 says, "taketh the lead."

Some Christians and even some ministers trespass the boundaries of sound doctrine. They do not abide in the doctrine of Christ. They do not stay with the principles of the oracles of God. They do not remain steadfast in the written scriptures. They go beyond sound doctrine, crossing over the boundary marked, "Danger Ahead." They venture into speculation, imagination, opinion, and wish-it-were-true thinking. Rather than carefully following the Holy Spirit and the Word of God, they, "take the lead," failing to realize that they are not qualified to take the lead.

Believers are not to lead the way in doctrine, but to follow in the way and be guided into all the truth. Some, however, especially those who have aggressive personalities and desire to be on the cutting-edge, end up *leading* in doctrine rather than *abiding* within the boundaries of sound doctrine. The Amplified Bible's rendering of II John 9 paints a forcible picture of this problem. It says,

> *"Any who runs on ahead [of God] and does not abide in the doctrine of Christ, who is not content with what He [Jesus] taught..."*
>
> II John 9 Amp

This scripture is an accurate depiction of the spiritual scene of this generation. The church is full of ministers who are aggressive, evangelistic, and vision oriented. These individuals love to be leaders. And this is not wrong. When it comes to the formulation of doctrine, however, these same individuals often run on ahead of God and trespass the boundaries of truth. This is hazardous to the spiritual health of the whole body of Christ.

A few years ago, I went snow skiing with a friend. We were enjoying the difficult runs of the mountain and having a good time. After a while, however, we were not content with the basic runs and began looking for something more exciting. At the edge of one run we noticed an orange boundary marker which forbade skiers to cross over. We skied up to that boundary marker, looked over, and saw deep untouched powder waiting for us. We crossed over.

Everything went good for a time. It wasn't long, however, till we began to tire. Before I knew what had happened my friend fell. "No problem," I thought, "he'll get up and we'll be on our way." Things did not go as I expected. The snow was so deep and so soft that my friend could not get himself back up. After waiting for a few minutes, I began to make my way to the place where he had fallen. It took me a long time to reach him and I exhausted myself getting there. Our problems were not over, however. I was not able to help him. We were in cool quicksand and getting nowhere fast. Eventually, my friend had to take off his skies and crawl on his belly all the way back to the boundary marker!

I was reminded of this story when considering the dangers of trespassing the boundaries of sound doctrine. Boundaries are posted for a reason. They are posted because those who are experts have determined that what lies on the other side is unsafe. When individuals trespass the boundaries of truth, it can be a long and difficult journey back to sound footing. Christians would do themselves a great favor if they would stay on the safe side of the boundary lines of sound doctrine as clearly laid out in the written scriptures.

The church of this generation often wanders dangerously close to and sometimes trespasses the boundaries of sound doctrine. Apparently, sound doctrine is not exciting and stimulating enough for what some call, "The church of the 90's." People want high stimuli. They want emotionally moving teaching and preaching. They have a hard time enduring the basic teachings of the written scriptures. They are like many who followed Jesus. Some followed only for the food — pure physical need. Some followed for the miracles — still a fleshly desire, but cloaked a little bit more in spiritual clothing. Only a few, however, followed for the truth and even these Jesus asked whether or not they were going to leave.

Concerning the response a believer should make to individuals who trespass sound doctrine, John said,

> *"If there come any unto you, and bring not this doctrine, receive him not into your house, neither bid him God speed: For he that biddeth him God speed is partaker of his evil deeds."*

II John 10

Those who are trespassing and teaching their unsound doctrines should not be received. They should not even be offered a, "God bless you." Those who bless and encourage the messengers of unsound doctrine are co-conspirators with them and in cooperation with the spread of error. This may be strong medicine, but it is the truth according to the Word of God.

THREE: RELIGIOUS DOCTRINES

The level of unsound doctrine called Religious Doctrines refers to the traditions of men. Religious doctrines are the result of men's attempts to interpret what God has said. Over time, these interpretations of God's Word are substituted for God's Word. They are elevated to a place of reverence and respect which supercedes reverence and respect for what God has said. These traditions spoil true spirituality by substituting man-made teachings for the Word of God.

Jesus' Disgust with Religious Doctrine

Jesus detested the religious leaders of His day because they were, "teaching for doctrines the commandments of men" [Matthew 15:6]. They taught their traditions as if they were truth and ignored the clear teachings of the written scriptures. By substituting their teachings for the doctrines of Word of God, they, "made the commandment of God of none effect" [Matthew 15:6].

This activity of substituting and exalting tradition above the written scriptures made Jesus angry. One time He reprimanded the religious leaders saying,

"Woe unto you, lawyers! for ye have taken away the key of knowledge: ye entered not in yourselves, and them that were entering in ye hindered."

Luke 11:52

The religious leaders took away the key of knowledge by teaching tradition rather than truth. Not only did they fail to enter into the things of God themselves; those they instructed could not enter in either! Unsound doctrine is spiritually debilitating. It keeps God's people outside of God's blessings and it makes Jesus angry!

On one occasion, the religious leaders, indignant with the behavior of Jesus' disciples, asked Him,

"Why do thy disciples transgress the traditions of the elders?"

Matthew 15:2

These religious leaders had exalted their traditions to the place where they thought they were sacred and could not be disobeyed. Jesus' reply to these religious leaders' question was,

"Why do ye also transgress the commandment of God by your tradition?"

Matthew 15:3

As far as Jesus was concerned, any teaching that was not strictly based on what God had said, that could not be prefaced by, "It is written," was a transgression against the commandment of God. Jesus still feels that way today. Any traditional teaching that transgresses what God has said in His Word must be judged as unsound and discarded!

The same question from the religious leaders and Jesus' answer to them is recorded in Mark seven. Here Jesus is recorded as saying this to the religious leaders,

"...laying aside the commandment of God, ye hold the tradition of men, as the washing of pots and cups: and many other such like things ye do...Full well ye reject the commandment of God, that ye may keep your own tradition."

Mark 7:8-9

Notice the two-part error of these religious leaders. They not only laid aside the commandment of God, they also held fast to the traditions. They set aside the commandments of God as children set aside toys they are bored with. Rather than reading and heeding the simple commandments of God, they entrenched themselves in an intellectual dissection of scripture. They revelled in their so-called revelation rather than humbling themselves in obedience to the truth.

Jesus chose strong words to reprimand these religious leaders. "Full well ye reject the commandment of God," He said. In an effort to maintain their own traditions, they rejected the Word of God. Like a man who falls out of a boat, but will not let go of his money-filled wallet in order to grasp a life-preserver, so these men held fast to their traditions rather than reaching out for the Word of God. They valued their own opinions so highly that they would rather clutch them and die than let go and live! Placing too much emphasis on the traditions of men and religious preferences is very danger-ous. Soon these unsound teachings will be reverenced as if they were Bible doctrine.

Religious Doctrine is Spiritual Leaven

Jesus warned His disciples to beware of the doctrine of the Pharisees and Sadducees saying,

> "...*Take heed and beware of the leaven of the Pharisees and of the Sadducees.*"
>
> *Matthew 16:6*

Initially, the disciples did not understand what Jesus meant by, "the leav-en of the Pharisees and of the Sadducees." They thought He was referring to the fact that they had forgotten to take bread on their trip. Because they failed to comprehend His message, Jesus addressed them again saying,

> "*How is it that ye do not understand that I spake it not to you concerning bread, that ye should beware of the leaven of the Pharisees and of the Sadducees?*"
>
> *Matthew 16:11*

When Jesus said this, the disciples understood that He was not speaking of physical bread and physical leaven, but of spiritual bread and spiritual leaven. Verse 12 says,

> "*Then understood they how that he bade them not beware of the leaven of bread, but of the doctrine of the Pharisees and of the Sadducees.*"
>
> *Matthew 16:12*

In Jesus' day, leaven was a sour dough in a high state of fermentation. When a little of this sour dough was mixed with a whole lump of regular dough, it spread its fermentation and caused the bread to rise. A little leav-en leavened the whole lump. Jesus compared religious doctrine to leaven because it was like truth that had fermented. When the leaven of religious doctrine was mixed with God's Word, the whole system of sound doctrine was spoiled.

Our modern leaven is yeast. Yeast is a bacteria which is mixed with dough to cause it to rise. When you buy a yeast-raised loaf of bread, you get a lot less bread than you think. Why? Because the yeast has caused the bread to be full of air-holes. If all the air was extracted from the loaf, you would discover that there is actually very little bread. In fact, one slice of unleavened bread has far more nutritional value than two or even three slices of leavened bread. Leavened bread tastes good and is easy to chew, but it is full of holes and full of hot air.

The leaven (or doctrine) of the Pharisees and Sadducees — the traditions and teachings they substituted for the commandments of the scriptures — sounded spiritual and made them appear spiritual, but they produced nothing spiritual. In fact, they hindered true spiritual growth. When all the tradition was stripped away, there was little Truth left. Jesus sounded forth a strong warning to his disciples concerning these religious traditions. He said, "take heed," and, "beware!" "Take heed," means to pay very close attention to something. "Beware," means to turn one's mind toward something by being on guard against it. Religious doctrine is dangerous to spiritual health. Believers must beware of it!

Example of Religious Doctrine

Jesus contended with a particular religious doctrine which said that if a person had extra finances and wanted to make a gift to the temple, they were free of the responsibility of supporting their parents. Jesus rebuked the religious leaders sharply concerning this unsound doctrine saying,

> *"Why do ye also transgress the commandment of God by your tradition? For God commanded, saying, Honour thy father and mother...But ye say, Whosoever shall say to his father or his mother, It is a gift, by whatsoever thou mightest be profited by me; And honour not his father or his mother, he shall be free. Thus have ye made the commandment of God of no effect by your tradition."*

> Matthew 15:3-6

This unsound doctrine sounded very spiritual. If one had extra money and wanted to give a special gift to God, then he would be free of the commandment which said to honor (financially support) his parents. This doctrine sounded so right, so spiritual. It is no wonder that most people thought it was right! After all, God is more important than parents, isn't He? Yes, He is! And because He is, these religious leaders should have obeyed His Word which **commanded** the honoring of parents rather than substituting their own spiritual sounding, but unsound doctrine for the Truth!

Jesus said to the religious leaders, "God commanded...But ye say." Holding fast to religious traditions causes one to transgress the commandments of the Word of God. If believers esteem the traditions of men as equal to or more important than the written Word of God, then the commandments of God will be ignored and the Word of God will become of no effect in their lives. Then Jesus will have to say to them,

"...ye made the commandment of God of none effect by your tradition."
Matthew 15:6

Jesus reprimanded the scribes and Pharisees, calling them hypocrites, for this very thing when He told them,

"...ye pay tithe of mint and anise and cummin, and have omitted the weightier matters of the law, judgement, mercy and faith..."
Matthew 23:23

The religious leaders of Jesus' day were very careful to keep their traditions, but they omitted the very matters God had commanded. Believers must be careful not to esteem the traditions of men above the commandments of God. If they do, they will judge the Word of God by their traditions rather than judging their traditions by the Word of God. They will ignore the Truth to preserve their traditions. They will honor the religious teachings of men rather than honoring the eternal Word of God. Their spiritual lives will be in jeopardy because the Word of God will be made of no effect.

The Traditions of Men

Paul warned the church at Colosse of the traditions of men saying,

"And this I say, lest any man beguile you with enticing words. For though I be absent in the flesh, yet I am with you in the spirit, joying and beholding your order, and the steadfastness of your faith in Christ...Beware lest any man spoil you through philosophy and vain deceit, after the tradition of men..."
Colossians 2:4-8

Rather than following persuasive arguments, philosophies of men, and good speeches, believers must remain steadfast in the faith. When Paul remarked about the "steadfastness of your faith," he was not referring to the faith by which believers are saved, but to that whole body of Christian beliefs called "the faith." To remain steadfast in the faith means to remain firmly rooted, resolute, and unwavering in those beliefs which are clearly specified in the written scriptures. It means to be well established in that body of teaching which is the sum and total of sound Christian doctrine.

The word "enticing" Paul used in this scripture to describe the words of men comes from the Greek *pithanologia*. This word signifies the employment of plausible arguments. Plausible arguments are logical and persuasive words meant to sound like truth, but intended to lead people away from the truth. Paul did not warn the believers in Colosse to be careful of words that were obviously unbiblical, but of words that were plausible. The Amplified Bible reads Paul's words this way,

> "I say this in order that no one may mislead and delude you by plausible and persuasive and attractive arguments..."
>
> *Colossians 2:4 Amp*

Some of the unsound traditions and teachings of men will be very attractive and persuasive. This category of unsound doctrine is extremely dangerous for believers. The words sound so right, so convincing, so rational, so practical, so spiritual. But they are not! Beware of religious doctrine. Because it is close to truth and sounds spiritual, it can be the most deceptive. After it has deceived you, it can be the most binding because it involves you in religious activities, satisfying your desire to be pleasing to God.

Some modern doctrines that could be included in this category of unsound doctrine called Religious Doctrine could include teaching which says it is wrong for women to wear make-up or cut their hair; teaching that says Christians must to go to church twice on Sunday; teaching which says that only certain lengths of hair or types of dress are acceptable; or teaching which says that certain kinds of Christian music are demonic.

Recently, a pastor spoke to me of a so-called full gospel church in his city. This "full gospel" church did not allow women to wear make-up and required them to wear their hair in a bun. Men and women had to sit on opposite sides of the church during the worship service. Black people were required to sit in the back of the church! You will be shocked by the name of this church. It was called The Whole Truth Tabernacle! I told the pastor that a more suitable name for that church would be The Selective Truth Tabernacle or The Very Little Truth Tabernacle.

Any traditional or religious teaching that distracts from the purity of God's Word, from the principles of the oracles of God's Word, from the principles of the doctrine of Christ, and from the foundations of pure doctrine must be carefully scrutinized. If found to be unsound, these teachings must be shunned.

FOUR: TANGENTS IN DOCTRINE OR IGNORANCE OF DOCTRINE

In this fourth category of unsound doctrine, I have combined two different, but related areas of unsound doctrine. The first area of unsound doctrine I have designated Tangents in Doctrine. The second area of unsound doctrine I have designated Ignorance of Doctrines.

Tangents in Doctrine

From the middle of 1988 through the end of 1989, the Holy Spirit was consistently speaking the word "tangents" in my spirit. At first, I did not understand what He was trying to show me. I continued to hear this word "tangents" in my spirit for months and then the Holy Spirit brought Ephesians 4:14 to my attention. It says,

> *"That we henceforth be no more children, tossed to and fro, and carried about with every wind of doctrine, by the sleight of men…"*
>
> *Ephesians 4:14*

By speaking the word "tangents" in my heart and then bringing Ephesians 4:14 to my attention, the Holy Spirit was showing me the spiritual condition of the body of Christ in this generation. He was showing me that believers were tangent oriented. Rather than coming to "full age" and growing up into the "measure of the stature of the fullness of Christ," believers have been like children tossed to and fro, literally "carried about" by winds of doctrine. They get hooked on one wind of doctrine and blow that direction for a while. Then they get excited about something else and blow that direction for a while. Rather than becoming increasingly solidified, grounded, and established in that body of foundational scriptural teaching called sound doctrine, believers have been pursuing tangents in doctrine.

Notice that Ephesians 4:14 does not say believers are blown about by winds of false doctrine. Though "winds of doctrine" could include false and corrupt doctrine, it primarily denotes doctrines that have been overemphasized, pushed to an extreme, or preached to the exclusion of other truths. This kind of unsound doctrine is just like the wind. It is hard to know where it comes from and difficult to determine exactly where it is going. It may blow hard in one direction for a short period of time and then stop or blow in a completely different direction. One thing we do know about wind, however, is that it affects us. According to Webster's dictionary, one of the definitions of wind is, "a prevailing influence." Winds of doctrine are often the prevailing, but unsound doctrinal influence of the day.

Another name for these winds of doctrine is "Tangents in doctrine." Webster says that a tangent is, "a straight line leading away from its proper point." A doctrinal tangent occurs when a particular Bible truth is emphasized to an excess and taught to the exclusion of other important doctrines. If this doctrinal tangent is pursued for very long, other doctrines will be discounted as unimportant. What is "a" truth will begin to be revered as "The" Truth. Whenever one doctrine is overemphasized or taught to the exclusion of other important doctrines, it is dangerous to spiritual health in the same way as eating only one kind of food is dangerous to physical health.

Webster's definition of "tangent" accurately depicts the current spiritual condition of the body of Christ. Rather than staying at their proper point and becoming increasingly sound, grounded, and solidified in that body of teaching called sound doctrine — those foundations and first principles of the oracles of God and of the doctrine of Christ [Hebrews 5:12-6:2] — believers are following doctrinal tangents away from the proper point. The proper point as concerns Christian doctrine is a balance of all the teaching of the written scriptures. Paul called it, "all the counsel of God" [Acts 20:27]. The writer of Hebrews called it, "the principles of the doctrine of Christ" [Hebrews 6:1].

Some ministers of this generation are guilty of pursuing tangents in doctrine. If the Holy Spirit gives them a revelation in a particular area, they think that their message is the missing key that will bring in the next revival. Sometimes they begin to preach their message exclusively. Soon all their disciples are "squeaking" the same message. In a short time there is a sound of a rushing wind reverberating throughout the body of Christ. It is not, however, the moving of the Spirit, but is the rustle of unsound spiritual leaders and their unsound doctrine. Jude called them, "clouds without water, swept along by the winds" [Jude12]. There is a whole lot of noise, a whole lot of stirring; there is even a cloud on the horizon. But the cloud is void of spiritual blessing.

Example of Praise and Worship

A few years ago there was a strong emphasis on the teaching of praise. Praise was preached as if it was the missing key to everything. Praise was the way to defeat the devil. Praise was the way to bring in the power of God. Praise was the way to win your city. Praise was the way to overcome fear and depression. Praise was the key to open every door. There was truth in all these teachings about praise. It was not false teaching, but was a tangent, a wind of doctrine. It was an emphasis that was needed, but which, in some cases, went beyond what the Word of God really teaches about praise.

A few years ago, I was ministering in a local church. In the middle of leading a song of worship, the Holy Spirit spoke through me in a word of prophesy. He said, "Praise is not a wave, but is a part of the great ocean of truth." He continued to inspire me to exhort the congregation not to forget the importance of praise and worship just because it was not being emphasized as much as it had been in the past.

Example of The Apostle and Prophet

One current tangent in doctrine is the unbalanced teaching about the role of the apostle and prophet. Some are pushing the place of these ministries to an extreme and causing confusion and instability in the church. For example, some twist the scripture in Ephesians two which says that believers are built upon the foundation of the apostle and the prophet. They say that if a local church doesn't have a prophet and an apostle functioning in it, they have a faulty foundation. This scripture does not mean, however, that local churches must be established by apostles and prophets. It means that believers and churches are spiritually built and established be the teachings of New Testament apostles and prophets who were given revelation from the Holy Spirit of the New Covenant [Ephesians 3:4-5]. These revelations can be found in the New Testament epistles. It is not the apostle, but the apostles' doctrine, that establishes believers [Acts2:42].

In 1983, the Holy Spirit told me that there would be a revival of the true apostolic and prophetic offices to the church. I recorded the word He gave me in my diary, but didn't teach on it then and still don't today. The Holy Spirit didn't tell me to teach this; He just told me. It was almost five years after the Holy Spirit spoke this word to me that I heard another reputable minister say the same thing. I didn't make the mistake so many would make if they had heard this word from the Holy Ghost. They would think that because the Holy Spirit showed them, they must be one of those called to be an prophet or apostle. They would travel throughout the body of Christ teaching that the problem in all the churches is that the apostles and prophets (themselves, of course) have not been given their rightful place. When the Holy Spirit enlightens a Bible truth, it does not mean that that particular truth must be forced to the forefront. Whatever teachings are true and in the timing of the Holy Spirit will find their place in the church without being propelled by the efforts of men.

Example of Refuting Spiritual Warfare

Recently, there has been a lot of teaching refuting the unsound teaching of excessive deliverance and spiritual warfare. This is not bad, but there is a danger that believers (especially ministers) will run to the other side of the issue and be on just as much of a tangent. As early as 1984, I observed particular ministers wandering in the direction of excessive deliverance. At that time the Lord gave me twenty reasons why their teaching on deliverance was unscriptural and dangerous for the body of Christ. I didn't preach against what they were doing, however, because the Lord didn't tell me to. He just showed me to keep me sound.

I can recall the very first time I heard teaching on militant prayer and the teaching about pulling down territorial demonic strongholds over cities. I knew immediately in my heart that it wasn't sound and wrote down scripture after scripture that proved it wasn't. I didn't preach against it, however, because the Lord didn't tell me to.

Now that some more well known ministers have addressed these doctrinal problems, however, other ministers, especially travelling ministers, will run to and fro throughout the earth proclaiming words of correction as if they got it from God themselves. In so doing, they will assist the devil in promoting even more confusion and instability. Some of them will push the pendulum so far back the other way that they will end up in the letter of the law. It is sad and unfortunate, but ministers are greatly to blame for the problem of doctrinal tangents and the resultant instability in the body of Christ.

The Lord told me several years ago to stay away from winds of doctrine and to stay with the prevailing wind of the Spirit. He said that if I did, I would reach my destination in time and intact. I just stick with the Bible and preach the messages God gives me to preach.

Example of Faith

Another true and foundational doctrine that some people pushed to a tangent was the teaching on faith. It is true that there is no doctrine more foundational in the Bible than, "faith toward God" [Hebrews 6:2]. Some, however, pushed this teaching too far and tried to make faith "the truth" instead of "a truth." They tried to apply faith to every area of their spiritual life. For example, I used to hear people say, "I'm just going to confess and believe that I have the mind of Christ." Christians cannot believe to have the mind of Christ. I Corinthians two teaches that believers **have** the mind of Christ because they have the indwelling of the Spirit of God. The way to "have the mind of Christ" is to listen to the Spirit of God.

Example of the Believer's Ministry

Another tangent in teaching in the last few years has been the emphasis on the believer's ministry. We have been taught that every believer should do the works of Christ. And that is true because Jesus said in John 14 that believers would do the same works He did. We have been taught that every believer can lay hands on the sick and they will recover. And that is true because, "these signs shall follow them that believe" [Mark 16:17]. This teaching must be balanced, however, or some believers will try to operate outside their own callings. When they do, they will not only become discouraged themselves, but will cause problems in the body of Christ.

Did you ever notice in the book of Acts that those who were sick tried to get in the shadow of Peter [Acts 5:15]? Why didn't they try to get in John's shadow? He was a believer, wasn't he? Or why didn't they try to get in the shadow of any believer? The reason the sick tried to get in Peter's shadow was because Peter was specially called and anointed, and therefore, noted for his healing ministry. Yes, all can pray for the sick. But some are specially called and anointed of God in that area and will, therefore, have much greater results.

There are a diversity of gifts, a diversity of administrations, and a diversity of operations [I Corinthians 12:4-6]. It is true that all believers can minister. It is also true, however, that there are diversities of ministries. A balance of the whole counsel of God's Word must be taught in this area of spiritual life or believers run away from a proper point of doctrinal soundness and drift away from stable Christian activity.

Example of Authority in the Ministry

In the recent past, there has been a strong emphasis of teaching on authority in the ministry. This teaching is not false or corrupt doctrine. If, however, believers are not taught about their own ability and responsibility to hear from God, to judge spiritual matters, and to know God themselves, there will be a problem of abused authority in the church.

I have heard many tragic stories of abused authority and have read dangerous statements which are the practical outgrowth of this teaching. Some teach, for example, that there is rank and order in the body of Christ and that believers need to submit to ministers. This is not necessarily false doctrine. Some, however, carry this a little further and teach that some ministers are Generals in the army of Christ. This teaching may still be within the boundaries of truth, but is drifting toward man-made ideas. Next someone will teach that if a General says, "Move," all the soldiers had better be ready to move. Now this teaching has drifted away from the proper point of sound doctrine and moved dangerously close to unsound doctrine. Someone else may push this teaching further by saying that if a General/Prophet is instructed by God to tell believers to give a certain offering, they had better obey him or God will not bless them. For example, a "General" might say, "God told me to tell you to make a sacrificial offering and you had better obey God!" You might ask yourself, "Could it really go that far?" Yes, absolutely. These words are a quote from a man with a television ministry! I heard it myself! And I am sure that I haven't heard the most radical gusts of this teaching.

Yes, we must teach about the five-fold ministry gifts and their authority in the church. But we must temper this teaching with other truths. We must teach that all believers are equal in the body. We must teach, as Jesus told His own apostles, that we are all brothers. We must teach that no scripture is of any private interpretation and that all believers can understand the Word of God themselves [II Peter 1:19]. And we must remind those who are called to the ministry that they are servants, not bosses! "Let this same attitude and purpose and humble mind be in you," said Paul, "which was in Christ Jesus" [Philippians 2:5 Amp]. No matter what the so-called highest ranking apostle in the body of Christ says, every believer must hold fast to the Word of God himself and follow the leading of the Holy Spirit himself.

Beware of Tangents

This category of unsound doctrine called "Tangents" is very dangerous because it doesn't just sound like truth, it is truth! It takes a careful spiritual eye and a trained spiritual ear to separate *a* truth from *the* truth. Those who are of full age will exercise themselves to discern both good and evil [Hebrews 5:14]. Discerning between good and evil not only refers to being able to discern between righteous and sinful lifestyle, but, as is clear from the context in Hebrews five, refers to being able to discern between sound and unsound doctrine.

Any truth can get out of hand if not balanced with and tempered by the whole counsel of the Word of God. If a truth is overemphasized and pushed to an extreme, the body of Christ will soon find itself in doctrinal error and spiritual trouble. A truth pushed to the extreme becomes error. Beware of tangents in doctrine. They can unsettle and even destroy sound spiritual life.

I am not saying, of course, that the Holy Spirit will not, at certain times, emphasize messages that are needed in the church. Jesus Himself spoke a current message to each of the young churches in Asia minor [Revelation 2 and 3]. Throughout history the Holy Spirit has re-revealed messages and truths that have been forgotten or abandoned. This does not mean, however, that believers should pursue every "new revelation." Neither should ministers teach a truth that the Holy Spirit is emphasizing at a particular season as if it was *the* truth rather than *a* truth.

There will be seasons when the winds of the Holy Spirit blow. Believers should know how to follow these winds of the Spirit and move with what God is doing in their generation. Doctrine, however, cannot be likened to winds, but to a rock. Concerning the foundational truth that He was the Christ, Jesus said, "upon this rock I will build my church" [Matthew 16:18]. A believer who is wise will dig deep till he finds the rock of sound doctrine and then lay his foundation there! When the floods, rains, and winds arise, he will remain unshaken! Why? He is founded on a Rock [Luke 6:48]!

The rock of sound doctrine is sure, steadfast, and unmovable. It does not shift like the wind. It does not swirl like the wind. It does not change direction from day to day like the wind. It does not alter in intensity like the wind. A rock is the same from day to day, from year to year, and even from century to century. The sound doctrines of the Word of God are this way. Heaven and earth will pass away, but forever the truths of God's Word are established!

Spiritual life can be influenced and refreshed by winds, but sound spiritual life is built upon the rock of the sound doctrines of God's Word. A shifting wind can never move a solid rock. But hidden in the rock of sound doctrine, believers will be secure from the winds of unsound doctrine! If you become established in the Word of God, the winds of unsound doctrine will never toss you to and fro! Sound doctrine, the teachings of the Word of God, is the Sure Rock we build our lives on!

The body of Christ must be careful in this hour about being tangent oriented rather than foundation oriented. Believers must be careful not to ride on waves of teaching, but to incorporate everything they learn into the whole ocean of truth. If believers ride waves, they will end up crashing on the shore. Unfortunately, it seems that whatever is new, different, and exciting is what people want. Tangents in doctrine keep believers *tossed* rather than *built*. Believers must quit being blown about like children and become established in sound doctrine.

Ignoring Important Doctrines

A second aspect of this fourth category of unsound doctrine is ignoring or excluding pertinent and essential doctrines. The result of ignoring or excluding basic Bible doctrines is that people will not grow to maturity and may be dangerously unbalanced in their spiritual lives.

Often this problem occurs when a true spiritual leader realizes that a particular truth has been ignored by the church. Responding to this realization, he begins to emphasize the particular truth that was formerly ignored. By so doing, he wakens the body of Christ to that area of teaching and gains a following. In the process of time, new churches with new pastors are born out the the particular emphasis of this man's ministry.

Unfortunately, the pastors and teachers that have oversight in these new churches fail to realize that although they were born again or became committed to God through the emphasis of a particular man's ministry, there is a Bible full of essential doctrines that must be taught in order for their sheep to be healthy. These young leaders often ignore or exclude any teaching that does not directly correspond with the emphasis of the man (or denomination) they follow. This same pattern has occurred over and over again throughout church history and is the fountainhead of hundreds of diverse denominations that emphasize varieties of doctrine. When ministers choose to ignore or exclude certain truths of God's Word, their churches and denominations will not be balanced.

Some ministers and churches ignore the teaching of healing. Although it is an obvious Bible truth, they don't want any part of it. Some ignore the baptism in the Holy Spirit and the manifestation of speaking in other tongues. When they exclude this doctrine from their teaching, they exclude that experience from their own lives and from the lives of those who follow them. Some ministers and churches don't want to teach what Jesus emphasized again and again about the sacrificial lifestyle of the true disciple. They may not deny that it is in the Bible, but they will not teach it because it is not popular and exciting. Some will not teach the clear and concise Bible message which instructs believers be content with what they have [I Timothy 6:8; Hebrews 13:5]. They ignore this uninspiring message and concentrate on prosperity.

Some won't preach the positive and some won't preach the negative. Some won't teach the sacrifice and some won't teach the reward. Some are so caught up teaching about the hereafter that they ignore teaching about how to have victory now. Others teach so much about victory now that people get earthly-minded and forget about heaven and eternity. No part of God's Word should be ignored or excluded. If it is, believers grow up unbalanced and out of proportion. Paul told the elders at Ephesus,

"...I kept back nothing that was profitable unto you...I have not shunned to declare unto you all the counsel of God."

Acts 20:20,27

Why did Paul say, "I have not shunned?" Why would he have reservations about teaching the whole truth? He had reservations because in declaring the whole counsel of God, he would have to say things that were hard to hear and not altogether fun and exciting. Perhaps he had to give instructions that challenged people's doctrines. Perhaps he had to bring correction that people did not want to hear.

Usually pastors and teachers know what their congregations want to hear and don't want to hear. Sometimes they will teach only those truths they know will be accepted because they fear that the people will dislike them, leave them, or even remove them. Unfortunately, job security and the praise of men tends to overshadow obedience to God and the preaching of the whole counsel of the Word of God. The true servant of God must live by the very same charge that Paul gave to young Timothy when he wrote,

"I charge [you] in the presence of God and of Christ Jesus, Who is to judge the living and the dead...Herald and preach the Word!...Whether it is convenient or inconvenient, whether it be welcome or unwelcome, you as preacher of the Word are to show people in what way their lives are wrong...convince them, rebuking and correcting, warning and urging and encouraging them, being unflagging and inexhaustible in patience and teaching."

II Timothy 4:1-2 Amp

CONCLUSION

We have very briefly studied four different categories of unsound doctrine. Every kind of unsound doctrine is dangerous because it leads believers away from the truth that will set them free. It leads them away from the foundation upon which spiritual life is built. It leads them away from the sound doctrines which will correct, encourage, enlighten, and strengthen their lives. Let's proceed now to learn where unsound doctrine comes from, what results from its promotion, and how to judge it accurately.

·~8~·

Sources of Unsound Doctrine

U nsound doctrine does not come from nowhere. It comes from some-where. In this chapter, we will study the sources of unsound doc-trine. I have divided the sources of unsound doctrine into three major categories: Unsound spiritual leadership in the church, Satan and seducing spirits, and Immature believers. Each of these, or any combination of these, can be a source or cause of unsound doctrine.

ONE: UNSOUND SPIRITUAL LEADERSHIP IN THE CHURCH

The primary source of unsound doctrine is individuals who are accepted as spiritual leaders in the church. False spiritual leaders, unsound spiritual leaders, and sometimes even truly called spiritual leaders can be guilty of inventing and promoting false and unsound doctrines. Unsound doctrine seldom comes into the church from outside gurus or secular leaders although their teachings may, to some degree, influence the doctrine of the church. The invention and promotion of unsound doctrine is primarily carried out by individuals who once were or are currently accepted as spiritual leaders within the church. This is the principal reason that unsound doctrine can so easily be introduced into and find pasture in the church.

FALSE SPIRITUAL LEADERS

False spiritual leaders are one source of false and unsound doctrine. When I speak of false spiritual leaders in this context, I am not referring to spiritual gurus from outside the church or those false leaders who claim no affiliation with the church. I am referring primarily to those who claim to be true spiritual leaders and gain acceptance in the church as spiritual lead-ers, but are false apostles, false teachers, and false prophets.

False Teachers and Unsound Doctrine

Peter spoke of the role of false teachers in introducing and promoting unsound doctrine in his second epistle. He said

"...there shall be false teachers among you, who privily shall bring in damnable heresies...And many shall follow their pernicious ways..."

II Peter 2:1-2

A false teacher is a person who, although he may claim to be a true teacher, teaches false and unsound doctrine. Peter reported that false teachers would be in the church and that they would secretly and carefully, "bring in damnable heresies." What does Peter mean when he says false teachers, "*bring in* damnable heresies?" He means that they are the inventors, the carriers, and the promoters of false doctrine. And to where do these false teachers *bring in* their false doctrine? They bring false doctrine into the church!

The Amplified Bible says that false teachers, "subtly and stealthily introduce heretical doctrines." False teachers carefully introduce unsound doctrines into the church so that they are difficult to detect. They introduce their unsound doctrines in such a favorable way that believers become familiar with them. They also mix unsound doctrine with sound doctrine so that over a period of time believers don't even realize that false doctrine has infiltrated their midst.

False teachers could be likened to drug dealers who introduce their "goods" in small doses accompanied by favorable rhetoric. They convince those they sell to that drugs are exciting, mind expanding, and stimulating. Drug dealers know that what they are selling will lead to dependence, bondage, and eventual death, but because they are skillful salesmen, they can peddle life-threatening substances without being rejected.

Concerning the efforts of unsound teachers, Peter said, "many shall follow their pernicious ways." Many will follow the unsound doctrine of false teachers. The "many" Peter was referring to are believers, not sinners. False teachers, when not recognized by the church as such, are a dangerous source of unsound doctrine.

False Apostles and Unsound Doctrine

The apostle Paul exposed the false apostles in Corinth as a source of unsound doctrine. In his second letter to that church, he spoke of the potential impact of false apostles who were preaching another Jesus and another gospel. He said,

"But I fear, lest by any means, as the serpent beguiled Eve through his subtilty, so your minds should be corrupted from the simplicity that is in Christ. For if he that cometh preacheth another Jesus…or another gospel…"

II Corinthians 11:3

Several verses later Paul clearly identified and labeled those who were preaching "another Jesus" and "another gospel" saying,

"…For such are false apostles, deceitful workers, transforming themselves into the apostles of Christ."

II Corinthians 11:13

False apostles disguised as ministers of righteousness gained entrance to the church in Corinth. Because they appeared to be true spiritual leaders, they were able to introduce "another gospel" and "another Jesus" without being refused. False ministers who disguise themselves as ministers of righteousness are a very dangerous source of unsound doctrine.

Paul depicted the close relationship between unsound doctrine and false spiritual leadership in Ephesians 4:14. There he wrote,

"That we henceforth be no more children, tossed to and fro, and carried about with every wind of doctrine, by the sleight of men, and cunning craftiness, whereby they lie in wait to deceive."

Ephesians 4:14

The Amplified Bible says,

"…tossed to and fro between chance gusts of teaching and wavering with every changing wind of doctrine, [the prey of] the cunning and cleverness of unscrupulous men, [gamblers engaged] in every shifting form of trickery in inventing errors to mislead."

Ephesians 4:14 Amp

False spiritual leaders invent doctrinal error. They are sly and cunning, waiting in hiding to mislead unsuspecting believers. They are one of the "fans" that start the winds of unsound doctrine blowing. Through the promotion of unsound doctrine, they mislead spiritual children and unsuspecting local churches.

False Prophets and Unsound Doctrine

The apostle John also exposed the relationship between false spiritual leadership and unsound doctrine. In I John 4:1, he wrote,

"Beloved, believe not every spirit, but try the spirits whether they are of God: because many false prophets are gone out into the world."

I John 4:1

John connected, "believe not every spirit, but try the spirits," and, "because many false prophets are gone out into the world," because there is an inseparable relationship between false teaching and false spiritual leadership. John warned his beloved not to believe every teaching they heard because false prophets were promoting doctrine inspired by evil spirits. False prophets, false apostles, and false teachers are inventors, promoters, and carriers of unsound and false doctrine.

Very seldom, however, do false teachers teach only unsound doctrine. Often they mix true and acceptable doctrine with their error. Because of this method, believers must be careful. Just because a so-called spiritual leader teaches some sound doctrine, it should not be assumed that everything they teach is right. Peter said that false teachers secretly and carefully introduce heretical doctrines. The way to successfully poison a person is by mixing poison with real food. False spiritual leaders are very subtle. It is with great care that they introduce unsound doctrine.

Heresies Come From Heretics

The church in Corinth had a serious problem with heretics and heresies. In his first letter to them, Paul exposed the significant relationship between heresies (unsound doctrines), heretics (unsound spiritual leaders), and sects (the unsound groups that result from the promotion of heresies). He wrote,

"Now in this...I praise you not...I hear that there be divisions among you...For there must be also heresies among you, that they which are approved may be made manifest among you."

I Corinthians 11:17-19

The heresies in Corinth were initiated and promoted by heretics who hoped, by teaching their heresies, to become leaders of their own groups. Heresies are the spiritual offspring of heretics. They are the false doctrines birthed and then promoted by false spiritual leaders. False doctrine comes from false spiritual leaders.

UNSOUND SPIRITUAL LEADERS

Unsound spiritual leaders, those who are not purposely false, but who are also not consciously striving for soundness, are another dangerous source of unsound doctrine. Unsound spiritual leaders include ministers with ungodly motivations, those who are not called to the ministry, religious leaders, and several other categories.

Ministers With Ungodly Motivations

Some unsound ministers, rather than allowing the two-edged sword of the Word of God pierce to their hearts and expose their wrong motivations and wrong activities, search for scriptures to justify themselves. This search commences the dangerous process of formulating doctrine to support personal opinions and personal desires. Ministers who are not afraid to twist the Word of God to validate their ungodly motivations are a dangerous source of unsound doctrine. They use their position to promote their doctrines and get what they want. Teaching their twisted doctrines not only validates their own ungodly motivations; it also attracts others with the same motivations who are looking for "Biblical" reasons not to change.

Jude referred to unsound spiritual leaders who were living ungodly and teaching unsound doctrine as those who had, "gone in the way of Cain" [Jude 11]. Notice what Cain did,

"And in the process of time it came to pass, that Cain brought of the fruit of the ground an offering unto the Lord...But unto Cain and to his offering he (the Lord) had not respect."

Genesis 4:3-4

God gave specific instructions to Cain and Abel concerning the presentation of offerings. Cain, however, substituted his way for God's Word. He brought the Lord an offering of the fruit of the ground instead of an animal sacrifice. By substituting his own opinion for the Word of God, Cain became a type for those who would follow in his way. By the time Jude wrote his epistle, it was understood that to go "in the way of Cain" meant to substitute personal opinions or doctrinal preferences for the clear Word of God. Unsound spiritual leaders who go the way of Cain are a common source of unsound doctrine.

A Wrong Financial Motivation

An unsound spiritual leader who desires riches and wants to justify this ungodly motivation will teach only the parts of the Bible which support the position that it is God's will for believers to prosper and increase. He will ignore, misinterpret, or misapply any scripture that warns believers to beware of riches and teaches them to be content with what they have. Notice the relationship between unsound teachers with a wrong financial motivation and their unsound doctrine from the words of Paul to Titus,

"...vain talkers and deceivers...teaching things which they ought not, for filthy lucre's sake."

Titus 1:10-11

Paul informed Titus that the reason certain so-called teachers were teaching their unsound doctrines was because of their ungodly motivation for money. In I Timothy six, Paul warned his other son in the faith, Timothy, of unsound men and their unsound doctrines concerning finances. Of these men he wrote,

> "...*men of corrupt minds, and destitute of the truth, supposing that gain is godliness: from such withdraw thyself. But godliness with contentment is great gain.*"
>
> I Timothy 6:5-6

The men Paul warned Timothy of wanted to be rich and so were teaching that financial prosperity was a sign of godliness and God's blessing. Their doctrine that, "gain is godliness," would obviously license them and those they instructed to pursue riches with God's approval. Paul, however, called those who promoted this false doctrine, "men of corrupt minds, and destitute of the truth." He corrected their false doctrine with the truth, saying,

> "*But godliness with contentment is great gain. For we brought nothing into this world, and it is certain we can carry nothing out. And having food and raiment let us be therewith content...*"
>
> I Timothy 6:6-8

Paul continued on to say that,

> "...*they that will (want to) be rich fall into temptation and a snare, and into many foolish and hurtful lusts, which drown men in destruction and perdition. For the love of money is the root of all evil: which while some coveted after, they have erred from the faith, and pierced themselves through with many sorrows.*"
>
> I Timothy 6:9-10

It is not a sin to be rich. There are Christians that God will abundantly prosper. There is, however, something *wrong* both with coveting riches and with teaching that being rich is a sign of godliness. There is also something very wrong with not teaching the whole counsel of God's Word concerning money! Paul concluded his instructions to young Timothy concerning money by telling him,

> "*But thou, O man of God, flee these things...*"
>
> I Timothy 6:11

Paul instructed Timothy in sound doctrine concerning his attitude toward money. He taught him that true gain was to be godly and to be content with the material blessings he already he had. Concerning the desire for riches, Paul's instructions were, "Flee!" This may not be your favorite teaching concerning finances, but it is the Truth! Ministers, however, who want to be rich will teach that financial gain is a sign of godliness. Undoubtedly, the same unsound teaching Paul warned Timothy of will have ready acceptance in our day because it validates Christians' desires to be rich.

A Wrong Motivation to Dominate Women

If men have a wrong motivation to dominate women, they can "prove" from the Bible that women are to submit to men. They will say, "The Bible teaches that men are the head over women." Actually, the Bible teaches nothing of the sort. The apostle Paul, speaking specifically of the marriage relationship, addressed the wife saying,

> "*Wives, submit yourselves unto your own husbands, as unto the Lord. For the husband is the head of the wife...*"
>
> *Ephesians 5:22-23*

Not only does this scripture not teach that men should be over women; it also does not teach husbands that they are the head over their wives. Notice that what Paul wrote about the husband being the head of the wife is not written to the husband; it is written to the wife! It is the Lord's instruction to the wife about submitting to her own husband. If husbands want to know what their place in the marriage is, they must read what Paul wrote to husbands. He wrote,

> "*Husbands, love your wives, even as Christ also loved the church, and gave himself for it...So ought men to love their wives as their own bodies...let every one of you in particular so love his wife even as himself...*"
>
> *Ephesians 5:25-33*

The only teaching relevant to men in Ephesians 5:22-35 is the instruction to husbands to love their wives in the same way that Christ loved the church. "But", you say, "I am sure that the Bible teaches that women should submit to men." No, it doesn't. The Bible instructs wives to submit to their own husbands. It is the wife's responsibility to fulfill the instruction to submit, not the husband's. If it was the husband's responsibility to make his wife submit, the Bible would say, "Husbands, make sure your wife submits." There is, however, nothing written to men in the Bible concerning the issue of submission in marriage.

Do you see my point? Unsound leaders who are motivated by self-interest can easily mislead believers and local churches with plausible arguments, misquoting, misinterpreting, and misapplying scripture. Wrongly motivated unsound spiritual leaders are not afraid to twist the Word of God for their own benefit.

A Wrong Motivation for Sexual Relations

An interesting Bible example of unsound doctrine being promoted by an unsound minister with a wrong sexual motivation is that of the gnostic teacher, Jezebel [Revelation 2:20-22]. This false prophetess, desiring leadership and power, promoted false doctrine. She taught that when Eve partook of the tree of the knowledge of good and evil she did not sin, but led the way into greater revelation. Jezebel then "proved" from this false premise that women had a greater capacity for spiritual experience than men.

Jezebel taught, however, that men could gain a deeper level of spiritual experience through sexual relations with women. This is how she was able to seduce Jesus' servants to commit fornication [Revelation 2:20]. She didn't seduce by putting on fancy makeup, fluttering her eyes, and acting like a prostitute. She seduced by teaching false doctrine! She taught that sexual relations were a doorway to heightened spiritual experience and greater knowledge. She validated sexual sin, teaching that fornication was permissible because the body and spirit were separate. She taught that what was done in the body could not affect the spiritual life. Men who wanted to involve themselves in sexual sin loved the opportunity afforded to them by this enticing false doctrine!

Recently, I heard about a pastor who became involved in a relationship outside his marriage. His extra-marital relationship continued for several months before his wife and congregation found out. His now divorced wife said that when she reflected back upon the sermons he preached during those months, she realized that he was strongly emphasizing the teaching that no matter what sin anyone committed, they could be forgiven. At the time he was teaching this she had thought to herself that his teaching did not seem balanced. Later she realized that he was preaching these things in order to justify the sin in his own life.

The church of this generation will have to face a flood of unsound doctrines that will be promoted in an attempt to validate sexual preferences. Many who have chosen a homosexual lifestyle have already twisted the Word of God to validate their sin. Their Biblical argument is, "God created me; therefore God loves me the way I am." These individuals have travelled a long way down the road of deception when they make God responsible for their unwillingness to obey His Word. If God said in His Word that homosexuality is a sin (and He did), then He will not create individuals to be homosexuals. The day that He acts against His own Word, He is no longer God!

The Bible teaches that those who have chosen a homosexual lifestyle "have turned the truth of God into a lie" and that "God has given them over to vile affections" [Romans 1:25-26]. Those who choose a homosexual lifestyle have chosen, as have any other persons who choose sin over obedience, not to retain God and His Word in their knowledge. Because of their willing disobedience, God gives them over to a reprobate mind to do things that are not fit to do [Romans 1:28].

The scriptures, both Old and New Testament are as clear concerning the homosexual or lesbian lifestyle as they are on any issue. This is not an obscure or gray area. In fact, the Word of God says that when women sleep with women, their activity is even, "against nature" [Romans 1:26]. Anyone who has studied human anatomy, or, for that matter, looked at the human body, knows that God designed and nature demands that a man go with a woman and a woman go with a man. Even the dogs, cats, and horses know this much!

Everywhere homosexuality is mentioned in the Word of God it is either listed with other sins and deeds of the flesh or condemned by God as sin. It is no more a lifestyle preference than would be a preference to lie, to cheat, to murder, or to commit adultery. Can you imagine someone saying, "I just prefer to get my vehicles by stealing them. Accept me the way I am?" Can you imagine a Christian saying, " I prefer to satisfy my sexual desires by sleeping with many different women. Accept me the way I am?" If homosexuality can be validated because, "God made me this way," then so can stealing, anger, alcoholism, pride, adultery, murder, or any other work of the flesh.

Some ministers, claiming to speak for God and desperate to validate their own choices, have, through teaching unsound doctrine, issued a license to others to pursue the homosexual lifestyle. These individuals who claim to be ministers of God are doing the same thing that God condemned false spiritual leaders in the Old Testament for doing. They are changing the Word of God to fit their own personal preferences and the preferences of those they teach. They are adjusting the truth to fit the times rather than adjusting their lives to fit the truth. Modern day so-called ministers of the gospel who justify homosexuality so that they don't have to feel guilty have not only lied to themselves and lied to their congregations; they have taken away the truth that can set homosexual men and women free!

Ministers with ungodly motivations will be sorely tempted to twist the Word of God to support and validate their desires. They are almost sure to develop and promote unsound doctrine. These ministers are a dangerous source of unsound doctrine.

Those Not Called to the Ministry

Another category of unsound spiritual leader that is a source of unsound doctrine are those individuals who wish they were called or suppose they are called to the full time ministry, but are not. Because they are not called to one of the five-fold offices in the church, they are not specially graced and anointed to set forth doctrine. Their teachings, therefore, will often be an unhealthy mix of truth and speculation. By esteeming themselves more highly than they ought, they cross over into an area of service they are not spiritually equipped to handle. The result is that they often promote teaching that is unsound and even false. Rather than establishing people in sound doctrine, they cause confusion. These individuals should accurately judge themselves according to Romans 12:3 because they have overestimated their calling.

With the calling to teach the Word as presented in Ephesians four — whether one is called to be an apostle, prophet, evangelist, pastor, or teacher — there is a complementary anointing, or grace, to teach. And while we must make it absolutely clear that no scripture is of any private interpretation and that all can understand the written Word, we must also understand that God **has** called certain individuals to teach the Word. Because He has called them to teach, He has also complemented them with a capacity both to comprehend and to transmit revelation. Paul wrote about his special grace to teach and preach in Ephesians three saying,

> *"If ye have heard of the dispensation of the grace of God which is given me to you-ward: How that by revelation he made known unto me the mystery…Which in other ages was not made known unto the sons of men, as it is now revealed unto his holy apostles and prophets by the Spirit…Unto me, who am less than the least of all saints,is this grace given, that I should preach among the Gentiles the unsearchable riches of Christ…"*

> *Ephesians 3:2-8*

I remember one meeting where I was laying hands on individuals by the direction of the Holy Spirit. About half way through the prayer line, I laid hands on a particular man. When I touched him, I knew instantly by the Spirit of God that he thought he was called to be a pastor. I also knew by the Spirit of God that he was not called to the ministry. I told him that he needed to reconsider what he thought he was called to do. He did not enter into the ministry and today is a sound believer and sound member in the church.

Some believers imagine themselves to be what they are not. Their inflated estimation of their own calling causes them to think that their teaching is right. In our day, individuals are calling themselves apostles, prophets, and all manner of other things. Certainly, some are, but others are simply individuals who desire those offices and crave the recognition and authority that comes with them. These individuals, because they are not called to these offices, are open to confusion and often become vessels of error. I have noticed that when individuals begin to call themselves something they are not, it is not long before they have wandered into unsound doctrine and are in spiritual trouble.

It is dangerous for individuals who are not called by God to full-time ministry to attempt to stand in a place of ministry and teach. It is dangerous for themselves and dangerous for those who listen to them. Not only are they not anointed to teach, but because they are outside God's will, they are open to the attacks and influences of the devil. By assuming a position they are not called to, they become a danger to the body of Christ.

Religious Leaders

Religious leaders — those who have secured positions of spiritual leadership, but hold fast to their traditions rather than to the Word of God — are also part of the group of unsound spiritual leaders who promote unsound doctrine. In fact, religious leaders are a most dangerous source of unsound doctrine because of all unsound spiritual leaders, they appear to be the most spiritual. Because they appear to be spiritual, they are respected by some as sound spiritual leaders.

Religious leaders' wrong doctrine and wrong interpretation of scripture can be affected to a large degree by their church background. If a minister grew up in the Catholic faith, he will have certain doctrines already established in his thinking. If a minister comes from a Pentecostal background, he will have certain doctrines and ways of thinking that are rooted in him. Unsound doctrines are perpetuated by religious leaders in the same way that Paul instructed Timothy to perpetuate sound doctrine. Timothy was to teach faithful men who would be able to teach other faithful men who would teach others, etc. In the same way, unsound doctrine passes from teacher to student and from generation to generation. Many religious leaders are simply faithful transmitters of the error of their teachers.

When the religious leaders of Jesus' day tried to validate their own views concerning divorce, Jesus answered them sharply saying, "have ye not read?" [Matthew 22:31]. Jesus shocked the religious leaders and, perhaps, all who heard Him, by asking them this incriminating question. These religious leaders prided themselves on being scripture experts, but they had abandoned scriptural authority. To refute their position concerning divorce, Jesus pointed them to what God established concerning marriage in the book of Genesis.

The religious leaders of Jesus' day promoted their unsound doctrines in place of the truth of the written scriptures. They exalted their interpretations of the Word of God above the truth of the Word of God and, thus, became a very dangerous source of unsound doctrine. The religious leaders did not *deny* the scriptures; they *misinterpreted* the scriptures! This is the reason Jesus so often and so pointedly warned the disciples to beware of the doctrine of Pharisees.

On one occasion the Sadducees, who did not believe in the resurrection, came to Jesus with a question about whose wife a woman would be in the resurrection who had married seven brothers. Jesus answered these religious leaders saying,

> "...Ye do err, not knowing the scriptures..."
>
> Matthew 22:29

The religious leaders of Jesus' day were unsound spiritual leaders who promoted unsound doctrine. Many religious leaders today do the same. Rather than accepting the Word of God as it is written and preaching and teaching it in a pure, unadulterated fashion, they promote opinions, traditions, and denominational thinking. Religious leaders are a very dangerous source of unsound doctrine.

TRUE SPIRITUAL LEADERS

You may ask, "How can you include sound spiritual leaders as a source of unsound doctrine?" Because, friend, everyone can make mistakes. Sometimes those who are truly called and rightfully accepted as spiritual leaders unintentionally wander from sound doctrine and promote their error. Though God has set ministers in the church to establish believers so that they will not be tossed to and fro by winds of doctrine, it is often ministers that keep the church upset. Some of the winds of unsound doctrine are formulated and fostered by truly called, but errant spiritual leaders.

Shortly after Peter received the great revelation from heaven that Jesus was the Christ, he was used by Satan as a mouthpiece. Peter, a truly called and anointed apostle, was at one moment inspired from heaven and at the next moment inspired by Satan. The most startling part is that he did not know the difference! One moment he received revelation from heaven and the next moment he transmitted Satanically inspired error! Believers must be awake, aware, and ready to judge because even sound ministers can promote error. Believers must not be fearful and paranoid, but must **always** be attentive and alert.

"But," you say, "if God really called someone to be a spiritual leader, could they ever become involved in and promote unsound doctrine?" Of course! Why do you think Paul wrote so extensively to Timothy and Titus about remaining sound in doctrine? Were they not called? Were they not anointed? Were they not church leaders and leaders of leaders? Yes, they were all these things! Paul warned them repeatedly, however, concerning soundness in doctrine because there was a possibility that they could fall into error themselves. It should be clear from what Paul taught Timothy and Titus that even the most sound spiritual leaders are susceptible to error and potential promoters of unsound doctrine.

Truly called, but sincerely wrong spiritual leaders are a most dangerous source of unsound doctrine. For various reasons they have wandered off course. Their sincerity, however, shines through their unsound teaching. This makes it very difficult for believers to judge them as unsound. Their sincerity is like the flavoring in children's medicine. Because the medicine tastes sweet, children will swallow it.

Believers must understand, for their own spiritual safety, that a minister can be sincere, but be sincerely wrong! Because sincerely wrong ministers are a dangerous source of unsound doctrine, believers must be willing to make objective examinations. Let's look now at the kind of sincere ministers who get into doctrinal error.

Ministers Who Will Not Study

Peter warned of individuals that wrest, or twist, scriptures. He said,

"...Paul...hath written unto you...in all his epistles, speaking in them of these things; in which are some things hard to be understood, which they that are unlearned...wrest, as they do also the other scriptures..."

II Peter 3:15-16

Ministers who are unlearned are those who will not, "study to show (themselves) approved unto God, a workman that needeth not be ashamed, rightly dividing the Word of truth" [II Timothy 2:15]. It takes discipline in study in order to, "rightly divide the Word of Truth." It takes discipline in study to interpret and teach scripture accurately. Ministers who will not study often twist the scriptures. They are careless, not thoroughly searching the scriptures, checking and rechecking what they teach. Their failure to study causes them to teach doctrine that is not accurate. When these sincere, but unlearned ministers gain places of spiritual leadership, unsound doctrine can easily and swiftly sweep into local congregations.

Some truths from the Word of God are not easy to understand. All truth can not be learned from a 15 page mini-book! Ministers must dig in and study. A minister must be a, "work-man." That is a man who works! If a man is called to teach the Word of God, he must, "labor in the Word and in doctrine." It is work to discipline oneself to take the time in study that is required in order to present the Word of God with accuracy, clarity, soundness, and vitality! If a minister is disciplined in his study, he will have no reason to be ashamed of his doctrine. Some ministers, however, will be ashamed when they realize that because of their laziness they have failed to bring forth the Word of God with accuracy, but have twisted scriptures, parroted others, and caused problems in the church.

Paul told Timothy to transmit his sound teachings to "faithful men" who were able to teach others [II Timothy 2:2]. Some men are not faithful to study and to prepare themselves. They refuse to bring their minds and their time into subjection to the will of God. Perhaps they fail to realize the seriousness of being a leader in the body of Christ. Perhaps they do not realize what profound problems can result in the church if their teaching is unsound. Those who will not study often misinterpret or misapply the Word of God.

Misinterpretation of the Word

Peter wrote in II Peter 1:20 that,

> "...no prophesy of the scripture is of any private interpretation."
>
> II Peter 1:20

The scriptures are interpreted by men. The word "interpretation" comes from two Greek words: *epi*, which means up, and *luo*, which means to loose. The word "interpretation" means to "loosen up." It denotes finding a solution or an explanation and literally means, "a release." To interpret the scriptures means to loosen the understanding of what the Holy Spirit has said through men.

One of the most important responsibilities of those called to the ministry is to "tread out the corn." Ministers are responsible to loosen the understanding of the words of God, formulate sound doctrine, and then teach it clearly. A minister's interpretation of the scriptures, however, can be right, wrong, or unsound. If a minister refuses to take time in study and prayer his interpretation of scripture will very likely be at least unsound.

Misapplying the Word

Scripture that is correctly interpreted, but then misapplied is also unsound doctrine. A prime example of the misapplication of a scripture is when Satan attempted to persuade Jesus to jump from a cliff by reminding Him of the ministry of angels as found in Psalms 91. "The angels will protect you," the devil said, "according to Psalm 91." And the devil was right. His interpretation of that particular scripture was very accurate.

The cunning part of the devil's temptation was that he misapplied this scripture. It is true that God's angels will watch over His people; they are ministers for those who are the heirs of salvation. This promise of protection cannot be applied, however, if one tempts God by putting himself in a dangerous situation. If one *falls*, the angels will come to deliver. If one *jumps*, however, the angels will not come.

One scripture that is often misapplied is the very familiar command to, "Love one another." This scripture has been so misapplied at times that even believers who willfully live in ungodliness have a scriptural basis for demanding acceptance. The scripture, "Love one another," cannot, however, be misapplied to mean that Christians must accept and fellowship with every other believer no matter what kind of lifestyle they are living. Although, "Love one another," does mean to care for one another and to be united with one another, the Bible also teaches that those who claim to be brothers, but persist in godless lifestyle are to be judged and disfellowshipped. Listen to Paul's words,

> "...I have written unto you not to keep company, if any man that is called a brother be a fornicator, or covetous...with such a one no not to eat...ye judge them that are within...put away from among yourselves that wicked person."
>
> I Corinthians 5:11-13

Believers are not required, because of, "Love one another," to accept and fellowship with other believers who insist on living in sin. Sound Christians are not to keep company with or even eat with those who persist in sin. Rather, these individuals are to be put out of the sound body. The misapplication of the scripture about loving one another can be just as dangerous as ignoring it or misinterpreting it.

Another example of misapplying scripture would be applying Jesus' teaching of, "Judge not, that ye be not judged," to every situation of spiritual life. Without studying that particular teaching in its context and comparing it with the whole counsel of God, one could assume that it was always wrong to make judgments. This misapplication of scripture will definitely lead to unbalanced teaching and unsound doctrine.

Ministers Who Overestimate Their Calling

From my own observation of ministry since 1980, I have concluded that there are two kinds of teachers in the body of Christ. (By teacher I am not referring only to the specific five-fold office of Teacher, but to anyone called to one of the five-fold offices, all of whom are primarily responsible to teach and establish doctrine.) One kind of teacher is called and gifted by God to dig out revelation himself, rediscovering and reestablishing truths in his generation. The other kind of teacher is primarily responsible to faithfully teach what others have dug out.

The second kind of teacher I mentioned is characterized by the "faithful men" Paul spoke to Timothy about. He said,

"*And the things that thou hast heard of me among many witnesses, the same commit thou to faithful men, who shall be able to teach others also.*"

II Timothy 2:2

Timothy was to entrust the teachings of Paul to faithful men. It was imperative that these men be faithful because they would be responsible to accurately transmit the sound teachings of Paul. Yes, they must be *able* to teach. But the first requirement was that they be *faithful* to accurately transmit Paul's sound doctrine.

Teachers who are not called and gifted to dig out revelation must be very careful. Although they are called to the ministry and are called to teach, they can create a tremendous amount of trouble by digging around in places where they are not spiritually equipped. They should stay within the boundaries of their callings and within their spiritual capacities and faithfully teach what others have rediscovered and reestablished.

I have listened to the teachings of ministers who tried to dig out revelation, but were not equipped to do so. Their revelations made me very nervous. Their doctrines were not sound. They should have concentrated on the basic teachings they had been established in themselves and left the digging to others.

Both kinds of teachers are necessary and important in the body of Christ and both are responsible to teach sound doctrine. Those, however, who are not called to dig out revelation, but are determined to do so, can be a source of unsound doctrine.

Ministers Who Have Zeal Without Knowledge

Sometimes, strange as it may seem, the urgent desire to do something great for God, to effect a radical change, and to make a great impact, can give rise to unsound doctrine. When ministers push too hard, they end up not only outside the boundaries of their own abilities, but outside the boundaries of sound doctrine. Rather than holding fast to the clear teachings of the Word of God, they rush into all kinds of unprofitable activities that look spiritual, sound spiritual, and give a sense to the mind and flesh that something spiritual is being accomplished.

Too much zeal mixed with too little knowledge gives rise to and sustains unsound spiritual activities and the doctrines that validate them. Undoubtedly, it is the zeal of modern-day ministers that has given rise to and sustained the contemporary teachings of militant prayer and spiritual warfare. Zealous ministers began to say, "There **must** be a key we are missing. There **must** be something we are not doing. We **must** do something more! We **must** shake the whole world for the kingdom and glory of God!" This kind of zeal throws caution to the wind. Overzealous ministers sense no need for caution when a dying world needs to be saved!

The desire to shake the whole world, even to radically effect cities, is honorable and noble. It is wonderful to be on fire for God and work to bring changes in the world. Zeal, however, must be mixed with knowledge in order to fulfill the will of God.

Think for a moment about Jesus' desire to reach the people of Israel. His heart cried out because of their spiritual condition and their eternal destination. These were the very people He came to seek and save! Don't you think He wanted to see the power of God change them? Of course Jesus wanted to see results in the lost sheep of the house of Israel. But most of them would not receive Him. Jesus could not change them. The most He could do is the most any of us can do. He sought the Father in prayer, moved by the direction of the Holy Spirit, and preached the truth by the anointing of the Spirit of God. When He had done that, He had done all He could do.

Do you remember how Jesus wept over the city of Jerusalem because they were missing the day of their visitation? Why didn't He pull down the stronghold of religious spirits over Jerusalem? Why didn't He do militant prayer? Why didn't He call for a praise gathering to praise down the strongholds? He did not do these things because the Word of God does not teach these activities in connection with winning people to God. The Word of God does not teach that whole cites can be claimed for God. The Word of God does not teach that if the spiritual strongholds over cities are pulled down, everyone will be free to receive the gospel. The Word of God does not teach that Jesus is Lord over cities.

How did Jesus teach His own disciples to respond if a particular city did not accept the gospel message? He taught them to shake the dust off their feet and go somewhere else [Matthew 10:14; Acts 13:51]. He didn't tell them to stay and pray. He didn't tell them to pull down the strong man over that city. He didn't tell them to praise until the glory fell. He didn't tell them to war in the heavenlies until they broke through.

Oh, I know these things sound so good. I wish myself they were true! But they are not in agreement with the example of Jesus or the teaching of Jesus. They are not in agreement with the example of Paul or the teachings of Paul. They are not in agreement with the example of Peter or the teachings of Peter. Quite simply, they are not in agreement with the Word of God.

What does the Word of God teach in connection with the salvation of the lost? The Word of God teaches us to be filled with the Spirit, to give ourselves to prayer, to follow the direction of the Holy Spirit, and to hold forth the Word of Life to people of every nation. We are to preach the gospel, proclaiming the good news of salvation, letting the seeds fall where they will. Then, if the ground is ready and good, there will come forth a harvest. We can sow and water, but the harvest is dependent upon the ground.

I do not fault ministers who want to shake cities and nations. I give them a round of applause for their zeal. Being zealous for the Lord is not wrong. Believers are to be fervent in spirit, serving the Lord. Zeal, however, **must** be coupled with knowledge! If it isn't, then much of the energy expended will be invalid and the doctrine of the church will become unsound.

Concerning Israel, Paul said that they sought after God with zeal, but did **not** find Him because they did not pursue after Him with knowledge [Romans 10:1-3]. Truly called ministers who are overzealous can be a source of unsound doctrine. Their desire is right, but their doctrine and activities are often unsound. Zeal is good, but zeal without knowledge is dangerous!

Evangelists and TV Ministers

Evangelists and T.V. ministers, because they are movers and shakers, tend to be more oriented toward the spectacular. They are more prone to stretch the Word of God in order to make it more exciting. They often promote winds of doctrine unconsciously by keeping believers hyped up about the next wave or the next move of God. These ministers, not realizing how much believers and younger ministers respect and follow their ministries, often do not understand the serious impact of their teachings.

Often these ministers desire to be on the cutting-edge of the move of God. They want to be on the forefront of spiritual exploration. They want to say something first, before another nationally known minister beats them to it. Because they want to be forefront and cutting edge, they are often willing to go beyond sound doctrine in order to be heard. Sometimes these ministers compete with one another. One stretches the truth a little. The next one stretches it a little further, making it even more exciting. The next one stretches it even further because everyone has already heard what the other ones said. Soon particular teachings are well outside the boundaries of what could be classified as sound Bible doctrine. Mark my words, the body of Christ will pay the price for these ministers' ambitions!

Even for the most sound spiritual leaders there is a temptation to look for something new or something different, something that will be interesting for the people. Even called and anointed spiritual leaders must be careful that their ambition to do great things for God does not push them toward unsound doctrine.

Ministers Who Are Novices

Being young in the ministry is not an excuse for teaching unsound doctrine. The young, however, because they are full of zeal and sometimes aggressive rather then teachable and humble, can be the perpetrators of unsound doctrine. Paul told Timothy,

"Let no man despise thy youth; but be thou an example of the believers, in word..."

I Timothy 4:12

Paul challenged Timothy, a young believer and young minister, to, "let no man despise thy youth." Why would someone despise Timothy's youth? They would despise his youth if he acted like a youth! If Timothy was foolish in doctrine and foolish in his spiritual life, people would not respect him as a spiritual leader. How could Timothy keep people from despising his youth? By acting like a spiritual adult!

In his instructions to Timothy about the selection of spiritual leaders, Paul warned him not to put an novice in office. He said,

"Not a novice, lest being lifted up with pride he fall into the condemnation of the devil."

I Timothy 3:6

A novice is one who is young in the faith. He is inexperienced in spiritual matters and susceptible to mistakes. If a novice gets lifted up in pride, he will assume that everything he thinks and teaches is sound.

Novices in the ministry, especially those who have zeal and charisma and can motivate people to action, can be a dangerous source of unsound doctrine. They can find quick success, get into pride, and lead people into error. They can overestimate themselves as did Satan, substituting their opinions for what God has said. Unsound doctrine can come from the young in ministry. Check carefully their doctrines and their attitudes.

Ministers Who Are Unstable

Others who are guilty of twisting the scriptures and being a source of unsound doctrine are the unstable [II Peter 2:16]. To be stable means to be firmly set, resistant to anything that tries to move or change you. Those who are unstable are moveable. They change opinions like a man changes his socks. They have not rooted themselves firmly in the truth and built up their resistance to unsound doctrine. Their instability makes them participants in the formation and propagation of unsound doctrine.

Unstable ministers will twist the scriptures to fit what they think God is doing now. An unstable minister might read a scripture like, "Behold I do a new thing" [Isaiah 43:19], and conclude that God has just spoken to him about a new move that is coming. A stable leader would realize that although God does emphasize certain truths at certain times, the particular scripture from Isaiah is specifically an Old Testament prophesy that foretells of the New Covenant.

Ministers Who Make Precedents of Particular Leadings of the Spirit

A common reason that ministers wander into and then become a source of unsound doctrine is because they make precedents out of particular leadings of the Holy Spirit. For example, the Holy Spirit may lead one minister to fast every Monday and pray for world peace. This minister cannot teach, however, that all believers must fast on Mondays and pray for world peace. Certainly, he can teach about fasting. Certainly, he can teach about prayer. He can even refer to his own experience. But he cannot make a doctrine of this particular leading of the Spirit.

A few years ago, one hour early morning prayer was very popular. This teaching was started by someone the Lord had dealt with concerning that kind of prayer. Soon, however, his message was being preached in churches as if it was a Bible doctrine. One pastor told me that people in his church became angry if exactly one hour was not spent in early morning prayer.

Then it became popular to pray and "call people in" to the church from the north, south, east, and west. I am certainly not going to tell you not to pray that prayer. I will inform you, however, that you cannot teach that kind of prayer as a Bible doctrine. If God told you and your church to pray this prayer, then pray it with all your might. But don't teach as a Bible doctrine what the Holy Spirit has impressed you to do.

Personally, I have very seldom prayed early in the morning. Personally, I have never used the Lord's prayer as my guideline for prayer. Personally, I have never called to the north, south, east, and west. I have never pulled down strongholds or warred with the devil in other tongues. Why? These are not Bible doctrines. Does this mean that I don't pray? Of course not. I pray because the Bible teaches me to pray. I pray prayers the Bible records and pray the way the Bible teaches to pray. I also pray about things and in ways that I feel impressed in my own heart to pray.

A few years ago, there was a teaching going around in the body of Christ that if Satan stole from you, you could believe God to get back seven times more. The scripture this teaching was based on came from one half of one verse from the book of Proverbs [Proverbs 6:31]. Because of this teaching, people sometimes asked me to agree with them to get back seven times what they had lost. I felt bad, but I could not agree with them in prayer. They were confused. Then I had to take time to instruct them in sound doctrine.

Perhaps the one who started this teaching was directed by the Holy Spirit to this particular scripture for a personal situation. A doctrine about getting back seven times more than what the devil has supposedly stolen cannot, however, be established on one half of one verse that is taken from the book of Proverbs and refers to a particular Jewish law.

In 1981, I was reading in the gospel of Luke about the dead boy from Nain that Jesus raised. When I came to the part where Jesus said to the dead boy, "Young man, I say unto thee, Arise," the Spirit of God leapt within me and said, "Young man, it is time for you to rise up and speak the things you know!" This was a word the Holy Spirit spoke to me from the written scriptures. It is not a Bible doctrine, however, and I would never teach it as a doctrine. It came from the written Word of God, but it was used by the Holy Spirit to speak to me in a special way for a special situation.

Conclusion

Ministers, whether false, unsound, or true, are a primary source of unsound doctrine. Those who are accepted and respected as spiritual leaders will have very little trouble introducing and promoting unsound doctrines to unaware believers.

Two: Satan, Seducing Spirits, And Demons

Unsound doctrine can be formulated and promoted both by Satan and by the seducing spirits and demons under his command. The Word of God makes it clear that Satan has the ability to suggest thoughts to peoples' minds. He put the thought in Judas' mind to betray Jesus to the religious community and then controlled his final actions [John 13:25]. In Acts five, Peter said to Ananias, "Why hath Satan filled thine heart to lie to the Holy Ghost." The Word of God also reveals that demons have the ability to influence the thoughts of men. The apostle Paul made this clear in his letter to Timothy informing him that seducing spirits and demons would influence the thoughts and, thereby, the doctrines of men [I Timothy 4:1].

SATAN

Satan's main mode of operation has always been deception. He is the father of lies [John 8:44] and the "deceiver of the whole world" [Revelation 12:9]. He has always been and will continue to be involved with the distortion, perversion, and masking of truth. His first words to the human race were, "Yea, hath God said" [Genesis 3:1]? The beginning of error is an uncertainty and a mistrust about the truth. A question, an unsettling thought, an, "Are you sure?" Satan asked Eve if God had really said that she and Adam could not eat of every tree in the garden. Eve considered his question about what God had said and by so doing opened a door that led to error and death.

Satan is a Master Deceiver. He is an expert in his field. He has the ability to suggest thoughts and questions to believers' minds. That is why the Word of God warns believers to be, "sober and vigilant," keeping a watch out for him [I Peter 5:8]. Just because one is knowledgeable in the Word of God does not mean that Satan will not attempt to deceive them. His deception will just be a bit more tricky, a little harder to separate out, and a little closer to truth. His deception, however, will be no less deadly!

Subtility, trickery, deception, cunning, falseness, untruth, fabrication — all these words describe Satan's mode of operation against God's people. It is through the use of disguises, crafty arguments, and twisted truths that he attempts to deceive the unsuspecting. It is through the perversion of truth, the distortion of truth, and the suppression of truth that he beguiles believers into false doctrine and spiritual error.

Jesus' Temptation

Immediately upon being anointed with the Holy Spirit in the river Jordan, Jesus was led by the Spirit into the wilderness. There he met the devil and his cunning temptations. Satan's first two temptations were straight-forward. Jesus responded to both of them saying, "It is written" [Luke 4:4,8]. Upon hearing these answers, Satan realized that Jesus was dependent upon the written scriptures. He quickly switched tactics and tempted Jesus by quoting from Psalm 91. Satan said,

> "...cast thyself down...For it is written, he shall give his angels charge over thee, to keep thee: and in their hands they shall bear thee up, lest at any time thou dash thy foot against a stone."
>
> *Luke 4:9-11*

Satan tempted Jesus to "cast thyself down" and explained that this action would be perfectly acceptable because it was written in the scriptures that the angels would come to rescue Him. Satan, cunning and wiley as he is, attempted to use the scriptures to lure Jesus outside the will of God and, therefore, outside the protection of God.

You see, the devil is sly. He knows the Word of God. And he will quote the Word of God out of context, wrongly divide it, and make every attempt to deceive believers by misusing it. If believers are knowledgeable in the Word of God, the devil will try to use the Word of God against them. The more acquainted believers are with the scriptures, the more they must be on guard, carefully interpreting and applying them.

Satan Works Through False Spiritual Leaders

Paul revealed something of the cunning and deceptive activities of Satan in a warning he gave to the church at Corinth. In this warning he said,

> "I fear, lest by any means, as the serpent beguiled Eve through his subtility, so your minds should be corrupted from the simplicity that is in Christ."
>
> *I Corinthians 11:3*

Paul said he was afraid for the believers in Corinth. He was afraid because of the possibility that Satan would deceive them and corrupt their faith in Christ. Paul would not have been afraid for these believers if Satan could not really deceive them. Did you notice the four words Paul used to describe Satan's possible methods of deception? He said, "lest by any means." Whatever means it takes to achieve the end of deception, Satan will try!

Paul warned these believers that as Satan had beguiled Eve so he would attempt to beguile them. It was, "through his subtility," said Paul, that Satan deceived Eve. One aspect of Satan's subtle deception was that he came in a body that was familiar and acceptable to Eve. He was also trying this tactic in Corinth.

In the church at Corinth, Satan was working through false apostles. Paul closely connected Satan's efforts to beguile [verse 3] with those who preached "another Jesus" and brought "another spirit" [verse 4]. The false apostles in Corinth were under the direct influence of Satan. They were "his ministers," said Paul [II Corinthians 11:15]. Satan supplied the plan and the message. His ministers — the false apostles — supplied the bodily disguise and the voice. To the church at Corinth, Satan came not as a wolf and not as a sheep, but as a shepherd!

Satan May Work Through Companions

Satan will not only attempt to mislead believers by influencing their thoughts directly and by speaking through false ministers. He will also try to work through individuals who would least likely be suspected as His messengers. Never forget that Satan is cunning and ruthless. He is determined to thwart the plan of God. He will not hesitate to speak through and work through even one's closest companions.

Near the time of His suffering and crucifixion, Jesus began to tell the disciples that He would, "suffer many things...and be killed, and be raised the third day" [Matthew 16:21]. What Jesus told His disciples was in perfect accord with the written scriptures. These truths had been prophesied of Him and were recorded in the Old Testament. Peter responded to Jesus' words, however, by saying, "Be it far from thee, Lord: this shall not be unto thee" [Matthew 16:22].

This "word" that Peter spoke was a very well calculated attempt by Satan to hinder the plan of God. Perhaps Jesus would accept Peter's words as a word from heaven. After all, only a short time ago Peter had received the revelation from the Father that Jesus was the Christ [Matthew 16:16]. Based on Peter's latest "revelation" Jesus could have thought to Himself, "Perhaps I don't have to suffer. Perhaps I don't have to die. God may be speaking to me through Peter."

Knowing the scriptures that were written of Himself, however, and being sensitive in the spirit, Jesus said, "Get thee behind me Satan" [Matthew 16:23]. He perceived that what Peter said was not from God, not according to the Word, and not even from Peter's own emotions, but was inspired by Satan himself. Jesus tested Peter's words, compared them with the scriptures, and found Satan himself behind them!

Do you see how subtle the devil is? He is sly as a fox. He did not *confront* Jesus. He *carefully approached* Jesus. He spoke to Him through one of his closest associates! Believers must be careful of their associations. If Satan knows you have absolute confidence in a person or a particular minister, he will try to use that person, unbeknownst to them or you, to lead you into unsound doctrine. It is **never** wise to absolutely trust the word or teaching of any man. Everything must be weighed against the scripture and tested by the witness of the indwelling Holy Spirit.

SEDUCING SPIRITS AND DEMONS

False and unsound doctrine can also proceed from Satan's cohorts — seducing spirits and demons. There are countless demon spirits subordinate to Satan. Some of these spirits have been assigned the task of misleading ministers and believers through the avenue of unsound and false doctrine.

We have already learned that Satan has the capacity to put thoughts into the minds of individuals. He did so with Peter, with Judas, and with Ananias and Sapphira. Satan, however, is nothing more than a fallen spirit. Demons, though less powerful than him, are also fallen spirits. Fallen spirits, whether Satan or the demons that work with him, have the ability to suggest thoughts to the minds of people. Paul confirmed this in his first letter to Timothy saying,

> *"Now the Spirit speaketh expressly that in the latter times some shall depart from the faith, giving heed to seducing spirits, and doctrines of devils..."*
>
> I Timothy 4:1

Paul said that some would depart from the faith by "giving heed to seducing spirits." To give heed means to pay attention to. The very fact that believers give heed to (listen to) seducing spirits confirms the truth that demon spirits have the capacity to communicate with human beings.

Demons and seducing spirits will attempt to teach "doctrines of demons" to believers to cause them to apostatize from the truth. Doctrines of demons are false teachings, ranging from faulty to fraudulent, that demons seek to impress upon the minds of the unsuspecting.

How Do Seducing Spirits Work?

Seducing spirits and demons can transmit unsound doctrines to believers in two ways. First, if a Christian is too open-minded and likes to consider other teachings along with the written Word, then demons and seducing spirits have an avenue of entrance to their minds. You may say, "Brother Guy, that makes me scared." Good! Then you will be very cautious with your thought life, studying carefully what the scriptures say and listening carefully to the voice of the Holy Spirit.

Second, seducing spirits can speak through the yielded mouths of false spiritual leaders, ministers, or other believers. The apostle John said,

"...believe not every spirit, but try the spirits whether they are of God; because many false prophets are gone out into the world..."

I John 4:1

Just as some men yield themselves to the Holy Spirit and speak the Word of God, so some men yield themselves to seducing spirits and speak error. There is a Spirit of Truth — He is the Holy Spirit. But there is also a "spirit of error" [I John 4:6]. The spirit of error inspires false prophets, apostles, and teachers who, in turn, teach error. Believers must be very discerning so that they will not be swayed by the words of men who are being inspired by seducing spirits.

In the Old Testament, lying spirits influenced the prophesies of false prophets. In one instance the Lord wanted to entice Ahab to engage in a battle that would bring about his fall. The Bible says,

"Then there came out a spirit, and stood before the Lord, and said, I will entice him. And the Lord said unto him, Wherewith? And he said, I will go out, and be a lying spirit in the mouth of all his prophets. And the Lord said, Thou shalt entice him, and thou shalt also prevail: go out, and do even so. Now therefore, behold, the Lord hath put a lying spirit in the mouth of these thy prophets..."

II Chronicles 18:20-22

In this account, lying spirits spoke through yielded false prophets. Through these human vessels, they spoke words which drew Ahab into battle and to his death.

How can believers combat seducing spirits and doctrines of demons? By knowing the written scriptures and by knowing the Spirit of Truth. "It is written," is the best defense against satanic thoughts and doctrines of demons. When a thought is inspired directly to your mind or when you hear someone else speak, you can check immediately to determine whether or not it agrees with the Word of God. Believers should also listen for the witnesses of the Holy Spirit that dwells in them. Because the Holy Spirit is the Spirit of Truth, He will not bear witness with false doctrine. If you are not immediately sure whether a thought or a teaching is sound or unsound, you must do a more thorough search of the Word of God and listen quietly and patiently for the guidance of the Holy Spirit.

THREE: IMMATURE BELIEVERS

The spiritual condition of the body of Christ plays a significant role in determining the doctrinal direction of the body of Christ. If believers are immature — always wanting something new, something different, something that justifies their lifestyle — they set the stage both for the deceptive activities of Satan and seducing spirits and for the wily activities of unsound leaders. Their lust for new teachings and new experiences and their boredom with sound doctrine is like an invitation to seducing spirits and cunning men. In Ephesians 4:14, Paul said that crafty and cunning men, "lie in wait to deceive." If believers wander down the road where these men are lying in wait, they will end up in spiritual trouble. Let's look at some of the dangerous spiritual attitudes believers can have which make them a catalyst for unsound doctrine.

Unhealthy Desire For Knowledge

One way that believers can be a cause, or catalyst, of unsound doctrine is by having an unhealthy desire for knowledge. An unhealthy desire for knowledge and its potentially dangerous consequences can be seen from the very beginning of time. Eve's desire for more knowledge was the weakness Satan preyed upon when he tempted her in the garden of Eden. In Genesis 3:1, he approached Eve and began to dialogue with her. First, he questioned God's instructions to her saying,

> "...Yea, hath God said, Ye shall not eat of every tree of the garden?"
>
> Genesis 3:1

Eve responded to Satan saying,

> "...We may eat of the fruit of the trees of the garden: But of the fruit of the tree which is in the midst of the garden, God hath said, Ye shall not eat of it neither shall ye touch it, lest ye die."
>
> Genesis 3:2-4

Then Satan lied to Eve, accusing God of withholding from her and Adam the knowledge that would make them like God. He said,

> "...Ye shall not surely die: For God doth know that in the day ye eat thereof, then your eyes shall be opened, and ye shall be as gods, knowing good and evil."
>
> Genesis 3:4-5

The opportunity to gain knowledge and be like gods was hard for Eve to ignore. Perhaps she thought to herself, "What if this is true? If I obey God's words, what would I be missing? Surely it couldn't hurt to investigate a little more?" Satan's explanation caused Eve to look at the tree of the knowledge of good and evil from a different perspective. This time she looked at the forbidden fruit, not from the perspective of the command of God, but from the perspective of her own desire to have knowledge and to be like God. Notice her new perspective of the tree,

> *"And when the woman saw that the tree was good for food, and that it was pleasant to the eyes, and a tree to make one wise, she took of the fruit thereof, and did eat, and gave also unto her husband with her; and he did eat. And the eyes of them both were opened..."*

> Genesis 3:6-7

Three things drew Eve to the forbidden fruit. First, the forbidden fruit stirred up the most basic human desire of hunger. She saw it was, "good for food." Second, the forbidden fruit attracted her eye. It was, "pleasant to the eyes." Third, she was drawn to the forbidden fruit because of her desire for knowledge. She saw that it was, "a tree to make one wise."

The name of the tree that God **forbade** Adam and Eve to partake of was, "The tree of the knowledge of good and evil." Christians sometimes wrongly think that only sexual sins, or lying, or having a temper are spiritually dangerous. But an unhealthy desire for knowledge, even an unbalanced desire to gain wisdom, can also be dangerous. Remember that it was the great wisdom and beauty of Lucifer that led to his pride, rebellion, and eventual overthrow. Eve's desire for knowledge was not, in itself, sin. She simply desired, "to know." But her desire for knowledge led to the abandonment of the words of God and to a very costly spiritual error.

The devil will always approach believers in whatever way he thinks he will be the most likely to succeed. He looks for what is *in* a person and then uses that trait to his advantage. Do you remember that when the devil came looking for Jesus, Jesus said, "He finds nothing in me?" There was nothing *in* Jesus that Satan could "hook on to." The devil will not approach maturing believers carrying a sign that says, "Hi, I'm Satan and I am going to deceive you." For those who know and love the Word of God, the devil will use the Word of God, suppressing parts of it and distorting other parts of it, in order to deceive.

A few years ago, a friend invited me to a particular group's meeting to test their doctrine and spiritual direction. When their meeting was over, my friend asked for my opinion. I said that I had enjoyed the teaching and could see there was a validity to the message, but that I had a check in my spirit because the group seemed to be very oriented on a mental level.

There seemed to be a hunger for profound knowledge, an appetite and craving for deep revelation. It was like a mental lust. Those who were teaching approached the Word of God like mathematicians who could not work enough equations or solve enough problems. They seemed intoxicated with revelation rather than seriously interested in the Word of God. Their attitude was mystic, as if they wanted nothing but knowledge. Their hunger for knowledge was "spiritually off." It was not pure. Something was unhealthy.

Eventually, spiritual pride and an elitist attitude settled in to this group. They thought that they were the only ones who had a real revelation of the truth. They began to look down on "simple" believers. When sound spiritual leaders offered advise and counsel, they became defensive. Eventually they dissipated and some of the leaders drifted further and further off, leaving the spiritual scene altogether. An unhealthy hunger for knowledge eventually led to this group's downfall.

Purpose of the Word

Paul wrote to Timothy about the real purpose of God's Word saying,

"Now the end of the commandment is charity out of a pure heart, and of a good conscience, and of faith unfeigned."

I Timothy 1:5

The Amplified Bible makes this truth a little clearer for us. It says,

"Whereas the object and the purpose of our instruction and charge is love which springs from a pure heart and a good (clear) conscience and sincere (unfeigned) faith."

I Timothy 1:5 Amp

The goal of the teachings of God's Word is threefold: Love out of a pure heart, a good conscience which proceeds from godly living, and unshakable faith in God. If believers use the Word of God to reach these spiritual goals, their efforts are lawful. If, however, believers use the Word of God to satisfy their hunger for knowledge, they will be susceptible to unsound doctrine.

The Word of God is **not** to be used is as another textbook for knowledge. Yes, the Word of God will make a man wise, but, "wise unto salvation" [II Timothy 3:15]. If believers have a wrong attitude concerning knowledge of the Word of God, they will be like those Paul wrote of who were, "ever learning, and never able to come to the knowledge of the truth" [II Timothy 3:7]. The little anecdote, "curiosity killed the cat," is quite true. An overbalanced desire for knowledge can be dangerous. Those who hunger and thirst for the simple truths of God's Word shall be filled. But those who simply hunger and thirst must be careful.

There is a simplicity to the gospel and we must maintain an attitude of simplicity in our study of it. We should stay with what is plain, clear, obvious, and foundational. When we have learned all the foundations, we should go back and put ourselves in remembrance of those truths, even if they are already established in us. The apostle Peter encouraged this approach to spiritual life when he wrote,

> *"Wherefore I will not be negligent to put you always in remembrance of these things, though ye know them, and be established in the present truth. Yea, I think it meet, as long as I am in this tabernacle, to stir you up by putting you in remembrance..."*

> *II Peter 1:12-13*

Paul confirmed this same approach when he wrote,

> *"To write the same things to you, to me indeed is not grievous, and for you it is safe."*

> *Philippians 3:1*

Peter said that he would put believers in remembrance of truths they were already established in. Paul said that it was *safe* for believers to be instructed and reinstructed in the basic truths and fundamental principles of the Word of God. A correct attitude toward the Word is important. A hunger for knowledge can open the door to unsound doctrine.

Lust For New

Sometimes the introduction of unsound doctrine into the church is a result of the lust believers have for something new. They want something different, something exciting, a new revelation. Believers' desire for emotions to be stirred and minds to be stimulated can push teachers of the Word toward unsound doctrine.

The children of Israel typified this spiritual problem by their boredom with manna. Manna was God's heavenly bread, specially prepared and specially sent to strengthen and maintain their physical life. Israel soon became bored with what God had prepared for them, however, and began to lust after and to ask for something new. After they complained and complained, God gave them what they wanted [Psalms 78:25-30]. Even then, however, they were not satisfied and continued to lust. The Bible says of Israel,

> *"...they waited not for his counsel, But lusted exceedingly in the wilderness, and tempted God in the desert. And he gave them their request; but sent leanness to their soul."*

> *Psalms 106:13-15*

Israel was not satisfied eating manna day after day. Although it completely met their physical needs, it didn't pacify their palate. Though God did not approve of their lust for something different, He allowed them to have flesh. Their belly's were indeed filled with flesh, but their souls became lean, sickened, and unhealthy.

Some believers are like the children of Israel. They are not content with the supernatural spiritual food God has sent from heaven. They are not satisfied with the sound doctrines of the Word of God. They want something dynamic, something explosive, something moving, something "anointed." And though God does not approve, He will permit. Just as He allowed Israel to have flesh to their own destruction, so He will allow believers to pursue their own doctrinal direction. Do not be deceived, however, into thinking that nothing will result from this carnal pursuit. Spiritual laws remain intact. Whatsoever a man sows, that shall he also reap. If unsound doctrine is sown into believers' hearts, spiritual weakness and confusion will follow.

Paul told Timothy that, "after their lust," believers would heap to themselves teachers [II Timothy 4:4]. Lust is nothing more than perverted desire. It is an overgrown desire which causes a person to sacrifice everything that is important in order to fulfill an immediate hunger. Lust will drive a person to activities and substances that he knows will ruin him. Lust demands, however, that he have it and that he have it now!

For example, a desire for sex is normal. A desire for sex all the time and in wrong ways with wrong people, however, is lust. Hunger, too, is normal. But an insatiable appetite, a desire to eat just to taste food, is a lust. It is a perverted desire.

Just as there is natural lust, there can be spiritual lust. A desire for the Word of God and for the moving of the Spirit of God is normal for a Christian. A craving for the supernatural and a desire to hear only exciting and stimulating teaching, however, is a lust. A craving for emotionally and mentally stimulating teaching and spiritual activity is a perversion of a sincere hunger for God and His Word.

Some believers lust after emotional messages, exciting teachings, and deep revelations. They know that these teachings are not good for them. They know that they will not profit them spiritually. They know that they could produce spiritual weakness. They know that they could lead to ungodly activity. But they don't care. They want what they want when they want it! The more that unsound teachers scratch their ears, the more they itch!

The pursuit of new doctrine and new spiritual experiences is not the way to, "go on with God." The Bible has more to say about holding fast to sound doctrine than it does about pressing on. Believers who are wise will hold fast to and walk in the light of the truths they already know. "Let us hold fast the profession of our faith without wavering," is the charge of the Word of God [Hebrews 10:23].

The modern day church is in danger of doctrinal unsoundness. We want new. We want more. We want different. We want exciting. If the preacher doesn't excite us, we are not happy. If he doesn't stir us, we criticize. If we are not stroked and stimulated, we complain. In the long run, we will have leanness in our souls. When believers demand something to satisfy their lust, they will be a catalyst of and then a partaker of vain, unprofitable, and even false doctrine.

Won't Endure Sound Doctrine

Paul warned Timothy that a time would come when people would not endure sound doctrine, but would have itching ears and turn away from the truth. He said,

> *"For the time will come when they (believers) will not endure sound doctrine; but after their own lusts shall heap to themselves teachers, having itching ears. And they shall turn away their ears from the truth..."*

II Timothy 4:3-5

When believers will not endure sound doctrine, it means that they will not listen to those who teach sound doctrine. Who will they listen to instead? They will listen to teachers who are willing to compromise the Word of God. When believers will not endure sound doctrine, they will, instead, heap to themselves teachers who will say what they want to hear. Their immature spiritual condition affords teaching opportunities to those who are willing to compromise the Word of God for a good offering. Scriptures will be misinterpreted and misapplied by teachers who are willing to scratch the itching ears of immature believers.

When believers refuse to endure sound doctrine, they can gain control of the spiritual direction of the church. Unsound and weak ministers can be swayed by the opinions and desires of these carnal Christians. Some spiritual leaders cannot handle the rejection which comes from those who don't want to hear sound doctrine. They would rather switch to what the people want to hear than fight for the sound doctrines of God's Word. This weakness in ministers contributes to the slide from sound doctrine into error and false doctrine.

Because ministers are supported by the offerings of those to whom they preach, there is tremendous pressure to be approved. If a pastor preaches doctrine his congregation doesn't like, they won't pay and he won't eat! His congregation may say, "If you don't preach what we like, we'll find someone who will." If the pastor will not yield to the immature congregation, they will dismiss him and heap someone else to themselves.

This same reality can apply to an evangelist or travelling teacher. They too feel the pressure to be approved in order to have the needs of their ministries underwritten. If people don't like their teaching, they will not give offerings. The success of their ministry appears to be dependent upon the approval of the people. It is easy to see how preaching, and, therefore, doctrine, can be heavily influenced by what believers want to hear.

Some ministers fear losing their ministries more than they fear God and value being approved of Him. Concerning those called to the ministry, however, Paul said,

"*Moreover, it is required in stewards (stewards of the mysteries of God), that a man be found faithful.*"

I Corinthians 4:1-2

It is not only required that ministers be faithful *to* preach. It is also required that they be faithful in *what* they preach! Those who are motivated more by their desire to be approved than because they are "valiant for the truth" [Jeremiah 9:3] are very susceptible to the opinions of men and are, therefore, spiritually dangerous.

John the Baptist did not try to brown-nose king Herod when the king was living in sin. He condemned the king's lifestyle even though it cost him his life. The truth divides. The Bible says of Jesus that there was a division among the people because of Him [John 7:43]. Jesus said that His teaching would even divide families [Matthew 10:35]. Those ministers who value being accepted by people more than they value ministering the truth will eventually compromise the Truth and become promoters of unsound doctrine.

It is **very possible** that the direction of the church be dictated, not by the Head of the Church, not by the Holy Spirit, not by eternal Truths and time-tested doctrine, and not even by God-ordained leadership, but by immature believers who won't endure sound doctrine! Immature believers are a catalyst of and, therefore, a source of unsound doctrine.

A Time of True Spiritual Hunger

There are times of true spiritual hunger. There are seasons when even unbelievers become tired with the pursuit of physical pleasure, tired with the pursuit of financial gain, and tired with the pursuit of mental competence. They have explored all these avenues, but are still hungry for God. They feel a simple and pure hunger for God, for His Word, and for His presence.

There have been and will continue to be seasons in time when there is a widespread hunger throughout the world and in the body of Christ for the things of God.

A season of true spiritual hunger is fantastic. It is a time when people turn to God and return to God. It is a time when the Spirit of God is moving and the Word of God is prevailing. A time of spiritual hunger can also, however, be a time of danger. In a time of spiritual hunger, Satan and would be spiritual leaders will attempt to take advantage of those who are truly seeking after God.

Have you ever come home hungry and gone to the refrigerator, gone to the pantry, searched through the cupboard, and not found anything to eat? Finally, you dug out an old stale bag of crackers and munched on them. When you are too hungry, you will eat anything, even foods that you would normally not consider fit to eat. People have been known to eat dog food, cat food, and many other unhealthy things I don't even care to mention when they were too hungry.

Before the advent of the desalinization of salt water, sailors used to have a serious problem. If they ran out of fresh water while at sea and became thirsty, they would drink salt water from the ocean. Drinking salt water only made them thirstier and more dehydrated. The thirstier they became the more they drank. And the more they drank the more dehydrated they became. The final result of trying to quench their thirst with salt water was that they died of dehydration.

I have had this same experience in the mental realm. Sometimes after I have been in a foreign country for a period of time, I get "hungry" to read something in English. I don't care what it is, I just want to read something. I look for anything that has some news or information in it just to read a little. Subjects and articles I would never consider reading when I am in my own country, I will read when I am "hungry."

This same principle of hunger can apply to the spiritual life. To those who are spiritually hungry, anything sounds good. The book of wisdom says,

> *"The full soul loatheth an honeycomb; but to the hungry soul every bitter thing is sweet."*
>
> Proverbs 27:7

When a person is spiritually hungry, he is open. He is open to God and open to the move of His Spirit. He is also, however, open to those individuals or that teaching that comes in God's name, but is unsound. To him, even bitter things are sweet. Openness to God is good, but an open mind is a vulnerable mind.

A time of spiritual hunger is a time of opportunity for Satan. Masquerading as an angel of light, he will espouse his doctrine. In this time of opportunity, he will commission his seducing spirits to plant seemingly spiritual thoughts in individuals' minds. In a time when there is a hunger for the Word of God, it will be the Word of God that Satan will use, in a twisted form, to mislead believers and undermine the health of the church. He will attempt, either on his own or through demon spirits, to influence those who have leadership positions in the church. He knows that misdirected leaders will aggressively propagate their unsound doctrines throughout the body of Christ.

A time of spiritual hunger is also a time of opportunity for would-be spiritual leaders. When people are open, looking for answers and desperate for God, they are easy prey. When a person is in this condition and a "spiritual leader" approaches them claiming to have answers, it is very possible that the hungry person will be swept along into the unsound spiritual leader's camp. The blind can lead the blind, but the blind can also lead hungry children!

A time of spiritual hunger is a time of refreshing, a time of returning to God and to His wonderful Word, and a time of growth in the kingdom of God. A time of spiritual hunger can also, however, be a dangerous time. A time of spiritual hunger can be a catalyst for unsound doctrine. In this time of spiritual hunger, Satan, seducing spirits, and unsound spiritual leaders will attempt to introduce and promote their unsound doctrines.

CONCLUSION

In this section we have examined some of the common sources and causes of unsound doctrine. We learned that unsound doctrine can come from spiritual leaders (both sound and unsound), from Satan and seducing spirits, and can even be inspired by the spiritual condition of believers. Wherever it comes from, unsound doctrine is dangerous for believers and for the church. Let's proceed now to study the dangerous results of the infiltration of unsound doctrine.

·~9~·
Results of Unsound Doctrine

At very best the teaching of unsound doctrine will produce nothing. At the very worst the teaching of unsound doctrine will overthrow believers' faith and cripple or destroy local churches. The results of unsound doctrine can range from unprofitable to mildly upsetting to catastrophic. Unsound doctrine is dangerous to the spiritual lives of believers, of local churches, and of the whole church of the Lord Jesus Christ. In this section we will study the negative results which can occur when unsound doctrine is taught and adhered to. Before we study the specific results of the infiltration of unsound doctrine, we will look at several basic reasons that unsound doctrine is so dangerous.

WHY IS UNSOUND DOCTRINE DANGEROUS?

Several times in my life I have cut down a large tree. I always experienced a moment of hesitation and a feeling of loss before starting to cut. In just a few minutes of time I would be undoing years of growth and development. What took many years to grow *up* would be cut *down* in a few minutes. I'm sure that individuals whose homes or businesses have been destroyed in a moment of time by a hurricane or an earthquake experienced a far greater sense of loss. What took them a lifetime to build was destroyed in a moment.

One of the great dangers of the infiltration of unsound doctrine is that what has taken years to establish in believers' lives and in local churches can be perverted or destroyed in a very short time. As it is true in the natural realm, so it is true in the spiritual realm: Tearing down takes far less time than building up! Unsound doctrine can swiftly shake up in minds, trouble souls, and bring catastrophe to whole local churches.

Another great danger of unsound doctrine is that it works from the inside, often coming from those who are accepted as spiritual leaders. Outside attacks are more obvious and most often resisted. Because they come from the outside, they tend to stir believers to action. Subtle inside attacks, however, are often not suspected and, therefore, often not detected. Most believers do not expect to be corrupted or misled by those they respect as spiritual leaders.

The corruption caused by unsound doctrine is not like the destruction caused by a storm or a war. The corruption caused by unsound doctrine would be better illustrated by the destructive activity of termites. Without notification, termites infiltrate foundations and begin to destroy. A house that appears immaculate on the outside may be being eaten up inside. Without any warning or obvious sign of corruption, the house may fall apart. Infiltration is the most subtle form of attack and, therefore, extremely dangerous.

Another reason unsound doctrine is so dangerous is because what people believe governs how they live. It has been said that people are what they believe. It is certainly true that Christians live their lives and govern their activities by what they believe. If, for example, one believes that it is a sin to wear makeup, they will not do it. If one believes that God is only a God of mercy, they will not be afraid to live in sin. If one believes that the Old Testament Sabbath Day is still holy, they will not work on Sunday. If one believes that Christians can not have demons, they will never suspect demonic influence in their life. If one believes that every problem is a demon, they will try to cast demons out of themselves and everyone else. If one believes, "Once saved, always saved," they may live ungodly, feeling that their eternal destiny is sure. If one believes that when they sin they lose their salvation, they will live in constant fear of going to hell. If one does not believe that the baptism in the Holy Spirit is for everyone, they will not speak in tongues.

Because Christian activity is based upon doctrine, unsound doctrine is very dangerous. If doctrine is unsound, spiritual life will be unsound. If doctrine is unhealthy, believers will be weak. If doctrine is false, Christians will live outside the will of God. It is impossible for believers to live sound Christian lives and fulfill the will of God if their doctrine is unsound!

Let's proceed now to study some of the specific dangerous results of unsound doctrine. We will start by studying the less dangerous results and proceed to the most dangerous results. Learning about these potentially dangerous results will motivate us to stay a safe distance from unsound doctrine.

ONE: UNSOUND DOCTRINE IS UNPROFITABLE

Unsound doctrine is, at best, non-beneficial. It won't do believers one bit of good. It is unable to bring any spiritual benefit. Listen to the instructions Paul gave to Titus concerning sound and unsound doctrine,

> "...these things I will that thou affirm constantly, that they which have believed in God might be careful to maintain good works. These things are good and profitable unto men, But avoid foolish questions, and genealogies, and contentions, and strivings about the law; for they are unprofitable and vain."
>
> Titus 3:8-9

Titus was to avoid foolish questions, genealogies, philosophies, and arguments because they, "are unprofitable and vain." The word "unprofitable" comes from the Greek *anopheles*. It is the negative form of the word which means, "to do good, or to benefit."

The word "vain" Paul used comes from the Greek *mataios* and means, "void of results." Unsound doctrine cannot produce positive spiritual results. It will not profit the hearer spiritually, mentally, emotionally, or physically. The teaching of unsound doctrine is in complete contrast to the teaching of sound doctrine which, according to Paul, is,

> "...profitable for doctrine, for reproof, for correction, for instruction in righteousness: that the man of God may be perfect, (fully matured and established) thoroughly furnished unto all good works."
>
> II Timothy 3:16-17

Sound doctrine is profitable for teaching, for correcting, and for instructing believers in righteousness. Sound doctrine can bring a believer to full maturity in the Lord and prepare him for any good work the Lord calls him to. Unsound doctrine, on the other hand, can doing nothing profitable for a believer. It is inefficacious and unproductive. It is empty of spiritual life and incapable of producing any spiritual blessing.

TWO: DISTRACTS FROM IMPORTANT DOCTRINES

Believers should give their attention to doctrine that is, "good and profitable for men." If they get caught up with doctrines that are unprofitable and empty of spiritual value, then those "first principles of the oracles of God" that are so essential for building a good foundation will be ignored. Unsound doctrine distracts believers from the important teachings and foundational doctrines that really matter. Notice this word of sound advice that Paul gave to Titus,

> "Not giving heed to Jewish fables, and commandments of men, that turn from the truth."
>
> Titus 1:14

Listening to fables and the commandments of men turns believers away from the truth. Rather than giving heed to unsound doctrine, believers should refuse profane and vain fables [I Timothy. 4:7], exercise themselves unto godliness [I Timothy 4:7], endure sound doctrine [II Timothy 4:3], be rooted and built up in Christ [Colossians 2:7], and become established in the unity of the faith [Ephesians 4:13]. If Christians will give their attention to sound doctrine, they will not waste energy striving over words that are vain and empty.

The Holy Spirit said to my heart one time, "There are things you need to *teach* on and there are things you need to *touch* on." If ministers spend precious time teaching on things that only need to be touched on, they will only have enough time to touch on the things they really should be teaching on.

In the spiritual life, as in almost every other area of life, first things must come first. There is teaching that is imperative, teaching that is essential, teaching that is important, teaching that is good, teaching that is acceptable, teaching that is unprofitable, teaching that is dangerous, and teaching that is destructive. Believers must involve themselves with that level of teaching that is imperative, essential, important, and good. If they ever become firmly settled and established in that level of sound teaching, perhaps God will permit them to go on to other teaching [Hebrews 6:3].

THREE: PRODUCES SPIRITUAL SICKNESS

Sound doctrine and unsound doctrine are opposite and, therefore, produce opposite results. The word "sound," as we learned, comes from the Greek word *hugiaino* and means, "to be healthy." From this word we get our English word "hygiene" which, according to Webster, means, "conditions and practices that contribute to disease prevention." The teaching of sound doctrine prevents spiritual disease and promotes robust spiritual health.

Unsound doctrine, on the other hand, is unhygienic. Rather than preventing sickness it contributes to spiritual sickness. Unsound doctrine could be called, "spiritually unhygienic." It fosters weakness and spiritual disease. If believers partake of unsound doctrine or live in the environment of unsound doctrine, there is a serious risk that they will become spiritually unhealthy.

In II Corinthians 11:3, the apostle Paul expressed his fear that the believers in Corinth would be corrupted by unsound teaching. He said,

> "But I fear, lest by any means, as the serpent beguiled Eve through his subtility, so your minds should be corrupted from the simplicity that is in Christ."
>
> II Corinthians 11:3

The word "corrupted" that Paul used means to destroy by introducing decay into something that was originally sound or healthy. Consider the illustration of tooth decay. If people are not careful to brush their teeth, decay will penetrate the enamel. This advancing decay will have to be drilled out and the tooth filled. If the decay is not drilled out, the teeth will become increasingly rotten and will need to be extracted. If rotten teeth are not extracted, the whole body can eventually be poisoned. That is why we "brush every day." It is to prevent decay from ruining our teeth and eventually affecting our whole body.

A Bad Diet Makes One Weak

If you want to remain healthy, you must be careful what you drink and eat. When I travel to less developed countries, the natives usually warn me not to drink the water because, "the water is unhealthy." What they mean is that the water is contaminated. If I drink it, I will become unhealthy. Unsound doctrine is contaminated. If you drink it, you will become sick.

If you want to stay healthy, you must be careful of what you eat. Junk food won't help you. Foods excessive in fats, salts, and other things definitely will not contribute to your health. Food laced with poison will kill you. The same principle is true in the spiritual realm. If you partake of unsound doctrine, you run the serious risk of becoming spiritually sick.

Some foods do not make people sick, they just don't provide any fuel for the body. People who don't eat nutritious foods feel run down and tired. One cannot regularly eat one piece of bread for breakfast, chips for lunch, and a greasy pizza for supper without feeling the ill effects of an unhealthy diet. In the same way, false doctrine (poison), corrupt doctrine (food that has unnecessary quantities of bad ingredients), fables and traditions of men (junk food with no value), or even excesses or ignorance of certain truths (the ignoring of certain food groups or eating too much of one thing) can make a person unhealthy.

Spiritual Gangrene

The infiltration of unsound doctrine is like a bacteria or a virus that weakens the healthy body. Paul told Timothy,

> *"But shun profane and vain babblings: for they will increase unto more ungodliness. And their word will eat as doth a canker."*
>
> II Timothy 2:16-17

Paul warned Timothy and the Holy Spirit warns us that unsound doctrine will, "eat as doth a canker (or gangrene)." Gangrene sets in when bacteria attacks a part of the body that has been cut off from the blood supply. Gangrene is not like a cut or bruise which hurts just one member of the body. It is an advancing disease; it is progressive. If allowed to gain a foothold in the human body, it will proceed, spreading to other members. Not only can gangrene damage members that are close to the originally infected member. Gangrene can poison the whole body.

Unsound doctrine, like gangrene, is an advancing disease. It is often introduced to the body through members who have alienated themselves from the blood supply of sound teaching and sound spiritual leadership. It usually gains a foothold in one member of the church and then advances to infect other members. Especially those members that are near — close friends, ministry associates, or followers of a particular ministry — are vulnerable to the same unsound doctrine. If not cut off, unsound doctrine will advance and infect the whole body. Though every member may not become dangerously sick or die, the whole body will feel the effects of doctrinal poison in its system.

The word "eat" that Paul used in II Timothy 2:17 to describe the effects of unsound doctrine is very interesting. It comes from the Greek phrase *nomen echo* which means, "to find pasture." This phrase was used in Greek writings of the spread of fire and of ulcers. False doctrine finds pasture in susceptible Christians and then spreads to other members in the body. Christians must raise their fences high, post their guards close together, and arm their alarm systems carefully. If they don't, unsound doctrine will sneak in and eat away at their vineyards until their fruit is devoured and they are spiritually bankrupt.

FOUR: SPIRITUAL HARVEST IS DEFILED

In Deuteronomy 22:9, God instructed Israel concerning the purity of their vineyards. He said,

> *"Thou shalt not sow thy vineyard with divers(different) seeds: lest the fruit of thy seed which thou hast sown, and the fruit of thy vineyard, be defiled."*
>
> Deuteronomy 22:9

If any unsound teaching is mixed with sound doctrine the spiritual harvest will be defiled. Bad seed produces bad fruit. Corrupt seed produces corrupt fruit. Due to the unavoidable law of sowing and reaping, it is impossible to sow the seeds of unsound doctrine into one's spiritual life and not reap a defiled harvest.

Jesus taught that the kingdom of heaven is like a man who cast seed into the ground. The seed eventually produced a harvest, but it was, "first the blade, then the ear, after that the full corn in the ear" [Mark 4:28]. From this parable we learn that it takes time for the seed that is sown to take root, more time before it shows a blade, and even more time before the fruit is produced. In time, unsound teaching will lead to wrong thinking and eventually corrupt individuals, churches, and even whole nations. By corrupt, I am not referring only to the rise of drugs and sexual promiscuity (although these fruits may follow), but am referring to the spiritual, emotional, and even economic corruption of individuals and nations.

For example, the people of what was once the Soviet Union are now reaping the harvest of over five decades of corrupt teaching. The spiritual, economic, political, and social life of that people cannot be turned around in one or two or even ten years. They need a complete purging of wrong teaching and then a lengthy process of re-education before a good harvest can be reaped.

On the other hand, the United States is still reaping a beautiful harvest because of the foundations of Judeo-Christian teaching. Although the United States does not necessarily have more intrinsic wealth than other nations, we have enjoyed a bountiful harvest? Why? Because we have had right teaching. Although wrong teaching and wrong thinking has certainly begun to take hold in this nation, the root of Judeo-Christian teaching is still bringing forth good fruit.

The effects of wrong teaching may not show up immediately. Be not deceived, however, God is not mocked. The truth of sowing and reaping cannot be changed. Whatever is sown will eventually be reaped. If right teaching and accurate doctrine is sown, there will eventually come a bountiful harvest of life and peace. If wrong teaching is sown, there will begin a process of spiritual corruption and decay that will conclude in ruin and spiritual destruction.

FIVE: BELIEVERS ARE UNSETTLED IN THEIR FAITH

In Ephesians 4:14, we find a very descriptive picture of the negative results of unsound doctrine. There we read,

> *"That we henceforth be no more children, tossed to and fro, and carried about with every wind of doctrine..."*

> *Ephesians 4:14*

When we read this scripture, we can see in our mind's eye the blowing of the wind, the churning of the waves, and the struggle of those who are caught in the storm. The word "tossed" that Paul used in this scripture is very interesting. It comes from the Greek *kludonizoma* and means to be tossed by a billow. A billow is a large wave which rises up out of the ocean. It is often created by a great wind and is capable of moving anything not securely moored to the ocean floor. Billows can destroy!

Sometimes, out of the ocean of truth, a particular teaching initiated by Satan, by seducing spirits, or by an unsound teacher swells up like a large billow. Those who are spiritual children, rather than resting in the quiet waters, are tossed by this billow of unsound doctrine. These dangerous billows of unsound doctrine can unmoor young believers from the Rock of Truth and toss them to and fro.

W. E. Vine says that the being tossed about Paul wrote of in Ephesians four is metaphorical of the unsettled condition of a mind agitated by one false teaching after another. This agitated mind lacks the firm conviction begotten by the truth. Spiritual children lack the firm and solid conviction and sure-footedness which comes from being established in the truth. They can, therefore, be dangerously shaken by winds of doctrine. Rather than being rooted in truth, they go to and fro, back and forth, in and out, up and down, blown about by unsound doctrine.

When winds of unsound doctrine blow, spiritual children suffer the most. Spiritual teenagers may blow for a short season with a wind of doctrine, but will not get "carried away" by it. Mature believers refuse to be moved by winds of doctrine. Spiritual children, however, are often carried away by every new word.

Sound spiritual life cannot built on winds. They must build on the Rock. Jesus did not say, "On this wind of doctrine — on this move of the Spirit, on this gust of current revelation, on this phase, on this fresh word from God — I will build my church." He said, " On this Rock, I will build my church." The church is built on revelations as basic as this: Jesus is the Christ, the Son of the living God. Local churches may be *birthed* in the winds of revival, but they must be *built* on the foundational doctrines of God's Word.

SIX: BELIEVERS GET CARRIED AWAY

Paul exhorted believers to, "be no more children, tossed to and fro, and carried about with every wind of doctrine" [Ephesians 4:14]. The writer of Hebrews issued a similar warning concerning unsound doctrine saying,

> *"Be not carried about with divers, and strange doctrines…"*
>
> *Hebrews 13:9*

The word "divers" simply means a variety. It is the same word used of those brought to Jesus who had, "divers diseases" [Matthew 4:24], of the divers trials of believers [James 1:2], and of the divers miracles of God which confirm the Word [Hebrews 2:4]. Believers are **not** to listen to or become involved with a variety of doctrines. The doctrines believers must hold fast to are those which proceed from that standard of truth called the holy written scriptures.

The phrase "strange doctrines" that the writer of Hebrews used could also be rendered "alien doctrines." Doctrines that are strange or alien are doctrines that have no place in the Christian life and experience. They are not part of the Word of God and should not be a part of Christian belief. Peter used the word "strange" in I Peter 4:12 when he said that fiery trials are *not* strange for the Christian. In other words, tests and trials *are* part and parcel of the Christian life and experience. Strange doctrines, however, should not be part of the Christian's life. If believers give attention to divers and strange doctrines, they will be carried away from sound faith and sound life rather than becoming and remaining steadfast, unmovable, firm, and unshakable.

SEVEN: BELIEVERS DON'T FINISH THEIR RACE

There are two major factors that can keep believers from finishing their spiritual race. First, if a believer is lazy and backslidden, if he has no zeal or endurance, he will not finish his race. This truth is rather obvious. A second factor is also important, however. If a believer is off course, he will not finish his race. This is one reason unsound doctrine is so dangerous. If believers follow it, they will be off course. If they are off course, it makes no difference how much zeal they have, how much energy they expend, or how much they persevere. They will not finish their race! In fact, running down the road of wrong doctrine with zeal and energy only carries believers further and further from their appointed destination!

I'm sure you are familiar with the conversion of the apostle Paul. He had studied the law under the tutorship of the great Gamiliel and was a distinguished scholar of the scriptures, excelling above his classmates [Acts 22:3]. Based on his faulty religious understanding, he was zealously persecuting Christians. Immediately prior to his conversion, he was on his way to Damascus to bind up believers there and bring them to Jerusalem to be punished. His zeal was noteworthy and his cause seemed righteous. His direction was clear and his mind was made up. He even had a commission from the chief religious leaders of his day! His doctrine, however, was wrong and, therefore, he was on the wrong road!

A most amazing thing, however, happened to Paul on the road to Damascus. He met the Way! He met the Truth! He met the Light! His former interpretation of scripture was completely realigned. His doctrine was transformed. From that moment on all his thinking and all his activity underwent a radical adjustment.

Robert Frost wrote a poem that is very interesting. It goes something like this:

Two roads diverged in a yellow wood
I took the road less travelled and
That has made all the difference.

It makes all the difference what doctrinal road believers are on. Wrong doctrine directs believers down roads that lead to trouble. The truth, on the other hand, sets disciples free, makes them strong, and carries them to their God-ordained destinations intact!

It is dangerous for believers to deviate from the course of truth. It can be likened to an airplane deviating from its proper flight plan. It doesn't make much difference in the first few minutes. But if the airplane continues off-course for its total flight time, it will finish a great distance from its proper destination. The faster the plane travels, the further off course it will be an equal amount of time.

Things are now moving swiftly toward the end of time. The pace seems to be accelerated in the body of Christ. Because of this increase of speed, believers must be extra careful. Teachings now spread through the body of Christ like wild-fire because of the advent of audio and video tapes, newsletters, television, and satellite. Because of this accelerated pace the body of Christ can get a long way off the course of sound doctrine in a very short time.

EIGHT: BELIEVERS FORFEIT THEIR RIGHTS

Listen to what Paul wrote to the church at Colosse,

"And this I say, lest any man should beguile you with enticing words...Beware lest any man spoil you through philosophy and vain deceit, after the tradition of men, after the rudiments of the world, and not after Christ."

Colossians 2:4-8

When Christians give heed to the enticing words, philosophies, vain deceits, and traditions of men, they are giving heed to unsound doctrine. One result of giving heed to unsound doctrine is that believers are "spoiled." This word is very interesting. It comes from the Greek *sulagogeo* and means to be carried off as the spoil of war. Believers who pay attention to unsound doctrine risk being carried away from sound doctrine and sound Christian life, the spoil of unsound doctrine's victory. They become the booty of doctrinal error, the acquisition of enticing words. In Colossians 2:18-23, Paul warned believers,

"Let no man beguile you of your reward...why...are ye subject to ordinances...Which all are to perish with the using after the commandments and doctrines of men?"

Colossians 2:18-23

The word "beguile" Paul used means to rob or to let someone else make a decision for you as an umpire. Those who listen to the commandments of men run the risk of being disqualified for the prize. The NIV Bible renders this scripture in such a clear way,

"Do not let anyone...disqualify you for the prize...These (doctrines of men) are all destined to perish with use, because they are based on human commands and teachings. Such regulations...lack any value in restraining sensual indulgence."

Colossians 2:18-23 NIV

Any doctrine based on human commands or teaching is destined to perish. The Word of God, however, "endureth forever" [I Peter 1:25]. Heaven and earth will pass away, but God's Word will never pass away [Matthew 24:25]. The truth is a rock you can build on forever, but the teachings and opinions of men will soon falter. If you have built upon them, you will perish with them.

For example, if believers are taught that being filled with the Holy Spirit and speaking with other tongues is of the devil, they will forfeit the great blessings and richness that accompany this experience. They will miss, "the refreshing...that causes the weary to rest" [Isaiah 28:11]. They will miss a great avenue of upbuilding and revelation [I Corinthians 14:2,4]. If believers are taught that some Christians are predestined by God to suffer with cancer and die at a young age, it will be almost impossible for them to exercise their faith for healing. To ask to be healed, according to their doctrine, would be to go against the will of God. If God is the source of their sickness, how can He be the source of their healing? Unsound doctrine robs believers of God's best and causes them to forfeit their full rights in Christ.

The unsound doctrines that the religious leaders substituted for and exalted above the written scriptures made Jesus angry. In one place, He reprimanded the religious leaders saying,

"Woe unto you, lawyers! for ye have taken away the key of knowledge: ye entered not in yourselves, and them that were entering in ye hindered."

Luke 11:52

The religious leaders of Jesus' day took away the key of knowledge by teaching tradition rather than scripture. Not only did they fail to enter into the things of God themselves; those they instructed could not enter in either! Unsound doctrine is spiritually debilitating. And it make Jesus angry!

Unsound doctrine undermines the purposes of God and robs believers of the full blessings of God. In fact, God's eternal plan for a relationship with man was almost destroyed by a lie! God's words, the Truth, keep men in proper relationship with Him, in proper relationship with one another, and out of relationship with sin and the devil. If God's words are corrupted, however, every relationship will be out of order.

NINE: BELIEVERS ARE SHAKEN IN FAITH

In his first letter to the church at Thessalonica, Paul wrote extensively concerning the second coming of Christ. In I Thessalonians 4:13, he wrote, "I would not have you to be ignorant, brethren, concerning them which are asleep." He then proceeded to instruct these believers concerning the resurrection of the dead at the second coming of Christ. He concluded his letter by sounding forth a note of confidence concerning these believers saying that he had no need to write to them of the times and the seasons because they had full understanding of the day of the Lord.

Something happened, however, to shake these believers' confidence concerning the resurrection. They were so shaken, in fact, that Paul had to write them a second letter to calm them down! What transpired in Thessalonica that so upset the believers there?

Apparently, false teaching concerning the second coming of Christ and the resurrection of the dead had swept into this church. Paul had to calm these believers with his second letter, assuring them that the day of Christ had not come and would not immediately come. He wrote,

"...*we beseech you, brethren...that ye be not soon shaken in mind, or be troubled, neither by spirit, nor by word, nor by letter as from us, as that the day of Christ is at hand. Let no man deceive you by any means...*"

II Thessalonians 2:1-3

The word "shaken" in this scripture refers to the loosening of a ship from its mooring by a stormy wind. Paul had anchored these believers in the Truth. He had moored them to the gospel. But winds of unsound doctrine were blowing in their region. The believers in Thessalonica were shaken in their minds because of these winds. Some were more than shaken; they were in danger of completely unmooring from the truth! Unsound doctrine and wrong teaching can shake believers' faith. If not dealt with in time, it can lead to a complete loosening from sound doctrine. Paul encouraged these believers to hold to the truth he had first delivered to them and charged them to let no man deceive them.

Paul encouraged these believers not to be "troubled." This word comes from Greek word *throeo*. It literally means tumult and came to mean, "a crying out." Webster says that a tumult is, "a turbulent uprising." When false doctrine sweeps into a local church things can become tumultuous. Arguments arise, confusion enters in, and convictions are shaken. If believers are not solidly anchored in the faith and full of strong convictions based on the Word of God, a real shaking can occur.

The Amplified Bible renders Paul's words to the believers at Thessalonica this way,

"...*we beg you, brethren, Not to allow your minds to be quickly unsettled or disturbed or kept excited or alarmed....*"

II Thessalonians 2:1-2 Amp

It is possible for believers to be unsettled in their minds by unsound doctrine because the mind is the place of reasoning. The devil tries to introduce unsound doctrines by dealing with believers' thoughts. Seducing spirits peddle their doctrines of demons in the mental market place. Clever unsound leaders present sharp and persuasive arguments. Believers must guard their minds by following their hearts. They must listen for the witness of the Spirit and hold fast to what is written. No matter how logical an argument sounds or how persuasive an individual is, if the teaching does not bear witness with the heart and agree with the scriptures, believers must refuse to move!

How did Paul finally respond to the trouble of unsound doctrine that invaded the church in Thessalonica? First, he reminded the church that when he was with them he had taught them all these things [II Thessalonians 2:5]. Then, he launched into a lengthy and sound doctrinal teaching concerning the time of the second coming of Jesus [II Thessalonians 2:3-14]. Next, he challenged these believers not to be moved from what he had taught before and then retaught the sound doctrine he had previously taught. He finished his instructions with these words,

"*Therefore, brethren, stand fast, and hold the traditions which ye have been taught, whether by word, or our epistle.*"

II Thessalonians 2:15

Paul encouraged these believers to "stand fast" and "hold" to what they had already been taught. These words describe a defensive position against something that is dangerous. Unsound doctrine is dangerous! It causes believers to be shaken in their minds and troubled in their faith. Whether it comes by listening to wrong spirits, by listening to wrong teachers, or by reading wrong teaching, unsound doctrine has the potential to shake up believers and local churches.

TEN: SPIRITUAL CATASTROPHE

In his second letter to Timothy, Paul instructed him to charge believers to stay away from words and teachings that were unprofitable and would subvert them. He said,

"Of these things put them in remembrance, charging them before the Lord that they strive not about words to no profit, but to the subverting of the hearers."

II Timothy 2:14

The word "subverting" that Paul used in this instruction to Timothy comes from the Greek word *katastrophe*. This word means to overturn or to overthrow. It also means to upset, to confute, and to ruin. It is from this Greek word *katastrophe* that we get our English word "catastrophe." Webster calls a catastrophe, "a great disaster." A catastrophe is not simply a disaster; it is a great disaster! It is an unexpected, undesired, and at times unredeemable disaster of grand proportions. In a moment of time, a catastrophe can destroy what took months and years to build and will take months and years to rebuild!

Unsound doctrine can cause catastrophe in the spiritual lives of those who follow it. Trouble is not expected or desired, but giving heed to unsound doctrine can result in serious and sometimes irreparable damage. In just a short time unsound doctrine can destroy what has taken months and even years to build. Just as a crop that is reaching harvest can be ruined by the unexpected infestation of insects, so a spiritual harvest can be ruined by the unexpected infiltration of unsound doctrine.

Overthrows the Faith of Some

Paul continued on to speak to Timothy of two particular men who were promoting unsound doctrine, saying,

"...of whom is Hymenaeus and Philetus; Who concerning the truth have erred, saying that the resurrection is past already; and overthrow the faith of some."

II Timothy 2:17-18

These two men had erred concerning the truth. Their unsound teaching, according to Paul, was overthrowing the faith of some. The word "overthrow" Paul used here is the same word he used a few verses later when he warned Timothy about words that "subverted." It is the word which means catastrophe.

When a believer's faith is overthrown by unsound doctrine, it does not just mean that they lose faith for a bodily healing or faith in the Father Who will provide. When a believer's faith is overthrown, it means that everything they believe is challenged! They become confused concerning their own convictions. They lose confidence, peace, hope, and faith. The effects of unsound doctrine can be catastrophic! The Amplified Bible renders Paul's words, this way,

> *"Who have missed the mark and swerved from the truth...They are undermining the faith of some."*
>
> *II Timothy 2:18 Amp*

To undermine means, "to weaken," or to, "work against in secret." The promotion of unsound doctrine works against and weakens the foundation of the Word of God that has been built in believers' spiritual lives. If believers do not inspect the doctrines they are entertaining, there may come a day when their houses will collapse. Solid spiritual houses cannot be built on faulty foundations!

In I Corinthians three, the apostle Paul wrote a warning concerning the materials used to build peoples' spiritual lives. He spoke of corruptible material like wood, hay, and stubble and of incorruptible material like gold, silver, and precious stones. He warned those who built that their work would be tested to find out what kind of material they used. If they used corruptible material, their work would burn. If they used incorruptible material, their work would stand. The person who built with corrupt material and, by so doing, hurt God's temple (corrupting it with false doctrines) would be destroyed by God [I Corinthians 3:15 Amp].

Unsound doctrine eats away at the sure foundation of the Word of God. Inspect your doctrinal house, my friends. Unsound doctrine will erode your foundation! "But," as the Amplified Bible says in the verse which follows Paul's warning about unsound doctrine,

> *"...the firm foundation [laid by] God stands, sure and unshaken..."*
>
> *II Timothy 2:19 Amp*

Eleven: Whole Churches Subverted

In his letter to Titus, Paul warned of the dangerous effects of unsound teaching. He wrote,

> *"For there are many unruly and vain talkers and deceivers...Whose mouths must be stopped, who subvert whole houses, teaching things which they ought not..."*
>
> Titus 1:10-11

It is very likely that when Paul wrote of "whole houses" being subverted, he was referring to small local churches that met in homes. In the early days of the church many local assemblies met in houses. For example, to the church at Colosse, Paul wrote,

> *"Salute the brethren...and Nymphas, and the church which is in his house."*
>
> Colossians 4:1

In his letter to the church at Rome, Paul wrote,

> *"Greet Priscilla and Aquila...Likewise greet the church that is in their house."*
>
> Romans 16:3-5

The word "subvert" Paul used in his warning to Titus comes from the Greek *antrepo* and means to turn up or to upset. W.E. Vine says that a second century papyrus illustrated this word by using the example of the complete upsetting of a family by the riotous conduct of one member. Just as whole families can be upset and torn apart by the activity of one riotous member, so whole churches can be overthrown by the promotion of unsound doctrine. The illustration of just one family member upsetting a whole family reminds me of the warning Paul gave to the elders at Ephesus. He cautioned them to watch out for individuals who would rise up in the midst of their own local body and by speaking perverse doctrine upset the whole local church [Acts 20:28].

Sound doctrine is both the foundation and the caretaker of Christian faith. Unsound doctrine brings mental distress and subverts believers. It can lead to ruin and destruction, eroding and upsetting believers' sure foundation. Unsound doctrine can subvert whole households and whole households of faith. Whole families and whole local churches, the two most foundational building blocks of the human race, can be turned upside down.

The Church at Antioch

The early church had problems maintaining doctrinal purity because every would-be leader wanted to promote his own doctrine. The young church of Antioch faced this test of unsound doctrine early in its spiritual life. Certain unauthorized men from the church in Jerusalem visited them and taught them that,

> *"Except ye be circumcised after the manner of Moses, ye cannot be saved."*
>
> Acts 15:1

This unsound teaching created a great dissension and great disputing in the church at Antioch. Eventually, Paul and Barnabas confronted these men and their doctrine. This issue was brought to full attention when Paul and Barnabas and certain others from the church at Antioch went up to the mother church in Jerusalem to discuss it [Acts 15:2]. By referring back the Word of God and leaning upon the help of the Holy Ghost, the leaders in the church at Jerusalem were able to settle the dispute and stop the advance of this unsound doctrine [Acts 15:4-23].

The false doctrine which had been promoted in Antioch created serious problems in that church. That this was true is obvious from the letter sent back with Paul to the church in Antioch. Listen to the words of the true spiritual leaders from Jerusalem,

> *"Forasmuch as we have heard, that certain which went out from us have troubled you with words, subverting your souls, saying..."*
>
> Acts 15:24

By the phrase, "subverting your souls," the spiritual leaders from Jerusalem were referring to the negative effects of false doctrine. The young believers were shaken up, troubled in their minds, and subverted in their souls. If Paul and Barnabas had not been there to contest the unsound doctrine, the future spiritual life of this church would have been in serious jeopardy. They could have lost their liberty in Christ, left the simplicity of the gospel, and came under bondage again to the law. This local church could have been ruined by false doctrine.

TWELVE: SOME DEPART FROM THE FAITH

"Now the Spirit speaketh expressly, that in the latter times some shall depart from the faith, giving heed to seducing spirits, and doctrines of devils..."

I Timothy 4:1

Unsound doctrine will cause "some" to depart from the faith. These "some" are believers. Unbelievers, having never been *in* the faith, could not "depart from the faith." One cannot leave a place he has never been. To be qualified to *depart* one must have been a resident somewhere. The "some" that shall depart from the faith are believers who were at one time established in sound doctrine and residents in sound local churches.

The word "depart" Paul used in this text comes from the Greek *aphistem* and can mean to revolt or to apostatize. Apostasy is the abandonment of a former allegiance or loyalty. Believers who give heed to false doctrine, no matter where it comes from, are in danger of abandoning their former allegiance to the pure Word of God and running after the inventions of men.

When Paul said, "some shall depart from the faith," he did not necessarily mean that believers would renounce their faith in Christ. The term "the faith" refers not only to the experience of salvation, but also to that set of beliefs, teachings, and doctrines which are the revelations of truth and the rule by which Christians live. Some who "depart from the faith" will not renounce their Christianity, but will leave sound doctrine and foundational principles and embrace strange doctrines and unsound spiritual practices.

The Spirit of God makes it very clear that in the latter days some believers will depart from the faith because they will entertain false doctrines. Their attention will no longer be on the scriptures. They will refuse to endure sound doctrine and hold fast to what they have been taught, but will give heed to seducing spirits and doctrines promoted by demons.

THIRTEEN: BELIEVERS LED AWAY FROM CHRIST

The apostle Paul was a fearless man. He was not afraid of the devil, not afraid of difficult circumstances, not afraid of persecution, of prison, or of lack. He faced every formidable situation claiming that he could do all things through Christ who strengthened him. This man who seemed to be without fear, however, had a great fear concerning the church in Corinth. What was Paul's fear concerning this church? His fear was that they would be corrupted and led away from Christ by false teachers and their unsound doctrines. Listen to his words,

"But I fear, lest by any means, as the serpent beguiled Eve through his subtilty, so your minds should be corrupted from the simplicity that is in Christ."
II Corinthians 11:3

The possibility that the believers in Corinth would be deceived and abandon their simple faith in Christ stirred fear in Paul's heart. The potential results of unsound doctrine not only includes the upsetting of believers and the undermining of their confidence in God. Unsound doctrine has the potential to so completely deceive believers that they leave the faith!

The word "beguile" Paul used in this scripture to describe both Eve's deception and the potential danger of false teaching is a very potent word. It comes from the Greek *exapatao* and is a strengthened form of a word which, itself, means deceive. To be "beguiled" meant to be thoroughly, or completely, deceived.

This is what happened to Eve. Satan thoroughly deceived her. As a result, both her's and Adam's relationship with God was broken. This is what Paul was afraid would happen to the believers in Corinth. He had already espoused these believers to Christ [II Corinthians 11:2]. Because of the influence of unsound doctrine, however, these believers were in danger not only of being corrupted, but of losing their relationship with Christ. Unsound doctrine can be completely spiritually devastating! It can draw men away from God!

When believers give heed to unsound doctrine, their minds can be corrupted. When their minds are corrupted, their relationship with God is threatened. The Amplified Bible renders Paul's words to the church at Corinth this way,

> *"But [now] I am fearful, lest that even as the serpent beguiled Eve by his cunning, so your minds may be corrupted and seduced from wholehearted and sincere and pure devotion to Christ."*
>
> *II Corinthians 11:3 Amp*

It is a problem when unsound doctrine causes questions to arise and minds to be shaken. It is a problem when unsound doctrine undermines faith and ruins the confidence of believers and local churches. But when unsound doctrine draws people away from their sincere and pure devotion to Christ, it is not just a problem; it is a time to be afraid!

The apostle Peter wrote of this same grave danger in his second letter. After writing about false teachers and their false teaching [II Peter 2:1-3] and of scoffers of the last days [II Peter 3:1-5], he gave his readers this strong word of warning,

> *"...they that are unlearned and unstable wrest, as they do also the other scriptures, unto their own destruction. Ye therefore, beloved, seeing ye know these things before, beware lest ye also, being led away with the error of the wicked, fall from your own steadfastness. But grow in grace, and in the knowledge of our Lord and Saviour Jesus Christ."*
>
> *II Peter 3:16-18*

Peter not only revealed that the unlearned and unstable wrest the scriptures to their own destruction, but warned believers to, "Beware lest ye also...fall from your own steadfastness." These believers were to be careful not do the same thing that the unlearned and the unstable do. They were to be careful not to "fall from (their) own steadfastness" by following after twisted scriptures and unsound doctrine.

To be steadfast means to be fixed and unyielding, firm in purpose and faith. What could possibly move a believer from that place? We know the devil will try, so we watch for him. We know laziness can, so we are careful of that. We know persecution could make us falter, so we purpose not to be moved by it. But did you know that error in the scriptures can move you from a place of steadfastness? Error in the scriptures can make you "fall from your own steadfastness." What can believers do to protect themselves from falling? Be careful with the interpretation of scripture, lean upon and trust in the grace of God, and grow in the knowledge of our Lord and Saviour Jesus Christ.

Peter said to these believers, "seeing that ye know these things *before.*" These believers were already aware that the unlearned and the unstable twisted the scriptures and that it resulted in their own destruction. Seeing that they knew this, how should they respond? They were to **beware** lest the same thing happen to them! Believers can fall from their solid stand on the Word of God and their solid relationship with God simply by not "bewaring" of error!

Perhaps you will say to me, "Brother Guy, this makes me a little afraid." Good! A little fear is good for you. It keeps you from doing dangerous things. A little fear concerning doctrine will keep you alert and restrain you from getting involved with anything detrimental to your spiritual soundness. Unsound doctrine is dangerous business!

FOURTEEN: GENDERS STRIFE AND DIVISION

In his second letter to Timothy, Paul wrote this about the danger of unsound doctrine,

> *"But foolish and unlearned questions avoid, knowing that they do gender strifes."*
> II Timothy 2:23

There was something Paul wanted Timothy to know and there is something God wants us to know. We should know that foolish and unlearned questions gender strife. The word "gender" simply means to beget or to birth. Unsound doctrine begets strife. Arguments, divisions, fights, and contentions are the progeny of unwholesome teaching.

Christians must avoid foolish and unlearned questions. The word "avoid" comes from the Greek *paraiteomai* and can mean to, "beg off," or to, "ask to be excused." This paints a picture in my mind of asking to be excused from a conversation with someone who is rude or overbearing. Although one may speak for a moment with that kind of person, as soon as possible he should excuse himself and find more intelligent and healthy company. Believers, too, should excuse themselves from unsound doctrine. If they encounter it they should say, "Excuse me. I must leave now."

Paul also instructed Timothy not to,

> *"…give heed to fables and endless genealogies, which minister questions, rather than godly edifying which is in faith…"*
> I Timothy 1:4

Fables and genealogies do not minister godly edifying, but raise more questions, more perplexity, and more arguments. The NIV says that unsound doctrines, "promote controversies."

The false teaching that the circumcisionists promoted in the young church at Antioch led to, "no small dissension and disputation" [Acts 15:2]. Because of their wrong teaching, Paul and Barnabas had to take a stand against these false teachers. When the question could not be settled between them, they had to spend time, energy, and money to travel to the church at Jerusalem and settle their trouble. Unsound doctrine is a root of dissension and strife, and can be very costly.

FIFTEEN: DIVISION IN LOCAL BODIES

Paul exposed the relationship between unsound doctrine and division in his first letter to the church at Corinth. He wrote,

> *"Now in this that I declare unto you I praise you not, that ye come together not for the better, but for the worse. For first of all, when ye come together in the church, I hear that there be divisions among you...For there must be also heresies among you..."*

> I Corinthians 11:17-19

Paul told this church that he had heard there were divisions among them. Then he said, "there *must* be also heresies among you." Paul understood that division was the fruit of heretical doctrine.

Where there is an intrusion of heresy into a local church, there will be a polarization of the members. Some will stay with the sound doctrine in which they were formerly established. Some will take hold with the self-willed opinions they prefer over the truth. It is the will of God, however, that local churches develop and maintain unity of the faith. Paul wrote this to the church at Ephesus,

> *"Till we all come in the unity of the faith..."*

> Ephesians 4:13

To the church at Philippi, Paul wrote,

> *"Fulfill ye my joy, that ye be likeminded, having the same love, being of one accord, of one mind."*

> Philippians 2:2

Peter wrote this in his first epistle,

> *"Finally, be ye all of one mind..."*

> I Peter 3:8

The only way to be of one mind and of one faith is to have one standard of truth. If heresies or any other kind of false doctrine enter in the result will be division. Those who deviate from sound doctrine will start factions. Paul warned the elders at Ephesus of this problem when he said,

"Also of your own selves shall men arise, speaking perverse things, to draw away disciples after them."

Acts 20:30

It is through speaking "perverse things" — distorted truth and unsound doctrine — that once established believers are led away from sound local bodies and into splinter groups. When unsound doctrine is espoused within a local church, divisions will follow. Wherever you find the unchallenged promotion of unsound doctrine, you will find divisions and church splits.

SIXTEEN: PRODUCES UNGODLY LIFESTYLE

In his letter to Titus, Paul exhorted him to constantly affirm the sound teachings he had learned. He wrote,

"...these things I will that thou affirm constantly, that they which have believed in God might be careful to maintain good works. These things are good and profitable for men."

Titus 3:8

One of the reasons Titus was to constantly affirm sound teachings was so that believers would be careful to maintain a godly lifestyle. Believers will live godly lives if they are instructed in and consent to sound doctrine. Paul revealed this truth in his explanation of the purpose of sound doctrine,

"Now the end (the intent and purpose) of the commandment is love out of a pure heart, and of a good conscience, and of faith unfeigned."

I Timothy 1:5

The sound teachings of the Word of God, if heeded, produce love out of a pure heart, a good conscience (which is the result of righteous living), and faith unfeigned. Healthy doctrine results in healthy Christian living. Proverbs 16:6 gives us a tremendous insight into this truth. It says,

"By mercy and truth iniquity is purged..."

Proverbs 16:6

Paul told Timothy that ungodly living — including lawlessness, disobedience, lying, stealing, whoremonging, murder, and perjury — was, "contrary to sound doctrine" [I Timothy 1:9-10]. There is an undeniable relationship between unsound doctrine and immoral living. Unsound doctrine produces ungodly lifestyle. If doctrine is wrong, lifestyle will be wrong. Paul revealed this truth in his second letter to Timothy saying,

"But shun profane and vain babblings: for they will increase unto more ungodliness."

II Timothy 2:16

The word "profane" designates that which lacks all affinity to God. The word "vain" means empty. The word "babblings" comes from two Greek words which together mean "empty sound." Profane and vain babblings are empty words devoid of spiritual substance. They must be shunned, Paul told Timothy, because of their dangerous spiritual effects.

Empty words, false doctrines, and unsound teachings will produce ungodly lifestyle. Notice the words "increase" and "more" in the above scripture. The word increase means, "to proceed further." Unsound doctrine leads individuals further and further down a path away from sound lifestyle. Unsound doctrine not only leads to ungodly lifestyle, however. It also defends and condones that lifestyle. It self-produces and increases unto more ungodliness. Notice what Paul wrote to the believers at Colosse,

"These (doctrines of men) are all destined to perish with use, because they are based on human commands and teachings. Such regulations...lack any value in restraining sensual indulgence."

Colossians 2:18-23 NIV

No level of unsound doctrine, whether completely false doctrine, religious doctrine, or a tangent in doctrine has the power to produce godly living. Any doctrine based on human reasoning lacks power to change men's lives or to restrain sensual indulgence. Rather, unsound doctrine leads to ungodly living.

The Churches of Revelation

In Revelation 2:13-18, Jesus rebuked the church at Pergamos because they held to the doctrine of Balaam. He said,

"...I have a few things against thee, because thou hast there them that hold the doctrine of Balaam, who taught Balac to cast a stumblingblock before the children of Israel, to eat things sacrificed unto idols, and to commit fornication."

Revelation 2:14

The doctrine of Balaam validated sexual promiscuity. This wrong teaching led to ungodly lifestyle in this church. Jesus rebuked this church for their wrong doctrine because it was the fountainhead of their ungodly lifestyle. His instruction was, "Repent." They were to repent not only of their ungodly lifestyle, but also of holding to the doctrine that gendered and permitted it. Jesus spoke to this same church about another doctrinal error, saying,

"So hast thou also them that hold the doctrine of the Nicolaitanes, which thing I hate."

Revelation 2:15

Jesus hated the doctrine of the Nicolaitanes because included in it was teaching on the community of wives and teaching which validated adultery and fornication. The obvious result of this unsound teaching was that the people committed fornication.

Jezebel promoted the same kind of unsound doctrine in the church in Thyatira. Jesus said that she taught and seduced His servants to commit fornication [Revelation 2:20]. Jesus' response to Jezebel's false doctrine and its results was very strong. He said,

"...But unto you I say, and unto the rest in Thyatira, as many as have not this doctrine, and which have not known the depths of Satan, as they speak; I will put upon you none other burden. But that which ye have already hold fast till I come."

Revelation 2:24

The ungodly lifestyle prevalent in the church at Thyatira was a result of false doctrine. The false doctrine of Jezebel did not lead this church to new heights with God, but plunged them into the "depths of Satan." This is an interesting use of words because the false gnostic teachers called their doctrine, "the depths of God." They tried to convince believers that their teachings were leading them into deeper things of God when they were actually leading them to the depths of deviant spiritual life!

Jesus exhorted the believers in the church at Thyatira who did not accept this false doctrine and, therefore, were not involved in the ungodly lifestyle of those who did, to remain established in sound doctrine and sound lifestyle. They were to hold fast and overcome!

Unsound doctrine is not an insignificant matter of minor consequences, but a matter of great seriousness! It can do much more than cause minor instability. Unsound doctrine can take believers down a road that leads to the depths of sin! Its rewards and its results are more and more ungodliness. False doctrine and the ungodliness it produces will grow in a local church body like disease grows in the human body. Unless judged and rejected, it will increase till the body is completely sick.

CONCLUSION

In this section we have briefly examined some of the negative and dangerous results of unsound doctrine. Some unsound doctrine is simply vain. It will produce no spiritual good whatsoever. Some unsound doctrine is dangerous. If accepted and followed, it can lead to spiritual sickness, to the undermining and shaking of faith, and to divisions within local churches. Some unsound doctrine is completely devastating. It can corrupt faith and deceive believers away from their relationship with Christ and with the truth of the gospel. All unsound doctrine is dangerous! Let's proceed now to learn how to judge doctrine in order to determine whether it is true or false, sound or unsound.

·~10~·
How to Judge Doctrine

A posture of carefulness concerning doctrine is especially important in these last days when false spiritual leaders will promote unsound doctrines and seducing spirits and demons will be active promoting doctrines of demons. Believers must be wise enough to know that not everything they hear will be right. They must also know how to judge doctrine and be prepared to hold fast to what is good and to let go of what is not good. In these last days, believers must not be careless; they must care more!

In these last days, believers will encounter doctrines that are in complete disagreement with the Word of God. Even young Christians with an elementary knowledge of the Word of God should be able to recognize blatantly false doctrine. Believers will also encounter erroneous doctrines. They may be based on a particular scripture, but not supported by the whole counsel of God's Word. This kind of unsound doctrine is not completely false, but neither is it sound.

Believers will encounter teachings that are religious traditions and the opinions of men. For example, they may hear a minister say, "Christians should not listen to this kind of Christian music." There is no scripture, however, to support anyone's theory about Christian music. Some ministers make the mistake of putting as much weight on their own opinions as they do on the written scriptures. This is unsafe and can lead to disputes and divisions.

Some teachings of the last days will be tangents in doctrine or, "winds of doctrine." Though these doctrines are not false, they will lead believers away from soundness by overstressing particular truths. Believers may also hear teachings about which they think, "That is not wrong, but it just doesn't matter!" I can say, "Amen," to that. Some ministers ignore the essential and emphasize the insignificant. Most Bible teachers would do themselves and those who hear them a great favor by staying with foundational teachings.

In section two we learned that one of the characteristics of the spiritual man is that he, "judges all things." The mature believer weighs what he hears, examines what he reads, tests the spirits behind teaching, and compares spiritual things with spiritual. Because he knows how to judge accurately, the spiritual man remains steadfast in the truth — unmoved by winds of doctrine, unshaken by error, and steadfast in God.

It is important that believers be equipped and qualified to judge the doctrines they hear. No doctrine should be exempt from scrutiny. No minister should be allowed to say, "This is the truth and if you don't see it this way, you are wrong." Because it is each believer's spiritual responsibility to judge doctrine, each believer must be educated in this area.

How can you recognize what is false doctrine and what is true doctrine? How can you distinguish between sound doctrine and unsound doctrine? How can you determine what is excellent teaching and what is corrupt teaching? How can you accurately judge doctrine? That is what we will answer in the rest of this chapter.

ONE: JUDGE BY THE WRITTEN SCRIPTURES

God inspired men to write His words because He was concerned that each believer possess an unchanging and perfect standard of truth. His purpose is very well portrayed by the words Luke chose to introduce his account of the life of Christ to Theophilus. He wrote,

> "It seemed good to me also, having had perfect understanding of all things from the very first, to write unto thee in order, most excellent Theophilus, That thou mightest know the certainty of those things wherein thou hast been instructed."
>
> Luke 1:3-4

This is how the Amplified Bible renders Luke's words,

> "It seemed good and desirable to me, [and so I have determined] also after having searched out diligently and followed all things closely and traced accurately the course from the highest to the minutest detail from the very first, to write an orderly account...[My purpose is] that you may know the full truth and understand with certainty and security against error the accounts (histories) and doctrines of the faith of which you have been informed and in which you have been orally instructed."
>
> Luke 1:3-4 Amp

Luke informed Theophilus that he had searched out the truth of Christ diligently and accurately from the highest to the most minute detail. He imparted these truths to Theophillus through writing. He gave him an "orderly account" and the "full truth." Luke's orderly account furnished Theophilus with certainty about what he believed, provided him with security against error, and offered him a clear understanding of the doctrines of faith.

Luke's explanation of why he wrote his letter characterizes God's motivation for inspiring men to write His words. God intended the written scriptures to be an orderly account of the truth from the highest to the most minute detail. He inspired the writing of the scriptures so that every Christian could know the full truth, have certain understanding, and be secure against error. The written scriptures, inspired by God and written by men, contain the full truth of the Christian doctrines of faith and are a believer's most certain security against doctrinal error.

The Scriptures — An Objective Standard

Final judgement concerning any doctrine must be decided on the basis of an objective standard of truth. The objective standard of truth for judging doctrine is the written scriptures. Christians must depend first and foremost upon this objective standard.

The written scriptures are the final standard of truth for all doctrine and all teaching in every place and for all time. Fads come and go, preferences change, opinions vary from generation to generation, but Truth remains steadfast. The scriptures cannot change; they cannot be altered. Heaven and earth will pass away, but God's words will never pass away [Matthew 24:35]. "For ever, oh Lord, thy word is settled in heaven," said the Psalmist [Psalms 119:89]. Every doctrine must be examined in light of the scriptures. Every teaching must be weighed against what God has already said. Concerning judging doctrine, believers must never wander from the written scriptures!

The written scriptures are plain, understandable, and unchanging. They are an eternal landmark by which all teaching must be measured and all doctrine judged. They are the final authority. If a doctrine does not agree with or conform to the written scriptures, it must be discarded as unsound. It is to the written Word of God that believers must be inexorably attached when examining and judging doctrine.

There is no more sure standard for judging doctrine than the written scriptures. They are absolute truth, making that which is not truth sordid by comparison. They are sound, healthy, and full of life, making teaching which is unsound sickly by comparison. They are perfect and pure, exposing that which is imperfect and impure. They are the light that discovers darkness in wrong teaching and unsound doctrine.

Although the written scriptures are an objective standard for judging doctrine, men's interpretations of scripture are subjective. It is certain, then, that there will be a diversity of interpretations concerning different subjects in the Word of God. One person may say, "This is what God showed me." Another may say, "This is what the Holy Spirit revealed to me." These individuals may be right or they may be wrong. Men's interpretations may even be in direct conflict. As much as possible, however, each believer must remain objective, allowing the Word of God be the final arbiter in all decisions concerning the soundness or unsoundness of particular doctrines.

The Scriptures — The More Sure Word

In II Peter one, the apostle Peter wrote about what he, James, and John had witnessed on the Mount of Transfiguration. In their mountaintop experience they heard the voice of God from heaven. "And this voice which came from heaven we heard," Peter wrote [II Peter 1:18]. They were also eyewitnesses of the glory of Jesus Christ when He was transfigured [II Peter 1:16]. On the basis of what he had seen, Peter could have claimed special spiritual status. Because he had heard the audible voice of God, he could have claimed to speak for God. The next words Peter wrote, however, were a loud and clear declaration about where men are to go for truth. He said,

> *"We have also a more sure word of prophecy; whereunto ye do well that ye take heed, as unto a light that shineth in a dark place, until the day dawn, and the day star arise in your hearts: Knowing this first, that no prophesy of the scripture is of any private interpretation. For the prophecy came not in old time by the will of man: but holy men of God spake as they were moved by the Holy Ghost."*
>
> II Peter 1:19-21

Peter declared that we have a **more sure word**. The "more sure word" he was referring to is the "prophesy of the scripture" that came when "holy men of God spake as they were moved by the Holy Ghost." Yes, Peter heard with his own ears the audible voice of God from heaven. Yes, Peter saw with his own eyes the glory of the transfigured Christ. But, he said, "We have also a more sure word!" Peter elevated, exalted, and emphasized the absolute surety and perfect soundness of the written scriptures. He declared that they were more sure than a visible manifestation of the glory of the Lord. He announced that they were a more solid foundation upon which to build than hearing God speak in an audible voice.

Why was Peter so careful to make this point? It was to insure that believers in every generation would not be led astray by the false doctrines of those who claimed to have had a special revelation or a supernatural visitation. You see, some will endeavor to justify their ministries and their teachings by claiming that they have heard from heaven. Some will say they have had a vision or special visitation from God. Peter **did** hear from heaven. Peter **did** see the glory of Christ. But he declared that the more sure word of the written scriptures was the ultimate authority.

Take Heed to the Scriptures

Peter did not simply announce that final truth was to be found in the written scriptures. He also urged believers to pay careful attention them! Concerning the more sure word of prophesy, he said,

"...whereunto (unto the scriptures) ye do well that ye take heed, as unto a light that shineth in a dark place, until the day dawn, and the day star arise in your hearts..."

II Peter 1:19

The written scriptures are a lamp unto our feet and a light unto our path [Psalms 119:105]. If believers walk in the light of the Word, they will not wander off the path of sound doctrine. The entrance of the truths of the scriptures bring light and give understanding even to the simple [Psalms 119:130]. Peter said that if believers would pay careful attention to the written scriptures, they would, "do well."

How long should believers give attention to the scriptures? "Until the day dawns," said Peter. Christians should give serious attention to the scriptures till all becomes clear, till their minds are renewed, till their thinking is sound. There is no reason for any Christian to be a doctrinal simpleton or susceptible to error. They must simply give adequate attention to the written Word of God.

Knowing This First

Included in Peter's exhortation about the absolute sureness of the written scriptures are these significant words,

"Knowing this first, that no prophesy of the scripture is of any private interpretation."

II Peter 1:20

The word "interpretation" Peter used in this passage comes from the Greek *epilusis*. This word literally means to "loosen up" and refers to solving, explaining, and releasing. The word "private" comes from the Greek *idios* which is a word that expresses what is one's own. The phrase, "private interpretation," refers to that solving, comprehending, and explaining which belongs to the elite or to a few special individuals.

The written scriptures, however, are **not** of any private interpretation! Because they were not inspired by men, they do not require special men to interpret them. Because they were written by *divine inspiration*, they are **not** of *private interpretation*. Interpreting the scriptures is neither the honor nor the responsibility of just a few special individuals. It is not the private privilege of the minister or the spiritual leader. The responsibility and the capability to interpret and grasp the truths of the scriptures belongs to every believer!

Immediately after informing believers that they could interpret the scriptures themselves, Peter wrote,

> "...there were false prophets also among the people even as there shall be false teachers among you...who privily shall bring in damnable heresies...And many shall follow their pernicious ways..."
>
> II Peter 2:1-2

Peter reported that false teachers would be among believers, introducing heresies and leading many away from sound doctrine. This is the primary reason Peter informed these believers that they could interpret the scriptures themselves. If they were not confident of this fact, they would have to put their trust in teachers, some of whom were false. They would, therefore, be susceptible to error.

If believers don't *know this first* — that they have the ability to interpret the Word of God themselves — they will abdicate their responsibility to judge doctrine and bequeath it to another. That another may be, as Peter wrote, a false teacher. He said,

> "And many shall follow their (the false teachers') pernicious ways..."
>
> II Peter 2:2

Many of the "many" who will follow false teachers and be misled by false doctrines are those who think that the scriptures are of private interpretation. Because they errantly suppose that only ministers are qualified to interpret the scriptures, they will not endeavor to understand the scriptures themselves. Rather than depending upon the Holy Spirit to help them interpret the Word of God, they will depend upon those who call themselves teachers. If believers abdicate their responsibility to interpret the Word of God and follow false teachers and their false teachings, they will end up in serious spiritual trouble.

I am sure that you don't want to be one of the many that follow false teachers and heretical doctrines. But what can you do? You can **know this first**! Know that the scriptures are not of private interpretation. Know that understanding the Word of God is not the sole privilege of those who call themselves teachers. Yes, God has set ministry gifts in the church to teach. Though we need these gifts, however, it is spiritually unhealthy to be too dependent on them. If believers are completely dependent on ministers there is a risk of error and the potential for abuse.

Do not make the mistake of thinking that you cannot understand the Word of God and accurately judge doctrine. The scriptures are written for you. They are open for your understanding and for your interpretation. If you don't come to grips with this truth, you will underestimate your ability to make correct judgments about doctrine and will continue to yield this responsibility to others.

Concerning judging doctrine the first principle you must become established in is that you can interpret the Word of God yourself! Who can interpret and understand the scriptures? YOU! Who is capable of judging the validity of doctrine? YOU! Who is responsible to judge doctrine? YOU! When you find the interpretation of a truth from God's Word and compare it with men's teachings, you may discover, as I have in some cases, that God's Truth and men's teachings don't always agree.

The Berean Christians

In the book of Acts we find a group of believers who are an excellent example of judging doctrine by the written scriptures. This group is the Berean Christians. The Bible says of them,

"These were more noble than those in Thessalonica, in that they received the word with all readiness of mind, and searched the scriptures daily, whether those things were so."

Acts 17:11

The Berean believers were, "more noble than those in Thessalonica." The word "noble" refers to being well-born, or of being in a higher class. The Berean believers were of higher Christian character than those in Thessalonica not only because they received the Word with readiness of mind, but also because they searched the scriptures daily to determine if what they were being taught was true.

Christians who are "more noble" — those who have a good spiritual constitution and are well educated spiritually — will exercise discretion concerning doctrine. They will take time to examine the teachings they hear. They will make an effort to test popular doctrines to determine if they agree with the Word of God. If Christians don't take time to examine the teachings they hear, it shows that they are missing something in their spiritual character. They have not progressed to the place where they can be called a "spiritual man."

The Amplified Bible says of the Berean Christians that they were, "searching and examining." They were doing what every Christian in every place and in every generation is responsible to do. They were researching, examining, and testing what they were being taught. They were igniting the fire of the Word under the teachings they were hearing to determine if they were the precious gold of God's Truth or the hay and stubble of men's fabrication. They were bringing the hammer of the Word of God to bear upon the doctrines they were hearing to determine if they were the Rock of Truth that could be built upon or the sands of men's philosophies [Jeremiah 23:29]. Let's notice several specific details about the spiritual activity of the Berean Christians that will help and challenge us.

They Searched

Acts 17:11 reports that the Berean Christians, "searched the scriptures." The word "searched" comes from the Greek *anakrino* and refers to the examining, weighing, testing, trying, and judging that Christians are responsible to do. This is the same word Paul used in I Corinthians 2:15 concerning the spiritual man who "judges" all things. The Berean Christians displayed spiritual maturity by judging the teachings they heard.

The fact that the Berean Christians searched conveys an attitude of seriousness and reveals that they put forth effort. They were not content to let words slip into their minds and hearts, but were concerned with being accurate and sound in what they believed. They were exercising responsibility for their own spiritual condition.

They Searched the Scriptures

The Berean Christians, "searched the scriptures." This is *where* they searched. Why did the Berean Christians search the scriptures? They searched the scriptures because the written scriptures are the final standard of truth for judging doctrine. The Berean Christians compared what they were being taught with the scriptures to determine if what they were being taught was true. Their greatest confidence was in the written Word!

Notice that the Berean Christians did not confer with other leaders or call around to see what brother so and so believed. They went directly to the Word of God and searched it out themselves. They compared what the teachers were saying to what God had already said. They put the teachings they were hearing side by side with the Word of God. If the teachings they were hearing were not in agreement with the Word of God, they were unsound doctrine.

Often when it comes to questionable doctrines the question everyone wants answered is, "Where does Brother So and So stand on this issue?" I realize that it is not wrong to have doctrines tested by someone who has proven themself in the ministry. The question my heart cries out to hear, however, especially from ministers, is not, "What does someone else say the Word says," but, "What does the Word itself say?"

Paul taught that the scriptures are profitable both for establishing and examining doctrine. He wrote this to Timothy,

> "...from a child thou has known the holy scriptures, which are able to make thee wise...All scripture is given by inspiration of God, and is profitable for doctrine, for reproof, for correction..."
>
> II Timothy 3:15-16

The scriptures are profitable for doctrine. They not only lead to sound doctrine, they also expose unsound doctrine. The scriptures will, "make thee wise," said Paul. When you are wise, you will be able to judge accurately. The scriptures are also profitable, "for reproof, for correction." If you begin to wander into unsound doctrine, the scriptures will correct you and put you back on the path of sound doctrine.

The Berean believers were spiritually mature. They went straight to the scriptures to judge what they were being taught. If what they were being taught *did* agree with the scriptures, they could rejoice. If what they were being taught *did not* agree with the scriptures, that teaching must be rejected!

They Searched the Scriptures Daily

The Berean Christians, "searched the scriptures daily." They were serious. They were diligent. They realized that their spiritual stability and their spiritual destiny was at stake. They searched the scriptures daily until they came to a sound conclusion. They were a living illustration of the instruction Paul gave Timothy to,

> "Study to show thyself approved unto God...rightly dividing the Word of truth."
>
> II Timothy 2:15

Do you know whose teaching these believers were examining and judging? They were examining and judging the teachings of Paul and Silas! The NIV Bible says of the Berean Christians that,

> "...they examined the Scriptures every day to see if what Paul said was true."
>
> Acts 17:11 NIV

Can you imagine judging Paul's doctrine? He was a chief apostle! He had been caught up into the third heaven! Sometimes believers suppose that certain teachers are beyond scrutiny. That kind of thinking, however, makes believers candidates for deception. If the Berean Christians judged Paul's teachings by the scriptures, then believers of this generation must judge the teachings they hear by the scriptures, no matter how reliable or respected the person who is teaching.

Christians cannot be lazy about doctrine. If they allow themselves to believe everything that anyone teaches, they will, without a doubt, end up in spiritual trouble. A noble Christian will be like the Berean Christians. He will go to the written scriptures and persevere in his examination of a teaching until he is sure himself whether the teaching is sound or unsound.

What the Berean Christians did is illustrative of the responsibility of every believer. No matter who is teaching, believers are responsible to carefully and diligently search out the true value of the teaching. Doctrine must be judged according to the scriptures!

The Early Church and the Written Scriptures

Very early in the book of Acts the local church at Jerusalem was confronted with a serious doctrinal question. The apostle Peter had visited the house of Cornelius, a Gentile, in contradiction to what the Jewish Christians in Jerusalem believed concerning association with Gentiles. There arose a sharp disagreement between the leaders in Jerusalem and the apostle Peter. After arguing this issue for some time, James said,

> "Men and brethren, hearken unto me: Simeon hath declared how God at the first did visit the Gentile, to take out of them a people for his name. And to this agree the words of the prophets; as it is written..."

> *Acts 15:13-15*

In making a decision concerning Peter's actions and a possible new doctrine, the leaders in Jerusalem weighed Peter's testimony, listened for the voice of the Holy Spirit [Acts 15:28], and looked carefully to the scriptures for a confirming witness. By taking this course of action, they set a pattern for the rest of the body of Christ in their generation and for the body of Christ in future generations. Yes, the actions of Peter were new; they were different. In fact, they flew straight in the face of the doctrine most Jews held fast to. But the scriptures, when searched carefully and open-mindedly, confirmed not only the single action of Peter, but revealed that God indeed intended to reach out to the Gentiles. The written scriptures were the final judge in the question.

The leadership in Jerusalem said concerning Peter's actions, "and to this *agree* the words of the prophets" [Acts 15:15]. Any doctrine or activity that cannot be confirmed by a specific scripture or by a precedent from the scriptures must be judged as invalid. If a doctrine has been appealed to the scriptures and judged by the scriptures as unsound, there is no higher court to which it can be appealed.

Getting Acquainted with the Scriptures

In Mark 12, the religious leaders questioned Jesus about the doctrine of the resurrection. Jesus made it very clear to these men why their doctrine was in error. He said,

"...Do ye not therefore err, because ye know not the scriptures..."

Mark 12:24

Because the religious leaders were not well acquainted with the scriptures, they were very prone to error. Error is the predictable consequence of not knowing the written scriptures. With no standard to appeal to, the quality of doctrine deteriorates. With no final measuring line, doctrine becomes inaccurate.

Paul wrote of two particular men who erred in doctrine concerning the resurrection. These two men, Hymaneaus and Philetus, taught that the resurrection had already passed. Concerning these men, Paul said,

"Who concerning the truth have erred..."

II Timothy 2:18

Why did these men err concerning the truth? Why was their doctrine unsound? Their doctrine was unsound because they ignored the word of truth and paid attention to, "profane and vain babblings" [II Timothy 2:16]. Anytime individuals ignore the written scriptures, they are prone to error.

The most important qualification for being able to judge doctrine *by* the scriptures is to *know* the scriptures. Here is a little phrase to challenge you as you prepare to judge doctrine: "*Know scriptures, No error!*" Let's consider three ways to know the scriptures better.

First: Read the Word of God

The simplicity of reading the scriptures is essential for becoming prepared to judge doctrine. If you only hear the Word of God in church, listen to tapes, or read books, then you are always hearing a man's interpretation of the Word. When you read the Word of God yourself, you only hear what God has said and what the Holy Spirit is showing you.

I can think of several times in my life that I heard teaching I was unsure of. Immediately, it seemed, three or four scriptures leapt to my remembrance. Sometimes the scriptures that came to mind confirmed what was being taught. I would think to myself, "That's right teaching." Sometimes the scriptures that came to mind contradicted what was being taught. Then I would think to myself, "That doesn't agree with the rest of scripture."

I remember being in a church service where a well known preacher quoted a phrase from the book of Proverbs and attributed it to Jesus. Not realizing his error, he asked the congregation, "How many of you know that Jesus said that?" I was shocked to see so many hands go up! Most of the congregation did not realize that the preacher was in error. Even more shocking, however, was that the preacher himself didn't know that he was in error! I knew immediately that he was wrong, however, because I have read and read the scriptures.

Can you see how easy it is for unsound doctrine to be introduced to the church? If someone we trust presents or promotes a particular teaching, we assume that what he is teaching is true. If, however, we take time to read the scriptures, they will speak to us, confirming or contradicting every teaching we hear.

Bring Me the Parchments

Paul loved to read the scriptures. At the end of his second letter to Timothy, he wrote,

"The cloak that I left at Troas with Carpus, when thou comest, bring with thee, and the books, but especially the parchments."

II Timothy 4:13

The parchments Paul referred to were most likely the Jewish scriptures or a copy of the Septuagint. Paul loved to read the Word of God himself and pointed his son in the faith, Timothy, to the Word he loved. He wrote this to Timothy concerning reading the scriptures,

"Till I come, give attendance to reading...to doctrine."

I Timothy 4:13

A few verses later, Paul said this to Timothy,

"Take heed...unto the doctrine; continue in them: for in doing this thou shalt both save thyself, and them that hear thee."

I Timothy 4:16

When believers pay close attention to the teachings of the scriptures, they save themselves and those they instruct.

Read in the Law

Even in the Old Testament, God stressed the importance of reading the scriptures. In Deuteronomy six, He spoke to the whole nation of Israel concerning the importance of reading His Word. He said,

"And these words...shall be in thine heart...And thou shalt bind them for a sign upon thine hand, and they shall be as frontlets between thine eyes. And thou shalt write them upon the posts of thy house, and on thy gates."

Deuteronomy 6:6-9

The people of Israel were to put the Word of God in a place where they could read it continually. It could be on their hands, in front of their eyes, on the posts of their houses, and on their gates. By reading the Word of God continually, they would be kept from wandering outside the will of God.

In Deuteronomy 17, God gave these instructions concerning those who would be kings in Israel,

"And it shall be, when he sitteth upon the throne of his kingdom, that he shall write him a copy of this law in a book out of that which is before the priests the Levites: And it shall be with him and he shall read therein all the days of his life..."

Deuteronomy 17:18-19

The king was to have his **own** copy of the scriptures written up to the point in time that he lived. He was to read these scriptures all the days of his life. If he did so his thinking would be sound, his lifestyle would be sound, and he would prosper and be blessed.

Have Ye Not Read?

Many times, when confronted with the error of religious leaders, Jesus asked the very pointed question, "Have you not read?" His question implied that if those who were questioning Him had read the scriptures themselves, they would not have been unsound in their doctrine. For example, when the Pharisees came to Him with questions about divorce, Jesus answered them,

"Have ye not read, that he which made them at the beginning made them male and female, And said, For this cause shall a man leave father and mother, and shall cleave to his wife: and they twain shall be one flesh?"

Matthew 19:4-5

When Jesus was riding into Jerusalem and the children were crying, "Hosanna," the religious leaders became very displeased. Jesus said to them,

"Yea; have ye never read, Out of the mouth of babes and sucklings thou has perfected praise?"

Matthew 21:16

When He finished teaching the parable of the wicked husbandmen and was giving the interpretation of it to the religious leaders, Jesus said,

> *"...Did ye never read in the scriptures..."*
>
> Matthew 21:42

Concerning the Sadducees' doctrinal error about the resurrection, Jesus said,

> *"But as touching the resurrection of the dead, have ye not read that which was spoken unto you by God..."*
>
> Matthew 22:31

One of the primary reasons the religious leaders were misinformed about the truth and in doctrinal error was that they did not read the scriptures. They spent far too much time reading and studying some rabbi's interpretation of the scriptures. They spent far too much time studying their own traditions. A major cause of their error in doctrine was that they did not read the scriptures!

When banks train their tellers to spot counterfeit money, they obligate them to handle hundreds and hundreds of real bills. Once they have become intimately acquainted with the real, the false is obvious. It is the same with the Word of God and unsound doctrine. If you will simply take time to read the Word of God and become intimately acquainted with it, what is false will be obvious. When you become well acquainted with the truth, error will be obvious! What Isaiah wrote in Isaiah 34:16 is choice encouragement: "Seek ye out the book of the Lord and read."

Second: Study the Word of God

If you study the Word of God, you will be in a safe position to examine, investigate, and correctly judge the doctrine you hear. Undoubtedly, this is one reason Paul told Timothy to,

> *"Study to show thyself approved unto God, a workman that needeth not to be ashamed, rightly dividing the Word of truth."*
>
> II Timothy 2:15

Timothy was not only a believer, but a young spiritual leader. It was absolutely necessary, therefore, that he be sound in doctrine. If he would discipline himself to study the Word of God, he would be able to rightly divide the word of truth and remain sound in doctrine. Then he would be approved by God, an excellent workman with no reason to be ashamed. There are several important elements in Paul's instructions to Timothy that we should consider.

Diligence in Study

The word "study" that Paul used in his challenge to Timothy comes from the Greek *spordazo*. This word means to be earnest and zealous, to hasten to do something, to exert oneself, and to persevere. It is often translated "diligence" or "endeavor." The Amplified Bible incorporates both the word study and the aspect of diligence in its translation of this passage,

"Study and be eager and do your utmost to present yourself to God approved (tested by trial), a workman who has no cause to be ashamed..."

II Timothy 2:15 Amp

Timothy was to be fervent and diligent in dividing the Word of Truth. He was to exert himself and persevere until he attained God's approval concerning his interpretation.

Jesus said that if believers would continue in His Word and become disciples (disciplined followers), they would know the truth [John 8:32]. Those who are diligent in their study of the scriptures will attain unto sound doctrine [I Timothy 4:6]. Those who are not diligent in their study of the scriptures will be susceptible to error. It takes diligence, effort, time, and consistency to be a true student of the Word.

Approved unto God?

Would you get an "A" from God if He tested your doctrine? Would He approve of your accurate interpretation or disapprove of your erroneous opinion? If God does not approve your doctrine, then what you believe is wrong and spiritually dangerous. When God does approve your doctrine, it is because you have come to the place in spiritual understanding and personal growth that He has ordained for you. When your doctrine is right and you are thoroughly matured, you will be ready for every good work.

It is not wise, however, to compare your knowledge of the scriptures with others' knowledge. There will always be those who know more than you know and will always be those who know less that you know. If you compare yourself with others, you will either feel condemned or you will become proud. Neither of these attitudes are godly. Just be diligent in the Word and be committed to study until you have a witness in your own heart that God would say to you, "Well done. Your doctrine is sound."

A Workman Not Ashamed

If you do not give the Word of God its rightful place in your life, you will be ashamed. You will be ashamed because God will not approve you. You will be ashamed because when the devil tests you, you will not be able to say, "It is written." You will be ashamed because when you need an answer to prayer, you will not know the promises. You will be ashamed because when the winds of life blow and the floods arise, your house will fall. You will be ashamed because you will not be able to hold your own ground when confronted with unsound doctrine.

Christians can choose between studying, rightly dividing the Word of truth, and being approved by God or being lazy and, therefore, ashamed. No believer, however, needs to be ashamed! Be diligent to study and you will become well-grounded in the solid teachings of the Word.

Rightly Dividing the Word of Truth

To rightly divide the Word of Truth means to deal accurately with the scriptures. In the Greek Septuagint this phrase was used of the godly directing of one's path [Proverbs 3:6; 11:5]. Rightly dividing the Word of Truth means to correctly interpret and correctly apply the truth. By so doing, believers will stay on the path of truth and not wander into speculation, opinion, or personal theory. The Amplified Bible's interpretation of this passage gives us further insight into what it means to rightly divide. It says,

"...*correctly analyzing and accurately dividing [rightly handling and skillfully teaching] the Word of Truth.*"

II Timothy 2:15 Amp

Paul would not have admonished Timothy to *rightly* divide the Word of Truth unless there was a possibility of *wrongly* dividing the Word of Truth. This realization should create within you a deep respect for the importance of accuracy in the Word of God. Rightly dividing the Word of Truth requires great care. Believers should never be hasty in their interpretation of it. Especially the young and zealous must be cautious in this area. Sometimes they jump to conclusions rather than becoming grounded in truth.

Always approach the Word of God with humility of heart, depending on the Holy Spirit to help you. Always be aware that you could get it wrong. At the same time, however, remember that no scripture is of any private interpretation. Not only can you can "get it;" you can "get it right!"

Third: Become Skillful in the Word

There is a very close relationship between skillfulness in the Word of God and spiritual maturity. The writer of Hebrews said that spiritual babies are, "unskillful in the word of righteousness" [Hebrews 5:13]. Those who have come to full age, however, are skilled in the word of righteousness. They have, "their senses exercised to discern both good and evil" [Hebrews 5:14]. Mature believers are not only able to determine what is sin and what is righteousness. They are also able to discern what is good doctrine and what is not good doctrine. A very distinguishing mark of spiritual maturity is skill and accuracy in the Word of God.

Believers should strive for skillfulness in the scriptures. In fact, after being born again for a certain amount of time, believers should be knowledgeable enough to teach the Word [Hebrews 5:12]. Unfortunately, however, many, rather than going forward and becoming skilled, become "dull in their hearing" [Hebrews 5:11]. When they regress, ministers must return to teaching the basic foundations of the oracles of God [Hebrews 5:12]. They cannot progress to deeper spiritual truths because of the condition of those they are instructing [Hebrews 6:3]. The result is that in a corporate sense, the body of Christ seldom gets past spiritual kindergarten.

Some Christians become nervous when we speak about a more serious study of the Word of God. They are afraid believers will turn into spiritually dead theologians. There is a significant difference, however, between being *mentally technical* and *spiritually precise*. There is no reason for Christians to be sloppy or unskilled in the Word of God. We should strive for the mastery and become masters. Even charismatic Christians would not suffer at all by becoming more accurate, precise, and skillful with the Word of God!

By way of illustrating the importance of being skillful in the Word of God, we can consider the modern soldier. This soldier may be issued the most advanced and effective weapon the army has. If, however, he does not know how to use the weapon, it is useless to him and, perhaps, dangerous to himself and others. So it can be with the Word of God. It is a sharp and powerful two-edged sword. If, however, believers do not know how to use the Word of God, it will be both useless to them and dangerous both to themselves and others. The flip side, however, is also true. The more skillful believers are with the Word of God, the greater will be the results when they wield it.

Jesus' Skillfulness in the Scriptures

Although Jesus was the Son of God, had a very intimate knowledge of and firm grasp of the written scriptures. He was not only able to quote the scriptures, He also knew the correct application. By the age of twelve, He was able to stump the religious leaders with his questions and answers. Being skillful in the scriptures kept Him sound in doctrine, sound in spiritual life, and sound in ministry.

His skillfulness in the written scriptures provided Jesus with a solution to every problem, an answer for every question, and a defense against every attack. For example, when He was confronted by the religious leaders because His disciples plucked corn on the Sabbath, He answered,

"Have you not read what David did, when he was hungered...How he...did eat the shewbread, which is not lawful for him to eat...or have ye not read in the law, how that on the sabbath days the priests in the temple profane the sabbath, and are blameless?"

Matthew 12:3

Jesus not only knew these Old Testament stories. He also knew their spiritual application. He interpreted these scriptures correctly and was able to apply them to a personal situation. Jesus remained free from the trap of religious doctrine because He was skillful in the scriptures.

When Jesus was challenged by the religious leaders concerning the issue of divorce, He answered with the scriptures saying,

"...Have ye not read, that he which made them at the beginning made them male and female, And said, For this cause shall a man leave father and mother, and shall cleave to his wife: and they twain shall be one flesh?"

Matthew 19:4-5

It did not take Jesus three hours to answer the religious leaders' question concerning divorce. He didn't hem and haw, beat around the bush, or skirt the issue. Because He was skilled in the scriptures, He was able to go straight to the heart of the matter.

When the religious leaders confronted Jesus because the young children were shouting, "Hosanna to the son of David," He responded,

"...Yea; have ye never read, Out of the mouth of babes and sucklings thou hast perfected praise?"

Matthew 21:16

Jesus quoted from Psalms 8:2 to validate the spontaneous worship of the children. Whenever a questionable situation arose or He was confronted with a particular teaching, Jesus could either refute it or validate it by the scriptures. He was able to bring forth a right answer for every question and a correct understanding of every situation.

We especially notice Jesus' skillfulness in the scriptures from the account of His temptation in the wilderness as recorded in Luke four. In response to Satan's first two temptations, Jesus answered, "It is written" [Luke 4: 4, 8]. He did not say, "Devil, I'm anointed," or, "Devil, I'm the Son of God!" Jesus depended upon the written scriptures to answer every temptation of the devil.

After failing twice to ensnare Jesus and twice hearing, "It is written," Satan changed his tactics and tried to deceive Jesus by twisting the scriptures. He tempted Jesus to jump from the pinnacle of a temple by referring to the ministry of the angels as recorded in Psalm 91. Satan said,

"For it is written, he shall give his angels charge over thee, to keep thee: And in their hands they shall bear thee up, lest at any time thou dash thy foot against a stone."

Luke 4:10-11

Satan used the scriptures in an attempt to trick Jesus. Jesus, however, was skilled in the written scriptures! Because He had studied diligently, He was aware that Satan had added the words, "at any time," to God's original promise of angelic protection. The promise of angelic protection did **not** apply to every situation. The angels would not, in fact, come, "at any time."

Jesus was also able to quickly consult with His heart to determine if other scriptures should be considered in this situation. He recalled the scripture in Deuteronomy 6:16 which warned against tempting God. If Jesus disobeyed this commandment by jumping, He could not expect the angels to bear him up.

Jesus *rightly divided* the scripture that the devil had *wrongly applied*. He informed the devil, in so many words, that the promise of angelic protection from Psalm 91 **did not apply** if He jumped! Then Jesus quoted the devil a scripture that **did apply** to jumping. He said, "It is said, Thou shalt not tempt the Lord thy God" [Luke 4:12]. Jesus' knowledge of the scriptures and his skill in rightly dividing them kept Him steadfast in the truth and in the perfect will of God.

In these last days, Satan will attempt to use the scriptures, in a twisted and misinterpreted way, to lead believers away from sound thinking and sound spiritual life. The doctrines promoted by demons will often sound very spiritual; sometimes even Biblical. The unsound doctrines promoted by false and unsound spiritual leaders will often be a mixture of truth and error or a twisting of truth. Believers who desire to step out into the arena of spiritual life and live in the perfect will of God in these last days must be skilled in the Word of God!

Five Basic Rules for Interpreting Scripture

Let's consider some valuable tips that will help us use the scriptures correctly when judging doctrine. These tips will help to ensure a correct conclusion from your efforts.

One: Must Be At Least One New Testament Scripture

There must be at least one clear New Testament scripture to support a New Testament doctrine. This may sound very simple, but it is very important. If there is not one clear and obvious New Testament passage to support what someone is teaching, their teaching is very likely wrong. If, in fact, there are only two or three New Testament scriptures to support an individual's doctrine, I would be very wary. If a doctrine was true, God would have made sure that it was clearly established in the New Testament. If there is not one solid New Testament scritpure to support a so-called New Testament doctrine, then keep your distance from that teaching.

Two: Must Quote Scripture Accurately

I remember being in a meeting and hearing a preacher quote something from one of Paul's epistles concerning a particular subject. After referring to what Paul had written, he began to give his interpretation. His interpretation was wrong. The reason his interpretation was wrong, however, was because he first misquoted what Paul had written!

It is very important to be accurate in quoting scripture. If a scripture is misquoted, the interpretation of that scripture will be wrong. Inaccuracy in quoting scripture can be dangerous! It can lead to wrong teaching, wrong doctrine, wrong thinking, and wrong living. Let's consider a couple examples.

A commonly misquoted scripture is Romans 8:1. Often preachers quote it like this,

> *"There is therefore now no condemnation to them which are in Christ Jesus…"*
> *Romans 8:1*

Some ministers go on from this inaccurate rendering of Romans 8:1 to teach believers that because they are in Christ, there is no condemnation for them. Is that really what Romans 8:1 teaches? Is that what the whole counsel of God's Word teaches? Actually, Romans 8:1 says this,

> *"There is therefore now no condemnation to them which are in Christ Jesus, who walk not after the flesh, but after the Spirit."*
> *Romans 8:1*

For believers who are walking after the Spirit, there is no condemnation. For believers who are walking in the flesh, however, there is condemnation. If they don't judge themselves, they will either be self condemned as Romans 8:13 says — "For if ye live after the flesh, ye shall die" — open to the attacks of Satan as I Peter 5:8 says — "your adversary the devil, as a roaring lion, walketh about, seeking whom he may devour" — or judged by God as I Corinthians 11:31-32 says — "if we would judge ourselves, we should not be judged. But when we are judged, we are chastened of the Lord, that we should not be condemned with the world."

Believers, be not deceived, God is not mocked. Whatever a man sows, he will reap [Galatians 6:7-8]. If believers walk in persistent disobedience, they are trampling under their feet the Son of God and counting the blood of the covenant an unholy thing. If they persist in their ungodly lifestyle, there is condemnation and much sorer punishment than those who disobeyed Moses received under the Old Covenant [Hebrews 10:29]. (By the way, some were killed without mercy!) The writer of Hebrews said it quite plainly,

> "...*Vengeance belongeth unto me, I will recompense, saith the Lord. And again, The Lord shall judge his people. It is a fearful thing to fall into the hands of the living God.*"
>
> *Hebrew 10:30-31*

Another very often misquoted scripture is II Corinthians 12:10. Most people quote it this way: "When I am weak, then He (God) is strong." Isn't this true? Isn't God strong on our behalf when we feel weak? Yes, He is and we praise Him for it. But you have missed the point. II Corinthians 12:10 does not say that when we are weak God is strong. It says,

> "...*when I am weak, then am I strong.*"
>
> *II Corinthians 12:10*

A lack of accuracy concerning this particular scripture will not throw one into the arena of dangerous spiritual error. It will, however, hinder one's understanding of the bestowal of God's grace. What Paul was really saying in this scripture was this:

> *When I am weak in my own human strength, Christ ministers grace to me. Through the infusion of His grace I am made strong. I am divinely equipped to do all things! I am equal to any task and ready for any problem that comes because Christ has strengthened me by grace.*

Do you see how important each word is? One or two misquoted words can change the meaning of the Word of God. Sometimes the results will not be significant, but there remains the possibility that wrong doctrine can arise simply from being inaccurate when quoting the written scriptures. Jesus demonstrated this principle in His rebuff to the Sadducees concerning their doctrine of no resurrection. He said to them,

> "*But as touching the resurrection of the dead, have ye not read that which was spoken unto you by God, saying, I am the God of Abraham, and the God of Isaac, and the God of Jacob? God is not the God of the dead, but of the living.*"
>
> *Matthew 22:31-32*

Notice the significance of the one word, "am." If this scripture said, "I was (past tense) the God of Abraham," then it could be assumed that Abraham had ceased to exist. But because this scripture said, "I am (present tense) the God of Abraham," it proved that Abraham was still alive. By dealing accurately with this one word, Jesus proved that Abraham was alive and confirmed the resurrection. Listen to the peoples' response to Jesus' simple, yet profound doctrine,

> *"And when the multitude heard this, they were astonished at his doctrine."*
>
> *Matthew 22:33*

Three: Check the Context

It is imperative when formulating or testing doctrine to pay the strictest attention to context. Very few passages of scripture can stand on their own. Most are a part of a whole thought. Some are a part of a whole book or a complete letter. If you ignore the context of an individual verse, what is written before and what is written after, you can make that scripture say anything you want it to say.

Perhaps you have heard this humorous linking together of two scriptures taken out of context, "Judas hanged himself...Go thou and do likewise." That, of course, is meant to be funny. Many times, however, scriptures are lifted out of their settings to support personal theories and erroneous opinions. By lifting passages of the Word of God out of their settings, anything can be proved. When scriptures are lifted out of context, they can be supporting evidence for unsound doctrine.

Some ministers are far worse than news reporters who, by isolating certain statements from a speech or an interview, make the person they have interviewed say anything they want said. Topical teachers can be especially prone to this error because they usually speak on a specific subject. To support their point they use scriptures from many different places. This is not wrong, but it can be dangerous. A true minister of the gospel will be very careful about lifting a scripture out of its context to prove his point.

I heard a teaching recently which asserts that one of the functions of speaking in other tongues is for casting out demons. The practical outworking of this teaching is that believers pray loudly and aggressively in other tongues thinking they will torment demons out of people. One scripture used to support this erroneous theory is I Corinthians 12:28. Here Paul said that there are, "diversities of tongues." Lifted out of context, this scripture can be made to say almost anything. If this scripture is dealt with honestly and in its context, however, it obviously refers to a specific ministry office that God has set in the church. Let's read this scripture in its proper context,

> *"And God hath set some in the church, first apostles, secondarily prophets, thirdly teachers, after that miracles, then gifts of healings, helps, governments, diversities of tongues. Are all apostles? are all prophets? are all teachers?...do all speak with tongues? do all interpret?"*
>
> *I Corinthians 12:28*

In the church there are a diversity of special offices and ministries. One of these ministries is the ministry of tongues and interpretation which is equal to prophesy. The way that this ministry functions is that one person speaks by the inspiration of the Holy Spirit in an unknown tongue and another person gives the interpretation of the unknown tongue by the inspiration of the Holy Spirit. Paul asked the question, "Do all interpret?" immediately after asking, "Do all speak with tongues?" because in this scripture he was referring specifically to the ministry gift of tongues and interpretation.

A very popular modern text concerning God's promise to meet financial needs is Philippians 4:19. It says,

"But my God shall supply all your need according to his riches in glory by Christ Jesus."

Philippians 4:19

Many quote this verse outside its context expecting God to give them a carte blanche financial miracle. If you read this promise in its context, however, you will realize that it was a promise made to believers who had already faithfully given of their financial means to the work of God. God will supply the need of those who have supplied the need of His kingdom.

Don't search for scriptures to support your theories or experiences. Just study God's Word and let your faithful study bring forth your doctrine. Be honest with the context of the scripture. Desire *truth* more than you desire *evidence* to support your theory. Always ask this question, "What did the writer and the Holy Ghost **really** mean in this scripture?" Don't be one of those who turn from the truth because it doesn't fit what you want to hear or wish was true. It is the will of God that all men, including you, come to a knowledge of the truth [II Timothy 3:7]. If you are desperate for a scripture to support your theory, you will be tempted to lift it out of its context. Then you will join that group of individuals called the unlearned and unstable who twist the scriptures [II Peter 3:16].

Four: Compare Scripture with Scripture

The whole counsel of the Word of God must be interviewed in order to arrive at completely accurate doctrine. This is why it is so important to read the *whole* Bible. A thorough knowledge of the scriptures brings a tremendous overview of the whole counsel of the Truth. When you have a superior overview of the Word of God, then the real meaning of each part is much more accurate. To know the whole, you must know the parts. But to comprehend each part, you must have a grasp of the whole.

It is important to compare scripture with scripture when examining particular doctrines. To compare means to examine so as to note the likenesses and differences of two or more things. The apostle Paul said that in his teaching he compared, "spiritual things with spiritual" [I Corinthians 2:13]. If someone uses a scripture to support his teaching, but you are unsure if it is valid, compare the scripture he used with other scriptures on the same subject.

For example, if someone taught that through prayer the power of God could be supplied to an individual or released in a situation, but only used the scripture from Acts12 where the early church prayed for Peter's release from prison, you should refer to other scriptures about prayer. Is there any other supporting evidence beside this one Bible example? Is the same pattern ever repeated? Do other scriptures about prayer indicate the same truth?

You could turn to James 5:16 and learn that the effectual fervent prayer of a righteous man does, in fact, avail much. You could turn to Paul's letter to the Philippian church where he reported that his imprisonment would turn to salvation through their prayers and the supply of the Spirit of Jesus Christ [Philippians 1:19]. You could refer to Acts four where the early church prayed for boldness. After they prayed, the building they were in was shaken. They were all filled with the Spirit and spoke the Word of God with boldness [Acts 4:29-31]. Without much study or effort one could locate at least three scriptures which support the teaching that prayer causes a release of the power of God for individuals and their circumstances.

If I heard someone teach that God could never send sickness or trouble, I would check out the whole counsel of scripture. Is there any Bible evidence that God could, in fact, send sickness? Is there any evidence that He can't? James said that every good and perfect gift comes down from the Father of lights Who cannot change [James 1:17]. Perhaps it is true that God can only send good and perfect gifts. What about king Herod, though? He refused to honor God and the angel of the Lord smote him with worms. It was not a demon that smote him, but an angel of the Lord [Acts 12:23]. What about Paul's words to Elymas the sorcerer that "the hand of the Lord is upon thee, and thou shalt be blind, not seeing the sun for a season" [Acts 13:11]. What about the awful past judgments of God upon the people of Egypt? What about the awful future judgement of God upon sinners as recorded in the book of Revelation. What about those in Corinth who were "weak and sickly," some even dead, because they did not judge their ungodly lifestyle and, thus, were judged of the Lord [I Corinthians 11:30-32]? Is it possible that God can send trouble, sickness, and disease? It seems that those who turn their hearts against God and are outside the covenant of blessing can receive something "not good" from the hand of God.

What is my point? Compare scriptures. Search the Word of God when you hear someone make statements about a particular subject. Does what you are being taught agree with other scriptures that deal with the same subject? Is a doctrine you have heard based on one isolated scripture or is it founded in the whole counsel of God's Word? Refer to the **whole counsel** of God's Word, not just to your favorite texts. Don't shy away from scriptures that appear contradictory to your's or someone else's opinion. Search for Truth!

Five: Accuracy in Interpretation

Finally, the Word of God must be accurately interpreted. Not only must the Word of God be accurately quoted and examined in the context where it was written, but the final interpretation must be accurate. When it comes to interpretation, however, there is always room for personal opinion. Two individuals can examine the same scripture and come up with two quite different interpretations.

In interpreting the Word of God, you must use your mind and your heart. Never put your mental conclusions before the guidance of the Holy Spirit, but do not ignore your mind. The Bible does not say to throw away your intellect, but to renew your mind. Intelligent Christians should have no trouble coming to a knowledge of the Truth. In fact, intelligence coupled with the power of the Holy Spirit is a formidable team!

Always approach the Word with reverence and care. It is God-breathed. It comes from His heart to your heart. Do not take lightly the words He has written. He certainly doesn't. Do not add to the Word or take away from it. If you do, you will find that in the middle of trying to understand the truth, you will be fighting against the Author of truth.

Pray for wisdom. We all lack it so we can all ask for it. Depend upon the Holy Spirit. Never approach the Word of God without yielding yourself to Him. He is the Spirit of Truth. He is the One Who inspired the Word. He can guide you into the Truth and give you the accurate interpretation of what He has inspired.

TWO: JUDGE BY THE WITNESS OF THE SPIRIT

Almost as important as interviewing the written scriptures in judging doctrine is listening to the witness of the Holy Spirit. The scriptures and the Holy Spirit cannot be separated. Not only were the scriptures inspired by the Holy Spirit as He moved upon men; they are also revealed by the Holy Spirit as He teaches men. The Holy Spirit is the Spirit of Truth. In order to stay sound in Truth, believers must stay in tune with the witness of the Spirit of Truth. The Holy Spirit cannot be ignored when judging doctrine!

The Holy Spirit — Author and Interpreter

Just a few pages ago we referred to the apostle Peter's declaration that the scriptures were not of private interpretation because they came by the inspiration of the Holy Ghost. Let's look at his words again, this time noting the important place of the Holy Ghost in interpreting the truth,

> "...*no scripture is of any private interpretation. For the prophesy came not in old time by the will of man: but holy men of God spake as they were moved by the Holy Ghost.*"
>
> *II Peter 2:20-21*

The scriptures, although dictated by men, were inspired by the Holy Ghost. Because they were written by Divine inspiration, they must be understood by Divine assistance. You see, no one understands more perfectly what any author means by a particular word or phrase than the author himself. If you want to know what an author really meant by something he wrote, ask him. If you want to know what the Holy Ghost meant by a particular scripture, ask Him.

When I was in college, I took a course in literature. Along with reading assignments were assignments to interpret what various authors meant by their writings. Though I always loved to read, I never enjoyed trying to interpret what the author really meant. How was I supposed to know what an author meant by, "The tree, standing against the elements of time, waved its laden boughs?" One student thought the author was saying life was difficult. Another thought the author was saying beauty could be found in all of life. To me it meant nothing more than that the tree's branches were waving in the wind! Sometimes I wanted to stand up in this literature class and shout to the esoteric teacher and his class full of would-be intellects, "This author probably wasn't trying to say anything, but if you really want to know, ask him!"

I recall, several years ago, visiting an art gallery. Some of the paintings in this gallery were for sale. I especially remember a large oil painting, approximately ten feet tall and four feet wide. The whole painting consisted of one pink stripe six inches wide that ran from top to bottom and one blue stripe three inches wide that ran from top to bottom. I cannot remember the specific title of this painting, but it was some kind of cosmic gibberish. I do, however, remember the price. It was $135,000.00!

Several people were milling about this painting with very serious looks on their faces. They were whispering together in low tones and giving "expert nods." I'm sure they were trying to determine what the artist was trying to say with this painting. I could have told them exactly what the artist was saying. He was saying, "Some dummy is going to buy this painting that took me three minutes to paint and doesn't mean a thing in the world, and I am going to be rich!"

One of the beauties and great realities of the New Covenant is that God has given the Author of the scriptures to every believer as a personal tutor. Because every believer has the Holy Spirit, every believer can be guided into all the truth and be accurate in doctrine and faith. Because the Word of God was *authored* by the Spirit, it can be *interpreted* by the Spirit to each person who has the Spirit. The word "interpretation," as we said earlier, means, "to loose" or, "to solve." The ministry of the Holy Spirit is to loosen the understanding of the Word of God to believers, bringing forth the explanation. Whoever has the Spirit of God can comprehend the Word of God and, therefore, has the ability to accurately discern and judge particular teachings to determine whether they are Biblically sound or unsound.

Jesus' Emphasis of the Holy Spirit

Immediately prior to His death and resurrection, Jesus instructed His disciples in several New Covenant truths He had not taught them before. Up to this time, He had not needed to instruct them concerning these truths because He was with them. When His departure became imminent, however, He began to prepare them for the New Covenant days that lay ahead. The New Covenant truths He taught them at this time are found in the gospel of John, chapters thirteen through sixteen. In John sixteen, Jesus said,

> "But these things (the things He taught in chapters 13-16) have I told you, that when the time shall come, ye may remember that I told you of them. And these things I said not unto you at the beginning, because I was with you. But now I go my way unto him that sent me..."

> *John 16:4-5*

In John 14, 15, and 16, Jesus referred to the New Covenant ministry of the Holy Spirit five times. He wanted to be sure that His disciples understood the significant place the Holy Spirit was now going to have in their lives. Up to this time Jesus had been the teacher. He had been the revealer of truth and the interpreter of the mysteries of God. After He left, however, and the New Covenant was inaugurated, they would have to depend upon the Holy Spirit.

By instructing His disciples about the ministry of the Holy Spirit five times in three chapters, Jesus drove home His point. The Holy Spirit would now fulfill the ministry of revealing truth and guiding believers into the truth. Let's note briefly several the things Jesus said about the ministry of the Holy Spirit.

John 14:16-17

> "And I will pray the Father, and he shall give you another Comforter, that he may abide with you for ever; Even the Spirit of truth..."
>
> John 14:16-17

Jesus promised the disciples that when He left, He would send "another Comforter." In order for there to be *another* Comforter, however, there had to be a *first* Comforter. Who was the first Comforter? It was Jesus Himself. For the disciples, Jesus was the Teacher. He revealed the Father. He spoke the truths of God. He interpreted the scriptures. He brought light, revelation, and guidance. For example, after teaching the parable of the Sower and the Seed, Jesus' disciples came privately to him and asked him concerning the meaning of the parable. Jesus told them that they were privileged to know the mysteries of the kingdom and then expounded to them in detail what the parable meant [Mark 4:1-25].

After His death and resurrection, but before His ascension, Jesus continued this aspect of His ministry. When He walked with the two disciples on the road to Emmaus, "beginning at Moses and all the prophets, he expounded unto them in all the scriptures the things concerning himself" [Luke 24:27]. After He departed from them and they realized He was Jesus, these two men said,

> "Did not our heart burn within us, while he talked with us by the way, and while he opened to us the scriptures?"
>
> Luke 24:32

Later, in His appearance to the eleven apostles, Jesus, "opened their understanding, that they might understand the scriptures" [Luke 24:45]. This revealing of truth and explaining of the scriptures was a vital aspect of the ministry of the first Comforter. Now, however, this Comforter would be leaving. The disciples felt anguish at the prospect of again being without a teacher, a helper, and a spiritual guide. The "another Comforter" Jesus promised to send, however, would fill the great empty place left when He departed. This Comforter would do just what Jesus did. He would guide the disciples into all the Truth.

John 14:26

"But the Comforter, which is the Holy Ghost, whom the Father will send in my name, he shall teach you all things, and bring all things to your remembrance, whatsoever I have said unto you."

John 14:26

The primary ministry of the Holy Spirit in the New Covenant is to teach believers the truth. He teaches the truth about God. He teaches truths of the Word of God. He teaches the truth about what God did for us in Christ. He teaches the truth about eternity. The Holy Spirit is responsible to teach us **all** truth. Jesus said, "he shall teach you **all** things." If we listen closely to our Teacher, we will do well on the test. There will be no reason to be ashamed or wish we had listened closer. We will be able to answer every true and false question correctly and score 100% on the test!

Jesus said that the Holy Spirit would, "bring all things to your remembrance, whatever I have said" [John 14:26]. The Holy Spirit not only gives us revelation of the truth; He also brings truths to our remembrance that we need at particular times. If we have read the Word and know it, the Holy Spirit can bring it to our memory and guide us into the truth by it.

The Holy Spirit is the greatest Teacher of truth. If you are willing to be a student in His classroom, you will do very well in the test of sound spiritual life. Perhaps you think, "But I'm just not that smart. I don't think I would be a good student." Don't worry. That is why God made sure you had the best teacher. Even poor students will do just fine if they are tutored by skilled and dedicated teachers!

Over and over again when I have been confronted with doctrine I was unsure of, the Holy Spirit has brought confirming scriptures or contrasting scriptures to mind. In a very few moments I would have my answer. The witness of the Word and the witness of the Spirit is convincing and true.

Recently, I was searching my heart for the witness of the Holy Spirit concerning a doctrine that was getting quite a bit of attention. I wanted to know if this doctrine and the move it gendered was of God. After being led to many scriptures which clearly revealed this doctrine to be unsound, I also heard the Holy Spirit say to my heart: "This is not a move of the Spirit. It is being perpetrated by men."

John 15:26

"But when the Comforter is come, whom I will send unto you from the Father, even the Spirit of truth, which proceedeth from the Father, he shall testify of me..."

John 15:26

In this passage, Jesus again referred to the Holy Spirit as, "the Spirit of truth." This name accurately describes the Holy Spirit's ministry. He guides believers *into* and to keeps believers *within* the boundaries of teaching that can be called the Truth. If believers learn to listen to and follow the Spirit of truth, they will abide in the truth and remain free from error.

The ministry of the Holy Spirit is to testify of the truth. To testify, or witness, means to tell what one has seen, heard, and knows. What better witness could we have than the Holy Spirit. He knows the truth because He is the Spirit of truth. He knows the Word of God because He inspired its writing. He knows the Father and the Son for He is one with them. He searches out the deep things of God and reveals them to us [I Corinthians 2:10]. If believers abide in harmony with the Spirit of truth, there will be no danger of doctrinal error.

By way of illustration, the Holy Spirit and truth could be likened to a tuning fork and a particular musical pitch. A tuning fork is designed to vibrate at a frequency which corresponds to a particular musical note. If a person plays the pitch which corresponds with the pitch of the tuning fork, it will begin to vibrate and make sound itself. When the right note is played, the tuning fork will respond. In a similar way, when the Truth is spoken, the Spirit of God who dwells in you will bear witness with that truth. When the truth is "played," the Spirit will bear witness!

This illustration can be reversed. Very often a tuning fork is struck first and the musical instrument must be tuned to the perfect pitch the tuning fork is resonating. If there are noticeable vibrations between the tuning fork and the instrument, they are not in tune. In the same way doctrine must be fine tuned to the Spirit of Truth. When there is not a witness of peace or harmony between teaching and the Spirit of Truth, we know that the teaching is "off pitch." The Truth and the Spirit of Truth always agree. To the discerning believer, the Truth has a Holy Ghost ring to it.

John 16:13

"Howbeit when he, the Spirit of truth, is come, he will guide you into all truth: for he shall not speak of himself; but whatsoever he shall hear, that shall he speak…"
John 16:13

The word "guide" used in this text comes from the Greek word *hodegeo*. This word means, "to lead the way." It is the same word the Ethiopian eunuch used when Philip asked him whether he comprehended what he was reading from the scriptures. The eunuch said,

"How can I (understand the scripture), except some man should guide me?"
Acts 8:31

The eunuch was reading the scriptures, but did not understand. He needed a guide. He needed someone to interpret for him what the scriptures really meant. He needed revelation of the truth. Philip became this man's guide. He started at the place in the scriptures where the eunuch was reading and preached the truth to him. The eunuch received the truth, was saved and baptized, and went on his way rejoicing.

In this same way the Holy Spirit will lead the way. He will lead believers into right teaching and sound doctrine. If you begin to wander off the path of truth, He will nudge you back. If you become unsettled because of false teaching, He will comfort you with the truth. Don't try to take the lead yourself. Don't drag the Holy Spirit into your unsound doctrine. In order to remain accurate in doctrine, you must learn to follow.

In the early days of the church, Christianity was called, "The Way." The Holy Spirit will not only lead into the way of truth, He will also lead into truths of The Way. Believers will be sound in "The Way" if they allow the Spirit of Truth to guide them.

The Spirit of Truth

Did you happen to notice that in these four passages, Jesus called the Holy Spirit the Spirit of Truth three times? This is very significant! Truth and the Holy Spirit cannot be separated. The Spirit of Truth inspired the Truth; the Spirit of Truth knows the Truth; the Spirit of Truth reveals the Truth; and the Spirit of Truth bears witness with the Truth. You cannot leave out the Holy Spirit when examining and judging doctrine to determine whether it is true or false!

The apostle John, a man who loved the truth and was deeply concerned with false teaching, said,

> "...And it is the Spirit that beareth witness, because the Spirit is Truth."
>
> I John 5:6

The Spirit and the Truth are one in being. They are in total agreement. If you follow the Spirit, you will walk in the truth. If you walk in the truth, you will be walking in the Spirit. If you are walking in something that the Spirit is not bearing witness with, then you are walking in error and with the spirit of error.

The Holy Spirit and Spiritual Discernment

To the New Covenant believer, God reveals mysteries and truths that were not revealed even to Old Testament prophets. He does so by the ministry of the Holy Spirit. Notice these important words of Paul concerning the revelatory ministry of the Holy Spirit,

> *"But God hath revealed them unto us by his Spirit: for the Spirit searcheth all things, yea, the deep things of God...Now we have received...the spirit which is of God; that we might know the things that are freely given to us of God...But the natural man receiveth not the things of the Spirit of God: for they are foolishness to him: neither can he know them, because they are spiritually discerned. But he that is spiritual judgeth all things, yet he himself is judged of no man. For who hath known the mind of the Lord, that he may instruct him? But we have the mind of Christ."*
>
> I Corinthians 2:10-16

Each believer has been given the Spirit of God that, "we might know the things that are freely given to us of God" [I Corinthians 2:12]. Christians should know truth from error. They should know sound from unsound. They should know right doctrine from speculation. How can they know? By the Holy Spirit, the Spirit of Truth, Who bears witness with their spirit. The Spirit of God is given to believers so that they can have accurate understanding of the truths, promises, instructions, and teachings of the New Covenant.

The Holy Spirit searches out even difficult truths, examining the deeper and more profound things of God and of His Word. What does He do with these insights? He reveals them to us! Even scriptures that are difficult to understand and have the potential to lead to error or confusion will be made clear by the Holy Spirit.

The Amplified Bible renders I Corinthians 2:14-15 this way,

> *"...the natural, non spiritual man does not accept...the gifts and teachings and revelations of the Spirit of God...and he is incapable of knowing them...because they are spiritually discerned and estimated and appreciated. But the spiritual man tries all things [he examines, investigates, inquires into, questions, and discerns all things]..."*
>
> I Corinthians 2:14-15 Amp

The natural man, the man who is not born-again and does not have the indwelling Holy Spirit, cannot understand, discern, or judge spiritual things. Why? Because, "they are spiritually discerned." They must be examined and judged in the spirit with the help of the Holy Spirit.

The spiritual man, however, is capable of discerning and judging spiritual things, including doctrine. Why? Because he has, "received the Spirit of God; that [he] might know." The spiritual man, the person who is born-again and has the Holy Spirit, "judgeth all things." He discerns, examines, weighs, understands, and comprehends all things. The things of God, truths of His Word and understanding of spiritual matters, are transmitted to and comprehended by the spirit of man with the help of the Holy Spirit.

Verse 16 concludes the thought of I Corinthians two,

"For who hath known the mind of the Lord, that he may instruct him? But we have the mind of Christ."

I Corinthians 2:16

Who is "him" in the question, "who hath known the mind of the Lord, that he may instruct him?" Is "him" the Lord? Should this question read, "Who has known the mind of the Lord that he may instruct the Lord?" No, "him" in this question refers to the spiritual man of verse 15. The question here is, "Who has known the mind of the Lord that he might instruct the spiritual man?" You see, because the spiritual man has the Holy Spirit and has learned to estimate, investigate, examine, and judge in spiritual matters, he is not dependent upon the instruction of another person. He is dependent upon His most excellent Teacher, the Holy Spirit.

The spiritual man has "the mind of Christ" because of the indwelling of the Holy Spirit. Therefore, he can judge, weigh, try, test, and examine all teachings and determine their true value. No one needs to be over him, instructing him at every step and in everything that relates to the Word of God and spiritual matters. Actually, just the opposite is true for, "we have the mind of Christ." Who is "we?" "We" is the men and women who are born again and indwelt by the Spirit of God. We can know the thoughts of God, the deep things of God, and the things freely given to us of God. We don't need to be spiritually dense, always dependent upon another person to lead us. We can be confident because we have the mind of Christ. How do we have the mind of Christ? We have the mind of Christ because we listen to the indwelling Holy Spirit!

Believer, you have the ability to make judgments concerning what doctrines are sound and what doctrines are unsound because the Holy Spirit dwells in you. By the witness of the Spirit, you can judge the validity of the doctrines you encounter. You do not always need another person or a minister to tell you what is right and what is wrong. Who has known the mind of the Lord to instruct you? You have the mind of Christ because you listen to the witness of the Spirit.

The Indwelling Anointing of Truth

The apostle John penned some very serious words concerning seductive false teaching and the Anointing of Truth. He wrote to his spiritual children to warn them both of unsound doctrine and unsound teachers. He informed them, however, that even if he had not written, the Holy Spirit would have alerted them to the potential danger of false teachings and kept them sound in the truth. In his first epistle, John wrote,

> *"These things have I written unto you concerning them that seduce you. But the anointing which ye have received of him abideth in you, and ye need not that any man teach you: but as the same anointing teacheth you of all things, and is truth, and is no lie, and even as it hath taught you, ye shall abide in him."*
>
> I John 2:26-27

When John said, "ye need not that any man teach you," he was not inferring that believers do not need to be taught by those God has called to the ministry. Rather, John was cautioning these believers not to be totally dependent upon teachers. If they were, they would be susceptible to false teachers and false teaching. These believers were to depend upon the Indwelling Anointing for all answers concerning men's teaching.

If believers are too dependent upon others to teach them and to decide for them concerning what is sound and what is unsound, then the door for error and abuse is open wide. Believers are not to be dependent upon fallible and possibly wrongly motivated persons, but upon the infallible anointing that abides within! If you want to know the truth, listen to the Holy Spirit. He is, "no lie," and He will tell no lies. The Indwelling Anointing, "is truth." The Holy Spirit does not just tell the truth, He *is* the truth!

Believers should be Spirit-led and right on track in all their judgments of doctrine. Romans 8:16 says,

> *"The Spirit itself beareth witness with our spirit, that we are the children of God..."*
>
> Romans 8:16

What does the Spirit bear witness with our spirit about? He bears witness about truths like, "We are the children of God," and we are, "heirs of God." The Word and the Spirit always agree. If the Holy Spirit does not bear witness with your spirit concerning what someone says the Word says, you must make a closer examination of what that someone is teaching. The Holy Spirit will bear witness with whatever the scriptures truly teach.

Because the Anointing of truth dwells in you, you can follow what is in your heart. Not what you hear in your head or in your emotions, but what bears witness with your spirit. If you hear teaching that is unsound, your heart will not bear witness with it any more than your body's immune system will happily accommodate a foreign substance.

The Indwelling Anointing — The Expert Witness

In I John 5:10, the apostle John wrote this,

"He that believeth on the Son of God hath the witness in himself..."

I John 5:10

Throughout this book we are learning about true and false doctrine and true and false spiritual leadership. "Is it true or false?" is the question we need to answer concerning doctrine. It is impossible, however, to make a correct judgement without evidence and expert testimony. Thank God, we have evidence and expert testimony concerning doctrine! The written scriptures are the evidence and the Holy Spirit is the expert Witness!

When a court is deciding the guilt or innocence of an individual, evidence is examined and witnesses give testimony. Often lawyers will call to the witness stand what they call an "expert witness." This is a person who is absolutely competent and completely trustworthy in his particular field. If, for example, a question must be answered concerning physical health, a doctor may be called as an expert witness. If a question must be answered concerning mental or emotional health, a psychiatrist or psychologist may be called as an expert witness. If a question must be answered concerning a gun used in a shooting, a weapons expert will be called to the witness stand. These expert witnesses are called to testify because they are considered ultimate authorities in their fields.

Concerning the Word of God, questions of doctrine, and matters of spiritual life, the Holy Spirit is The Expert Witness! Because God knew that questions would arise concerning doctrine and other spiritual matters, He called the Holy Spirit to the witness stand! The Holy Spirit is already sworn in. He has already promised to tell the whole truth and nothing but the truth. He is already in place, sitting upon the witness stand of our hearts, ready to testify as an expert witness concerning the truth or error of any teaching.

The Holy Spirit — Our Alarm

There are men who will attempt to lead sound believers into unsound doctrine. There are seducing spirits who will attempt to lure believers into doctrines of demons. But God has already pre-arranged for that eventuality! He put an automatic alarm within us that warns us!

The Holy Spirit is the all-efficient means of enabling believers to possess a knowledge of the truth. Learn to listen to the Holy Spirit. Check your own heart. Even an ancient Old Testament man named Elihu said, "there is a spirit in man: and the inspiration of the Almighty giveth them understanding" [Job 32:8]. The writer of Proverbs said that, "the spirit of man is the candle of the Lord" [Proverbs 20:27]. It is in your spirit, by His Spirit, that God will shine the Light and keep you in the light.

The Indwelling Anointing will teach you and guide you. Learn to recognize His voice. The Anointing that is in you, "is truth, and is no lie." If you follow the Anointing within you, you will remain in the truth and free from every lie.

THREE: DID JESUS TEACH IT?

If you hear teachings that Jesus did not teach or that contradict what Jesus taught, you should be very cautious. Of course, there were truths Jesus did not teach in His short earth ministry; especially the fuller revelation of New Covenant truth. But if a teaching does not conform to what Jesus taught, especially if it contradicts something Jesus taught, it is most likely error. Sound doctrine will **never** be in conflict with the teachings of Jesus!

In His final words to the disciples, often called the great commission, Jesus said,

"Go ye therefore, and teach all nations…Teaching them to observe all things whatsoever I have commanded you…"

Matthew 28:19-20

When the disciples went forth into the world to minister to all nations, they were to teach what Jesus had taught them. The writer of Hebrews confirms the paramount place of the teachings of Jesus saying,

"God…Hath in these last days spoken unto us by his Son…"

Hebrews 1:1-2

In the Old Testament, God revealed Himself and His Word through the prophets. The words of the prophets were the teachings of God. In these last days, the New Covenant days, God has spoken to us through His Son. Jesus was the full revelation of the Word of God and the full expression of the will of God. If you pay close attention to His teachings and carefully follow His lifestyle, false doctrine and unsound spiritual life will be easy to recognize.

The apostle John wrote,

"Whosoever trangresseth, and abideth not in the doctrine of Christ, hath not God. He that abideth in the doctrine of Christ, he hath both the Father and the Son."

II John 9

By the phrase, "the doctrine of Christ," John was referring not only to teachings *about* Jesus, but to the teachings *of* Jesus. The Amplified Bible confirms this saying,

> *"Anyone who runs on ahead [of God] and does not abide in the doctrine of Christ [who is not content with what He taught] does not have God..."*
>
> II John 9 Amp

John was very stought with these words. He declared that anyone who was not willing to submit to what Jesus taught, who was not content with His teachings, was without God. Paul confirmed John's words in his instructions to Timothy about what he should teach. He wrote,

> *"If any man teach otherwise, and consent not to wholesome words, even the words of our Lord Jesus Christ, and to the doctrine which is according to godliness; He is proud, knowing nothing..."*
>
> I Timothy 6:3-4

The "words of our Lord Jesus Christ," or the "doctrine of Christ" as John called it, are wholesome words. His teachings are right. They are godly and life-giving. They are a standard by which other teaching must be judged. The great apostle Paul, when leaving the elders at Ephesus, confirmed his own lifestyle and challenged theirs with the words of Jesus saying,

> *"I have shewed you all things, how that so labouring ye ought to support the weak, and to remember the words of the Lord Jesus, how he said, It is more blessed to give than to receive."*
>
> Acts 20:35

Some teachers are not content with the simplicity of what Jesus taught and, therefore, do not consent to, or agree with, what Jesus taught. They want something more and so they invent something more. The result is that they wander into unsound doctrine.

For example, in the past few years teaching about the authority of the ministry has been very popular. Some ministers love this teaching and even misuse it because it gives them a place of position over people. But what did Jesus teach about ministry? Did He ever include the aspect of authority when teaching His disciples about ministry? I am sure you remember what Jesus said when certain of His disciples were pulling for position. He warned them not to seek after position and insisted that they demonstrate the heart of a servant [Matthew 20:20-28].

It has become popular in these days for those in the ministry to declare their office. If one thinks he is called to be a teacher, he says, "I am a Teacher." If one thinks he is an apostle, he says, "I am an apostle." But what did Jesus say about this taking of titles to one's self? He said,

"But be not ye called Rabbi [or Teacher]: for one is your Master, even Christ; and all ye are brethren."

Matthew 23:8

Am I saying that one cannot say what God has called them to be in the ministry? No. Paul declared many times, "I am an apostle." He only made this declaration, however, because the Father and the Lord Jesus Christ had made it first. The point I want to make here is that believers must always examine carefully any teaching which is different than the teachings of Jesus. Always ask, "Did Jesus teach it? Did Jesus do it?"

The current strong emphasis on militant prayer and pulling down demonic strongholds over cities should be examined in this light. Did Jesus ever identify or pray against demons over cities? Did He ever teach His disciples to pray this way? Is there any indication of this kind of activity in His teaching or His ministry? I believe you will find that aside from casting demons out of possessed individuals, Jesus never took an offensive posture against the devil or his demons.

Several years ago I preached at a local church. After I finished teaching, I turned the service back over to the pastor. He gave an invitation for people to come forward for a time of personal ministry. During this time a man who had lost finances in an unfair business deal came forward for prayer. In a very aggressive tone the pastor said, "Well, we're just going to take back what the devil has stolen, bless God, and get what's ours!" He also made statements like, "It's time for Christians to fight for what is theirs." Then he began to pray for the man in a very aggressive manner, commanding finances to come back to him.

When this pastor began to pray, I sensed a kind of sickly feeling in my spirit. Something was not right. I began to search my heart for the witness of the Holy Spirit. Almost immediately the Holy Spirit brought the teaching of Jesus concerning this kind of situation to my remembrance. This is what Jesus taught,

"But I say unto you, That ye resist not evil...if any man will sue thee at the law, and take away thy coat, let him have thy cloak also."

Matthew 5:39-40

What had happened to the man who came for prayer was obviously evil. He was clearly wronged in a financial matter. But Jesus taught His disciples not to resist evil. Christians are not to fight for their personal rights, extracting an eye for an eye and a tooth for a tooth, even when wronged by sinners. Yes, in the Old Testament an eye for an eye and a tooth for a tooth was right. But many of the teachings of the Old Testament have been super-seded by the truths Jesus taught.

This man's pastor should have instructed him to love his enemy, bless the man who stole from him, and pray for the one who despitefully used him. Then this man could have demonstrated that he was a child of his heavenly Father Who does good to all, the just and the unjust. He would have been perfect as his Father in heaven is perfect [Matthew 5:44-48]. If this man had released his enemy through love, forgiveness, and prayer, the door would have remained open for God to bring about true vindication and justice. Paul taught believers this very same truth concerning personal jus-tice saying,

> *"Dearly beloved, avenge not yourselves, but rather give place unto wrath: for it is written, Vengeance is mine; I will repay, saith the Lord...Be not overcome of evil, but overcome evil with good."*
>
> Romans 12:19-21

Shortly after my wife and I moved into the house we now live in, some-one came through a window at night and stole one hundred dollars from my office desk. I prayed for that person, asking God to minister to them because they obviously were in great spiritual need. The very next day my travel agent called to tell me that an airline special had just come up and I could exchange the ticket for my flight to Arizona for one that was one hundred dollars less! You see, God will repay. We are not to avenge ourselves.

It is quite possible that you don't like this teaching of Jesus. You may ask, "What happened to the militant church? What happened to aggressive prayer that takes what belongs to us? Don't Christians have rights too?" All I can say is that you must realize that not all the teachings of Jesus, or of the rest of the Word of God for that matter, are easy. Any teaching that Jesus did not teach or that is not in agreement with what Jesus taught must receive a thorough investigation.

FOUR: DID PAUL OR ANOTHER FOUNDATIONAL APOSTLE TEACH IT?

The original apostles were the instruments of God to bring forth revelation of the New Covenant. They were specifically equipped, as Paul said of himself in Ephesians 3:3-5, to bring forth revelation. Paul wrote,

> *"...by revelation he made known unto me the mystery...Whereby when ye read, ye may understand my knowledge in the mystery of Christ. Which in other ages was not made known unto the sons of men, as it is now revealed unto his holy apos-tles and prophets by the Spirit."*
>
> Ephesians 3:3-5

Just as the Spirit of God moved upon Old Testament men, inspiring them to set down in writing the words that God was speaking, so He inspired New Testament men with revelation which they set down in writing. He selected specific men to understand and to set forth in a clear and orderly way the life and ministry of Christ and the mystery of redemption and salvation through Christ. He chose men to lay foundations of truth, accurately writing of the life and ministry of Christ and clearly communicating the fullness of the work of salvation. These revelations were taught orally in the early church, communicated through epistles, and have been handed down to us through the apostles' writings and teachings. The apostle Paul said of himself,

> "...I am made a minister, according to the dispensation of God which is given to me for you, to fulfill the word of God (to preach it in its fullness), Even the mystery which hath been hid from ages and from generations, but now is made manifest to his saints: To whom God would make known what is the riches of the glory of this mystery among the Gentiles; which is Christ in you, the hope of glory: Whom we preach, warning every man, and teaching every man in all wisdom..."
>
> Colossians 1:25-28

Paul was specially chosen, as were several others, to communicate the mystery of the gospel in its fullness to the saints of God. He was called to preach the full revelation of the work of Christ and to establish believers in the mystery of the gospel. He said of himself and others in I Corinthians 4:1,

> "Let a man so account of us, as of the ministers of Christ, and stewards of the mysteries of God."
>
> I Corinthians 4:1

The physician Luke, a man who knew of Christ from the very beginning and travelled extensively with the apostle Paul, introduced his writings this way,

> "...I have...searched out diligently and followed all things closely and traced accurately...from the highest to the minutest detail from the very first, to write an orderly account...[my purpose] is that you may know the full truth and understand with certainty and security against error the accounts (histories) and doctrines of the faith..."
>
> Luke 1:34 Amp

The early church became established in doctrine through the teachings of men who were called by God to be stewards of the mysteries. New believers depended upon the teachings of the apostles. Acts 2:42 says of the early church that they,

> "...continued steadfastly in the apostles' doctrine..."
>
> Acts 2:42

Because these early apostles were chosen and specially anointed by God to set forth foundational revelation of the mystery of the gospel and other spiritual truths, we must always compare current doctrine with what they said. Paul told the believers in Ephesus that they were, "built upon the foundation of the apostles and prophets" [Ephesians 2:20]. This does not mean that every local church must have a functioning apostle and prophet. It means that believers and local churches are established upon the foundational teachings of the early apostles and prophets. Any current doctrine that conflicts with what the early apostles taught must receive a thorough examination.

Paul adamantly opposed any teaching that conflicted with his. To the church at Galatia he said this concerning men whose teachings contradicted his,

"...there be some that trouble you, and would pervert the gospel of Christ. But though we, or an angel from heaven, preach any other gospel unto you than that which we have preached unto you, let him be accursed."

Galatians 1:7-8

For emphasis, Paul repeated himself in the very next verse,

"As we said before, so say I now again, if any man preach any other gospel unto you than that you have received, let him be accursed."

Galatians 1:9

This is very strong language! Paul damned anyone, any human minister or angelic messenger, that preached or taught anything contrary to the gospel he preached and taught. Twice he said that if anyone preached another gospel let him be, "doomed to eternal punishment" [Galatians 1:9 Amp]. The Cottonpatch version of the Bible renders Paul's words this way,

"If anyone preaches a different message than I preached, let that person go to hell."

Galatians 1:8 Cottonpatch

That is very strong punishment for just preaching and teaching unsound doctrine, don't you think? Should a person should be condemned to hell for teaching unsound doctrine? Perhaps unsound doctrine is more dangerous than you thought!

Paul also wrote this to the church at Corinth of those who preached different doctrine than he did,

"For if he that cometh preacheth another Jesus, whom we have not preached..."

II Corinthians 11:3-15

As far as Paul was concerned, anything that did not agree with what he taught, or contradicted what he taught, was dangerous.

Sometimes ministers will say, "The Lord told me to teach," or, "The Holy Spirit showed me." Some will even say, "I had a vision and God told me to tell you." If, however, you can not find a basis for what they are teaching in the writings of Paul or one of the other foundational apostles, their doctrine is calling for a very careful inspection.

The apostle John wrote this concerning the epistle we call the book of Revelation,

> *"For I testify unto every man that heareth the words of the prophecy of the book, If any man shall add unto these things, God shall add unto him the plagues that are written in this book: And if any man shall take away from the words of the book of this prophecy, God shall take away his part out of the book of life, and out of the holy city, and from the things which are written in this book."*
>
> Revelation 22:18-19

God's attitude concerning men who add to or take away from what He supernaturally inspired men to write is obvious. He will not tolerate it! If men are teaching doctrines that the early apostles did not teach, whether by adding to or taking away, you must be careful!

FIVE: BEWARE OF OLD TESTAMENT DOCTRINE

Beware of contemporary teaching based on types and shadows or even isolated scripture verses from the Old Testament. Old Testament stories and examples can be interpreted and used in almost any way one fancies. In fact, almost any Old Testament story could be used to illustrate almost any New Testament teaching. Old Testament stories or specific Old Testament scriptures can complement New Testament doctrine, but they cannot be the foundation or sole scriptural support for a New Testament doctrine.

Rightly Dividing the Word at the Cross

One absolutely essential fact that believers must be aware of is that there is a profound difference between the Old and New Covenants, between the Old and New Testaments. The teachings of Jesus and the revelation of the mystery of the New Covenant have fulfilled Old Testament prophesies and superseded Old Testament teachings. For example, in His sermon on the Mount, Jesus said,

> *"Ye have heard that it hath been said (in the Old Testament), An eye for an eye, and a tooth for a tooth: But I say unto you, That ye resist not evil…"*
>
> Matthew 5:38-39

Jesus' teaching concerning retribution superseded and cancelled the Old Testament teaching on this matter.

Concerning Sabbath day observance, the Old Testament law said that no work of any sort could be done. To work on the holy day of rest was sin against the law of God as specified in the ten commandments. In the New Testament, however, the apostle Paul said,

> "*One man esteemeth one day above another: another esteemeth every day alike. Let every man be fully persuaded in his own mind. He that regardeth the day, regardeth it unto the Lord; and he that regardeth not the day, to the Lord he doth not regard it…*"
>
> Romans 14:5-6

If a man sinned in the Old Testament, he paid for his own sin with a special offering. Even then, however, his sin was only covered, not forgiven. In the New Testament, men receive full pardon and cleansing from their sin through faith in the saving work of the sacrificial Lamb, Christ Jesus.

Old Testament scriptures cannot be imported into New Testament thinking. If they agree with the New Testament, they can be used to support a doctrine. But Old Testament scriptures **cannot** be used as a foundation for New Testament doctrine.

Old Testament Stories

There was a teaching that went around recently that was based on the Old Testament story of Moses' death and Joshua's call to leadership. Some ministers were using this story to teach that God was trying to do something new in this generation and older ministers would have to step aside and make room for young ministers. This story was being used by some young ministers as a "scriptural example" to sway people toward their leadership.

This teaching, however, is not sound doctrine. At the very best it is dangerous speculation. At the very worst it is false, divisive, confusing, and destructive. You cannot take pictures out of the Old Testament and build teachings around them no matter how spiritual or exciting they sound!

The truth of the matter concerning the story of Moses and Joshua is that when Moses was finished with his ministry, God retired him. He was not pushed out by an uprising led by Joshua. It is also true that when the spiritual leaders of our day are finished, God will retire them. Young and militant ministers who desire and strive for spiritual position are in danger of the same judgement that Koran, Dathan, Ibiram, and their followers suffered when they tried to take leadership from Moses. If you want an Old Testament story to illustrate what is happening today with some of the aggressive young leaders, just look to that story!

If you are a minister and think you are a "Joshua" destined to take spiritual leadership in your generation, then grow up in God and learn to serve. In the New Testament it is the servants who are the true spiritual leaders. God will **not** choose ambitious and aggressive youngsters for positions of spiritual leadership. Not only would it ruin their lives; it would upset the whole body of Christ. If you want to be a Joshua, stay in the tent of meeting with God while Moses fulfills his ministry. When it is your turn to lead, God will let you know.

Another popular modern day teaching taken from an Old Testament story is based on the words Jehoshaphat declared to the children of Israel before they went up to battle. He said,

> "...Believe in the Lord your God, so shall ye be established; believe his prophets, so shall ye prosper."
>
> II Chronicles 20:20

Some ministers wrongly use this scripture to encourage people to do what they say. Ministers especially like to use this "teaching" when speaking about money. I have heard men on the television give a "word of prophesy" about an amount of money people should send in and then use this scripture to justify their "prophesy" and motivate people to respond. If a minister's words carry so little authority that he has to entice people to give by using this scripture, he had better go back to the closet!

Recently, I was browsing through one man's book on the subject of money. He used this scripture from II Chronicles 20 to authenticate his teaching. He said that one of the main causes of financial problems in the body of Christ was that believers did not listen to God's prophets. If they would listen to God's prophets, he said, they would prosper. Then he said that if believers didn't listen to what anyone else said, he was one prophet that they had better listen to.

In the Old Testament prophets were the oracle of God to the people. Not only did they deliver those words which would later become the written scriptures; they also delivered specific advice for special circumstances. The New Testament ministry of the prophet is not the same. First of all, New Testament prophets do not speak forth words which will later be part of the written scriptures. Secondly, although a New Testament prophet may prophesy specific instructions, each believer has the Holy Spirit themselves and must follow His voice first.

A good New Testament example of this truth can be found in Acts 19-21. The apostle Paul had purposed in his own spirit, by the direction of the Holy Spirit, to go to Jerusalem. In every place he went, however, disciples prophesied to him of the trouble he would encounter in Jerusalem and tried to persuade him not to go. In Acts 21:10, Agabus, a man respected as a prophet and one who had prophesied accurately in times past of the world wide drought [Acts 11:28], took Paul's girdle and prophesied to him of the trouble he would encounter in Jerusalem. Did Paul listen to this prophet and prosper? No, he went to Jerusalem because that was the direction he had in his own heart by the Holy Spirit.

Beware of any contemporary teaching that is founded solely on types and shadows or even partial scriptures from the Old Testament. If one is teaching sound doctrine based on a New Testament scripture and uses an Old Testament story to support his doctrine, or to give an illustration, that is fine. Any doctrine, however, that is based on Old Testament stories and cannot be substantiated by New Testament teaching is wrong.

SIX: BE CAUTIOUS OF NEW MOVES

Believers must beware of tangents in teaching. Especially charismatic Christians would do well to be cautious in this area. Because they are excited about the things of God, they are often too influenceable. Rather than getting grounded in the Word of Truth, they jump from move to move, from wave to wave. I call this "Spiritual surfing." Spiritual surfers are usually either "high" or "crashed."

The problem with riding waves of doctrine is that believers eventually crash on the shore. Then they have to pick themselves up, dust themselves off, and paddle back out into that great ocean of truth called the Word of God. It is important to remember that a wave is nothing more than water that surges upward for a moment before it becomes part of the ocean again.

It is not wrong to move with the flow of the Holy Spirit. If He is emphasizing something for a season, be open to Him. Don't be afraid to move. A good surfer, however, knows when to get off the wave. He knows when the wave has done all it can do and is heading for a confrontation with the beach. A good surfer stays in the water. And a sound believer, though he may catch an exciting wave now and then, builds his life in the scriptures.

A few years ago, while ministering at a particular church, the Holy Spirit said something through me in a word of prophesy that caught my attention. It was something I had not really considered before. He said, "Praise and worship is not a wave, but is simply a part of the whole ocean of truth that you need to be established in and maintain in your spiritual walk." What the Holy Spirit said in this word of prophesy about the teaching of Praise and Worship is true of any particular teaching from God's Word. Although it may be emphasized for a season, just as a wave rises briefly above the level of the rest of the ocean, it is simply a part of the whole ocean of truth we need to be established in.

When the apostle Paul visited Athens and realized that the city was, "wholly given to idolatry," he began to dispute in the synagogue and preach in the market place. When some of the local philosophers heard him teaching, they desired to know his doctrine. They took him to Mars Hill and said, "May we know what this new doctrine, whereof thou speakest is?" These men were bored with their own theories and curious about the new; they were always looking for a different twist. The Bible says of these men that,

> "...all the Athenians and strangers which were there spent their time in nothing else, but either to tell, or to hear some new thing."
>
> Acts 17:21

New is always stimulating, but new is not always right! New is always exciting, but new is not always true! Be careful of those who are always talking about a "new move," or are promoting a, "new teaching that God is bringing forth."

What God wants to do in our generation is the same as He has wanted to do in every generation. The Holy Spirit wants to do in this generation the same things He did in the book of Acts and has wanted to do in every generation. The Head of the church, the Lord Jesus, has no new plans. His first plan is the right plan. Stick with the Word and you will stick with the truth. Keep looking for "new" and you may wander into speculation and come under the influence of false and unsound spiritual leadership.

Beware of the pendulum swing in doctrine. There is always a tendency to overemphasize what has been ignored and then later to ignore what was, for a season, emphasized. Thus, believers remain tossed to and fro by the unpredictable gusting of the wind. Don't follow gusts of wind. Stay with the prevailing wind of God's Word.

SEVEN: HAS IT BEEN TAUGHT BEFORE?

Recently, there have been quite a few "new" doctrines in the church. It is important to discover whether these "new" doctrines have been taught before in church history. If they have been taught before, what kind of response did they receive from the sound spiritual leaders of the day? Some unsound doctrines, you see, surface on a regular basis. It is valuable, therefore, to learn what happened in the church the last time they came around.

Because people desire new, exciting, and different, there is often a pressure placed on ministers that they cannot handle. In order to keep their ministries exciting, cutting-edge, and forefront, they feel compelled to come up with new teachings. This is very dangerous. Too easily ministers can wander away from fundamental and sound doctrine in order to stay on the cutting-edge of spiritual developments.

If what someone is teaching has never been taught in church history, examine that teaching very carefully. Yes, truths can be lost that need to be recovered. Yes, there are doctrines that get shelved or closeted that need to be brought out again. When Martin Luther taught, "The just shall live by faith," he was declared a heretic. The doctrine of justification by faith, however, is the very foundation of the whole Christian faith. It was prophesied in the Old Testament and taught by the early apostles and early church fathers.

If a doctrine has never been taught before in church history, be careful. Be a spiritual man and examine the doctrine to determine whether it is valuable or even valid. Always ask, "Is this a time-tested Bible doctrine or is this a completely new doctrine?" "Has this been taught before in church history?" "If this doctrine has been taught before, what was the response to it from sound spiritual leaders?"

EIGHT: EXAMINE THE FRUIT

Unsound doctrine obstructs spiritual growth and leads to spiritual sickness. If, therefore, a certain teaching undermines faith, makes believers spiritually sick, or is counter productive to true spiritual growth, it is very likely unsound doctrine. The apostle James asked this question,

> "Doth a fountain send forth at the same place sweet water and bitter? Can the fig tree, my brethren, bear olive berries? either a vine, figs?"
>
> James 3:11-12

If the fruit is bad, you can be certain that the root is bad. If the water is bitter, you can be sure that the well is polluted. Likewise, if the fruit of a particular teaching is bad, then without a doubt the teaching is unsound.

Paul taught Timothy that the scriptures were "profitable." This word means, "an advantage, a benefit, or useful." Sound doctrine is profitable, not destructive. The sound doctrines of God's Word set men free. If the teachings you are hearing do not give you an advantage, if they hurt rather than help or take away rather than add to, they cannot be the sound doctrines of scripture. If a teaching does not benefit your spiritual growth, you must check it carefully.

Paul told Timothy to avoid foolish and unlearned questions, knowing that they do gender strifes [II Timothy 2:23]. If a particular teaching produces strife and division, it is unsound doctrine. Because I travel to many local churches, I know personally that some teachers cause division, strife, and confusion almost every place they go. The fruit of their doctrine is not unity, peace, edification, and confidence. The fruit of their teaching is division, confusion, frustration, and fear.

Some places where I have travelled recently, I have observed activities which are the result of the current teaching on militant Christianity. In these places, I have not seen an increase in any Christian virtue except zeal. Baby Christians think they are really doing something for God because they pray loud, praise loud, and wave their fists at the devil. They are not mature enough to realize that their activity is fleshly. When I say their activity is fleshly, I do not mean that it is sin. I simply mean that it is useless. The devil cannot see their fists shaking and cannot hear the volume of their voices. If volume made a difference in the effectiveness of prayer, then we should all pray through P.A. systems!

Unsound doctrine produces sickly Christian thinking and living. If you find sickly Christian thinking and living, you can be sure that unsound doctrine is at its source. If believers are not growing strong, steady, and balanced, you know the teaching material is inferior. It is reasonable to conclude that if a teaching does not produce spiritual strength, confidence in God, hope for the future, joy in the Holy Ghost, and personal peace, then it is not the life giving truth of the Word of God. Any so called Bible doctrine that undermines confidence in God, robs peace, steals joy, or leads to religious works, demands a closer look.

Nine: Discuss Your Questions With A Minister

Sometimes teaching you hear will not bear witness with your spirit and will seem to contradict scripture, but you may not be able to determine with certainty that it is unsound doctrine. Others who follow this teaching may appear to be sound, but you are having a hard time determining its validity.

At this point it is allowable and often very beneficial to discuss this teaching with someone you have confidence in both concerning their doctrine and their spiritual life. For most individuals this person will be their pastor. Sometimes, however, it does occur that a pastor himself gets caught up in strange doctrines. If this happens, you may have to find a spiritually mature person somewhere else.

There are two or three individuals that I highly respect in their relationship with God, their soundness in doctrine, and their effectualness in ministry. Every time I have approached them with a question concerning a particular teaching, they have had the same question and have been seeking an answer themselves. We have been able to discuss, share scriptures, and to sense together the witness of the Spirit even as the early church leaders did when they wrote to the Gentiles concerning their decision on a particular doctrine that, "It seemed good to the Holy Ghost and to us" [Acts 15:27].

Ministers who are of sound faith, who know God, who know the Word of God, and who know the witness of the Spirit can be a very important part of reaching a sound conclusion concerning questionable doctrines.

CONCLUSION

In this chapter we have learned several of the most important means of judging doctrine. If you have a firm grasp of the written scriptures and know the witness of the Holy Spirit, you should have no trouble remaining sound in doctrine. If you hear, read, or in any way encounter doctrines that are questionable, employ these methods for judging and you will soon know whether to hold fast to that doctrine or to avoid it.

If, after you have examined a doctrine, you are not sure whether or not it is sound, then wait and relax. You won't miss God. And don't let anyone tell you that you will! If you are actively pursuing your relationship with Him, growing in your knowledge of His Word, and sincerely desiring to be in step with what He is doing in your generation, He won't leave you behind. Trust Him! Trust the Spirit He has given you! If He found you when you were His enemy and "took you along," He certainly will not abandon you now!

Section Four

Judging Leadership

II Peter 2:1-2

"There shall be false teachers among you...and many shall follow their pernicious ways."

·~11~·
Identifying Unsound Spiritual Leadership

F alse teachers, false prophets, false apostles, false pastors, and false evangelists have been part of the spiritual scene of the church since the days of the first apostles. It was a problem then, it is a problem now, and it will especially be a problem in the last days.

In every generation there will be men who purposely or unknowingly cause believers to stumble in their spiritual lives by leading them away from sound churches, sound leadership, and sound doctrine. This will continue to occur because of the tactics of Satan and because of the self-serving nature of man. The opportunity for power, position, recognition, and money are strong temptations. Satan even attempted to seduce Jesus with these temptations. The closer we move to the end of this age, the greater will be the proliferation of false teachers and their false teaching.

Concerning individuals who cause His children to be offended, Jesus said,

"Woe to the world because of offenses! for it must needs be that offenses come; but woe to that man by whom the offense cometh."

Matthew 18:6-7

Jesus said, "it must needs be that offenses come." Offenses will come. Some false leaders will be successful. Some true children of God will be misled and misused. Some believers will depart from the faith because of the activity of false leaders. Offenses will come, but, as Jesus said, "woe to that man by whom the offense cometh!"

There are several facts we should be aware of as we begin this section on judging spiritual leadership. First, false and unsound spiritual leaders will be on the spiritual scene in increasing numbers as we approach the end times. There will be many that will deceive many. Second, false and unsound spiritual leaders will so cleverly disguise themselves that were it not for the warnings issued in the Word of God, they would operate unsuspected and undetected and be successful in their endeavors. Third, if false and unsound spiritual leaders go unsuspected, undetected, and not confronted, it will be to believer's and local church's loss in every way: spiritually, mentally, emotionally, and financially.

CATEGORIES OF UNSOUND SPIRITUAL LEADERSHIP

Not all false spiritual leadership can be described with one sweeping statement. Just as there are different categories of unsound doctrine, so there are different categories of unsound spiritual leadership. Some unsound spiritual leaders openly promote other religions, claiming no relationship to Christ. Some unsound spiritual leaders claim allegiance to Christ and the gospel, but promote obviously false doctrine. Some unsound spiritual leaders come from outside the church; some arise from within the midst of a sound body. Some unsound spiritual leaders are purposely wrong; some are sincerely wrong. All unsound spiritual leaders, however, have this in common: They are dangerous to believers and to the church! Unsound spiritual leaders draw believers away from sound bodies, away from sound doctrine, away from sound spiritual leaders, and, thus, away from spiritual soundness and spiritual health.

To help you identify unsound spiritual leaders, I have classified them into four categories. These categories range from obviously false spiritual leaders who promote false religions to spiritual leaders called the sincerely wrong. There are three basic questions we will answer concerning unsound spiritual leadership that will help to distinguish each category. These three questions are:

First: What is their personal relationship with Jesus Christ and with the gospel? Are they unsaved, are they backslidden from the truth, or are they saved and sincere about the Lord?

Second: Do they operate outside the church or do they identify themselves with the church? Do they operate within local bodies or outside local bodies?

Third: What is their intention? Are they aware of the results of their unsound activities? Do they know that their teachings are outside the boundaries of sound Bible doctrine? Are they intentionally misleading believers or are they unaware that their teaching is unsound and that they are upsetting believers' lives?

Let's begin our study of the four different categories of unsound spiritual leadership. Be careful to note the answers to the three questions mentioned above at the summary of each category.

ONE: FALSE LEADERS WHO PROMOTE FALSE RELIGIONS

The first and most obvious unsound spiritual leaders are "False Leaders Who Promote False Religions." These false spiritual leaders have not accepted Jesus Christ as their Saviour or even as the Saviour. They do not confess that He is the Son of God come in the flesh or believe that He is the Saviour of the world. Some false spiritual leaders may acknowledge Him as a spiritual teacher or as one of the many prophets of God. Others may not acknowledge Him at all.

False spiritual leaders who promote false religions do not pretend to promote the gospel of Jesus Christ. They do not come in Jesus' Name or claim allegiance to Him. They do not accept the gospel message or believe that the Bible is the infallible Word of God. To some false spiritual leaders the Bible is just one of many books that contain spiritual truth. Others have no relationship with the Bible and do not refer to it at all. False spiritual leaders who promote false religions do not claim to be part of the body of Christ in order to gain acceptance. In fact, most of them have no past relationship with the church.

Some Are Convinced Their Message is Right

Some false spiritual leaders who promote other religions have become entrenched in completely false doctrine. They are convinced that what they teach is right. Somehow they have become completely deluded. They may be following another false leader who is very convincing. They may be following a supernatural voice they heard or vision they saw. They may be following the reasoning of their own unregenerate minds. For whatever reason, they have become steeped in their own false doctrine and are actively promoting it.

Some Are Motivated by Carnal Rewards

Some false spiritual leaders who promote false doctrine and other religions are motivated purely by the carnal rewards of leadership. They pretend to be teachers of truth, but hope for nothing more than to get what belongs to their followers. They espouse, promote, and live what they know to be a lie simply because it brings them financial income. They recruit lost individuals by promising leadership, security, peace, and family.

The lost individuals who get involved with these leaders and their cults are happy make the sacrifices of personal responsibility and financial means in exchange for the acceptance and identity they so desperately crave.

Some false spiritual leaders desire nothing more than sexual relations. Their "gospel" is a no-holds-barred gospel. They lust after the carnal rewards which come when they "preach" their doctrines and pretend to be spiritual leaders. Often they have women and even men available to them whenever they want. The men and women who have "been enlightened" to their "truth" are willing to serve their spiritual leader in this way.

Some Are Deceived by Satan

Some false spiritual leaders who promote false doctrine and other religions have been thoroughly deceived by Satan and are operating under the strong influence of demon spirits. The founders of several well known false religions claim to have been visited by angels of light. It could be true that they experienced an angelic visitation. Their visitation, however, was not from God or one of His angels. It was either a visitation from Satan who had transformed himself into an angel of light or a visitation from one of his demons who had transformed themselves to appear as an angel of light.

Through the avenue of angelic visitation Satan has, in the past, gained access to future false leaders' lives and, thereby, affected generations with the false doctrines he transmitted to them. It should be no surprise to us that he will continue employing this tactic. Paul warned the church at Corinth about the ability of Satan to transform himself into a messenger of truth. He said,

"And no marvel; for Satan himself is transformed into an angel of light."
II Corinthians 11:14

If Satan could fill the heart of Judas to betray Christ, fill the heart of Ananias and Sapphira to lie to Peter and the Holy Ghost, and put words in Peter's mouth to distract Jesus from His mission, he can certainly influence the thoughts of those who are not committed to Christ and to the truth of the Word of God. Paul warned the churches of Galatia to beware of unGodly angelic visitations when he said,

"But though we, or an angel from heaven, preach any other gospel unto you than that which we have preached unto you, let him be accursed."
Galatians 1:8

Paul implied, through these words, that spirits can transmit false doctrine to men. No doubt some false spiritual leaders have been influenced by demon spirits that presented themselves as bearers of truth.

False Christs and False Prophets

Jesus warned the disciples of false spiritual leaders in His discourse on the end times. He said,

"Then if any man shall say unto you, Lo, here is Christ, or there; believe it not. For there shall arise false Christs, and false prophets, and shall shew great signs and wonders; insomuch that, if it were possible, they shall deceive the very elect."

Matthew 24:23-24

Jesus said there would be "false Christs." The word "christ" simply means anointed or specially chosen of God. There will arise on the spiritual scene in the last days false spiritual leaders who claim to be specially chosen and anointed of God. They are false christs. Jesus also said there would arise "false prophets." A true prophet is one who speaks to the people on behalf of God. There will arise on the spiritual scene in the last days those who claim to speak for God, but do not. Their message will not be in agreement with God's written Word. They are false prophets.

These false spiritual leaders will rise up on the spiritual scene attempting, and sometimes succeeding, to draw people after them. They are leaders because people follow them. But they are false leaders, false christs, and false prophets. They are not anointed of God, but say they are (they are false christs). They do not speak for God, but say they do (they are false prophets). Their intention, especially those who operate under the inspiration of Satan and demon spirits, is to deceive the very ones that God has called unto himself.

How Do They Deceive?

False spiritual leaders use whatever means possible to draw people into their cults. Some promise sexual freedom, peace, or holistic lifestyle. Some motivate by fear. Some simply claim that their religion and teaching is "up to date." Some claim to be specially chosen to deliver "truth" to a waiting world. Others claim to be leaders of true religions and may even have a "Bible" that "God" gave them. Mormons and Jehovah's Witnesses fall into this category.

The devil works through false spiritual leaders using his favorite tactics. He attempts to raise the question in peoples' minds, "Has God really said?" He endeavors to lead people toward a place where their perception of God and of the truth is more "open minded." Motivated by Satan, false spiritual leaders will attack the Bible as far too narrow and irrelevant for the modern man and woman. They will endeavor to lead people away from the simplicity of what God has said into a more "inclusive and enlightened faith."

Several years ago my wife helped to introduce a young woman to the Lord. After this young woman was saved, she wanted to be filled with the Holy Spirit and had a sincere desire to follow the Lord. In a very short time, however, she drifted far away from the truth and became involved with a false cult whose leader claimed to be an alien. When she became involved with this false cult she came under a strong spirit of seduction.

The teachings and the activities of this false cult in no way resembled the teachings of the Word of God. In fact, everyone in this cult was sexually involved with one another. Eventually the leader, who claimed to be an alien and was supposedly immortal, died of AIDS.

Recently, my wife received a letter from one of this young woman's friends. The letter said that this young woman had appeared on a national talk show telling of her involvement with this cult and speaking of her fear that she, too, may be infected with AIDS. The letter requested of my wife that she try to contact this young woman and minister to her in the hope that she would return to the Lord and be restored.

It seems almost unreal, doesn't it, that a Christian (even a baby) would get involved in something so strange? Would a sane person really believe that an alien had come to earth to establish a spiritual group? Yes, it happened! It happened to a young lady who had received the Lord, but had not yet become established in the truth.

Don't think for a moment that just because someone is saved the devil and his false leaders won't attempt to mislead them. Adam and Eve were perfect in God and had heard the truth. But Satan, disguised as an angel of light, led them away from the truth and into spiritual death. If a person knows the truth, the devil and false leaders will use the truth, in a twisted or lifted-out-of-context form, to seduce them away from the Word of God and from the sound body of Christ.

As we approach the end days, some false spiritual leaders will even work miracles and show special signs. Jesus said they would, "show great signs and wonders; insomuch that, if it were possible, they shall deceive the very elect" [Matthew 24:24]. Through signs and wonders some false leaders will "prove" that they are the true representatives of God.

A New Approach

Recently, I have noticed that more familiar and well established false religions like Mormonism, Jehovah's Witnesses, some Eastern religions, and even the New Age movement have modified their methods of promotion. Some of these cults are now trying to appear associated, even if loosely, with

Christianity. They are using words and phrases familiar to Christians. Some even say that they follow Jesus. They will not tell you, however, that they believe He is one of the Ascended Masters or one of many true prophets. False cults are beginning to promote the teachings of their religion in a more deceptive fashion.

In the past, if I met individuals promoting false religion in the airport and I informed them I was a Christian, they would turn away, not wanting me to witness to them. Now when I tell them, "I am a Christian," they say, "I am too." When I say, "I believe the Bible," they say, "I do too." They identify with believers to gain entrance. They look for an open door, a susceptible mind, a seeking person. They disguise their inward motivation by their outward presentation.

The Mormon church is now promoting their Book of Mormon on television, claiming that it is an account of the further ministry of Jesus in His post-resurrection appearance to the American Indians. They are calling it, "another testament of Christ." The young woman who appears in the television advertisement is very lovely and speaks of her tender affection for the Savior. She says that she wants to know more about Jesus and encourages people to buy "another book" which speaks of the Saviour she loves. The footage of the advertisement is soft-focussed and the voices are gentle. This creates an aura of peace and well being.

Recently, the leader of a large cult in Montana was being interviewed on a national talk show. This woman claimed to believe the Bible and to believe in Jesus Christ as Saviour. She also confessed, however, to believe in reincarnation and in other "spirit-guides." It is well known that these "integrated" cults are attractive to disillusioned Christian who have not received good grounding in the Word of God or had solid spiritual leadership.

False spiritual leaders are becoming more and more cunning, introducing their teachings in more subtle ways. If believers listen to their teachings, they will likely hear words and phrases they recognize. Then they will become curious to hear more teaching. For example, the advertisement of the Mormon church concerning "another testament of Christ" could easily stir the curiosity of a young Christian. Just as curiosity and the desire for deeper knowledge led Adam and Eve away from the simple truth of God's words, so individuals today could be led away from the simplicity which is in Christ to another gospel and to a more "advanced religion."

False spiritual leaders who promote other religions, though they are obviously false, are potentially dangerous to believers and to the church. If they were not dangerous, Jesus and other New Testament leaders would not have issued warnings about them. False spiritual leaders are dangerous because they claim special revelation and often have charismatic personalities. Some, because they are convinced they are right, are very convincing. Some, because they are inspired and empowered by Satan himself, have a strong seducing influence. False spiritual leaders will especially be successful in deceiving and misleading babes in the Lord. Let's summarize this category of false spiritual leadership by answering the three questions we listed earlier.

Summary

Answer to Question One: False spiritual leaders are not saved and do not claim any allegiance to Christ or to the Bible.

Answer to Question Two: False spiritual leaders do not pretend to identify with the church; they operate outside the sound body of Christ.

Answer to Question Three: The intention of false spiritual leaders is to draw individuals, including Christians, into their cults and profit from them. They will use any means to do so.

Two: Antichrists

The second category of unsound spiritual leadership is called "Antichrists." This is a designation the apostle John conferred upon individuals who had apostatized from the sound body of Christ and were promoting false teaching in their attempt to seduce believers away from sound local bodies. John's epistles contain several warnings concerning these unsound spiritual leaders called antichrists. It was because antichrists were dangerous that John warned his spiritual children to beware of them. In his first epistle, he said,

> *"Little children, it is the last time: and as ye have heard that antichrist shall come, even now are there many antichrists…These things have I written unto you concerning them that seduce you."*
>
> I John 2:18, 26

Although antichrists are obviously false, they can be dangerous to the church. They are seductive and cunning. They are motivated by spirits of error and inspired by lying spirits. They intend to seduce believers away from the truth and away from sound local bodies.

Antichrist — antichrists

In the scripture we just read, John wrote,

> *"…ye have heard that antichrist shall come, even now are there many antichrists…"*
>
> I John 2:18

Near the time of the second coming of Jesus there will be falling away and Antichrist will be revealed. In II Thessalonians 2:3, Paul called Antichrist, "that man of sin," and, "the son of perdition." He will lead those who, "received not the love of the truth." Those who follow him, "believe a lie," and, "believed not the truth" [II Thessalonians 2:4,12]. Antichrist will oppose God and oppose the truth. He will be inspired and empowered by Satan himself. Through deceptive words and the working of signs and wonders he will draw to himself those who believe his lies.

The Antichrist is yet to come. Even now, however, the spirit of Antichrist is operating in the world through many antichrists. These antichrists once knew the truth, but drew back from the truth and willingly yielded themselves to lies and to seducing spirits. They now seek, through the employment of persuasive words, to draw others into their error and under their spell. There is more than charisma and the art of persuasion behind their words, however. There is a supernatural force working through them. This is why John warned his spiritual children to "test the spirits" of those who claim to speak for God. Concerning the spirits that motivate and speak through false prophets, John said,

> "...this is the spirit of antichrist, whereof ye have heard that it should come; and even now already is it in the world."
>
> I John 4:3

False spiritual leaders called antichrists are motivated and inspired by the spirit of antichrist which is already at work in the world. This is a spirit of error that leads men into error [I John 4:6]. This is a demonic power, an occult force, working through yielded vessels and speaking through yielded lips. The goal of the spirit of antichrist and the goal of antichrists is to keep unbelievers from the truth and to draw believers away from the truth.

Once Part of the Sound Body

One factor that distinguishes this category of unsound spiritual leadership from the first category is that antichrists once held to the truth and were part the sound body of Christ. They apostatized, however, both from the truth and from the sound body. In his first epistle, John wrote,

> "Little children...there many antichrists; whereby we know that it is the last time. They went out from us, but they were not of us: for if they had been of us, they would no doubt have continued with us..."
>
> I John 2:18-19

John said concerning antichrists that they, "went out from us." He also said, "if they had been of us, they would no doubt have continued with us."

John's words clearly indicate that at one time these unsound spiritual leaders had been, or at least had presented themselves as, committed members within a sound local body. They "went out," however, and began promoting error.

Antichrists are ungodly men who abandon their place in God and their place in the body of Christ. Peter compared these unsound spiritual leaders, as did Jude, with the "angels that sinned" [II Peter 2:4]. Like the angels that sinned, these unsound spiritual leaders, "kept not their first estate." The Amplified Bible says of fallen angels that they, "did not keep their own first place of power, but abandoned their proper dwelling place" [Jude 6 Amp].

They Deny That Jesus is the Christ

Antichrists deny that Jesus is the Christ. The apostle John wrote,

> "Who is a liar but he that denieth that Jesus is the Christ? He is antichrist, that denieth the Father and the Son. And every spirit that confesseth not that Jesus Christ is come in the flesh is not of God: and this is that spirit of antichrist, whereof ye have heard that it should come; and even now already is it in the world."
>
> I John 2:22; 4:3

In his second epistle, John wrote,

> "...many deceivers are entered into the world, who confess not that Jesus Christ is come in the flesh. This is a deceiver and an antichrist."
>
> II John 7

John called these unsound spiritual leaders "antichrist" because they are against Christ and against the gospel message which proclaims salvation through faith in Him alone. They oppose the message of Christ, the very heart of the gospel message, and the person Christ, the only Rock upon which the church can be built. They are opposed to the truth which Peter so boldly confessed: "Thou art the Christ, the Son of the living God."

Antichrists do not deny that there is a God or that Jesus existed, but they do deny that Jesus was God manifested in the flesh. They do not deny that Jesus was born, but they do deny the virgin birth. They do not deny that Jesus was a spiritual man, perhaps even a prophet of God, but they do deny that He is the Christ, the Saviour of the world. Antichrists have abandoned the most foundational doctrines of the Christian faith and are, therefore, far outside the boundaries of truth.

Peter was likely referring to this category of unsound spiritual leader when he wrote,

"But there were false prophets also among the people, even as there shall be false teachers among you, who privily shall bring in damnable heresies, even denying the Lord that bought them..."

II Peter 2:1

Peter was not referring to false spiritual leaders who promote other religions when he wrote of, "false teachers among you, who privily shall bring in damnable heresies." The false spiritual leaders of the first category operate outside the church. The false teachers Peter referred to were operating among believers, perhaps even within a local church. They were purposely attempting to introduce damnable heresies into the church.

One of the damnable heresies these false teachers were promoting was, "denying the Lord that bought them." Apparently these false teachers had, at one point in their lives, espoused faith in Christ. They had accepted the gospel message and Jesus' wonderful work of salvation. Now, however, they were denying the Lord that bought them and attempting to introduce this damnable heresy into the church. The false teaching which denies Jesus is Christ and Saviour is one of the distinct identifying messages of antichrists.

Why Do They Leave?

There could be several reasons why antichrists apostatize from the faith and leave the church. Perhaps they become bored with the simplicity of the gospel message. Perhaps they become "more enlightened." Perhaps they begin to doubt the deity of Christ, considering Him just one of many prophets. Perhaps the gospel message becomes too narrow and they err from the faith because they want a broader gospel.

Peter and Jude compared unsound spiritual leaders with the inhabitants of Sodom and Gomorrah who left righteous living for sensual pleasure [II Peter 3:5-6; Jude 7]. Some antichrists may abandon Christ and the gospel message and leave the church for personal pleasure and personal gain. For whatever reason, antichrists deny the Lord that bought them, apostatize from sound local bodies, and promote their error, attempting to mislead believers.

How Do They Deceive?

Antichrists deceive by teaching that a relationship with God can be had apart from faith in the saving work of Christ. They speak of God, but teach that each person must find their own way to Him. They deny the foundational gospel message which insists that only through faith in the work of Christ can one come unto the Father. They promote spirituality, but not Christianity. They promote a form of godliness, but deny the power of God unto salvation which is the gospel of Jesus Christ.

Antichrists raise questions in the minds of believers by mocking well defined Christian doctrine. They attempt to lead sound believers away from the instructions of Christian life by making those teachings look old fashioned and narrow. Christians, for example, who hold firmly to the teachings of God's Word may be labeled as narrow-minded or old fashioned. Christians who oppose the intrusion of New Age teaching into schools may be labeled as paranoid. Believers who refuse to accept homosexuality as a God-approved lifestyle may be labeled homophobic. Those who take a stand against sin may be accused of not loving people.

Some antichrists, though they have left the sound body, may use the fact that they were once part of a local body as a drawing card. Some may still claim to be part of the body of Christ. Others may claim that the only reason they left the church was because God gave them "deeper revelation." The apostle John, however, in the typical boldness of a true apostle, said that because "they went out from us...they were not of us." Stay away from them, John warned. They want to seduce you away from Christ, away from sound doctrine, away from the sound body, and away from true spiritual leadership.

The unsound spiritual leaders called antichrists are very accurately portrayed by Jesus' warning of "wolves." He said,

> "Beware of false prophets, which come to you in sheep's clothing, but inwardly they are ravening wolves."
>
> Matthew 7:15

Jesus said of false prophets that they, "come to you." Antichrists, though once within the flock, now approach the flock from outside. They are experts, however, (perhaps because they were once in the church) at concealing their identity and their intentions. They come, "dressed up as sheep" [Matthew 7:15 Amp]. Whereas false spiritual leaders who promote other religions make no pretense to be Christian, antichrist wolves pretend to be sheep. For this reason Jesus said, "Beware."

The apostle Paul also warned of wolves who would come from outside the church and damage the flock. To the elders at Ephesus, he said,

> "For I know this, that after my departing shall grievous wolves enter in among you, not sparing the flock."
>
> Acts 20:29

Paul spoke of grievous wolves as those that, "enter in among you." By saying that they, "enter in among you," Paul revealed both that these false spiritual leaders come from outside the sound body and that they seek to gain an entrance into the local body. Antichrists often proselyte in local churches.

The believers and elders in Ephesus heeded Paul's warning concerning grievous wolves. We know this because at a later time Jesus commended the church in Ephesus for recognizing and judging the false apostles who tried to infiltrate their church. He said,

"...thou hast tried them which say they are apostles, and are not, and hast found them liars..."

Revelation 2:2

Antichrists are liars. They lie about who they are and they promote lies. John confirmed this when he wrote,

"Who is a liar but he that denieth that Jesus is the Christ? He is antichrist..."

I John 2:22

Many Antichrists in the Last Days

In his second epistle John wrote,

"...many deceivers are entered into the world, who confess not that Jesus Christ is come in the flesh. This is a deceiver and antichrist."

II John 7

He also wrote,

"Little children, it is the last time...now are there many antichrists; whereby we know that it is the last time."

I John 2:18

In the last days — the days which began on the day of Pentecost and will conclude when Jesus comes again, but are especially upon us now — there will be an increase in this category of unsound spiritual leader. There will be "many antichrists," said John. There will be many false spiritual leaders who, at one time, identified themselves with the church and with Christ, but are now trying to lead Christians away from sound doctrine, sound local bodies, and sound spiritual leadership.

Just as Antichrist will, "(oppose) and (exalt) himself above all that is called God," and will show himself, "that he is God," so the many antichrists of the last days will also oppose God and the message of the gospel of God. They will grow bolder and more blatant as we approach the second coming of Christ. They will make a mockery of those who live godly in Christ. They will denounce the values of righteous living as archaic. They will put down champions of righteousness as "Victorian dictators" and raise themselves up as the new oracles of freedom. They will blaspheme the lifestyle teachings of Christ, calling them antiquated, and promote their opinions in place of the gospel. Rather than calling sin, sin, they will call it a, "lifestyle preference." In the same breath they will credit God with creating them the way they are!

In these last days, antichrists will be a gale force wind that unmoors nominal Christians from their foundations. "Truth" will become relevant, changing as each new situation or ungodly desire arises. As truth shifts, people will lose their mental, emotional, and spiritual equilibrium; they will no longer have a sure footing. Right will become wrong and wrong will become right. Black and white will mix with a dull gray arising. Believers who are not aware and prepared could be swayed in their minds as they compare their yielded lives to the wild and free "Do what you want to do" lifestyle of these self-proclaimed end time messengers.

Who Are Antichrists?

What will these antichrists look like? Most of them will present themselves as some kind of spiritual leader. They will claim to know God (even now many like to talk about "God") and will have a form of spirituality. Some of them will call from outside the church, challenging committed church members to abandon their outdated commitments to Bible commandments. Some of them will preach from the lofty pulpits of dead churches, validating the ungodly lifestyles of their members in order to maintain their membership. They will all present themselves as oracles of truth and spiritual guides to those who are without direction. Many of them will look right, talk right, and dress right. Were it not for the warnings of "wolves in sheep's clothing," many of them would go unsuspected.

Some lesser antichrists may come in the form of well known athletes, television personalities, or music stars who claim to have God in their life, but refuse to adhere to the plain teachings of scripture concerning Christian lifestyle. One very well know athlete recently discovered that he was HIV positive. On a late night talk show he speculated that his disease might be part of "God's plan for his life." In a very emotional and sincere manner he said that God had been good to him and that he planned to dedicate his life to helping young people by speaking out about sexual activity and the problem of AIDS. His intended message, however, is shocking in light of the fact that he acknowledges God. He is going to encourage young people to practice safe sex!

This man is well known, well liked, and extremely influenceable. Therefore, he is a leader. I feel compassion for him because of his physical condition. I must, however, speak the truth concerning this man. He is not working for God. He is working against God and against the commandments of God's Word! In a very real sense he could be labeled an antichrist because he promotes a "spirituality" that is unattached to the born-again experience and unattached to the commandments of Jesus Christ.

Last night, I watched the American Music Awards on television. After listening to several of the acceptance speeches by artists who won awards, I became indignant. Almost without exception these artists said, "I want to thank God because He is the who made this possible." These carnal artists thanked God for their ability to sing raunchy songs and create sexually explicit music videos!

A particular group won an award for a "single." One group member came to the podium without a shirt on. Another member said, "I thank God, for without Him we could not have done this." You may be shocked by the title of the song they won an award for and could not have done "without God." The title of their song was, "I Wanna Sex You Up." Is God inspiring new lyrics these days? This is absurd! These individuals speak the name of God with their lips, but refuse to honor Him with their lives! They claim that God is part of their life, but are "anti-Christ" because they refuse to accept and obey Jesus' teachings.

Some other lesser antichrists may include so-called experts in counseling and social issues. Some of these individuals have studied for years to find the truth. They refuse, however, to acknowledge the Truth. They will not agree with or promote what God has already spoken. These so-called experts surface quite regularly on popular talk shows presenting their "enlightened" positions on very serious issues. Almost without fail their positions on critical issues are based on human reasoning and at odds with the truth of God's Word. Any person in the audience who attempts to draw attention to even a simple Bible truth receives an immediate, "Boo," accompanied with thumbs-down gestures. These fools, claiming to be wise, resist the truth and lead others in their error.

Music artists, sports heros, and social experts, although they make no claim to be spiritual leaders, do qualify as spiritual leaders. They are leaders because people, especially the young, follow them. They are spiritual leaders because they influence peoples' spiritual lives. By promoting their gradually regressing values, they influence others, even believers, to move farther and farther away from the plain teachings of the Word of God.

Beware of Antichrists

Believers must beware of this category of unsound spiritual leadership called antichrists. Antichrists know exactly what they are doing. They are not sincerely wrong or making honest mistakes. They are, as John boldly declared, "liars." They allow their consciences to be seared and then promote what they know is not truth in order to seduce believers and make personal gain.

Antichrists, although they are obviously unsound spiritual leaders, have the potential to mislead believers and negatively influence local churches. This is why John warned his spiritual children concerning them. And this is why the Holy Spirit made sure that John's words of warning concerning antichrists have travelled through time to us who live in these last days.

Summary

Answer to Question One: This category of unsound spiritual leadership called antichrists once claimed allegiance to Christ; they once believed in and accepted His saving work. Now, however, they deny that Jesus is the Son of God come in the flesh and have abandoned the foundational truths of the gospel message.

Answer to Question Two: Antichrists are those who were once part of a sound local body. "They went out from us," however, and now operate outside the church. They do, however, attempt to seduce believers away from sound local churches.

Answer to Question Three: These unsound spiritual leaders fully intend to seduce believers away from sound local bodies and sound spiritual leadership. They intend to build their own followings, profiting from those they seduce.

THREE: UNSOUND TEACHERS AMONG US

The third category of false spiritual leadership is "Unsound Teachers Among Us." Unsound teachers among us believe in Jesus Christ. They do not promote other religions or deny Christ and the gospel message as do false spiritual leaders that promote other religions. They do not deny the deity of Jesus, His saving work, and the basic gospel message, and have not abandoned the faith or apostatized from the sound body as do antichrists.

Unsound teachers among us come in Jesus' name claiming to called of God and claiming to be true ministers of the Word. Some of them may, in fact, have been originally set apart and anointed of God for the work of the ministry; they may have had authentic callings from God upon their lives. Some of them may have even answered that call for a season and gained a place of leadership in the body of Christ. For a variety of reasons, however, these individuals have erred in doctrine and in spiritual life. Because of their unyielding attachment to unsound doctrine, they are dangerous both to themselves and to the rest of the body.

Unsound teachers among us do not teach against the Bible. They do not reject Christ or deny the basic gospel message. They do, however, invent and promote false and unsound doctrines. They preach Jesus, but he is, "another Jesus." They preach the gospel, but it is a twisted gospel [II Corinthians 11:4]. They preach a message that sounds spiritual and is convincing, but is perverted [Galatians 1:6-9].

Unsound teachers among us, although they may be saved, have motivations that are not pure. Their ministries and their doctrines are tainted. They are not afraid to misuse the Word of God if it brings them what they want. They are willing to, "[handle] the Word of God deceitfully" [II Corinthians 4:2]. They twist the scriptures to fit their own opinions and lead people into their error. Often they know that their doctrines are not sound, but their own desire for personal gain keeps them from repenting and changing.

Unsound teachers among us are seldom submissive to true spiritual leadership. In fact, they are often renegades from sound churches or other sound organizations. They become a rule unto themselves, refusing to submit to anyone or anything except their own opinions. When sound leaders speak a word of correction to them, they either cry, "Persecution," or run away to a place where their corrupted seed can find a more suitable environment for growing.

Unsound teachers among us are accepted by some believers as sound teachers and sound spiritual leaders. If believers did not accept them, they could not be "among us." Because they are accepted, they have a place to propagate their unsound doctrines. Often, over a period of time, they develop their own followings and, so, become the founders of spiritually and doctrinally errant churches. Because unsound teachers among us can be mistaken for true spiritual leaders, they are a dangerous source of unsound doctrine.

They Operate In Our Midst

Paul accurately typified this third category of unsound spiritual leadership in his warning to the elders of the church at Ephesus. He said,

> "Also of your own selves shall men arise, speaking perverse things, to draw away disciples after them. Therefore watch…"

> Acts 20:30-31

Paul not only warned the elders in Ephesus of wolves who would come from outside the church, but also of men who would rise up in their own midst. Men who raise themselves up in the midst of sound bodies, promote their unsound doctrines, and draw away their own band of disciples are unsound teachers among us.

The church at Ephesus was not the only church that faced this problem of unsound teachers in their midst. Many of the early churches had to deal with this category of unsound spiritual leader. Paul warned the church in Corinth of false apostles who had gained entrance into and a foothold in their midst. The reason he warned them was to, "cut off occasion from them which desire occasion" [II Corinthians 11:12]. Paul exposed the false apostles in Corinth, hoping to prevent them from gaining a stronger foothold in that local body.

In his letter to Titus, the apostle Paul spoke of this dangerous category of unsound spiritual leader saying,

> "...there are many unruly and vain talkers and deceivers...whose mouths must be stopped, who subvert whole houses, teaching things which they ought not, for filthy lucre's sake."
>
> *Titus 1:10-11*

Paul called unsound teachers, "vain talkers and deceivers." It is clear that they had a teaching position in the church because Paul said they, "subvert whole houses, teaching." These unsound teachers were teaching things which they should not teach. Although both the motivation and the teaching of these individuals was wrong, they were accepted by some in the church as true spiritual leaders.

The unsound teachers Paul referred to in his warning to Titus were not outside gurus who were promoting false religions or antichrists who had denied Christ and apostatized from the faith. If they had been in this category of unsound spiritual leader, Paul would not have instructed Titus to correct them, but to expose them and mark them. Note, however, what Paul instructed Titus to do,

> "...rebuke them sharply, that they may be sound in the faith."
>
> *Titus 1:13*

Paul's instruction to Titus to rebuke these unsound teachers indicates that there was a chance for them to repent of their error and return to sound spiritual sense.

Hymaneaus and Philetus

Paul informed Timothy of a man named Hymanaeus and his departure from the faith. He wrote,

> "...some having put away concerning faith have made shipwreck: Of whom is Hymanaeus...whom I have delivered unto Satan, that he may learn not to blaspheme."
>
> *I Timothy 1:19-20*

Hymaneaus was once sound in life and doctrine, but he, "put away concerning faith." He not only shipwrecked in faith and ruined himself, however. He was also blaspheming. The word "blaspheme" comes from two Greek words which mean, "to injure," and, "speech." To blaspheme means, "to injure with speech." Hymaneaus was shipwrecking other believers with his teaching. He was passing on his false doctrines, spreading them throughout the body and overthrowing the faith of others. Apparently, Paul had attempted to correct Hymaneaus. Because he had no success, he had to deliver him to Satan.

In his second letter to Timothy, Paul referred again to Hymanaeus. He also spoke of a man named Philetus, one of Hymenaeus' cohorts in promoting false doctrine. Both of these men had erred from the truth and were promoting their error in the church. Concerning these false teachers, Paul said,

"And their word will eat as doth a canker: of whom is Hymenaeus and Philetus; Who concerning the truth have erred..."

II Timothy 2:17-18

Paul was bold to call the names of Hymaneaus and Philetus and confront their error. They had swerved from the path of sound doctrine and sound life and were spreading their false doctrines like a deadly poison throughout the body of Christ. Because of the potential danger of their activities, Paul called their names.

False Teachers in Antioch

The church at Antioch was birthed when believers scattered by the persecution in Jerusalem passed through Antioch and preached the gospel. People received the gospel message, were born again, and a church started. In its first year of existence both Paul and Barnabas spent a considerable amount of time teaching there.

Early in the life of this local church, however, there was trouble. Certain men came from the church at Jerusalem and taught the new believers in Antioch that unless they were circumcised according to the teaching of Moses, they could not be saved [Acts 15:11]. This message, of course, was a perversion of the truth and completely contrary to Paul's message of justification by faith in Christ alone. These so-called teachers from the church at Jerusalem were able, however, to introduce false teaching to the sound body of believers in Antioch and undermine their faith.

These unsound teachers had no commission from the true spiritual leaders at Jerusalem [Acts 15:24]. Because they came from the mother church at Jerusalem, however, they were accepted as elders in the faith and esteemed as more spiritually advanced. Evidently, the believers at Antioch gave no thought to the possibility that these men might be unsound. Because they came from a sound local body and presented themselves as true ministers of the gospel, it was easy for them to gain entrance to the church in Antioch.

The young believers in Antioch willingly received these "certain men" from Jerusalem who taught doctrines that conflicted with the teachings of Paul and Barnabas. Fortunately, Paul and Barnabas were in Antioch when this error was introduced. If they had not been there, this new church would very likely have fallen prey to false doctrine and forfeited their liberty in Christ.

Paul and Barnabas withstood the false teachers who came from Jerusalem until they agreed to take the question to the mother church in Jerusalem. After discussing this doctrinal issue at length, the spiritual leaders in Jerusalem determined that it seemed good to them and to the Holy Ghost not to lay this burden of circumcision on the Gentile believers [Acts 15:28]. They sent a letter to the church at Antioch, introducing their final decision this way,

> *"Forasmuch as we have heard, that certain which went out from us have troubled you with words, subverting your souls, saying, Ye must be circumcised, and keep the law: to whom we gave no such commandment..."*
>
> Acts 15:24

The men from the church at Jerusalem who invaded the church in Antioch are a good example of, "false teachers among us." They came in Jesus' name, were part of a sound local body, and were teaching from the scriptures. These men were readily accepted as spiritual leaders by the young believers in Antioch and had a wide open door for promoting their unsound doctrine. They did precisely what Paul warned the elders in the church in Ephesus about. The result of their false teaching was that they undermined and upset the spiritual life of the believers in Antioch.

Heretics

Unsound teachers among us include individuals that Paul called heretics. In his letter to Titus he wrote,

> *"A man that is an heretick after the first and second admonition reject; Knowing that he that is such is subverted, and sinneth, being condemned of himself."*
>
> Titus 3:10-11

A heretic, according to Paul, "is subverted and sinneth." According to W. E. Vine, the word "subverted" that Paul used in this passage means, "to be turned inside out and to change completely." A heretic is person who was formerly sound in faith and doctrine and held a place of respect and influence in the church. This person, however, changed completely and departed into unsound doctrine. Although he changed completely and left sound doctrine, he may yet command a place of respect and influence in the church. Some may still look to him as a spiritual leader. For this reason heretics must be warned of and dealt with.

Paul instructed Timothy that heretics were to be admonished. They were to be corrected by being put in remembrance of the truth. If, after the second admonition, they refused correction, they were to be rejected. The word "reject" Paul used in his instruction to Titus is, in other places, translated, "avoid." If a heretic will not receive correction, he must be pointed out to members of the church and they must avoid him. If a heretic is allowed to continue functioning in the church, he will lead others into his unsound doctrine.

The heretic Paul wrote to Titus about was not a false spiritual leader who promoted false religions. He was not an antichrist who blatantly denied Christ and the gospel. He was a former sound member of the church who changed completely and was now promoting unsound doctrine. This unsound teacher in the church was to be admonished by a true spiritual leader in the hope that he would repent of his wrong doctrine and come back to his spiritual senses. This man was still salvageable. Only if he twice refused to accept correction was he to be marked and avoided.

There is not much hope for false spiritual leaders who promote false religions. Their reasoning is darkened and their spiritual eyes blinded. Neither is there much hope for antichrists. They have already rejected Christ and the gospel and will not be able to find a place of repentance. There is, however, hope for unsound teachers among us. Although many of their doctrines are wrong and their activities are detrimental to the body of Christ, God will give them the opportunity and the time to repent.

Beware of Unsound Teachers Among Us

Unsound teachers who gain entrance into a church or an association or who rise up within a church or an association are very dangerous. They are more difficult to recognize than the promoters of false religions and antichrists. They look right, sound right, act right, and even operate within the sphere of a sound body or organization. They are often, for a season, perceived as true spiritual leaders.

260 •⌒• *True or False – Judging Doctrine and Leadership*

Because unsound teachers among us are accepted, at least for a season, as part of a sound local body, they have a "temporary license" to promote unsound doctrine. Just as the believers at Antioch did not suspect the "teachers" who came from the church at Jerusalem, so believers today do not suspect some who may actually be unsound teachers among us. Because they are "among us," many will follow them.

Believers should not be surprised that unsound teachers will be in our midst. It was so in the Old Testament, it was a reality in the early church, and it will be a problem in these last days. Many will rise up from inside the ranks of sound bodies and sound organizations and become the promoters of perverted and unsound doctrine. If believers accept them, churches will be weakened.

Summary

Answer to Question One: Unsound teachers among us have professed faith in Christ. They are Christians although they do not hold fast to sound doctrine.

Answer to Question Two: Unsound teachers among us operate within the church body and may even be accepted members of sound organizations or local churches.

Answer to Question Three: Though unsound teachers among us are saved, their hearts are often not right and their intentions are usually wrong. They do not intend to build up believers and build up the kingdom of God. They intend, rather, to lead believers away from sound local bodies, away from sound doctrine, and into their sectarian groups.

FOUR: SINCERELY WRONG MINISTERS

The last category of unsound spiritual leadership is "Sincerely Wrong Ministers." Sincerely wrong ministers are spiritual leaders in the body of Christ who have embraced and are promoting some unsound doctrines. They do not reject the gospel and promote other religions as do our first category of unsound spiritual leaders. They have not turned away from Christ and the gospel message as do the antichrists. They are not false teachers among us who have become unsound in the faith and are knowingly teaching false doctrines. The sincerely wrong are ministers who have become unsound in particular doctrines, but do not realize that their doctrines are unsound. Because they suppose that their unsound doctrines are right, they promote them with conviction.

Sincerely wrong ministers are convinced that they are right. They are sure they have discovered a truth everyone else missed. They are sure that the unsound doctrines they teach are Biblical and sound. They are sincere, but they are wrong!

The sincerely wrong are not like wolves that disguise themselves in sheep's clothing and intentionally deceive. The sincerely wrong are more like misdirected shepherds. They lead the sheep into poor and sometimes dangerous pastures. Their hearts are right; they desire to do the will of God and want to be a blessing to people. They do not have ill intentions or purposely deceive. They have, however, wandered into doctrinal error and are guilty of misleading sheep.

Sincerely wrong ministers will not usually ruin churches or destroy believers. They are, however, unsound and can lead believers into unsound doctrine and unsound spiritual life. At the very least, the teachings of the sincerely wrong will distract believers from the foundational truths they need in order to become established and settled in Christian faith and life.

Sincerely Wrong Ministers Transgress Doctrine

The apostle John very accurately pictured this category of unsound spiritual leadership in his second epistle when he wrote,

"Whosoever transgresseth and abideth not in the doctrine of Christ…"

II John 9

The best manuscripts of II John have the Greek word *proago* for "transgresseth." This word is often translated, "go." It means, "to go before," or, "to lead the way." The Revised Version's marginal reading of II John 9 translates transgresseth as, "taketh the lead."

Sincerely wrong spiritual leaders seek to lead in doctrine rather than to abide within the boundaries of sound doctrine. They cross over the boundary line marked, "Danger Ahead." Rather than carefully following the guidelines of the scriptures and listening to the voice of the Holy Spirit, they, "take the lead," forgetting that they are not qualified to take the lead. The Amplified Bible translates John's words this way,

"Any one who runs on ahead [of God] and does not abide in the doctrine of Christ — who is not content with what He taught…"

II John 9 Amp

Sincerely wrong ministers "run on ahead [of God]." They are "not content with what He (Jesus) taught" [II John 9 Amp]. Rather than teaching clearly defined doctrines, they push the limits and often go beyond the limits of sound doctrine. Although there is a wealth of sound doctrine to teach, they cannot wait for the next revelation or the next "prophetic word." I have heard some ministers say, "I cannot wait for what God is going to do next!" These ministers, because they can not wait, do not wait. Consequently, they are candidates for error and potential unsound spiritual leaders.

What Do They Teach?

Sincerely wrong ministers do not promote blatantly false doctrines. Often the unsound doctrines they teach are an extreme emphasis of a particular truth. For some reason they become obsessed with a particular message and wander away from the center of truth. When they wander too far away from truth, it can be very difficult for them to get back. Pride enters in and they become the champions of their own doctrines, heroic defenders of their error. If another minister brings them a word of correction, they will accuse him of not walking in love.

It is likely that every believer has been influenced by, or at least heard the teaching of, a sincerely wrong unsound spiritual leader. At the beginning of the charismatic revival, for example, many denominational ministers attributed speaking in other tongues to Satan. Some ministers still believe this false teaching. Teaching this doctrinal error will not keep believers out of heaven, but it will keep the power of heaven out of believers! Ministers who believe and teach this error are not false spiritual leaders or antichrists; they are sincerely wrong.

Ministers in one particular denomination teach that if a person is not baptized in water, he cannot be saved. These ministers are sincere. They are convinced that what they teach is right. They are, however, wrong. Their teaching is not biblical, does not lead to faith, and genders fear and works. I'm sure that if the apostle Paul was alive in this generation, he would deal with these sincere, but injurious ministers the same way he dealt with the circumcisionists of his day.

When I was of high-school age, my brother and I questioned our pastor about the gifts of the Spirit. We wanted to know what they were and why we did not hear about them in our church. We were told that they had passed away when that which was perfect (the canon of scripture, he said) had come. When we pressed this issue a bit more, our pastor informed us that he would not discuss this area of the Bible. This man was sincere. He was an honest and good man. He did not, however, know or teach the truth about the gifts of the Holy Spirit.

A modern day example of sincerely wrong ministers teaching outside the boundaries of Bible truth is the misuse of II Corinthians 10:4. This scripture says,

"...For the weapons of our warfare are not carnal, but mighty through God to the pulling down of strongholds..."

II Corinthians 10:4

Some sincerely wrong modern day ministers have pulled this scripture out of its proper context, lifted out the one phrase, "pulling down of strongholds," and built a whole movement upon it. The thrust of this movement is the so-called pulling down of demonic strongholds over cities through militant prayer and praise.

Recently, I heard a minister on Christian talk show speaking about pulling down strongholds. In the course of his conversation with the host, he was asked how a Christian could discern what demonic strong man was ruling over a city. This minister answered that a Christian could discern the prevailing strong man over a city by simply observing what sinful activities were prevalent in that city. He used Miami, Florida as an example. He said that because Miami had a very bad drug problem, it was obvious that the ruling spirit over that city was the spirit of Pharmicai.

The word "Pharmicai" he used to identify the ruling spirit over Miami is evidently the Greek word from which we get our word pharmacy. I must admit that when this man spoke of the "spirit of Pharmicai" that ruled over Miami, I did not think he was serious. After a moment, however, I realized he was. His explanation sounded very spiritual, especially because he used a Greek word. His explanation, however, was unsound, having no precedence in the scriptures. Perhaps the only reason Miami has a drug problem is because it is a port city and a doorway to South America.

Currently, some ministers are travelling to major cities and "warring against the strongholds" in those cities. All their prayer and militant praise is directed against the devil. Some of these individuals are very forceful. Some shout till they lose their voices. Some actually dress up in military fatigues! They are trying to accomplish by the strength of the flesh what can only be accomplished in the Spirit. Their intentions are noble and their zeal is commendable, but their doctrine and their activities are unbiblical. They are sincerely wrong.

So-called spiritual leaders who are aggressively teaching and promoting this kind of spiritual warfare are teaching doctrines that Jesus, Paul, and other New Testament leaders never taught. Jesus taught His disciples that if they preached the Word of God in a particular city and were rejected, they should shake the dust off their feet and go to another city [Luke 10:8-16]. He didn't instruct them to pull down hindering strongholds. Jesus informed the local church in Pergamos that they lived in the city where Satan had his seat. Jesus never suggested, however, that they pull down the strong man over their city. He did, however, instruct them to correct two doctrinal errors in their church [Revelation 2:13-16].

When Paul came to Athens and saw the whole city given to idolatry, he didn't pray or praise down strongholds. He, "preached unto them Jesus, and the resurrection" [Acts 17:16-17]. When he came to Ephesus, well known for its worship of the goddess Diana, Paul did not pull down the demonic strong woman over that city or praise down strongholds. He preached and taught the Word of God for two years. Acts 19:20 records that "mightily grew the word of God and prevailed." When persecution forced the early believers out of Jerusalem, God didn't tell then to go back to their city and capture it for Him. They just left! Jesus wept over this same city because He could do nothing for their spiritual condition.

Some sincerely wrong ministers simply get hyped up and excited in their preaching and veer from sound teaching into unsound teaching. They are like a person who is driving a car, but not watching the road. I heard one minister who was preaching faster than he could think say that most teenagers are demon possessed and need deliverance. That is silly. There may be a few that need deliverance, but definitely not most. In the heat of his message, however, this minister made an unsound sweeping statement. If not corrected, this could lead his church into a doctrinal extreme and unprofitable spiritual activity. This minister is not a false teacher; he is sincerely wrong.

Some sincerely wrong ministers teach that every Christian has a demon. Every problem, whether it be fear, lust, anger, or overeating is attributed to a demon. The only solution, according to these ministers, is ongoing deliverance. Some teach that Christians need deliverance checkups every few months.

How I wish this doctrine was true! Christian life would be so simple if all we needed was an occasional deliverance session. We wouldn't have to crucify the flesh. We wouldn't have to "mortify the deeds of the body" [Romans 8:13]. We wouldn't have to discipline ourselves at all. When the demon making us act a certain way was cast out, we would be free in that area.

This doctrine, however, is not true. It is not in agreement with the teachings of Jesus or of any other New Testament teacher. Those who teach this doctrine and carry out the naturally corresponding activities have transgressed well beyond the boundary line of sound doctrine. They may be very sincere, but they are very wrong!

Spiritual Children Playing Church

Sincerely wrong spiritual leaders are often like mischievous children. They are always instigating some kind of mischief, always "pressing their luck," always up to something new. And they lead other children into their mischief. This is not because they are *bad* children. It is because they *are* children. Children love whatever is exciting and new. They become bored with the same toys and the same games. They are constantly getting into things that they should not get into. This is the nature of a child. This is why children cannot raise children.

When I see what some ministers do in the name of God and hear some of the things they teach, I often think to myself, "It is nothing more than spiritual children playing church." Some individuals who gain leadership positions in the body of Christ are not qualified to be spiritual leaders. They are sincere, but they are children themselves. The body of Christ needs adult leadership! It needs sound leaders who can pass on spiritual soundness and health to those who are still children.

Some Will Receive Correction — Some Will Not

Some sincerely wrong spiritual leaders will not receive correction. If another minister offers a suggestion or correction concerning their doctrine, they will label that minister as a persecutor of the righteous. If a sound minister questions their teachings, he will be considered a tool of the devil to hinder the new move of God. These leaders are "right." They have heard from God and that is the final word on the subject.

Others may be open to correction and instruction as was a New Testament teacher named Apollos. When Aquila and Priscilla heard Apollos preaching, they recognized that he did not know all the truth. He was not completely wrong. He was just missing part of the truth and didn't realize it. Aquila and Priscilla, "expounded unto him the way of God more perfectly" [Acts 18:26]. Apollos received their correction, adjusted his teaching, and became an even more excellent minister of the truth of God.

Beware of the Sincerely Wrong

Though sincerely wrong ministers may not have ungodly ambitions, they are not a positive influence, but a negative force in the body of Christ. Rather than being good ministers of Christ, they assist in promoting instability in the church. This is unfortunate because some of them have honest hearts and good intentions. Good intentions, however, do not produce sound local bodies!

Sincerely wrong ministers usually start out in the Word of God, but they finish outside the boundaries of sound doctrine. They do not intentionally promote error, but they do promote error!

Sincerely wrong ministers are dangerous for several reasons. First, they are dangerous because they are ministers within the sound body of Christ. They look, sound, and act like ministers should look, sound, and act. They may be respected as spiritual leaders. In fact many of them have authentic callings and anointings upon their lives. Some are sincerely wrong pastors of local churches. Some are sincerely wrong travelling teachers. Some are sincerely wrong evangelists. Some are sincerely wrong apostles and prophets.

Second, sincerely wrong ministers are dangerous because of their sincerity. They do not just pretend to be sincere. They are sincere! They believe they are called of God and sound in doctrine. Because they are convinced that they are right, their presentation is completely convincing. It is said that the best salesman is the one who believes in his product and uses it himself. This is also true of sincerely wrong ministers. When believers perceive the genuine sincerity of the sincerely wrong, they let down their guard.

Individuals in this final category of unsound spiritual leadership will very likely not be suspected as unsound spiritual leaders. If they are not recognized, however, and judged as unsound, believers will ignorantly follow them in their error.

Summary

Answer to Question One: Sincerely Wrong Ministers are saved and have a personal relationship with God. They err in doctrine, however, not holding fast to the written scriptures.

Answer to Question Two: Sincerely wrong ministers operate within sound local bodies. They may be respected members, even leaders, of sound church organizations.

Answer to Question Three: The intentions of sincerely wrong ministers are not evil. Most often they are innocent in their motivation, sincerely desiring to serve God and to help people. They are deceived, however, either by their own reasonings or by demonic influence, and become deceivers of others.

CONCLUSION

Not all unsound spiritual leadership is the same. They have varying relationships with Jesus Christ, varying levels of involvement with the church, and varying intentions. They promote different levels of unsound doctrine, employ different methods of deception, and have different degrees of awareness concerning their own identity and activity.

All false and unsound spiritual leaders share one common trait, however. They are dangerous to believers and to the church. Their doctrines and their spiritual activities gender unsettledness, error, confusion, and division. They can cause spiritual disaster both to individual believers and to local churches.

For believers and local churches the most dangerous categories of unsound spiritual leadership are the last two. These are the "Unsound Teachers Among Us" and "Sincerely Wrong Ministers." Because these unsound spiritual leaders profess faith in Christ, operate in the midst of the sound body, and claim to be teachers of the Word, they may be readily accepted as sound leaders.

·~12~·
Why Do Once Sound Leaders Err?

*I*n our previous chapter we studied four categories of unsound spiritual leadership. Three of those four categories were comprised of individuals who were formerly sound in spiritual life and part of the church. Undoubtedly, some of the individuals in these three categories were formerly sound spiritual leaders. Some may have had significant followings and experienced success in the ministry. Some may have done marvelous things for God and seemed destined for a life of great service in the kingdom of God. For various reasons, however, these once sound members left the sound body of Christ, departed from sound doctrine and sound spiritual life, and became the promoters of unsound doctrine and unhealthy spiritual activity.

Why did these individuals get off the mark spiritually? Why did they become unstable? Whey did they abandon sound doctrine? Why did and why do once sound leaders leave sound doctrine, sound spiritual life, and sound local bodies and become the promoters of unsound doctrine and unsound spiritual life? In this chapter we will explore some of the reasons answering the question, "Why do once sound spiritual leaders err?"

ONE: THEY GIVE HEED TO SEDUCING SPIRITS AND DOCTRINES OF DEMONS

In these last days, some sound ministers will leave sound doctrine and sound spiritual life because they will give heed to seducing spirits and doctrines of demons. Paul warned Timothy of this in his first letter saying,

> "Now the Spirit speaketh expressly, that in the latter times some shall depart from the faith, giving heed to seducing spirits, and doctrines of devils; Speaking lies in hypocrisy..."

> I Timothy 4:1-2

The word "expressly" Paul used concerning the Holy Spirit's warning comes from the Greek *rhetos* and means, "in stated terms." The Amplified Bible uses the word "distinctly." The Holy Spirit has sounded forth a clear warning concerning the latter days. His prophetic word will come to pass. According to Him, some believers (including ministers) will depart from the faith because they entertain thoughts and doctrines promoted to them by demon spirits.

Just as the Holy Spirit endeavors to guide believers *into* the truth, so seducing spirits endeavor to draw believers *away* from the truth. One of their primary activities in the latter days will be to woo believers (especially ministers) away from sound doctrine. After once sound ministers embrace and become entrenched in unsound doctrine, they become promoters of it. They will, Paul said, "[speak] lies in hypocrisy." After becoming unsound themselves, they become the devil's accomplices.

It may be hard to comprehend that a sound minister could embrace a doctrine of demons. We must understand, however, that the devil's accomplices are extremely cunning and deceptive. They do not seduce with doctrines that are obviously contrary to sound doctrine. They seduce with doctrines that appear very spiritual. Only by deceiving in this careful way is it possible for them to lead sound ministers away from the truth.

Both of the doctrines of demons Paul cited as examples could find ready acceptance in our day. Consider, for example, the demonic doctrine of forbidding to marry. It is not hard to imagine that in these latter days seducing spirit will try to influence ministers with "deep spiritual thoughts" like, "We are so close to the end of time that it would be better not to marry." A minister may hear this thought, wrongly conclude that he has received a fresh revelation from heaven (a now word from the Holy Spirit), and begin to promote this demonic revelation.

Can you see how a charismatic minister could hear a demonic teaching like this, wrongly conclude that it was a word from the Lord, and set out to promote his "new message from the throne for this generation?" He might preach, "God needs a young army of totally sold out believers in this hour! To fulfill that calling we must be undivided in our attention. In these last days we should not marry! Give yourself completely to the Lord! Go all the way for God!" If you hear a "spiritual leader" forbidding young people to marry because of the closeness of the end of time, be sure to run away. Why? He has given heed to and is promoting a doctrine of demons!

Recently, I heard a very similar doctrine of demons. A young couple had been strongly advised by their minister not to have children because it was the end times. The man had an operation and now the young couple cannot have children. This, too, is a doctrine of demons being promoted by so-called ministers!

A second doctrine of demons Paul mentioned to Timothy was the teaching to abstain from meats. This teaching and other teachings about diet could also find ready acceptance at this time. This teaching, however, is a doctrine of demons. It sounds spiritual, but is in direct conflict with the Word of God. Notice Paul's words of corrective instruction concerning this teaching,

> "...God has created (meats) to be received with thanksgiving of them which believe and know the truth. For every creature of God is good, and nothing to be refused, if it be received with thanksgiving: For it is sanctified by the word of God and prayer."

> *I Timothy 4:3-5*

Christians who "know the truth" can eat meat and enjoy it as a gift from God. Every creature God has made is good and can be eaten. Nothing need be refused. Of course, believers must use wisdom, temperance, and self control in their diets just as they use wisdom, temperance, and self control in every area of life. But any food can be eaten if it is received with thanksgiving and sanctified by the Word of God and prayer. That is the truth concerning Christians and food. Following his words of correction, Paul told Timothy,

> "If thou put the brethren in remembrance of these things (specifically right teaching about marriage and about food), thou shalt be a good minister of Jesus Christ, nourished up in the words of faith and of good doctrine, whereunto thou hast attained."

> *I Timothy 4:6*

Timothy was to put the brethren in remembrance of sound doctrine and warn them of teachings that were unsound. He was to keep himself and those he ministered to "in the words of faith" and in "good doctrine." If he refused unsound doctrines and taught the truth, he would be, "a good minister of Jesus Christ." Good ministers *hold fast* to words of faith and good doctrine and promote them in the church. Ministers who *let go* of the words of faith and good doctrine and give heed to seducing spirits and doctrines of demons become unsound themselves and the promoters of unsound doctrine.

The two unsound doctrines Paul cited as examples of doctrines of demons confirm the fact that doctrines of demons are seldom far out and obviously false. On the contrary, many of them sound very spiritual. In order to have any chance of being embraced by ministers who are born of the truth and walking in the truth, doctrines of demons must sound like the truth. The unsound doctrines promoted by demons and seducing spirits will not only not sound dangerous; they will often sound very spiritual.

It is not impossible that truly called and sound leaders in the church, without even being aware of what is happening, give heed to the whispered thoughts of seducing spirits. Not every thought that comes into ministers' minds comes from God. Satan and his demon spirits also have the ability to introduce thoughts into ministers' minds.

This happened to Judas, one of Jesus' hand picked disciples. He was chosen to be one of the twelve apostles. He had obtained a part in that ministry. He had been specially chosen to a place of significant spiritual leadership [Acts 1:17, 20]. But Satan was successful in infiltrating his thoughts. What started as a Satanically inspired thought concluded with Judas abandoning his spiritual position and becoming the arch enemy of Jesus Christ and a traitor to the kingdom in which he had once served. Luke 22:3-4 says,

> *"Then entered Satan into Judas surnamed Iscariot, being of the number of the twelve. And he went his way, and communed with the chief priests and captains, how he might betray him (Jesus) unto them."*
>
> Luke 22:3-4

Satan did not suddenly force himself upon Judas at this moment. He had been speaking to him for some time about this idea. He continued to tempt Judas with thoughts of self-gain and personal recognition until he gave in. Only when Judas yielded to these thoughts did Satan take over. Then Judas, "went his way." This is exactly what happens when ministers yield to the doctrines inspired by demons and seducing spirits. They literally go their own way rather than staying in The Way and in the truth.

The Influence of Lying Spirits

In II Chronicles 18 there is an interesting Old Testament example of the influence of lying spirits. In this story the Lord wanted to entice king Ahab to engage in a battle that would bring about his fall. It was finally determined that a lying spirit speaking through the mouths of false prophets would be the means to Ahab's enticement. The true prophet Micaiah revealed what transpired in the realm of the spirit preceding the false prophesying of the false prophets. He said,

> *"Then there came out a spirit, and stood before the Lord, and said, I will entice him. And the Lord said unto him, Wherewith? And he said, I will go out, and be a lying spirit in the mouth of all his prophets. And the Lord said, Thou shalt entice him, and thou shalt also prevail: go out, and do even so. Now therefore, behold,*

the Lord hath put a lying spirit in the mouth of these thy prophets…"

II Chronicles 18:20-22

A lying spirit successfully influenced king Ahab's prophets. Under its inspiration, they errantly prophesied concerning the battle he was considering, promising him victory. The prophet Micaiah then prophesied the truth and revealed the influence of the lying spirit upon the false prophets. This revelation stirred up the anger of one false prophet named Zedekiah. He hit Micaiah and then asked this question,

"…Which way went the Spirit of the Lord from me to speak to thee?"

II Chronicles 18:23

The prophet Zedekiah did not realize that he had been influenced by a lying spirit rather than by the Spirit of God. Apparently he had become overconfident and assumed that everything he "heard" was from the Spirit of God. He did not, therefore, discern the source of his inspiration. He did not realize he had yielded to a lying spirit. Micaiah answered Zedekiah's request for an explanation by telling him,

"…Behold, thou shalt see on that day when thou shalt go into an inner chamber to hide thyself."

II Chronicles 18:24

What happened to the prophets of Ahab is a vivid picture of what can happen to New Testament leadership. Sound spiritual leaders, if they do not spend time in the closet (in the Word and in prayer), become spiritually dull and, therefore, susceptible to voices other than the voice of God and spirits other than the Spirit of God. If they entertain and then yield to false spirits, they become the promoters of doctrines of demons. Most often these ministers do not even suspect that their doctrine is not from God.

Some ministers, because they have heard from God in the past, forget that they could be misled. They assume that all their thoughts are divinely inspired and, therefore, fail to consider the possibility that some of their doctrines could be wrong. Because of an "I'm right" attitude, these ministers can be easily deceived by seducing spirits.

The Holy Spirit has sounded out a clear warning concerning the latter days activity of seducing spirits and demons. They will be effective in misleading some ministers into unsound doctrine and unsound spiritual life. Those who are misled into unsound doctrine will then become promoters of the unsound doctrines they have embraced.

TWO: THEY OVERESTIMATE THEMSELVES

Some once sound ministers begin their descent from spiritual soundness by esteeming themselves too highly. They suppose themselves to be prophetic leaders, pace-setters in the body of Christ. They imagine that they have come onto the spiritual scene as special envoys from heaven, bringing the current directive from the throne of God. When they begin to think, speak, and act this way, many who are looking for that kind of dynamic, heaven sent leader believe them, thus reinforcing their errant thinking. Their ministries grow in number, confirming their elevated opinions of themselves.

Some ministers become deluded in their minds concerning their spiritual capacities and their importance. As far as they are concerned there is no need for them to question themselves and certainly no need for them to listen to the warnings of others. They are called and anointed of God and they are right. That is the end of the discussion! When ministers step out beyond their proper limit, however, they become fascilitators of instability in the body of Christ and risk becoming the promoters of false doctrine.

Paul gave this solemn spiritual admonition to the believers at Rome,

"For I say, through the grace given unto me, to every man that is among you, not to think of himself more highly than he ought to think; but to think soberly, according as God hath dealt to every man the measure of faith."

Romans 12:3

Paul warned all believers, including ministers, not to think of themselves more highly than they ought to think, but soberly, according to what God had dealt to them in the way of gracing, gifts, and spiritual abilities. Ministers must estimate themselves honestly, according to the proportion of their calling and gifting from God. They should think soberly — rationally and sound mindedly. They must be especially careful, said Paul, not think too highly of themselves.

It is possible for a minister to become so intoxicated with his own gifts and anointings (whether real or imagined) that his thinking is no longer sober. He has estimated himself to be far more than he really is. His imagination, rather than his sober mind, has given the final verdict on his calling. If this individual maintains a distance from true spiritual leaders and shields those who follow him from true spiritual leaders, he will meet very little resistance to his charade. Unfortunately, those who say they are more and act like they are more are often received as more.

When ministers assume that they are spiritual giants specially commissioned by God in their generation, they also assume that their doctrines and opinions are right. They assume that every voice they hear is the voice of the Holy Spirit and every new thought they think is revelation from heaven. At this point they are extremely vulnerable to error.

I heard one young minister say that God told him he was called to be the leader of a special, very mature remnant. When I heard these words I thought to myself, "Doesn't God realize how dangerous it is to say those words to a zealous young novice?" The fact of the matter is that this minister heard exactly what he wanted to hear. By crediting God with the "word of prophesy," however, he validated his own ministry and heightened people's perception of him. After all, God called him to lead a special remnant with a special assignment. This kind of elite and "We're the only ones following God" attitude is very dangerous. This man, in his aggressive pursuit of spiritual leadership, overestimated his own calling and his own spiritual capacity and may well have taken his first step toward unscriptural thinking and unspiritual activity.

Outside One's Commission is Dangerous Territory

Some ministers are not content within the limits of their commission. Rather than faithfully serving God in the gifts He has allotted to them, they presume to be more, say they are more, and convince people they are more. When ministers reach beyond the limits of their callings, they venture outside their jurisdictions, outside the will of God, and beyond their spiritual capacities. At this point they are prime candidates for error.

In II Corinthians 10:13-15, Paul expressed his personal concern about going beyond what he was called and anointed to do. His words concerning the limitations of his commission are profound. Especially those who are called to the ministry should listen carefully. Paul wrote,

> *"But we will not boast of things without (or outside) our measure, but according to the measure of the rule which God hath distributed to us...For we stretch not ourselves beyond our measure...Not boasting of things without (or outside) our measure..."*

II Corinthians 10:13-15

Notice how the Amplified Bible reads,

> *"We, on the other hand, will not boast beyond our legitimate province and proper limit, but will keep within the limits [of our commission which] God has allotted us as our measuring line...For we are not overstepping the limits of our province and stretching beyond our ability...We do not boast beyond our proper limit...still within the limits of our commission."*

II Corinthians 10:13-15 Amp

Notice that in speaking of his divine commission, Paul repeatedly used the word "limits." He did not speak about stretching out into greater callings and greater anointings. He was not constantly pressing for more. He purposed, rather, not to extend beyond the limits of his commission. His commission from God was the absolute and final measuring line by which he planned and evaluated all his ministry activity.

To every minister God has given a commission, a divine calling. That commission not only specifies what a minister is anointed to do, but also specifies what that minister is not anointed to do. Paul, a wise minister, said that he was not, "overstepping the limits of (his) province and stretching beyond (his) ability." Those who overstep the limits of their commission also stretch beyond their ability. When they stretch beyond their God-given ability, they become susceptible to error.

Within one's commission there is a grace and an anointing. Outside one's commission, however, there is no anointing. When a minister steps outside his commission, he steps outside his anointing and becomes susceptible not only to the devil and his schemes, but also to the inflated thoughts of his own mind. Some ministers have transgressed the boundaries of sound doctrine and entered into unsound spiritual activity because they stretched beyond their spiritual capacity.

Desiring To Be Teachers

In his first letter to Timothy, Paul spoke of individuals who were pressing for a place of spiritual leadership. He wrote,

> *"From which some having swerved, have turned aside unto vain jangling; Desiring to be teachers of the law; understanding neither what they say, nor whereof they affirm."*

> I Timothy 1:6-7

The Amplified Bible's translation of this text is revealing. It says,

> *"But certain individuals have missed the mark...[and] have wandered away...They are ambitious to be doctors of the Law...but they have no understanding either of the words and terms they use or of the subjects about which they make [such] dogmatic assertions."*

> I Timothy 1:6-7 Amp

This is an accurate description of some who become unsound spiritual leaders. They have a personal ambition to be spiritual leaders, but they do not understand the meaning of the words they speak or comprehend the subjects about which they claim to be experts. Consequently they have "swerved aside" into vain jangling and unsound doctrine.

The word "swerve" Paul used in this text means, "to miss the mark." It is the same word he used to describe the dangerous error of two formerly sound men, Hymenaeus and Philetus. Concerning these two men, Paul said,

"Who concerning the truth have erred (swerved)...and overthrow the faith of some."

II Timothy 2:18

The fact that these men swerved away from the truth reveals that they were once sound in the truth. They had not discontinued their spiritual journey, but had turned onto a wrong road. When they left the path of truth, they became unsound ministers. Those who trusted their leadership also left the path of truth and took the road of error with them.

It is no small thing for individuals to take titles to themselves and try to stand in places of spiritual leadership they are not called to. Outside one's calling is a dangerous place. David, even though he was anointed to be king over Israel, stayed within the will of God while Saul finished his time in office. Because David did this, he prospered. Absolum, on the other hand, was judged by God because he attempted to usurp an office he was not called to. During the days of Moses' leadership, Korah and his followers died for the same reason. They, too, had tried to take a place of leadership they were not called to. Modern day ministers who aspire to be more than God has called them to be will not only fall into error themselves, but will be instruments of offense, confusion, and unhealthy doctrine in the body of Christ.

These Seldom Receive Correction

It is very unlikely that a minister who overestimates himself and gets involved in unsound spiritual life will suspect, much less admit, that he is wrong. "No," he will say, "not me. I couldn't be wrong. I've heard from heaven. Look at the results! Look at how large a church I have built. Look at how many people buy my books. Look at how many people love my ministry. I couldn't be wrong!"

Paul instructed Titus to reject a man who remained a heretic after two admonitions. Then he said,

"...he that is such is subverted, and sinneth, being condemned of himself."

Titus 3:11

The word "subverted" means to change completely. Paul's words to Titus concerned individuals who were once sound leaders, but had changed completely, embracing unsound doctrine and unsound spiritual life. It is clear that Paul expected some heretics to refuse correction because his instructions to Titus provided a course of action to take for those who did so.

When unsound ministers esteem themselves more highly than they should, it is very difficult to bring them correction. Because they regard themselves as spiritually superior, everyone else is regarded as spiritually inferior and, therefore, not qualified to help. If someone does confront their revelation, they fall back on the "fact" that they are called to such and such an office and are, therefore, right. Often they are afraid to face the reality that they are not all they think they are.

Those who think they could never be wrong are in a very dangerous spiritual condition. Paul said in I Corinthians 10:12,

> "...let him that thinketh he standeth take heed lest he fall."
>
> *I Corinthians 10:12*

Ministers should remember that God used a simple donkey to keep the prophet Balaam from death! Many times the simple and sincere have far more honest and accurate spiritual vision than those who suppose they are greatly anointed!

THREE: PUSHED BY UNDEVELOPED BELIEVERS

Not only do ministers who overestimate themselves get off the track of sound doctrine and spiritual life. Ministers who are exalted and lifted up by the believers who follow them are also in danger of wandering from the path of sound spiritual life.

It can occur that believers elevate ministers higher than the ministers themselves can handle. When believers persist in praising and flattering the ministers they follow, pride can set in. In I Corinthians 4:6, Paul wrote to the church at Corinth about their tendency to exalt ministers. He said,

> "And these things, brethren, I have in a figure transferred to myself and to Apollos for your sakes; that ye might learn in us not to think of men above that which is written, that no one of you be puffed up for one against another."
>
> *I Corinthians 4:6*

The Amplified Bible's rendering of this scripture is more clear. It says,

> "Now I have applied all this [about parties and factions] to myself and Apollos for your sakes, brethren, so that from what I have said of us [as illustrations] you may learn [to think of men in accordance with Scripture and] not to go beyond that which is written; that none of you may be puffed up and inflated with pride and boast in favor of one [minister and teacher] against another."
>
> *I Corinthians 4:6 Amp*

The believers in Corinth were puffing up their favorite ministers against other ministers. They were saying things like, "You are a much better teacher than so-and-so." This kind of practice on the part of believers can eventually cause ministers to be puffed up about themselves. Paul instructed the believers in Corinth,

> *"So let no one exult proudly concerning men [boasting of having this or that man as a leader]..."*
>
> I Corinthians 3:21 Amp

It is a very strong human tendency to praise other men. But the praises of the people do not help the pride problem of those in the ministry. And pride sets ministers up for a fall!

Some of the greatest ministers of the near past fell into spiritual error because of this very problem. For example, John Alexander Dowie, a man who had a fantastic healing ministry and was at the forefront of ministry in his own generation, fell into error because he yielded to those who were trying to convince him that he was Elijah. When he began to think he was, he became lifted up in pride and fell into error. It was only a short time before he passed off the scene.

Some ministers make the dangerous mistake of surrounding themselves with flatterers. They would rather be continually reassured of their importance than confronted about their shortcomings. Flatterers, however, will not tell ministers the truth because they will be dismissed from the inner circle. Instead, they stroke ministers with their words, telling them how wonderful they are. Ministers eventually become convinced by these flatterers that they are, indeed, wonderful. From that moment their fall from soundness is not far away.

Every minister of God should include in his list of friends those who have nothing to gain by flattering and nothing to lose by telling the truth. These true friends will help keep ministers honest and out of the ditch of unsound spiritual activity and unsound doctrine.

FOUR: NOT CAREFUL WITH THE SCRIPTURES

Sometimes spiritual leaders get off in doctrine and spiritual life because they are careless with the Word of God. This problem is prevalent in our time, especially among charismatic ministers. Many are pushing the limits of what could reasonably be called sound doctrine. One minister will twist a scripture a little bit and the next one will push it a bit further until, without even realizing what has happened, whole areas of teaching are well outside the boundaries of what could honestly be called sound doctrine. Ministers who do not handle the Word of God carefully are often the inventors and promoters of unsound and even false doctrine.

Paul spoke often of handling the Word of God in a sincere, honest, and careful manner. In II Corinthians 4:2, he said,

"But (we) have renounced the hidden things of dishonesty, not walking in crafti-ness, nor handling the word of God deceitfully..."

II Corinthians 4:2

Ministers must be very careful when handling the Word of God. They should stay with what is clear, obvious, and sound. If ministers don't persist in the basics, they tend to drift over into unsound doctrine.

For example, I heard one minister comment concerning Jesus' teaching that believers could command the sycamine tree to move and "it should obey you" [Luke 17:6]. This minister said that Jesus was not teaching that the tree would obey faith-filled words, but that our faith would obey our command and go move the tree. He said, "You can just relax and let your faith go do the work of moving the tree." Not only is this contrary to what this scripture obviously means and contrary to the way it has been correctly interpreted for years — that faith filled words can move mountains — but I must ask, "What is the point of trying to dig out something different from every scripture?" These kind of mental gymnastics do not lead to soundness in doctrine.

Ministers should not dig so hard looking for a new twist on every sub-ject. By so doing, they run the grave risk of twisting and distorting doc-trine. They end up handling the Word of God in flippant manner. Pushing the limits on scriptural interpretation leads to unsound doctrine. Ministers should also examine and scrutinize their doctrines in light of the whole counsel of God's Word. Has their doctrine been approved by God? Do they even care whether or not their doctrine is sound or are they more con-cerned with whether people like their teachings and follow their ministries? Do they want to hear God say, "Well done," or do they want to hear people to say, "Wow!"

Will Not Study

Some ministers fall into error because they will not study. Because they will not study, they have nothing with which to compare what they think the Holy Spirit is showing them. They also have nothing with which to compare what they hear other ministers teach. If they would study diligently and become well acquainted with the Word of God, they would immediately recognize unsound doctrine. The Word within them would speak to them and arrest their thoughts and imaginations. Most sincerely wrong leaders have not studied the Word till God approved their doctrine. Rather than *wrestling* with the Word of God until they develop a strong grasp of doctrine, they *wrest* the Word and come up with winds of doctrine [II Peter 2:16].

Paul told young Timothy,

> *"Study to shew thyself approved unto God, a workman that needeth not to be ashamed, rightly dividing the word of truth."*
>
> *II Timothy 2:15*

The word "study" in this passage actually means, "to be diligent." Paul exhorted Timothy to be diligent in his preparation to be a workman. He was to be persistent in study until God approved his doctrine! If ministers are not diligent with the Word of Truth there remains the possibility that they will wrongly divide it. It is seldom a problem that unsound ministers deny the Word of Truth. The problem is that they wrongly divide the Word of Truth!

This is where the unsound teachers who negatively affected the church in Antioch missed it. They were teaching believers that they should be circumcised, "after the manner of Moses" [Acts 15:1]. These unsound teachers were not denying the Word. They were wrongly dividing the Word. They failed to realize that there is a great division between the Old Testament and the New Testament and that the Word of God must always be divided at the cross. They failed to realize, therefore, that Old Testament circumcision had been done away in Christ. They had scriptures to prove their point, but because they were wrongly dividing the Word, they concluded in error.

Timothy was to be diligent in rightly dividing the truth so that he would be a, "workman that needeth not to be ashamed." If ministers do not rightly divide the Word of Truth there will come a day when they will be ashamed. It may be in this life. A day may come when they realize they have been wrong and have deceived themselves and misled countless others. In this moment they will be ashamed. If not in this life, then at the judgement they will be ashamed when the books are opened and they realize that rather than building with gold, silver, and precious stones, they have built with wood, hay, and stubble. Their works shall burn. They will be saved, but as by fire [I Corinthians 3:12-15].

Failure to diligently study the Word of God is a principal reason that ministers get off into unsound doctrine. They only know part of the Word and they only know the Word in part. Therefore, not only can Satan use the Word to lead these individuals off, but in their own minds they can get off.

One of my great concerns for the church of this generation is that ministers, especially in charismatic circles, will not study. Too much is available to them. Books abound. Magazines give them messages. Television, cassettes, and videos give them "revelation." They have no idea what it means to take a subject, or even one text of scripture, and wrestle with it, pray over it, and meditate upon it till they truly understand. Many of our modern day ministers have a very limited revelation of the whole counsel of the Word of God. They understand a few pet doctrines and favorite scriptures, but are bankrupt when it comes to the full counsel of God. When our spiritual leaders are thus educated, they are a risk rather than a boon to the body of Christ.

They Pray More Than They Study

Sometimes ministers get into trouble because they pray more than they study. Now please don't misunderstand me. Prayer is absolutely essential; especially vital for those called to the ministry. The early apostles said that they would not leave prayer or the ministry of the Word [Acts 6:2,4]. Paul spoke very often of his life of prayer. Ministers, however, who spend all their time "in the Spirit" and have a limited knowledge of the Word of God will be prime targets for the enemy to seduce with strange doctrine and thinking.

When ministers concentrate on prayer without having a real grasp of the whole counsel of God, they can formulate and hold to thoughts that do not agree with the Word of God. Some of these thoughts will come from their own unrenewed minds. Some will be inspired by Satan or his demons. If, on the other hand, ministers become grounded first in the written Word of God, they will have something with which to compare what they hear in prayer. They will be able test their "revelations" against the written Word of God.

Women should be extra careful in this area of prayer because they are naturally constituted with a greater sensitivity both spiritually and intuitively. This is why women are usually the first in the family to be saved and filled with the Holy Spirit. Because women are by nature more spiritually sensitive, they often give themselves to prayer more than men do. Just as they are more sensitive to the Spirit of God, however, they can be more sensitive to other spirits. For this reason, they can be more susceptible to deception.

A part of Paul's first letter to Timothy concerned women who were vying for spiritual leadership and usurping authority. These women were likely part of the sect of gnostics. They thought and taught that they had a greater capacity for spiritual revelation than men. They believed that Eve, by partaking of the tree of the knowledge of good and evil, had entered into and then led Adam into a greater level of experiential spiritual knowledge. Paul informed Timothy, however, that in the beginning Eve was deceived and, being deceived, was in the transgression [I Timothy 2:14]. Eve did not enter into more spiritual knowledge by partaking of the tree of knowledge of good and evil. Rather, she was deceived, fell into spiritual death, and then led Adam into spiritual death.

Undoubtedly, Satan approached Eve rather than Adam because she was the more susceptible of the two. She was more open to spiritual influence. It is likely that Paul had this very thought in mind when he told the believers in Corinth,

> *"For this cause ought the woman to have power on her head because of the angels."*

> I Corinthians 11:10

Paul suggested here that it was profitable for a woman to be under authority because of the angels. The "angels" Paul was referring to were not the ministering angels of God, but the seductive angels of Satan. Paul's point in this case was that submission was spiritually safe for women because of their susceptibility to seducing spirits.

Paul instructed Timothy not to allow women to usurp authority over the men [I Timothy 2:2]. He did not write this instruction because it is wrong for women to be in the ministry, but because the gnostic women of his day had yielded themselves to unsound doctrine and sinful practices and were promoting their brand of spirituality in the church.

This does not mean, by any means, that women cannot be called to the ministry or to prayer. Women should, however, exercise caution because of their greater sensitivity to spiritual things. A woman's greater sensitivity can be used to tremendous advantage if it is balanced with a strong foundation in the scriptures as a safe guard. If women in the ministry do not study, however, they will be primary target of the attacks of Satan and his seducing spirits.

Ministers should consider Jesus as an example of the importance of knowing the written scriptures. When he was twelve years old he had a command of the written Word of God that astonished even those whose whole life was devoted to the study of it. He launched His ministry by quoting from Isaiah 61. When he faced the devil, He relied strictly upon the written scriptures. "It is written," was His defense against the words of the devil. When confronted by religious leaders, He continually referred them to the scriptures, not to His own opinions. Many, many times He prefaced His responses to them saying, "Have you not read?" Certainly, Jesus knew how to be in the Spirit. He spent much time in prayer and in special fellowship with the Father. But He also had a deep knowledge and a strong personal grasp of the doctrines of the written scriptures.

Don't Wait on God to Get Their Own Revelation

In the book of Jeremiah the Lord said this concerning false leaders,

> *"...I am against the prophets...that steal my words every one from his neighbor."*
> Jeremiah 23:30

Some ministers, rather than being students of the Word and the Spirit just preach what they hear other ministers preach. Ministers should not get their "word" from other ministers. They are called to be preachers, not parrots!

I can recall several times in the past years hearing well respected ministers declare something they thought the Holy Spirit was emphasizing. In a very short time every pastor and every travelling minister was saying the same thing. They were not saying it because they heard it from God themselves, but because someone they respected in the ministry said it. Ministers who only repeat what other ministers teach (to appear as if they are "in the know") are out of spiritual order!

Often these "parrot-ministers" misinterpret or misunderstand what the ministers they are mimicking really said. They preach his message, but it is misinterpreted. When they spread this misunderstanding, they cause confusion and problems in the body of Christ. I can think of many times, especially in my own overseas travels, that I have encountered believers who were confused because of what some minister said another minister said. This is sad!

Some ministers are so wrapped up in preaching "hot" and "cutting-edge" messages that they forget to listen to the Spirit of God themselves. A recent example of this truth was the message, "We are the Joshua Generation." I either heard or read that statement so many times over a two year period that it was almost comical. Did all the ministers who preached this message get it while they were alone in their prayer closets? I think not! No, what happened is that they heard one of their favorite ministers say it and saw that it got a good response. Then they started saying it. Then others heard them and started saying it. Then someone wrote a book. And this teaching spread throughout the whole body.

In 1983, I heard a number of ministers "declare" that the next year was going to begin the great outpouring and moving of God's Spirit that we had been waiting for. I'm not sure where it got started, but it seemed like everyone was saying it. I had a different witness, however, in my own spirit. I felt that what the Spirit of God was saying was that we were in a time of building. I felt that we were in a season when God was giving local churches time to prepare themselves by becoming established in the Word of God. Because that was in my own heart, that was the course I followed for a number of years in my own teaching to local churches.

Ministers must get in their own prayer closets, listen to the Holy Spirit themselves, and quit getting their messages from their "neighbors." They must stand in the counsel of the Lord and listen. Some have been so busy "declaring" what they have heard other ministers say that they don't realize they have long since stepped beyond the boundaries of what God told them to say.

The Road To Error

Many times the road to error is a long and complicated one. Often it is a gradual slipping away that occurs over time. Let's consider briefly one of the very basic routes that ministers take to the destination of doctrinal error.

Often the road to error begins with a particular doctrinal *Emphasis*. A minister will deal with one area of truth in a primary way and on a continual basis. The importance of this truth is magnified above the importance of other areas of truth. As this truth is pushed to the forefront, it becomes a distinguishing mark of that man's ministry. As this truth is given attention over an extended period of time, it begins to become The Truth rather than A Truth.

When this one truth is taught and emphasized too much other areas of truth are ignored or even snubbed as unimportant. Now the minister has moved into an area of *Excess*. Other truths are discounted as unimportant or brushed aside because they are "not what God is emphasizing now." Webster says that "excess" is an amount beyond what is required or appropriate. Too much emphasis being placed on one specific area of truth is excess.

If a minister keeps travelling this direction, he begins to be obsessed with this one area of truth. Now, more than simply overemphasizing a truth, the truth is being warped, stretched, and wrested beyond the boundaries and limitations of the Word. Scriptures are twisted and shaped to fit the "doctrine" he is obsessed with. This minister has now entered into an area of *Extreme*. All truth is now perceived and interpreted through "extreme glasses." Emotional involvement begins at this point and a defensiveness against correction begins to enter in.

When ministers hold fast to their extreme views and refuse to accept correction they are only one step from complete doctrinal *Error*. Their doctrine is now well beyond the boundaries of the written scriptures. What began as an interest in and an emphasis of a particular truth has digressed to the place where doctrine is completely unsound.

When a minister's error becomes apparent, other believers will begin to notice and may attempt to bring correction. When other members of the Body of Christ extend a loving hand to help balance the error, ministers and their followers will resist. They will claim that the devil is persecuting them because they have arrived at a new truth and are the leaders of the next move of God. Rather then recognizing the gentle hand of the Holy Spirit, they see those who try to help as instruments of the devil, persecuting them for their great revelation. They may also think that those who attempt to bring correction are jealous. The "persecution" they receive is, to them, the proof that they are right.

Because this group feels they have stepped into a greater revelation, or a revelation that the rest of the body of Christ "cannot see," they develop an *Elitist* attitude. They say, "We see truth, praise God, that others cannot see." They say, "Bless the hearts of those who persecute us. They can not see the light." This attitude of pride makes it almost impossible to reach those who are errant. Even God cannot help them.

Five: Zeal Without Knowledge

Paul said of Israel that they, "have a zeal for God, but not according to knowledge" [Romans 10:2]. Israel pursued salvation, but they pursued it outside the boundaries of truth. Paul said they, "going about to establish their own righteousness, have not submitted themselves unto the righteousness of God" [Romans 10:3].

Some over zealous ministers are like the nation of Israel. They have zeal without knowledge. They are sincere about accomplishing something for God, but are trying to do the work of God outside the boundaries of the Word of God. Rather than submitting to the truth, they are running after results. They keep pressing buttons and pulling levers hoping one of them will save the world.

Zeal without knowledge is not only vain, it is dangerous. Unfortunately, ministers who are very zealous will often not take the time to study. If they would just slow down and become grounded in the Word of God, they could remain within the boundaries of sound doctrine and spiritual activity. The Lord said of false prophets in the Old Testament that,

> "I have not sent these prophets, yet they ran: I have not spoken to them, yet they prophesied. But if they had stood in my counsel, and had caused my people to hear my words, then they should have turned them from their evil way, and from the evil of their doings."

> *Jeremiah 23:21-22*

There are ministers running in our generation who have not been instructed to run and are not anointed to run. God has not spoken anything special to them, but because they want to be special they are "prophesying." They are declaring, "God said this," and "God said that." But what God really says of these unsound spiritual leaders is, "I have not spoken to them."

Some ministers are so busy trying to win the race that they don't take time to read the roadmap. Do they have energy? Yes! Plenty of it! But energy is not the only component for spiritual success. You see, it takes the same amount of energy to drive down the wrong road as it does to drive down the right road. Some ministers are running further and further away from the path that is lit by the Word of God. The longer they run, the further they get away from the truth!

Some young energetic ministers who talk and preach about "moving out with God" and "exploring new territory" remind me of the early settlers of the United States. These early settlers were young and restless, zealous and unrestrained. They set out to conquer! Not only did they not know where they were going, however. They were also unprepared for what they would encounter on the way.

Being too ambitious or too hasty is dangerous in spiritual life. It has caused some who were truly called of God to become unsound leaders. Some individuals get what they think is a revelation from heaven on Monday and are preaching it on Tuesday! You will find this problem most prevalent among young ministers. This does not mean, of course, that a young minister cannot be accurate in the Word. Young ministers, however, because they lack the wisdom which comes through experience, must be sure they do not lack the wisdom which comes from a thorough knowledge of God's Word!

Those who are zealous, but truly called of God must temper their zeal with knowledge. "Wait on the Lord" is a good word for these ministers. Some of them, if they go into their closets, will discover, as did the false prophets of Micaiah's day, that the Spirit of the Lord is not inspiring their bold declarations of, "Thus saith the Lord." Overzealousness can lead to spiritual instability and unsound doctrine.

SIX: LUST FOR SOMETHING NEW

Some ministers err in doctrine and spiritual life because they are always looking for something new. They get bored preaching the same old message. They feel a need to relight the fire and get people stirred up. And so they look for, or listen for, something new. Any new thought that tickles their ears, they run with saying, "God is doing something new," or, "This is a new move of the Spirit." Because of their unstable spiritual personalities, they easily fall prey to counterfeit things. Ministers should remember: New is not always true!

The continual need for stimulation, for something new, different, or exciting, is a sign of spiritual immaturity. The body of Christ cannot afford to have immature spiritual leaders. It is a problem when believers will not endure sound doctrine. But when those who are called to be spiritual leaders will not endure sound doctrine, the church is certainly headed for trouble!

I have heard a few "exciting new revelations" that some popular modern day ministers are promoting. Some are well outside the boundaries of safe and sound doctrine. They certainly are new revelations. So new even God hasn't heard them yet!

At different times in history men, through the help of the Holy Spirit, have indeed rediscovered truths from God's Word. As these rediscovered truths were preached revivals resulted. Revival, however, is a renewing of something that has laid dormant. It is a rekindling of something that has been lost. Revival is not a creation of something new.

The next new thing that will come on the scene will be the new heaven and the new earth. At this time of reformation God will make all things new. "Behold," He said, "I make all things new" [Revelation 21:5]. Whatever God will do in this generation, He has already done before. Whatever God does in this hour will be precedented in the written scriptures. Those who insist on finding something new will undoubtedly conclude their search in spiritual error!

SEVEN: A PERVERTED DESIRE FOR KNOWLEDGE AND SPIRITUAL EXPERIENCE

Some ministers have a perverted desire for knowledge. Paul wrote in his letter to Timothy that some men are, "Ever learning, and never able to come to the knowledge of the truth" [II Timothy 3:7]. When ministers are too hungry for knowledge, they will go digging for it like a prospector digs for gold. If they dig long enough they will find something. But it could be fool's gold! This was the mistake the early gnostics made. Their hunger for spiritual experience led them past the Word of God and into sexual perversion in the hope of gaining spiritual knowledge.

Several years ago I was invited by a friend to a meeting held by certain ministers. My friend had some questions about their teaching and wanted me to check it out. I found their teaching to be basically Bible-based, but sensed that for them the gaining of revelation was like the head-rush of solving a mathematical problem. I mentioned to my friend that for these ministers the discovery of knowledge was almost like a mental high. Although I could not disagree with what they taught that particular night, I had a sense that I should avoid further meetings. In a short time their meetings digressed and eventually their ministry closed down.

It is not safe to pursue revelation for revelation's sake. Paul told Timothy that the end, or the purpose, of the Word of God is, "charity out of a pure heart, and of a good conscience, and of faith unfeigned" [I Timothy 1:5]. Knowledge has a purpose. But the pursuit of knowledge for the sole purpose of gaining knowledge will lead to error.

Other ministers have a hankering for the supernatural. They keep pushing and pushing, wanting to move out in the realm of the spirit. But "moving in the spirit" is not necessarily the same as moving with God. A perverted desire for the supernatural and an overbalanced hunger for manifestations can be spiritually debilitating. Those who aggressively pursue spiritual experiences will be accommodated!

I remember that in the early years of my ministry I heard many ministers make this statement, "There is nothing I love more than the anointing." When I heard these statements the Holy Spirit within me would say, "Never love the anointing more than you love God or you will get off."

Recently, a friend of mine who leads a prayer group told me that a group of young and excited Christians had come to join her. She asked me about a particular situation that had arisen in their prayer time. Often she felt like the zealous young believers were fighting with her for control of the direction of prayer. She said they were like "spiritual mavericks." They were untamed and untrained. They just wanted to, "move out in the Spirit." I told her that until they were established more in the Word of God it would be better not to let them pray like this. It could be dangerous.

Some ministers are just "hungry." They have lusty personalities. They love food, they love sex, they love money, and they love spiritual power. This is why some very anointed men also have serious problems with diet, money, and sex. Hunger for power, hunger for anointing, and hunger for the supernatural can easily lead ministers down the road of spiritual error. Because they are anointed and seem to move easily in the gifts of the Spirit, people are often attracted to their ministries. Unfortunately, these kind of ministers are often not disciplined in their own spiritual lives.

Some sound spiritual leaders, called of God and gifted by God, are drawn away from sound doctrine and sound spiritual life because of their appetite for power, for knowledge, or for spiritual experience. Their appetite is that something "in them" that the devil finds and then hooks them with.

Ministers who are too hungry are candidates for all kinds of spiritual mistakes. Physical hunger caused Esau to trade his precious birthright for a single bowl of pottage! A strong hunger is like an open door. Something is going to come through. When ministers pursue knowledge and spiritual experiences, they open themselves up for deception.

CONCLUSION

We have studied briefly a few of the reasons once sound spiritual leaders get off course spiritually and become unsound spiritual leaders. Many of these individuals are ignorant of their error. They have made honest mistakes, missed the mark, and wandered away from sound doctrine. They are, nevertheless, dangerous to the church. Their error will not send men to hell, but it will keep believers from a full and balanced expression of spiritual life in Jesus Christ.

·~13~·
What Do False Spiritual Leaders Want?

In the previous chapter we examined reasons why some once sound spiritual leaders depart from sound doctrine and become unsound spiritual leaders. We learned that many of them unintentionally swerve into false doctrine and become unsound. They do not intend to become unsound. They are not deliberately errant. Without realizing what has happened they become unsound and the promoters of unsound doctrine and unsound spiritual activities.

There are false spiritual leaders, however, who abandon sound doctrine and sound spiritual life because of ungodly motivations. They intentionally promote unsound doctrine and unsound spiritual practices because they know it will bring them personal advantage. They knowingly twist and misapply the Word of God in order to deceive unsuspecting believers and get what they want. They know who they are and they know what they want. They conceal their intentions, however, by transforming themselves into ministers of righteousness. They are wolves hiding either in sheep's wool or shepherd's clothing.

What is it that motivates false spiritual leaders? What is the impetus behind their efforts? What do they want? What motivates them to teach unsound doctrines and promote activities that are detrimental to the body of Christ? In this chapter we will answer these questions. We will look to the Word of God to discover what inspires false spiritual leaders to their unsound spiritual activities. Understanding the motivation of false spiritual leaders will help us to recognize them and accurately judge them if they come into our midst or cross our paths.

ONE: THEY WANT PERSONAL FINANCIAL GAIN

One of the primary factors that motivates false spiritual leadership is the desire for money. Some are motivated purely by the prospect of personal financial gain. Everything they teach, every action they take, and every relationship they pursue is done with the thought in mind, "How will this profit me?"

Money — A Directing Force

Jesus made a very strong point when He told His disciples," You cannot serve God and mammon (money)" [Matthew 6:24]. In making this statement, Jesus not only called for a choice between God and money, but revealed that God and money are, in fact, the two primary gods that people serve. You may ask, "How is it that people serve money?" People serve money when every decision is based upon and every activity dictated by how things will turn out financially. When money dictates decisions, alters directions, and determines the activities of men's lives, then money is their god.

Many false spiritual leaders serve the god of money. Rather than being motivated by obedience to God and compassion for people, they are motivated by the possibility of making money. The result of their lust for money will be their own sorrow and the corruption of healthy believers and healthy local churches.

Paul made a very strong and revealing statement when he said, "the love of money is the root of all evil" [I Timothy 6:10]. This statement is strong even when it stands by itself. When it is read in its proper context, however, it is both revealing and damning concerning false and unsound spiritual leaders! This statement about the motivating power of the love of money is part of a stern warning Paul gave Timothy about the money motivated evil activities of false and unsound spiritual leaders!

Money itself is not the source of evil activity; it is not inherently evil. Rather, it is the love of money, the desire to have more money, that is the root — the source, the birthplace, the inspiration, the motivation — for all evil activity. The potential for personal profit is one of the most powerful motivating factors behind evil activities.

Do you wonder why the use of illegal drugs is so hard to control? It is because the distribution of drugs is a money making business. Take away the opportunity for financial profit and the business of drug dealing will be stripped of its power. Do you wonder why there is a problem with pornography? It is because pornography is a big money business. Take away the potential of profit and the pornography industry will collapse. Imagine any evil activity and you will find that a desire for money is the source of its inspiration.

The love of money, said Paul, is the inspiration for *all* evil. Being a false prophet, a false apostle, a false teacher, a false pastor, or a false evangelist is evil. The apostle John confirmed this in his second epistle saying that any person who bids a false teacher Godspeed, is, "partaker of his evil deeds" [II John 11]. Teaching unsound doctrines and feigning power with God is evil. Pretending to be a spiritual leader and misusing believers is evil. It is evil because it is contrary to the Word of God. It is evil because it destroys lives, upsets churches, and leads to spiritual sickness and moral decay. False spiritual leaders are evil and their activities are evil. Very often it is the hope of obtaining money that is the impetus behind the evil activities of false spiritual leaders.

Certain teachers of Paul's day would not consent to sound doctrine. One of their unsound doctrines stated that financial gain was a sign of personal godliness and of God's blessing. Concerning these unsound ministers, their love of money, and their unsound doctrine, Paul told Timothy,

> *"But they that will be (want to be) rich fall into temptation and a snare, and into many foolish and hurtful lusts, which drown men in destruction and perdition. For the love of money is the root of all evil: which while some coveted after, they have erred from the faith, and pierced themselves through with many sorrows. But thou, O man of God, flee these things..."*

> I Timothy 6:9-11

These false teachers Paul spoke of coveted money. They wanted to be rich. They would not, "consent to wholesome words, even the words of...Jesus," but taught that, "gain is godliness" [I Timothy 6:3, 5]. Rather than being content with "food and raiment" these men aspired to be rich [I Timothy 6:8-9]. Their love of money dictated the activities of their lives and shaped the doctrines they taught.

Paul challenged Timothy how to respond to the temptation of financial gain. He said,

> *"But thou, Oh man of God, flee these things..."*

> I Timothy 6:11

The true minister of God must not only not love money; he must flee from the desire for it! It is too strong a temptation to be meddled with. Too easily one can be snared and then drowned by money's intoxicating power. Too easily the prospect of financial gain can become the motivation for every teaching and every activity.

They Covet the Wealth of the Flock

In issuing His strong warning concerning false spiritual leaders, Jesus depicted them as ravenous wolves. He did not pretty the picture or soft focus His vivid and concise description. He purposely made His warning forceful and His description startling to arrest our attention and make us a cautious and discerning people. Listen to His warning,

"Beware of false prophets, which come to you in sheep's clothing, but inwardly are ravening wolves."

Matthew 7:15

Webster says that a wolf is a fierce, flesh eating wild animal of the dog family. Jesus did not, however, just call false leaders "wolves." He called them, "ravening wolves." The word "ravening" comes from the Greek *harpar* and means pillage, robbing, or extortion, all words which denote the forceful or illegal taking of money. "Extortion" is the offense of obtaining money or anything valuable by the means of threat or force. The description of false spiritual leaders as ravening wolves is not pretty. It depicts persons who are hungry for believers' possessions and will find a way to get them, even if they have to dress up like a true minister. By calling false ministers, "ravening wolves," Jesus revealed their evil motivation and their voracious hunger for the sheeps' goods.

False spiritual leaders view the sheep in terms of their own potential financial advantage. They come to a flock to take. They do not care for the sheep, will not feed the sheep, will not protect the sheep, and will not lay down their lives for the sheep — all things that a true shepherd would do. They will not live with the sheep, eat with the sheep, sleep with the sheep, or endure hardship with the sheep. They do not even think of the sheep except when they are hungry. Their all consuming thought is, "I am hungry." Their god — the directing force of their life — is their belly. They are always devising ways to take from the flock in order to satisfy their own hunger. When they see the sheep, their mouth waters. They know that their hunger will be satisfied if they can get into the flock.

The Hireling Serves for Wages

Some false spiritual leaders could be described as hirelings. Jesus spoke these words about the hireling,

"...he that is an hireling, and not the shepherd, whose own the sheep are not, seeth the wolf coming, and leaveth the sheep, and fleeth: and the wolf catcheth them, and scattereth the sheep. The hireling fleeth, because he is an hireling, and careth not for the sheep."

John 10:12-13

The Amplified Bible says,

> *But the hired servant — he who merely serves for wages…when he sees the wolf coming deserts the flock and runs away…Now the hireling flees because he merely serves for wages and is not himself concerned about the sheep — cares nothing for them.*

> *John 10:12-13 Amp*

The hireling, "merely serves for wages." He enlists in the shepherding business for the sole purpose of making money. He aspires to leadership not because he cares about the sheep, but because he cares about the pay.

They Want Yours

In his letter to the church at Corinth, Paul, after defending his own apostleship and exposing those who were false apostles, said,

> *"…I will not be burdensome to you: for I seek not yours, but you…"*

> *II Corinthians 12:14*

Paul was not seeking these believers' goods, he was seeking their good. He was not pursuing their finances, he was pursuing them. He did not endeavor to win their confidence so they would trust him with their money, he endeavored to espouse these believers as a pure bride to Christ. He did not seek what they had, he sought them and their spiritual well-being.

In the short phrase, "I seek not yours, but you," we perceive the motivation of a true minister of Christ. A true minister does not concern himself with how he is going to be blessed by the people. He does not attempt, through the preaching of the Word or any other method, to take what the people have. He is concerned solely with the well-being of the believers to whom he ministers.

In the short phrase, "I seek not yours, but you," we can also fathom the ungodly motivation of false ministers. False spiritual leaders, "want yours." They want what believers have! They want to profit by their association with them. They hope to make personal gain by their spiritual position over believers. False ministers do not seek the welfare of the people, but their own welfare. They do not devise ways to be a blessing, but devise ways to get blessings. They covet believers' goods and will use sheep's clothing, even going so far as to transform themselves into ministers of righteousness, to get it!

A true minister shares the attitude of Paul, who said,

> *"…I will very gladly spend and be spent for you…"*

> *II Corinthians 12:15*

This is the heartbeat of a true spiritual leader. He will spend and be spent with no demand for repayment. His attitude is, "No matter what it costs me, I am going to serve the people." A false minister, on the other hand, wants the people to spend for him. His attitude is, "No matter what it takes, I am going to profit from these people."

In this same chapter of scripture, Paul asked the believers at Corinth,

"Did I make gain of you by any of them whom I sent unto you?"
II Corinthians 12:17

Paul did not make personal financial gain by his relationship with the believers in Corinth. He did not even ask this church to take care of other ministers he sent to bless them. Rather, he was willing to sacrifice so that the people would be blessed.

A true minister of the gospel is motivated first by the calling of God and second by compassion for the people. He seeks ways to bring believers into the fullness of their blessings in Christ. He diligently studies, prays, teaches, and does whatever else needs to be done in order to bring the power, the love, and the blessings of God to the people. His primary vision is to present spiritually matured believers to the Lord.

A false minister will prepare messages precalculated to persuade the flock to feed him. Rather than preaching the Word and enriching the flock spiritually, emotionally, and physically, he devours the flock to sustain his own life and to underwrite his own vision. He wants the flock to provide him with a big house, a new car, new clothes, and a decent income. On top of that, he wants the flock to finance his ideas and ambitions. He has no concept, as does the true minister, that he works for the Great Shepherd and that his primary responsibility is to take care of the sheep.

Teaching for Financial Gain

Concerning deceivers and false ministers, Paul said,

"...(they teach) things which they ought not, for filthy lucre's sake."
Titus 1:11

The false teachers Paul wrote to Titus about were in error for two reasons. First, they were in error because they were teaching false doctrine. Second, they were in error because their motivation for teaching was wrong. Their motivation for teaching was personal gain. These men sought to profit through the ignorance of God's people. Paul told Titus that one of these false teachers said of his own kind that they were, "liars, idle and lazy gluttons" [Titus 1:12 Amp]. These false teachers were "lazy." They wanted something for nothing. They were "gluttons." They only wanted to fill their own bellies with food. And they were "liars." It was by lying that they obtained what they coveted.

False teachers attempt to profit financially by capitalizing on the sincere ignorance of God's people. Rather than teaching the truths of the Word of God as the Holy Spirit inspires their hearts, they teach whatever works out in the end to bring them financial gain. They teach what they should not teach and do so in order to profit financially.

Filthy Lucre

Paul was very strict concerning the place of money in the ministry. In his first letter to Timothy, he spoke about the qualifications for spiritual leadership. In order for a person to qualify even for the office of deacon, he must be, "not covetous," and could not be, "greedy of filthy lucre" [I Timothy 3:3, 8]. The words "not covetous" that Paul used come from the Greek *aphilarguros* and mean, "not money-loving." In his letter to Titus, Paul said that a bishop could not be, "given to filthy lucre" [Titus 1:7]. Paul instructed both Timothy and Titus that no individual could be put in a position of spiritual leadership, could not even be a deacon in the church, if he loved money. Why? Because the love of money motivates men to evil activities.

The apostle Peter also warned the elders he was responsible for concerning their attitude toward financial gain through the ministry. He said,

"The elders which are among you I exhort...Feed the flock of God...not for filthy lucre, but of a ready mind..."

I Peter 5:1-2

These elders were to do the work of the ministry with no thought of making financial gain. Rather, they were to be of a "willing mind." They were to feed the flock of God and fulfill the will of God regardless of how it was working out financially for them. They were to be ready for good times and for rough times. They were to be ready to obey God no matter how good or how bad it looked. They were to be ready to serve the flock whether it profited them or not! This is the attitude and mind set of the true minister of Christ.

The elders were not to minister to gain "filthy lucre." Have you ever wondered why, when referring to financial gain from the work of the ministry, the Word of God always calls money, "filthy lucre?" Money is called filthy lucre in this case because anything a minister says or does that is premeditated to profit himself financially thoroughly taints whatever has been gained! The money that comes from the hand of God through others to meet a minister's needs is clean and pure. Money, however, that is gained through any activity of ministry that is pre-calculated to bring financial profit, is filthy in the sight of God! It is corrupted, dirtied, soiled, and polluted.

This does not mean that God will not bless ministers through the sheep they minister to. It is, in fact, a New Testament principle that those who preach the gospel should be sustained by those they preach to. Those who feed a flock should drink of the milk of the flock. Those who plant a vineyard should eat of the fruit of it. Those who plow should plow in hope and those who thresh should thresh in the hope of being a partaker [I Corinthians 9:7-10]. There is a great difference, however, between drinking the milk of the flock and devouring the sheep!

The apostle Paul displayed an exemplary attitude concerning finances in his letter to the church at Philippi. He wrote this concerning their financial gifts,

> *"For even in Thessalonica ye sent once and again unto my necessity. Not because I desire a gift: but I desire fruit that may abound to your account."*
> *Philippians 4:16-17*

Although Paul rejoiced to receive financial blessing from this local body, he was most concerned that they be blessed. He did not desire a gift for himself, but desired that fruit would abound to their account. This is the heart of a true minister. He willingly receives blessings from the sheep, but his primary concern is that the sheep receive a blessing and have fruit credited to their account.

They Make Merchandise of Believers

Concerning the covetousness of false teachers, Peter said,

> *"And through covetousness shall they with feigned words make merchandise of you..."*
> *II Peter 2:3*

The word "covetousness" Peter used comes from the Greek *pleonexia* and literally means, "a desire to have more." False teachers are not motivated by a calling from God, by the desire be a blessing, or even because they like to teach. They are motivated by the desire to have more money! They teach what they teach because they are covetousness. They misuse Bible doctrines, twist the scriptures, and sometimes even fabricate doctrines in order to get believers' money.

These men, said Peter, "[will] with feigned words make merchandise of you." To teach with "feigned words" means to speak words that are pre-calculated to produce a certain response. False teachers don't teach because they see the need believers have to be instructed in particular Bible doctrines. They don't teach a specific message because they are inspired by the Spirit of God to teach it. What they teach is based upon what they have pre-determined will cause believers to respond financially to them. They will preach whatever will catch believers' attention. They teach their unsound doctrines and believers give them their money.

The phrase, "make merchandise," according to W. E. Vine, signifies, "to travel for business and to make gain." False leaders do whatever they do, whether speaking or pretending miracles, in order to make financial gain from believers. They will schedule conferences, report happenings, write books, sell tapes, do newsletters, or request finances through the mail. In whatever way possible they will "travel to you" to get your money.

None of the activities I have mentioned above are wrong in themselves. It is the intention of the heart that matters. If the intention of the heart is to use every available means to bless the people of God, then the activity is allowable. If the objective is to edify, build up, encourage, and enlighten believers in the Word of God, then the activity is permitted.

I participate in some of these activities myself. I travel to many places, speak in churches, record music albums, write books, and send out newsletters. My motivation is to use every vehicle possible to fulfill the ministry God has given me. I search for means to establish and strengthen believers in local churches and to minister blessing to the body of Christ.

Unsound ministers, however, do what they do to make personal gain. Always at the forefront of their minds is the question, "How will this prosper me?" Recently, I was preaching at a particular church. After the service, a woman bought some of our materials. As she was walking away from our book table, I happened to notice that she was carrying a book by a well known and respected minister and author. I was shocked to notice the price tag on his paperback book. It was over $12.00!

I know what it costs to produce a paperback book and can estimate how long it would take a minister of this man's reputation to recover his production costs. Maybe his book cost a little more to produce than my books, but to charge over $12.00 for a paperback book is exorbitant. Personally, I would call this making merchandise of the people.

That may sound too strong to some of you, but it is no stronger than what Peter and Paul said. You must remember that the body of Christ does not exist to support ministers. Rather, ministers have their being and possess whatever gifts God has endowed them with for the purpose of giving to the body of Christ. No minister of the gospel should do anything, whether it be writing a book, producing a music album, sending out a newsletter, or preaching a particular message, based on what it will produce financially for him. A true leader flees from the temptation to use people for financial gain. A false leader, on the other hand, retails the gospel for his own financial profit.

Examples of Using Gifts for Gain

The opportunity to make gain is enticing. The temptation to compromise just a little to get just a little more is often overpowering. This temptation, even if resisted once, will certainly surface again. The temptation to use the pretense of being a minister to make financial gain from God's people is strong.

The Way of Balaam

An Old Testament prophet named Balaam had a problem with financial temptation. On one occasion, because he was respected as a prophet and had power with God through his words, a king named Balak tried to entice him to curse Israel. He sent the elders of Moab and Midian in an attempt to retain Balaam. The Bible says that the elders of Moab and Midian approached Balaam with, "the rewards of divination in their hands" [Numbers 22:7]. They asked him to prophesy cursings on Israel and offered him financial remuneration to do so. Balaam, however, refused this first invitation according to what God had already spoken to him.

When Balak heard that Balaam had refused, he sent more honorable princes to Balaam with this message,

> "...Let nothing, I pray thee, hinder thee from coming unto me: For I will promote thee unto very great honour, and I will do whatsoever thou sayest unto me: come therefore, I pray thee, and curse me this people."
>
> *Numbers 22:16-17*

Balaam answered with these words,

> "...If Balak would give me his house full of silver and gold, I cannot go beyond the Word of the lord my God, to do less or more."
>
> *Numbers 22:18*

Though Balaam resisted at first, however, the temptation to profit by using his ability to speak for God was overwhelming. He kept asking God to let him go till God gave in. On his way, however, an angel of the Lord withstood him and spoke a message from God. He said,

> "...I went out to withstand thee, because thy way is perverse before me..."
>
> *Numbers 22:32*

The word "perverse" that the angel of the Lord spoke can also be inter-preted, "headlong." Balaam was pushing headlong into trouble. He was being drawn outside the perfect will of God and seriously contemplating using his God-given gifts to advance his own financial standing.

Now the practice of using one's gifts for personal financial gain is called, "the error of Balaam." Jude said of false spiritual leaders who were introduc-ing false doctrine that they, "ran greedily after the error of Balaam for reward" [Jude 11]. The apostle Peter wrote of false teachers that they,

> "...have forsaken the right way, and are gone astray, following the way of Bal-aam...who love the wages of unrighteousness..."
>
> II Peter 2:15

Because Balaam had an affection for money, it was almost sure that at some time he would be "turned" to misuse his gift for his own advantage.

Gehazi

Perhaps you are familiar with the story of how Elisha the prophet healed Namaan of incurable leprosy [II Kings 5]. After Namaan was healed, he offered to bless Elisha with financial reward. Elisha, however, refused to take financial reward in payment for the power God had entrusted to him.

Elisha recognized the dangerous temptation of using the power of God for personal gain. If he accepted payment for being used by God, he would be embarking upon a trip that would lead to his own spiritual ruin. Not only would he begin to take advantage of people, but his own desire for financial gain would grow and his love for God would grow cold. Eventually, his enjoyment of the things of the world would overtake him. He would lose his power with God and lose his favor with God.

Elisha's servant Gehazi, however, was not as pure in his motivation. He recognized and took advantage of an opportunity for personal profit. After Namaan and his troop left, Gehazi ran after them and told Namaan that two young men had come to visit. Elisha needed some extra money and cloth-ing. Could Namaan help? Namaan, of course, responded by giving Gehazi the goods he asked for.

When Gehazi returned from meeting with Namaan, Elisha confronted him. Gehazi lied about meeting with Namaan, but Elisha said, "Went not mine heart with thee when the man turned again from his chariot to meet thee" [II Kings 5:26]. Elisha saw the activity of Gehazi in the spirit. Then Elisha said to Gehazi,

> "...Is it a time to receive money, and to receive garments, and olive yards, and vineyards, and sheep, and oxen, and menservants, and maidservants?"
>
> II Kings 5:26

Elisha grasped the reality that his purpose on earth was not to accumulate things, but to do the will of God and serve people. He was not motivated by a desire to meet his own needs, but by the desire to do the will of God. True ministers grasp this reality. False ministers will not consider it. They continually scheme, as did Gehazi, how to "receive money."

Young Woman With a Spirit of Divination

In Acts 16, we read about a young woman who followed Paul and his companions declaring that they were servants of the most high God. Verse 16 says,

"And it came to pass, as we went to prayer, a certain damsel possessed with a spirit of divination met us, which brought her masters much gain by soothsaying..."
Acts 16:16

The young woman that followed Paul and his companions was possessed of a demonic spirit. By that spirit she was able to divine the future. Certain men who recognized this spiritual (not Godly) gift had brought this young woman under their employment. They used her and her supernatural gift to profit themselves. The Bible says that by her soothsaying she, "brought her masters much gain." Spiritual gifts, whether of God or by occult power, can be employed to bring financial gain.

A Minister's Misuse of the Word of Knowledge

I heard a well know minister tell a story of another minister who was specially used of God in the word of knowledge. Although this minister moved in the Spirit and helped people, he also yielded to familiar spirits. By yielding to familiar spirits, he learned things about people and used this knowledge for his own advantage.

In one case this minister described a particular piece of jewelry and its location accurately and then told the man it belonged to that the Lord was saying to give it to him. The man who owned the jewelry, seeing a supernatural gift in operation, did not suspect that the minister was yielding to familiar spirits to make personal financial gain. He gave the minister the piece of jewelry thinking that this minister was moving in the gifts of the Spirit.

Freely Give

In every occupation of life it is right that a person be paid for his efforts. For those called to the ministry, however, the command is, "Freely you have received, freely give." The ministry is not a money making business. It is, rather, a vocation based upon obedience to God and the promise of eternal reward. The gifts and anointings of God are never to be used to bring personal gain. What ministers have been freely given of God in the way of special gifts are to be freely used for the benefit of those in need.

Those who love money cannot be true spiritual leaders. God will not endorse them. The spiritual and financial welfare of His sheep are at stake. The possibility that a money-loving person will abuse His flock is a risk God is not willing to take. His people were purchased at a great expense. He will not allow some money hungry imposter to take advantage of His people and profit by them.

You may say, "But I know people in the ministry who love money and aspire to be rich." Yes, I'm sure you do. But I can guarantee you that they have built their own ministries and will not be approved by God for long. He may allow them to minister for a season, hoping to bring them to growth and correction. But He will not for very long tolerate those who take from His flock to satisfy their personal desires.

TWO: THEY WANT THEIR OWN DISCIPLES

A desire to make personal disciples is another strong motivating force which drives the deceptive and unsound spiritual activities of false spiritual leaders. Some men want men to follow them. They would rather be kings in their own kingdoms than servants in God's kingdom. These false spiritual leaders draw believers away from sound local bodies, away from Holy Spirit ordained leadership, and after themselves.

True spiritual leaders obey the great commission of Matthew 28:18-20. They go forth into all the world for the singular purpose of making disciples of Christ. They work for the advancement of God's kingdom by preaching the simple message of the gospel. They speak the truth of God's Word and depend upon the Holy Spirit to draw men to Christ.

False spiritual leaders follow their own ambitions and desires. They do what Jesus accused the religious leaders of His day of doing. They traverse land and sea to make one disciple for themselves. Listen to Jesus' stout words against these false leaders,

> "Woe unto you, scribes and Pharisees, hypocrites! for ye compass sea and land to make one proselyte, and when he is made, ye make him twofold more the child of hell than yourselves."
>
> Matthew 23:15

Whereas the calling of true spiritual leadership is to make disciples of Christ, false spiritual leaders want to make personal disciples. In whatever way possible, whether through perverse teaching, through promises of position, by downgrading true leaders, or by a combination of these things, false spiritual leaders attempt to draw disciples unto to themselves.

Satan's Rebellion

The ungodly motivation to have a personal kingdom was first conceived in Satan. He was not content with the position God had assigned him. He desired more power and personal allegiance. To get this allegiance he lifted himself up against God and persuaded one third of God's angels to follow him. Through careful deception (which, no doubt, included the promise that in his kingdom they would have far greater power and authority than they had in God's kingdom) Satan convinced these angels to follow him. He, "drew the third part of the stars of heaven" [Revelation 12:3]. This is exactly what Paul said unsound leaders would do. He said they would *draw* disciples after themselves.

Satan achieved his ambition to have followers. Through the power of persuasion he became god of the kingdom of darkness. He became Beelzebub — lord of the flies [Matthew 12:27]. He became the prince over the powers of the air [Ephesians 2:2] and lord over demonic spirits [Ephesians 6:12]. He is also god to those who reject Jesus Christ as Saviour. Satan is lord, however, of a doomed kingdom. His brief rise to leadership is swiftly coming to an end.

Korah's Rebellion

Jude cited Korah, an Old Testament man who competed for a position that was not his, as an example of unsound spiritual leadership. He said that false spiritual leaders, "perish in the gainsaying of Core" [Jude 11]. Korah was a well known and respected man who lived in the time and under the leadership of Moses. Korah, however, was an ambitious and driven man who desired to have a more prominent position in Israel. He wanted to have his own kingdom and his own disciples. By speaking against God's ordained leadership and stirring up a desire in others for greater position, he was able to gather a band of his own disciples and lead a rebellion against Moses. We read this about his insurrection in the book of Numbers,

> "Now Korah...took men. And they rose up before Moses, with certain of the children of Israel, two hundred and fifty princes of the assembly, famous in the congregation, men of renown."
>
> *Numbers 16:1-2*

The Bible says that Korah, "took men." How did he take them? No doubt a promise of position and the prospect of greater advantage caused these already well known and famous men to desert Moses and align themselves with Korah. Korah understood that one of the principal ways to gain followers is to give them titles and positions in the new kingdom.

Korah is a type of false spiritual leadership. He was not content with his position. He wanted recognition. He did not want to be under someone else's authority, but wanted others under his authority. Korah was outside the will of God. He was pushing against what God had ordained. He was unsound and leading others into his error. Korah's wrong activities were motivated by his personal ambition to have his own disciples.

The Apostle John's Warning

The apostle John wrote to his spiritual children to warn them of false leaders who had departed from the sound body and were attempting to draw disciples after themselves. He said,

> *"...even now there are many antichrists...They went out from us, but they were not of us...These things have I written unto you concerning them that seduce you...And now little children, abide in him (in Christ)..."*

> *I John 2:18, 19, 26, 28*

The false leaders John called antichrists were once part of a sound local body. They went out, however, from the body and were attempting to seduce believers to join them. The apostle John's final word of instruction to his spiritual children in this context was, "And now little children abide in him" [I John 2:28]. Believers are to be disciples of Christ. They were loved by Christ, saved by the gospel of Christ, established in Christ, and are to remain steadfast to Christ. False spiritual leaders, however, attempt to seduce believers away from Christ and make personal disciples for themselves.

Paul's Warning to Elders in Ephesus

In Acts 20:28-31, the apostle Paul warned the elders in Ephesus to beware of ambitious men who would rise up within their local body and try to draw away believers after themselves. He said,

> *"Also of your own selves shall men arise, speaking perverse things, to draw away disciples after them."*

> *Acts 20:30*

Paul forewarned the elders at Ephesus that men from their own congregation would speak perverse things to draw disciples after themselves. The Greek word translated "perverse" means, "to turn away from." To speak perverse things means to teach things that will cause individuals to turn away from a path they are already following. False leaders speak words — whether false doctrines, negative words about true spiritual leaders, or just words of enticement — that are intended to turn the sheep away from true shepherds, away from sound doctrines, and into their own pastures.

Paul's Problem With the Judaizers

In almost every local church he started, Paul had problems with a band of unsound teachers called the Judaizers. The Judaizers didn't start any churches of their own, but proselyted among other men's converts. They perverted the gospel of Christ, teaching believers that they could not be saved unless they were circumcised according to the law of Moses. They tried to convince believers of their doctrine and, thus, draw them into their party.

The proselyting activity of the Judaizers was a primary concern of Paul and gave rise to his letter to the churches of Galatia. The believers in those churches had already given heed to "another gospel" and, "were removed from him that called (them) into the grace of Christ unto another gospel" [Galatians 1:6]. They had been drawn away from sound doctrine and from sound leadership by unsound spiritual leaders who wanted their own disciples.

False Leaders Seduce Sound Disciples

Some sound believers will follow false spiritual leaders just as a large number of angels followed Satan and as prominent men followed Korah. You may be asking yourself, "Is it really possible for believers to be misled and tricked into following a false leader?" Yes, absolutely. We just mentioned that one third of all God's created angels followed the devil in his revolt. These angels were not ignorant. They were the creation of God, His appointed servants. Yet they were deceived! We also learned that some of the most prominent men in Israel were drawn away by Korah in his rebellion against Moses.

Deception, you see, is deceptive. It is the absolute intention of false spiritual leaders to persuade individuals to follow them without realizing that they are being deceived. I don't know what Satan said to God's angels to entice them, but he must have been very persuasive. He must have made some very enticing promises. I don't know, either, what Korah said to the men of renown and reputation in Israel to persuade them to follow him. I can only assume that he made promises of position and prestige. If these men had foreseen the end of their folly, I am sure they would not have followed this false spiritual leader.

The same sinful desire to gain personal disciples that motivated Satan, that motivated Korah, and that motivated the false spiritual leaders that Paul, John, and Jude warned of, motivates false spiritual leaders of our day.

Those who are not called by God to lead, but desire to lead, will lift them-selves up in the midst of sound local bodies and campaign for their own dis-ciples. They will present their own platforms, hoping to draw individuals after themselves so that they can establish their own kingdoms.

THREE: THEY WANT A PLACE OF AUTHORITY

False spiritual leaders are just what their title says they are. They are individuals who want to be spiritual leaders, who act like spiritual leaders, who convince others they are spiritual leaders, but who are **not** spiritual leaders! False spiritual leaders are those who want leadership, pull for lead-ership, and often rise to leadership, but are not called to leadership in the body of Christ.

These individuals transform themselves for the same reason Satan trans-formed himself when he beguiled Eve. Why did Satan transform himself? Why did he tell a deceptive lie? Was is just for the fun of masking himself in a disguise? Was it for the enjoyment of telling a lie? No. Satan gained no satisfaction from the act of transforming himself. He got no excitement from telling a lie.

The act of transforming himself and telling a lie was a means to the end Satan desired. He wanted to be lord over! His intention was to gain lord-ship over Eve and Adam and, in reality, over the plan of God. He wanted to gain a position and then use that position for his own advantage. Satan succeeded in his plan. Through deception he gained authority over Adam and Eve and over the human race.

It is no surprise that false ministers, Satan's ministers as Paul called them, desire the same thing. They want power over people. They want authority and position.

True spiritual leaders use their abilities and gifts to serve people. Peter instructed the elders he wrote to exercise oversight in the flock of God not, "as being lords over God's heritage," but as, "examples to the flock" [I Peter 5:3]. False leaders, however, operate on Satan's system. Any gift or personal endowment they possess will be used to gain position over people. A false apostle, a false prophet, or a false teacher, though he may speak familiar words and seem to do the right things, is motivated by the same desire as Satan. He wants to be lord over people.

False leaders, once they gain a position, will exercise the rights of their gained position. Paul said of the false apostles that had gained a foothold in Corinth that they,

"...bring you into bondage...devour you...take of you...exalt himself...smite you on the face..."

II Corinthians 11:20

False leaders, after they have lied to believers, drawn them away with unsound doctrine, promoted themselves, lived a hypocritical lifestyle, and gained a reputation, will begin to exercise their authority. By gaining a place in the local church and in believers' personal lives, they have gained the opportunity to be lord over. Believers should always remember this: No one — no man, no demon, not Satan, and not even Jesus — can exercise authority over you unless you give them permission.

They Love the Preeminence

In his third epistle, the apostle John wrote to a particular church that had refused to let him come to visit. In this church there was a man named Diotrephes. Diotrephes evidently had a position of authority in that church and was the person who had refused to let John come. John wrote to that church saying,

"I wrote unto the church: but Diotrephes, who loveth to have the preeminence among them, receiveth us not."

III John 9

Diotrephes, said John, loved to have the preeminence. The word "preeminence" comes from two Greek words which translated mean "love" and "first." The Amplified Bible renders John's words this way,

"...Diotrephes, who likes to take the lead among them and put himself first, does not acknowledge my authority and refuses to accept my suggestion or to listen to me."

III John 9 Amp

Diotrephes, "likes to take the lead," said John. Because he loved the lead, he put himself first. He used his position to forbid a true spiritual leader from coming and blessing the people. Perhaps Diotrephes was afraid that he would lose status when the people became acquainted with John and recognized what a true spiritual leader really looked like. Perhaps he was afraid of being exposed for who he really was — a man with ambitions who loved position.

Jesus' Words About Preeminence

Jesus addressed the wrong motivation of striving for preeminence to His own disciples. On one occasion James and John came to Him and said,

"...Master, we would that thou shouldest do for us whatsoever we shall desire...Grant unto us that we may sit, one on thy right hand, and the other on thy left hand, in thy glory."

Mark 10:35-37

In response to their desire for and struggle to gain preeminence, Jesus told His disciples that it was sinners who jockeyed for positions and schemed for a place of preeminence among themselves. He said,

"...Ye know that they which are accounted to rule over the Gentiles exercise lordship over them; and their great ones exercise authority upon them. But so shall it not be among you: but whosoever will be great among you, shall be your minister: And whosoever of you will be the chiefest, shall be servant of all."

Mark 10:42-44

In the world system, said Jesus, those who are leaders exercise lordship and authority. Concerning those called to minister in God's kingdom, however, Jesus said, "so shall it not be among you" [Matthew 20:26]. True spiritual leaders do not contend for authority or seek a preferred position.

False spiritual leaders love to be first and, therefore, strive, by whatever means possible, to be first. Rather than humbling themselves to serve, they raise themselves up to rule. They want to be leaders and so they take the lead if possible. They aggressively pursue their desire to have position over people.

False spiritual leaders covet recognition and love the privilege of position. Their intense desire to be important causes some of them to foster new movements based on unsound doctrine. They become the spearheads of sectarian movements and splinter groups. They are the cause of church splits and of divisions and strife.

FOUR: THEY DESIRE THE PRAISES OF MEN

Another strong motivating factor of false apostles, prophets, teachers, and other false leaders is the desire for glory, praise, and adulation. They seek the approval of men rather than the commendation that comes from God. They love the praise, glory, and honor that true leaders refuse to accept. They often claim special anointing and special favor with God and, thereby, become recipients of the glory that belongs to God alone.

A true spiritual leader will not receive praise for any fruit which comes from his ministry. He realizes that although he may sow and water, it is God who gives the increase. He realizes that neither "is he that planteth anything, neither he that watereth" [I Corinthians 3:7]. He realizes that whatever he has in the way of natural or supernatural gifts comes from God.

Therefore, the praise and the glory belong only to God. True spiritual leaders refuse to accept the glory and praise that belong only to God the Father and to Jesus.

Peter Refused to Accept Praise

In Acts 3 we find the familiar story of the lame man at the gate called Beautiful who was healed by the apostle Peter. Following this great miracle of healing, Peter had two opportunities to receive the praise of men. Immediately following the healing of the lame man, the Bible reports that,

> *"...all the people ran together unto them in the porch that is called Solomon's, greatly wondering."*
>
> *Acts 3:11*

The people were amazed by the miracle they had witnessed. They were in awe. Their attention was riveted on Peter. Who was this man with such power? When Peter perceived the attitude of the people and realized that they were about to give him the glory, he said,

> *"...Ye men of Israel, why marvel ye at this? or why look ye so earnestly on us, as though by our own power or holiness we had made this man to walk? The God of Abraham, and of Isaac, and of Jacob, the God of our fathers, hath glorified his Son Jesus... And his name through faith in his name hath made this man strong, whom ye see and know: yea, the faith which is by him hath given him this perfect soundness in the presence of you all."*
>
> *Acts 3:12-16*

Before the people could give him credit for this great miracle, Peter turned their attention to Jesus and to the power of His Name. "Do not look at us," Peter said. "The man was healed, not through our power or holiness, not because of who we are or what we have. This man was healed because of the power of God which is available through faith in the name of Jesus. Don't look to us; look to Jesus."

Peter had a second opportunity to advance his own name and gain personal recognition because of this miracle. When the religious leaders heard about the miracle, they apprehended Peter and the other disciples and put them in prison. The next day the rulers, elders, scribes, and high priest came together to question him. They asked him, "By what power, or by what name, have ye done this" [Acts 3:7]? If Peter had wanted to gain a name for himself and advance his own position with people, this would have been a perfect opportunity. Peter, however, answered with these words,

> *"...Ye rulers of the people, and elders of Israel, If we this day be examined of the good deed done to the impotent man, by what means he is made whole; Be it*

known unto you all, and to all the people of Israel, that by the name of Jesus Christ of Nazareth, whom ye crucified, whom God raised from the dead, even by him doth this man stand here before you whole."

Acts 3:9-10

Peter refused to take any credit for the great miracle. He said, "Be it known unto you all...that by the name of Jesus...doth this man stand here before you whole." Peter wanted to be sure that the people knew the source of healing power and knew, therefore, Who was to be the recipient of the praise. Like Peter, true spiritual leaders do not look for ways to gain praise. If people try to give them praise, they will stop it as quickly as possible.

Peter's Refusal of Special Honor

In Acts 10 we find another occasion where the apostle Peter could have allowed himself to receive special honor. A Gentile named Cornelius had been visited by an angel who told him to send to Joppa for a man named Peter. This man Peter, said the angel, "will tell thee what thou oughtest to do" [Acts 10:6]. In the mind of Cornelius this Peter, whoever he was, must be a very special person. After all, God sent an angel and the angel recommended Peter! Peter must be a man who had special status with God.

When Peter arrived at the house of Cornelius, "Cornelius met him, and fell down at his feet, and worshipped him" [Acts 10:25]. Peter, however, esteeming himself as a servant of Christ, took hold of Cornelius' arm, stood him up quickly, and said, "Stand up; I myself also am a man" [Acts 10:26]. Peter refused to be honored as anything more than a fellow man. He could have taken just a moment to enjoy the feeling of being reverenced by Cornelius and his household. He could have said nothing and left the impression that it was right for them to "honor the man of God." Peter immediately corrected the situation, however, making sure that God received the glory.

Paul and Barnabas Refused to Accept Worship

While preaching the gospel one day at Lystra, Paul noticed an impotent man in the crowd. This man had been lame from birth. Perceiving that this man had accepted the message of salvation and possessed the faith to be healed, Paul commanded him, "Stand upright on thy feet" [Acts 14:9]. Responding to the command of Paul, this man, "leaped up and walked" [Acts 14:10]. When the people saw this great miracle, they began to cry out, "The gods are come down to us in the likeness of men" [Acts 14:11]. They were ecstatic about the demonstration of power and wanted to make a special sacrifice to Paul and Barnabas.

At this point Paul and Barnabas could have allowed themselves to be lifted up. They could have taken advantage of the people. They could have said to themselves, "Now here is an opportunity to get something for our services. If these people want to lay down, let's walk on them." Notice, however, the response of Paul and understand the heart of a true minister of the gospel,

> *"Which when the apostles, Barnabas and Paul, heard of, they rent their clothes, and ran in among the people, crying out, And saying, Sirs, why do ye these things? We also are men of like passions with you, and preach unto you that ye should turn from these vanities unto the living God..."*
>
> Acts 14:14-15

Rather than receiving the praises of men or enjoying, even for a moment, that sense of power one feels when people applaud, Paul cried out that he was simply a human being like they were. He refused to let them esteem him as anything more than a "[man] of like passions with them." He made it very clear that he was not a great man, but simply a man who knew a living God. Paul sought to turn the attention of the people away from himself to God.

This is the attitude of a true minister. He will always discourage people from esteeming him as great man and will direct all the praise and the glory back to God. False leaders, however, love to be praised. They love to be flattered and highly esteemed. Rather than humbling themselves, they exalt themselves, pretending to be some great spiritual person so that the people will honor and respect them. It is the will of God, however, that, "no flesh should glory in his presence" [I Corinthians 1:29].

Ministers Receiving Praise

I recall being in a meeting where, when a certain minister took the pulpit, people began to applaud. It was obvious that the people were enamored by him. They thought he was significantly spiritual. They esteemed him as special. It seemed to me that this minister enjoyed the praise. He certainly did not try to discourage it. I cannot say for sure that he enjoyed the moment of admiration because I cannot truly know his heart. In my own spirit, however, something felt wrong. It was a kind of nauseous feeling.

I also recall being in a meeting where, in the process of introducing a certain minister, the person doing the introduction went on and on about how great this man was in God, how much he had done for God, etc. I could sense that the minister being introduced was very uncomfortable with the praise he was given. He never said a word about it or made any kind of facial expression to indicate that this was so, but I could sense that the praise made him very uncomfortable. And that is the response of a true minister. A true minister is uncomfortable with praise.

Recently, I was watching a minister preach on television. He was pulling very hard for finances and preaching strongly, especially to the television audience. At one point in his message, the camera came behind him and gave a view of the audience from over his shoulder. When this happened, I saw a man standing up facing the audience. When the preacher made a good point this man would lift his hands. On this cue the audience would begin to applaud. How far we have come! And how far will we go?

FIVE: THEY WANT TO BE ESTEEMED AS SPIRITUAL

Some unsound ministers want to be esteemed as spiritual men. They love to be considered as anointed of God. They love to be admired and savor the advantage that comes when people consider them special ministers of God.

Exalt Themselves

Concerning the false apostles who had gained a foothold in the church at Corinth, Paul said that they, "exalt themselves" [II Corinthians 11:20]. How does a minister exalt himself? By saying things and doing things, perhaps even by pretending things, in order to cause people to perceive them to be more than they really are. You see, if people esteem a minister highly, then praise and glory will be their response. Unsound spiritual leaders will say certain things and act in certain ways to elevate people's perception of their spiritual stature. In this way, they draw to themselves the attention they crave.

Paul spoke of the false ministers in the church at Corinth as those who were, "puffed up." He wrote that he would come shortly to Corinth to know "not the speech of them which are puffed up, but the power" [I Corinthians 4:18]. This aspect of being "puffed up" makes me think of balloons. Balloons are made out of a specific amount of material, but by puffing them up with air they can be made to look much bigger than they really are. No more material has been added to the makeup of the balloon, but the impression is much greater.

Some unsound ministers are like balloons. They puff themselves up with slick speeches and pass themselves off as something BIG. But when you take away all the persuasive talk, all the smooth speech, and all the hot air, they are not made up of much true spiritual material. Paul was going to

Corinth not to listen to the speeches of the false ministers, but to discover their power. He was not interested in how smooth they could speak, but in whether or not there was any true spiritual power operating in their lives.

Extra-Spiritual Religious Leaders

It was concerning this issue of presenting oneself as extra-spiritual that Jesus constantly confronted the false spiritual leaders of His day. These religious leaders made a show of spirituality by praying long prayers in public, by blowing trumpets in the streets when they paid their alms, and by putting on sad countenances when they fasted [Matthew 6:1-16]. They also requested to be called "Rabbi." All these activities were carefully calculated to cause people to esteem them as spiritual. Jesus said concerning these hypocrites, "all their works they do for to be seen of men" [Matthew 23:5]. These unsound spiritual leaders pretended to be spiritual in order to gain the admiration of men.

They Love Titles

Unsound spiritual leaders love to take titles to themselves or to be given titles by those who follow them. These titles serve to separate them from the "common Christian" and give them spiritual status. They love to be called, "Bishop." They love to be called, "the man of God." They love to be called, "prophet."

Jesus taught His disciples a much different attitude concerning ministry. He said,

> "But be ye not called Rabbi: for one is your Master, even Christ; and all ye are brethren. And call no man your father upon the earth: for one is your Father, which is in heaven. Neither be ye called masters: for one is your Master, even Christ."
>
> *Matthew 23:8-10*

Jesus taught His disciples that they should not allow people to call them "Rabbi," or "Master," or "Father." They should not allow people to give them titles that represented spiritual status. The attitude of their minds was to be this: Jesus is the Master and we are all brethren [Matthew 23:8]. True spiritual leaders retain in the forefront of their thinking the reality that all believers, themselves included, are brethren. Jesus concluded His short teaching about true spiritual leadership by speaking to the disciples about the attitude of a true minister,

> "…he that is greatest among you shall be your servant. And whosoever shall exalt himself shall be abased: and he that shall humble himself shall be exalted."
>
> *Matthew 23:11-12*

Compounding the problem of ministers loving titles is that people love to have a king. They love to put titles on individuals and then identify themselves with that person. They will say things like, "So and so is one of the greatest pastors in this move of God and, by the way, we go to his church." They may say, "So and so is an end-time General and he wants us to work with him." Through giving titles and then identifying with those who have been given the titles, individuals seek to gain a certain level of prominence themselves.

Paul had to caution the believers in Corinth along these very lines because they were puffing up ministers. He said,

> *"...no one of you (should) be puffed up for one against another...what hast thou that thou didst not receive? now if thou didst receive it, why dost thou glory, as if thou hadst not received it?"*

I Corinthians 4:6-7

Ministers that allow and enjoy being called "Bishop," or "Father," or "General," or "Doctor," or "Cutting-edge Leader," or any other title that gives them status in the body of Christ and status over people, are on dangerous ground. Those who take titles unto themselves or allow people to give them special status can too easily abuse and misuse the precious flock of Christ. The love of titles can easily lead them to the place where they will have to be abased by the Lord.

I know true and forefront spiritual leaders who request that they be introduced as "brother." I also know unstable ministers who cover their books and brochures with unearned titles like, "Dr. So and So," and want to be introduced as such. Others self-assign titles to themselves like "prophet" or "apostle."

Someone might say, "Well, Paul called himself an apostle." Yes, he did. Before he called himself an apostle, however, he was called to be an apostle. He always wrote, "Paul, an apostle of Jesus Christ by the will of God" [Ephesians 1:1; Galatians 1:1; II Corinthians 1:1]. There is a significant difference between being called by God to be something and calling yourself something!

True spiritual leaders carry within themselves a strong revelation of the truth that aspiring to be great in God means aspiring to be called, "Servant." They do everything in their power to keep people from esteeming them as anything other than "brethren in the Lord." They realize that the greatest in the kingdom of God is not the man with the highest title, but the man who serves the best!

The Mind Set of the True Minister

All believers, including ministers, should, in lowliness of mind, esteem others as better than themselves [Philippians 2:4]. The Word of God says,

"Let this mind be in you, which was also in Christ Jesus..."

Philippians 2:5

The phrase, "let this mind be in you," simply means, "Think this way." Ministers especially should think like, act like, and possess the attitude of Christ. What was Jesus' attitude in His ministry? From this same passage in Philippians, the Word of God says,

"(He) made himself of no reputation, and took upon him the form of a servant...he humbled himself..."

Philippians 2:7-8

True spiritual leaders follow the example of Jesus. He was "meek and lowly in heart" [Matthew 11:29]. True spiritual leaders will present themselves in humility and meekness, not seeking the praise and admiration of men. The Word of God says of Moses, the greatest Old Testament prophet and one of the most powerful men of God that ever lived, that he was, "very meek, above all the men which were upon the face of the earth" [Numbers 12:3].

In these days, ministers, rather than humbling themselves to serve, seek avenues to lift themselves up, sometimes even spending thousands of dollars to establish their reputations and make a place for themselves. They do market research. They create high powered advertisements using words like, "One of the strongest anointings of the 90's," or, "Operates under a heavy prophetic anointing," or, "Stands on the cutting edge of the move of God." All these kinds of phrases are calculated to create an image of power.

Some of the so-called forefront ministers of our generation need desperately to humble and correct themselves before they are judged of the Lord. We are on this earth to serve one another with our special gifts and anointings and to preach the gospel to the lost. We are not here to build reputations and make a place for ourselves in the church history books! Would to God that ministers would live by the principles of the Book that they so boldly claim to preach!

Six: They Want Power

Some unsound spiritual leaders simply love power. They love the feeling of being able to move an audience with their words. They love to be the one laying hands on people and demonstrating the power of God. They don't want to be a blessing; they want to be the one doing the blessing. I have heard ministers remark that they love nothing more than the anointing. That is a very dangerous attitude. The gifts of God can easily be abused if ministers develop a passion for the power of ministry.

It is very natural that a person who is used in supernatural ways will be elevated in everyone's eyes. The power of God gives them power with people. Hebrews 7:7 says,

> *"And without all contradiction the less is blessed of the better."*

Hebrews 7:7

There is no disagreement with the truth that the lesser individual is blessed of the greater individual. The person doing the blessing is always esteemed as greater than the person being blessed. Unsound spiritual leaders like the power to bless because it makes them the "better."

Simon the Sorcerer

In Acts 8:9-24 we find the story of Simon the sorcerer's conversion. Before his salvation he, "used sorcery, and bewitched the people of Samaria, giving out that himself was some great one" [Acts 8:9]. Simon presented himself as "some great one" and the whole city of Samaria gave heed to him, from the least to the greatest, saying of him, "This man is the great power of God" [Acts 8:10]. When the people of Samaria heard Phillip preaching the gospel of truth, however, they were converted to Christ.

Simon also believed in Christ, not only because of the message of the gospel, but also because of the, "miracles and signs that were done" [Acts 8:13]. Simon was not, however, instantly sanctified. He still had wrong thinking and unregenerate motivations and desires. When he saw that the apostles laid hands on people and the people were filled with the Holy Ghost, he offered the apostles money saying,

> *"...Give me also this power, that on whomsoever I lay hands, he may receive the Holy Ghost."*

Acts 8:19

Peter rebuked Simon saying,

> *"...Thy money perish with thee, because thou has thought that the gift of God may be purchased with money. Thou has neither part nor lot in this matter for thy heart is not right in the sight of God. Repent therefore of this thy wickedness, and pray God, if perhaps the thought of thine heart may be forgiven thee. For I perceive that thou are in the gall of bitterness, and in the bond of iniquity."*

Acts 8:20-23

Although Simon had been saved, he still had a sinful desire for power. He had given up his power of sorcery when he was saved, but now he wanted to have the power of God. He wanted it, however, for the wrong reasons. He did not want the power of God so that he could bless the people of God. He wanted the power of God because he wanted to be the one doing the blessing!

Simon, the former sorcerer, would have been a dangerous and unsound spiritual leader because he loved power. His heart, said Peter, was not right. He could have moved in the power of God, but would have, at some point, abused this power because of his wrong motivation.

It is very possible for individuals to be saved and yet bound by motivations and desires that are not of God and are, therefore, spiritually dangerous. Peter told Simon that his heart was not right in the sight of God and that he must repent of his wicked thoughts. What were his wicked thoughts? His wicked thoughts were his desire to have the power to get people filled with the Holy Ghost through the laying on of hands.

"But," you may say, "isn't that a good desire?" It depends entirely upon why one wants that power. If one desires to have the power of God so that he can advance God's kingdom and be a blessing to people, his desire is good. But if one wants power and spiritual gifts so that he can be the one doing the blessing, then his heart is not right in the sight of God and he must repent!

The More Excellent Way

After teaching about the gifts of the Spirit, membership in the body of Christ, and offices in the church, Paul counseled the believers in Corinth to, "covet earnestly the best gifts" [I Corinthians 12:31]. To covet means to desire what belongs to someone else. Concerning special gifts and special endowments it is permissible to covet what you see operating in someone else. There is, however, as Paul said, a more excellent way.

To be motivated by love is the most excellent way. Loving God (wanting to see His kingdom advanced) and loving people (truly desiring to see their needs met) is the very highest motivation for desiring the gifts and endowments of God. This makes one a very safe minister. Ministers who are motivated by love will never use their gifts or their authority for anything but for edification. This is what Paul meant when he said,

> *"For though I should boast somewhat more of our authority, which the lord hath given us for edification, and not for destruction…"*
>
> II Corinthians 10:8

The purpose of any gift or endowment from God is not to profit the minister, not to bring him glory, power, or money, but to edify the body of Christ. Wanting the power of God just to have the power of God is not wrong. But it is certainly not the most excellent way. If one *desires* power just because they *love* power, there always remains the possibility that they will use the gifts and power of God for their own advantage.

CONCLUSION

False and unsound ministers engage in their unsound activities for a variety of reasons. Some simply want money. Some desire to be leaders and so seek after followers. Some love authority and want to be lords over God's flock. Some love the admiration which accompanies position. Some want power. Men who consider how their gifts can be used to raise money, to bring them attention, or to give them special recognition and titles, are certainly not qualified to be spiritual leaders.

·~14~·
How Do False Spiritual Leaders Get What They Want?

*I*n our previous chapter we discovered what false spiritual leaders want. We learned about their *motivations*; why they do what they do. In this chapter we will learn about false spiritual leader's *methods*. We will answer the question, "How do false spiritual leaders get what they want?"

FALSE SPIRITUAL LEADERS DECEIVE

Although there are a wide variety of methods false spiritual leaders use to get what they want, no matter what specific method they employ it will always fall under the general heading of deception. Deception is the *means* to the false spiritual leader's *end*. Everywhere you find a warning concerning false spiritual leadership in the New Testament, you will find some form of the word deception.

Jesus foretold the end time deceptive activity of false spiritual leaders in His response to the disciples' question concerning the end times. He said,

"...take heed that no man deceive you...For many shall come in my name...and shall deceive many..."

Matthew 24:3-4

Paul also spoke prophetically of the end time activity of false spiritual leaders and their employment of deception in his second letter to Timothy,

"This know also, that in the last days perilous times shall come...But evil men and seducers shall wax worse and worse, deceiving and being deceived."

II Timothy 3:1,13

Paul's word to Timothy is a very accurate description of false ministers. They are deceivers who will get worse and worse as we move toward the end days. They will not only be deceiving, but will be being deceived themselves! If you had to choose one word that summarized the activities of false spiritual leaders, the word "Deception" would be the hands-down choice!

Satan's Method — False Spiritual Leaders' Method

The apostle Paul associated the deceptive activities of false ministers and the deceptive activities of Satan. Notice this comparison in his second letter to the church at Corinth,

> *"For such are false apostles, deceitful workers, transforming themselves into the apostles of Christ. And no marvel; for Satan himself is transformed into an angel of light. Therefore it is no great thing if his ministers also be transformed as the ministers of righteousness..."*
>
> II Corinthians 11:13-15

In this message, Paul identified false apostles as, "his (Satan's) ministers." It was not surprising, he said, that false apostles deceived by pretending to be apostles of Christ because this is the same method Satan employs. He transforms himself into an angel of light.

Deception is the primary strategy Satan employs to gain advantage over both unbelievers and believers. This has been his *modus operandi*, his method of operation, since the very beginning. In fact, this is how he first gained lordship over the human race. It was not through warfare or physical force, but through the power of deception. Satan continues to deceive those who remain ignorant, be they saved or unsaved. To whatever level he can deceive, to that level he can maintain control over individuals.

Speaking of the "son of perdition," the Antichrist yet to come who, being empowered by Satan, will so effectually deceive the world, Paul wrote,

> *"And then shall that Wicked be revealed...Even him, whose coming is after the workings of Satan with all power and signs and lying wonders, And with all deceivableness of unrighteousness..."*
>
> II Thessalonians 2:9-10

The phrase, "all deceivableness of unrighteousness," signifies all manner of words and deeds designed to deceive. The Antichrist will operate in the same way as Satan. His "coming is after the workings of Satan." He, too, will be a deceiver. But, as the apostle John revealed, there are already many antichrists at work in the world [I John 2:18]. These many antichrists operate in the same way as Antichrist will operate. Their every word and every deed is calculated to deceive.

False spiritual leaders, having the same aspirations as Satan and the Antichrist, use the same strategy to achieve their goals. Deception is the means to their end. To whatever level they can deceive, they can exercise control and take what they want. How do false spiritual leaders get what they want? Through deception!

Understanding Deception

The word "deception" is a fairly common word in the English language. The New Testament, however, translates several different Greek words to the English "deceive." There are also several other Greek words that convey a similar meaning. A quick look at some of these word will enhance our concept of deception, especially as relates to false spiritual leadership.

False Impression

One of the words translated to the English "deceive" is the Greek *apate*. This word means, "that which gives a false impression, whether by appearance, statement, or influence." False spiritual leaders deceive by disguising their outward appearance, by using deceptive words, or by any other means that gives a false impression.

The Webster's English dictionary corroborates this definition saying that a deceiver is a person who studiously undertakes to pass himself off for what he is not. Deception is purposeful misrepresentation. It is habitual and intentional fraud. False spiritual leaders get what they want by giving a false impression of who they are by appearance, by words, and by activities.

All-working

The word translated "subtility" that Paul used in II Corinthians 11:3 when warning believers of false apostles comes from the Greek *panourgia* and literally means, "all-working." This word is always used negatively in the New Testament. False spiritual leaders are "all-working." They will do anything, say anything, and pretend to be anything in order to deceive.

The word "subtility" signifies craftiness and unscrupulous activity. It is translated "cunning craftiness" in Ephesians 4:14 where Paul wrote of men who, "lie in wait to deceive." The word "subtility" represents more than being temporarily tricked, as by the sleight of hand. It denotes being thoroughly convinced or brain-washed of a particular position or doctrine.

False and unsound spiritual leaders will use any means possible to deceive and mislead believers. Paul told the church at Thessalonica,

> "...be not soon shaken in mind, or be troubled, neither by spirit, nor by word, nor by letter as from us...Let no man deceive you by any means..."
>
> II Thessalonians 2:2-3

Paul warned these believers not to be troubled or deceived whether by spirits, by word, or by a letter which false teachers claimed came from himself.

Brainwash

In his letter to Titus, Paul said,

"...for there are many unruly and vain talkers and deceivers...teaching things which they ought not..."

Titus 1:10-11

Here the word "deceivers" literally means mind-deceiver. To be deceived is to be convinced that something is right when, in fact, it is wrong. Deception is a sin against common sense. Some ministers are both deceived and deceivers. They are wrong, but think they are right. They are deceived, but don't know it. They want so badly to be right that they convince themselves they are right. Because they are convinced they are right, they endeavor to lead others into their error.

Lead Down the Wrong Path

To deceive can mean, "to cause to wander from the right path." This meaning comes from the Greek word *plane* used by Paul in Ephesians 4:14. Here he was writing of spiritual children who are misled by, "the sleight of men...whereby they lie in wait to deceive." When Paul said that false spiritual leaders, "lie in wait to deceive," he revealed that what they do is intentional; they deceive on purpose. False spiritual leaders misrepresent themselves and lie, carefully corrupting doctrine and slyly introducing wrong teachings, for the purpose of leading believers down the path of error. They watch for and attempt to lead susceptible individuals from the path of spiritual soundness into deception, confusion, and error.

Sleight of Hand

The word "sleight" Paul used when he spoke of the "sleight of men" comes from a Greek word that denotes dice-playing. Metaphorically this word signifies trickery and sleight of hand. The Amplified Bible helps to bring out this idea. It says,

"So then, we may no longer be children, tossed [like ships] to and fro...[the prey of] the cunning and cleverness of unscrupulous men, (gamblers engaged) in every shifting form of trickery in inventing errors to mislead."

Ephesians 4:14 Amp

False spiritual leaders are like professional gamblers. Some of them have been around for a long time. They know all the tricks. They know how to bluff their way through. They are experts at sleight of hand. Just as the eye can be deceived by an expert at sleight of hand, so believers can be drawn into unsound doctrine by expert spiritual deceivers. The Amplified Bible says of these men that they, "(invent) errors to mislead" [Ephesians 4:14 Amp]. They can make believers think they have a hand full of doctrinal aces when, in fact, they are spiritually and morally bankrupt! Because deception is their business, they are experts at it.

Seduce

The word "seduce" is a strong and suggestive word which accurately describes the activity of false spiritual leaders. The apostle John used this word when warning his spiritual children of the false spiritual leaders he called antichrists. In his first epistle, he wrote,

"These things have I written unto you concerning them that seduce you."

I John 2:26

To be seduced is to be led astray. It is to be persuaded to go against the conscience of your own heart and to depart from what you were previously established in as a standard for your life. To be seduced is to have your conscience overcome by good sounding words or by an outward appearance.

For false spiritual leaders to successfully seduce believers they must present themselves as harmless. They must paint a very favorable picture of themselves. They must convince believers that they want the best for them and would not hurt them. "We have your best interests in mind," they say. Their words sound so right. Their intention, however, is to lead believers away from sound leadership, away from sound doctrine, and away from sound bodies.

Vagabonds

The apostle John warned of deceivers in his second epistle. He wrote,

"For many deceivers are entered into the world, who confess not that Jesus Christ is come in the flesh. This is a deceiver and an antichrist."

II John 7

The word translated "deceiver" in this scripture is the Greek *planos* which depicts an imposter of the vagabond type. A vagabond is a person who moves from place to place without having a home base.

Some false spiritual leaders are vagabond types. They are like seeds in the wind. They blow along till they come to a place where conditions are suitable for putting down roots. They look for a place where people are not prepared for an imposter. They wander along from church to church and from group to group till they find a place where their doctrine can take root.

Often this is a young church or a place where the pastor is not guarding his flock. Often this is a place where people are not aware of the danger of false spiritual leaders and are hungry for something new and exciting.

Thoroughly Deceived

The possibility of deception and the consequent disastrous results made Paul afraid for the church at Corinth, the churches of Galatia, the church at Thessalonica, and, very likely, all the churches he was involved with. In his second letter to the church at Corinth, he expressed his fear saying,

"But I fear, least by any means, as the serpent beguiled Eve through his subtility, so your minds should be corrupted from the simplicity that is in Christ. For if he that cometh preacheth another Jesus, whom we have not preached, or if ye receive another spirit which ye have not received, or another gospel..."

II Corinthians 11:3

The word "beguiled" that Paul used in this text comes from the Greek *exapatao*. It is a strengthened form of *apatao* which means means deceived. "Beguiled" is intensive and means to be thoroughly deceived, to be completely fooled. Writing of Eve's deception in I Timothy 2:14, Paul used this same strong word. Thorough and complete deception is precisely what false spiritual leaders hope to accomplish. They want to completely hoodwink believers.

Paul also used the strong word *exapatao* (beguile) when he wrote to the church at Thessalonica to comfort them concerning some false teachers' doctrine about the second coming of Christ. He wrote,

"Let no man deceive (exapatao) you..."

II Thessalonians 2:3

Deception is the means false spiritual leaders use to achieve their end. It is their absolute intention to persuade individuals to follow them, but not realize what they are getting themselves into. There are, however, many specific methods of deception that false spiritual leaders use. Let's proceed now to examine some of the specific methods of deception.

ONE: DISGUISE THEMSELVES IN SHEEP'S CLOTHING

One of the primary ways false leaders deceive is by disguising themselves in sheep's clothing. By so doing, they conceal their inward motivation and true identity. Because of the very realistic possibility that believers could be deceived by this method, Jesus warned His disciples saying,

"Beware of false prophets, who come to you dressed as sheep, but inside they are devouring wolves."

Matthew 7:15 Amp

In order for false spiritual leaders to persuade believers to follow them, they must convince them that they are something different than what they really are. What better place to start than with that which is immediately perceptible. False spiritual leaders realize that very few believers will take the the time to look past the external and the obvious. This lack of scrutiny makes it easy for them to deceive by simply wearing familiar clothing.

False spiritual leaders deceive believers by covering their inward motivation with "garments" that are familiar. They come, "dressed as sheep," Jesus said. They look like sheep, act like sheep, and sound like sheep. From all outward appearances they are sheep. This is the reason Jesus warned believers to, "Beware of false prophets." It is because most false prophets do not look like false prophets. It is because most wolves do not look like wolves.

The method of putting on outward clothing to disguise one's inward motivation is as old as Satan himself. In his first calculated encounter with the human race, he came in a clever disguise. He presented himself in a way that both hid his inward motivation and was readily acceptable. Satan's successful deception and the consequent fall of the whole human race began with the outward "clothing" he put on!

Recently, there was a news report about several households that had been victimized by criminals dressed up as policemen. These men would come to the front door of a home and simply ring the doorbell. When the residents of these homes looked out and saw men in police uniforms, they did not suspect their motivation for being there. Their only thought was, "Open the door, it's the police." Once the residents opened the door and invited the "policemen" in, the "policemen" were able to exercise force and take what they wanted.

Why did these criminals go to people's homes? To steal their stuff! How did they get in? By dressing up in the clothing of men who are commissioned and authorized to protect and serve. These residents would have been wise to ask a few more questions and check a little closer before granting these "policemen" entrance to their homes.

Recently, I was at my parent's home. When I walked into the kitchen, I noticed a lovely bowl of green apples on the table. Because I was hungry, I went straight to the table and grabbed one. I was shocked to discover that it was a fake. I was so disappointed. What looked so real was found to be fake upon closer examination. In the same way, if believers are too hungry they may grab something that looks good and take a big bite before checking carefully. If they do, something far worse than disappointment will be the outcome.

In a very famous historical battle, an army devised a very clever plan to invade and overtake a city. Rather than bringing a direct attack, they pretended to make peace with the city. To prove their "good" intentions, they built a large, beautiful wooden horse and presented it as a gift. To the inhabitants of the defending city it seemed to be a time for celebration. They had won a victory and received a beautiful gift.

Little did the men of that city know, however, that the empty belly of the Trojan horse was filled with enemy soldiers. After darkness fell, the soldiers hidden inside the horse climbed out. They killed the city guards and opened the gate for the rest of their army to come in. Through a carefully calculated deception they were able to overthrow the city and gain the rule. What appeared to be a gift and was received as a gift turned out to be a means of destruction. What was outwardly and visibly acceptable cloaked an inward and deadly force.

Recently, I watched an afternoon talk show. On this particular day the host was interviewing men who preferred to dress as women. These men looked like, acted like, and sounded like women. Unless they took off their clothes, one would never know that they were not women! One man's disguise was so clever that he actually convinced another man to marry him! It wasn't till their wedding night that his true identity was uncovered!

How Jacob Deceived Isaac

An Old Testament man named Jacob deceived his father by disguising himself in "sheep's clothing" [Genesis 27:1-40]. Jacob's intention was to steal his brother Esau's birthright. His means was to disguise himself as his brother. Jacob was successful in deceiving his father Isaac and pilfered the birthright and blessing that belonged to Esau. There were several factors that contributed to Jacob's successful deception.

First, Jacob was successful because Isaac was old and blind. It was not by choice that Isaac was blind, but he was, nevertheless, blind. His physical condition made it far easier for Jacob to deceive him. Because he could not see, he had to rely on less accurate senses.

There is a natural seeing and there is a spiritual seeing. If believers have poor spiritual eyesight, they are more susceptible to deception. Believers must be sure that at all times their spiritual eyes are open and their spiritual ears are sensitive. If believers do not remain spiritually keen, they are candidates for deception.

Second, Jacob was successful because Isaac gave more attention to how Jacob felt than to Jacob's voice. When Jacob first spoke, Isaac was sure it was the voice of Jacob he heard. In fact, this was the reason Isaac asked to feel him. After he felt Jacob, Isaac said,

> *"The voice is Jacob's voice, but the hands are the hands of Esau."*
>
> Genesis 27:22

When Isaac felt and smelled Jacob, he was deceived. The Bible says that Isaac, "discerned him not because his hands were hairy" [Genesis 27:23]. Isaac checked several times, but in the final analysis he trusted more in the outward feel than in the voice he heard. He did not discern Jacob's intention because Jacob felt and smelled like Esau. Jacob's outward clothing concealed his true identity.

Believers must pay very close attention to what people say and to the spirit and the attitude behind what they say. Beware of those who try to move you by feelings. Beware of those who want you to get very close to them. Sometimes it is difficult to discern from too close! Listen objectively to the voice. Try the spirits. The "feel" may entice you, but the voice must be that of the Holy Spirit. Jesus said, "My sheep know my voice, and I know them and they follow me" [John 10:27]. Even if you don't have perfect spiritual vision, you can still recognize the voice. Never rely too much on how one makes you feel.

Third, Jacob was successful in his deception because Isaac was expecting and waiting for Esau to come. And "Esau" came. Because Jacob came disguised as Esau at a time when his father was expecting Esau, he had a very good chance to make his deception work.

Believers who are looking for a new word from the Lord or are restless to "move on with God" must be very careful. This is a prime time for false spiritual leaders disguised as true spiritual leaders to take advantage of you. It is not spiritually healthy to always look for something new. A time of expectancy is also a time of spiritual vulnerability. Isaac was ripe for deception by a false Esau because he was expecting Esau.

Disguised as a Loyal Friend

Satan came to Jesus one time disguised as a loyal friend. Jesus had recently been speaking to His disciples about His impending suffering and death. These soon coming events were very traumatic for Jesus. His flesh and His mind recoiled. That a part of Him wanted to turn back from the will of God is evident from His words and His emotional condition in the garden of Gethsamene.

Knowing that God had a plan of redemption and desiring to thwart that plan, Satan attempted to mislead Jesus through a vessel that He would not suspect as Satanic. Through the mouth of one of Jesus' closest companions came the Satanically inspired plea, "Be it far from thee, Lord: this shall not be unto thee" [Matthew 16:22].

Because of his close relationship with Jesus, Peter was shocked by Jesus' words about His coming suffering and death. He was emotionally unsettled. Therefore, he was not prepared for the thought that came to him and which, without examining, he spoke out of his mouth. Peter did not check his thought to determine whether or not it was in accord with the written scriptures. He did not examine what he was about to say to determine if it proceeded from his own emotions, hopes, and wishes or from the inspiration of God. Because Peter was close to Jesus, because his emotions were unsettled by what Jesus had just said, and because he was impulsive by nature, he was an convenient vessel for Satan to speak through.

It was Satan's intention, by speaking through Peter, to put a stumbling block in the way of the plan of God. He made a very serious and calculated attempt to entice Jesus to abandon His suffering and death. The words that came out of Peter's mouth were intended to pull on Jesus' soul. A part of Him was already drawing back from His impending suffering and death. Now, in addition to the recoiling of His soul, words being spoken by a close friend were further influencing him to draw back from the plan of God. Jesus, however, was keen in the Spirit and committed to the prophesies of the scriptures concerning Himself. Even at this moment of great emotional trauma, He was not unprepared for the schemes of the enemy. Because Peter's words were not in agreement with the witness of the written scripture and the witness of the Spirit, Jesus quickly discerned the inspiration of Satan.

In response to Peter's words, Jesus said, "get thee behind me Satan" [Matthew 16:23]. Satan, a master of disguise, had disguised himself in the body and behind the words of Peter. He came to Jesus as a companion and a disciple. Peter was the sheep's clothing Satan put on to deceive Jesus and hinder the plan of God.

Satan and his ministers are very cunning. They will disguise themselves in whatever covering they think will most readily be accepted. Never think for one moment that Satan will not use those close to you to entice you into error. Why will he use them? Because they are the ones you would least likely suspect to be in error or to lead you into error. Your soul is knit to your friends. You have a deep affection for them. There is a bond of loyalty between you. For this reason you can be blinded to the error they espouse. It is not impossible that those who you love and respect, even friends or family members, may unknowingly slip into error and be used by the devil to lead you into the same error. For this reason believers must cultivate and maintain a keenness to the witness of the Holy Spirit and cultivate and maintain a strong grasp of the scriptures. Be on the alert, especially when emotions and personal ties are involved.

Does Love Always Mean Acceptance?

It is very dangerous when false spiritual leaders come dressed up as sheep because believers feel obligated to accept other "sheep." The body of Christ has been instructed so much about the importance of love and acceptance that it has become the unpardonable sin to ignore someone or turn them away. After all, God accepts everyone doesn't He? No, as a matter of fact, He doesn't. And you should not either!

The teaching of love and unity tends to produce a relaxed posture between believers. This can be very good, but it can also be an open door of opportunity for false and unsound spiritual leaders to infiltrate sound local bodies. Anyone who refuses to accept another "sheep" will be accused of not walking in love and of promoting division in the body of Christ. We live in an hour, however, when we must be cautious. There is no need to be paranoid, but we must be watchful. The teaching of love and unity is wonderful, but it can also be dangerous. Associations can draw you upward in God, but they can also draw you off course.

The apostle John's first epistle is a perfect example of the important spiritual balance between love and discernment. He teaches in a clearer and stronger way than any New Testament writer about the importance of loving one another. Running parallel with his strong theme of love, however, are equally strong words of caution concerning those who claim to be spiritual leaders, but are seducers. Love and acceptance is important, even paramount in the church. But John said, "I have no greater joy than to hear that my children walk in truth" [III John 4]. Walking in love is important, but equally important is walking in truth. To accept, in the name of love, every person who claims to be a fellow-believer is spiritual ignorance!

Beware of Sheep!

The putting on of external disguises to conceal one's true identity and inward motivation is the most basic and oldest method false spiritual leaders use to gain acceptance by individuals who would otherwise reject them. Outward appearances can be very deceiving. Seldom can persons or matters be thoroughly and accurately comprehended without a closer examination. False spiritual leaders will disguise themselves so carefully that were it not for the serious warnings of Jesus and other New Testament leaders, believers would not discern them.

Do not be too afraid of those who look like wolves. They are obvious and, therefore, easily avoided. Be wary of those who look like sheep. They may be wolves in sheep's clothing! Remember this for it is as true in the spiritual realm as it is in the natural realm: The better the disguise, the less chance there is of being discovered.

False spiritual leaders will purposefully disguise themselves in order to get into the midst of the flock and devour the sheep. Don't be naive and think that no person would do this. They will! The Bible tells you so. Don't be ignorant or gullible, especially in these end times. Be wise as serpents. That is the admonition of Jesus.

Two: Transform Themselves Into Ministers Of Righteousness

Not only do false leaders disguise themselves as sheep; some transform themselves into shepherds! They display themselves as ministers of righteousness, misrepresenting their true nature and motivation. In this way they are able to creep unsuspected into local churches and gain a foothold in believers' lives. Perhaps the most deceptive way false spiritual leaders deceive believers is by presenting themselves as true spiritual leaders.

The false apostles who gained a position of leadership in the church at Corinth were described by Paul as those who transformed themselves into ministers of righteousness. He clearly exposed and marked these deceitful workers for the whole church saying,

> "For such are false apostles, deceitful workers, transforming themselves into the apostles of Christ. And no marvel; for Satan himself is transformed into an angel of light. Therefore it is no great thing if his ministers also be transformed as the ministers of righteousness..."
>
> II Corinthians 11:13-15

The word "transform" that Paul used in this text comes from two Greek words. The word *meta* implies change and the word *shema* refers to the outwardly perceptible mode and shape. The meaning of the word transform is, "to change the outward appearance," or, "to augment or alter what is perceived." The Amplified Bible says of false ministers that they, "masquerade as apostles." They come disguised as someone they are not.

It is not surprising that false ministers transform themselves because, "Satan himself is transformed into an angel of light" [II Corinthians 11:15]. In the Garden of Eden, Satan came to Eve in a form that was familiar and acceptable to her. Eve did not suspect Satan when he approached her because he had so carefully altered his outwardly perceptible shape. He not only came in a body that was familiar and acceptable to Eve, he also represented himself as an interpreter of the words of God. Although he twisted God's words, he did it in such a way as to sound as if he was giving the real meaning of what God had said. He transformed himself into an angel of light and a minister of truth.

Paul wrote to the church at Corinth because he was afraid that just as Satan transformed himself and deceived Eve, so the false apostles who had transformed themselves would deceive the believers at Corinth. Paul was afraid the church would be led away from truth and spiritual stability by men who claimed to be apostles and acted like apostles, but were false apostles.

Think about the words, "transform themselves." The false apostles in Corinth were not unintentionally misunderstood by the believers there. They purposely transformed themselves. They deliberately masqueraded as true apostles in order to gain entrance to that local church and make personal gain. Using the cloak of hypocrisy, they spoke lies and lorded over lives. They were not suspected, however, because from all appearances they were true ministers.

False spiritual leaders alter their outward appearance, hoping to be perceived as true ministers. They look like, act like, and talk like true ministers. They come as shepherds, pretending to care for the sheep. They use all the right buzz words. They "love the Word" and want to "flow with the move of God."

In every generation there will be men who transform themselves into ministers of Christ. Wherever there is a true people of God there will also be false ministers who will abuse and take from them by presenting themselves as spiritual leaders. The Word of God and the history of the church validate this reality. People of wisdom, however, will learn from the Word and learn from the past and avoid being deceived by false spiritual leadership.

THREE: THEY USE ENTICING WORDS

Another primary way false spiritual leaders seduce is by their use of words. Almost all false leaders are word experts. They have learned how to use words to work their way into leadership positions. They are convincing and charismatic, able to draw people into their movements with persuasive words. They seduce believers away from sound bodies by speaking untruth in a very persuasive way. Paul warned of these kind of men saying,

"And this I say, lest any man should beguile you with enticing words."

Colossians 2:4

The word "beguile" Paul used in this verse means, "to deceive by means of false reasoning." The phrase "enticing words" suggests the use of persuasive speech in contrast to demonstrating true spiritual power. By the masterful use of words, false and unsound spiritual leaders manipulate, deceive, coerce, sway, and bring under control those who listen to them.

In Ephesians 5:6, Paul warned the believers at Ephesus saying, "Let no man deceive you with vain words." To the church at Colosse he said, "Beware lest any man spoil you through philosophy and vain deceit" [Colossians 2:8].

Word Experts

Spiritual word experts could be likened to our modern day lawyers. Lawyers are experts at arguing cases. It is often true, however, even in legal court cases, that right does not prevail. Often it is the best presentation, be it right or wrong, that prevails. Some lawyers argue and win cases for defendants they don't even believe.

When I was in college, I heard an interesting story about a young man on the debate team. This young man was assigned to defend a particular position. He took that position, argued his case, and won. Then they switched him over to the opposite side of the debate. He took the opposite position, argued it, and won again! Who knows what he really believed. He was a word expert and could prove either side.

Recently, I was a guest on a Christian television program speaking about the importance of discernment in doctrine and spiritual leadership. In the course of the program the host shared with me that he and his wife had recently encountered unsound teaching. They had organized a Bible study in their home and invited a certain person to do the teaching. In a short time, without realizing what had happened, they had been drawn into doctrine that was unsound. Although they had a check in their spirits about what was being taught, the person doing the teaching was very convincing. His explanations sounded so right that the host and his wife were persuaded. In time, however, they realized that they had been drawn into unsound teaching and terminated the Bible study.

Many Christians who have been seduced by unsound spiritual leaders had an early warning in their spirit, an alarm or a bad feeling about that person. At the same time, however, there was a fleshly pull, convincing words, and an implication from the false teacher that if one didn't believe their teaching they were spiritually ignorant. Through the art of persuasion false spiritual leaders convince believers to override their conscience. Word experts can present their doctrinal cases in such convincing ways that even when the Spirit of God is warning that their doctrines are not sound, believers find themselves being persuaded.

Through Feigned Words

The apostle Peter said this concerning false teachers' use of words,

"...there shall be false teachers among you...And through covetousness shall they with feigned words make merchandise of you..."

II Peter 2:1-3

The word "feigned" means, "formed, molded, or fabricated." To teach with feigned words means to speak words that are pre-calculated to produce a certain response.

Motivated by fleshly desires, false teachers will, with fabricated doctrines and pre-planned speeches, make merchandise of believers. They will experiment with different teachings to find what gets the best response. They may practice different emotional displays and vocal levels. I have heard ministers talk about how to "work your audience." They learn which buttons to push, which words to say, what facial expressions to use. I even heard of one minister who offered to teach another minister how to cry at will in order to get people to respond.

Words Are Bait

Concerning false teachers, Peter wrote that they,

"...cannot cease from sin; beguiling unstable souls..."

II Peter 2:14

The word "beguiling" that Peter used comes from the Greek *deleazo* and means to lure or to catch by the use of bait. False ministers go fishing for men with snaring words. They use words to draw believers to themselves just as a fisherman uses bait to draw fish to his hook. Those who are not sensitive to the Holy Spirit or have not been warned to beware often "take the bait" and end up in the fisherman's boat. A good looking worm can make even a dangerous hook look appetizing!

The word "beguile" can also be translated allure or entice. Peter said of false leaders that when they,

> "...*speak great swelling words of vanity, they allure through the lusts of the flesh...*"
>
> II Peter 2:18

Jude wrote concerning false leaders that,

> "...*their mouth speaketh great swelling words...*"
>
> Jude 16

How is it that false leaders allure? It is with, "great swelling words of vanity." The word "swelling" is an adjective. It means excessive weight or size and is used especially of arrogant speech. False teachers do not just use swelling words, however. They use "great swelling words." We know from this phrase that false teachers, like politicians, attempt to appear as experts in their fields by the use of complicated and enticing rhetoric.

The words of unsound spiritual leaders are, however, "words of vanity." They are empty of any spiritual value. They cannot produce. Unlike the Word of God which gives life, bears fruit, renews minds, and saves souls, the words of false teachers only tickle the ears, excite the emotions, and puff up the head. Listening to these kinds of words is like swallowing air. For a short time the stomach feels full. But there is no food value and there will be no growth or strengthening.

Word Experts Prey on the Simple and Unstable

False spiritual leaders prey on the simple or the young in Christ because they are easy targets. In Romans 16:17-18, Paul said,

> "*Now I beseech you brethren, mark them which cause divisions and offenses contrary to the doctrine which ye have learned and avoid them. For they that are such serve not our Lord Jesus Christ...and by good words and fair speeches deceive the hearts of the simple.*"
>
> Romans 16:17-18

Paul spoke here of unsound spiritual leaders who "deceive the hearts of the simple." How do unsound spiritual leaders deceive the *hearts* of the simple? They do so by playing word games with their *heads*. They use convincing words and enticing speeches — "good words and fair speeches," Paul called them. Their words are tools of deception used to sway people. The simple, especially, are not hard to sway. They are often naive and pure hearted, not educated to the ugly reality that a "spiritual leader" would deceive them.

In his letter to Titus, Paul warned of false teachers saying,

"For there are many unruly and vain talkers and deceivers, specially they of the circumcision: Whose mouths must be stopped, who subvert whole houses, teaching things..."

Titus 1:10-11

Paul labeled these false teachers as "deceivers." This word comes from the Greek *phrenapates* and literally means "mind-deceiver." How did these false spiritual leaders deceive peoples' minds? With enticing teaching! Their teaching was not truth, but because it was presented in a skillful and convincing way, they were able to persuade believers that it was truth. Rational teaching, even if it is not truth, can be convincing to the rational mind.

The words of seducers are like weapons. With them they intimidate those who do not excel in the mental realm. One who is mentally sharp and convincing can win arguments even when he is wrong. His mental ability gives him power over those who are less adpet. Often the simple cannot defend their convictions against the verbal skills of false leaders.

Beguile Unstable Souls

In II Peter 2:14, Peter said concerning false teachers that they, "(beguile) unstable souls." The Knox translation says,

"They know how to win wavering souls to their purpose."

II Peter 2:14 Knox

The New English Bible says,

"...they captivate the unsteady ones..."

II Peter 2:14 NEB

The unstable are usually spiritual pushovers for false spiritual leaders. The unstable are not rooted and grounded in the Word of God. These unsteady individuals are already teetering and, thus, easy to upset. When unsound spiritual leaders present themselves as experts and tell the simple, "This is right," the simple will usually agree.

Heresies

In order to draw disciples away from sound bodies and into their groups, false leaders must teach something different than what is being taught in the sound body. If false leaders submitted to and promoted the truth, they would no longer stand out as different. Their teaching would be the same as everyone else's. Without different doctrine, false leaders could not establish their own followings. When, however, they espouse their opinions in the place of the truth they cause divisions in the church and the formation of new splinter groups of which they are leaders. The teaching of heresies is a primary means to establishing their own followings.

There is an inseparable relationship between false leadership, heresies, and sects. This inseparable relationship is very clear in Paul's words of correction to the church at Corinth. He wrote,

> "...when ye come together in the church, I hear that there be divisions among you...For there must be also heresies among you, that they which are approved may be made manifest among you."
>
> I Corinthians 11:18-19

False leaders invent and promote heresies. Heresies give rise to factions and sects. In between false leaders and new sects are heresies. The promotion of heresies is a means false leaders use to get to the end of having their own followings.

The True Minister Verses the False Teacher

True spiritual leaders preach and teach the simple Word of God and trust the power of the Holy Spirit to affect the hearts of men. False spiritual leaders speak convincing words hoping to mislead sincere individuals into their parties. The true spiritual leader can boldly say with Paul,

> "For our exhortation was not of deceit, nor of uncleanness, nor in guile: But as we were allowed of God to be put in trust with the gospel, even so we speak; not as pleasing men, but God, which trieth our hearts. For neither at any time used we flattering words, as ye know..."
>
> I Thessalonians 2:3-6

The purposeful use of enticing words was something that Paul refused in his own ministry. In I Corinthians 2:1-4, he said,

> "And I, brethren, when I came to you, came not with excellency of speech or of wisdom...For I determined not to know anything among you save Jesus Christ, and him crucified...And my speech and my preaching was not with enticing words of man's wisdom..."
>
> I Corinthians 2:1-4

Paul refused the temptation to draw people to himself with persuasive words. Instead, he preached the pure Word of God and let the Spirit of God draw men to the truth.

FOUR: THEY MISUSE THE WORD

Another way false spiritual leaders seduce disciples is by misusing the Word of God. Knowing that Christians depend upon and trust the scriptures, they use the scriptures in a deceitful manner to mislead believers.

Paul, a true minister of the gospel, said that he would not use the Word of God in a deceitful manner. He had,

> "...*renounced the hidden things of dishonesty, not walking in craftiness, nor handling the word of God deceitfully...*"
>
> *II Corinthians 4:2*

According to W.E. Vine, the word "deceitfully" Paul used here means to, "ensnare especially by mingling the truths of the Word of God with false doctrines or notions, and so handling it deceitfully." Some false ministers handle the Word of God deceitfully and, thus, ensnare individuals. They lure people into corrupt doctrine and unhealthy teaching using the Word of God as bait.

A true and honest minister, Paul refused to distort the Word of God for his own advantage. He would not pre-plan how to sway his hearers. In II Corinthians 2:17, he said,

> "*For we are not as many, which corrupt the word of God: but as of sincerity, in the sight of God speak we in Christ.*"
>
> *II Corinthians 2:17*

The word "corrupt" that Paul used in this text is very interesting. It means to deceive and to adulterate the Word of God, but includes the broader meaning of doing so in order to make dishonest gain. False spiritual leaders who corrupt the Word of God do so in order to profit personally.

This word "corrupt" also signifies being a peddler or a huckster. A huckster is a person who deals in anything whatsoever in order to make base gain. He will do anything for personal advantage. False spiritual leaders are hucksters. They will do whatever they must do to make a "sale," including misusing the Word of God. They are like the peddlers of the old west who marketed magical cure-all potions until they were discovered and run out of town.

Paul said that he did not "hucksterize" the Word of God, but handled it with all sincerity in the sight of God. He didn't twist it, misteach it, misinterpret it, or in any way compromise it in order to benefit himself. He said, "we are not as many, which corrupt the word of God" [II Corinthians 2:17]. Apparently there were many individuals in Paul's day who misused the Word of God for their own advantage. This will also be true in the last days. Many unsound spiritual leaders will use the Word of God for their own personal gain.

They Use the Word Unlawfully

Paul wrote to Timothy of false leaders who desired to be teachers of the law. In this context he said,

"But we know that the law is good, if a man use it lawfully."

I Timothy 1:8

There is absolutely nothing wrong with the scriptures, even with the Old Testament law. The law is only good, however, if a man use it lawfully. Some false teachers do not use the scriptures lawfully. Rather than using the Word of God to edify believers and build the kingdom of God, they use it as a means to build their own kingdoms. They use it as a weapon in their own war. They twist the truth and then teach it for their own advantage. They pervert the scriptures and then use the scriptures to persuade others to join them. Paul warned the elders at Ephesus of this very activity saying,

"Also of your own selves shall men arise speaking perverse things, to draw away disciples after them."

Acts 20:31

The word translated "perverse" in this scripture means twisted or distorted. False leaders seldom promote blatant false doctrine. If they did, they would not be accepted. Rather, they twist the Word of God, misapply the Word of God, or mix the Word of God with other teachings. Rather than studying the Word of God in order to become established in true doctrine, false teachers search for passages of scripture to support their erroneous doctrines. This misuse of the Word of God is very effective for influencing young or uneducated Christians.

The Judaizers Misused the Word

In Acts 15 we read that certain false teachers from the church in Jerusalem went to Antioch and attempted to influence believers into their brand of doctrine. These Judaizers used the scriptures to "prove" their doctrine. They wrongly divided the Word of Truth in their endeavor to bring New Testament believers under submission to the Old Testament covenant of circumcision. By the careful use of Old Testament scriptures, these false teachers were successful in swaying the hearts and subverting the souls of young believers.

Paul said of the false teachers called the Judaizers that they, "pervert the gospel of Christ" [Galatians 1:7]. They perverted the truth in order to bewitch believers and bring them into bondage. They used the scriptures to gain positions in local churches. They did not, however, rightly divide the word of truth [II Timothy 2:15]. Their application of Old Testament law to New Testament freedom in Christ was an abuse of the scriptures. By using the scriptures, however, they were able to make significant inroads into some local churches.

FIVE: THEY SEDUCE WITH ZEAL

In Galatians four, Paul expressed his fear concerning the spiritual condition of the churches in Galatia due to the zealous activity of the Judaizers. In verse 11, he said,

"I am afraid of you, lest I have bestowed upon you labour in vain."

Galatians 4:11

Paul was afraid that the young converts in Galatia would be carried away by the proselyting fervor of the Judaizers. He was afraid that the hours of teaching and prayer he had invested into their lives would be undone by the high energy false teachers they were listening to. The churches were being affected, but not in a good way. In verse 17, Paul said this concerning the false teachers in Galatia,

"They zealously affect you, but not well..."

Galatians 4:17

The Amplified Bible says,

"These men [the Judaizing teachers] are zealously trying to dazzle you — paying court to you, making much of you; but their purpose is not honorable or worthy or for any good. What they want to do is to isolate you [from us who oppose them], so that they may win you over to their side and get you to court their favor."

Galatians 4:17 Amp

The false teachers influencing the churches of Galatia were "on fire." They were aggressive and persuasive in promoting their version of the gospel. They were trying to dazzle the young believers with their zeal for spiritual things.

Zeal is not wrong. In fact, Paul told the churches in Galatia that it was a good thing to be zealously affected. But, he said in verse 18, it is good to be, "zealously affected always in a good thing." The believers in Galatia were being affected by the zeal of the Judaizers, but not in a "good thing." Wrongly mistaking the zeal of the Judaizers for spirituality and a deeper spiritual commitment, they thought they were "going on with God." They thought they were in the "next move."

Proselyting zeal must not be mistaken for Christian fervor! Those who have a new twist and a "deeper revelation" are often very zealous to spread their message. They are thrilled with their own movement. They promote their gospel with energy and enthusiasm. Their enthusiasm can be very con-tagious. It is transmitted to others just as fire spreads from dry tree to dry tree.

Believers must be careful of those who exhibit a zeal to "go on with God" and to "get into the next move." If there is no real next move, then those who are zealously pursuing it become court jesters for the devil's enter-tainment. The devil laughs at the church because again he has side-tracked believers away from the central calling of the church which is to preach the simple gospel and make disciples of all nations. As the devil laughs and the world laughs, the church continues on in its grave ignorance, unwilling to suspect, much less admit, that they may be wrong.

The Power of a Charismatic Personality

Recently, I heard of a man who caused one of the biggest Savings and Loan bankruptcies in the United States. This man had, in a very short peri-od of time, squandered two billion dollars of bank money on parties, boats, travel, art, and other personal interests. He pushed the bank into irrecov-erable debt.

When the history of this man was finally investigated, it was discovered that he was a con. Everywhere he had been in the past few years he had bankrupted businesses and cheated people. This man, however, gave great speeches and offered seemingly innovative ideas about how to make a great profit for the bank. Because this man talked like a leader, he was accepted as a leader. Because he marketed himself as a leader, he was accepted as a leader. Without knowing who he was or where he came from, people allowed him a leadership position!

Some people in the church want charismatic leaders and so they allow charismatic individuals to "take" leadership positions. Without investigating their past, without examining their home life, without questioning their doc-trine, and without listening to the Holy Spirit, they gave them a place. They want a dynamic leader who is going to take them into great and mighty things! Like Israel, they want a king.

A short time ago, I was watching a minister preach on national televi-sion. I lost count of how many times he said that he was mightily anointed of God and that tremendous things were happening "right now" in the spirit. He kept saying, "A mighty river of financial miracle working power is going out over the people right now." When he said that God had specially anointed him and that a wave of financial miracle working power was flow-ing, people began to applaud and cheer. He had them! Of course, if they wanted to participate in the financial miracle wave, they had to give a sac-rificial gift into his ministry, "right now in Jesus name!"

Was God really in that? I seriously doubt it. The amazing thing is that most people don't know what is from God and what is not from God. They just believe whatever the preacher says because he claims to be, "mightily anointed of God."

The man I watched on television said that he was a prophet of God and proclaimed that what he prophesied was certainly going to come to pass. It would have been very interesting to do a poll of those who were in that meeting to see if they received a financial miracle. Of course, when this man does his next program, he will take testimonies from those who did have some kind of a miracle. When he interviews them, it will give credence to his ministry. Have you ever wondered why television ministers don't interview those didn't receive a miracle? Believers need to quit being so naive!

Unsound ministers who are charismatic and exhibit flash and pizzazz make true and sound leaders seem dull by comparison. This was a problem the apostle Paul dealt with continually, even in the churches he established. Paul was a true servant. He was willing to lay down his life for the church. He worked with his own hands rather than being a burden to the churches. Because of his servant attitude, however, some believers thought Paul was weak. After encountering the demanding, aggressive, and persuasive false spiritual leaders, Paul seemed dull and spiritually impotent by comparison.

Let's Go On With God

Zealous false leaders often promote a kind of getting high on following God. "Let's go on with God," they say. Often these zealous false leaders equate participation in their activities with "going on with God." They convince believers that if they participate in the things they call "spiritual," they will become spiritual. But this is not true. A truly spiritual person will naturally do spiritual things.

Some ministers who talk and preach about moving out with God and exploring new territory remind me of the early settlers of the United States. They were young and restless, zealous and unrestrained. They set out to explore and conquer. Unfortunately, many of these young and zealous explorers died. Sure, they were visionaries; sure they were zealous. But they were poor leaders because they didn't even know where they were going themselves! And the individuals they inspired through zeal, hype, words of excitement, and promises of fame followed them in their folly.

Only on rare occasions — specifically when the house of His own Father was being perverted — did the zeal of the Lord overtake Jesus. Otherwise He was not a naturally inspiring leader. He did not set the world on fire with His preaching and hyped up meetings. Often He could be found quietly instructing the disciples on the side of a mountain or addressing a crowd from a boat.

This is the reason Jesus was despised and finally rejected of men [Isaiah 53]. It was because He was not a dynamic leader. It was because He did not push people or force His program. He was a solitary man, usually soft spoken, Who brought forth the truths of heaven like gems set on a pillow of silk. He ministered the Word of God for three and a half years and invited people to follow Him. Those who had spiritual ears heard and followed. As for the rest, He let them go their own ways.

Yes, our Lord is a warrior, but not in the way we think. He is not a warrior like Rambo. Some modern day ministers are guilty of trying to create the same Jesus that the people of Bible days were trying to create. They wanted a dynamic king. They wanted someone who was forceful and domineering. But Jesus came as a servant.

It is Jesus' earth ministry that true spiritual leaders are to emulate and imitate. Let me repeat that: It is Jesus' earth ministry that true spiritual leaders are to emulate and imitate! In His earth ministry, Jesus humbled Himself to serve. That is why God could anoint Him with the Spirit without measure. Because Jesus was totally dedicated as a servant to God and a servant to the people, God could trust Him with His full anointing.

False and unsound spiritual leaders may indeed zealously affect believers, but not in a good thing. They will try to get believers involved with and turned on to the things that they teach. They will endeavor to get them excited and enthusiastic, but not in things which bring true spiritual profit. Zeal without knowledge is empty activity. It is dangerous because it takes the place of true spirituality.

FIVE: THEY SEDUCE BY A DISPLAY OF POWER

Speaking of false spiritual leaders and the last days, Jesus said,

"...false Christ's (those who pretend to be anointed) and false prophets (those who claim to speak for God) shall arise, and shall shew signs and wonders, to seduce, if it were possible, even the elect."

Mark 6:22

Another way that false leaders will attempt to deceive in these last days is through the use of signs and wonders. For believers, signs and wonders are most often considered to be a confirming testimony from God that a message or messenger is of Him. The devil and his ministers are very cunning, however. They will imitate God to mislead believers. This is why

God has given us the Holy Spirit. Within us, He will witness concerning what is and what is not truth and who is and who is not true. No matter what kind of supernatural manifestation you see and no matter how anointed or mighty in the Spirit a minister appears, if you have a check in your heart concerning that person, wait and watch!

In the book of Acts there was a false spiritual leader called Simon the Sorcerer. He maintained power over the people of his city through special signs and wonders. They perceived him as, "the great power of God" [Acts 8:10]. Simon the Sorcerer's supernatural powers validated his claim to leadership.

I heard the story of one evangelist who required people to register at the door for his crusades. They were to put their names and addresses on a special form and include what miracle they needed from God. Halfway into his evening sermon the evangelist would begin to call out people's names and addresses, telling them exactly what miracle they needed from God. It was later discovered that this "supernatural" information came from the registration cards, not from the Holy Ghost.

I heard a similar story of a minister who wore a hearing device in his ear while he preached. His wife would read information to him from prayer cards while he was on stage. Operating in this spectacular "anointing" always drew people's attention! This man was pretending to be moving in the word of knowledge, but it was all a scam! With his simple imitation of the supernatural he was able to deceive the simple and get their offerings.

SIX: THEY PLAY ON FLESHLY DESIRES

Some unsound ministers play upon people's fleshly or emotional desires. They know what people want or need and then become that in order to attract people to themselves.

The "We Love You" Approach

One way unsound spiritual leaders play upon people's fleshly desires is with a seductive "we love you so much" attitude. Unsound ministers who seduce in this way usually reach out to those who are hurting and unaccepted. Many people are desperate for love; they are desperate to find acceptance in some group; they need to belong somewhere. False ministers gladly fulfill these individual's need for acceptance. The thick love smoke screen they create and then hide behind can be very difficult to see past. Their false love is a dangerous spiritual trap from which escape is almost impossible.

It is important for believers to realize that identical external actions can be birthed out of completely opposite motivations. Whereas true ministers reach out to people in true compassion because the love of Christ compels them, false ministers reach out with false compassion because people's need for love and acceptance will cause them to open the door to their lives. False ministers who approach with false love are preying upon people's deepest and greatest need. They are fishing with a "hook" that many will swallow!

The seductive love approach that some false ministers use is dangerous for several reasons. First of all, it is dangerous because the ungodly motivation behind the "love" is very difficult to detect. The poison is hidden in so much honey that is is virtually impossible to detect. Second, the love approach is dangerous because soul ties are quickly established between those who "love" and those who need love. Even when an individual discovers that the false minister does not really love them, it is very difficult to sever the relationship. Third, this love approach is dangerous because when an unsound minister reaches out to someone in love, perhaps even takes care of that person for a season, he obligates that person to him. If that person tries to leave, the false minister will hold the fact that they helped them as a lever against them. "We helped you when you were desperate," they will say. "Are you going to desert us now?"

Prey Upon a Weakness in the Flesh

Another way that unsound leaders seduce believers is by preying upon a lust in their flesh. They may draw believers in by offering them more freedom than other "stiff and old fashioned churches." They may draw believers in by flaunting money and success. Believers hope by hanging around these ministers to get rich too. Some unsound ministers may even offer sexual freedoms that fit more with the times than with the Word. They will validate people's sinful desires through unsound teaching. They will assist them in overriding their consciences.

This is how a harlot seduces. By displaying herself in an enticing way, she causes one's fleshly desires to overrule common sense. A harlot will not tell someone that if they go with her it will destroy their family, waste their finances, ruin their reputation, and perhaps give them an irreversible disease. She exclaims that everything is OK. She pretends to care and may even say, "I love you." The whole time, however, she despises the person she seduces, thinking only of the money she will take. Whatever she has to say or has to be to get a person's money she will say or be. She becomes what a person wants in order to get what they have.

False spiritual leaders will do the same. They will find out what buttons to push to get believers to respond. What are believers looking for? Are they looking for words from God? We have them. Are they looking for love and acceptance? We have that. Are they looking for signs and wonders? We have that. Are they looking for emotional attachments? We have that too. Are they looking for sexual liberty? You can be free here. False spiritual leaders become what believers want in order to get what they have.

The woman Jezebel, a false prophetess from the church at Thyatira, was a seducer. Jesus said this concerning her,

"...thou sufferest that woman Jezebel, which calleth herself a prophetess, to teach and to seduce my servants to commit fornication..."

Revelation 2:20

Jezebel led believers astray both in doctrine and in lifestyle. She called herself a prophetess, but was a prostitute. She not only used convincing teaching, but also pulled on men's sexual desires in order to draw them to herself. She was not only persuasive and convincing; she was enticing.

This method of deception is a common theme of mystery movies. In these movies a beautiful woman is always in cahoots with a gangster. She disguises herself and uses her beauty to entice a good guy. She says the right words, puts on the right eyes, and acts the right way. Her outward gestures conceal her true motivation. By seduction, she attaches herself to the good guy. Her intention is to capture him and deliver him to the bad guy.

If you have ever watched a movie like this on television you may have found yourself wanting to shout to the good guy on the screen, "Hey, watch out! Don't listen to her! She's working for the bad guy." The good guy, of course, can't hear you. And even if he could, he would not listen. He's been hooked. He won't find out the truth about that woman until it's too late.

I'm sure that at times God feels like a person watching a mystery movie. He sees the whole picture. He knows what goes on behind closed doors. He knows the heart of the one dressed up like a real minister. Fortunately, however, when God shouts, "Don't follow them," we can hear and heed His warnings!

Play Upon a Desire for Knowledge

The name of the tree that God forbid Adam and Eve to partake of was, "The tree of the knowledge of good and evil." God had transmitted to Adam and Eve the knowledge that He wanted them to have. What He had told them was all they needed to know. Eve should have been satisfied with the knowledge God had deemed necessary for her. But she had a fascination with knowledge. Satan was able to deceive Eve by playing upon her desire for greater knowledge.

The people of Israel are a pertinent example of this problem. God decided to feed them seven days a week with heavenly bread called manna. This bread alone was to be their diet. Through this heavenly meat God would sustain and strengthen them. Israel, however, became bored with manna and began to lust for something more. Their lustful desire for more was fulfilled, but they died.

A strong desire for more — for something new, for something different — can be an open door for false leaders. If they sense that believers love knowledge, they will claim to have deep revelation.

I spoke with a man several days ago who was hungry and thirsty for revelation from the Word of God. His desire was so strong that he was hiding away from people and only studying the Word. He was desperate to learn. He told me that sometimes he would read and study for seven or eight hours a day trying to comprehend the Word of God. One time he became so frustrated with his lack of revelation that he punished himself by staying up for 24 hours to pray and study.

When I visited this young man, he was in need of help. He was in a dangerous spiritual condition. He would have been ripe for picking by some unsound spiritual leader. Fortunately for him, some of his friends were praying and God directed him to me and another sound minister. I told this young man to relax. I told him that study and prayer are not the revealer of truth, but that the Holy Spirit is the Revealer of Truth. I told him that if he would simply be sincere and faithful, the Holy Spirit would reveal to him truths he needed to know when he needed to know them. I told him that just as Jesus did not teach His disciples everything at one time, so God would show him a bit at a time what he needed to know and what he could comprehend and make use of. I told him that if he dug too hard he would find something, but it would be fool's gold. Revelation must be received with meekness, not aggressively pursued.

In his generation, Paul had to deal with gnostic men and women who were always seeking for heightened spiritual experience. They were always looking for deeper knowledge, a further revelation beyond what was written. Some gnostic women leaders claimed that when Eve partook of the tree or the knowledge of good and evil she did not sin, but gained greater spiritual revelation. These gnostic women teachers were encouraging other women, and men also, to seek further experiential spiritual knowledge even through sexual relationships. It was this problem that led Paul to tell Timothy,

"But I suffer not a woman to teach, nor to usurp authority over the man...Adam was not deceived, but the woman being deceived was in the transgression."
                                                                    I Timothy 2:12-14

Eve did not gain greater spiritual insight by partaking of the tree of the knowledge of good and evil. She was deceived and sinned. Her hunger for knowledge made her a willing student to the angel of light who came to interpret the words of God to her. Satan opened a door that God had closed by saying, "God doth know that in the day ye eat thereof, then your eyes shall be opened, and ye shall be as gods" [Genesis 3:4]. Eve wanted to see; she wanted her eyes to be opened. And they were! But her revelation was not from God and did not lead to godliness. Her revelation was of Satan and led to spiritual death!

A desire for knowledge beyond the limits that God has determined is dangerous. A hunger to see more is something "in you" that false spiritual leaders can find and use against you. If they discover you are hungry, they know the smell of food will bring you to the table. Without caution, you may sit down and begin to eat. As hunger caused Esau to forfeit his birthright, so spiritual hunger may lead you to forfeit your stability in God. Never be too hungry to make a careful examination of those who feed you!

SEVEN: CALL THEMSELVES SOMETHING

Some false ministers exalt and commend themselves in their attempt to draw people to themselves. They "commend themselves" and "(compare) themselves among themselves" [II Corinthians 10:12]. They boast beyond their true assignment and give good testimonies about themselves. They say, "I'm an apostle," or, "God has given me a message for this hour," or, "You can either listen to me or miss God." In a short time, everyone is saying about these individuals what they say about themselves.

Jesus referred to false apostles who tried to get into the church at Ephesus as those who, "say they are apostles, and are not" [Revelation 2:2]. These false spiritual leaders called themselves apostles, but they were liars. In Revelation 2:20, Jesus, referring to another false minister named Jezebel, said,

"...thou sufferest that woman Jezebel, which calleth herself a prophetess..."
                                                                    Revelation 2:20

Jezebel called herself a prophetess and was received as such by much of the church. Her successful deception began with what she called herself.

Paul wrote of the false apostles in Corinth that they, "exalt themselves" [II Corinthians 11:20]. He said, of himself, however, and of other men that he worked with that they would not,

> "*...make ourselves of the number, or compare ourselves with some that com-
> mend themselves...*"
>
> *II Corinthians 10:12*

A few months ago a pastor told me about a Christian talk show program
he had watched on television. A minister being interviewed on this talk
show said of himself that he was one of ten true prophets currently alive in
the earth. I am shocked that anyone would have the courage to say that
about themselves. The unfortunate reality is that many will say of this man
exactly what he has said of himself. Because he called himself a prophet and
acts like a prophet, they will call him a prophet and receive him as such.

I am Christ

In Matthew 24:4-5, Jesus spoke this warning concerning false spiritual
leaders,

> "*...Take heed that no man deceive you; For many shall come in my name, say-
> ing, I am Christ; and shall deceive many.*"
>
> *Matthew 24:4-5*

Notice that Jesus did not say false spiritual leaders would say, "I am
Jesus," or, "I am Jesus Christ," or, "I am the Son of God." He said they would
say, "I am Christ."

The designation "Jesus" is a proper name. It was the Son of God's earth-
name. Others have since had that name although they were not Jesus of
Nazareth the son of Joseph and Mary. The designation "Christ," however,
is not a proper name. It simply means, "Anointed One." The title "Jesus
Christ" simply means, "Jesus the anointed One."

The word "Christ" in Matthew 24:4-5 is spelled with a capital "C." This
capitalization, however, was added by the translators. Christ could be spelled
with a small "c." This would be more accurate because when Jesus said that
many would come saying, "I am christ," He was not primarily referring to
individuals who would actually claim to be Him — Jesus Christ of Nazareth
— but to individuals who would claim to be anointed of God. False
prophets and teachers who Jesus said would come declaring, "I am christ,"
will not be claiming, "I am Jesus Christ the Savior of the world," but will
be claiming, "I am called and anointed of God."

Think about it for a moment. If a person approached you claiming to
be Jesus Christ of Nazareth, the Son of God, would you receive him? Most
likely not. You would probably think the man was crazy. If someone
approached you, however, whether in person or by some other medium, and
said, "I am specially called of God," or, "I am anointed in a special way,"

would you receive him? There is a good chance you might. In fact, you may be inclined to believe him. If he was convincing enough you might even follow his ministry.

When Jesus warned the disciples to beware of individuals who say, "I am christ," He was warning them to be on the alert for men who would deceive by presenting themselves as true ministers. In these end days, believers must beware of those who claim to be specially called and divinely anointed. Some of those who do will be false prophets, false apostles, and false teachers.

They Glory After the Flesh

Some false spiritual leaders use claims of natural achievements to convince believers that they are qualified as spiritual leaders. They, "glory after the flesh" [II Corinthians 11:18]. They may say things like, " I used to work for so-and-so's ministry," or, " I went to such and such a Bible school." They may claim to be a friend of pastor so-and-so or use their number of years in the ministry as a validating factor. Some use the title "Doctor" to help raise their status in people's eyes. Some false leaders simply start organizations, vote themselves in as president, and thus create their own status.

The church at Corinth was in serious danger of following after false apostles who claimed to be true apostles. Because of this critical situation, Paul was forced to boast of his own apostleship and his own qualifications. He did not boast because he wanted to raise his personal profile and draw believers to himself. He boasted only because he was willing to do whatever was necessary to keep these believers in the will of God. Four times in II Corinthians eleven he apologized for boasting because it so embarrassed him to compete for God's people this way. Listen to his words,

> *"Would to God ye could bear with me a little in my folly: and indeed bear with me…That which I speak, I speak it not after the Lord, but as it were foolishly, in this confidence of boasting. Seeing that many glory after the flesh, I will glory also."*
>
> II Corinthians 11:1, 17-18

Paul made it clear to these believers that he was not speaking by inspiration — he was not speaking "after the Lord" — but was boasting only in order to keep them sound in the faith and following sound spiritual leadership. The false apostles in Corinth were boasting of their qualifications and thus validating their ministries in the eyes of the believers. Paul competed with these false apostles by playing their game. He said that if anyone was qualified for the ministry on the basis of fleshly reasons, he was. He then apologized twice more for boasting, saying,

> *"...Howbeit whereinsoever any is bold, (I speak foolishly,) I am bold also...*
> *Are they ministers of Christ? (I speak as a fool) I am more..."*
> II Corinthians 11:21-23

Paul, a true minister of Christ, had no desire to boast of his natural qualifications in order to validate his own ministry. In fact, he was embarrassed to do so. False spiritual leaders, however, will use claims of natural qualifications and fleshly achievements as a means of drawing believers after themselves. By commending themselves and giving themselves titles, false and unsound spiritual leaders gain attention and gain a following.

EIGHT: CLAIM SPECIAL SPIRITUAL EXPERIENCE

Some false and unsound spiritual leaders flaunt their supernatural experiences or even manufacture experiences in order to gain attention and validate their ministries. Their supernatural experiences are the "proof" that they are of God. By claiming to have special revelation or by claiming to have had a supernatural experience, they seek to leave the impression that they are specially called by God. Their claims of supernatural experiences are calculated to authenticate their "calling" to be a spiritual leader.

Unsound spiritual leaders sometimes use claims of special spiritual experiences because these experiences cannot be judged. Who can say whether they had a vision or not? Who can say whether or not the Lord spoke to them? Who can say whether or not they saw an angel? Because another person's spiritual experiences are difficult to judge, believers are put in a very awkward position when so-called spiritual leaders use them to validate their callings.

It is possible for unsound ministers to paint an unrealistic picture in people's minds about how anointed they are. People are vulnerable; they are gullible. And people love the incredible. True ministers refuse to use these tactics. Rather, they emphasize the truth that they are a Christian brother or sister; a fellow servant of Christ. They remind people that they are no more than what people see them or hear them to be. Even angels of God who brought special messages said to men who bowed down,

> *"...See thou do it not: for I am thy fellowservant, and of thy brethren the*
> *prophets, and of them which keep the sayings of this book: worship God."*
> Revelation 22:9

God Told Me

Some ministers attempt to validate their teachings by simply saying, "God told me." They claim that what they are saying is what the Spirit of

God is saying. Often, however, they are only attempting to validate their vain words.

Just this week, I was watching a Christian television program. After showing preaching from a particular meeting, the preacher came on live to appeal for money. His ministry, he said, was heading deeper and deeper into debt and he needed immediate help. Then he said that he had been praying and the Lord told him that there were 1000 people who would give $1000.00 each.

This man claimed to have heard from God. He said that God spoke to him. And, of course, God does speak to people. That is not out of the ordinary. This man, however, was attempting to validate his request for money because, "God told me."

Why is it that God always speaks in round figures? Why didn't He tell this man that there were 876 people who would give varying amounts ranging from $32.76 to $13,789.98? And if 1000 people were going to give $1000.00 anyway, why should God tell this man at all? What good does it do him to know how many are going to give and how much they are going to give? It is far more likely that this man was trying to persuade people to give to his ministry by claiming that God had spoken to him.

Paul Refused to Flaunt His Experiences

In II Corinthians 11 and 12, Paul was obligated to boast of his calling and apostleship in order to maintain his spiritual position in the church at Corinth and, "cut off the claim of those who would like to claim that they work on the same terms that we do" [II Corinthians 11:12 Amp]. He had to shut the door on the false apostles who were attempting to get a foothold in the church.

After he finished testifying of the many experiences he had in his ministry and the incredible hardships he had endured, Paul began to speak of his supernatural experience of being caught up into the third heaven. He introduced this validating supernatural experience by saying,

> *"True, there is nothing to be gained by it, but [as I am obliged] to boast I will go on to visions and revelations of the Lord."*
>
> II Corinthians 12:1 Amp

Paul began to speak of the visions and the revelations he had received from the Lord. He spoke of how he had been, "caught up into the third heaven...and heard unspeakable words, which it is not lawful for a man to utter" [II Corinthians 12:2-4]. He could have continued on to detail this divine experiences and he would have been telling the truth, but he stopped short, discontinuing his boasting by saying,

> *"Should I desire to boast, I shall not be a witless braggart, for I shall be speaking the truth. But I abstain (from further boasting of divine experiences and visions and revelations from God) so that no one may form a higher estimate of me than [is justified by] what he sees in me or hears from me."*
>
> II Corinthians 12:6 Amp

Paul could have gone on and on boasting of his supernatural experiences in the Lord and he would have been telling the truth. He refrained, however, so that no one would think any more highly of him than what they saw him to be in his own Christian life or heard from him when he spoke.

In refusing to boast, Paul demonstrated the attitude of a true minister of the gospel. A true minister will not flaunt his experiences with God. In fact, he will usually regard them as so personal, special, and holy, that he will be hesitant to speak of them except as the Lord commands and as it will be a benefit to the body of Christ. Even if he speaks of his experiences the true spiritual leader will emphasize the fact that he is no greater than any other believer, but that it was simply the will and purpose of God to visit him or speak to him in such a way. He will insist that he did not have a supernatural experience because he is special and neither is he special because he had a supernatural experience. He will humble himself, behave as a brother in the Lord, and give all the glory to God.

A true minister plays it straight. Even if God has used Him in special ways and given him special insight and revelation, even special spiritual experiences, he does not flaunt these experiences to heighten his respect among people. A true minister does not glory in those things that others cannot measure. He is content to be judged by what people see him to be and hear him to be. He purposes to conduct himself in such a way that people form their opinion of him not by what he claims to have seen, but by what they see and hear him to be themselves.

In defending his ministry, the apostle Paul always referred people to his lifestyle among them. He validated his ministry, not by claims of special experience, but by things that could be judged. Notice his words,

> *"Giving no offense in any thing, that the ministry be not blamed: But in all things approving ourselves as the ministers of God, in much patience, in afflictions, in necessities, in distresses, In stripes, in imprisonments, in tumults, in labours, in watchings, in fastings; By pureness, by knowledge, by longsuffering, by kindness, by the Holy Ghost, by love unfeigned..."*
>
> II Corinthians 6:3-6

The reason false spiritual leaders refer to special experiences rather than to their godly lifestyle, their commitment to the flock, and to their sufferings for the sake of the body, is because rather than being a benefit to the body of Christ they have actually benefited from the body of Christ. They have not lived the life of a servant and so cannot validate their ministry on that evidence. In fact, if they were judged on that evidence, they would be found "not guilty" of being true ministers. Unsound ministers prefer being esteemed as spiritual giants because of some spiritual experience over being esteemed as servants to people.

NINE: THEY SPEAK AGAINST TRUE SPIRITUAL LEADERS

Sometimes false leaders attempt to divide the flock and draw people after themselves by speaking against true spiritual leadership. They sow the seeds of discord hoping to harvest disciples. Paul asked the believers in Galatia this question,

"Who hath bewitched you that you should not obey the truth?"

Galatians 3:1

To "bewitch" means both to slander a person and to mislead individuals. The false teachers that bewitched the churches of Galatia did exactly this. They slandered Paul and his doctrine of justification through faith casting a shadow of doubt upon the hearts of the believers in Galatia. After bringing accusations against Paul and raising doubts concerning his doctrine and leadership, they presented themselves as true spiritual leaders. By "bewitching" they were able to persuade believers to accept their false doctrine.

False spiritual leaders often undermine true leadership by raising questions about how they lead or what they say. They will twist words, emphasize real or invented weakness in the leader, and lift themselves up in the eyes of those they seek to mislead. By speaking against Holy Ghost ordained overseers, they credit themselves.

False spiritual leaders will also attempt to introduce dissatisfaction within the body. They will test the waters to determine who is swayable; who is dissatisfied. They will pick out those who are looking for something new or something different and begin to draw them under their teaching. These false leaders will point out in a very "spiritual" manner what they see as wrong in the church; especially with the pastor. Often they will attempt to make believers discontent with their current spiritual leaders by emphasizing the faults or weaknesses of that leader.

They may say things like, "God is doing so much more than what is happening in your church." Or they may say, "Your pastor just isn't flowing with the new move of God." Sometimes they say cunning spiritual things like, "You really need to take some special time of prayer for your pastor because he is just not seeing what God is really doing." They will make any number of statements to create dissatisfaction in the people. They hope to turn believers away from the one that the Holy Spirit has made overseer in that flock. Because of what they say and how they act, these false spiritual leaders are often perceived as true spiritual leaders. In a short time a small splinter group can form within a local body and a foothold be gained.

This is precisely the problem Paul had with the church at Corinth. When he left there, others began promoting themselves as spiritual leaders. They spoke against Paul, saying that he was not a true apostle and that he operated, "according to the flesh" [II Corinthians 10:2]. Paul wrote his second letter to the church at Corinth to defend his apostolic calling to this church and to expose those who were really false apostles.

False spiritual leaders are not afraid to slander God-ordained and anointed spiritual leaders in order to raise themselves up as experts in spiritual matters. After slandering true leaders, raising questions and doubts concerning them and the truth itself, they will offer themselves as guides and leaders.

TEN: THEY ARE FORWARD AND DEMANDING

Often false spiritual leaders are forward and demanding. They simply push their way into churches. Anyone who would dare to question them is made to feel like a spiritual dunce. Paul reminded the church at Thessalonica of his gentle attitude among them when he said,

> "But we were gentle among you, even as a nurse cherisheth her children: So being affectionately desirous of you, we were willing to have imparted unto you, not the gospel of God only, but also our own souls, because ye were dear unto us."
>
> I Thessalonians 2:7

Some ministers force themselves on believers by putting themselves forward as authorities in spiritual matters. When they act like spiritual authorities, many believe that they are. Those who are demanding and aggressive are often esteemed as spiritual and regarded as leaders. Those who are gentle and meek, on the other hand, are often despised and ignored. Their meekness is mistaken for weakness. My observation, however, is that those who act bold, demanding, and so sure of themselves are often trying to convince people that they are something they really are not.

Recently, I heard of a young couple who left an unsound church after attending there for 17 years. Following their exodus they received numerous letters which told them they were reprobate, that God was finished with them, and that they were damned to hell. I heard another young woman say on national TV that when she had questioned her pastor concerning church finances, he told her that if she asked anymore questions, she would be damned to hell.

Isaiah said of Jesus that He was, "despised and rejected of men" [Isaiah 53:3]. Why did people despise Jesus? They despised Him because He was not the dominating, aggressive, powerful king they wanted. He was a servant. He was meek and lowly of heart. Though He was God's true anointed minister, He was despised and then rejected.

The apostle Paul was rejected by the church at Corinth. He said to them, "The more abundantly I love you, the less I be loved" [II Corinthians 12:15]. Paul's meekness was mistaken for weakness and so he was slighted. The church at Corinth, however, accepted false apostles who were demanding. The apostle Paul said it this way,

> "For ye suffer, if a man bring you into bondage, if a man devour you, if a man take of you, if a man exalt himself, if a man smite you on the face."
>
> II Corinthians 11:20

People have a tendency not to receive true, honest, and sincere ministers, but to receive those who come in their own name, exalting and promoting themselves. Some believers feel comfortable when demanding false ministers exercise their authority. Something in them feels safe when they are lorded over. They feel secure with a dominant leader. Jesus expressed this reality when He said,

> "I am come in my Father's name, and ye receive me not: if another shall come in his own name, him ye will receive."
>
> John 5:43

ELEVEN: THEY IDENTIFY WITH ORGANIZATIONS

Sometimes false leaders attempt to expand their doctrine and find doors of entrance into a local churches by identifying themselves with churches or organizations. Because associations are often happy to increase their membership, they are not always careful in their scrutiny of those who apply. It is not difficult, in a brief examination or written application, for a false or unsound spiritual leader to paint a nice picture of himself. If he can gain acceptance into an organization, he can get into local churches.

False spiritual leaders who want to get into a particular stream of ministry will use all the familiar "buzz words." If they want entrance into the Assembly of God churches, they will speak and act like Assembly of God people. If they want to be accepted in Baptist churches, they will speak "Bapteese." If they want to be accepted by Word of Faith churches they will speak the Word of Faith language.

I remember hearing the story of a young man who joined a particular organization. At first everyone was so excited about him joining. He had come from another part of the country and was committed to evangelizing in an area that really needed evangelists. In a short time, however, there came back reports that he was claiming to be an apostle and causing division in local churches. When his background was investigated it was discovered that he had already established a negative reputation for himself. When the leader of the organization tried to rectify the problem, the young "apostle" lost his temper and shouted about control.

False spiritual leaders may also claim to be associates or friends of true and accepted spiritual leaders. They will use names like one uses keys to open doors to the places they want to get in to. They may say, "I know so and so." They may say, "I spoke in so and so's church, so I should come to your church." They look for a ticket into local churches. By claiming to be "hooked up" with other respected leaders, false ministers can ride well accepted coat tails into local churches and church organizations.

The false apostles who wanted a foothold in the church at Corinth claimed to be affiliated with Paul and other true apostles. They claimed to work on the same terms. Their claim of companionship was their ticket into the church. Paul, however, took issue with the claim of these false apostles saying,

> *"But what I do I will continue to do…in order to cut off the claim of those who would like…to claim that in their boasted [mission] they work on the same terms that we do. For such are false apostles…counterfeits…"*
> *II Corinthians 11:12 Amp*

Paul said he would cut off the claim of the false apostles who said that they worked on the same terms as he did. They lied about their association with Paul in order to get into the church.

Earlier in this same letter to the church at Corinth, Paul asked a question which reveals one of the tactics of the false apostles who gained entrance into that church. He asked,

> *"Do we begin again to commend ourselves? or need we, as some others, epistles of commendation to you, or letters of commendation from you?"*
> *II Corinthians 3:1*

When Paul asked whether he needed a letter of commendation "as some others," he was referring to a method false spiritual leaders used to get into churches. They would obtain or forge a letter of recommendation from some other minister who had contact with the church they wanted to get in to. By so doing, they had instant credibility and an open door into the churches. Paul claimed that his "letter of recommendation" was the fruit of his ministry.

Paul revealed this same tactic in his second letter to the church at Thessalonica. He encouraged these believers not to be troubled by spirit, by word, or, "by letter as from us" [II Thessalonians 2:2]. Some false ministers were sending out letters of recommendation and claiming that they came from Paul. By "riding Paul's coattails," they attempted, and often succeeded, in getting into local churches.

CONCLUSION

False spiritual leaders employ various methods to get what they want. These include dressing up in sheep's clothing, coming as true ministers, misusing the Word of God, and other methods which we have studied in this chapter. False spiritual leaders will come disguised as the very move of God if they think you will follow! Every specific method is calculated to deceive and to hide the inward motivation. By carefully deceiving, false spiritual leaders hope to gain a position with people and profit by their position.

·~15~·
Results of False Leadership

The results of the activities of false and unsound spiritual leaders can range from detrimental to devastating. Due to their influence, some believers will be temporarily unsettled. Others will be robbed mentally, emotionally, spiritually, and financially. Some believers will let go of sound doctrine and sound spiritual life. Others may completely apostatize from the faith and shipwreck as did Hymaneaus and Philetus. There are no positive results from the influence of false and unsound spiritual leaders, only varying degrees of negative results. False and unsound spiritual leaders, if allowed a place of influence, will always weaken and sometimes even destroy believers and local churches.

Because false and unsound spiritual leaders invent and promote false and unsound doctrines many of the results of their activities are the same as the results of unsound doctrine that we studied in Section Three. There are, however, other negative results produced by the activity of false and unsound spiritual leaders. In this chapter we will explore some of those negative results. We will discover that the unsound activities of false spiritual leaders affect believers, local churches, and the reputation of God and the gospel. Becoming aware of these negative results will further educate us concerning the danger of false and unsound spiritual leaders and, as I have said before, put us in an aware and defensive spiritual posture.

ONE: THE FLOCK IS NOT FED

God has set ministry gifts in the body of Christ to bring the saints to maturity. They help bring believers "unto the measure of the stature of the fullness of Christ" [Ephesians 4:13]. They help to equip them "for the work of the ministry, for the edifying of the body of Christ" [Ephesians 4:12].

When true spiritual leaders hold a place of leadership in a church the sheep come to maturity and are prepared to do their part in the church.

Even in the Old Testament it was essential to have spiritual shepherds to lead and feed the sheep. Notice the kind of leadership God intended for His people to have in the Old Testament,

> *"And I will set up shepherds over them which shall feed them: and they shall fear no more, nor be dismayed, neither shall they be lacking, saith the Lord."*
>
> Jeremiah 23:4

The shepherd's primary responsibility is to feed the flock. When the flock is properly fed, the sheep will fear no more, they will not be dismayed, and they will not be lacking. Their faith will be strong, their hope will be intact, and their needs will be supplied. This all comes through proper feeding. Notice this promise from God to His flock,

> *"And I will give you pastors according to mine heart, which shall feed you with knowledge and understanding."*
>
> Jeremiah 3:15

It is with spiritual knowledge and understanding that a true shepherd feeds the flock of God. The pastors, or shepherds, that minister this way are according to the heart of God.

The very least that will occur if a false or unsound spiritual leader gets a foothold in the church is that the flock will not be fed. If the sheep are not fed, they will not come to spiritual maturity. They will not be prepared to do the good works God has ordained for them. They will also be susceptible to spiritual attack. Their lack of knowledge will make them vulnerable both to the storms of life and to the devouring activities of Satan and his cohorts.

These negative results were addressed by God Himself in His judgement of the unsound spiritual leaders of Jeremiah's day. He said,

> *"Son of man, prophesy against the shepherds of Israel, prophesy, and say unto them, Thus saith the Lord God unto the shepherds; Woe be to the shepherds of Israel that do feed themselves! should not the shepherds feed the flocks? Ye eat fat, and ye clothe you with wool, ye kill them that are fed: but ye feed not the flock."*
>
> Ezekiel 34:2-3

In this word of judgement, God asked a question. He said, "should not the shepherds feed the flocks?" This is the prime responsibility of the true shepherd. Under the rule of an unsound spiritual leader the flocks will not be fed.

Feed My Sheep

In John chapter 21 we find the account of Jesus' commission to Peter to feed the sheep. Three times Jesus asked Peter, "Simon, son of Jonas, lovest thou me?" Three times Peter answered, "Yea, Lord; thou knowest that I love thee." Each time Peter answered this way, Jesus responded by instructing him, "Feed my sheep" [John 21:15-17].

By instructing Peter three times, "Feed my sheep," Jesus was impressing upon his heart that feeding the sheep was his life-time vocation. Peter was called to the ministry. He was called to work for the Lord. And what was the essence of his calling? He was to feed the flock. Yes, Peter had a healing ministry. Yes, he was an apostle to the Jews. Yes, he had a place of spiritual authority in the local church at Jerusalem. But burned deep into his consciousness by the thrice repeated instructions of Jesus was the reality that he was called to nurture and feed the flock.

That this message was, in fact, burned very deeply into the consciousness of Peter is evident from his words to elders who came under his spiritual authority. He charged them with these very same instructions saying,

> "The elders which are among you I exhort...Feed the flock of God which is among you."
>
> *I Peter 5:1-2*

The same instructions that Jesus gave to Peter and that Peter gave to other spiritual leaders, Paul gave to the Holy Ghost ordained leaders in the church at Ephesus. When he was preparing to depart from them for the last time, he charged them,

> "Take heed therefore...to all the flock over the which the Holy Ghost hath made you overseers, to feed the church of God, which he hath purchased with his own blood."
>
> *Acts 20:28*

Local churches need to be fed spiritual food. False spiritual leaders, however, because they are not called of God, are not equipped to feed the sheep. When false or unsound spiritual leaders are allowed to gain a place of leadership, the flock will not be fed.

TWO: BELIEVERS HINDERED FROM FULL TRUTH

Those who make the mistake of following unsound spiritual leaders will be hindered from entering into the knowledge of God and, thus, hindered from entering into the full blessings of God. They will forfeit spiritual, mental, emotional, and physical prosperity. They will leave the straight, narrow,

and level road of truth — the road that leads to more light and more life —
and become bogged down in the quagmire of religious tradition.

It is not God's will that believers are hindered in any way. False spiritual
leaders, however, get in the way of the will of God. They are a roadblock
in the way of believers' destiny to stand, "perfect and complete in all the will
of God" [Colossians 4:12]. Paul warned of the hindering force of false spiritual leaders in Rome when he said,

> "Now I beseech you, brethren, mark them which cause divisions and offenses
> (stumblingblocks and traps) contrary to the doctrine which ye have learned; and
> avoid them."
>
> Romans 16:17

This word "offenses" Paul used comes from the Greek *skandalon*. This
word is used of anything that hinders or causes to fall by the way. False and
unsound spiritual leaders are an offense to believers. They get in the way
of sound faith, unswerving hope, unfeigned love, and every other quality that
can be identified with spiritual growth and sound faith.

When unsound spiritual leaders hide the truth from believers, they hold
them back from the full blessings of God. This has been a grave sin of the
leadership of some denominational churches. Many believers have been
steeped in the narrow teachings of their own denominations rather than
established in the full counsel of the Word of God. Consequently, they have
missed out on the "full gospel." They have been limited by their leadership.
They have been stifled rather than stimulated; they have been repressed
rather than inspired.

On one occasion, Jesus issue this stern judgement upon the religious
leaders of his day,

> "Woe unto you, lawyers! for ye have taken away the key of knowledge: ye
> entered not in yourselves, and them that were entering in ye hindered."
>
> Luke 11:52

The room of revelation is richly furnished. In it are the blessings of freedom that truth provides. The door is oiled and waiting to swing open. But
so-called spiritual leaders have taken away the key in order to keep power
over the people.

I grew up in a mainline denominational church. I never heard about
the baptism in the Holy Spirit. I never heard that God was willing to heal.
I never heard about lifting my hands and praising God. What I was taught
was not necessarily wrong, but Bible truths that would have been a great
blessing to me were withheld.

I was hindered from entering into greater blessings because important truths were ignored by the spiritual leadership I trusted. Some of these spiritual leaders were honestly ignorant themselves. Others were afraid to even entertain thoughts of "full gospel" truths because their position in the church would have been at risk.

Believers must make their own choices. They must not to yield the responsibility of spiritual matters to those who call themselves spiritual leaders. Why? Because if the leaders they submit to are not true spiritual leaders, they will forfeit the full blessings and freedom that result from knowing and walking in truth.

Christian friend, do not be lazy and allow others make all your spiritual decisions. That is spiritual communism. Think for yourself. Be responsible for your own life. You have the Holy Spirit and the written word of God. You have the ability and the responsibility to judge and discern for yourself. You need not, as John said, that any man should teach you. This does not mean, of course, that you do not need to be taught. It means that it is never spiritually healthy to be completely dependent on others. Being completely dependent on another makes you susceptible to deception and error.

THREE: BELIEVERS LOSE THEIR FULL REWARD

In his letter to the church at Colosse, Paul wrote,

"Let no man beguile you of your reward..."

Colossians 2:18

The word "beguile" Paul used in this warning comes from the Greek verb *katabrabeus*. This verb, commonly used in sporting events, referred to an umpire's decision against a racer. Paul warned the believers at Collosse to beware of false teachers who would attempt to disqualify them from receiving the prize that belongs to those who hold fast to sound doctrine and sound spiritual life. They should not let others, especially unsound and false spiritual leaders, make decisions for them in spiritual matters. If they did, they risked forfeiting the full blessings that belong to those who maintain spiritual stability. The Amplified Bible renders this verse from Colossians this way,

"Let no one defraud [cheat] you by acting as an umpire and declaring you unworthy and disqualifying you for the prize..."

Colossians 2:18 Amp

When athletes participate in sporting events, they voluntarily submit themselves to the decisions of the judge, the umpire, or the referee. If the umpire says, "Out," they are out. If a referee says, "Out of bounds," they are out of bounds. In spiritual life, however, it is foolish to allow others, especially those who are not true spiritual leaders, to be umpires and call us, "Out!"

Paul said that false spiritual leaders defraud believers of their prizes by acting like umpires. They discourage believers from receiving the blessings that belong to them by rendering judgements against them. They tell believers, "Well, you can't expect God to answer your prayers every time." They say, "Sometimes you just have to do what feels right for you." They make a mockery of obedience by saying, "Listen, have fun while you can, before you get to old." In varying ways, false and unsound spiritual leaders attempt to keep believers away from God's will and God's blessings.

Don't let any man be the final umpire in your spiritual life. No man has the right to call you safe or call you out. That right belongs to God alone. Don't let another man decide against you. If God is for you, don't let false leaders be against you.

Four: Doctrinal Error

One of the very obvious results of the activities of false and unsound spiritual leaders will be the infiltration of unsound doctrine into the church. Where you find false and unsound spiritual leaders, you will find false and unsound doctrine. They cannot be separated.

Peter said that false teachers bring damnable heresies into the church [II Peter 2:1]. Paul warned the elders at Ephesus that unsound men would arise in their local church and speak perverse things to draw away their own disciples [Acts 20:30]. Of the false apostles who gained a foothold in Corinth, Paul said they were preaching another Jesus and another gospel [II Corinthians 11:4]. Paul told Timothy that false leaders would give heed to and then promote doctrines of devils [I Timothy 4:1-3]. Paul informed the churches of Galatia that the false teachers who were misleading them had perverted the gospel [Galatians 1:6-9]. And the apostle John, when warning his spiritual children of those who would seduce them, referred to teaching that was not the truth [I John 2:18-27].

In the book of Jeremiah, God spoke these words of indignation against those who caused His people to err,

> "Behold, I am against them that prophesy false dreams, saith the Lord, and do tell them, and cause my people to err by their lies, and by their lightness; yet I sent them not, nor commanded them: therefore they shall not profit this people at all, saith the Lord."
>
> Jeremiah 23:32

False spiritual leaders cause believers to err both by their lies and by their lightness. Some unsound spiritual leaders purposely lie in order to lead God's people into error. They know their teaching is unsound, but covet the results of their unsound teaching. Other unsound spiritual leaders cause God's people to err through their lightness. Because they do not take seriously the responsibility of claiming to speak on God's behalf, they do not prepare themselves accordingly. Consequently, their teaching may include truth and error.

Some ministers do not take nearly seriously enough what it means when they claim to speak on God's behalf! Nowadays there are many self-proclaimed prophets running to and fro throughout the earth teaching others how to prophesy or how to be prophets. Soon there will be hundreds of spiritual children peeping, "Thus saith the Lord," throughout the body of Christ. Some of these so-called prophets and their disciples do not take nearly seriously enough what it means when they declare, "Thus saith the Lord," at the conclusion of their so-called inspirations. Those who claim to be speaking for the Lord had better have it right! I Peter 4:11 says,

"If any man speak, let him speak as the oracles of God…"

I Peter 4:11

This is a tremendously limiting factor in vocal ministry! It puts restrictions on everything a person says. If a man speaks, he must speak what God is speaking. He cannot say more and he should not say less. If he does, he has wandered outside God's will, outside divine inspiration, and over into the imaginations and vain impressions of his own imperfect thoughts. Those who claim to be speaking for God had better be sure they are saying what He is saying. Otherwise, they may be in danger of judgement themselves!

FIVE: BELIEVERS FALL IN THE SPIRITUAL DITCH

Speaking of unsound religious leaders, Jesus said,

"Let them alone: they be blind leaders of the blind. And if the blind lead the blind, both shall fall into the ditch."

Matthew 15:14

In this scripture, Jesus referred to religious leaders as, "blind leaders of the blind." In another place He called them, "blind guides" [Matthew 23:16]. The designation "blind guides" is a contradiction in terms, but Jesus used this obvious play on words to make a strong point. False and unsound spiritual leaders act like they know where they are going. Because they cannot see, however, they soon abandon the path of truth and light and fall into a ditch, halting not only their own spiritual progress, but also the progress of those who have foolishly followed them. The destination of blind guides and all that follow them is a spiritual ditch.

The word "ditch" that Jesus used to describe the destiny of unsound spiritual leaders and those who follow them would be better translated "deep hole." Especially in this modern century "deep hole" gives a more appropriate image to the danger of following unsound spiritual leaders than "ditch." When we who live in this modern time think about a ditch, we imagine a grassy incline off the side of the road. Although going into the ditch is certainly not as safe as staying on the road, it is not always disastrous. It is possible to drive into the ditch and come out again with minimal damage. I have done that a couple times myself! It is also possible to make forward progress, although obviously limited, while in the ditch.

A deep hole, however, is dangerous. It is a deep place. It is a small place. It is a dark place. It is a scary place. It is almost impossible to get out of a deep hole without outside assistance. And in the deep hole it is impossible to make forward progress!

Even in the Old Covenant the activity of unsound spiritual leaders was damaging. To the Old Covenant priests who backslid from the will of God and departed from His ways, God said,

> "For the priest's lips should keep knowledge, and they should seek the law at his mouth...But ye are departed out of the way; ye have caused many to stumble at the law; ye have corrupted the covenant of Levi, saith the Lord of hosts."
>
> Malachi 2:7-8

God said of these unsound priests of the Old Covenant that they had caused many to "stumble at the law." Not only had they departed "out of the way" themselves, but being esteemed as spiritual leaders, they "caused many to stumble," leading them away from the way of God and into a spiritual ditch.

Some who follow false spiritual leaders into the deep hole of spiritual error will never come out. They will become accustomed to the dark and prefer to stay there. Others will be fortunate enough to be dragged out of the deep hole by the prayers and commitment of other believers. Damage, however, will have been done and time lost. Walk carefully upon the narrow road of sound spiritual life because the ditch is deep and dark!

SIX: CHURCHES GO BACKWARDS SPIRITUALLY

Paul did not waste any time coming to the point in his letter to the churches of Galatia. Following a brief introduction he wrote,

"I marvel that ye are so soon removed from him that called you into the grace of Christ unto another gospel."

Galatians 1:6

The churches of Galatia were being affected by the proselyting activity of false spiritual leaders called the Judaizers. These men were a constant trial to Paul and to the churches which he birthed in the Spirit and established in sound doctrine. They constantly endeavored to bring young churches into bondage by persuading them to be circumcised according to the law of Moses. Paul contended with their teaching and warned the young churches of Galatia saying,

"Stand fast therefore in the liberty wherewith Christ hath made us free, and be not entangled again with the yoke of bondage."

Galatians 5:1

Rather than leading believers to spiritual growth, the Judaizers were entangling them in fleshly practices which satisfied a religious bent, but brought no spiritual growth. They were not teaching them the truth that would set them free and keep them free. They were teaching religion that would bring them back under a yoke of bondage. Continuing on, Paul wrote,

"Ye did run well; who did hinder you that you should not obey the truth?"

Galatians 5:7

After being saved, the believers in Galatia were becoming established in the truth and running well. They were making progress. They were overcoming. They were walking in victory. They were growing up into Christ in all things. Something happened, however, to threaten their spiritual progress. They were being hindered from walking in the truth.

The word "hinder" Paul used in this text is particularly enlightening. It comes from the Greek *enkopto* and refers to impeding a person's progress by breaking up the road or by placing an obstacle in the path. This word is very revealing concerning both the method and the results of the activity of unsound spiritual leaders.

False and unsound spiritual leaders break up the road. They steal parts of the truth and leave dangerous potholes, making it very difficult for believers to run. They also put up obstacles in the path, reducing believers' forward progress and increasing their frustration. It is very difficult to run on a broken up road or on a road filled with obstacles. False spiritual leaders do not help believers to progress, but hinder them, even pushing them backwards.

In Galatians 5:9, Paul said this of the negative influence of unsound spiritual leaders,

"A little leaven leaveneth the whole lump."

Galatians 5:9

The Amplified Bible says,

"A little leaven [a slight inclination to error, a few false teachers] leavens the whole lump [perverts the whole conception of faith, or misleads the whole church]."

Galatians 5:9 Amp

How aptly stated! Just a little wrong teaching from a few false teachers can pervert the whole conception of faith and mislead the whole church. It doesn't take much to make an impact. A little leaven can affect the whole lump!

Paul concluded his specific words of warning about the false spiritual leaders called the Judaizers in verse ten. Here he said,

"...he that troubleth you shall bear his judgment, whosoever he be."

Galatians 5:10

The Amplified Bible says,

"...But he who is unsettling you, whoever he is, will have to bear the penalty."

Galatians 5:10 Amp

False teachers trouble and unsettle believers. Through the power of persuasion, they draw believers away from the truth, thus hindering them from walking in freedom and liberty. False and unsound spiritual leaders are a hindering force.

Young Churches of This Generation

Just as the young churches Paul started faced an onslaught from false spiritual leaders, so many young churches, young ministers, and young believers in this generation will face the attempted intrusion of false spiritual leadership. Especially the young and the not yet stable are prime candidates for persuasive and oftimes overbearing and aggressive unsound spiritual leaders.

God is moving in this hour by His Spirit. All throughout the world people are coming into the kingdom. All throughout the world new churches are springing up. Concurrent with the moving of God's Spirit and the birth of new churches will be a continual attempt by Satan and false spiritual leaders to enter in and dominate these young churches. False spiritual leaders will attempt, as did the Judaizers of Paul's day, to bewitch the young, hinder their growth, deter their progress in the truth, and entice them away from true spiritual leadership. They will take advantage, if allowed, over the young and ignorant. This is why a warning must be sent out! Young believers must beware and true spiritual leaders must confidently take their place!

SEVEN: LOCAL CHURCHES CANNOT FULFILL THEIR VISION

When false or unsound spiritual leaders gain a position in a local church, that church will either be side-tracked from its vision or wounded to the place where it cannot fulfill its vision. The devil enjoys it when local churches get into such a spiritual mess that they abandon their God-given visions.

In Revelation two, Jesus addressed the local church at Thyatira because it had allowed a false prophetess to have a position of spiritual leadership. Because of Jezebel's ungodly influence, this local church had reached a point of spiritual crisis. Jesus spoke strong words of correction to this church, concluding His word to them by saying,

> "I will put upon you none other burden. But that which ye have already hold fast till I come."
>
> Revelation 2:24-25

What did Jesus mean when He said that He would put on this local church, "none other burden?" He certainly was not referring to a burden of sin or depression. He certainly did not mean a burden of sickness, disease, or some other negative thing. What did Jesus mean?

In one of His brief addresses to His disciples, Jesus said,

> "Take my yoke upon you...For my yoke is easy, and my burden is light."
>
> Matthew 11:29-30

A "yoke" was the device oxen wore over their necks which enabled them to pull a plow and work in the field. When Jesus told His disciples, "Take my yoke upon you," He was issuing them an invitation to work in His kingdom. By saying, "my yoke is easy, and my burden is light," He was assuring His disciples that the work He had for them to do would not be too heavy for them.

In His message to the church at Thyatira the word "burden" referred to a specific assignment Jesus had given to this local church. Just as individual believers have special callings and assignments, so local churches are given specific assignments. Different congregations are called to accomplish different works at different seasons and in different places. Jesus referred to this church's assignment as a "burden" because it would take commitment, dedication, and sacrifice in order to fulfill it. Churches that are stronger and more mature will be given greater "burdens." They will be given more responsibility.

Jesus said to this local church, however, that He would put upon them, "none other burden." There would be no additional assignment from the Head of the church. Why was this? It was because this church could not handle additional responsibility. They had been unsettled, misled, and weakened by the false spiritual leadership of Jezebel. Because of their spiritual condition, they were not capable of handling more than their original vision. All their spiritual efforts would be needed to rebuild and maintain spiritual stability. Jesus was telling this church, "Because of what you have allowed to happen in your midst, you are not capable of handling any further assignment. Just hold fast to the assignment I have already given you till I come." What Jesus had already instructed this church to do would be the totality of their vision. They were to hold fast to and labor in that vision till He came again.

When false spiritual leaders get a foothold in local churches, the churches will be weakened and may even fall apart. Just as a sick or injured man cannot win a marathon and may not even by able to run in it, so local churches that have been weakened by unsound spiritual leaders will not be able to fulfill their God-given visions. Even if the unsound spiritual leaders are discovered and judged, the churches that have been devastated by their influence will have to put all their efforts into rebuilding spiritual soundness. It may be years before they are ready to launch out again into the plan of God.

EIGHT: BELIEVERS AND CHURCHES SUBVERTED

Hymenaeus and Philetus were two false spiritual leaders who caused trouble in Paul's day. These men had erred from the truth, shipwrecked their own lives, and were busy promoting their false doctrines. The result of their proselyting efforts was that the faith of some believers was overthrown. Paul wrote,

"...Hymenaeus and Philetus; Who concerning the truth have erred, saying that the resurrection is past already; and overthrow the faith of some."
II Timothy 2:17-18

The word translated "overthrow" in this scripture is the Greek word *katastrophe*. A catastrophe is more than a difficult situation. It is more than an irritant or a temporary aggravation. A catastrophe is a disaster!

The results of the influence of false and unsound spiritual leaders upon the lives of believers and local churches can be disastrous! In a very short time what took years to establish can be weakened and destroyed. Foundations of faith can be eroded, souls vexed, relationships broken, questions raised, doubts stirred, and confidences shaken. Attitudes can be altered, hopes can be dashed, and lifestyle can be negatively influenced. When believers give place to false or unsound spiritual leaders, catastrophe can result.

The results of the activities of false and unsound spiritual leaders could be likened to the destructive effects of a hurricane. Houses that took years to build can be destroyed in a few moments of time. Some of the damage can be repaired. Many houses, however, will be completely ruined and have to be abandoned or replaced.

Young Believers Completely Unsettled

In Ephesians four, Paul painted a picture which accurately portrays one of the negative results of the influence of unsound spiritual leaders. He wrote,

> "...*no more children tossed to and fro, and carried about with every wind of doctrine, and by the sleight of men, and cunning craftiness, whereby they lie in wait to deceive...*"

Ephesians 4:14

If believers follow after false spiritual leaders, adhering to their teachings and following their example, they will be tossed to and fro, unsettled and shaken in the Christian faith. They will no longer be guided by Truth. They will no longer be led by the the Good Shepherd. They will not feed in green pastures. They will not lay down beside still waters. They will not be led in paths of righteousness. They will not dwell under the shadow of the Almighty. They will not hide themselves in the Rock. Rather than being anchored in the protective harbour of Truth, they will be tossed to and fro by the wind and the waves.

Spiritual children suffer the most from the influence of unsound and false spiritual leaders. Just as in the natural realm children are very often the innocent victims of the deviant activities of evil men, so it is true in the spiritual life. Young believers are not yet securely established in the Word of God. They are just beginning to recognize the voice of the Spirit. They are still basking in the afterglow of their new found life in Christ, unaware that trouble already waits at their door. Even if these children recognize that something is amiss, they are not prepared to defend themselves against wily unsound ministers.

Paul warned Titus of this grave danger of unsound spiritual leaders, saying this,

"Whose mouths must be stopped, who subvert whole houses, teaching things which they ought not, for filthy lucre's sake...rebuke them sharply..."

Titus 1:11-13

The word "subvert" Paul used in this scripture comes from the Greek *anatrepo*. It means to upset or to overthrow. A popular second century illustration of this word was the complete upsetting of a family because of the riotous activity of one of the family members. This illustration accurately depicts both the activity and the results of false and unsound spiritual leaders.

Paul told Titus that whole houses were being subverted by the activity of false teachers. By "whole houses" he was referring not only to natural families, but also to spiritual families, to local churches which, in those early times, met in homes. When once sound members of the church became unsound and began to behave in spiritually deviant ways, they upset the whole church family.

One Rotten Apple

When I was younger, I often heard adults quote short anectodes. Sayings like, "A stitch in time saves nine," and, "Haste makes waste," were very familiar. As I grew older, I began to realize that these sayings were not just cute, but were succinct statements of time-tested wisdom.

One of these familiar phrases which very aptly applies to the potential effects of unsound spiritual leaders is, "One rotten apple spoils the whole bushel." It is a natural law that rottenness, if contacted, will defile what is healthy. Sickness and rottenness is contagious, health is not contagious. If you put one rotten apple in a bushel full of good apples, the many good apples will eventually become rotten. If you put one sick person in a room full of healthy people, the many healthy people will become sick. Corruption perpetuates itself.

The law that rottenness defiles what is healthy is not, however, only a natural law. It is also a spiritual law. Paul said that, "a little leaven leaveneth the whole lump" [I Corinthians 5:6]. He was referring in this case to the corrupting influence in a local church of one unsound member. It is amazing how damaging and detrimental negative elements can be. A local body of believers — a local spiritual family — can have good teaching, sound doctrine, and good leadership, but be upset and unsettled by the deviant activity of just one unsound teacher.

Souls are Subverted

In Acts 15, the spiritual leaders from the church in Jerusalem wrote a letter to the church in Antioch concerning certain false teachers that had come to them from Jerusalem. They wrote,

> "...*Forasmuch as we have heard, that certain which went out from us have troubled you with words, subverting your souls, saying...*"
>
> *Acts 15:23-24*

False teachers bring trouble with them, even causing souls to be subverted. What does it mean that souls are subverted? In this context, the word "soul" refers, in general, to a person's spiritual life. The word translated "subvert" comes from the Greek *anaskeuazo. Ana* means up. *Skeuos* means a vessel. To subvert means to upset, or overturn, a vessel. The phrase, "subverting your souls," signified the upsetting and putting in jeopardy of a person's spiritual life and sound faith.

When believers submit themselves to true spiritual leaders, listening to their teaching and following their life of faith, they will come to maturity, stand perfect and complete in all the will of God, and be vessels of honor. If, however, believers submit themselves to false or unsound spiritual leaders, their lives will be turned upside down. Vessels which God intended to establish in the faith, fill with His love, grace with His glory, and use for His service will be overturned and the faith, love, glory, and anointing will run out!

The word "subverting" used in this text also referred, in a military context, to the plundering of a town. When a town is plundered, it is burned and all its precious goods are stolen. If false spiritual leaders gain entrance into the "town" of local churches, they will plunder them. They will take the goods, burn the people, and then go on to the next place. False and unsound spiritual leaders can rob a whole church of its precious goods; its peace, its faith, its love, and its unity.

This same word "subverting" was also used in Bible times of going bankrupt. If believers allow false spiritual leaders to run the business of their spiritual lives, they will go bankrupt. Occasionally believers will be able to declare bankruptcy and reorganize their lives under other leadership. Many times, however, believers will literally go under. Unsound spiritual leaders defraud believers of spiritual richness and stability. They never add anything to a church, but rob true richness in God.

NINE: FLOCKS ARE SCATTERED

A flock that takes years to build up can be wounded and scattered in a short span of time by cunning wolves. In Jeremiah 10:21, God spoke of the condition that resulted in His flock because of the activity of false spiritual leadership,

> *"For the pastors are become brutish, and have not sought the Lord: therefore they shall not prosper, and all their flocks shall be scattered."*
>
> *Jeremiah 10:21*

God said that the pastors, or the shepherds, were brutish. This meant that they cared only about base pleasures. They wanted food, they wanted money, they wanted sexual pleasures. Spiritually they were boorish. They did not seek the Lord and they did not bless the flock. Because of this, they did not prosper and all their flocks were scattered.

When a pastor or any other minister becomes unsound, caring only about his own hunger and his own wants, then he will not prosper in any spiritual qualities and the people he leads will be scattered. In Jeremiah 23:1-2, the Lord said this,

> *"Woe be unto the pastors that destroy and scatter the sheep of my pasture! saith the Lord…Ye have scattered my flock, and driven them away, and have not visited them…"*
>
> *Jeremiah 23:2*

Rather than ministering to the flock and pursuing them in love, unsound spiritual leaders scatter the flock and drive the sheep away. We see this result of the activity of false spiritual leaders in the words God spoke to the shepherds in the book of Ezekial. He said,

> *"Son of man, prophesy against the shepherds of Israel, prophesy, and say unto them, Thus saith the Lord God unto the shepherds; Woe be to the shepherds of Israel that do feed themselves! should not the shepherds feed the flocks? Ye eat fat, and ye clothe you with wool, ye kill them that are fed: but ye feed not the flock. The diseased have ye not strengthened, neither have ye healed that which was sick, neither have ye bound up that which was broken, neither have ye brought again that which was driven away, neither have ye sought that which was lost; but with force and with cruelty have ye ruled them. And they were scattered, because there is no shepherd: and they became meat to all the beasts of the field, when they were scattered."*
>
> *Ezekial 34:2-5*

False spiritual leaders do not strengthen the diseased or heal the sick. They do not bind up those who are broken or search out those who have wandered from the fold. Rather than serving the people, they rule them with "force and cruelty." Because of this improper treatment, the sheep run from the shepherds. They become confused and weakened, prey for the enemy. Because there is no true shepherd, they become, "meat to all the beasts of the field."

It is popular nowadays for pastors to tell their flock, "Well, if you don't like it here go somewhere else!" Rather than leading their flocks to quiet waters and feeding them what they can handle, they push the sheep to join them in their "big visions." The sheep become discouraged by the lack of true love, by the multitude of mistakes, and by the harsh attitudes. Recently an individual remarked to me, "Why should I go to church week after week just to be yelled at?" The pastor of the church he was attending was driving the sheep away. True shepherds will make great efforts to gather the sheep together and feed them in love.

TEN: FLOCKS ARE DEVOURED

The false minister cares more for his own prosperity than he does for the prosperity and success of the flock. Consequently, the sheep will suffer. It is even possible that they will be "slaughtered" for the lust and ravening appetite of the wolf. At the very least they will be spiritually poor. At the worst they will be spiritually, emotionally, and financially bankrupt. Unaware flocks are a smorgasbord for hungry wolves. Listen to God's stout words against unsound Old Testament leaders,

> "Thus saith the Lord God unto the shepherds; Woe be to the shepherds of Israel that do feed themselves! should not the shepherds feed the flocks? Ye eat the fat, and ye clothe you with wool, ye kill them that are fed: but ye feed not the flock."
>
> Ezekiel 34:2-3

These unsound Old Testament spiritual leaders, rather than feeding the flock, fed themselves. They ate the fat of the flock. They clothed themselves with the wool of the flock. They consumed the people's goods! They disguised their intentions, used their positions, and profited at the expense of God's flock!

A true minister gives his life for the sheep. Because he does, the sheep become strong and produce milk, both for themselves and for the sustaining of the shepherd. False spiritual leaders, however, devour the sheep. If they gain places of spiritual authority, flocks will be bankrupted and devoured materially, emotionally, and spiritually. Unsound spiritual leaders, rather than laying down their lives for the sheep, demand that the sheep lay down their lives for them.

The church at Corinth allowed false apostles to devour them, to rob them of their substance, and to take from them. Paul, warning the believers of these false spiritual leaders, said,

"For you suffer (allow)…if a man devour you, if a man take of you…"

II Corinthians 11:20

The word "devour" in this text comes from the Greek *katesthio*. It is made up of two words. *Kata* signifies intensive and *esthio* means to eat up. False spiritual leaders consume the goods of the flock. W.E. Vine remarks that in the context in which Paul used "devour," it meant to demand financial maintenance. Jesus used this same word in Matthew 23:14 in reference to the religious leaders' forcible devouring of widows' houses. They used their spiritual position to "rightfully take for the work of God" and left poor widows financially bankrupt.

Paul also said of the false apostles in Corinth that they, "take of you." This is an interesting phrase because in the King James Version the words "of you" are in italics. This indicates that they are not in the original text. Literally, Paul said of false apostles that they "take." The false apostles in Corinth did not invest in the church. Rather, they demanded financial restitution.

Souls Devoured

The Lord, speaking of the devouring activity of false prophets in Ezekiel, said,

"There is a conspiracy of her prophets in the midst thereof, like a roaring lion ravening the prey: they have devoured souls; they have taken the treasure and precious things…"

Ezekiel 22:25

False leaders consume people. They not only devour finances; they also devour souls. They take, as did Old Testament false prophets, the "precious things." They demand finances for the "church vision," taking up tithes, offerings, special offerings, sacrificial offerings, and faith offerings. They also demand to be taken care of themselves. When they take, take, take, they not only bankrupt the people of God financially, but devour their souls, causing them to become embittered.

Recently, I preached at a church that had received an number of new members from a neighboring local church. The pastor told me why these members had left the other church and come to his church. A few months earlier a supposed spiritual overseer had been to that church to speak. While he was there, he told the pastor that he needed to get his members to sign up on a church role and commit their tithes to the church. If they wouldn't commit their tithes, this "leader" said, they could not be members in the church. This so called spiritual leader stirred up an ungodly motivation in this pastor for financial blessing.

The pastor, influenced by this unsound spiritual leader, began to demand finances for himself. He demanded a new car and some other things. He went so far as to demand to know what salary his people made so he could be sure they were paying their tithes. Needless to say, these church members were wounded. The pastor was demanding their finances rather than ministering to their needs.

ELEVEN: DECEPTION LEADS TO DESTRUCTION

After establishing the church in Corinth and then teaching there for one and a half years, Paul departed. Some time after his departure this local church opened its doors to false apostles, giving them a place of spiritual authority. The apostle Paul, knowing the potential outcome of a relationship with false apostles, notified this church in clear and strong language of the potential devastation they were facing. He wrote,

"...I fear, lest by any means, as the serpent beguiled Eve through his subtility, so your minds should be corrupted from the simplicity that is in Christ."

II Corinthians 11:3

The word "beguile" Paul used in this text comes from the Greek *exapatao*. This word is a strengthened form of the word translated deceive and means to be thoroughly deceived. The meaning of this word, however, refers not only to the actual deception, but includes the pain and confusion that always results from believing a lie. Paul used this word when referring to how, "sin deceived (him) and slew (him)" [Romans 7:11]. Deception always opens the door to destruction.

The word "subtility" Paul used in this text means craftiness. This word does not signify a temporary tricking as by the sleight of hand, but represents a thorough convincing; a brainwashing that persuades people of a particular position or doctrine.

The word "corrupt" Paul used in this text to describe what would happen to believers' minds because of the deceptive activity of false spiritual leaders comes from the Greek *phtheiro*. It means to destroy by the means of contamination and bring into a worse state. Spiritual corruption is a result of associating with those who have denied the truth and hold to false doctrine.

Paul was afraid that the believers in Corinth would be thoroughly deceived and corrupted in their minds by the subtility and craftiness of false apostles. He was afraid that what Satan did to Eve, false apostles would do to the believers in Corinth.

What did Satan do to Eve? First, he thoroughly deceived her. He came as an angel of light, as a minister of truth, as an interpreter of the words of God, as one who would open Eve's eyes. Because Satan was so well disguised, Eve was convinced of his good intentions and willingly, even happily, accepted and followed his counsel.

Second, through deception Satan became lord over Eve. Her relationship with God was severed. Her relationship with Adam was poisoned. Her own mind was darkened. She came under the power of sin and death. Truth was forfeited and so was her freedom. On the heels of deception came destruction!

Paul knew that danger lay ahead for the believers in Corinth if they allowed themselves to come under the control of false spiritual leaders. The least that would happen is that they would forfeit God's best. The worst that could happen is that they would abandon the truth, abandon their relationship with Christ, and come under the lordship of false spiritual leaders. The outcome of a relationship with false spiritual leaders can be devastating. Deception can lead to destruction.

TWELVE: DIVISIONS AND DEVASTATION

The most subtle, yet devastating force that can be brought to bear upon any kingdom is trouble from the inside. The most destructive force that can be levied against a local church is division from within. In Matthew twelve, Jesus revealed this truth saying,

> *"Every kingdom divided against itself is brought to desolation; and every city or house divided against itself shall not stand."*
>
> Matthew 12:25

Notice that Jesus said, "Every kingdom...every city or house." "Every kingdom" includes the kingdom of God. "Every house" includes families and local churches. When false spiritual leaders gain a foothold in a local church, division will result. And division, said Jesus, leads to desolation.

Division within a local body can lead to spiritual bareness. What begins with unsound leadership and unsound doctrine can lead to the dissolving of once sound local churches. Churches that had a divine destiny — that were intended to impact their communities, that were intended to be bastions of truth and love in their cities, that were to be champions for the lost, that had already withstood the outward attacks of persecution and the years of hardship in laying foundations — can end up in division and spiritual ruin because of the influence of unsound spiritual leadership.

Unity of Spirit, unity of love, and unity of faith made the early church effectual in its outreach to the world. As long as true spiritual leaders maintained leadership, the early churches maintained unity and prospered spiritually. When unsound teachers and false apostles infiltrated the local churches, they were divided and desolated and their impact in the world was greatly diminished.

Mark Those Who Cause Divisions

Because of the self-consuming power of division, Paul warned the church at Rome to mark those who caused it. He wrote,

> *"Now I beseech you, brethren, mark them which cause divisions and offenses contrary to the doctrine which ye have learned; and avoid them. For they that are such serve not our Lord Jesus Christ, but their own belly; and by good words and fair speeches deceive the hearts of the simple."*
>
> *Romans 16:17-18*

There is little doubt that Paul was warning the church in Rome of unsound spiritual leaders when he earnestly appealed to them to mark and avoid those who fostered divisions. By marking and avoiding false spiritual leaders, they could spoil the seeds of division and maintain spiritual soundness and unity of faith and vision.

Paul warned the church at Rome because if unsound spiritual leaders were allowed a place in their midst, divisions would result. Members would be set against members. Ministers would be exalted against other ministers. Small fires would be kindled as each faction defended their favorite teacher to the bitter end. These small fires, fanned by the winds of Satanic inspiration, would grow until the whole flock was consumed.

Division in Corinth

Paul addressed the problem of division in his first letter to the church at Corinth. He said,

> *"For ye are yet carnal: for whereas there is among you envying, and strife, and divisions, are ye not carnal, and walk as men? For while one saith, I am of Paul; and another, I am of Apollos; are ye not carnal?"*
>
> *I Corinthians 3:3-4*

The strife and divisions in the local church at Corinth resulted because some members of the church preferred Paul and some preferred Apollos. Not only did certain believers prefer one of these two spiritual leaders, however. They came to strife and division over them! Paul, in the typical style of a true spiritual leader, downplayed his own importance and the importance of Apollos saying, "Who then is Paul, and who is Apollos, but ministers by whom ye believed" [I Corinthians 3:5]. He corrected this local church saying, "let no man glory in men" [I Corinthians 3:21].

If following sound ministers can lead to strife and divisions within a local church, imagine the problems that will arise when believers follow false spiritual leaders! False ministers will not, as did Paul, point believers away from themselves and to Christ. Rather than directing the attention of believers away from themselves, false spiritual leaders will pull for the attention and admiration of believers and will be catalysts for strife and division.

Later in his letter to the church at Corinth, Paul wrote,

> "For first of all, when ye come together in the church, I hear that there be divisions among you..."
>
> *I Corinthians 11:18*

These believers were still coming together as one church. They had not yet split. In the midst of their apparent "coming together," however, they were "coming apart." The divisions within this local church were a direct result of the heresies promoted by unsound spiritual leaders. We know this is so because in the very next verse, Paul said,

> "For there must be also heresies among you, that they which are approved may be made manifest among you."
>
> *I Corinthians 11:19*

Paul said, "If there are divisions, there must be heresies." By teaching heresies false leaders were "made manifest," or came to a place of prominence, within the local body. When they came to prominence, individuals within the local church began to follow them. Without heresies there can be no divisions. But without false teachers there can be no heresies. False teachers are the source of the heresies which lead to divisions within local bodies.

Because of ongoing division, internal strife, and deviant spiritual activity, this local church incurred judgement from the Lord. The final result was that some were sick and weak and some even died in the Lord! All this was a result of following unsound spiritual leadership! These believers should have judged themselves, said Paul. Then they would not have been judged and chastened of the Lord [I Corinthians 11:31-32]. Not only should they have judged themselves, however. They should also have judged the spiritual leaders who led them to their wrong lifestyle. The inappropriate lifestyle, shameful activity, and division in this local church was a consequence of following unsound spiritual leadership.

THIRTEEN: BELIEVERS DRAWN AWAY FROM TRUE LEADERSHIP

Paul warned the Holy Ghost ordained leaders at Ephesus to beware of unsound individuals within their flock who would raise themselves up to draw disciples away after themselves. He said,

"Also of your own selves shall men arise, speaking perverse things, to draw away disciples after them."

Acts 20:30

Another one of the very dangerous results of the activity of false and unsound spiritual leaders is that when believers follow unsound spiritual leaders, they are drawn away from Holy Ghost appointed and Holy Ghost anointed leaders. They are led away from the protection and care of sound pastors and sound local bodies.

The word perverse Paul used in this scripture can mean, "turned aside." False spiritual leaders want to turn believers away from the path of soundness to another path. They will speak perverted words and use the Word of Truth in a distorted way to lead believers away from the path of truth and onto a side road which just happens to lead straight to their camp!

Recently, I heard a story from a young couple who are members of a sound charismatic fellowship. Not long ago, they told me, a young couple had started to attend their church. This couple seemed very loving and charismatic and quickly became acquainted with members in the church. Before long they were inviting church members to their home for worship and Bible studies. Some of the people of that local congregation were very excited. Something new was going on.

The young couple's home Bible study grew quickly. There were exciting times of worship along with special times of prayer and ministry. Even the pastor of the church was excited about what was going on. In time, however, this young couple began to criticize the leadership in that local church. They insinuated that the pastor and others were not really with it spiritually. They, of course, presented themselves as very spiritually advanced.

The couple who told me the story related to me that although this new couple seemed to be on fire for the Lord and that many in the congregation, including the pastor, were excited, something just did not click for them. They could not enjoy this couple's Bible study. At times they could not even stay in the same room while the ministry was going on. They could not put their finger on what was bothering them. They just had a funny feeling.

Because they felt so unsettled about this young couple, they encouraged the pastor to check their background. When the pastor called some of the churches this couple said they had been involved with, every pastor reported that they had caused trouble in the church. When this information was revealed the members of the church began to separate themselves from this young couple. In a short time the young couple left the church and, I'm sure, began to search for a foothold somewhere else.

Without realizing exactly what was happening, the couple who told me this story were sensing something that was hidden by an outward adorning of "sheep's clothing." The witness of their hearts, however, prompted further investigation. The further investigation revealed that the hesitation they sensed about the young couple was justified.

The couple who told me this story refused to be pulled in by this charismatic couple. It was a benefit to their own spiritual lives, a benefit to the members of that congregation, a benefit to the reputation of the pastor, and a benefit to the ongoing spiritual stability of that local congregation. This situation could have developed to the place where people left the sound fellowship to run with this more charismatic couple. If they had, it would have led not only to their own spiritual trouble, but could have caused a split in that church, contention and heartache between believers, and even the ruin of a perfectly sound local work.

A Congregation Within a Congregation

When false spiritual leaders rise up within a local church and draw disciples after themselves there often develops a congregation within a congregation. This happened in the local church at Thyatira. By calling herself a prophetess and using her physical attributes as a woman to empower her teaching, Jezebel was able to attract believers to herself. Because of her influence, there developed a congregation within a congregation.

That this was true is obvious by how Jesus addressed the local church in Thyatira. First, He spoke about Jezebel, her followers, and their destination. Then He spoke to those in the congregation who had not followed Jezebel, saying,

> *"But unto you I say, and unto the rest in Thyatira, as many as have not this doctrine and which have not know the depths of Satan..."*

> *Revelation 2:24*

The "you" and the "rest in Thyatira" that Jesus spoke to were those in the congregation who had not followed Jezebel. It is clear that this congregation had within itself a smaller congregation that followed Jezebel.

FOURTEEN: BELIEVERS BECOME TENTATIVE TOWARD TRUE SPIRITUAL LEADERS

False and unsound spiritual leaders present themselves as true ministers. They look like ministers, act like ministers, and talk like ministers. When a believer follows a false or unsound spiritual leader, they will have a negative experience with a "minister." It will not be unlikely, then, that they will mistrust true ministers who look like, act like, and talk like the false ministers who imitate them.

This same dilemma occurs in other areas of life. If, for example, a young woman dated several athletes and they all mistreated her, she would be tentative about any athlete who asked her for a date. Her bad experience with a few athletes would make her tentative about all athletes. In the same way, if a school boy had bad experiences with several of his teachers, he would likely be tentative about all other teachers. This is how humans defend themselves against recurring bad experiences.

If believers fall prey to the deceptive activities of false spiritual leaders and then come to their senses, realizing they have been deceived, they will become tentative toward true spiritual leadership. If they have been burned, tricked, or mistreated by "spiritual leaders," they will not risk that eventuality again. They will be very wary, suspecting all ministers of wanting what the unsound minister wanted. If a true spiritual leader told them, "I love you," they would immediately think, "What do you want from me?"

FIFTEEN: SPIRITUAL INTERBREEDING

If false spiritual leaders are confronted and exposed by true spiritual leaders, they sometimes abandon their efforts to proselyte and turn inward. They become leaders of very exclusive groups under their control. These groups, most often local churches, are not open to any outside influence. They errantly perceive themselves as a special remnant that God has favored with extra revelation. They don't realize this same fatal error has been repeated hundreds and hundreds of times in the history of the church!

Because a false spiritual leader exercises control over his followers, they have no other option but to interbreed with each other. When they "mingle" only with one another, however, all their spiritual children are spiritually retarded. These spiritual children are incapable of breaking out beyond the very narrow borders defined by their spiritual leaders. Only when a special move of the Spirit comes can some of them break away from unsound spiritual leaders and be set free.

Even mainline denominational churches can be guilty of this kind of control. When I was in high school, I began to participate in an openly evangelical para-church ministry. When I did this, my family came under the serious scrutiny of our local church leadership. Anything outside our denominational boundaries was considered unnecessary and even dangerous.

The same situation occurred when I chose a private college that was not affiliated with our denomination. Because of my decision, I was considered a rebel. It is always healthy to be open to outside influence, but it is certainly not spiritually healthy to be completely ingrown!

Sixteen: Ungodliness

The spiritual condition of the people of God is very dependent upon the spiritual condition of those who are accepted and respected as leaders. This is so because spiritual leaders are not only teachers, but are standards and examples of spiritual life. If the leader says or does something, the rest of the body of Christ will say and do the same thing. Spiritual children will emulate and imitate those they consider to be spiritual leaders. Sheep follow those they consider to be shepherds.

I have had the opportunity to visit in many peoples' homes. It always amazes me how much the children are a reflection of the parents. If the parents are calm, the children are calm. If the parents are loud, the children are loud. Occasionally, I have been in someone's home when the children misbehaved. Sometimes the parents say, "I don't know where they get that!" I have often been tempted to respond, "I do!"

A few years ago, I was ministering in a particular foreign country. While in that country, I observed that many of the pastors and congregations worshipped God in the same way. They lifted their hands in a certain way. They stepped forward in a certain way. They stood in a certain way. I found this to be very interesting.

A few weeks later I visited the church and Bible school that many of these pastors had either graduated from or had a close affiliation with. During the time of worship, I glanced over at the man who was the founder and president of the school. In that moment I knew precisely why all the pastors worshipped the same way. They were all imitating him! Now, no matter where I go in the world, if I see an individual worship in that way, I know he or she has a connection to that church and Bible school.

One of the responsibilities of true spiritual leaders is to hold high the standard of godly living both through teaching and preaching and through personal example. True spiritual leaders will preach a message and live a life of obedience and commitment. Those who follow them will emulate their spiritual life and be obedient and committed.

Because believers emulate and imitate those they follow, false and unsound spiritual leaders are a dangerous source of spiritual direction. Because the source of direction is ungodly, those fed by the source will be ungodly. Because the well is polluted, the water will be bad. Because the root is corrupt, the fruit will be corrupt.

In Jeremiah 23:15, God revealed this relationship between unsound spiritual leadership and unrighteous living. He said,

> "...for from the prophets is profaneness gone forth into all the land."
>
> Jeremiah 23:15

Profaneness is immorality, unholiness, and ungodliness. It was "from the prophets", God said, that profaneness had gone forth into all the land. By "prophets" God was not referring only to those who stood in the office of the prophet, but to all spiritual leaders who were called to represent Him to the people. If a spiritual leader is profane, those who follow him will, most likely, be profane.

The church in Thyatira is a startling example of the ungodly influence of false spiritual leadership. From her place of leadership, the false prophetess Jezebel taught and persuaded Jesus' servants to, "commit fornication and to eat things sacrificed unto idols" [Revelation 2:20]. Notice the words of judgement Jesus spoke concerning this woman,

> "Behold, I will cast her into a bed, and them that commit adultery with her into great tribulation, except they repent of their deeds. And I will kill her children with death..."
>
> Revelation 2:22-23

Jezebel was a source of ungodly living in the church at Thyatira. Those who accepted her as a spiritual leader emulated her doctrine and lifestyle. Jesus called those who followed Jezebel, "her children." They were her children, not by natural birth, but by spiritual association. Because they looked like her, acted like her, and followed her, they were her children.

Believers will take on the spiritual attributes of those they choose as spiritual leaders. If they choose godly and righteous leaders, they will live godly and righteous. If they choose ungodly and profane unsound spiritual leaders, they will become ungodly and profane themselves.

SEVENTEEN: DECEIVED AWAY FROM PURE DEVOTION TO CHRIST

Because he was a true spiritual leader, Paul's desire was to establish believers in faith and love and prepare them as a beautiful bride for Christ. He had a grave concern for the believers in Corinth, however, because they were allowing themselves to come under the influence of false spiritual leadership. In his second letter to the church at Corinth, he said,

"For I am jealous over you with godly jealousy: for I have espoused you to one husband, that I may present you as a chaste virgin to Christ. But I fear, lest by any means, as the serpent beguiled Eve through his subtility, so your minds should be corrupted from the simplicity that is in Christ."

II Corinthians 11:2-3

Paul reminded the believers in Corinth that he had espoused them to one husband as a chaste virgin to Christ. The terms Paul used referred to the Bible-days custom of giving virgins special care to ensure that they were educated and kept pure for marriage.

By espousing the believers at Corinth to Christ, Paul characterized the calling of all true spiritual leaders. True spiritual leaders are called to help believers beautify themselves in faith and love. They are called to educate believers in the truth and prepare them for the marriage. They are called to help believers keep themselves pure for Jesus. True spiritual leaders do not strive for the affection of believers, but help them mature in their affection for Christ.

Paul was afraid, however, for the believers in Corinth. He was afraid that just as Satan had beguiled Eve with lies, seduced her away from the truth, and destroyed her relationship with God, so false apostles would deceive them away from the truth, and spoil their relationship with Christ. Although he had introduced these believers to Christ by his gospel and established them through his teaching, Paul was afraid that they would abandon their full commitment to Christ and give allegiance to false apostles.

False spiritual leaders don't want to help believers love someone else. They want believers to love them! They want devotion. They want praise. They want admiration. They want finances. They want to "sleep" with believers! They are the seducers the apostle John warned of who attempt to entice believers away from pure devotion and full hearted commitment to Christ into a relationship with themselves.

Believers, both individually and corporately, are the espoused bride of Christ. His shed blood was the dowry that purchased us. We have given our promisary word to Him. We are engaged to Christ. He is the waiting husband and we are the bride in preparation. The full hearted and undivided devotion of the church belongs to Christ, not to men! Believers must be careful not to be drawn away from their love relationship with Christ into an affair with seducers!

The apostle John expressed this concern for his spiritual children. He was afraid that their relationship to Christ would be violated by false spiritual leaders. Because he was concerned, he warned them saying,

> *"These things have I written unto you concerning them that seduce you...And now, little children, abide in him (Christ); that, when he shall appear, we may have confidence, and not be ashamed before him at his coming."*
>
> *I John 2:26-28*

John warned his spiritual children to beware of seducers who would lure them away from Christ and instructed them, "abide in Him." Why did John give this seemingly obvious instruction to abide in Christ? Because seducers will attempt to entice believers away from devotion to Christ. This is a potential spiritual danger!

If believers abide in Christ, John said, they will not be ashamed when He comes again. Some believers, however, will be ashamed at the second coming of Jesus. They will be *saved*, but they will be *ashamed*. They will be ashamed because they allowed themselves to be seduced away from their pure devotion to Christ by those who were false or unsound spiritual leaders. They submitted themselves to unsound men rather than staying totally committed to Christ. They were like a wandering bride. They played around a little, letting men take advantage of them.

EIGHTEEN: THE REPUTATION OF THE GOSPEL DAMAGED

One of the terrible results of the activity of false spiritual leaders is that the reputation of God, of the gospel, and of the church is damaged. The unsaved, especially, are not able to separate between spiritual leaders who are sound and those who are unsound. Anyone who claims to be a minister is equally a minister in their estimation. All "spiritual leaders" are lumped together into one big group.

Notice what Peter said happens when believers follow the pernicious ways of false teachers,

> *"But there were false prophets also among the people, even as there shall be false teachers among you...And many shall follow their pernicious ways; by reason of whom the way of truth shall be evil spoken of."*
>
> II Peter 2:1-2

The way of truth is not evil spoken of because of the activity of outside false spiritual leaders such as those involved with cults or other religions like Islam or Mormonism. The way of truth is evil spoken of because of "false teachers among you" — those who either were in the past or are presently identified with the church. Unsound spiritual leaders and those who follow them bring the church, the truth, and even God and the Lord Jesus Christ a bad rap.

Recently, I heard a well-respected minister say that when ministers get off into excess or false doctrine it scares intelligent people away. This is exactly what the apostle Peter meant. When unsound teachers in our midst introduce heretical doctrines, the result is that the "way of truth is evil spoken of." Intelligent people, both believers and unbelievers, get turned off to God and to the church because of unsound ministers who identify themselves with the church of Jesus Christ and claim to be true ministers.

Who is it that will speak evil of the way of truth because of the activity of unsound spiritual leaders? Will strong and established believers? No. Will reputable and sound ministers? No. The two groups of individuals that will speak evil of the way of truth are those who so desperately need the truth! These two groups are the unsaved and baby Christians.

The unsaved simply assume that anyone who claims to be "of God" and a part of the church is "of God" and part of the church. When they observe the abuse, mismanagement, deception, and selfishness of "spiritual leaders," they speak evil of ministers, of the church, and of God. Baby Christians and spiritual children will also speak evil of the way of truth. If they are misled or misused by unsound ministers, they will be turned off to God and to the Christian life.

False teachers and other unsound spiritual leaders bring disrepute upon the church, upon the Way of Truth, and upon true spiritual leaders. This is one reason false teachers and unsound spiritual leaders must be marked. The salvation of unsaved individuals is at stake. The stability of young believers is at stake.

A Good Reputation With Sinners

Those who are perceived as spiritual leaders influence people's perception of God, of the Lord Jesus, and of the Christian life. It is the will of God that ministers have a good testimony even with the unsaved. Concerning the selection of a person to a position of spiritual leadership, most likely that of a local pastor, Paul told Timothy,

"Moreover he must have a good report of them which are without [the unsaved]; lest he fall into reproach and the snare of the devil."

I Timothy 3:7

Those called to spiritual leadership must have a good report with the unsaved. This, of course, blows the "spiritual" theory that ministers must lead the pack of radically saved believers who talk strange and act in strange ways in order to be a "peculiar people." Nowadays, those in places of spiritual leadership want to impress both the saved and the unsaved with how radical they are for God. Most often, however, their radical activities are nothing more than an attempt to appear spiritual to other believers and other ministers. Radical and strange activities in no way display one's measure of spirituality!

True ministers must know how to relate to and win the unsaved. The Word of God says that he who wins souls is wise. The converse of this is also true. Those who turn away souls from God, either by word or activity, are fools!

Paul said that those who hold a place of spiritual leadership must have a good report with those outside the church so that they don't, "fall into reproach." The word reproach means disgrace, embarrassment, or shame. The minister is, in the minds of the unsaved, a representative of the church and of the Lord Jesus Christ. If he falls into reproach, the unsaved will not be the least interested in God. Rather, they will have a negative perception of the church and of God.

What is the "snare of the devil" Paul warned Timothy about? The snare of the devil is the scheme of Satan to bring disrepute to the gospel and to the Lord Jesus Christ by enticing ministers into strange doctrines and strange activities. The devil will take advantage of unstable ministers or play upon a minister's personal weakness and lead him down a path that is not only ungodly, but that turns others off to God. The plan of the devil is to keep the unsaved from being saved by making God and the truth unattractive. What better way to keep people from being saved and turned on to God than to snare spiritual leaders into strange doctrines and weird activities.

Christians Who Follow Unsound Ministers

Not only will the way of truth be evil spoken of because of the bad reputation of false ministers. It will also be evil spoken of because of the ungodly lifestyle of those who follow unsound leaders. The apostle Peter said,

"Many shall follow their (the false minister's)lascivious ways by reason of whom (the many who follow false ministers) the way of truth shall be evil spoken of."

II Peter 2:2

Those who follow false teachers will be misled, corrupted, and so out of spiritual order, that when the unsaved encounter them, they will lose any interest they had in Christianity. In fact, they will speak evil of Christianity. Disrepute comes to the gospel message and to the church of the Lord Jesus Christ when believers follow unsound spiritual leaders in their strange doctrines and unsound lifestyle.

Some believers follow unsound leaders in their unsound spiritual activities because they want so badly to be "spiritual." According to Peter, believers are a "peculiar" people. The word "peculiar," however, which some use as an excuse to be strange and extremely radical, simply means to be "set apart." Believers are set apart for God. Of course, they are not to act like the world. Some believers think, however, that if they don't act far out and do strange things, they are not really sold out to God. They feel lukewarm. They feel like God won't be pleased with them.

Even the unsaved realize that some of the "spiritual" things believers are involved with are weird. It is a sad testimony for the church when sinners recognize before believers when doctrine and Christian activity has gone beyond the limits!

CONCLUSION

We have explored briefly the results which unsound spiritual leaders bring to believers, local churches, and to the reputation of the gospel. I'm sure you noticed that no good fruit results from their activity. The very least that will occur from contact and relationship with unsound spiritual leaders is that believers will get nothing. The worst that can occur is that faith is shaken or destroyed and that believers or whole local congregations experience spiritual, mental, emotional, and financial bankruptcy.

·~16~·
What Happens to False Spiritual Leaders?

ot only do false spiritual leaders affect believers and local churches. False spiritual leaders affect themselves! They backslide in their own lives because of the error of their teaching and bring upon themselves the possibility of judgement and destruction. They not only open a door to Satan through error and pride, but swiftly catch the attention of God, of the Head of the church, and of true spiritual leaders.

In this chapter we will learn what happens to false spiritual leaders. In the first part of the chapter we will learn that sometimes false spiritual leaders destroy themselves. In the second part of this chapter we will learn that sometimes false spiritual leaders are judged by God.

ONE: FALSE SPIRITUAL LEADERS DESTROY THEMSELVES

Concerning the activity and results of false spiritual leadership, Peter said,

"...they that are unlearned and unstable wrest, as they do also the other scriptures, unto their own destruction..."

II Peter 3:16

Those who twist the scriptures do so to "their own destruction." Destruction in this scripture does not refer to ceasing to exist, but indicates the loss of well-being, of being wasted. When false and unsound spiritual leaders distort the truth, they make it impossible for themselves to remain sound. They suffer the very same consequences in their lives that they cause in others. Jesus said that when the blind lead the blind, they both fall into the ditch. Blind leaders fall into the same deep hole that they lead others into.

Paul said this concerning the false teachers Hymeneaus and Alexander,

"Holding faith, and a good conscience; which some having put away concerning faith have made shipwreck: Of whom is Hymenaeus and Alexander..."

I Timothy 1:19-20

These two men shipwrecked in the faith because they refused to consult the map when charting their course. If they had consulted the map, they would have known where the dangerous reefs were, hidden just below the surface of the water. These unsound spiritual leaders, however, by putting away faith and a good conscience, ruined themselves. False spiritual leaders cannot possibly attain or maintain sound spiritual health because their chosen doctrine and lifestyle are wrong.

Self-Condemned

In his letter to Titus, Paul said that a heretic who refused to be admonished and delivered from error was, "subverted, and sinneth, being condemned of himself" [Titus 3:11]. False spiritual leaders who will not accept correction are not unlike sinners who will not accept the message of salvation. Help is available for them. Because they refuse to acknowledge the truth, however, they refuse to deliver themselves from the judgement that is fit for their activity. They can not be helped because they will not be helped. Because they refuse correction, they are beyond redemption. When heretics refuse to accept correction, they pronounce a guilty sentence upon themselves.

In our chapter called "What do False Leaders Want?" we learned that one of the wrong motivations of false spiritual leaders is the desire to be rich. Notice the fatal outcome of their love of money,

"But they that will (want to be) be rich fall into temptation and a snare, and into many foolish and hurtful lusts, which drown men in destruction and perdition. For the love of money is the root of all evil, which while some coveted after, they have erred from the faith and pierced themselves through with many sorrows. But thou, O man of God, flee these things."

I Timothy 6:9-11

Paul said that because these false spiritual leaders desired to be rich, they fell into, "temptation and into a snare; and into many foolish and hurtful lusts." The end result of their love and pursuit of money was that they erred from the faith and pierced themselves through with many sorrows. These men destroyed themselves! Because they insisted on pursuing carnal gain, they guaranteed for themselves a harvest of corruption.

In His parable of the sower and the seed, Jesus referred to "the deceitfulness of riches" as one of the weeds that grows up and chokes the Word of God. What is the deceitfulness of riches? It is the lie which says that if you get rich you will be happy. Some once sound spiritual leaders have been corrupted because they believed this lie. Once they had fruit in their lives. The love of money, however, choked out any fruit they had, leaving them spiritually barren and a threat to others.

Because of the desire to be rich, even once sound ministers can wander off into unsound doctrine and wrong spiritual activity. Balaam was a perfect example of this. He loved the wages of unrighteousness and was willing to sell his soul and misuse his gift from God to get it. God, knowing that Balaam's pursuit of riches would lead to his own destruction, did his best to warn Balaam. He even opened the mouth of Balaam's donkey to arrest his attention. Balaam, however, finally conceded to his lust for money and erred in the faith. Now the abandonment of truth for the love of money is called, "The error of Balaam" [Jude 11].

Elisha's servant Gehazi is another example of the destructive end of the love of money. His lust for money motivated him to lie to both Nathan and Elisha. Gehazi's end was not pretty. He died of the dread disease, leprosy. Not only did his love of money affect him, however. His offspring was sentenced with him in the curse of leprosy [II Kings 5:20-27].

Peter brought forth this same truth when he said concerning false spiritual leaders that they, "wrest the scriptures to their own destruction" [II Peter 3:19]. Unsound spiritual leaders nullify their own freedom when they abandon the truth. They cancel their own opportunity for eternal life when they deny Christ and leave the paths of righteousness. They forfeit their opportunity to receive when they engage only in taking. If they would heed the scriptures and be doers of the Word, they could be blessed in all their deeds. But when they wrest the scriptures, they make it impossible for God to bless them.

Oppose Themselves

Paul, writing to Timothy of the potential end of false spiritual leaders, said

"In meekness instructing those that oppose themselves; if God peradventure will give them repentance to the acknowledgement of the truth; And that they may recover themselves out of the snare of the devil, who are taken captive by him at his will."

II Timothy 2:25-26

Paul told Timothy that false spiritual leaders "oppose themselves." This reveals that the confusion of false spiritual leaders is initially self-inflicted. When ministers deviate from the truth, they cross over into Satan's territory and run on paths where he hunts. If Satan snares them, if they come under his influence, he can manipulate them at his will. Unless they escape back to the protective territory called Truth, they will remain under his influence.

Paul told Timothy to, "(instruct) those that oppose themselves." Though they opposed themselves and were on the road of error which led to destruction, they were still salvageable. There was still a possibility that they would acknowledge the truth (which also means that they would admit their error), come to repentance, and, by so doing, break the deceptive hold that the devil had upon their minds and hearts.

Abandoned to the Destructive Forces of Darkness

In both of his letters to young Timothy, Paul mentioned a man named Hymenaeus. This man had not only abandoned sound doctrine and ship-wrecked in his own life, he was also promoting his error and overthrowing the faith of others. In his first letter to Timothy, Paul said this about Hyme-neaus,

"...some having put away concerning faith have made shipwreck: Of whom is Hymenaeus and Alexander; whom I have delivered unto Satan, that they may learn not to blaspheme."

I Timothy 1:19-20

Hymeneaus made two wrong decisions that made him prey to the destructive forces of darkness. First, he abandoned the faith himself. Although this choice produced spiritual shipwreck in his own life, there were no immediate physical or emotional consequences. Second, he began to promote his error. This second decision made Hymeneaus a threat to the body of Christ. When he began to promote his error, he quickly caught the attention of God and of true spiritual leaders. His decision to promote error made Hymeneaus dangerous enough to the body of Christ that he had to be given over to Satan for physical and emotional destruction.

In a very similar case, Paul turned a young man from the church in Corinth over to Satan. To the church at Corinth, he wrote,

"To deliver such an one unto Satan for the destruction of his flesh, that the spirit may be saved in the day of the Lord Jesus."

I Corinthians 5:5

The young man in Corinth was turned over to Satan for the destruction of his flesh because he would not judge himself. His sinful lifestyle was a threat to the whole church at Corinth. "A little leaven leaveneth the whole lump," said Paul, concerning the sinful lifestyle of this young man. He instructed the church at Corinth to purge out the leaven and not to keep company with fornicators [I Corinthians 5:7, 10].

Paul turned the false teacher Hymeneaus over to Satan because he was blaspheming; he was promoting false doctrine. There is little doubt that Hymeneaus experienced emotional and physical trauma as a result of being turned over to Satan. If he would not listen to his own heart, would not listen to the Holy Spirit, and would not listen to true spiritual leadership, perhaps he would listen to his own sickened body. Sometimes the only way obstinate men will listen is when they have pain in their bodies.

Hymeneaus was turned over to Satan for the destruction of his flesh for two reasons. First, he was turned over to Satan in the hope that he would come to his own spiritual senses and return to sound faith and Christian life. The destruction of his flesh would hopefully catch the attention of his mind and heart. Second, and more importantly, he was turned over to Satan so that his strong negative influence in the church would be broken.

Hymeneaus' promotion of false doctrine was very dangerous to the church. Paul said that his teaching would, "eat as doth a canker" [II Timothy 2:17]. Before his false teaching could spread and affect the whole body, Hymeneaus had be stopped. This is why Paul turned him over to Satan for the destruction of his flesh. Even Satan can be a tool of God in bringing correction and halting wrong spiritual activity.

Some ministers of this generation would do well to study the end of former ministers who abandoned sound doctrine and died at a very young age. Some of them were turned over to Satan for the destruction of their flesh. Does this mean that God did not love them? No. Does this mean they did not go to heaven? No. What, then, does it mean? It means that God could not afford to let them go any further in their promotion of unsound doctrine! They had to be stopped for the sake of the spiritual destiny of the church. They were abandoned to the forces of darkness for the destruction of their flesh so that they would no longer poison the church with unsound doctrine and mislead believers into unsound spiritual life.

Those who promote false doctrine are at serious risk. They will soon be abandoned by God to the destructive forces of darkness. They may still be saved, but it will be, "as by fire" [I Corinthians 3:15]. Their physical life, however, is in jeopardy.

End According to Their Works

The final destination of false spiritual leadership will be according to their works. Whatever they have sown, they will reap. Paul, writing to the church at Corinth about the false apostles in their midst, said,

"Therefore it is no great thing if his ministers also be transformed as the ministers of righteousness; whose end shall be according to their works."

II Corinthians 11:15

What is the destination of false spiritual leaders? Their destination is the same as their works. Because their works are evil, so will their destination be evil. Because their work is to corrupt, so shall their end be corruption. Because their work is to destroy the temple, so shall their own temples be destroyed. Because they have wrongly labored for carnal gain, they shall of the flesh reap corruption and destruction. Because they have twisted the scriptures and abandoned the truth, God gives them up to the thoughts of their own reprobate minds and allows them to engage in activities which lead to their own death. False spiritual leaders will reap what they sow!

Their End is Destruction

In the third chapter of Philippians, Paul was admonishing the believers to follow after him and other spiritual leaders who were godly. Then he reminded them with "weeping" of what he had "told them often" about false spiritual leaders. He said,

"...they are the enemies of the cross of Christ: Whose end is destruction, whose God is their belly, and whose glory is in their shame, who mind earthly things."

Philippians 3:18-19

The end of those who are enemies of the cross of Christ is destruction. This sobering truth if verified by the writer of Hebrews. Referring to those who "were once enlightened, and have tasted of the heavenly gift, and were made partakers of the Holy Ghost, And have tasted of the good word of God, and the powers of the world to come," but who had fallen away, the writer said,

"But that which beareth thorns and briers is rejected, and is nigh unto cursing; whose end is to be burned."

Hebrews 6:8

According to the writer of Hebrews, those who are born again and drink of the rain of the goodness of God and bring forth fruit for God will be blessed [Hebrews 6:7]. Those, however, who bear "thorns and briers" will be rejected. In fact, they are nigh unto cursing! They are at risk of eternal damnation! Those who were once saved, but have now rejected the truth and promoted error are in a very dangerous condition. They risk being rejected, cursed, and burned!

Their Folly Will be Revealed

Paul wrote to Timothy of false spiritual leaders who were, "ever learning and never able to come to the knowledge of the truth." He said these men, "resist the truth," are, "men of corrupt minds," and are, "reprobate concerning the faith." He then compared these false spiritual leaders to two men who resisted Moses saying,

"Now as Jannes and Jambres withstood Moses, so do these also resist the truth..."
II Timothy 3:8

Though you cannot find the names Jannes and Jambres in the Old Testament, it is agreed among Bible scholars that these men were two chief magicians of Egypt who withstood Moses by performing the first three plagues that Moses performed. Moses performed these plagues by the power of God. The Egyptian magicians performed these plagues by occult power. After Moses' first three plagues had been duplicated by the magicians, it was not sure that Moses had really been sent by God. The plagues were to be the proof that he was, in fact, sent by God, but the magicians of Egypt were able to produce them also. When it came time for the fourth plague, however, the lesser power of the magicians became evident. The Bible says,

"And the magicians did so with their enchantments to bring forth lice, but they could not...Then the magicians said unto Pharaoh, This is the finger of God..."
Exodus 8:18-19

For a season false ministers may be able to convince people that they are operating in the power of God. In time, however, their folly will become evident. Concerning the false spiritual leaders he compared to the Egyptian magicians Jannes and Jambres, Paul said,

"But they shall proceed no further: for their folly shall be manifest unto all men, as their also was."

II Timothy 3:9

False leaders will proceed some distance. For a time they may be able to hide behind words or behind feigned power. For a time they may appear to be true spiritual leaders. It will soon become obvious, however, that they have been playing games with people. As it was discovered of Jannes and Jambres so it will be discovered of false spiritual leaders that there is no true power of God behind what they say or do. There will be no true deliverance. There will be no setting free. There will be no real joy or peace. In time, the lie of false spiritual leaders will be exposed.

False spiritual leaders may make some initial headway, but, "they shall proceed no further." God will make sure they are exposed. As Aaron's rod-turned-serpent swallowed up the magician's rods-turned-serpents, so shall the truth of God swallow up the lies of false leadership. Though false spiritual leaders may operate in devious and deceptive ways for a season, their intentions will soon be brought to light. All their endeavors will be exposed by the breaking forth of the confirming power of God!

Pass Off the Scene

Often sincerely wrong spiritual leaders gain a strong following in their early days. When they are exposed as unsound, however, their momentum is slowed and they begin to fade off the spiritual scene. Some unsound spiritual leaders abandon the ministry altogether. Rather than admitting they were wrong and going back to a place of beginning, they abandon the call of God. Some who were sincerely wrong, but wrong nonetheless, become very bitter toward other spiritual leaders, toward the church, and even toward God. Sometimes they turn inward and die. This only goes to further show that what they were involved with was not a move of the Spirit, but was something gendered and carried by the strength of their own personalities.

A wise man named Gamaliel, a doctor of the religious law who lived in the early days of the church, had some very sound words of wisdom concerning religious movements and their leadership. He warned the religious leaders of his day not to fight against the apostles in case they were, in fact, of God. He said,

> "For before these days rose up Theudas, boasting himself to be somebody; to whom a number of men, about four hundred, joined themselves: who was slain; and all, as many as obeyed him, were scattered, and brought to naught. After this man rose up Judas of Galilee in the days of the taxing, and drew away much people after him: he also perished; and all, even as many as obeyed him, were dispersed. And now I say unto you, Refrain from these men, and let them alone: for if this counsel or the work be of men, it will come to naught: But if it be of God, ye cannot overthrow it; lest haply ye be found even to fight against God."
>
> Acts 5:36-39

Whatever is truly of God cannot be overthrown. If God is behind it, it will continue to carry on throughout generations. The opposite is also true. If a movement is not of God, it will fail. When the man who is carrying the movement is gone, the movement will be gone. Occasionally there may remain a very small remnant who hold fast to the unsound teachings of a false leader, but when the power behind the movement is dead, the movement will be dead.

TWO: FALSE SPIRITUAL LEADERS WILL BE JUDGED BY GOD

Ever since God first called a people unto Himself, He has had to deal with the destructive influences of false spiritual leaders. Ever since He uttered His first instructions, there have been individuals standing ready to distort and deceive. Of all the individuals who have walked or do walk the face of this earth, there are none that God has less tolerance of and stricter punishment for than false and unsound spiritual leaders. Those who pervert His words and negatively influence His people are at great risk!

Old Testament Unsound Leaders

In the books of Jeremiah and Ezekiel, God spoke words of forthcoming judgement against the spiritual leaders in Israel because of their negative and destructive influence upon His people. To Jeremiah, He said,

> *"For both prophet and priest are profane; yea, in my house have I found their wickedness, saith the Lord. Wherefore their way shall be unto them as slippery ways in the darkness: they shall be driven on, and fall therein: for I will bring evil upon them, even the year of their visitation, saith the Lord...they caused my people Israel to err...Behold, I will feed them with wormwood, and make them drink the water of gall: for from the prophets of Jerusalem is profaneness gone forth into all the land."*
>
> *Jeremiah 23:11-15*

God said, "in my house have I found their wickedness." The false leaders He was speaking against were not prophets of Baal or the prophets of other foreign gods. God was speaking against those He had called and given a place of spiritual leadership in Israel. They were called to lead the nation in righteousness and truth. But in the midst of His own people and in the very place where true ministry was to be performed — "in [His] house" — God found the wicked activity of those who had departed from godliness and become unsound spiritual leaders.

Notice the attitude and intended judgement of God concerning these false prophets and priests. He said their ways would be, "slippery ways in the darkness." Confusion of mind and dimming of reasoning follows those who persist in promoting unsound doctrine and deviant spiritual activity. They will not walk with sureness and confidence. Because God abandons them, they fall victim to the unsound reasonings of their own carnal and reprobate minds. The path of false spiritual leaders will grow dimmer and more slippery.

God said concerning these unsound spiritual leaders that He would, "feed them with wormwood, and make them drink the water of gall." He also said that He would bring evil upon them; upon the prophet and the priest. Why would God do this? Because these unsound spiritual leaders caused His people to err. You see, the people of God look to the ministers of God for direction. If ministers give the wrong directions, God's people will either be injured in the way or arrive at the wrong destination. God will not allow false spiritual leaders to continue sending His people down roads that lead to defeat and death! When unsound spiritual leaders draw the people of God away from spiritual soundness, God will bring judgement upon them. In Jeremiah 23:1, He said this,

> "Woe be unto the pastors that destroy and scatter the sheep of my pasture! saith the Lord."
>
> *Jeremiah 23:1*

Can you feel the attitude of God against these unsound spiritual leaders? "Woe to them," He says. Why does God say, "Woe be unto the pastors?" He says this because a day of reckoning will come and they will be found wanting. The reward of their wrong spiritual leadership will be harsh! The judgement they will receive will cause them to weep, to cry, to mourn, to be in anguish, to suffer, to be in misery, to be afflicted, and to experience torment. False spiritual leaders are going to wish one day that they had never misled the people of God.

We also perceive God's attitude toward Old Testament false spiritual leaders in the book of Ezekiel. In one place He said to Ezekiel,

> "Son of man, prophesy against the shepherds of Israel, prophesy, and say unto them, Thus saith the Lord God unto the shepherds; Woe be to the shepherds of Israel that do feed themselves! should not the shepherds feed the flocks...ye feed not the flock. The diseased have ye not strengthened, neither have ye healed that which was sick, neither have ye bound up that which was broken, neither have ye brought again that which was driven away, neither have ye sought that which was lost; but with force and with cruelty have ye ruled them...Therefore, O ye shepherds, hear the word of the Lord; Thus saith the Lord God; Behold, I am against the shepherds; and I will require my flock at their hand."
>
> *Ezekiel 34:2-10*

God was against the shepherds that fed themselves rather than feeding the flock. He was against them because they did not strengthen or heal the flock. He was against them because they did not pursue those who had drifted away, but were responsible for driving them away! He was against them because rather than serving the flock, they ruled the flock. And they did that with "force and cruelty." God was against them and would require His flock at their hand. He would ask them concerning His flock and recompense them for their works. A day of judgement would come and it would be rough!

God was against those who said they spoke for Him, but lied. Of these individuals, God said,

> "Behold, I am against the prophets, saith the Lord, that use their tongues, and say, He saith. Behold, I am against them that prophesy false dreams, saith the Lord, and do tell them, and cause my people to err by their lies, and by their lightness; yet I sent them not, nor commanded them..."
>
> Jeremiah 23:31-32

God was against those that said, "He saith," but He didn't even send them. God was against those who took lightly the fact that they claimed to be speaking on His behalf, but were speaking errors and lies. God was angry with those unsound spiritual leaders because they caused His people to err by their lies. What would He do with these unsound spiritual leaders? He said,

> "...I will even punish that man and his house."
>
> Jeremiah 23:34

God did not long tolerate the unsound activity of unsound spiritual leaders who claimed to be speaking on His behalf. Because of His great mercy, He may have temporarily withheld judgement, hoping they would repent. But the day of judgement was not far off! God said He would punish that man and his house.

In another place, God said this about false prophets,

> "Thus saith the Lord God; Woe unto the foolish prophets, that follow their own spirit, and have seen nothing! Therefore thus saith the Lord God; Because ye have spoken vanity, and seen lies, therefore, behold I am against you, saith the Lord God. And mine hand shall be upon the prophets that see vanity, and that divine lies: they shall not be in the assembly of my people, neither shall they be written in the writing of the house of Israel, neither shall they enter into the land of Israel...Because, even because they have seduced my people..."
>
> Ezekiel 13:3-10

The foolish prophets that followed their own inclinations, listened to the thoughts of their own minds, and then spoke those things as if they were from God, were in serious trouble. They would not be allowed to remain in the midst of God's people. Their names would not be named with those who followed after God and were a blessing to the people. They would not partake of the blessings of the promised land of Israel. They would be out-casts from God and cut off from the promises they pretended to promote. Why would they have this kind of outcome? Because they had seduced God's people.

New Testament Unsound Leaders

In Revelation chapters two and three, Jesus began His address to each of the seven churches by saying, "I know your works." Hebrews 4:13 says that, "all things are naked and opened unto the eyes of him with whom we have to do." God the Father and Jesus the Head of the church know exactly what is going on in the church scene. They know what is happening in each local church. They know who are sincere and honest ministers and they know who are wrongly motivated, but disguised ministers. Wolves in sheep's clothing may fool the sheep, but they do not fool the great Shepherd of the sheep!

The Protective Nature of the Father

Fathers have a natural affection for their children and will protect them at all costs. If Johnny gets thrashed by the town bully, Johnny's father will be paying the bully a visit. God is a heavenly father and believers are His children. He has very strong protective feelings toward them and will not allow carnally minded so-called ministers to defraud them of His blessings and love.

Although God does appoint spiritual leaders to serve His people, He closely monitors those leaders' activities. He does so for the safety of His people. Because ministers are human, there always remains the possibility that they will misuse their positions.

When so-called spiritual leaders prey upon the Father's children, they incur His wrath and mark themselves for judgement. If the Father watches over each sparrow and knows their individual needs, He will certainly know when one of His own children is at spiritual risk.

God is in the intervention business where His children are concerned. He will not long tolerate the negative and spiritually debilitating activity of false spiritual leaders. Only His great mercy and unlimited compassion stays His immediate judgement of false and unsound spiritual leaders.

Jesus' Attitude

As Head of the church, Jesus is responsible for the church. He will care for and watch over her. Every activity that occurs in each local church will be scrutinized and evaluated by Him. If things are in their proper spiritual place, He can rejoice and commend that church. If things are out of line, He will be alerted and take whatever action He deems necessary. First, He will deliver a message by the Holy Ghost to that church and watch for their response. If the church does not heed His word, judge themselves and their leadership, and make the necessary changes, He will judge the false spiritual leaders and make the corrections Himself.

In one of His teaching sessions, Jesus very clearly expressed His feelings concerning those who offend the little ones that believe in Him. Listen to His stought words,

> "But whoso shall offend one of these little ones which believe in me, it were better for him that a millstone were hanged about his neck, and that he were drowned in the depth of the sea. Woe unto the world because of offenses! for its must needs be that offenses come; but woe to that man by whom the offense cometh!"
>
> Matthew 18:6-7

The Amplified Bible says,

> "...whoever causes one of the little ones to stumble and sin — that is, who entices him, or hinders him in right conduct or thought..."
>
> Matthew 18:6-7 Amp

Whoever causes a believer (especially a baby Christian) to stumble and fall is in serious trouble. Jesus said it would be better for that person if a millstone was placed around his neck and he was thrown into the depth of the sea. The judgement this offender will receive from God will be far worse than a heinous natural death! It would be better for him to die a gruesome and frightful death *before* he had the opportunity to offend one of Jesus' children than to receive the judgement of God *after* he offended one of Jesus' children! Let me tell you something about the judgement of God against those who abuse His people: It will not be pleasant!

Note these sobering words of Jesus concerning Judas Iscariot,

> "...but woe unto that man by whom the Son of man is betrayed! it had been good for that man if he had not been born."
>
> Matthew 26:24.

With these words, Jesus confirmed the eternal destination of the man who betrayed Him. Judas Iscariot left his calling in the ministry and betrayed Jesus for the carnal reward of a few pieces of silver. This one decision cost him dearly. He could not come to repentance. The judgement of God was upon him! His eternal destination was sealed! Although he had been called by Jesus and had worked for the kingdom of God, his one deviant action insured his eternal destiny in hell.

Jesus' feelings toward false spiritual leaders are made very clear in His address to the church of Thyatira. This church had allowed a false prophetess to operate in their midst rather than judging her. Notice what Jesus said about this false prophetess,

> *"And I gave her space to repent of her fornication; and she repented not."*
>
> Revelation 2:21

Jesus dealt with this false prophetess' heart and gave her an opportunity to repent and change her ways. Jesus is so merciful! Even though this woman was seducing His servants to commit fornication, He gave her an opportunity to repent and be spared of impending judgement. Because she would not repent, however, Jesus said,

> *"Behold, I will cast her into a bed, and them that commit adultery with her into great tribulation...And I will kill her children (her spiritual offspring) with death...and I will give unto every one of you according to your works."*
>
> Revelation 2:22-23

Just as Jesus gave Jezebel time to repent, so He will give the false teachers of this generation an opportunity to repent. But just as He meted out severe punishment when Jezebel failed to repent, so He will meet out severe punishment upon the false spiritual leaders of our day who refuse to repent.

Jesus is not only the Head of the church, He is also the Husband of the Bride. Anyone who, rather than faithfully preparing His bride for Him, attempts to fraternize with her will be in serious trouble. Paul had a burning vision to present the church as a chaste bride to Christ. He was jealous over the church with a godly jealousy. Anyone who tried to turn the bride away from her husband had to contend with a jealous Paul. And anyone who messes with the bride of this generation will not only have to deal with true and zealous spiritual leaders, they will also have to deal with an angry Groom and His Father!

Paul's Attitude

In Galatians 1:8-9, Paul, writing by the unction of the Holy Spirit, expressed in very strong terms his feelings toward those who preached a message different than the pure and unadulterated gospel he preached. His stout words not only reveal his indignation against unsound spiritual leadership; they also reveal the indignation of the Holy Spirit. Note these strong words of judgement Paul deemed worth uttering twice,

> *"But though we, or an angel from heaven, preach any other gospel unto you than that which we have preached unto you, let him be accursed. As we said before, so*

say I now again, if any man preach any other gospel unto you than that ye have received, let him be accursed."

Galatians 1:8-9

Paul made a strong and perfectly clear statement. One translation of the Bible renders his stout words against false spiritual leaders this way: "may (they) be damned" [Galatians 1:8-9 Phi]. Paul's heart, as a pure sounding board, resonated the feelings of the Father and the message of the Holy Spirit concerning false spiritual leaders. Those who teach and promote a perverted gospel are in danger of being cursed by God. They purchase to themselves damnation. Their eternal destiny is in the balance. The Amplified Bible says they are, "doomed to eternal punishment." Their evil deeds will take them straight to and straight through the gates of hell if they do not repent!

Those who pervert the gospel and promote their perversion are in danger of the judgement of God. Yes, God is a God of mercy. But when men adulterate His pure Word, hurt His children, mislead His blood-purchased possession, and plow illegally in His vineyard, they shall incur His wrath!

Concerning the false leaders that were influencing the churches of Galatia, Paul also wrote,

"I wish those who unsettle and confuse you would [go all the way and] cut themselves off!"

Galatians 5:12 Amp

In these words we sense the indignation of a true spiritual leader. Paul wished that the Judaizers who wanted to cut the Galatian believers in circumcision would cut themselves off! Paul expressed no compassion for those who were promoting unsound doctrine and unsound spiritual activity. He agreed with the apostle John's words and did not wish them God-speed except in the sense that God would speedily remove them from the scene!

By saying he wished the Judaizers would be "cut off," Paul made a striking play on words. The Judaizers who were troubling the churches in Galatia taught believers that they needed to be circumcised. They were attempting to bring them under subjection to the Old Testament, teaching that faith in Christ was not enough. Paul was very bold and forthright concerning these false leaders. In so many words, he said, "These false leaders want to cut you, but I wish they would just cut themselves off!"

These strong and damning words may not sound like the response of a spiritual leader. Don't forget, however, that these words not only came from a true and compassionate spiritual leader; they also came by divine inspiration. Perhaps you have not yet comprehended how dangerous unsound spiritual leadership is. Perhaps you have not yet understood how concerned God is with the spiritual well being of His own children.

There is nothing so close to the heart of God as His own people. He purchased them with a great price; not with gold or silver, but with the precious blood of His own Son. He will not allow some self-centered false minister to come in and cause His flock to be plundered, misled, or destroyed. If He has to cut out the "leaven" in order to spare the "lump," He will do so!

God Will Destroy Those Who Hurt His Temple

In his letter to the church at Corinth, Paul made it very clear that, "other foundation can no man lay than that is laid, which is Christ Jesus" [I Corinthians 3:11]. The foundation of the church is the revelation of Jesus Christ. Not only, however, is the foundation material important. It is also important what the rest of the building is built with. Every man who has any influence in the body of Christ will have his work tested to see what kind of material he built with. If his work stands the test, he will be rewarded. If, however, his works burn, he will suffer loss [I Corinthians 3:15].

Why is it such a serious issue what material is used in building the church? It is serious because the church is God's house. Notice Paul's question to the church, in Corinth,

> "Know ye not that ye are the temple of God, and that the Spirit of God dwelleth in you?"
>
> I Corinthians 3:16

The Amplified Bible renders Paul's words this way,

> "Do you not discern and understand that you [the whole church at Corinth] are God's temple (His sanctuary), and that God's Spirit has His permanent dwelling in you — to be at home in you [collectively as a church and also individually]?"
>
> I Corinthians 3:16 Amp

Any person who has any part in building the temple of God must be very careful. When they affiliate themselves with the church, they are involving themselves with the object of God's eternal affection. The church is His chosen nation; His special people. He does not take it lightly if ministers build with bad material. And He certainly does not take it lightly if false spiritual leaders tear apart the work of others! Those who do so are in danger of the wrath of God. "But," you say, "I thought God was a God of love." Yes, He is. He cares deeply for His children and for His church. This is precisely why ministers must deal very carefully with His church!

In the next verse, Paul made a very strong statement concerning God's attitude and His action against those who hurt His church. He wrote,

"If any man defile the temple of God, him shall God destroy; for the temple of God is holy, which temple ye are."

I Corinthians 3:17

In this potent scripture we can appreciate God's strong bias toward the church and His anger against those who hurt it. He is against anyone who does anything that leads to spiritual breakdown in the church. If someone destroys His temple, God will destroy that person. The Amplified Bible's rendering of this scripture is good because it emphasizes the activity of unsound ministers. It says,

"If anyone does hurt to God's temple or corrupts [it with false doctrines] or destroys it, God will do hurt to him and bring him to the corruption of death and destroy him. For the temple of God is holy — sacred to Him — and that [temple] you [the believing church and its individual believers] are."

I Corinthians 3:17 Amp

The local church at Corinth was being infiltrated by false apostles. Paul's words, therefore, were not only a statement of truth concerning God's feelings and sure action against false leadership. They were also an ominous warning to the false apostles who had assumed a place of leadership in that church.

Why will God destroy those who destroy the temple? Because, "the temple of God is holy." This does not mean that the church is perfect. It means that the saints in every local church have been specially set apart for God. They are His people. He loved them; He bought them; He called them; He saved them; and He has a place prepared for them. These people called "the temple" have the mark of God upon their lives. If anyone meddles with what belongs to God, they are on very dangerous ground!

God will bring retributive destruction upon the offender guilty of violating His body through false doctrine and unsound leadership. He will corrupt him by sending whatever judgement fits the crime. Woe be to that man! Because his offense is grievous his judgement will be severe! Marring a local church by leading it away from holiness of life and purity of doctrine incurs God's retributive destruction.

The Eternal Destiny of False Spiritual Leaders

Writing of false leaders "who crept in unawares" and were misleading a sound body with unsound teaching, Jude said these things,

"For there are certain men crept in unawares, who were before of old ordained to this condemnation, ungodly men...Woe to them! These are spots in your feasts of charity, when they feast with you, feeding themselves without fear: clouds they

are without water, carried about of wind; trees whose fruit withereth, without fruit,
twice dead, plucked up by the roots; Raging waves of the sea, foaming out their own
shame; wandering stars, to whom is reserved the blackness of darkness for ever."

Jude 4-13

Somehow false spiritual leaders had crept into this sound local body and
been accepted as true spiritual leaders. They even participated in this local
body's feasts of charity. Notice, however, the judgement Jude pronounced
upon them. He said that they were, "ordained to condemnation," and that
for them, "is reserved the blackness of darkness for ever" [Jude 13].

Jude referred to these false leaders as, "wandering stars." They were
meant to shine for the Lord. They were supposed to be ministers of light,
holding forth the Word of Life in a dark place. But they wandered from
their proper place. The natural stars stay in their place in obedience to the
Word of God's power. Some ministers, however, leave the course God has
assigned them and mislead the church. When they do so, they purchase to
themselves damnation.

The phrase, "the blackness of darkness," that Jude used is very potent.
W.E. Vine says that "blackness" refers to the gloom of the regions of the lost.
Moffat's translation calls this place "the nether gloom of darkness" and says
that it has been reserved eternally for false spiritual leaders. Very interestingly, the same word is used by Jude in verse 6 (there translated "darkness")
to foretell the eternal destination of the angels who sinned in the beginning.
He said that,

"...the angels which kept not their first estate, but left their own habitation, he hath
reserved in everlasting chains under darkness unto the judgment of the great day."

Jude 6

I'm not sure exactly what the "blackness of darkness" is, but I can guarantee you that it is not a place in heaven! False spiritual leaders who infiltrate and upset local churches are in danger of eternal darkness!

In his epistle, Jude referred to three groups of individuals who were
destroyed by God because they left their divine calling. He referred to these
groups to illustrate the fact that God would not hesitate to judge and destroy
false and unsound spiritual leaders. By putting the church in remembrance
of these three groups and their judgments, Jude hoped to put the fear of God
in them and in the false ministers in their midst.

The Children of Israel

Jude wrote first about the children of Israel, saying

"I will therefore put you in remembrance, though ye once knew this, how that the Lord, having saved the people out of the land of Egypt, afterward destroyed them that believed not."

Jude 5

Although God had chosen Israel, loved them, and delivered them from Egypt, He destroyed them when they rebelled against His Word. It was not that God no longer loved Israel. He gave them warning after warning and opportunity after opportunity to repent and walk in His commandments. He acted in great mercy and patience, hoping they would abandon their evil ways and walk in obedience to His Word. After numerous opportunities were given, however, and Israel failed to repent, God destroyed them.

The Angels That Sinned

Jude wrote second about the destiny of the angels that sinned. He said that just as these angels left their first calling and were judged of God, so false leaders who abdicated their first calling in order to indulge themselves in wicked desires and lusts of the flesh would be judged of God. The Amplified Bible gives a very clear meaning of this text,

"And angels that did not keep (care for, guard and hold to) their own first place of power but abandoned their proper dwelling place, He has reserved in custody in eternal chains (bonds) under the thick gloom of utter darkness until the judgement and doom of the great day."

Jude 6 Amp

The angels that followed Satan in his rebellion were created by God and given a place of responsibility. They served faithfully in the perfect will of God for a time, but then abandoned their first place of power and followed Satan in his rebellion. These angels did not stay within the boundaries of God's will; they did not remain within their appointed sphere of authority. Although they had served faithfully, perhaps for millions of years, by their single act of disobedience they purchased to themselves eternal damnation. Once they lived and worked within the perfect will of God. Now, however, they have only the wrath of God to look forward to.

Sodom and Gomorrah

Jude's third example was the complete destruction of the cities of Sodom and Gomorrah. He reiterated in this verse that the destruction of these cities was an example for New Testament believers. He said,

"Even as Sodom and Gomorrah, and the cities about them in like manner, giving themselves over to fornication, and going after strange flesh, are set forth for an example, suffering the vengeance of eternal fire."

Jude 7

Sodom and Gomorrah were two normal ancient cities. At some point in time, however, they began to yield themselves to the lusts of their flesh. It is very likely that they continued for years in their sin, digressing to the place where they were totally corrupted. Only after they had abandoned a righteous lifestyle and persisted till they were totally degradent did God judge and destroy them.

God Will Abandon False Spiritual Leaders

The false spiritual leaders Jude wrote about started out in the will of God. They had been part of the body of Christ. They had been saved and walked in the way of righteousness. They were, very likely, spiritual leaders. As did the angels that sinned, however, these men left their first place. They, too, "abandoned their proper dwelling place." They left the path of righteousness, gave themselves over to fleshly lusts, and began to infiltrate the sound body with their filth and false teaching. They, too, put themselves in danger of the judgement and wrath of God.

The point Jude wanted to drive home in his three examples was that God was not incapable of abandoning those who abandoned Him. This also included those who were specially chosen by Him, as was Israel. This included those who were specially created by Him and set in positions of authority, as were the angels. This included those who abandoned righteous living and perverted their neighbors, as did Sodom and Gomorrah. And this included, as Jude was purposing to illustrate, unsound spiritual leaders who had abandoned the faith and were leading others astray. The unsound spiritual leaders Jude wrote of were in danger not only of being rejected by God, but of coming under the consuming fire of His severe vengeance.

Jude did not quit here, however, but prophesied further judgement for false ministers,

> "And Enoch also, the seventh from Adam, prophesied of these (false leaders), saying, Behold, the Lord cometh with ten thousands of his saints, To execute judgement upon all, and to convince all that are ungodly among them of all their ungodly deeds which they have ungodly committed, and of all their hard speeches which ungodly sinners have spoken against him. These are murmurers, complainers, walking after their own lusts; and their mouth speaketh great swelling words having men's persons in admiration."

> Jude 14-16

Far back in time, Enoch prophesied of false spiritual leaders when he spoke of the coming of the Lord and His exacting judgement. When Jesus comes again, He will not only smile upon the saints. He will also execute judgement upon false spiritual leaders and make clear to each person exactly where they were wrong. False spiritual leaders will pay a price at the judgement day for their unsound and wrong spiritual activities.

False Spiritual Leaders and Their Sure Judgement

The apostle Peter also wrote quite extensively of the punishment awaiting false spiritual leaders. In his second letter, he wrote this concerning false ministers,

"...*whose judgement now of a long time lingereth not, and their damnation slumbereth not. For if God spared not the angels that sinned, but cast them down to hell, and delivered them into chains of darkness, to be reserved unto judgement; And spared not the old world...And turning the cities of Sodom and Gomorrah into ashes condemned them with an overthrow...The Lord knoweth how to...reserve the unjust unto the day of judgement to be punished...these...shall utterly perish in their own corruption; And shall receive the reward of unrighteousness...to whom the mist of darkness is reserved forever...*"

II Peter 2:4-17

This promise of judgement concerns the "false teachers among you" that Peter introduced in II Peter 2:1-3. These false teachers were feasting in the midst of the sound body [verse 13]. They were, "cursed children," Peter said, "which have forsaken the right way, and are gone astray" [verses 14-15]. These had once, "escaped the pollutions of the world through the knowledge of the Lord," but they had become, "entangled again" [verse 20]. These false teachers once knew "the way of righteousness," but had turned away from it [verse 21].

It is very apparent that these false spiritual leaders had once walked with the Lord and walked in the way of truth. Now, however, "Forsaking the straight road they have gone astray" [II Peter 2:15 Amp]. These false leaders will be judged by God with a very harsh judgement. It will be no less harsh than the judgement of the angels that left their rightful place. It will be no less severe than the complete desolation of Sodom and Gomorrah. It will be no less devastating than the complete destruction of the world in the time of Noah.

These false leaders, you see, had known the right way. They chose instead, however, the rewards of unrighteousness. Although they had abandoned the faith, they were using their knowledge of the truth and their past relationship with the church as a means of misleading believers and profiting themselves. The judgement of these once sound believers turned false spiritual leaders will be very swift and very stiff!

False teachers, said Peter, are reserved unto the day of judgement to be punished. They will be rewarded for their sin. They will utterly perish in their own corruption in this life and pay for their sin in eternity. They are damned, cursed by God, and their judgement is not far off. They will "receive the reward of unrighteousness" [verse 13] and for them is reserved a place called, "the mist of darkness" [verse 17]. In this place of darkness they shall spend eternity.

What About Love?

The judgement of the Lord may appear, at first glance, to be cruel and unloving. Judgement, however, is right and absolutely born of love. God is love. And because He is, He will not for very long allow self-seeking and hungry false spiritual leaders to continue in their evil deeds. After all, why should the body of Christ pay for the sins and perverted ways of false spiritual leaders? Why should churches be divided and subverted just so that one false spiritual leader can be "loved" by God? Why should the faith of righteous children be shaken while the false spiritual leader grows fat? Why should the wolves eat and the sheep starve? False spiritual leaders will be judged by a God of love!

False and unsound spiritual leaders will always be warned. Because many of them were once members of the sound body of Christ and may still profess faith in Christ, the heart of God goes out to them and He delays His judgement. Just as He gave Israel opportunity after opportunity to return to Him before He gave up and delivered them into captivity and destruction, so He will give false spiritual leaders an opportunity to repent and return to righteous living and right doctrine. Even if a temporary judgement of the flesh must be rendered, there is still hope in the heart of God that some false leaders will come to repentance. Perhaps His judgement will bring to their attention the seriousness of their wicked ways.

If false spiritual leaders fail to heed the warnings of God, they will be judged. If there was no judgement, there could be no repentance or turning away from wrong activity. If false leaders were not warned of impending judgement and then judged when they refused to repent, they would continue on in their promotion of destructive doctrine and deviant activity. If false spiritual leaders could manage to persist in wrong doing without reaping a compensatory harvest, they would do so. Judgement is often the only option false spiritual leaders leave God.

CONCLUSION

The Lord judges false spiritual leaders, not only in the hope that they will repent and return to godly living themselves, but even more so for the purpose of maintaining spiritual health in the body of Christ. When the spiritual health and the spiritual destiny of the church or of local churches is in jeopardy, God must render judgement. If the whole lump is at risk, the little leaven will be purged out!

If you are a minister and this teaching makes you afraid, then I am satisfied. The truth has been heard and received. Spiritual leadership is nothing to be trifled with. If you are called to be a shepherd of the sheep, then you have had entrusted to you that which means the most to God! You would be wise to train well and to maintain the very highest standards in the truth and in the Spirit. Don't make yourself an enemy of God by misleading the church!

·~17~·
How to Judge Spiritual Leadership
Part One

U p to this point, we have covered a lot of ground concerning spiritual leadership. We have learned who they are, what they want, and how they get what they want. We have studied the negative and sometimes disastrous results that can occur when false spiritual leaders gain access to believers' lives and get a foothold in local churches. We have also discovered what happens to false spiritual leaders themselves; both what they bring upon themselves and the judgement of God upon them.

In this section we will study the different ways to judge those who claim to be spiritual leaders. It is very unlikely that you will ever employ every method I have included when examining a person to determine whether they are a true or a false or unsound spiritual leader. By studying these methods, however, and by knowing what to watch out for, you will avoid being taken by surprise by false spiritual leaders and will, therefore, avoid the negative and disastrous results which could occur if you followed them.

ONE: EXAMINE THEIR DOCTRINE

One of the very simplest and most basic ways to judge spiritual leaders is to examine the doctrines they teach. If those who claim to be teachers, apostles, prophets, or any other ministry gift teach and promote sound doctrine, there is a good chance they are sound spiritual leaders. If, however, those who claim to be teachers, apostles, prophets or any other ministry gift teach and promote unsound doctrine, they are likely unsound spiritual leaders and should be examined further. Just as holding fast to and teaching sound doctrine is a distinguishing mark of sound spiritual leaders, so holding fast to and teaching unsound doctrine is a distinguishing mark of unsound spiritual leaders.

There is an inseparable relationship between sound doctrine and sound spiritual leadership. Paul exhorted Titus, a young spiritual leader, to have uncorrupt doctrine and sound speech [Titus 1:9; 2:7-8]. He was to, "speak...the things which become sound doctrine" [Titus 2:1]. The spiritual leaders that Titus was to ordain in every city were to, "hold fast the faithful word" [Titus 1:9]. If they did not hold fast to sound doctrine, they were not qualified to be spiritual leaders. Paul gave similar instructions concerning sound doctrine over and over again to young Timothy. Paul charged him to, "Preach the Word," even when people didn't want sound doctrine [II Timothy 4:1]. He was to hold fast to sound words and continue in the holy scriptures. He was to study and rightly divide the word of truth and shun false doctrine [II Timothy 1:13; 2:15-16; 3:14-17].

Just as there is an inseparable relationship between sound doctrine and sound spiritual leadership, so there is an inseparable relationship between unsound doctrine and unsound spiritual leadership. Peter said that false teachers bring damnable heresies into the church [II Peter 2:1]. Paul said that wolves would arise in the midst of local churches and speak perverse words [Acts 20:30]. Of the false apostles that attempted to get a foothold in Corinth, Paul said they were preaching another Jesus and another gospel [II Corinthians 11:4]. Paul told Timothy that false leaders would give heed to and then promote doctrines of devils [I Timothy 4:1-3]. Paul informed the churches of Galatia that the false teachers who were misleading them had perverted the gospel [Galatians 1:6-9].

As long as those who claim to be spiritual leaders hold fast to and teach sound doctrine, they pass the most basic test of sound spiritual leadership. If, however, those who claim to be spiritual leaders teach unsound doctrine, they fail the most basic test for sound spiritual leadership. One of the most basic ways to judge whether a teacher is true or false, sound or unsound, is to judge his doctrine.

Take Heed to the Scriptures

In his second letter, Peter highlighted the very close relationship between unsound doctrine and false teachers. After recounting his experience on the mount of transfiguration, he wrote,

> "We have also a more sure word of prophecy; whereunto ye do well that ye take heed, as unto a light that shineth in a dark place...Knowing this first, that no prophecy of the scripture is of any private interpretation. For the prophecy came not in old time by the will of man: but holy men of God spake as they were moved by the

Holy Ghost. But there were false prophets also among the people, even as there shall be false teachers among you, who privily shall bring in damnable heresies..."
II Peter 1:19- 2:1

It was because of the surety that their would be false teachers in their midst that Peter encouraged believers to take heed to the scriptures. He said, "there shall be false teachers among you, who privily shall bring in damnable heresies...and many shall follow" [II Peter 2:1-2]. The point Peter was making to these believers was simple, yet very crucial to their spiritual stability. His point was this: "If you take heed to the scriptures, you will be able to recognize false teachers." If believers know the scriptures and recognize sound and unsound doctrine, they will be able to judge those who claim to be teachers.

Peter pointed believers to the written scriptures to prepare them for two types of false spiritual leaders. First, there will be those who claim to be spiritual leaders because they have had a supernatural experience. They may say they heard the voice of God or profess to have had a vision. By calling the scriptures, "a more sure word of prophesy" — thus elevating the witness of the scriptures above hearing a voice from heaven or seeing a vision — Peter forever established that agreement with the written scriptures is a far more important requirement for true spiritual leaders than claiming to have had a supernatural experience.

Second, there will be those who will simply pose as teachers and begin to carefully introduce heresy and unsound doctrine into the sound body. If believers are not grounded in the scriptures, they will not recognize the heresies and unsound doctrines false teachers teach and will not, therefore, suspect the person who is teaching.

Because false spiritual leaders often conceal their identity, sometimes by claims of supernatural experience and sometimes by posing like true ministers, they can be very difficult to recognize. It is almost impossible, at times, to judge their motives, especially if they are hidden beneath a disguise of spirituality. Their doctrine, however, can be judged. If one who claims to be a spiritual leader teaches unsound doctrine, he is likely unsound and should undergo further examination. It is that simple.

Are They Going the Way of Cain?

In his epistle, Jude wrote of false spiritual leaders who were introducing false doctrines into the church. One way he characterized these false teachers was by saying that, "they have gone the way of Cain" [Jude 4]. What did Jude mean when he said that these false spiritual leaders went the way of Cain?

Early in the book of Genesis, God gave instructions to Cain and Abel concerning their offerings. When Cain brought his offering to the Lord, rather than bringing the fruit of the ground as God had commanded, he brought a lamb. In so doing, Cain substituted his own thoughts, his own opinions, and his own ways for God's words.

When ministers teach and promote doctrines which have no precedent in the Word of God, they go the way of Cain. Cain's works, say the Bible, were evil. His works were not evil because there was something defective with his offering. His works were evil because he was outside the boundaries of God's words concerning the offering. Those who go the way of Cain by abandoning what God has said disqualify themselves as sound spiritual leaders.

Example of Judging Doctrine

The area of deliverance is a popular modern theme. Let's consider what some ministers are teaching concerning deliverance to see if they would qualify as sound spiritual leaders or if they should be investigated further.

Concerning the area of demon possession, I heard one man refer to the Old Testament story of Rebekah and the unborn twins struggling in her womb. In this story, Rebekah asked the Lord about the conflict she felt in her womb. The Lord answered that there were two nations in her womb and that the younger would rule the elder [Genesis 25:22-23]. The man who was teaching about deliverance cited this Old Testament story to "prove" that even before birth, babies have demons in them. He said that the reason the twins were fighting in Rebekah's womb was because the two demon spirits in them were fighting.

Does this sound absurd? Some believers accept it as the truth. Only one good thing can be said about this kind of teaching. It makes it quickly obvious that this man and his teaching must be further investigated.

Some teach that the blood of Jesus must be pled over a demon possessed person in order to cast the demon out. Where does the Bible say that? If this is the only way they come out, how did the disciples cast them out before Jesus shed His blood? No, the truth is that demons come out when men exercise authority over them. The disciples were given authority cast out devils in Jesus' Name. When they exercised that authority, they obtained results. In the New Covenant, every believer has been given authority to cast out demons in Jesus' Name. When believers exercise their authority through faith in the Name of Jesus, demons will come out. Jesus said, "In my name shall they cast out devils" [Mark 16:17].

Some teach that believers should ask demons their names. Jesus only asked a demon it's name one time, although several times He did identify demons by the gift of discerning of spirits. Some teach that believers should cast devils into the lake of fire or into the abyss. Jesus, however, made it quite clear that when a demon goes out of a person, it wanders around in a dry place seeking another lodging. Sometimes the demon that is cast out returns to the very place it was cast out of [Matthew 12:43-45]. Believers cannot cast a demon into the abyss or into the lake of fire. If we could, the earth could cleansed of demons. The time, however, has not yet come for their final sentencing [Matthew 8:29].

Some ministers are currently teaching that demons are driven out by intercession or by warring against them in other tongues. They teach believers to torment demons by speaking to them in other tongues till they come out. There is, however, no scripture to support that teaching and no scriptural example. Demons are not driven out over time. The Bible does not teach that we war them out, wear them out, coax them out, or irritate them out. The Bible teaches that we cast them out in Jesus' Name! The truth of the matter is that Jesus, our example in ministry, never even prayed over a demon-possessed person. He simply commanded the demons to leave, and they did!

You see, it is not difficult to judge those who claim to be spiritual leaders. Simply check their doctrines against the Word of God. Compare what they teach and what they do with what God has already said. This is a very basic method for judging spiritual leadership. If those who claim to be spiritual leaders go the way of Cain by teaching doctrines that cannot be confirmed by the Word of God, then they must be suspected of being, at the least, an unsound spiritual leader. Further investigation is definitely required.

Sound Doctrine or New Moves?

It is important to determine whether the teachings of those who claim to be spiritual leaders is based on time-tested and well proven Bible doctrines or on some "new revelation." If you find that their teachings are primarily based on "something God is saying right" now, be cautious. Always teaching, promoting, or doing something new is a sign of spiritual immaturity.

The last new thing God said He would do until the time when He makes all things new, was to inaugurate the New Covenant. He prophesied of this in the Old Testament saying, "Behold, I do a new thing" [Isaiah 43:19]. Everything else that God will do between now and the second coming of Jesus, He did in the early church and in church history. Of course, I know that the early church did not have radio and television, but I am not speaking in terms of the medium of communication, but in terms of the message being communicated. God is the same. The gospel message is the same. The doctrines of the Word of God are the same. The gifts of the Spirit are the same.

Why do some ministers push for new moves and new revelation? Often it is because they are bored and discontent without continual stimulation. A continual need for change and constant activity, however, reveals a spiritual deficiency; a lack of the true internal working of God's Word and the Holy Spirit. It also reveals that ministers are discontent with sound doctrine. They are bored with ministering the Word of God by the inspiration of the Spirit. A constant need for something new is a sign that a minister is at least immature.

Sound ministers preach the sound doctrines clearly laid out in the Word of God. Remember that in his strong charge to Timothy, Paul told him to, "Preach the Word" [II Timothy 4:2]. The responsibility of true spiritual leaders is to settle believers, not to drag them from new move to new move and from wave to wave. If ministers take believers anywhere, it should be from faith to faith, from glory to glory, from truth to truth, from strength to strength, from victory to victory, and from babyhood to full age!

Soul Ties and the Two-Edged Sword

Be especially attentive to the written scriptures when you are judging a person with whom you have a close spiritual relationship. Because of your deep affection for them, your soul can be knit to them. If questions ever arise in your heart about the direction they are going spiritually, it may be very difficult for you to separate between truth and your emotions; between what the Holy Spirit is saying and what your soul is saying. This is a time when you must depend upon the written Word of God. The writer of Hebrews wrote,

> "For the word of God is quick, and powerful, and sharper than any two edged sword, piercing even to the dividing asunder of soul and spirit..."
>
> *Hebrews 4:12*

The word translated "dividing" in this text comes from the Greek *merismos* which means a division or a partition. This dividing ability of the Word of God is very important when judging spiritual leadership. It can divide between the thoughts and feelings of your soul and the thoughts and impressions of your spirit.

It could happen, for example, that a friend in the ministry or someone you respect in the ministry moves in a questionable spiritual direction. You sense in your spirit that their direction is not right. On the other hand, because you respect and love them and don't want to forfeit your relationship with them, your soul is saying something else. Your feelings for that person are speaking to you and the Holy Spirit is speaking to you. It can be very difficult in this situation to discern what is coming from your spirit and what is coming from your soul.

This is when you must go to the unchanging and objective standard of the written scriptures. It will help you to discern what thoughts are proceeding from your soul and what thoughts are coming from your spirit. Whatever thoughts agree with the scriptures are coming from your spirit by the Holy Spirit. Whatever thoughts and feelings cannot be confirmed by the Word are coming from your soul. If that friend or close associate is teaching doctrine or doing things that are not in agreement with what is already written in the Word of God, then no matter what you feel for them, you must conclude that what they are teaching or doing is unsound. It makes no difference how you feel, how persuasive they are, or how much they pull on your heart-strings. If they are out of harmony with the written Word, they are wrong.

When you cannot, because of your closeness to an individual, discern between your spirit and your soul, go to the objective standard of truth, the written scriptures. Emotions are subjective. What you think the Holy Ghost is saying is also subjective. The written scriptures, however, are not subjective. They are objective. It is written! It is settled! It is a fact! The truth is eternally established and clearly spelled out in black ink on white pages. When you cannot, because of emotional involvement, discern between your spirit and your soul, let the Word of God divide and separate out for you what is and what is not Truth.

Cultivate and maintain a strong grasp of the scriptures. Be on the alert, especially when emotions and personal ties are involved. Never think for one moment that those close to you could not lead you into error. And don't think for one moment that Satan won't attempt to use those close to you to entice you into error! Why will he use them? Because they are the ones you would least likely suspect to be in error or to lead you into error. Because your heart is knit to them and your soul is tied with them, you can be easily blinded to the error they espouse. It is not impossible, however, for those you love and respect, even friends or family members, to unknowingly slip into error and be used by the devil to lead you into the same error.

TWO: FOLLOW THE WITNESS OF THE SPIRIT

In order to be accurate in the Christian life, it is absolutely essential to know the witness of the Holy Spirit. He has been given as a gift to believers so that they can know "all things." As it is true in all other areas of Christian life, so it is also true in this area of judging spiritual leaders: It is imperative to know the witness of the Spirit! In this section we will study what the apostle John taught in his first epistle about the relationship between the Indwelling Anointing of the Holy Spirit and recognizing false spiritual leaders. Some scriptures that are familiar to you will take on new meaning as we examine them in the context in which they are written.

An Unction from the Holy One

In his first letter to his spiritual children, the apostle John revealed the vital relationship between the indwelling Holy Spirit and recognizing false spiritual leaders. He wrote,

> "...*even now are there many antichrists; whereby we know that it is the last time. They went out from us, but they were not of us: for if they had been of us, they would no doubt have continued with us: but they went out, that they might be made manifest that they were not all of us. But ye have an unction from the Holy One, and ye know all things.*"
>
> I John 2:18-20

Referring to the false spiritual leaders he called antichrists, John said, "They went out from us." These false spiritual leaders were formerly members of a sound local body. John stated, however, that because they went out from the body, they proved that they were not really of the body.

"But," John said in verse 20, "ye have an unction from the Holy One and ye know all things." Notice that John's statement begins with the word, "But." "But" is a word of contrast and in this case relates what John said in verse 20 about the unction of the Holy One and what he said in verses 18-19 about antichrists. John said that the antichrists where recognizable because they departed from the sound body. "But," he said, they could have also been recognized by listening to the unction of the Holy One. Because believers have an unction from the Holy One, the indwelling witness of the Holy Spirit, they can know who is false and who is not false even before they expose themselves by departing from the body.

What John wrote about the "unction from the Holy One" was written in direct context with his warning about false spiritual leaders. He was encouraging these Christians to depend upon that unction. If they followed it, they would know "all things," especially, in this context, they would know who were false spiritual leaders. By being sensitive to the unction that God put within them, they could know who were antichrists even before they revealed themselves by departing from the sound body. It is good to know who are false and unsound *after* they have exposed themselves, but it is far better to know *before* they expose themselves!

Believers have an internal witness. Believers have an unction from God that speaks to them. This internal witness, the Holy Spirit, will alert believers to false spiritual leaders even before they expose themselves.

The Anointing that Abides Within

John repeated this very same truth just a few verses later saying,

"These things have I written unto you concerning them that seduce you. But the anointing which ye have received of him abideth in you, and ye need not that any man teach you: but as the same anointing teacheth you of all things, and is truth, and is no lie, and even as it hath taught you, ye shall abide in him."

I John 2:26-27

John told his spiritual children that the reason he had written was to warn them of false spiritual leaders. "But," he said, "the anointing which ye have received of him abideth in you, and...the same anointing teacheth you of all things." Again, John used the word "But" to make a point. He said that he had written his spiritual children to inform them about false spiritual leaders, but even if he had not written, the anointing would have warned them! The anointing would have testified within them as to which teachers were true and which teachers were false.

The Indwelling Anointing will point out those who look like sheep, but are wolves dressed in sheep's clothing. The Indwelling Anointing will tell believers, "That individual is not what he pretends to be or says he is." The Indwelling Anointing will reveal to believers who is of the truth and who is not of the truth. John said,

"...ye need not that any man teach you; but as the same anointing teacheth you of all things, and is truth..."

I John 2:27

By the words, "ye need not that any man teach you," John did not mean (as some errantly think) that believers don't need to be taught by true spiritual leaders. What John meant was that believers should not be completely dependent on spiritual leaders, but should learn to listen to and be dependent upon the indwelling anointing of the Holy Spirit. If believers are not confident in the indwelling anointing, they will have to accept another person's word as truth. If believers are dependent on teachers, they will be susceptible to false teachers. If believers are dependent on men, they are targets for deception. Believer must put their first and full confidence in the Indwelling Anointing, the Spirit of Truth, Who has been sent to lead and guide them into the truth.

What does the Indwelling Anointing teach believers? The anointing, said John, teaches believers that they should, "should abide in Christ" [I John 2:27]. Abiding in Christ is the opposite of following false spiritual leaders. Abiding in Christ refers not only to staying saved, but also refers to remaining firmly established in the doctrine of Christ. If the Indwelling Anointing teaches believers to "abide in Christ," then it will also alert them to anyone who would endeavor to draw them away from Christ.

The Anointing is Truth

The "anointing teacheth you of all things, and is truth," said John [I John 2:27]. In saying this, John tied the Truth and the Holy Spirit into a knot so tight that the two cannot be separated. The Spirit that indwells believers is Truth. He is the Spirit of Truth. Because He is the Spirit of Truth, He not only recognizes Truth, but also recognizes those who are of the Truth and those who are not of the Truth. He recognizes and points out these individuals for the benefit of believers.

Do you recall the tragic story of Ananias and Sapphira as recorded in Acts chapter five? This couple sold a parcel of land and agreed together to lie to the apostles about how much they sold it for. When Ananias brought the money to the apostle Peter and told him that it was the whole amount of the sale of the land, Peter knew instantly by the witness of the Holy Spirit that Ananias was lying. Listen to what Peter said to him,

> *"...Ananias, why hath Satan filled your heart to lie to the Holy Ghost?"*
>
> *Acts 5:3*

Notice that Peter did not say, "Ananias, why did you lie to me?" He said, "Ananias, why did you lie to the Holy Ghost?" Peter and the indwelling Holy Spirit were inseparable. When Ananias spoke, the Spirit of Truth within Peter did not bear witness with his words. Peter did not need to fast and pray. He did not need to consult the city records concerning the sale of that piece of land. He knew immediately, by the witness of the Anointing of Truth that abided within him, that Ananias was lying.

The Holy Spirit is like an internal bell and truth is like a hammer. When truth is spoken, the Holy Spirit resounds within. The anointing that abides within, said John, "is no lie." It will not bear witness within you either of lies or of liars. The anointing within you will always bear witness *with* those who are of the Truth, and will bear witness *against* those who are not of the Truth.

The Holy Spirit is like a metal detector in an airport. When false spiritual leaders come all dressed up in ministers' clothing, the Holy Spirit detects their hard heart and alerts us immediately that there is something dangerous inside! He sounds an alarm in our spirit, informing us that trouble lies ahead if we follow that person.

The Holy Spirit is a one hundred percent accurate, right every time, "Wolf-ometer." And where is He? He, "abideth in you." Believers must learn to listen to their hearts. If we will pay attention to The Anointing that abideth within us, He will teach us all things. Specifically, He will teach us who is of God and who is not of God.

What John wrote in this second chapter of his first epistle concerning the unction from the Holy One [verse 20] and the anointing which abides within [verse 27] was written directly in the context of discerning false spiritual leaders. Although ministers commonly use these verses in reference to the teaching ministry of the Holy Spirit, that is not exactly what John meant to teach. What John revealed in these verses about the ministry of the Holy Spirit is that He will alert believers to false ministers and seducers. The Indwelling Anointing, said John, will show believers who is and who is not of the Truth.

Greater is He That is in You

John associated the ministry of the Holy Spirit and the discerning of false spiritual leadership at another place in his first epistle. In chapter four, he wrote,

> *"Ye are of God, little children, and have overcome them: because greater is he that is in you, than he that is in the world."*
>
> I John 4:4

Believers often use this scripture to stand against the devil or to believe for victory in difficult circumstances. Their thinking is that Christ in them is greater than the devil in the world. This interpretation and use of I John 4:4 is not necessarily wrong. This scripture must, however, be read in its proper context. It is written in the context of teaching about false prophets [verse 1], of testing spirits to discern whether or not they are of God [verse 1], and of teachers that are not of God [verse 6]. When understood in its proper context, this scripture takes on a whole new meaning.

"Ye are of God," said John to his spiritual children in verse four, "and have overcome them." Who is the "them" John is referring to that believers have overcome? "Them" are the false prophets motivated by wrong spirits that John said to, "believe not...but try" [I John 4:1]. "Them" are the teachers motivated by the "spirit of antichrist" that are "of the world" [I John 4:3, 5]. "Them" are the spirits that are "not of God" [I John 4:3]. "Them" are the "spirit[s] of error" [I John 4:6]. Notice what the Amplified Bible says,

"*Little children, you are of God...and have [already] defeated and overcome them [the agents of antichrist]...*"

I John 4:4 Amp

And notice the New English Bible's rendering of this verse,

"*But you, my children, are of God's family and you have the mastery over these false prophets...*"

I John 4:4 NEB

The "them" in I John 4:4 that believers overcome is not sickness, disease, depression, or financial difficulty. "Them" are false spiritual leaders and the spirits of error that motivate them.

How are believers able to overcome "them?" How are they able to overcome false prophets, false teachers, the spirit of antichrist, and spirits of error? According to John, believers are able to overcome them because someone greater than false spiritual leaders and spirits of error lives in them. John said,

"*Ye...have overcome them because greater is he that is in you, than he that is in the world.*"

I John 4:4

It is "because" the greater one is in them that believers can overcome false spiritual leaders and spirits of error. But who is this "greater one?" The greater one that lives in believes is the Spirit of God! And what does the Greater One do? He enables believers to overcome false spiritual leaders!

John speaks of the Holy Spirit in believers as the Greater One. But who is He greater than? He is greater than the spirit of antichrist that is operating in the world. He is greater than the seducing spirits of error that work through false ministers. He is greater than false prophets and other false spiritual leaders. The Holy Spirit is greater; He more effectual, more skillful, and more dedicated to leading believers into and keeping them in the truth than seducing spirits and false spiritual leaders are dedicated to leading believers into error. Therefore, the Greater One will prevail! He will keep believers in the truth. False spiritual leaders and the seducing spirits that motivate them will fail in their attempts to lead Spirit-sensitive believers into error!

We have already learned that the way false spiritual leaders overcome believers is through deception. But how do believers overcome the false spiritual leaders who are trying to overcome them? Believers overcome false spiritual leaders by recognizing and avoiding them! Believers overcome false spiritual leaders because the Greater One in them exposes false spiritual leaders and the seducing spirits that motivate them.

Greater is the Holy Spirit that indwells believers than the false spiritual leaders who are in the world. False spiritual leaders will attempt to overcome believers through clever deception. But believers will overcome false spiritual leaders and their clever deceptions by the help of the Holy Ghost that lives in them! This is the true meaning of, "Greater is he that is in you, than he that is in the world!"

Believers Have the Witness in Themselves

Near the end of his first epistle, John said,

> *"He that believeth on the Son of God hath the witness in himself."*
>
> *I John 5:10*

The Holy Spirit is the "Eye"-witness that indwells believers. He sees what we cannot see. He knows what we could not possibly know. He searches the hearts of men and reveals to believers who is and who is not of God. The Indwelling Witness tells the truth, the whole truth, and nothing but the truth!

Believers should not always look outside themselves for the answer. They should not always ask someone else, "Do you think this teacher is sound?" They should not always look to someone else for confirmation. The most important witness is the Witness that abides within us. His name is the Holy Ghost.

I can think of many instances over the past fifteen years when they Holy Spirit has witnessed to my spirit concerning certain spiritual leaders. At the time He witnessed to my heart, there was no other way to know that something was "off" except by His witness.

A few years ago I became acquainted with a certain minister who was uniquely used of God in the gifts of the Spirit, had a fast growing ministry, and was gifted in music. I enjoyed his ministry and considered pursuing a relationship with him. Each time I thought that direction, however, I had a check in my heart. The thoughts of my heart were, "I don't know what it is, but there is something wrong about him." To tell you the truth, one of the witnesses I had in my spirit was that he had a problem with lust. Around that same time, this minister attempted to recruit one of my friends into a leadership position in his organization. When my friend asked me what I thought he should do, I told him, "Avoid him, he wants to build his own empire." This was the witness of the Spirit that I had.

Unfortunately, the witness I had concerning this individual was right. The things that were wrong in his life eventually surfaced. At the time, however, there was no way to know he was unsound except by the witness of the Spirit. Hindsight is 20/20. We can all avoid unsound ministers when their "unsoundness" surfaces. But believers can have 20/20 hindsight *now* by listening to the witness of the Spirit!

There is another minister I have known of for years. He is a nice man and in the ministry today. The very first time I heard him speak, however, something in me said, "Something is not right. I don't know what it is, but I would not follow him." This did not mean that I didn't like his personality or disliked the suit he was wearing. I just had a kind of nauseous feeling in my belly; a mild "yucky" feeling is the best way I know how to say it. I wondered if he had sexual problems. A few years after I first heard this minister speak and had that check in my spirit, he divorced his wife and left his family.

A number of years later my wife happened to go to an evening meeting where this man was speaking. When she came home from the meeting she told me that she would never go to another meeting where this man was speaking unless I was along. She told me that he had looked at her in very strange ways and thought he had a problem with lust. I had never spoken a word to her about this man, but ten years later she had the same witness about him.

The Holy Spirit will witness these kinds of things to you concerning ministers. It is not to *expose them*, but to *protect you*. It is to keep you from getting involved with those who will hurt you. How can you know things that are hidden? By the witness of the Holy Spirit. He knows all things. He will lead you into all the truth and show you things to come [John 16:13]. Some of the "things to come" He will show you is what will happen if you involve yourself with certain ministers.

Which Holy Ghost Should I Listen To?

A very interesting situation took place in the the the life of the apostle Paul that underscores the necessity of knowing the witness of the Spirit for ourselves. Paul had purposed in the Holy Spirit and was "bound in the spirit" to go up to Jerusalem [Acts 19:20; 20:24]. He had counseled with the Holy Spirit and settled the direction of God for that season in his life. In every city Paul travelled through, however, disciples perceived by the same Holy Ghost that he would encounter persecution in Jerusalem. Because of what the Holy Spirit was witnessing about Paul's imminent trouble, the disciples in these cities tried to persuade Paul not to go up to Jerusalem [Acts 21:4-14]. They said,

> "...when we heard these things, both we, and they of that place, besought him not to go up to Jerusalem."
>
> Acts 21:12

These believers were moved by compassion and moved to action concerning Paul's impending danger in Jerusalem. Because of what they sensed in the Spirit, they pulled hard on Paul not to go to Jerusalem. Notice, however, what Paul said,

> "Then Paul answered, What mean ye to weep and to break mine heart? for I am ready not to be bound only, but also to die at Jerusalem for the name of the Lord Jesus."
>
> Acts 21:13

When these disciples realized that they could not persuade Paul to change his plans, they said, "The will of the Lord be done" [Acts 21:14].

Paul was at risk of being pulled outside the boundaries of the will of God, not by his enemies, but by those who cared for him the most! The disciples in each city heard correctly what the Spirit of God was witnessing, but they misinterpreted His message. Their motivations were sincere, but their interpretation was wrong. Their feelings for Paul clouded their interpretation. They never checked to determine if the reason the Holy Ghost had witnessed to them about Paul's upcoming trouble in Jerusalem was so that they could be part of praying for him in his trouble.

Despite the pleading of these believers, Paul remained faithful to what the Spirit of God had directed him to do. He knew that bonds and afflictions awaited him, but said, "none of these things move me" [Acts 20:24]. The only thing that moved Paul was what God had already said to him by the Spirit. Paul's ability to properly discern the voice of the Spirit and not be moved by his relationship with other believers enabled him to fulfill the will of God.

Several years ago there was a "wind of doctrine" that swept through some parts of the body of Christ. I was a part of the body that had an opportunity to catch that wind. I was quite sure by the teaching of the scriptures that this doctrine was not sound, but because many other ministers were following after it, I had to check closer. Rather than following the direction everyone else seemed to be going, I simply said, "Holy Spirit, is this of God or not?" Immediately, I heard Him say, "This is not a move of the Spirit, but is being propagated by men." Although other leaders in the body of Christ were saying, "This is the move of God and you had better join in," I had a different witness in my heart and stayed with that. In time, it turned out that the witness I had from the Holy Spirit was right.

The Spirit of Truth — The Spirit of Error
Of false spiritual leaders, the apostle John said,

> *"They are of the world...the world heareth them. We are of God...he that knoweth God heareth us. Hereby know we the spirit of truth, and the spirit of error."*
> *I John 4:5-6*

False spiritual leaders who are motivated by seducing spirits are, "of the world." Those who hear and follow them are of the world. But believers are "of God." Because we are God's children, "God hath sent forth the Spirit of His Son into our hearts" [Galatians 4:6]. Because the Holy Spirit lives in our hearts, we are able to recognize the spirit of error and the spirit of truth [I John 4:6]. The Spirit of Truth within us not only recognizes error and those who are motivated by spirits of error, however. He also recognizes Truth and those who are motivated by God.

In his letter to Titus, Paul spoke of false teachers as "deceivers." This word literally means "mind-deceiver." False spiritual leaders will play games with believers' minds. They will offer convincing reasoning and seemingly airtight arguments. Because of this, believers' minds could be deceived. Their brains could be brain-washed. Their emotions could be swayed. But their spirit, by the Holy Spirit, knows the truth! Even if an argument seems 100% convincing, if you have a check in your heart, give it a more thorough examination.

If you are born of God, you are capable of discerning between spiritual leaders that are of God and spiritual leaders that are not of God. Don't be afraid of being misled. You can discern the spirit of Truth and the spirit of error. You can overcome the devil's tactics to seduce you through unsound spiritual leaders. Rejoice and fear not, but simply be aware and listen to the Greater One, the Spirit of Truth, the unction, the anointing which ye have received. If you do, you will overcome every attempt of Satan and false spiritual leaders to mislead you!

THREE: TEST THE SPIRITS
Another important method for judging those who claim to be spiritual leaders is to test the spirits behind them. The apostle John instructed his spiritual children to do this very thing when he wrote,

> *"Beloved, believe not every spirit, but try (or judge) the spirits whether they are of God; because many false prophets are gone out into the world."*
> *I John 4:1*

What did John mean when he instructed his spiritual children to, "try the spirits?" Primarily, John was referring to identifying the motivating spirit behind one who claims to be a spiritual leader. This motivating spirit will either be the Spirit of God Who inspires true spiritual leaders or a demonic entity which inspires false spiritual leaders. Secondarily, it is important to discern the attitude that motivates those who claim to be spiritual leaders. Let's look closer at these two aspects of testing the spirits.

Influencing Spirits

John warned his spiritual children to "believe not," but to listen with a healthy skepticism to the teaching of those who claimed to be spiritual leaders. It was important that believers realized that not everyone who was speaking in the name of God was speaking by the inspiration of God or for the benefit of the kingdom of God. John instructed these believers to test and by testing to determine whether or not the spirit that was inspiring a specific minister was the Spirit of God or a lying spirit.

By instructing his spiritual children to, "try the spirits...because many false prophets are gone out into the world," John vitally linked false prophets and antichrist spirits. He revealed that many false prophets and other false ministers are influenced and inspired by demonic spirits. Even some sincere ministers occasionally yield to spirits that are not of God. Seducing spirits look for men with open minds and open mouths and attempt to speak through them by putting thoughts in their minds and words in their mouths.

It is very interesting that the apostle John told believers *to* test the spirits, but never instructed them *how to* test the spirits. This indicates that the believers John wrote to knew exactly what he was referring to when he told them to, "try the spirits." Evidently they knew how to judge. They knew how to discern the spirits behind those who claimed to be leaders. Testing spirits should not be a foreign spiritual activity to any believer. If we are "spiritual men" — if we are grounded in the truth of God's Word, sensitive to the voice of the Holy Spirit, and have our "senses exercised to discern both good and evil" — then examining, testing, and judging in spiritual matters should be a normal part of our lives.

The Voice Behind the Voice

Believers must listen with a discerning ear to the voice behind the voice of those who speak. The sheep will recognize the voice of the True Shepherd even when He speaks through undershepherds. If they do not recognize the voice that is speaking, they will not follow. Concerning the sheep and the voice of the shepherd, Jesus said,

"...he that entereth by the door is the shepherd of the sheep...and his sheep follow him: for they know his voice. And a stranger will they not follow, but will flee from him: for they know not the voice of strangers."

John 10:2-5

Why do the sheep follow the true shepherd? They follow because they know the voice. The inverse is true concerning false shepherds. The sheep will not follow them. In fact, the sheep will flee from the false shepherd. Why will the sheep flee? Because they do not recognize the voice.

Earlier we studied the story of how Jacob deceived his father Isaac and stole Esau's birthright. Jacob successfully deceived his father by dressing up to feel and smell like Esau. You will recall, however, that Jacob's voice almost spoiled his deception. When he spoke, Isaac was sure that the voice he heard was Jacob's voice. Isaac said,

"The voice is Jacob's voice, but the hands are the hands of Esau."

Genesis 27:22

Why did Isaac think that the voice he heard was Jacob's voice? Because he had heard Jacob's voice a thousand times over the years. Even though Jacob certainly tried to make his voice sound like the voice of Esau, there were certain qualities and a certain style that could not be disguised. Isaac, however, errantly decided to rely more on what he smelled and on what he felt than what he heard. The primary reason Isaac did not discern the false "Esau" was because he didn't trust his own ears!

On Christmas Eve a couple years ago, my younger brother was elected to dress up as Santa Claus and bring gifts for the children. He put on the familiar red suit, stuffed a pillow under his shirt, taped a white beard and moustache in place, and donned a red cap. All the children, of course were very excited. Santa Claus had come to visit them. None of them wondered who was behind the beard and moustache. It was Santa Claus.

A very interesting thing happened, however, when "Santa" began to speak. His own boy, less than two years old, cried out, "Daddy!" It made no difference that my brother had dressed himself up and tried to disguise his voice. When he spoke, his young son recognized his voice!

Even if you don't have perfect spiritual vision, you can recognize unsound spiritual leaders by their voice. If Isaac would have trusted his ears, he would not have been deceived. In the same way, if believers trust their spiritual ears, they will not be deceived. "But how will I know the voice of a wrong spirit," you ask? The answer is quite simple. Become familiar with the voice of Jesus and the voice of the Holy Spirit by reading the Word of

God and listening to your heart. Any voice that does not sound like Theirs must be suspected.

A few years ago a minister I respect started wandering down a road of error. Although I suspected for some time that something was not right, I can recall the moment when I was sure. I was listening to a cassette tape of him speaking and I said to myself, "That's not him!" Yes, it was his natural voice, but it was not him. I called a good friend of mine and asked them to listen to the tape. I told them, "It is not so-and-so speaking. I'm not sure what's gotten hold of him, but something is motivating him beside the Spirit of God. There is something else behind him." This minister, unbeknownst to himself and others, had yielded to something that was not of God. You could even sense it in his voice. When someone is being motivated by a spirit that is not of God, you will often have an immediate question mark in your spirit. Sometimes, however, it may take a little more time and investigation to be sure. For example, when one of my three brothers call me on the phone, I usually know immediately which brother it is. It may be something they say, how they say it, or just the tone quality of their voice that helps me determine it is. Sometimes, however, it is not as easy to discern. Because their voices are similar, they can disguise themselves as one of the other brothers. If I made a quick judgement about which brother it was, I might be wrong. If, however, I take the time to listen for just a few moments, I can always determine which brother it is.

Pay close attention not only to what people say, but also to the voice they speak with. Don't allow yourself to be caught up in an emotional response or be swayed by convincing words. Listen carefully with the ears of your spirit. The "feel" of an unsound spiritual leader may entice you, but if the voice is not that of the Holy Spirit or of the Good Shepherd, do not follow, but flee away.

A Lying Spirit

Earlier, we studied an interesting Old Testament account about the influencing power of lying spirits. In II Chronicles 18, we read that the Lord wanted to draw king Ahab into a battle that would bring about his fall. A spirit came before the Lord and said,

> "...I will go out and be a lying spirit in the mouth of all his prophets..."
> II Chronicles 18:20

It was by the inspiration of this lying spirit that 400 prophets prophesied to king Ahab that he would win the battle. The prophet Micaiah, however, prophesied by the inspiration of the Spirit of God that king Ahab would be defeated in battle and would die. Which prophets were right? Was Micaiah right or were the other prophets right? They both claimed to be prophets. They both claimed to speak for God. They both gave a word that could be right. The final responsibility for deciding which prophets were speaking by the Spirit of God fell on the shoulders of king Ahab. His decision in this case would mean either life or death.

This same situation can occur in the church. Two different ministers, each claiming to speak for God, can deliver opposite messages. Who is responsible to discern which minister is telling the truth? Believers are responsible. Each believer must discern for himself who is speaking for God by the inspiration of the Spirit of God and who is speaking for the devil by the inspiration of false spirits. Depending on which minister a believer follows, it could mean peace and growth or confusion and loss.

A few years ago my wife was in a large meeting where the leaders were making a very strong pull for finances. In response to the encouragement to give, many individuals were bringing their jewelry to the front of the church. My wife said that she felt a strong pull to give her very nice watch in the offering, but at the same time sensed a very quiet witness from the Spirit of God not to give. She said the witness of the Spirit felt just like a little drop of rain in her spirit. She refrained from giving because she was able to separate between the Holy Spirit and whatever other kind of spirit was operating there. She is thankful to this day that she did not give away her watch. She knows she would have missed God.

It can happen that ministers bring forth accurate information by the inspiration of familiar spirits. Sometimes ministers use this "gift" to validate their ministries and gain people's confidence. Earlier in our study I related the story of a minister who knew, by the revelation of a familiar spirit, that a certain man had a valuable piece of jewelry hidden in a certain place. He told the man where the jewelry was hidden and then said that God wanted the man to give it to him. The man gave this minister the jewelry because he assumed that if the minister knew about the piece of jewelry, it must have been revealed to him by the Spirit of God. This man should have checked closer. He should have tried the spirit by which that minister was receiving supernatural information. It would have saved him a lot of money.

When Peter rebuked the Lord concerning his eminent death, Jesus recognized immediately that he was speaking by the inspiration of Satan. Although Peter's lips were moving, it was Satan who was speaking. Jesus saw past Peter, heard past his words, and discerned the source of his inspiration. It was a spirit most definitely not of God! Listening carefully and discerning the spirit behind the voice will keep believers in the middle of the will of God!

Attitudes

When we test the spirits behind those who speak, we must not only discern whether an individual is being motivated by the Spirit of God or a demonic spirit, but also test their attitude. In II Timothy 2:7, Paul said,

> *"God has not given us a spirit of fear; but of power, and of love, and of a sound mind."*
>
> II Timothy 2:7

Paul, writing in II Corinthians 4:13, said

> *"We having the same spirit of faith..."*
>
> II Corinthians 4:13

Having a spirit of faith doesn't mean that a spirit with the name "Faith" lives in you. It means that you have an attitude of faith, the character of faith, the heart of faith; you are faith motivated. Having a spirit of love does not mean that a literal spirit named "Love" lives in you. It means that because the love of God has been shed abroad in your heart, you are empowered to love. When Paul told Timothy that God had not given him a spirit of fear, he was not referring to a literal spirit named "Fear." He was exhorting Timothy not to be ashamed of the gospel or ashamed of him because God had given him supernatural resources — faith, love, and a sound mind.

In these cases the word "spirit" does not refer to a spiritual entity, whether an angel or demon, but to a heart attitude. It refers to the character qualities a person exhibits, the spiritual posture one carries himself with. It represents those qualities present in an individual's spiritual personality.

The spirit, or attitude, of a person reveals whether they are connected to a Godly source or a Satanic source. If, for example, a person exhibits a spirit of faith, it is because they are connected to God and in fellowship with His Word. If a person has a spirit of love, it means that they are connected to the source of love. If, on the other hand, a person has a spirit of pride, it means that He is out of touch with God and His Word and listening to Satanically inspired thoughts.

There is a very clear example of this sense of the word "spirit" in the gospel of Luke. When the time for Jesus' crucifixion was nearing, He "set his face to go to Jerusalem" [Luke 9:51]. One of the cities He entered on the way did not receive Him because He was obviously destined for Jerusalem. When James and John saw this, they were angered and asked Jesus,

> *"Lord, wilt thou that we command fire to come down from heaven, and consume them, even as Elias did?"*
>
> Luke 9:54

Jesus responded to their display of anger by rebuking James and John. The Bible says,

> *"But he turned, and rebuked them, and said, Ye know not what manner of spirit ye are of."*

Luke 9:55

By the words, "ye know not what manner of spirit ye are of," Jesus did not mean that James and John had suddenly become possessed by an evil spirit. He meant that God was not the source of their angry feelings. The thoughts they thought and the emotions they felt and displayed toward the people of this city were not the kind of thoughts and feelings Jesus had. Their feelings of anger and their desire to render judgement was not godly. They had yielded to a vindictive attitude rather than an attitude of love and compassion. By rebuking James and John and saying, "ye know no what manner of spirit ye are of," Jesus was revealing the ungodly source of the ungodly attitude of the Sons of Thunder.

Why is it important to test the attitude, or the spirit, behind those who claim to be spiritual leaders? It is important because when believers submit themselves to a person to receive instruction, they learn from them in two ways. First, and obviously, they learn from the specific material the teacher teaches. Second, however, and not so obvious, they learn by the attitude of the teacher. When believers submit themselves to someone for instruction, they not only learn what that person knows, they also become what that person is. Believers learn as much by who a teacher is as by what a teacher says.

A minister may have right doctrine, but have a negative, condemning, or prideful attitude. If you choose this person as a spiritual leader, you will find yourself becoming negative, condemning, or prideful. Both a minister's words and his spirit (attitude) will influence you. You will emulate those you admire, as a son does his father. Follow those of Godly character and Christlike spirit. Avoid those in whom you perceive ungodly attitudes and characteristics. Avoid those who display a wrong spirit.

When you test the spirit behind one who claims to be a minister, discern if he is motivated by the Spirit of God or a spirit of error and also observe what attitude he is of, whether Christlike or fleshly. If you know the Word of God and listen to the voice of the Spirit, you will be able to discern the voice of a stranger. Any time you hear a voice that is unfamiliar or sense an attitude that is unfamiliar, take a cautious position and make time for further investigation.

FOUR: BY THEIR FRUITS YE SHALL KNOW THEM

Although believers possess the Spirit of God, it is not always simple to discern the hidden motivations of another man's heart. For this reason, believers must be prepared to examine the fruit of those who claim to be spiritual leaders. Jesus emphasized this important method for judging those who claimed to be spiritual leaders when He warned His disciples of false prophets. He said,

> *"Beware of false prophets, which come to you in sheep's clothing, but inwardly they are ravening wolves. Ye shall know them by their fruits."*
>
> *Matthew 7:15*

It is not always possible to perceive a person's true spiritual identity. Are they true or false? Are they sound or unsound? What is their real intention? What is their real motivation? What is their hidden agenda? How can I discover what is hidden beneath the surface?

Jesus revealed how to discern the hidden "root" of mens' lives. He said that the root could be known by the fruits. As is the fruit, so is the root. Believers can identify a person's true inward spiritual character by examining their outward fruits. If a tree bears apples, it is an apple tree. If a tree bears cherries, it is a cherry tree. If a tree bears lemons, it is a lemon tree. You can know the root by the fruit. You can know a minister's true inward self by his fruits.

Jesus continued to speak about the direct relationship between a minister's true spiritual character and the fruit of his life, saying,

> *"...a good tree cannot bring forth evil fruit, neither can a corrupt tree bring forth good fruit."*
>
> *Matthew 7:18*

A corrupt tree will bring forth evil fruit. If the fruit is good, it is because the tree is good. If the fruit is bad, it is because the tree is bad. It is that simple. Judging a minister's fruit is one of the simplest and most practical ways to know whether he is true or false, sound or unsound.

Continuing in the same theme, Jesus said,

> *"Wherefore by their fruits ye shall know them. Not everyone that sayeth unto me, Lord, Lord, shall enter into the kingdom of heaven; but he that doeth the will of my Father. Many will say to me in that day, Lord, Lord, have we not prophesied in thy name? and in thy name have cast out devils? and in thy name have done many wonderful works? And then I will profess unto them, I never knew you: depart from me, ye that work iniquity."*
>
> *Matthew 7:19-23*

This scripture is not meant, as some use it, to put fear in believers' hearts that they will be rejected by Jesus when He comes again. This scripture does not mean that those who work for the Lord all their lives, but wane at one point in their love for Jesus will be turned away. This scripture does not refer to luke-warm Christians or to those who have attended church all their lives, but never made a personal decision for the Lord. This scripture refers to false spiritual leaders.

The some who say, "Lord, Lord," who have prophesied in Jesus' name, and who have worked miracles, are false prophets and false spiritual leaders. Don't automatically trust a person who says that Jesus is their Lord. Don't automatically follow those who prophesy and then say, "Thus saith the Lord." Don't automatically follow those who cast out devils and do miracles. Check their fruits! They may be false prophets or other false spiritual leaders; those that work iniquity, as Jesus said.

It is very important, because of the time that we live in, to realize the importance of what Jesus said. Just because a minister claims to be prophesying by the Spirit of God does not mean that he is. Just because a minister displays supernatural manifestations does not mean that he is of God. Just because someone casts out a devil does not mean that he is a sound spiritual leader. Just because a minister advertises himself as, "An anointed, cutting-edge leader in this end time move of God," it cannot be automatically concluded that he is even called of God.

Be careful of those who are pursuing the advancement of their reputations by exaggerating the fruit of their ministry. Be bold to check them out yourself. Go to a meeting. Listen to them minister. Is their fruit the fruit of righteousness, love, and of the Holy Spirit? Or is their fruit the fruit of showmanship and carefully planed emotional impact and advertising skill? Do not be afraid to examine the fruit of a minister you are considering submitting yourself to. You must examine them! You are a fool if you don't. By examining their fruits, you will be able to determine if they are a good tree or a corrupt tree.

The Fruit Exposes the Root

Why did Jesus teach His disciples to examine the fruit of those who claim to be spiritual leaders? Because fruit is visible, perceivable, and judgeable. It is the outward and visible expression of what is at work inwardly and invisibly. The nature of the fruit reveals the nature of the root. You cannot always see what is "underground" in someone's life. The fruit on the branches, however, is obvious and irrefutable evidence. If you can't uncover the root, look at the fruits.

In the natural realm, fruit is what the average person must see in order to determine what a tree is. If, for example, a common person looked at a grove of fruit trees in the winter season, he would not be able to identify the various trees. If, however, this person looked at the same grove of trees in the fruit-bearing season, he could point to each tree and confidently identify it. He could say, "The peach tree is the one with peaches on it. The apple tree is the tree with apples." Even young children can identify trees by their fruit.

This same principle applies in the spiritual realm. Some believers are not so skilled in the Spirit that they can instantly perceive the spiritual character of another person. And remember: False leaders are disguise experts. They practice disguising their true motivations. When their fruit comes forth, however, even spiritual children can identify true and false spiritual leadership.

Judging the Fruit of Personal Life

Notice that the Paul argued the validity of his apostleship by citing the fruit of his personal lifestyle. He said,

"Giving no offense in anything, that the ministry be not blamed: But in all things approving ourselves as the ministers of God, in much patience, in afflictions, in necessities, in distresses, in stripes, in imprisonments, in tumults, in labours, in watchings, in fastings, By pureness, by knowledge, by longsuffering, by kindness, by the Holy Ghost, by love unfeigned, By the word of truth, by the power of God, by the armour righteousness, on the right hand and on the left..."

II Corinthians 6:3-7

Paul pointed to the fruit of his personal life as a significant validating factor concerning his true calling to the ministry. He called the attention of his readers to the display of fruit from his personal life in order to approve himself as a true minister of Christ.

A true spiritual leader must be spiritually developed. And true spiritual development is measured first and foremost by the display of the fruit of the Spirit. A true minister validates his own calling by bringing forth the fruits of righteousness. False ministers, on the other hand, attempt to validate their ministries by good words, by saying they are anointed, by saying, "Lord, Lord," and even by working miracles. If you listen to what they say, you will believe they are a true minister. But if you watch how they conduct their lives, you will know they are not. By their fruits you will be able to judge whether individuals are true spiritual leaders or a false spiritual leaders.

When judging the fruit of a person's life to determine whether or not they are a true spiritual leader, you must examine the fruit of their home life.

Paul made it quite clear in his instructions to Timothy and Titus concerning choosing spiritual leaders that a candidate's home life was a significant consideration. A man who was being considered for a place of spiritual leadership was to be the husband of one wife, given to hospitality, could not have a temper, and must be able to rule his own house and his own children [I Timothy 3:2-13; Titus 1:5-9].

What is the fruit of a minister's home life? Has he abandoned his family? Has he divorced his wife so that he can "fulfill his ministry?" Has he abandoned his own children? Oh, his eyes may fill with water and his voice resonate with compassion when he tells you that he loves you. But if he has abandoned his own children, what makes you think he won't abandon you?

Are his words cruel and cutting when he's not "on stage?" Does he have a temper? Does he demonstrate true love in daily life or is he just lovy-dovy when he is in the pulpit? Is he longsuffering or does he lose his patience quickly if things don't go his way? Is he kind and gentle or is he rough and unsympathetic? Is he irritable and touchy or is he easy to be entreated? Does his presence bring peace and comfort or does his life bear the fruit of constant turmoil, distress, and trouble?

Ministers who exhibit little fruit of the Spirit in their home life and personal life are not necessarily false spiritual leaders, but they certainly disqualify themselves as sound spiritual leaders. One of the primary requirements for a spiritual leader is to be an example of spiritual maturity. If a minister is spiritually immature, he cannot be a sound spiritual leader. There is a great difference, you see, between being a Bible teacher and a spiritual leader.

The Fruit of Ministry

When judging the fruit of a person's life to determine whether or not they are a true spiritual leader, you must also examine the fruit of their ministry. Do people become established and settled under their ministry or are people upset and unsettled? Are people becoming established in sound doctrine or are they running after new things year after year? Does this minister promote unity or cause division? Do churches grow or split under his ministry?

If you want to know if a man's ministry is sound, examine the people (the fruit) that follow his ministry. Are those who follow him stable or flaky? Do those who follow him develop a Christ-like nature or do they remain spiritually immature? Paul said that the believers in Corinth were the seal of his apostleship. The spiritual results in their lives were the proof of his calling. The Amplified Bible puts Paul's words like this,

"Am I not an apostle…Are you [yourselves] not (the product and proof of) my workmanship in the Lord? Even if I am not considered an apostle (a special messenger) by others, at least I am one to you; for you are the seal (the certificate, the living evidence) of my apostleship in the Lord — confirming and authenticating it. This is my [real ground of] defense— my vindication of myself— to those who would put me on trial and cross examine me."

I Corinthians 9:1-3

The believers at Corinth were the fruit that proved Paul was a true apostle. They were "living evidence." Paul said that the ripening fruit of his ministry — saved and transformed lives — was his "real ground of defense" against those who accused him of being a false apostle. His fruit was the "product and proof" of his ministry.

What is the consensus of opinion concerning a particular man's ministry? Do some like him and some dislike him? Is there a general report that he is a blessing or are there conflicting reports, some good and some bad? Why would there be negative reports about this man? What is the source of these negative reports? Paul told Titus that if he was a good minister and sound in doctrine, no one would have anything bad to say of him [Titus 2:8].

Does this minister make disciples of Christ or disciples of himself? Do people talk more about him than they do about Jesus? Is he tangent-oriented, running with whatever is popular, or does he bear the same fruit year after year? Does he jump from plan to plan and from idea to idea, never quite sure what the Lord is saying? Does he keep his word and swear to his own hurt in fulfilling obligations or does he "get a new word from the Lord" every time he wants to make a change?

The apostle Paul offered extensive teaching and spiritual advice in his letter to the church at Rome. In the final chapter, he made a plea to this church saying,

"Now I beseech you, brethren, mark them which cause divisions and offenses contrary to the doctrine which ye have learned; and avoid them."

Romans 16:17

Those who bear the fruit of division are very suspect as unsound spiritual leaders. They are not serving Christ, but their own appetites. They should not be followed, but avoided. If a man bears the bad fruit of division in his ministry, he is likely an unsound spiritual leader.

Importance of Patience

At times, it may be difficult to clearly discern what the Spirit of God is witnessing about a person. You may not be sure what spirit is behind their words. Even their doctrine may be borderline. It may not be false, but neither is it obviously sound. If you are unsure about a person, then watch and wait. In time, fruit will appear. When it does, you will know exactly what the tree is. You will know whether it is good or corrupt.

Patience is a very important factor when judging a tree by its fruits. If you are unsure of the identity of a particular tree, just wait. In time, the fruit will tell you the truth. A tree may declare, "I am a peach tree." It may have a label on it that says, "Peach tree." It may be in the middle of a grove of peach trees. It may even be trimmed like a peach tree. But if this tree eventually bears lemons, you know without a doubt that it is a lemon tree!

This same truth applies in the spiritual realm. If you are unsure about someone who presents themselves as a true minister, wait and watch. Some will declare, "I am an apostle," or, "I am a teacher." They may look like ministers and associate with reputable ministers. They may look, talk, and act like ministers. If they bear corrupt fruit, however, you know without a doubt, no matter what they say, that they are unsound or false.

Patience is important when judging ministers because some false spiritual leaders will demand that you accept them immediately. They will make you feel like something is wrong with you if you hesitate to agree with them. They imply that you are spiritually ignorant if you don't "hook up" with them. Be patient, however, and wait on those who demand that you accept them immediately. Give them a season to prove their claims by bringing forth good fruit. Don't worry, you won't miss God. And you may avoid serious error and spiritual tragedy!

What Comes Out in the Squeeze?

People are often like sponges. It can be hard to know what is inside until they are squeezed. I heard a story about a young minister which is an excellent illustration of this truth. This young minister desired to be a member of a particular ministerial association. He displayed all the fruit, said the right words, did the right things, and connected with the right people. He appeared to be of the same spirit and of the same vision as the other ministers in this organization and was, therefore, welcomed with open arms.

In a very short time, however, reports of division and strife began to filter in from local churches. Apparently, this young man was taking some very bold positions and was calling himself an apostle. He was upsetting local churches and attempting to draw people after his ministry. When the president of the association confronted this young so-called apostle, he became hostile and verbally abusive, even shouting on the phone. When he was squeezed, bad fruit juices flowed out.

A Final Word on Examining Fruit

As you watch for and examine the fruit of the personal lives and ministries of those who claim to be spiritual leaders, remember these things:

First: A true spiritual leader can make honest mistakes. There may be a time or two when he operates in the flesh and seems to bear a piece of bad fruit. He may say something he should not say or do something he should not do. One mistake or one bad piece of fruit, however, is not enough evidence to condemn a man as a false spiritual leader. Even a good tree may have one or two sour apples from time to time. A true spiritual leader, however, one who is called by God and sound in spirit, will consistently, though not perfectly, bring forth good fruit. The majority of the fruit of his life and his ministry will be good.

Second: Even a truly called, truly anointed, and completely sincere minister can be misrepresented by people who don't like him or who feel threatened by him. Stephen, a true and effectual minister in the early church, was accused by false witnesses. These false witnesses were paid to testify against him because the religious leaders feared Stephen [Acts 6:8-13]. Both Jesus and Paul were accused of being false spiritual leaders. None of these men, however, were false leaders. Just because you hear one or two negative reports about a minister, do not conclude that he is false. He may have been misrepresented by those who fear him or do not like him.

Third: An unsound minister can bring forth some good fruit. They may show some signs and wonders and some of their teaching may be acceptable. The effect of their consistently bad fruit, however, will eventually spoil what little good they had. Just because you see a few pieces of good fruit does not mean that a minister is sound. He may display a few good apples on the top to convince you to buy the whole bushel!

Fourth: Don't look for just one fruit or one result from a minister's life. Don't look for one good work or one mistake. Jesus said, "By their fruits (plural) ye shall know them" [Matthew 7:19]. What do they consistently bear? Do they produce unity or division? Peace or strife? Do they serve or dominate? Do they give or take? Are they faithful or sporadic? Do they teach sound or unsound doctrine? When judging a ministers by his fruits, be sure to examine all his fruits.

FIVE: THE SIGNS OF AN APOSTLE

Looking for the evidence of supernatural signs is another means of judging spiritual leadership. When John the Baptist asked whether or not Jesus was the awaited Messiah, Jesus responded,

"Go and shew John again those things which ye do hear and see: The blind receive their sight, and the lame walk, the lepers are cleansed, and the deaf hear, the dead are raised up, and the poor have the gospel preached to them."

Matthew 11:4-5

Jesus claimed that the miracles and healings He performed were a sign that He was called and anointed by God. The works He did were proof of who He was. Jesus said, "Go and shew John again those things which ye do hear and see." In another place, Jesus encouraged those who were having difficulty believing His words to believe Him because of His works [John 14:10]. Signs and wonders help people "see" who is and who is not of God. God not only performs supernatural signs and miracles to deliver those in need, but also to sanction men's ministries.

That signs and wonders are a validating "stamp of approval" from God is confirmed by the apostle Peter in Acts two. There he said this concerning Jesus' supernatural ministry,

"Ye men of Israel, hear these words; Jesus of Nazareth, a man approved of God among you by miracles and wonders and signs, which God did by him in the midst of you, as ye yourselves know..."

Acts 2:22

Peter said the "miracles and wonders and signs" that God did through Jesus were a clear validation of Jesus as "approved by God."

Just as Jesus offered His works as proof that His words were true, so did the apostle Paul. He wrote this to the church at Rome about the signs and wonders God did through his ministry,

"For I will not dare to speak of any of those things which Christ hath not wrought by me to make the Gentiles obedient, by word and deed..."

Romans 15:18

How were the Gentiles persuaded to become obedient to the gospel message? It was by Paul's words and by the mighty deeds that God did through him. The deeds that Paul did were the proof to the Gentiles that he was speaking on God's behalf. Paul clarified more precisely what these deeds were in the very next verse. He said,

"Through mighty signs and wonders, by the power of the Spirit of God..."

Romans 15:19

That signs and wonders confirm a man's ministry is also clear in Paul's defense of his apostleship to the church at Corinth. In his second letter, he said,

"Truly the signs of an apostle were wrought among you in all patience, in signs, and wonders, and mighty deeds."

II Corinthians 12:12

The "signs of an apostle," according to Paul, were, "signs, and wonders, and mighty deeds." Supernatural signs and miracles can attest to and confirm the validity of a person's call to spiritual leadership. This truth is also confirmed in the second chapter of Hebrews. There we read,

"...so great salvation; which at the first began to be spoken by the Lord, and was confirmed unto us by them that heard him; God also bearing them witness, both with signs and wonders and with divers miracles, and gifts of the Holy Ghost, according to his own will..."

Hebrews 2:3-4

The writer of Hebrews confirms that God bears witness to the gospel of salvation with signs, wonders, and divers miracles. These special manifestations of His power are visible proof that a man is truly called of God and that His message is true. Signs, wonders, and miracles are God's "stamp of approval," especially made visible for the unbeliever or for the doubting Thomas.

A Note of Caution

Not only can supernatural signs confirm that a man's ministry is truly from God, however. They can be also be used by false spiritual leaders to deceive and mislead. Signs and wonders, therefore, cannot be the sole consideration when judging a man's ministry. Working miracles or moving in the supernatural gifts of the Spirit is not the final proof that one is a true or sound spiritual leader.

I know of ministers who, while living an adulterous life, were flowing in the gifts of the Spirit. The fact that they were displaying gifts of the Spirit concealed the serious spiritual problems in their own lives. A man who commits adultery on a regular basis is obviously disqualified as a spiritual leader. Because he can temporarily flow in the supernatural, however, he may be able to "confirm" that he is sound and stable.

It is important to remember that supernatural events can transpire apart from the power of God. Satan and evil spirits can also work through individuals to perform special signs. The Egyptian magicians, for example, were able to duplicate, by occult power, the first four plagues that God brought on Egypt. The performance of these supernatural signs was not, however, proof that they were of God. Simon the sorcerer also operated in occult power before his conversion. By his sorcery he bewitched the people of

Samaria and was able to control a whole city. The Bible says that all the people of that city, from the least to the greatest, gave heed to him thinking that he was, "the great power of God" [Acts 8:9-11]. His supernatural manifestations led men to think that he was endorsed by God.

Jesus warned that in the last days false prophets and unsound spiritual leaders would use signs and wonders as a tool of deception. He said,

> *"For there shall arise false Christs, and false prophets, and shall shew great signs and wonders; insomuch that, if it were possible, they shall deceive the very elect. Behold, I have told you before..."*
>
> Matthew 24:24-25

False spiritual leaders will not only deceive unbelievers with miracles and special signs and wonders. They will also attempt to deceive the very elect. Believers must be careful when it comes to the area of signs and wonders. It can be difficult to refuse a person who has such power. Signs and wonders can confirm a man's calling to spiritual leadership, but they must not be the sole consideration.

CONCLUSION

In this chapter we have studied five primary ways to judge those who claim to be spiritual leaders to determine if they are true or false, sound or unsound. It is unlikely that you will need to employ all these methods in each situation. Most often, by testing in one or two of these areas you will be able to make an accurate judgement. In the next chapter we will continue in the same theme of how to judge spiritual leaders, but will consider some very practical questions to ask concerning those who claim to be spiritual leaders.

·~18~·
How to Judge Spiritual Leadership
Part Two

I n our previous chapter we considered five basic methods for judging to determine if one who claims to be a spiritual leader is true or false, sound or unsound. In this chapter (a continuation of last chapter) we will consider several basic questions to ask concerning those who present themselves as spiritual leaders. The answers to these questions will help to determine whether a person is a true spiritual leader or not.

ONE: IS HE WILLING TO SACRIFICE FOR THE CHURCH?

People often ask, "What is the real test of whether one is a true apostle or other ministry gift? Is it whether or not they have signs and wonders in their ministry? Is it whether or not they had a vision? Is it their ability to start churches? What does a true apostle look like? What does a true prophet look like? How can I judge whether or not a man is really a spiritual leader who has been called by God and is operating correctly in his calling?"

The apostle Paul was often put in the position of having to defend his apostleship. Because many of the churches that he founded opened their doors to false apostles and false teachers, he was compelled again and again to prove that he was a true apostle. How did Paul validate his calling and prove his apostleship?

The primary way Paul defended his calling and validated his own ministry was by emphasizing the sacrifices he made for the sake of the church. Time and time again he stressed that his willingness to make personal sacrifices was the proof that he was a true spiritual leader.

Paul's Proof of His Calling

In his first letter to the church at Corinth, Paul wrote,

"Am I not an apostle?...are ye not my work in the Lord? doubtless I am to you. Mine answer to them that examine me is this..."

I Corinthians 9:1-3

What was transpiring in the church at Corinth was like a contest. The false apostles who had gained a foothold in the church at Corinth had "examined" Paul and then accused him to the church of being a false apostle. Paul, on the other hand, was defending himself and accusing the false apostles in Corinth of being false apostles. Who was true and who was false?

Paul was forced to defend his apostleship to this church. How would he prove that he was the true apostle? How would he prove that he was a true spiritual leader called by God? Paul proved that he was a true apostle, a true spiritual leader, by presenting to the believers at Corinth a long list of sacrifices he had willingly made for their benefit. He began his defense by saying, "Mine answer to them that question me is this," and then said,

"Have we not the right to our food and drink [at the expense of the churches]? Have we not the right also to take along with us a Christian sister as wife...Or is it only Barnabas and I who have no right to refrain from doing manual labor for a livelihood [in order to go about the work of the ministry]?...What soldier at any time serves at his own expense? Who plants a vineyard and does not eat any of the fruit of it? Who tends a flock and does not partake of the milk of the flock? Does not the law endorse the same principle? For in the Law of Moses it is written, You shall not muzzle an ox when it is treading out the corn. Is it [only] for oxen that God is having a care? Or does He speak certainly and entirely for our sakes? [Assuredly] it is written for our sakes, because the plowman ought to plow in hope, and the thresher ought to thresh in expectation of partaking of the harvest...If we have sown [the seed of] spiritual good among you, [is it too] much if we reap from your material benefits?"

I Corinthians 9:4-11 Amp

If you did not read that scripture, go back and do so. All the statements Paul made and the questions he asked concerned rights that he had as a true minister of God. Notice, however, how Paul concluded his defense,

"...we have never exercised this right, but we endure everything rather than put a hindrance in the way..."

I Corinthians 9:12 Amp

Everything Paul wrote in I Corinthians 9:1-23 was written to defend his calling to spiritual leadership, to prove he was an true apostle called by God. What was his defense? How did he prove his apostleship? By declaring his willingness to sacrifice for the benefit of the church and to serve the people at no cost to them. In verse 19, Paul said, "I made myself servant unto all, that I might gain the more." In verse 23, he concluded his whole argument in this section by saying, "And this I do for the gospel's sake."

Although it is right that those who, "preach the gospel should live of the gospel," Paul would not use these rights. He would not in any way hinder the gospel by giving people grounds to accuse him. Whatever it cost him to fulfill his ministry to the church, he was willing to pay.

A true spiritual leader is concerned first and foremost with the advancement of the gospel and the steadfast adherence to it by those to whom he ministers. He will make whatever sacrifices and commitments are necessary to accomplish that goal. He is willing to make personal sacrifices, deep commitments, and difficult choices in order to see that God's flock is established and enriched.

In his second letter to Corinth, Paul again defended his apostleship to the believers and the false apostles in Corinth. He did not want to — he said, "I speak as a fool" — but the spiritual destiny of the church at Corinth was at stake. If they abandoned the leadership of Paul and followed false apostles, they would be overthrown in their faith and end up in spiritual catastrophe. Again, Paul's primary line of defense was a bold declaration of his willingness to make sacrifices for the sake of the gospel and for the benefit of the church. Listen to how one of the greatest apostles of all time defended his apostleship,

> "*Are they ministers of Christ? (I speak as a fool) I am more; in labors more abundant, in stripes above measure, in prisons more frequent, in deaths oft. Of the Jews five times received I forty stripes save one. Thrice I was beaten with rods, once I was stoned, thrice I suffered shipwreck, a night and day I have been in the deep; In journeyings often, in perils of water, in perils of robbers, in perils by mine own countrymen, in perils by the heathen, in perils in the city, in perils in the wilderness, in perils in the sea, in perils among the brethren; In weariness and painfulness, in watchings often, in hunger and thirst, in fastings often, in cold and nakedness. Beside those things that are without, that which cometh upon me daily, the care of all the churches.*"

II Corinthians 11:23-28

Again, I quoted this whole passage for a reason. Paul was making a point. He was notifying the church at Corinth that his willingness to endure all these hardships for the sake of the church was the proof that he was a true apostle. With Paul, I want to drive home this point: A true spiritual leader has at the top of his list of priorities and responsibilities that he will pay the cost for the benefit of the church! A willingness to sacrifice for the sheep is one of the most distinguishing personality traits of a true shepherd. In II Corinthians 12:14-15, Paul said,

> *"...I seek not yours, but you: for the children ought not to lay up for the parents, but the parents for the children. And I will very gladly spend and be spent for you..."*

> *II Corinthians 12:14-15*

This is the heart attitude of a true minister. He will lay up an inheritance for the spiritual children. He will spend and be spent for the benefit of the church. And because of his genuine and deep love for those to whom he ministers, he will do so gladly.

A willingness to make sacrifices and to endure hardships, even to go without if necessary, is one of the most fundamental character traits of a true spiritual leader. Whereas unsound ministers love the pay and false spiritual leaders covet the pay, true spiritual leaders are willing to pay! They are willing to lay down their lives for the benefit of the church! This is one of the greatest tests for determining whether or not a man is a true spiritual leader. A man who is willing to serve the people of God no matter what it costs him is a true spiritual leader. A man who is not willing to sacrifice for the flock, but wants the flock to sacrifice for him, is certainly not a true spiritual leader.

TWO: DOES HE HAVE A SHEPHERD'S HEART?

A number of times over the years I have heard ministers give this general teaching: "A pastor has a pastor's heart, but evangelists, teachers, and other ministry gifts don't have a pastor's heart." Evangelists, they say, come in and tear the people up and then the pastor has to put them back together. Teachers, they say, only love to study and teach; they don't really care about the people. Prophets are categorized as bold and direct and always rough on the people. Apostles supposedly love to start churches, but don't want to stay with the people once the church becomes established. This kind of teaching and thinking about the ministry, however, is nothing more than carnal thinking. It is not only unbiblical, but it is dangerous because it becomes self-fulfilling.

The truth is that all those truly called to the ministry *must* have a shepherd's heart. I will say that again because it is so important: All those truly called to the ministry must have a shepherd's heart! It is as simple as this: If a man does not have a shepherd's heart, it means that he does not care about the sheep. And if a man does not care about the sheep, he is automatically disqualified as a spiritual leader! When you are examining a man to determine if he is a true, unsound, or false spiritual leader, look to see if he has the heart of a shepherd. Let's take a few moments to discover what the Word of God has to say about the true spiritual shepherd.

Shepherd or Hireling?

Some who manage to gain places of leadership in the church are not true shepherds, but hirelings. Jesus said this concerning the difference between a shepherd and a hireling,

> *"...the good shepherd giveth his life for the sheep. But he that is an hireling, and not the shepherd, whose own the sheep are not, seeth the wolf coming, and leaveth the sheep, and fleeth: and the wolf catcheth them, and scattereth the sheep. The hireling fleeth, because he is an hireling, and careth not for the sheep."*
>
> John 10:11-13

The Amplified Bible says,

> *"But the hired servant — he who merely serves for wages...when he sees the wolf coming deserts the flock and runs away...Now the hireling flees because he merely serves for wages and is not himself concerned about the sheep — cares nothing for them."*
>
> John 10:12-13 Amp

A hireling is not concerned about the sheep; he "cares nothing for them." When the flock is producing and trouble is far away, he does his job and enjoys his wages. But when trouble comes, he flees because he, "is not himself concerned about the sheep." A hireling only stays to serve the sheep when the pay is worth the trouble.

A true shepherd, on the other hand, is prepared to give his life for the sheep. He will stay with the flock no matter what comes, whether good times or bad times. The true shepherd cares deeply for the sheep and is also very aware of his responsibility and accountability to the Owner of the sheep.

The Heart of the True Shepherd

The apostle Peter wrote these challenging words to the elders he was responsible for,

> *"The elders which are among you I exhort...Feed the flock of God which is among you, taking the oversight thereof, not by constraint, but willingly; not for filthy lucre, but of a ready mind; Neither as being lord's over God's heritage, but being ensamples to the flock."*
>
> I Peter 5:1-3

There are several truths from these words of Peter that will help us understand the true shepherd's heart.

The Flock is God's

A true shepherd views the flock as God's property. He realizes, as Peter affirmed twice in the above passage, that believers are "the flock of God" and "God's heritage." He does not forget that he is an undershepherd, called and entrusted by the Owner with the responsibility of caring for His sheep. He does not view the flock in terms of his own potential for profit. To him, the flock is a responsibility, not an opportunity.

Feed the Flock

A true shepherd realizes that his priority is to feed the flock. He does not expect the flock to feed him. He does not exploit the flock to fulfill his own vision. He does not take from the flock for his own financial gain. Neither does he use the flock as an audience for his own philosophies and vain opinions. Prevalent in the mind of the true shepherd is the importance of feeding the flock.

Shepherds Live Among the Sheep

A true shepherd does not see himself over the flock, but among the flock. Peter said, "The elders which are among you," and, "the flock of God which is among you." The shepherd lives among the sheep and the sheep live with the shepherd. The apostle Paul confirmed this truth in his instructions to the elders in Ephesus. He said,

> "Take heed therefore unto yourselves, and to all the flock, over the which the Holy Ghost hath made you overseers…"
>
> Acts 20:28

Someone might say, "See, Paul told the elders in Ephesus that the Holy Ghost set them over the flock." It may appear that way from a simple reading of this scripture. If, however, you were to investigate the word "over" that Paul used in this passage, you would discover that it comes from the Greek word *en* which, in over two thousand other places in the New Testament, is translated "in." This passage is the only place in the New Testament that *en* is translated "over." According to Paul, shepherds are *in* the flock, not *over* the flock.

Oversight

Peter told the elders to, "(take) the oversight." W.E. Vine says concerning the word "oversight" that it is not a matter of assuming a position, but of doing one's duties. A true shepherd understands that spiritual oversight is not a right over people, but a responsibility to people. Over-sight means to see over, not to rule over. A true shepherd will exercise spiritual oversight; he will over-see, not over-rule. This means that he will watch out for the well-being of the sheep.

Not By Constraint, But Willingly

A true shepherd does not watch over a flock because he is forced to, but is of a willing mind. He is eager to serve the sheep in whatever way the Lord chooses. He does not serve because the Lord forces him to or because men expect him to. Willingly He serves God. Willingly He serves people.

Not for Filthy Lucre, But of a Ready Mind

A true shepherd is of a ready mind. He is ready for good times, ready for rough times. He is ready for peace, ready for the storm, ready for times of plenty, and ready for shortage. It makes no difference. His commitment to service is not based on his pay. He has prepared his mind and is ready to serve God's flock no matter what it costs.

Not as Lords, But as Examples

The Amplified Bible says that shepherds should not be, "arrogant, dictatorial and overbearing...domineering over those in your charge...but being examples — patterns and models of Christian living" [I Peter 5:3 Amp]. A true spiritual leader will exhibit true godliness and Christ-like character. He will display the fruit of the Spirit and true humility. He will be an example, a standard of Christlikeness, for the flock in which God has made him undershepherd.

When you look for a true spiritual leader, look for a man with the heart of a shepherd. Look for a man who cares about the sheep, not who cares about himself. Look for a man with a pastor's heart, whether he is called to the office of the pastor or to one of the other ministry offices. A true minister is a shepherd who will lay down his life for the sheep.

THREE: DOES HE HAVE THE HEART OF A SERVANT?

Over and over again, Paul prefaced his letters to the churches with a phrase that revealed his true spiritual character. He wrote,

> *"Paul, a servant of Jesus Christ, called to be an apostle..."*
>
> RomaOns 1:1

> *"Paul and Timotheus, the servants of Jesus Christ..."*
>
> Phillipians 1:1

> *"Paul, a servant of God and an apostle of Jesus Christ..."*
>
> Titus 1:1

Paul saw himself as a servant with a specific calling to be an apostle. A true spiritual leader will have this same attitude. He will both perceive himself and present himself as a servant called to a specific assignment. A true pastor's attitude, for example, should be, "I am a servant of Christ who has been called to be a pastor." A true prophet's attitude should be, "I am a servant of Christ called to be a prophet." A true spiritual leader will not draw attention to his office, but to his attitude of service.

If there is a continual emphasis on the authority of an office, it can lead to a wrong attitude and open the door for abuse. When, on the other hand, the emphasis is upon the attitude of being a servant, ministers remember who they really are in the body. They are not authorities over, but servants unto. Paul wrote this to the church at Corinth,

"For though I be free from all men, yet have I made myself servant unto all, that I might gain the more."

I Corinthians 9:19

True spiritual leaders see themselves first as servants to God and to the Lord Jesus Christ, second as servants to the church, third as servants to other ministers, and last as anointed to stand in a particular office in the church.

Although Jesus taught and emphasized this most basic principle concerning ministry, it seems to have been forgotten in our generation. Modern day ministers often seek success and preferred position. They forget that the word "minister" does not mean boss, but servant. When James and John forgot who they were and sought preeminence among the other apostles, Jesus reminded them about the required attitude of true spiritual leaders. He said,

"Ye know that they which are accounted to rule over the Gentiles exercise lordship over them; and their great ones exercise authority upon them. But so shall it not be among you: but whoever will be great among you (a true spiritual leader) shall be your minister (servant). And whosoever of you will be the chiefest, shall be servant of all."

Mark 10: 42-45

In the secular world system, those who rise to leadership exercise authority over others. They use their gifts and abilities to get a position and then use their position to get their way. Among spiritual leaders, however, "so shall it not be." True spiritual leaders use their gifts and abilities to serve others in order that others will be edified, built up, and prosperous. It is absolutely essential that spiritual leaders adopt this servant attitude and let it govern their anointing, rather than allowing their anointing to determine their attitude.

The Servant's Towel

Immediately prior to His death, Jesus gave His disciples an unforgettable lesson in serving. After partaking of the Last Supper together, Jesus stood up in the midst of the disciples and prepared Himself to wash their feet. He took off His robe and donned the towel of a servant. He prepared a basin full of water. Then He knelt down and began to wash the disciples' feet [John 13:1-12].

The significance of washing feet was that this was the lowliest task of the day. In our time, it would be comparable to taking out someone's garbage, mopping someone's floor, or washing someone's clothes. There was nothing mystical about the fact that Jesus washed feet. And there is nothing spiritual about having a "foot washing service" in church. The point of the matter was that Jesus was willing to serve in the most common way. Let's consider for a moment the symbolism in what Jesus did.

First, Jesus took off His own robe. He, "laid aside his garments" [John 13:4]. This is symbolic of the laying aside of personal identity, rights, position, and status. Then He took the towel of a servant and put it on. He, "took a towel and girded himself" [John 13:4]. This is symbolic of identifying one's self as a common servant with no emphasis on the outward appearance. Next, Jesus poured water into a basin. This is symbolic of the preparation and use of special gifts and abilities in ministry (service). Special talents and spiritual endowments should be considered servant's tools, not spiritual status symbols. Finally, Jesus knelt down and ministered to His disciples. When He was finished, He said,

> *"Know ye what I have done unto you? Ye call me Master and Lord: and ye say well; for so I am. If I then, your Lord and Master, have washed your feet; ye also ought to wash one another's feet. For I have given you an example, that ye should do as I have done to you."*

> *John 13:12-14*

Jesus is the ultimate standard for New Testament ministry. And He said, "I have given you an example, that ye should do as I have done to you." So many ministers want to identify with the Mighty Healer, with the Great Teacher, with the One Who could discern the presence of evil spirits and perceive the thoughts of men. Very few, however, want to identify with Jesus the Servant. I am afraid that many of our prestigious and sophisticated modern day ministers would cringe at the thought of taking off their "robes" and donning the "servant's towel." After all, isn't "the man of God" supposed to be served? Jesus, however, said, "I have not come to be served, but to serve." Any minister who comes to be served rather than to serve has come in the wrong spirit.

Ministers Who Want To Be Served

The modern day attitude that ministers should be served by the sheep is a stench to God. Some so-called ministers demand limousines, five-star motels, specified offerings, and then expect all their expenses to be paid. How do I know this? Because I have spoken with pastors who were "required" to pay the way for these men! Let me say something that some modern day, cutting-edge, super-anointed preachers and so-called spiritual leaders might not like: The body of Christ does not need any more generals. It needs servants! There is no room for spiritual hierarchy in the body of Christ! It would be good for some ministers to remember that servants have no rights!

Often so-called spiritual leaders expect churches to serve them with money. Some demand, for example, that the body of Christ get behind their vision or their project because, "It's not my vision, it's God's vision for the body." By using spiritual language, they con money out of the hands of innocent people. Listen minister friends, if God has given you a vision, then let Him underwrite it. Don't pressure the body of Christ to underwrite your vision. Believers do not exist to serve ministers!

And let me say a word to itinerant teachers. It is not the responsibility of local churches to serve you by underwriting your ministry. This is wrong thinking! If your vision is really from God, then let Him underwrite it. If your vision is your own, then underwrite yourself. If you want to put pressure somewhere, put it on God and expect Him to meet your needs. Years ago the Holy Spirit said to me, "God has the ability to supply the means to do the work." God will pay for the construction of His own house! If He is not supporting you, then you must not be working on His house!

I say this because I have heard stories of travelling ministers being angry because local churches did not give them enough money. I have also heard reports of itinerant ministers who call pastors and say, "I really need a meeting because my finances are in bad shape. Could I come and preach in your church?" Ministers, you should not ask for meetings because you need money! Where did you receive your spiritual education? Are you really called to the ministry? If you are, then you are called to serve, not to be served by local churches.

There is only one reason you should go to any local church. It is to serve the people of God with whatever gifts God has entrusted to you. If, after you have edified the people, you are blessed financially through that local church (and they should minister carnal things to you if you gave them anything spiritual), then rejoice. If the church doesn't give you anything, then rejoice even more because you have a wonderful opportunity to see your needs met from some other supernatural source. You will never have financial miracles if you demand payment for your service!

Recently, a pastor told me about a minister who wanted to be a pastor to pastors. This man called pastors from a particular area together for a special meeting. At this meeting he made a great show of being a servant to these pastors. When it came to the bottom line, however, he asked all the pastors to commit ten percent from their churches to underwrite his ministry. He said that if they didn't, he could not fulfill his calling. This is not the attitude of a servant. This is the attitude of a business man!

When you are examining a man to determine whether he is a true spiritual leader or an unsound or false spiritual leader, you must examine his attitude. Does he display the attitude that he is called by God to serve or does he display the attitude that he is someone special in God who should be served? Especially beware of those who demand to be served. You see, in true New Testament church leadership there are no kings; there are no great men. There are only servants who are gifted to help the body of Christ. Never forget that the greatest minister is the servant of all. When you examine a man to determine whether or not he is a true spiritual leader, look for the heart of a servant.

FOUR: DOES HE HAVE THE HEART OF A FATHER?

True spiritual leaders will care for believers with gentleness and tenderness as a father would care for his own children. This "father heart" of the true minister is especially obvious in the writings of the early apostles. The apostle John, for example, frequently called those he was an apostle to, "little children." This is a term of endearment, a term of great affection. In I John 2:1, he wrote,

> "My little children, these things I write unto you..."
>
> I John 2:1

In eight other places, John referred to the believers he was writing to as, "little children." In II John 4, he said,

> "I have no greater joy than that my children walk in the truth."
>
> II John 4

The apostle Paul also had a father heart toward believers. He watched over, protected, and nourished his children in the faith. In I Corinthians

4:14, he warned the believers at Corinth concerning false teachers who were coming into the church, saying,

> *"I write not these things to shame you, but as my beloved sons I warn you. For though ye have ten thousand instructors in Christ; yet have ye not many fathers..."*
>
> I Corinthians 4:14-15

False and unsound spiritual leaders are like Day Care workers. Most Day Care workers don't work in a Day Care Center because they care about each child; they work there is because it is a job. Their work is motivated by pay, not by love.

True spiritual leaders, however, have the compassion of a loving parent for those to whom they minister. To them, each believer is precious in his or her own way. A true leader is willing to invest his whole life in his spiritual children with no thought of return and no remorse about sacrifice. Notice what Paul wrote to his spiritual children in Corinth,

> *"...I will not be burdensome to you: for I seek not yours, but you: for the children ought not to lay up for the parents, but the parents for the children. And I will very gladly spend and be spent for you..."*
>
> II Corinthians 12:14-15

Paul spoke, as would a parent, of his willingness to spend and be spent for these believers' benefit. He desired to lay up spiritual blessings for them. Parents who truly love their children will sacrifice for schooling, for music lessons, for athletic equipment, or for anything else their children need. They willingly spend to make sure that their children get the very best!

Recently, I was watching the winter Olympic games on television. In one segment of the programming, a former Olympic gold medalist and well known figure skating champion was being interviewed. Behind the scenes of his seeming storybook rise to fame was a single mother who happily worked menial jobs to pay for his many years of skating instructions. Her greatest reward after years of personal sacrifice was the achievements of her son. The apostle Paul expressed these same feelings concerning those whom he served, saying,

> *"...my dearly beloved and longed for, my joy and crown...For ye are our glory and joy."*
>
> Phillipians 4:1; I Thessalonians 2:20

Good natural parents are willing to lay down their lives for the success of their children. It is amazing, however, that things can get so turned around in the church! Some ministers calculate how to entice the children to give to them. "How am I going to get blessed," they wonder? "What's in it for me," they ask? It is not right, however, in spiritual life that the children take care of the parents! Paul said, "the children ought not to lay up for the parents, but the parents for the children."

Occasionally, my wife and I watch a certain television talk show. One afternoon, the talk-show host did a program about children who took care of their parents. It was amazing how confused and messed up some of the parents were! Their children were more mentally and emotionally stable than they were! In fact, the parents on this program were looking to their children for help in making decisions! These children were forced to take the place of responsibility abdicated by their parents. You could see, however, that the children were not qualified for this role and had suffered greatly without parental guidance.

A true spiritual father will not abandon his children. He will be like the father of the prodigal son. Even if his son has run off with the inheritance, he will watch every day for him to come home. And when the son comes home, he will run out to greet him with arms and heart open wide.

A true father does not place unreasonable demands upon his children. He is encouraging without being unrealistic in his expectations. He does not provoke his children to wrath by demanding superior performance in every "event." He is longsuffering and patient while he waits for his children to become adults.

A real father makes time for his children. He is not selfish. He is not untouchable or unreachable. His ears are open to the cries and the questions of his children. If he does not know how to answer a question or deal with a problem, he seeks his own Father for direction. When you look for a true spiritual leader, look for a man with the heart of a father.

FIVE: DOES HE HAVE A PREVAILING ATTITUDE OF HUMILITY?

A true spiritual leader has a prevailing attitude of humility. To the church at Philippi, Paul wrote,

> "Let nothing be done through strife or vainglory; but in lowliness of mind let each esteem other better than themselves...Let this mind be in you (learn to think this way), which was also in Christ Jesus: Who, being in the form of God...made himself of no reputation, and took upon himself the form of a servant..."
>
> *Phillipians 2:3-7*

The Amplified Bible says,

> "Let this same attitude and...[humble] mind be in you which was in Christ Jesus. Let Him be your example in humility. Who, although being essentially one with

God and in the form of God [possessing the fullness of the attributes which make God]...stripped himself [of all privileges and rightful dignity]..."

Phillipians 2:5-7 Amp

Although Jesus came to earth in the form of man, He was God. He was anointed with the Spirit without measure. He worked great signs and wonders. His life was perfect and sinless. If anyone had reason to boast, He did. But Jesus, in the fashion of a true spiritual leader, humbled Himself and took on the form of a servant. Although He was Master, He was willing to humble Himself. All believers, including ministers, are exhorted by the Word of God to do the same.

When people asked John the Baptist, heralded by Jesus as the greatest prophet born of women, who he was, he humbly replied,

"I am the voice of one crying in the wilderness..."

John 1:23

John said, "I am only a messenger; I am only a signpost pointing you to Christ." This was the attitude of the great prophet, John the Baptist. He didn't make up a brochure telling of his past exploits, boasting of how many people he had prophesied to or who they were. He refused to exalt himself or consent to titles that would have been perfectly true. Rather, he turned the attention of people to Jesus. I wonder sometimes about our modern day ministers who, instead of making themselves of no reputation and serving the people with humility, spend thousands of dollars to build reputations, promoting and advertising themselves to the top of the ministry heap.

Recently, I heard a minister preaching on television. He got excited, preached some things he thought were pretty good, and then said to the audience, "Now that's good preaching, isn't it?" The congregation didn't respond enough for his satisfaction, so he repeated in a little stronger voice, "Isn't it?" Still, they did not give him enough reaction so a third time, with a demanding voice, he said, "Isn't it?" Then the audience applauded him. If this minister really thought he preached good, when he returned to his own home or motel room he should have humbly lifted his hands and thanked God for inspiring him and allowing him to be a vessel of honor. When you look for a true spiritual leader, look for a man who carries himself with meekness and humility.

Six: Does He Meet The Qualifications For Being A "Bishop?"

Paul instructed both Timothy and Titus concerning the qualifications for spiritual leadership in the church. To Timothy, Paul wrote concerning "bishops." To Titus, he wrote concerning "elders." Most likely, Paul was referring to men who were being considered for the role of pastor in a local congregation. Without a doubt, however, these requirements apply to any place of spiritual leadership in the church. The requirements Paul listed were very strong. They serve, however, to separate between those who simply want to be bosses and those who are willing to make the commitments necessary to be true spiritual leaders. Let's read the requirements Paul wrote to Timothy,

> *"A bishop then must be blameless, the husband of one wife, vigilant, sober, of good behavior, given to hospitality, apt to teach; Not given to wine, no striker, not greedy of filthy lucre; but patient, not a brawler, not covetous; One that ruleth well his own house, having his children in subjection with all gravity; (For if a man know not how to rule his own house, how shall he take care of the church of God?) Not a novice, lest being lifted up with pride he fall into the condemnation of the devil. Moreover he must have a good report of them which are without; lest he fall into reproach and the snare of the devil."*
>
> I Timothy 3:2-7

Blameless

A true spiritual leader must not have a bad reputation. The Amplified Bible says that he must, "give no grounds for accusation but must be above reproach" [I Timothy 3:2 Amp]. One who seeks to be a spiritual leader must be serious minded and watchful, especially over his own life and his own affairs. He must be sober-minded, leading a sensible, well behaved, and disciplined life. He should not be given to excess in any area of life where he could be accused, whether it be food, jewelry, cars, homes, or any other area. By living moderately a true spiritual leader keeps the door of accusation closed.

Is He Hospitable?

True spiritual leaders must be willing to entertain people in their homes. The Amplified Bible says that they should show love for and be a friend to believers. I have heard the teaching which says that ministers should maintain a distance from the people because otherwise the people will lose respect for them. Some cite the familiar phrase, "Familiarity breeds contempt." Familiarity only breeds contempt, however, if one is contemptible. If a minister is a hypocrite, not walking in the light he preaches, people will feel contempt for him. If, however, a minister lives what he preaches, people will be even more challenged by him because they see that what he preaches is real in his own life!

Some so-called spiritual leaders of this generation hide in their houses. I have even heard of pastors who will not allow members of their congregations to come to their homes. Some say, "I must have a place to be myself." Who are you? Who is your real self? Do you need a place to, "flesh-out?" There should be nothing ministers do in the privacy of their own homes that the congregation could not see. Perhaps the problem is that our so-called spiritual leaders are not what they pretend to be and need places to relax from the facade they wear among the sheep.

Certainly, ministers need time to rest away from the people. Certainly, ministers should have their own home life with their own family. Certainly, there may be a few things that a minister does in his own home that are not sin for him, but might cause a weaker member of the church to stumble. Hospitality stands, however, as a Bible requirement for spiritual leadership!

Is He Money Hungry?

Another of the essential qualifications for spiritual leaders is that they cannot love money. Paul made this point twice saying, "not greedy of filthy lucre" and "not covetous" [I Timothy 3:8]. True spiritual leaders are not motivated by money. They do not covet what others have, especially those they minister to. A true spiritual leader is motivated primarily by his calling from God and by his compassion for people. He will preach the Word of God based on what the Head of the Church is directing and based on what he senses the people need. To be motivated by a desire for "base gain" is far too low for a true minister to stoop. True spiritual leaders set high spiritual standards; they don't follow low ones.

It is dangerous to follow ministers who love money for at least three reasons. First, if a minister is money motivated it warps everything he preaches. He does not preach messages that are inspired by God to change believers' lives. He preaches messages that are inspired by his desire to get money. Second, if a spiritual leader is money hungry, it is very possible that he will fall into temptations and snares and become reprobate to the things of God himself [I Timothy 6:9-10]. One of Paul's co-workers named Demus left him and left the will of God because of his love of worldly things [II Timothy 4:10]. If you are following a spiritual leader who loves money and he falls into temptation, you may fall with him. Third, if a spiritual leader is money hungry, he will con believers' money away from them. He will make them believe they are giving to God. The truth, however, is that all "God's money" will be spent on his personal desires. Believers should never follow a man who is money hungry!

Examine His Family

In listing the qualifications for spiritual leadership, Paul drew a relationship between the natural family and the family of God. He said that if a man could not manage the affairs of his own home, he was not qualified to manage the spiritual affairs of others. One translation of this scripture says that if a man cannot control his little family, how will he be able to look after a congregation of God's people. This is, perhaps, a qualification that not many would consider in this generation. It stands firm, however, as a part of the unalterable truth of the Word of God. Let's read this qualification for spiritual leadership,

"One that ruleth well his own house, having his children in subjection with all gravity. For if a man know not how to rule his own house, how shall he take care of the church of God."

I Timothy 3:4-5

Paul cited this same qualification for leadership in the list he gave Titus. He said that a spiritual leader must,

"...[have] faithful children not accused of riot or unruly."

Titus 1:6

To be a true spiritual leader, one must rule well in his own home first. This qualification is very, very sobering, especially in light of our modern standards of godliness. A true spiritual leader knows how to minister to, care for, and guide the affairs of his own home and own family. His children love him, respect him, and listen to him. He holds a place of honor in his own home, not by force, but by virtue of who he is and how he lives.

When looking for a true spiritual leader ask, "What is the man's home life like?" Does he care for his family when he thinks no one is watching? Does his own family love and reverence him? Is he insensitive to his wife and irritable with his children or is he long-suffering and patient? Are his children unruly or are they mature and obedient? Are his children subject to him or do they resent him because he is a hypocrite, living one life at home and another in the pulpit?

Is He a Novice?

Paul told Timothy that a novice was not to be set in a place of spiritual leadership in the church. If a novice was given a place of authority, there was a danger that he would be lifted up in pride and fall into the condemnation of the devil. If this occurred, a young man called and anointed by God could be ruined by the wiles of the devil before he had a chance to mature. If God inspired Paul to tell Timothy not to put novices in an office in the church, then He certainly will not put novices in a place of spiritual leadership Himself.

True spiritual leaders have a few years of spiritual experience. This does not mean that it is impossible for a spiritual leader to be young in age. "Young" and "novice" are not synonymous terms. Both Titus and Timothy were young men when Paul began to give them spiritual responsibility. It is possible for a person to be qualified for a place of spiritual leadership at a young age. It is still important to be careful of young ministers because they have not yet made all the mistakes they are going to make. It is not always enjoyable to be the one that the young gain their experience on.

It is possible for young individuals to be spiritually developed to the place where you could follow them as a spiritual leader. But remember: God will not put a novice in an office. Check the spiritual maturity of the young before you submit yourself to them.

SEVEN: DOES HE STUDY AND PRAY?

In Acts six, we read that the church in Jerusalem had grown to the place where the apostles could no longer do all the work of the ministry. So that they could give themselves to their primary calling to pray and minister the Word, they instructed the disciples to pick out seven men who could perform the ministry of serving the tables. Of themselves, they said,

"But we will give ourselves continually to prayer, and to the ministry of the Word."

Acts 6:4

A true spiritual leader will give himself to prayer and to the ministry of the Word. He will not just pray occasionally, or pray only in emergencies, or pray just to get sermons. The Word and prayer will be vital aspects of his life. Prayer and personal study should equal, if not supercede, the spiritual leader's ministry of teaching and preaching. True spiritual leaders pray. False spiritual leaders prey.

In Ephesians 2:11-19, Paul reminded the believers in Ephesus that they were being built up into a spiritual house for a habitation of God through the Spirit. The next words Paul uttered were, "For this cause" [Ephesians 3:1]. Then he expounded for eleven verses about his ministry of teaching and preaching for the cause of building up the saints [Ephesians 3:1-11]. Paul prefaced his prayer in Ephesians 3:14-19 with the same words. He wrote,

"For this cause I bow my knees unto the Father of our Lord Jesus Christ, of whom the whole family in heaven and earth is named."

Ephesians 3:14-15

For what cause did Paul pray? The cause for which Paul prayed was the same cause for which he preached and taught! It was to build up believers into a holy temple. He not only ministered the Word. He also gave his life in prayer for those to whom he ministered. The working together of these two spiritual endeavors caused believers to be established and matured. "For this cause" Paul preached and "For this cause" Paul bowed his knee.

Paul revealed this same spiritual principle in his letter to the church at Colosse. He told them that he had been called and graced by God to preach the Word of God in its fullness and to make known to the saints the mystery of the gospel. He said that he preached and taught in order to present every man perfect in Christ [Colossians 1:24-28]. Note, however, the next thing Paul wrote,

"Whereunto I also labor, striving according to his working, which worketh in me mightily. For I would that ye knew what great conflict I have for you..."

Colossians 1:29-2:1

Notice Paul said, "Whereunto I also labor." "Also" implies, "In addition to." In addition to preaching and teaching, Paul did something else. He said he also labored and strived. What was this other labor Paul involved himself with? What was the striving he did? This other labor and striving Paul was referring to was the praying he did for those to whom he ministered the Word! Paul, being an honest and sincere spiritual leader, did not just preach hot messages. He did not just razzle-dazzle crowds at hyped up conferences. He did not just carry on like a showman on the stage. He poured out his life and strived with God in prayer for those to whom he ministered.

We note this same life of commitment to prayer in a true spiritual leader named Epaphras. Not only did Epaphras bring the gospel to those in Colosse [Colossians 1:7]; he also prayed fervently for them. Listen to Paul's description of Epaphras's praying,

Epaphras, who is one of you, a servant of Christ, saluteth you, always labouring fervently for you in prayers, that ye may stand perfect and complete in all the will of God. For I bear him record, that he hath a great zeal for you...

Colossians 4:12-13

Notice how the Amplified Bible renders this verse,

"Epaphras...always striving for you earnestly in his prayers, [pleading] that you may — as persons of ripe character and clear conviction — stand firm and mature (in spiritual growth) convinced and fully assured in everything willed by God. For I bear him testimony that he has labored hard in your behalf..."

Colossians 4:12-13 Amp

Nowadays preachers love to preach and teachers love to teach. They enjoy the pulpit. They like being in the lead. Many of them, if they were not preachers, would have been showmen, actors, and actresses. They like being up front. They like the anointing. They like to tell people what to do. But true spiritual leaders are not just committed to the pulpit. They are also committed to study and to prayer! Why? Because to them the people of God are not just an audience; they are a spiritual responsibility!

Ruling well as a true spiritual leader includes treading out the corn of the Word — laboring in the Word and doctrine — before feeding it to the people [I Timothy 5:17-18]. Being a true spiritual leader also includes laying down one's life in prayer for those to whom one is called to minister. When you look for a true spiritual leader, don't look for the man with red hot sermons. Look for the man with red kneecaps!

EIGHT: IS HE AMBITIOUS?

Be careful of men who are ambitious. You could be the means to their end. Rather than serving you, you may end up serving them and become the means by which they fulfill their own desires. Spiritual leaders who are truly called of God and on the right path will be motivated by divine commission, by divine grace, and by divine compassion.

Paul as an Example

Paul wrote something very interesting to Timothy about why he was saved and called into the ministry. He said,

> "...for this cause I obtained mercy, that in me first Jesus Christ might shew forth all longsuffering, for a pattern to them which should hereafter believe on him"
>
> I Timothy 1:16

Paul was saved, not just to be delivered from hell, but also to be a pattern for believers and ministers. If you study his life, you will discover that his motivation for ministry was sincere and pure. He had no intent of personal gain, no desire to be famous, no visions of gaining power or prestige, and no plans to profit from those to whom he ministered. Paul had no personal ambitions.

Paul was primarily motivated by his divine commission (his calling to the ministry), his divine gracing (God's ability working in him), and his divine love (a constraining compassion for those destined for destruction). Recognizing that Paul is a pattern for true ministers, let's look at these three areas of motivation in his ministry.

Divine Commission

Paul wrote this to Timothy in his second letter,

"Who hath saved us, and called us with an holy calling...according to his own purpose and grace..."

II Timothy 1:19

Paul recognized, above all other things, that he was called with a holy calling according to God's purpose. His life belonged to God. He was an apostle, "by the will of God" [Ephesians 1:1]. He was a chosen vessel called to preach to the Gentiles, to kings, and to the children of Israel [Acts 9:15]. If God directed him to go somewhere he went [Acts 16:9-10]. Paul was not disobedient to his heavenly vision [Acts 26:19]. He finished his course [II Timothy 4:7].

Divine Gracing

To the churches in Galatia, Paul wrote this concerning his calling and gracing,

"...the gospel of the uncircumcision was committed unto me... For he (God) that wrought effectually in Peter to the circumcision, the same was mighty in me toward the Gentiles...And when (they) perceived the grace that was given unto me..."

Galatians 2:7-9

The Amplified Bible renders Paul words this way,

"For He...motivated and fitted me and worked through me..."

Galatians 2:7-9 Amp

Not only was Paul called by God and entrusted with the assignment to carry the gospel to the Gentiles; he was also supernaturally equipped by grace. God was, "mighty in (him) toward the Gentiles." Paul was "motivated and fitted" by divine grace. In Ephesians, he wrote this of the special inworking of grace God had dispensed to him,

"If you have heard of the dispensation of the grace of God which is given me to you-ward (to me for you)...I was made a minister, according to the gift of the grace of God given unto me by the effectual working of his power...Unto me is this grace given, that I should preach among the Gentiles..."

Ephesians 3:1, 7-8

Paul recognized that he was divinely graced by God to be a benefit to others. By God's grace he was made a minister. In I Corinthians 15:9-10, Paul revealed that his labors were motivated and sustained by the grace at work within him. He wrote,

"…I laboured more abundantly than they all: yet not I, but the grace of God which was with me."

I Corinthians 15:9-10

Paul was motivated and enabled to labor abundantly by divine grace. His impetus and his direction in ministry came from his divine gracing.

Divine Love

Paul was also motivated by love. In his second letter to the church at Corinth, he wrote,

"For the love of Christ constraineth us…"

II Corinthians 5:14

Paul's own experience of Christ's love and his understanding of God's plan to redeem humanity stirred his heart toward people. He was "constrained." In another place, this word is translated, "pressed in spirit." Love was a driving force behind Paul's ministry.

This element of compelling compassion is often missing in our modern ministries. Some are motivated by their own visions or their own ambitions. Some are even motivated because they love to preach and move in the Holy Spirit. When a minister covets the anointing and the power of God more than he loves the people, however, there will be problems. Paul said it this way,

"…covet earnestly the best gifts: and yet shew I unto you a more excellent way."

I Corinthians 12:31

I Corinthians thirteen is called the love chapter. It applies to all of Christian life. Did you ever notice, however, that this love chapter is strategically located between two chapters that deal with ministry and with the moving of the Spirit in local churches. Why is this love chapter located between two chapters devoted to ministry? Because the possibility of a wrong motivation in ministry and the consequent abuse of people is so great. Personally, I am wary of those ministers who only love to preach and love to feel the power of God, but are not concerned about people. When I sense a thirst for power, but perceive no divine love, I see red lights.

It is not wrong, of course, to covet the things of the Spirit of God. Paul urged believers in I Corinthians 12:31 to, "covet earnestly the best gifts." It is permissible to be thus motivated. But I will show you a more excellent way, Paul said! The most excellent motivation for ministry is the motivation of love.

Why is the way of love the more excellent way? It is the more excellent way because when a minister is motivated by love he will not abuse others to satisfy his own desires. Any aspect of ministry that is exercised outside the motivation of love, whether it be preaching, taking care of the poor, or moving in the gifts of the Spirit, is obnoxious. It is like a clanging symbol and it produces no true spiritual benefit.

If a minister is truly called of God and on course spiritually, you should be able to recognize that the motivating forces behind his ministry are obedience to his divine calling, the motivating power of grace working in him, and a compelling compassion for people. True spiritual leaders are not motivated by personal ambition, by their own visions, by desires for recognition, or by competition with other ministers. Personal ambition in the ministry is not the unpardonable sin, but it can be spiritually dangerous. If you perceive any ambition in a spiritual leader it should be an ambition to obey God and an ambition to serve people!

NINE: IS HE PUSHY AND DEMANDING?

Often false spiritual leaders push people to join them in their vision. If someone doesn't go along with their program, they treat them in a rude, abusive, and vindictive way. By acting like this, they attempt to leverage power over people. Paul said of the false apostles at Corinth that, "they smite you in the face" [II Corinthians 11:20]. Beware of ministers who mistreat you. It is very unlikely that they are true spiritual leaders.

Notice the words of judgement God pronounced on Old Testament unsound spiritual leaders,

> *"Woe be to the shepherds of Israel...The diseased have ye not strengthened, neither have ye healed that which was sick, neither have ye bound up that which was broken, neither have ye brought again that which was driven away, neither have ye sought that which was lost; but with force and with cruelty have ye ruled them."*
>
> *Ezekiel 34:2-4*

Unsound ministers often motivate through fear. They make statements like, "This is God and you had better not miss it!" They may say, "If you don't get in with us, God is not going to use you in these last days!" Some of these so-called leaders imply, and some openly declare, that if you don't come to their little group and do it their way, you'll never get help. What does that say about the God they claim to serve? Stay away from ministers who try to push or pull you into their programs through fear.

I know a man who was a good pastor. The first church he pioneered was a good work of around 125 people. His congregation was being established in the Word of God and there was a good flow of the Holy Spirit. Unfortunately, several different "spiritual leaders" got involved in his life. One called himself an apostle and I'm not sure what the others thought they were at the time, although now one of them now calls themselves an apostle. Rather than helping this man and encouraging him in his work, they told him how much help he needed and how unprepared he was for the ministry. They destroyed his self-esteem, ruined his confidence, and convinced him that he was unqualified to minister. This man ended up being "trained" by the so-called spiritual leaders who convinced him that he needed more training.

What these so-called spiritual leaders really did was break this man down so they could make him again in their image. I don't think this man could even stand on his own now. He has become attached to and dependent on these other "spiritual leaders."

Something is wrong when good, solid, effectual servants of Christ are swept away by self-proclaimed apostles, prophets, and prophetesses who declare that their messages and ministries are of God. If the truth be known, the personal lives and ministries of many of these self-proclaimed spiritual leaders are a mess.

I remember being at a particular meeting several years ago where a minister who is a self proclaimed apostle put their arms around me in an embrace and said, "Your one of ours." Being a nice person I didn't say anything, but in my own mind I thought, "No, I'm not one of anybody's!"

This same minister had previously asked me to speak at one of their meetings even though I wasn't really involved with their "movement." I never considered it at the time, but now I wonder if they were trying to pull me in to their circle by involving me. When I ministered for them, they tried to get me to move in the gifts of the Spirit after I had spoken. They kept saying, "You have a word, brother." They wanted me to move out in the gifts of the Spirit, but there was nothing the Holy Spirit was saying. Finally they gave up and I never heard from them after that.

Recently, a young single woman told me about the female singles director at her church. This singles director demanded to be involved with every relationship in her singles group. She told the singles that dating was not right. She confronted those who dated with strong words telling them that they had a problem with lust. If two individuals in her group seemed to like each other, she tried to break up the relationship.

This woman was enforcing her opinions concerning relationships on the young singles in her church and was probably being praised as a spiritual leader because of her strong stand. A strong stand on shaky ground, however, is completely invalid! If what a person promotes is not in the Word of God, then they cannot enforce it as if it was. Guidelines on relationships can be given and young people must be challenged to holiness, purity and modesty. No one, however, can dictate in other believers' lives. These kind of individuals just want to be in control.

I heard of a case where the pastor of a local church insisted that his members sign a role to show their dedication to him and to his vision. If they didn't sign the role, they could not be considered a part of the local church. This pastor demanded that people align with him and his vision or leave. This is absurd! This man is not a spiritual leader. He is a fearful dictator.

These kind of unsound spiritual leaders proclaim themselves authorities and then expect everyone to submit. They cannot tolerate what they call rebellion. Anyone who won't comply with them and submit to their authority is "in rebellion." Submission, however, is voluntary on the part of the person submitting. If you do not feel called to submit to one who claims to be a spiritual leader, you should not do it.

If you determine that a person is not to be your authority in spiritual life and that person is, in fact, a true spiritual leader, they will probably be glad that they don't have one more soul to be accountable for. They will encourage you to follow the Lord and follow the leading of your own heart. They may tell you that they think you are making the wrong choice, but will make it clear that the decision concerning who you submit to is between you and God.

An unsound spiritual leader, however, will not be happy that you do not submit to him. He may accuse you of abandoning your "spiritual parents." He may tell you that you are "missing God." He may "prophesy" your failure if you leave him or his organization. He may call you a defector. I've heard of cases where nasty letters were written, calling people unfaithful. I've even heard of cases where so-called spiritual leaders became so angry that they shouted at people or threw their Bibles.

These uncalled, unsound, self-appointed leaders cannot tolerate those who are stable and don't need constant attention and direction. They love to be leaders and do not like it when others do no submit to them. The angry response they give when their leadership is questioned proves that they are not true spiritual leaders. Paul told Timothy that one of the qualifications a bishop was that he should, "Not soon [be] angry." True spiritual leaders have their tempers and their emotions under control.

Don't let people control you by making you think they know more than you know or by manipulating you through fear. Be led by the Word and guided by the Holy Spirit. God is big enough to help you if you are off the mark. He corrects and chastens His children. He who has begun a good work in you will complete it. You began in the Spirit and will come to maturity in the Spirit. God will continue to work in you both to will and to do His good pleasure.

TEN: DOES HE CALL HIMSELF SOMETHING?

Believers must be wise enough to realize that just because someone calls themselves something is not the proof that they are. In fact, those who proclaim to be something often are not! Many who flaunt titles or make special claims to leadership are not at all what they say they are.

"But," you say, "Paul boasted of his apostleship." Yes, he did. But only when he was forced to do so in order to keep certain local churches from coming under the control of false leadership. When he felt compelled to boast of his apostleship he said things like, "bear with me in my folly" and "I speak foolishly." He was embarrassed at the thought of boasting in his calling. He was even hesitant to relate how he was caught up into the third heaven and heard, "unspeakable words, which it is not lawful for a man to utter" [II Corinthians 12:4]. In fact, Paul went no further than to briefly mention his heavenly experience. He abstained from citing his supernatural experiences, saying,

> *"Should I desire to boast, I shall not be a witless braggart, for I shall be speaking the truth. But I abstain [from it] so that no one may form a higher estimate of me than [is justified by] what he sees in me or hears from me."*
>
> II Corinthians 12:6 Amp

In the style of a true and mature spiritual leader, Paul was willing for people to judge him by what they saw and heard themselves. He encouraged them to listen to his words and observe his life and then judge for themselves. He would not use claims of visions or supernatural experiences to validate his ministry

False spiritual leaders, however, make claims of special callings and claims of special experiences. They say things like, "God called me to be an apostle," or, "God set me in this office." Some may say that God appeared to them in a special vision. But did God really call them to the ministry? Are they what they say they are? You must make your own decision. Do not allow yourself to be pressured into taking someone's word about themselves as absolute truth.

It is interesting that in both instances where Jesus spoke of false leadership in His address to the seven churches in Revelation, those who were false leaders had called themselves something. To the church in Ephesus, Jesus said,

"...thou has tried them which say they are apostles, and are not..."
Revelation 2:2

These false spiritual leaders had declared that they were apostles. That was their testimony about themselves. They were not apostles, however, but liars! To the church in Thyatira, Jesus said this concerning the false prophetess Jezebel,

"...that woman Jezebel, which calleth herself a prophetess..."
Revelation 2:20

Jezebel called herself a prophetess and many of the people of that local church accepted her as such. She was not, however, a prophetess, but a seductress!

In both of these passages, those who proclaimed themselves to be spiritual leaders were not what they said they were. There is a great difference between being called by God to be something and calling one's self something.

Jesus warned His disciples to beware of the many in the last days who would come saying, "I am christ." This warning referred to false leaders who would claim that they were something in the ministry. They would say, "I am anointed by God...I am called by God...I am this...I am that."

The body of Christ in this generation must be careful of accepting someone as a spiritual leader just because they call themselves something. Just because an individual pins a name tag on themselves that says Billy Bob, it is not necessarily true that he is Billy Bob. In fact, nowadays, he might well be Emmy Lou!

Be very careful of those who call themselves something. Paul instructed young Timothy, "make full proof of thy ministry" [II Timothy 4:5]. If a man claims to be called of God, let him prove it with his fruit. Be careful, too, of those who "prove" they are called of God by claiming to have had visions and special revelations. How can you judge whether that person had a vision or not? A healthy skepticism will keep you spiritually safe. Always remember that just as a person has the right to call themselves something, so you have the right to examine the validity of their claim.

ELEVEN: DOES HE WIN YOU WITH THE WORD OR WITH WORDS?

A true spiritual leader never wanders far from the written scriptures. His emphasis will always be on the Word. It will be the foundation of his ministry, the central point and the boundary lines for every message. It will be the guideline for his own life and activities. If he wins you, it will be with the Word, not with enticing words and fancy rhetoric.

The early apostles preached the Word of Truth by the inspiration of the Holy Spirit. They did not rehearse their messages. The Bible says of Stephen that the people could not resist the spirit and the wisdom by which he spoke [Acts 6:10]. The spirit he was speaking by was the Holy Spirit. If you study his message, you will see that he was not speaking pre-planned words; he was speaking directly from the scriptures [Acts 7:2-52].

The "word of faith" was the message Paul preached [Romans 10:8]. He preached the scriptures both to the saved and the unsaved [Acts 26:22-23]. He reported that when he preached the gospel, he did not do it with, "enticing words of men's wisdom," but by the inspiration of the Holy Spirit. This insured that the faith of those who heard his message would not rest in the cleverness of his words, but in the power of God [I Corinthians 2:4-5]. Paul instructed young Timothy, a pastor and a leader in the early church, to, "Preach the Word" [II Timothy 4:2].

The Holy Spirit spoke this word to me one time and I wrote it down in my personal diary,

Declare My Word, says the Lord
Don't try to persuade
Simply speak to those who will hear
And I will make the way

Declare My Word, says the Lord
Do it by the Spirit
And you will be amazed
By the results in those who hear it

Declare My Word, says the Lord
Speak the truth in love
And I will confirm that which you speak
By My Spirit from above

For I know what My people need
And that's what I'll give to you
Words of Life to feed my sheep
Words of Love, strong and true

March 29, 1985

A true spiritual leader does not depend upon enticing words or the power of persuasion. He does not depend upon convincing arguments to sway people. He depends upon the power of the Holy Spirit to bring the Word of God to the hearts of men. He always endeavors, even though he has prepared himself by studying the Word of God, to speak by the inspiration of God. He lives by I Peter 4:11 which instructs,

"If any man speak, let him speak as the oracles of God..."

I Peter 4:11

False spiritual leaders, on the other hand, attempt to win people with their words. Peter said that they make merchandise of believers, "with feigned words" [II Peter 2:1-3]. This word "feigned" represents a real point of delineation between true teachers and false teachers. "Feigned" means something pre-planned, as from a mold or a cast. The teaching of false spiritual leaders is pre-calculated to produce a desired response. Every message is premeditated to persuade the hearer.

False ministers attempt to persuade peoples' minds through the power of cunning speech. They will play act, saying just the right words, to tweak emotions. Their ministries are an exercise in manipulation. They ascertain what words and what actions people will respond to and then plan their speeches and gestures accordingly. They know when to get loud and when to be soft, when to shed a tear and when to shout. I even heard of one minister who offered to show another minister how to cry at will in order to get a response from the people. Is that unbelievable to you? Well, my friend, it is true! Be wise as serpents.

Watch Out For the Man With the Silver Tongue

In his letter to the churches of Galatia, Paul referred to the power of persuasion, saying,

"Ye did run well; who did hinder you that ye should not obey the truth? This persuasion cometh not of him that calleth you."

Galatians 5:7-8

Through skillful arguments and the motivation of fear, false teachers persuaded the churches of Galatia to come under bondage to the law. Paul declared, however, that this "persuasion" was not from God. It did not come from the One who had called them.

False teachers can be very persuasive! Some are like expert salesmen. They have learned the art of persuasion. They know how to use words to move people. They can persuade believers to buy their "product" and then take their money for it. Like an expert salesman, they can sell believers things they do not need!

A few years ago my wife took a study course from a particular sales training company. This company had carefully studied what triggered peoples' responses. They had become such sales experts that they told my wife, "If you follow our presentation word for word you will make three sales for every twenty contacts. It's guaranteed." Why could they say that? Because they had learned how to push peoples' buttons.

It can be difficult at times to discern between the working of the Holy Spirit upon our hearts and the working of men's persuasion upon our emotions. This is precisely the reason that God's Word, especially in the New Testament, warns us again and again of false spiritual leaders. If we are not careful and do not know how to judge, there is a chance we will be taken advantage of by spiritual hucksters and suffer physically, emotionally, spiritually, and financially.

You must learn how to recognize when someone is messing with your emotions and when someone is speaking by the power of the Spirit. Do the ministers you follow appeal to and direct you to the scriptures? Are their messages solidly based upon the Word of God? Do they preach and teach the Word of God with simplicity and humility? Or do they attempt to move you with emotional stories and enticing words?

TWELVE: DOES HE POINT PEOPLE TO CHRIST?

One of the character traits of false spiritual leaders is that they want their own disciples. A prominent trait of a true spiritual leader, on the other hand, is his concern that believers are espoused solely to Christ. He will be concerned that their allegiance is to Jesus rather than to himself. He will make every effort to present Christ to believers and believers to Christ. Paul said this to the believers in Corinth that were being drawn away from Christ by false apostles,

> "...I am jealous over you with a Godly jealousy: for I have espoused you to one husband, that I may present you as a chaste virgin to Christ. But I fear..."
>
> II Corinthians 11:2-3

Paul's mission as a true spiritual leader was to prepare a people to present to Christ. He always had this vision in the forefront his mind. He saw himself as a sign-post that pointed men to Christ. He was, therefore, very concerned and jealous when the believers in Corinth began to give allegiance to false apostles.

In Acts 20: 28-31, Paul warned the spiritual leaders from the church at Ephesus to watch out for men who would rise up from within their own flock, "speaking perverse things, to draw away disciples after them." It is characteristic of unsound spiritual leader to draw people toward themselves. If you encounter spiritual leaders who are always attempting to draw people into their groups, always trying to build organizations, and always trying to get others to "hook up with them," be very careful. Beware of those who seek to build a following with themselves at the lead or create an organization with themselves at the center. Trouble will only be a short distance ahead.

One pastor told me about a strange experience he had along these lines. One day two pastors from a particular ministerial organization called him and asked if they could come to visit. Thinking that they desired to fellowship with him, he invited them to his home. After visiting for only a short time, however, it was very apparent that the only reason these pastors had come to visit was to recruit him to their organization. They persisted, insisted, and tried to persuade him to join the ministerial organization they were in. This pastor, however, felt no leading from the Lord to do so and kindly explained this to the other pastors. They finally gave up trying to convince him and stood up from the table to leave. After escorting these pastors to the door and bidding them goodbye, the pastor returned to his table only to discover that they had left money there as a final enticement to join their organization.

True spiritual leaders do not attempt to draw men unto themselves, but labor to draw men to Christ. True spiritual leaders follow the example of John the Baptist. When his disciples began to worry about his waning popularity due to the fact that Jesus had come on the scene, he responded with a calm assurance and a sense of reality about who he was and who Christ was. John said, "He must increase, but I must decrease" [John 3:30]. Because he was a true spiritual leader, John was concerned that even his own disciples knew and followed Christ.

THIRTEEN: DOES HE SPEAK AGAINST OTHER SPIRITUAL LEADERS?

Some unsound ministers, desiring position and respect, attempt to raise their spiritual profiles by speaking against other older and time-tested ministers. These unsound ministers, however, must be weighed in the balance themselves. Even if their teaching is accurate, their haughty and presuming spirit and proud attitude disqualifies them for true spiritual leadership. They are a dangerous risk to those who follow them.

In the Old Testament a man named Korah was jealous of Moses and Aaron and wanted more authority in the congregation. He attempted to raise himself up by putting Moses down. He spoke these words against Moses,

> *"Ye take too much upon you, seeing all the congregation are holy, everyone of them, and the Lord is among them: wherefore then lift ye up yourselves above the congregation of the Lord?"*
>
> Numbers 16:3

Korah and his men were not content in their calling. They wanted more respect, more admiration, and a greater position. To get it, they put down Moses and brought attention to themselves. Moses responded to Korah and those who stood with him by reminding them that they already held a position of responsibility in Israel and should not seek for more than they were called to be.

God did not tolerate this attitude of aggressiveness and self-advancement. He instructed Moses to tell the congregation to get away from the dwelling place of Korah, Dathan, and Abiram. The congregation was to,

> *"...Depart...from the tents of wicked men, and touch nothing of theirs, lest ye be consumed in all their sins."*
>
> Numbers 16:26

Moses then said to the congregation,

> *"...if the Lord make a new thing, and the earth open her mouth, and swallow them up, with all that appertain unto them, and they go down quick into the pit; then ye shall understand that these men have provoked the Lord."*
>
> Numbers 16:30

This terrible disaster came to pass as Moses said. The ground opened up and swallowed Korah, his possessions, and all the men that followed him.

At times, judging spiritual leadership takes a great deal of spiritual discernment. Korah was not a false prophet from the outside, but a discontent and ambitious man who already held a position of spiritual leadership in the congregation. He was already being used of God and had respect from the congregation. Korah, however, wanted more! To gain position, he spoke against and even confronted God's true spiritual leader.

This rebellious attitude started with Korah, spread to Dathan and Abiram, and then to 250 other men who already had positions in Israel and were noted as "famous" in the congregation. God was provoked with these men because they sought positions He had not appointed them to and did so by speaking against His anointed leadership. The final result of this incident was the death of at least 14,953 men.

What God said to the congregation of Israel concerning their relationship with Korah is good advice for believers concerning those who exalt themselves by speaking against God-ordained and anointed leadership. God told them, "Depart...from the tents of wicked men, and touch nothing of theirs, lest ye be consumed in all their sins" [Numbers 16:26]. Keep a safe distance away from those who speak against true spiritual leaders. God will not advance these individuals to leadership positions in the church. He may not even tolerate them!

A Correct Attitude for Ministers

David is a beautiful example of a man who was truly called of God, but had a deep respect for God's current anointed leader. Even after he was anointed by God to be king, David would not touch Saul. Although Saul had already been judged as undeserving of the throne and David had already been anointed to stand in his place, David would not usurp God's place in judgement. When the time was right, God removed Saul from the scene Himself.

This is the character of a true leader. Even if God has called him to the forefront in leadership, he waits till God raises him up. He will not seek to gain spiritual recognition by speaking against God-ordained spiritual leaders. He will be patient and meek, waiting on the Lord and respecting and revering those ministers who have labored before him in the Lord.

Follow spiritual leaders like David. Follow those who faithfully do the will of God without pressing for position. If you follow those who are wise in God, stable in life, humble in attitude, and meek in spirit, you will have the opportunity to come to spiritual maturity yourself. If, on the other hand, you follow position seekers, those who are not content without recognition and attention and who will speak out against true and established leadership to get it, you run the grave risk of perishing with them in their spiritual folly.

FOURTEEN: DOES HE NEED TO BE NEEDED?

Some individuals enter the ministry to fulfill their own need to be needed. They are unfulfilled, empty, lonely, and insecure. They are lost without people who need them. Just as the Bible says that sheep are scattered without a shepherd, so some shepherds are lost without sheep. Without a congregation, some ministers would be totally lost; they would feel useless.

True spiritual leaders are not dependent upon the people they minister to for fulfillment. They are happy and fulfilled in God. They are rich in their own spiritual lives and minister out of a position of stability and contentment rather than from a need to be needed. They are available when people need them, but are not dependent on someone needing them to be fulfilled.

Unsound spiritual leaders endeavor to keep believers dependent on them. They don't want believers to become stable in the Word and confident in God. After all, what will they do if someone doesn't need them anymore? These unsound ministers are like selfish parents. They say that they love their children so much they can't release them. This is selfish and soulish. It is not because of love, but because of their own personal insecurities and their underdevelopment that these ministers can't let their children go. They need their children. They feel lost without them.

A true spiritual leader endeavors to bring people to the place where they are able to stand on their own. Like a good parent, he will help his spiritual children, but his goal is to make them independent of him and dependent on God and His Word. He will lead them and guide them, but looks forward to the day when they can stand strong in God themselves.

Do the leaders you follow say, or does their attitude suggest, that to get what you need from God, you will have to come to them? Do they say things like, "Come to us and we will pray and then God will heal you?" Why don't these leaders teach you to pray to your Father in Jesus' name and expect the Father to grant your request.

Watch out for those who say things like, "You need to come to us for prayer," or, "You need to come to us or you can't be delivered." Watch out for so-called spiritual leaders who want to keep you dependent on them. Watch out for those who have a mediator mentality. Jesus is the only Mediator between the Father and man and He has already mediated. We are the children of God. We must establish and develop our own relationship with God.

FIFTEEN: DOES HE PROMOTE SPIRITUAL PRIDE?

Beware of ministers who portray an elitist attitude. Beware of those who think they have a revelation no other group has. Ministers who have this kind of attitude have built a wall of spiritual pride so high around themselves that even God can't climb over. They are imprisoned in their own narrow minded opinions.

Do the ministers you follow say or imply things like, "We have what no other group has," or, "Bless their hearts, but they are ignorant. We'll pray for them that God will open their eyes?" Do they say, "We are specially chosen for this revelation. We see what others cannot see."

This attitude of being specially chosen almost always ends in the abuse of those who are not in your little group. It lends itself to a feeling of special rights and special privileges. In fact, some have such "deep revelation," they don't even think they have to live by the Word. Beware of those who portray this kind of spiritually elite attitude.

SIXTEEN: IS EVERYTHING "IN THE SPIRIT?"

Do the ministers you follow say things like, "A lot happened in the Spirit tonight," or, "Things are really happening right now in the spirit realm." Of course, things transpire in the realm of the spirit that we cannot see with our physical eyes. And there are definitely times when prayer or praise produces changes in the realm of the spirit that will not be seen in the natural realm till a later date. But are things really happening when these ministers say they are? How can you know for sure? Or do you just have to believe them because they know and you don't? That is a dangerous position. You are open for deception and abuse if you believe something just because the person in charge said so.

Did you really pull down spiritual strongholds over the city tonight? The leader said you did. But did you? I don't know if you did or not. Was what happened in the service really a manifestation of the Holy Spirit or was it something manufactured and pushed along by the will of men? Was the word of prophesy that someone gave you of God or not? And what if you say that you don't agree with the leader? Will you automatically be labeled as a rebel?

The Emperor's New Clothes

Perhaps you remember the story of the Emperor's new clothes. In this story, the emperor of a nation wanted to have an outfit of clothing that was different from what anyone else in the kingdom had. The tailor who was chosen to make this outfit knew he could not please the emperor, so he deceived him. He made no outfit, but claimed that the invisible outfit he "made" was more beautiful than anything anyone had seen before. The tailor dressed the emperor up in the "outfit" and made a great show about how beautiful it looked. The emperor left the tailor's shop thrilled with his new clothing.

That same day a parade was scheduled. The emperor, of course, wanted to display his beautiful new outfit. He made an announcement about his new clothes and then marched through the city streets. All the people of the city, afraid to admit that the emperor was naked, participated in the lie. They were afraid they might be wrong. Finally, however, a boy who was too young to pretend, cried out, "The emperor is naked!" The whole crowd, released by the young boy's declaration of the truth, began also to cry out, "The emperor is naked!"

This same kind of situation can occur in the spiritual life. Some ministers claim that things are happening "in the Spirit" just to persuade you to stay with them. They present themselves as spiritual experts and make you feel like spiritual children. Because they carry themselves with authority, believers are afraid to disagree with them. Many, therefore, play the game just like the people did with the emperor. Only when someone dares to stand up and declare that what the minister is doing is false are people released to express what they suspected from the very first, but were afraid to say.

If a person's ministry is based to a great degree on the intangible realm and they have no scriptural proof or fruit to support what they say is happening, follow your own heart. Do not abdicate your responsibility to judge.

SEVENTEEN: ARE YOU SOUL-TIED?

It can happen that ministers who led you to God or led you further into the things of God wander away from spiritual soundness. You must realize that no matter how close a friend they are or what they have done for you in the past, you are not obligated and indebted to them for a life-time. I've heard people praising spiritual leaders by saying things like, "We owe them our life." I believe ministers will be rewarded for what they have sowed into your life, but you do not owe them your life and you are not obligated to follow them for a life-time. If you think this way about any minister, your thinking is unhealthy. Always remember, as Paul said, that it was Christ who died for you and it is to Christ that you owe your life. Ministers are simply servants by whom you believed or by whom you were blessed.

Especially if you are the pastor of a church, you must be aware of this principle. You may feel obligated to the person who led you into the things of God. It is important, of course, to be thankful to that person. If, however, they have wandered away from sound doctrine, you will have to put your responsibility to your flock before your feelings for this person. Don't forget that God has raised you to a place of spiritual leadership and given you responsibility for the lives of those in your own congregation.

Wanting to be a faithful friend to one who has helped you in the past does not release you from your responsibility to watch out for the flock now entrusted to your care. What your "friend" might say in your pulpit (since having him in your pulpit is as good as saying that you agree with his doctrine) could greatly influence the spiritual life of your congregation. I know of ministries and local churches that have suffered from the influence of unsound doctrine and unsound spiritual activity because pastors felt obligated to their "friends" even though they had wandered down the path of error. Truth is more important than loyalty!

EIGHTEEN: ARE YOU JUDGING BY HIS FOLLOWING?

Don't judge the validity of a person's ministry by whether or not they have a large following. Don't be conned by the hype, the excitement, and the noise of the crowds. And don't fall for the false statement, "This many people can't be wrong." The truth is that the many are often wrong! Remember, it was a crowd of many sincerely wrong individuals, stirred to action by rabble-rousers, that crucified Jesus.

Many Christians follow whoever is the most charismatic rather than whoever is the most spiritual. And most Christians, like sheep, simply follow the sheep ahead of them. Don't take your cue from other sheep. They may all be headed for a fatal leap off the cliff. Take the time and make the effort yourself to find a sound spiritual leader.

From Paul's epistles, we realize that in many of the churches he started, believers followed after false spiritual leaders. Although Paul was a true and dedicated spiritual leader, many believers were not interested in him because he was not forceful. He said this to the church at Corinth,

> "…the more abundantly I love you, the less I be loved."
>
> II Corinthians 12:15

Even Jesus, the greatest and most sound minister that ever lived, was left with only a few hundred followers when He finished His earth ministry.

People will follow charismatic leaders whether they are right or wrong. The fact that people follow someone's ministry in no way proves, confirms, or even indicates that a person's message or ministry is sound. Do not judge a man's ministry by the size of his following. Judge him in the ways that you have learned in these last two chapters.

CONCLUSION

In these last days it is important to be led by those who are truly called of God and who are walking carefully and faithfully in their calling. This is an hour when men are evil and self-interested. Your spiritual health and spiritual destiny are at stake. Who you follow will, to a substantial measure, determine who you are. Choose a spiritual leader who will lead you to maturity, to soundness, to spiritual riches, and to a steadfast relationship with Jesus and with the Father God.

Section Five

Conclusion

II Peter 3:16-18

"Ye therefore, beloved...beware lest ye also, being led away with the error of the wicked, fall from your own steadfastness."

·~19~·
To Believers

We have covered an extensive amount of material in this study. We have learned about Satan's latter day's strategy against the church. We have learned that believers are responsible to judge doctrine and spiritual leadership. We have learned where unsound doctrine and unsound spiritual leaders come from and the dangerous results which occur when believers embrace them. We have also learned how to judge doctrine and spiritual leadership. In this final section we will present some practical advice to believers in general and then to those called to the ministry.

WATCH!

The presence of false doctrine and the activity of false spiritual leadership will be very much a part of the spiritual scene of the last days. Because this is true, you must expect it! Do not be surprised or unprepared when you encounter unsound doctrine. Do not be surprised or unprepared when you encounter false spiritual leaders. Remain on guard. Watch, beware, and keep alert! Unsound doctrine will be promoted in these last days. Unsound spiritual leaders will endeavor to mislead you in these last days. Take heed! You have been foretold!

Remember that Paul wrote this to young Timothy concerning unsound doctrine and the last days,

"Now the Spirit speaketh expressly, that in the latter times some shall depart from the faith, giving heed to seducing spiritus, and doctrines of devils…"

I Timothy 4:1

Remember also that Paul wrote this to Timothy concerning false spiritual leadership and the last days,

"This know also, that in the last days perilous times shall come…evil men and seducers shall wax worse and worse, deceiving and being deceived."

II Timothy 3:1,13

If you do not expect to encounter false doctrine and false leadership, you will not watch. To *watch* is a different spiritual attitude than to *look*. To *look* means to actively search for something. To *watch* simply means to keep alert so that if something does come, you will see it. If you do not watch for unsound doctrine and watch for false spiritual leadership, you risk being a victim of deception.

BELIEVE NOT!

The words, "believe not," are a safe starting point for every believer. Don't believe everything you hear. Don't believe every person you encounter. No matter how nice, how gentle, or how "spiritual" they seem, don't automatically believe everything. The apostle John wrote,

> "Beloved, believe not every spirit, but try the spirits whether they are of God: because many false prophets are gone out into the world."
>
> I John 4:1

"Beloved," said John, "believe not." This is a warning! These words are meant to put believers at mental and spiritual attention! This is a word of caution about gullibility, about ignorance, and about being susceptible to spiritual deception. John's words are a warning to believers in every generation to test teachers and teaching.

Most believers have been taught to believe the best of each person and not to be critical or judgmental. And this is not wrong teaching. It must, however, be carefully tempered with John's strong message of, "Believe not!" When it comes to embracing doctrine or following spiritual leadership it is important to remember that your own spiritual life is at risk. What you listen to and who you submit to can make the difference between being strong and established or being tossed to and fro, a spiritual mess. It is indeed true that believers are sheep. But even sheep should know better than to eat poison grass or to follow a wolf to his den!

Believer, believe not everything you hear! Some of it will be doctrines of demons. Believe not everything you hear! Some of it will be the carefully contrived words of deceptive men who want what you have. Believe not everything you hear! Some of it will be the unsound doctrine of sincere, but wrong spiritual leaders. If you follow unsound doctrine, you will become spiritually unsound.

Believer, believe not everyone you hear! Some individuals are false ministers who intentionally promote false doctrine. Believe not everyone you hear! Some false ministers want to make gain from you. Believe not everyone you hear! Some ministers don't know what they are talking about themselves! If you follow the blind, you will end up in the ditch!

WISE AS SERPENTS

In one place, Jesus spoke these words of instruction to His disciples,

"Behold, I send you forth as sheep in the midst of wolves: be ye therefore wise as serpents and harmless as doves."

Matthew 10:16

In their heart attitude and personal motivation the disciples were to be gentle. Concerning their spiritual perception, however, they were to be as sharp and cunning as serpents; they were to be on constant alert. Why was it so important that they be "wise as serpents?" It was because they were in the "midst of wolves!"

The book of wisdom confirms this instruction of Jesus with an insight that is very pertinent for New Testament believers concerning carefulness in the spiritual walk. Note these words,

"The simple believeth every word: but the prudent man looketh well to his going."

Proverbs 14:15

The foolish man believes everything he hears. A prudent and wise man, on the other hand, is very careful about his steps. He cautiously ponders the path he will take and carefully considers the places he will go. His eyes and ears are wide open. He is alert and vigilant concerning his own goings.

Believers must not be afraid or unwilling to think! I remember speaking to a pastor about a particular doctrinal direction I saw some ministers going. I told him I was very hesitant about going that particular direction myself. The response I saw in his face was, "Who do you think you are?" As it turned out, however, I was right and the ministers who were going that particular doctrinal direction were wrong. The Bible does not instruct believers to cut off their heads, but to renew their minds. A sharp mind coupled with a sensitive heart will make believers a difficult target for unsound doctrine and false spiritual leaders.

HOW TO RESPOND TO DOCTRINE

Doctrine guides the thinking, governs the activities, and determines the fruit of believers' lives. Sound doctrine is profitable. It keeps believers and local churches steadfast in faith, accurate in truth, knowledgeable of God, and safe from the devil's attacks. Sound doctrine will bless, encourage, and sometimes even excite, but it can also cut to the heart and expose secret motivations, unrenewed thoughts, wrong attitudes, and ungodly conduct [Hebrews 4:12]. It is the light which exposes darkness, the two-edged sword that cuts going in and cuts coming out.

Those who involve themselves in sound doctrine will flourish spiritually. Those who read and heed the good Word of God will be blessed in all their deeds [James 1:25]. They will come to full maturity and be completely outfitted to do the good works God calls them to do [II Timothy 3:16-17]. If a believer is careful to establish himself in sound doctrine, he will make noticeable spiritual progress. Paul told Timothy to,

"...give attendance to reading, to exhortation, to doctrine...Meditate upon these things; give thyself wholly to them; that thy profiting may appear to all."

I Timothy 4:13

Believers must be careful to maintain sound doctrine. Meditating upon it, giving yourself to it, and paying attention to it will be profitable both for you and for those who hear and follow you.

Walk in the Truth

The apostle John had a tremendous love for believers and for the church. He is known as the apostle of love and often referred to believers as his children. John not only had a tremendous love for believers, however. He also had a tremendous passion for truth. In fact, nothing rejoiced his heart more than to hear that his spiritual children remained in the truth. Listen to John's words in his second letter,

"I rejoiced greatly that I found of thy children walking in the truth..."

II John 4

John rejoiced greatly when he heard that believers walked steadfastly in the truth! If this was the response of an earthly spiritual father, it must also be the response of the Holy Spirit, of Jesus, and of our heavenly Father when we walk in the truth. In his third letter, John wrote,

"For I rejoiced greatly, when the brethren came and testified of the truth that is in thee...I have no greater joy than to hear that my children walk in the truth."

III John 3-4

John rejoiced greatly when he heard that the truth remained in his spiritual children and rejoiced again when he heard that they walked in the truth! He said he had no greater joy than to hear that his children walked in the truth.

John had a passion for the truth and a profound concern that his spiritual children walked in it. In fact, if you asked this great apostle, "John, what is most important in my spiritual life?" he would tell you, "Walk in love and walk in the truth!"

Endure Sound Doctrine

The apostle Paul warned Timothy that a time would come when believers would not endure sound doctrine. He said,

> "For the time will come when they will not endure sound doctrine; but after their own lusts shall they heap to themselves teachers, having itching ears; And they shall turn away their ears from the truth…"
>
> II Timothy 4:3-4

In this passage the word "endure" comes from the Greek *anecho* and means to "hold to." Sound doctrine requires enduring; it must be held to. Evidently sound doctrine will not always be fun and exciting. Fun things, you see, do not have to be endured. They can be enjoyed! To remain spiritually sound requires an attitude of "holding fast" to sound doctrine. Believers must endure sound doctrine even if it requires work and discipline.

Study and Shun

Paul told Timothy,

> "Study to shew yourself approved unto God, a workman that needeth not to be ashamed, rightly dividing the Word of truth. But shun profane and vain babblings for they will increase unto more ungodliness. And their word will eat as doth a canker…"
>
> II Timothy 2:15-17

Paul instructed Timothy in two contrasting responses toward two kinds of doctrine. Concerning the Word of truth, Paul exhorted Timothy to study. Concerning profane babblings, Paul admonished Timothy to shun. This is a tremendous spiritual posture and attitude for believers to take: *Study and Shun.* *Study* God's Word and be accurate in your interpretation of it. *Shun* unsound doctrine. If you hear it or contact it in any other way, turn around and don't involve yourself with it.

Study

The word "study" actually means to be diligent. Those who are diligent and careful in dividing the Word of Truth will be approved by God. They will be approved by God because their interpretation of His Word will be right. Those who are diligent and careful in their dividing of the Word of Truth will not need to be ashamed. They will not have to look back on their lives and wish they had gone a different doctrinal direction. Those who are diligent and careful in their dividing of the Word of Truth will be right in their interpretation of what God has said and will, therefore, be sound in their spiritual lives.

Shun

The word "shun" comes from the Greek *periistemi*. This word is built on the Greek word *histemi* which means to stand. A person can stand in many ways. He can stand up straight, he can face forward, he can lean over backwards, etc. To "shun" means to stand in such a way as to avoid. It gives the sense of turning one's back to something.

Have you ever been speaking with someone and said something they didn't like? Perhaps this person turned their back to you and crossed their arms. Their posture was saying, "I refuse to listen to you"! It was saying, "I will not allow myself to hear what you say!"

To shun gives the mental picture of giving someone the cold shoulder. If you face someone directly, you invite them into your territory by exhibiting a certain measure of vulnerability. But if you turn your shoulder, your body language tells the other person that they are not welcome to get to know you. An emotional and mental wall of defense is acted out in body language.

By instructing Timothy to shun unsound doctrine, Paul was telling him what kind of spiritual posture he should take concerning teaching that could not be classified as sound doctrine. Timothy was to turn his back to it, avoid it, show disinterest in it, and ignore it. He was to turn around and walk away giving a clear sign that he was not interested. He was to maintain a defensive posture so as not to be drawn into unprofitable teaching.

Notice that the positive act of *study* is something done alone. To *shun* means to avoid discussions with others over unimportant tits and tats. In this there is an important spiritual insight for believers. We must get in our own closets, get out our own Bibles, and listen to the Holy Spirit ourselves! We must study until we have a witness in our hearts that we have a solid grip on the basic truths of God's Word.

HOW TO RESPOND TO SPIRITUAL LEADERSHIP

It is not only important which doctrines a believer holds to, whether true or false, sound or unsound. It is also very important which men or women believers recognize as true spiritual leaders. It is important because believers not only follow the doctrines of those they esteem as true spiritual leaders; they also take on their spiritual character. It is absolutely essential, therefore, that believers approve those who are truly ministers of God and mark those who are unsound or false.

Approve True Ministers

In his first letter to the church at Corinth, Paul approved Timothy and instructed the believers there to receive him as a sound minister. He wrote,

"Now if Timotheus come, see that he may be with you without fear: for he worketh the work of the Lord, as I also do. Let no man therefore despise him: but conduct him forth in peace, that he may come unto me: for I look for him with the brethren."

I Corinthians 16:10-11

Just a few verses later, Paul approved the ministry of Stephanas, saying,

"I beseech you, brethren, (ye know the house of Stephanas, that it is the firstfruits of Achaia, and that they have addicted themselves to the ministry of the saints,) That ye submit yourselves unto such..."

I Corinthians 16:15-16

Paul not only approved the house of Stephanas, but even urged the believers to, "submit yourselves unto such." What did Paul mean by this phrase? He meant that believers should recognize and submit themselves to true ministers who were willing to lay down their lives to serve.

In this same context, Paul referred to several other ministers. He acknowledged their ministries himself and exhorted the church in Corinth to do the same. He said,

"I am glad of the coming of Stephanas and Fortunatus and Achaicus: for that which was lacking on your part they have supplied. For they have refreshed my spirit and yours: therefore acknowledge them that are such."

I Corinthians 16:17-18

Paul again instructed the believers in Corinth to, "acknowledge them that are such." The believers in Corinth were to recognize and appreciate true ministers.

In the book of Acts we read that the brethren in Ephesus wrote a good testimony to the brethren in Achaia concerning the ministry of Apollos. The Bible says,

"And when he (Apollos) was disposed to pass into Achaia, the brethren wrote, exhorting the disciples to receive him: who, when he was come, helped them much which had believed through grace..."

Acts 18:27

The believers in Ephesus acknowledged Apollos as a true and effectual minister and recommended him to the believers in Achaia. The believers there received him as such and greatly benefitted from his ministry.

Near the end of Paul's letter to the church at Rome, we find a long list of individuals and ministers that he commended and recommended to that church. Lets' notice some of the things he wrote concerning these true ministers. In Romans 16:1, he wrote,

> *"I...commend to you Phebe our sister, which is a servant of the church which is at Cenchrea...That ye receive her in the Lord...and that ye assist her in whatsoever business she hath need of you: for she hath been a succourer of many, and of myself also."*
>
> Romans 16:1-2

In verse three, he wrote,

> *"Greet Priscilla and Aquila my helpers in Christ Jesus: Who have for my life laid down their own neck: unto whom not only I give thanks, but also all the churches of the Gentiles."*
>
> Romans 16:3-4

In verse seven, he wrote,

> *"Salute Andronicus and Junnia, my kinsmen, and my fellowprisoners, who are of note among the apostles, who also were in Christ before me."*
>
> Romans 16:7

In verses twelve and thirteen, he wrote,

> *"Salute Tryphena and Tryphosa, who labour in the Lord. Salute the beloved Persis, which laboured much in the Lord. Salute Rufus chosen in the Lord..."*
>
> Romans 16:12-13

Paul acknowledged and approved those ministers who were truly called of God and were fulfilling their ministry with the right attitude and corresponding good fruit. He encouraged other believers and local churches to do the same. They were to recognize, acknowledge, and approve true ministers one to another.

Mark Those Which Cause Divisions

Immediately following his words of kindness and commendation concerning sound ministers, Paul wrote this to the church at Rome,

> *"Now, I beseech you, brethren, mark them which cause divisions and offenses contrary to the doctrine which ye have learned; and avoid them."*
>
> Romans 16:17

Paul instructed these believers to, "mark them which cause divisions." The word "mark" comes from the Greek *skopeo* and means to watch, to contemplate, and to look at. Paul warned the believers at Rome to watch out for ministers who taught contrary doctrines and caused divisions within the church. Not only were they to watch out for unsound ministers. If they recognized them, they were to "avoid them."

Paul's words about marking those who caused divisions were serious spiritual advice. He anticipated that believers would come into contact with unsound ministers who would negatively affect their spiritual lives. Precaution should be taken; carefulness should be exercised. Notice how the Amplified Bible renders this scripture,

> "I appeal to you, brethren, to be on your guard concerning individuals who create dissensions and difficulties and cause divisions, in opposition to the doctrine — the teaching — which you have been taught. [I warn you to turn aside from them, to] avoid them."
>
> Romans 16:17 Amp

Paul's words were a warning to be on guard concerning ministers who created dissensions. Believers were to "turn aside" from and avoid divisive so-called spiritual leaders. In the next verse, Paul revealed who these individuals were who caused divisions and clarified what they wanted. He said,

> "For they that are such serve not our Lord Jesus Christ, but their own belly; and by good words and fair speeches deceive the hearts of the simple."
>
> Romans 16:18

Those who caused divisions and promoted contrary doctrines were unsound spiritual leaders. These men did not serve Christ, but served their own appetites and low desires. With ingratiating and flattering speeches they beguiled the hearts of the unsuspecting and simple-minded. Paul made it clear that so-called ministers who stir up strife and division and promote false doctrine must be marked and avoided.

Do Not Bid False Teachers God-speed

Concerning the response believers should make to those who trespassed sound doctrine, the apostle John said,

> "Whosoever trangresseth (goes beyond) and abideth not (does not stay) in the doctrine of Christ, hath not God...If there come any unto you, and bring not this doctrine receive him not into your house, neither bid him Godspeed: For he that biddeth him Godspeed is partaker of his evil deeds."
>
> II John 9-11

The apostle John warned his spiritual children not to receive into their house those who transgressed doctrine. They were not to fellowship with these individuals. Their error was too contagious; it was too easily transmitted. John also told his spiritual children not to bid individuals that transgress doctrine, "Godspeed." They should not even be told, "God bless you." Basically, John warned against any association with those who carried unsound doctrine. Though John's words may not, at the first, sound like an expression of Christian love, they really are. If believers love their own lives in Christ, love the truth, and love the body of Christ, then they must refuse any person that carries spiritual sickness.

Parents follow this rule in the natural realm. If their little Johnny wants to go to little Billy's house to play, but little Billy has measles, they don't let little Johnny go, do they? No, of course not. Because they love their little Johnny, they refuse to allow him to fellowship with little Billy. The same principle is true in spiritual life. It is unwise to involve one's self with a person who is known to be spiritually sick. Because the negative so easily corrupts, believers must mark false spiritual leaders and refuse to associate with them.

GET YOUR FULL REWARD

In II John 7-10, John expressed concern that his spiritual children remain firm in God and firm in faith and doctrine. If they did so, they could receive their full reward. In verse eight, he gave this warning to believers,

> *"Look to yourselves, that we lose not the things which we have wrought (gained), but that we receive a full reward."*

> *II John 8*

John was concerned. He wanted his spiritual children to walk in the full reward of the sound spiritual life. He wanted them to walk in the full benefits of their salvation as promised in the written scriptures. John, therefore, warned believers, saying, "Look to yourselves." They were to be on guard for their own spiritual well-being, watching out for unsound doctrine and watching out for unsound spiritual leaders. If they were not on guard, they risked losing what they had gained in their lives from the sound teachings of God's Word. By looking to themselves, watching over their own spiritual lives, and being on the alert for unsound doctrine and unsound spiritual leadership, these believers could receive and walk in their full reward!

·~20~·

To Ministers

The body of Christ of this generation desperately needs true spiritual leaders. We need spiritual leaders who have a personal relationship with God, who know the voice of the Holy Spirit, and who are well grounded in the truth of the scriptures. We need spiritual leaders who are not just *followers* of other spiritual leaders, but who are *peers* with other spiritual leaders. We need spiritual leaders who are not afraid to ask questions and who are capable of producing answers. We need spiritual leaders who will hold fast to the truth even if everyone stands against them, but who are not so proud that they will not let go of their opinions if they are shown to be wrong by the Word of God. We need spiritual leaders who will honestly interpret and preach the Word of truth whether it is to their personal advantage or disadvantage. We need spiritual leaders who are more zealous for the truth than they are ambitious to build their ministries.

In this final chapter we will issue a few challenges to those who are called by God to the full-time ministry. Hopefully these challenges will not only teach ministers, but will also inspire ministers to reach out, reach up, and reach within themselves for a new standard of Godly excellence in their own ministries.

EXAMINE YOUR DOCTRINES

Ministers, examine your doctrines. It is no small matter to be one who is promoting wrong or twisted doctrine. You must heed the warning of Paul who said, "let every man take heed how he buildeth" [I Corinthians 3:10]. Don't forget that every time you minister to people you are impacting the temple of God! Perhaps the words of David to his son Solomon concerning building the Old Testament temple would be appropriate to read. David said,

> *"...and the work is great: for the palace is not for man, but for the Lord God. Now I have prepared with all my might for the house of my God the gold..and the silver...and the brass...and the iron...and the wood; onyx stones...glistering stones...and all manner of precious stones, and marble stones in abundance. Moreover, because I have set my affection to the house of my God, I have of mine own proper good, of gold and silver...I have prepared for the holy house..."*

I Chronicles 29:1-3

As David said of the Old Testament temple, so it is true of the New Testament church. The work is great, for the temple is not for man, but for the Lord God! David prepared for the building of the temple. Not only did he carefully set aside the wealth of the nation of Israel for building, but because he had set his affection upon the temple of the Lord, he had set apart his own wealth for its building.

Ministers, ask yourselves these questions: Where is your affection? Is it set upon making gain for yourself or is it set upon building something strong and beautiful for the Lord? Are you building with gold, silver, and precious stones — with excellent material that has cost you something? Or are you building with hay and stubble — with material that you picked up for nothing from along side the roadway or in an empty field? Are you building with material that another man purchased through faithful study and dedicated prayer? Or have you sacrificed your own time and effort to dig out precious building material? Remember that "the temple of God is holy" [I Corinthians 3:17]. It is dedicated, set apart, and precious unto the Lord. Take heed how you build!

The Lord had some very strong words to say through the prophet Ezekiel concerning the building practices of the spiritual leaders of his day. Not only did God say they had seduced His people; He also said,

> *"...one built up a wall, and, lo, others daubed it with untempered mortar. Say unto them which daub it with untempered mortar, that it shall fall...So will I break down the wall that ye have daubed with untempered mortar, and bring it down to the ground, so that the foundation thereof shall be discovered, and it shall fall...Thus will I accomplish my wrath upon the wall, and upon them that have daubed it with untempered mortar, and will say unto you, The wall is no more, neither they that daubed it..."*

Ezekiel 13:10-15

These spiritual leaders built a wall with untempered mortar. They did not want to pay the price or make the effort to build with that which would stand for generations. Their main concern was to give the impression that they were building something sound. But God saw past the outward appearance. He inspected the wall that these so-called spiritual leaders built and promised to break it down, revealing its weakness.

Ministers, it is always safe to question yourself concerning doctrine. Always double check your teachings. If you are a member of a ministerial association or follow another minister closely, don't just accept their teaching as the final word on every subject. Study the Word of God yourself. Labor in the Word and in doctrine yourself. If you are called to feed the flock, then you are also called to tread out the corn!

Sometimes it can be profitable to ask other ministers or even other believers who are sound in the faith what they think of your teaching. Don't, however, ask the people who love and follow your ministry for their opinion. They cannot tell you the truth because they have accepted your teaching as right. Don't ask those who have personal advantage in mind by being in relationship with you. They won't tell you the truth because they are afraid you will dismiss them from your inner circle. And don't ask the flatterers who tie themselves to you by stroking you with syrupy words. They will tell you only what they think you want to hear. Ask someone who truly knows the Word of God, who is sound in doctrine, and who will not be afraid to tell you the truth. If you are wrong or unsound in your doctrine in a particular area, their advice will afford you the opportunity to make adjustments before it's too late!

MINISTERS OF THIS GENERATION

Some current spiritual leaders are like surfers that try to ride every so called "wave of the Spirit." These spiritual surfers end up crashing on the shores of unsound doctrine, but simply paddle back out to catch another wave. To them the thrill of the ride is more important than making true spiritual progress and helping others make true spiritual progress. Other ministers of this generation are like uneducated sailors. They suppose that if they can just catch the wind of the day, they will be carried to the forefront of the ministry pack. A wise sailor, however, sets his sails to take full advantage of the predictable prevailing winds. He knows that the short term gusts will certainly change or stop.

Especially young and aggressive ministers should be concerned about their doctrine. Just as Paul carefully instructed and warned young Timothy and young Titus concerning doctrine, so young ministers of this generation should be very careful concerning doctrine. Young ministers, you should be on the alert so that you do not become, as was the impulsive Peter, an unwilling tool of the enemy. As a novice, you should be careful so that you do not become lifted up in pride and fall into the condemnation of the devil. Do not think more highly of yourself than you ought to think, but soberly, in accordance with what God has dealt to you.

Some ministers of this generation need to do a very serious examination of the doctrines they are teaching to see if they will stand the examination of the intense, dividing, searching, and illuminating Word of God. Some are twisting scriptures to support their exciting new revelations. Some are lifting scriptures out of their proper context. Others have departed from the Word of God altogether and are offering man-made philosophies and comforting rhetoric in its place. I believe it can be very fairly stated that many of the ministers of this generation are dangerously uneducated in the full counsel of God's Word. They are captivating speakers, classy entertainers, and slick salesmen, but lack the depth of knowledge required to be true spiritual leaders who can build strong, steadfast, and enduring churches!

RETURN TO STUDY AND PRAYER

The words that God spoke to and through the Old Testament prophet Jeremiah concerning unsound spiritual leadership are very pertinent for spiritual leaders in every generation. Let's read a few of the things God said. In Jeremiah ten, He said,

> "For the pastors are become brutish, and have not sought the Lord: therefore they shall not prosper, and all their flocks shall be scattered."
>
> *Jeremiah 10:21*

Notice that God said, "the pastors are become brutish." To be "brutish" means to have low standards, to be crude and course, to be undignified and common. These pastors did not start out brutish, however. They *became* brutish. They digressed from a higher spiritual plane to the lower spiritual condition of brutishness. And why did this occur? It was because they had not sought the Lord! The final result was that they did not prosper in their own lives and the flocks they had spiritual responsibility over were scattered.

In Jeremiah twenty-three, God said,

> "I have not sent these prophets, yet they ran: I have not spoken to them, yet they prophesied. But if they had stood in my counsel, and had caused my people to hear my words, then they should have turned them from their evil way, and from the evil of their doings."
>
> *Jeremiah 23:21-22*

These unsound spiritual leaders were operating on their own whims. They had not been sent by God. They had not been spoken to by God. Therefore their activities produced no benefit for the people. If they had stood in God's counsel and spoken the words He gave them, they could have turned the people from their wicked ways and into the way of life. Ministers must take time to wait upon the Lord!

Just a few verses later, God said,

> *"...I am against the prophets...that steal my words every one from his neighbour."*
>
> Jeremiah 23:30

God requires ministers to get their own messages directly from Him. Notice that He said these unsound prophets stole His words from their neighbors. It was not because these prophets were speaking a false message that God was angry with them. It was because they borrowed another man's revelation! God requires of the ministers He calls that they wait upon Him themselves and receive those messages He wants them to speak.

True spiritual leaders must maintain times of personal study and personal prayer. The spiritual leaders in the early church in Jerusalem had a strong recognition of this important aspect of ministry. When there was a lack in ministry in that local church, they refused to abandon their priority of prayer, study, and preaching. I am sure they were *willing* to serve the neglected widows, but they realized it would not be *right* for them to do so because it would encroach upon their first calling. In response to this needed area of ministry, they said,

> *"...It is not reason (not right) that we should leave the word of God, and serve tables."*
>
> Acts 6:2

These early spiritual leaders realized that it was not right for them to abandon the Word of God, both their study of it and their preaching of it, in order to serve the widows. Their clear recognition of priorities was confirmed just two verses later as the apostles again said,

> *"But we will give ourselves continually to prayer, and to the ministry of the word."*
>
> Acts 6:4

We live in very busy times. Not only does the simple business of living seem to take more time every year, but the business of ministry has become more and more complicated. Not only is this true, but the emphasis of ministry in this generation seems to be on meetings. Christian life and meetings have become so intertwined that few ministers could live their spiritual lives outside the context of a meeting.

There should be much more to the spiritual life of ministers than meetings and preaching. It was not in a meeting that the apostle John received the revelation of the end times. It was not in a meeting that Paul received his revelation. It was not in a meeting that God revealed to Peter that He would reach out to the Gentile nation. Those who are called to be spiritual leaders must have personal time for study, for prayer, and for their own devotional life.

GUARD THE FLOCK!

Before his departure from the church at Ephesus, Paul warned the elders concerning false spiritual leadership and exhorted them to a particular course of spiritual responsibility. He said to them,

> "*Take heed therefore unto yourselves, and to all the flock, over the which the Holy Ghost hath made you overseers, to feed the church of God, which he hath purchased with his own blood. For I know this, that after my departing shall grievous wolves enter in among you, not sparing the flock. Also of your own selves shall men arise, speaking perverse things, to draw away disciples after them. Therefore watch, and remember, that by the space of three years I ceased not to warn every one night and day with tears.*"

Acts 20:28-31

The responsibility Paul issued to the elders of this local church was twofold. First, they were to feed the flock by ministering the Word of God. Second, they were to maintain a careful watch for any destructive forces that would come against that local body, guarding the flock both from the *infiltration* and from the *uprising* of false spiritual leadership.

It is often true of ministers, especially of pastors, that their tenderheartedness makes it difficult for them to confront men or women who are a danger to the local church. They are afraid to refuse these kind of people a place in their churches. The result is that rather than protecting the sheep from wolves, they try to help the wolves!

Ministers have a responsibility to the flock over whom the Holy Spirit has set them. No tenderheartedness or gentleness can overrule their God-given responsibility of protecting the sheep. Pastors, you have authority over your local congregation. Your authority comes from God. If He set you in a place of leadership, then it is necessarily true that you have authority in that place. Do not be weak when it comes to wolves or unsound doctrine. When a bear tried to get into David's flock, he killed it. When a lion tried to get into David's flock, he caught it by the beard and killed it. It is not your responsibility to convert or to guide wolves. It is, however, your responsibility to guard the flock!

In warning the church at Ephesus, Paul put the elders at attention. He directed their minds toward the issue of guarding their flock and put them in a defensive spiritual posture. His final exhortation on this subject is very revealing. He said,

> *"Therefore watch and remember, that by the space of three years I ceased not to warn everyone day and night with tears."*
>
> Acts 20:31

"Watch and remember." "Watch and remember." "Watch and remember." For three years Paul warned the spiritual leaders of this local church concerning false spiritual leadership. For three years he, "ceased not to warn everyone day and night." Issuing warnings concerning false spiritual leadership never left Paul's spiritual instruction agenda concerning this local church. If Paul taught about and warned about this issue day and night for three years, it should be very, very obvious to modern day ministers that the infiltration and uprising of false spiritual leadership is extremely dangerous to the life of local churches!

When are wolves able to enter from the outside into a local flock? When are men able to rise up in the local church and usurp authority? These things happen when there is a weakness in true spiritual leadership! Paul told the elders at Ephesus that when he left wolves would attempt to enter in among them and men would attempt to rise up from among them. He knew this would happen when he, a true and strong spiritual leader, left. When there is a void in true leadership, it will be filled by false leaders.

Ministers, especially pastors, must be willing to point out false doctrine and unsound spiritual leadership. This is not always an easy thing to do. Sometimes when a true leader points out error and makes scriptural corrections, the false leaders cry out, "They are not walking in love!" Sometimes they say, "We are being persecuted! The last move always persecutes the new move!" In any way possible, false leaders will try to make true spiritual leaders look like the bad guys. This is why it is so important that whole congregations know the Word of God and the witness of the Spirit of Truth themselves. If things ever come to a showdown between a true spiritual leader and a false spiritual leader, the congregation may be forced to make a choice themselves.

INSTRUCT THOSE WHO OPPOSE THEMSELVES

Not every Christian is called upon to make the same response to unsound doctrine and unsound spiritual leadership. Those who are called to leadership positions in the church have a greater responsibility to attempt to help those who are unsound in doctrine and spiritual life. Through meekness and gentle instruction they are to attempt to help those who oppose themselves. If these individuals have not gone too far into unsound spiritual life, God may be able to open their eyes. If they are able to see the error of their ways, they can repent and acknowledge the truth.

Concerning the responsibility of the spiritual leader, Paul told Timothy,

> *"And the servant of the Lord must not strive; but be gentle unto all men, apt to teach, patient, In meekness instructing those that oppose themselves; if God peradventure will give them repentance to the acknowledging of the truth; And that they may recover themselves out of the snare of the devil, who are taken captive by him at his will."*

II Timothy 2:24-26

Satan loves to trap believers in false and unsound doctrine because it causes them to "oppose themselves." Because they refuse the truth, they forfeit their freedom. Because they refuse sound doctrine, they forfeit their own spiritual soundness. By refusing to acknowledge the truth, they chart their own course to spiritual sickness, weakness, and possible destruction. Those who are involved in unsound doctrine are working against their own spiritual stability. If they are sincerely ignorant, God will "give them repentance." If, however, they are willfully ignorant, proud, and hard-hearted, they will reject the opportunity to repent and will be beyond God's help.

The word repentance Paul used when he spoke of repenting and acknowledging the truth comes from the Greek *metanoi*. This word means "to perceive afterwards." It represents a change of mind and purpose that is a change for the better. Hopefully, those involved in false doctrine will repent and acknowledge the truth when carefully and gently instructed by true spiritual leaders.

Through the able and patient instruction of Timothy and other sound ministers, Paul hoped that some unsound believers would recognize that the teachings and spiritual activities they were holding to were wrong. Those who recognized their error and repented would, "recover themselves out of the snare of the devil." The *snare* of the devil is his use of false teachings which produce instability, questions, strife, fear, uncertainty, and unsound spiritual life. Those who repented would be restored to a place of soundness in spiritual life.

True spiritual leaders should make an attempt to help those who have wandered into or even purposely embraced unsound doctrine. Through the means of instruction, they should make an effort to bring them back to the road of truth. Some believers will repent of their unsound doctrine by acknowledging the truth. This is a day of rejoicing for God and for the church!

CONFRONT UNSOUND SPIRITUAL LEADERS

True spiritual leaders may be called on by the Lord, as were Titus and Timothy, to instruct false teachers who opposed themselves. True spiritual leaders may be called on by the Lord to rebuke unsound spiritual leaders in the hope that they will abandon their false teaching. True spiritual leaders may be called on by the Lord to mark false spiritual leaders for all believers to see. True spiritual leaders may also be called on by the Lord to reject unsound spiritual leaders. Not every minister may be called upon this way, but the Lord will surely speak to those who are sound and experienced about taking a place of authority in determining what is and what is not sound doctrine and who is and who is not a sound spiritual leader.

Concerning teachers who were teaching unsound doctrine, Timothy was to charge them before the Lord not to do so. Paul said,

> *"As I besought thee to abide still at Ephesus...that thou mightest charge some that they teach no other doctrine..."*
>
> *I Timothy 1:3*

Timothy was to take a position of spiritual authority over those who were promoting false and unsound doctrine. He was to "charge some" not to teach unsound doctrine. To "charge" is not a suggestion. It is not the offering of timid guidance. To charge means to command adherence. Timothy was to tell those who promoted unsound doctrine, "Don't do it!"

Some ministers may be called on by the Lord to expose and mark unsound ministers so that believers do not become swept up in their error. Paul was not afraid to call the names of those who were unsound in his generation. In his first letter to Timothy, he said,

> *"...some having put away concerning faith have made shipwreck: Of whom is Hymenaeus and Alexander; whom I have delivered unto Satan, that they may learn not to blaspheme."*
>
> *I Timothy 1:19-20*

In his second letter to Timothy, he wrote,

> *"...of whom is Hymenaeus and Philetus; Who concerning the truth have erred..."*
>
> *II Peter 2:17*

The apostle John was also not afraid to name names. In his third epistle, he identified a man named Diotrephes as one "who loveth to have the preeminence among them" [III John 9].

True spiritual leaders may also be called on by the Lord to boldly confront those who refuse to acknowledge the error of their way. Paul gave Titus this challenging instruction,

"A man that is a heretic after the first and second admonition reject; knowing that he...is subverted..."

Titus 3:10-11

Titus was to admonish and rebuke the heretic in an attempt to persuade him to let go of unsound doctrine and come back to the truth [Titus 1:13]. If he would not receive correction, however, he was to be rejected from the local church. Why must he be rejected? Because the promotion of unsound doctrine by heretics can lead to spiritual catastrophe!

Paul also told Titus this concerning false teachers,

"...rebuke them sharply, that they may be sound in the faith."

Titus 1:13

As we learned in our chapter on the significant place of sound doctrine, the word "rebuke" signifies a confronting kind of reprimand and the word "sharply" means to speak in a manner that cuts. Titus was to boldly confront unsound teachers. As William's translation says, he was to, "continue correcting them severely!" This was no pleasant or simple task for Titus and it will not be a pleasant or simple task for modern day spiritual leaders. It must be done, however, because whole local churches are at risk when unsound teachers teach their unsound doctrines!

IF THEY ARE NOT AGAINST ME, THEY ARE FOR ME

There is one more matter ministers must be careful of. They must be careful of labeling other ministers who don't do it their way as false. Ministers must not think or say, "They don't do it like we do in the Assembly of God church, so they can't be of God." Ministers must not think or say, "They don't do it like we do in the Word of Faith churches, so they can't be of God."

There are many different ways to serve the same bread of Life. Be careful not to be critical of ministers or churches who do it different than you. If their doctrine is wrong, that, of course, is a whole other issue. I am quite concerned, however, that some ministers are crusaders for their way, or for the way of their organization. If someone doesn't fit within the narrow confines of their way, they label them as not of God.

On one occasion, John came to Jesus and told Him that he and the other disciples saw another person casting out devils in Jesus' name. "We forbad him," said John, "because he followed not with us" [Luke 9:49]. Notice Jesus' response to John,

"Forbid him not: for he that is not against us is for us."

Luke 9:50

Ministers, you must understand that there is more than one way to do the same thing. In this hour, some ministers will need to be very careful not to embrace the very wrong thinking that their way is the only way, or even the best way, to do things. Pride goeth before a fall.

Paul made it very clear to the church at Corinth that if one said, "I am of Paul," and another said, "I am of Apollos," (both who were true ministers) they were carnal and spiritual babies. I am afraid, however, that we have some of that kind of thinking in this hour. Ministers, you must follow Jesus!

A LAST WORD

Being a spiritual leader is not an easy task; it is not a pleasure trip through life. The spiritual life of the church depends upon its spiritual leaders. The success of the kingdom of God depends upon its spiritual leaders. The plans and purposes of God depend upon His spiritual leaders. If you are called to be a spiritual leader, if you are called to the full-time ministry, you have a very serious responsibility to fulfill! You will need help, but God's grace is enough!

To order books and tapes by Guy Duininck,
or to contact him for speaking engagements,
please write:

Master's Touch Ministries
P.O. Box 54026
Tulsa, OK 74155